Lecture Notes
in Business Information Processing   516

Series Editors

Wil van der Aalst , *RWTH Aachen University, Aachen, Germany*

Sudha Ram , *University of Arizona, Tucson, AZ, USA*

Michael Rosemann , *Queensland University of Technology, Brisbane, QLD, Australia*

Clemens Szyperski, *Microsoft Research, Redmond, WA, USA*

Giancarlo Guizzardi , *University of Twente, Enschede, The Netherlands*

LNBIP reports state-of-the-art results in areas related to business information systems and industrial application software development – timely, at a high level, and in both printed and electronic form.

The type of material published includes

- Proceedings (published in time for the respective event)
- Postproceedings (consisting of thoroughly revised and/or extended final papers)
- Other edited monographs (such as, for example, project reports or invited volumes)
- Tutorials (coherently integrated collections of lectures given at advanced courses, seminars, schools, etc.)
- Award-winning or exceptional theses

LNBIP is abstracted/indexed in DBLP, EI and Scopus. LNBIP volumes are also submitted for the inclusion in ISI Proceedings.

Yiliu Paul Tu · Maomao Chi
Editors

E-Business

New Challenges and Opportunities for Digital-Enabled Intelligent Future

23rd Wuhan International Conference, WHICEB 2024
Wuhan, China, May 24–26, 2024
Proceedings, Part II

 Springer

Editors
Yiliu Paul Tu 🅾
University of Calgary
Calgary, AB, Canada

Maomao Chi
China University of Geosciences
Wuhan, China

ISSN 1865-1348   ISSN 1865-1356 (electronic)
Lecture Notes in Business Information Processing
ISBN 978-3-031-60259-7   ISBN 978-3-031-60260-3 (eBook)
https://doi.org/10.1007/978-3-031-60260-3

This Springer imprint is published by the registered company Springer Nature Switzerland AG
The registered company address is: Gewerbestrasse 11, 6330 Cham, Switzerland

If disposing of this product, please recycle the paper.

Preface

The 23rd Wuhan International Conference on E-Business (WHICEB), an AIS-affiliated annual conference, took place from May 24 to 26, 2024, in Wuhan, China. The conference hosts were the School of Economics and Management, China University of Geosciences, Wuhan, China, and Baden-Württemberg Cooperative State University Heidenheim, Heidenheim, Germany. The organizers were The Center for International Cooperation in E-Business, China University of Geosciences, Wuhan, China, the School of Information Management, Wuhan University, China, and the College of Business Administration, Ningbo University of Finance & Economics, China. The conference was sponsored by the Association for Information Systems (AIS), the China Association for Information Systems (CNAIS), the China Information Economics Society, and Wuhan University of Communication.

WHICEB is dedicated to advancing scholarly research and fostering networking opportunities within the e-business sector and related fields. Our goal is to catalyze academic inquiry and business innovation by facilitating discussions on e-business, global finance, and the imperative for ongoing innovation. This conference aims to showcase cutting-edge research, solutions, and methodologies that leverage the Internet as a powerful tool for global commerce. The digital age presents a myriad of challenges, from technological hurdles to behavioral adaptations, marketing strategies to data analytics, and concerns over efficacy to security. In recent years, the ABCD Technology—big data, cloud computing, artificial intelligence, and blockchain—has sparked a new wave of innovation across manufacturing, business, education, and personal life sectors. This digital and intelligent transformation is paving the way for a novel digital economy growth model, redefining "Internet Plus" applications, and enabling businesses to reinvent their models from the ground up. In response to this digital and intelligent trend, companies are actively engaging with new challenges, thereby generating numerous research opportunities.

This year's conference theme, "New Challenges and Opportunities for a Digital-Enabled Intelligent Future," is designed to ignite robust academic and corporate engagement by integrating e-business and information technology in our increasingly digital and intelligent landscape, alongside fresh insights and discoveries in service, marketing, and operational management reform. The conference sought to highlight groundbreaking scientific research in fields enabled by artificial intelligence, foster cross-disciplinary studies, and share experiences from various nations and regions. These proceedings encompass 16 tracks and will be indexed appropriately. The selected best papers from the proceedings will be recommended to international academic journals including but not limited to the following: Electronic Commerce Research and Applications, Electronic Markets, Electronic Commerce Research, Internet Research, Journal of Organizational and End User Computing, Journal of Information & Knowledge Management, International Journal of Networking and Virtual Organizations, and Journal of Systems and Information Technology.

The research papers in these proceedings went through a double-blind peer review process. Papers were accepted based upon a clear research methodology and contributions to the knowledge of e-business including but not limited to case studies, experiments, simulations, and surveys. The efforts made by our track chairs in reviewing submissions are really appreciated, which ensures the quality of the proceedings. On behalf of the conference organization, we thank them for their professional diligence. They are: *Xing Wan, Jiangnan Qiu, and Lin Jia*, Advancing Digital Education; Innovations, Challenges, and Opportunities; *Yaobin Lu, Ling Zhao, and Jiang Wu*, Artificial Intelligence & IoT(AIoT) Enabled Business Innovation; *Yi Wang, Yuan Sun, and Si Shi*, Artificial Intelligence and New Ways of Working; *Guoyin Jiang, Xiaodong Feng, and Wenping Liu*, Computing and Complexity in Digital Platforms; *Dongxiao Gu, Jia Li, and Yiming Zhao*, Data Science and Smart Social Governance; *Zhongyun (Phil) Zhou, Yongqiang Sun, and Xiao-Ling Jin*, Digital Enablement and Digital Governance; *Xiaobo (Bob) Xu, Weiyong Zhang, and Fei Ma*, Digital Innovation and Social Impact; *Ping Wang, Xiuyan Shao, and Cong Cao*, Disruptive Technologies and Digital Transformation; *Xiaoling Li, Lu Wang, and Qing Huang*, E-business Strategy & Online Marketing; *Rong Du, Hongpeng Wang, and Peng Wang*, Emerging e-Commerce Initiatives Enabled by Advanced Technologies; *Shaobo Wei, Xiayu Chen, and Hua Liu*, Emerging Technologies and Social Commerce; *Nannan Xi, Hongxiu Li, Juho Hamari, and Juan Chen*, Engaging Technologies; *Zhaohua Deng, Tailai Wu, and Jia Li*, Healthcare Service and IT Management; *Haichao Zheng, Yuxiang Zhao, and Bin Zhu*, Human-Computer/AI Interactions; *Hefu Liu, Meng Chen, and Zhao Cai*, Information Systems and Operations Management; *Zhao Du, Ruoxin Zhou, and Shan Wang*, Transformative Digital Innovations: Education, Sports, and Entertainment.

This year, we received a total of 354 submissions, from which 107 papers successfully secured acceptance for publication. This results in an acceptance rate of approximately 30.79%. Our proceedings are structured across three volumes. Each paper included in these volumes has undergone a rigorous review process, involving a minimum of three double-blind reviews conducted by members of the Program Committee. Again, we express our sincere appreciation to all members of the Program Committee for their invaluable contributions, unwavering support, and dedicated efforts throughout this process.

April 2024

Yiliu Paul Tu
Maomao Chi

Organization

Conference Co-chairs

Jing Zhao
School of Economics and Management, China University of Geosciences, China

Juergen Seitz
Baden-Württemberg Cooperative State University Heidenheim, Germany

Doug Vogel
Harbin Institute of Technology, China

Publication Chairs and Proceedings Editors

Yiliu (Paul) Tu
University of Calgary, Canada

Maomao Chi
China University of Geosciences, China

Program Committee

Chairs

Weiguo (Patrick) Fan
University of Iowa, USA

Zhen Zhu
China University of Geosciences, Wuhan, China

Members

Yukun Bao
Huazhong University of Sciences & Technology, China

Zhao Cai
University of Nottingham Ningbo, China

Cong Cao
Zhejiang University of Technology, China

Juan Chen
Anhui University of Finance and Economics, China

Meng Chen
Soochow University, China

Xiayu Chen
Hefei University of Technology, China

Xusen Cheng
Renmin University of China, China

Zhaohua Deng
Huazhong University of Sciences & Technology, China

Rong Du
Xidian University, China

Zhao Du
Beijing Sport University, China

Xiaodong Feng
Sun Yat-sen University, China

Qiang Wei	Tsinghua University, China
Shaobo Wei	University of Science and Technology of China, China
Jiang Wu	Wuhan University, China
Tailai Wu	Huazhong University of Science & Technology, China
Nannan Xi	University of Vaasa, Finland
Huosong Xia	Wuhan Textile University, China
Wenlong Xiao	Chang Gung University, Taiwan RoC
Xiaobo (Bob) Xu	Xi'an Jiaotong-Liverpool University, China
Ying Yang	Hefei University of Technology, China
Jinmei Yin	Nanjing University of Aeronautics and Astronautics, China
Ming Yi	Central China Normal University, China
Shuping Zhao	Hefei University of Technology, China
Yiming Zhao	Wuhan University, China
Yuxiang Zhao	Nanjing University of Science and Technology, China
Haichao Zheng	Southwestern University of Finance and Economics, China
Zhongyun Zhou	Tongji University, China
Ling Zhao	Huazhong University of Sciences & Technology, China
Weiyong Zhang	Old Dominion University, USA
Ruoxin Zhou	University of International Business and Economics, China
Bin Zhu	Oregon State University, USA

Session Chairs

Kanliang Wang	Renmin University, China
Jinghua Xiao	Sun Yat-sen University, China
Rong Du	Xidian University, China
Xiangbin Yan	Guangdong University of Foreign Studies, China
Yi Jiang	China University of Geosciences, China

Organization Committee

Chair

Yao Zhang	China University of Geosciences, Wuhan, China

Secretary-General

Fei Wang   China University of Geosciences, Wuhan, China

Members

Jiang Wu   Wuhan University, China
Shangui Hu   Ningbo University of Finance & Economics,
                                    China
Yating Peng   China University of Geosciences, Wuhan, China
Jing Wang   China University of Geosciences, Wuhan, China
Qian Zhao   China University of Geosciences, Wuhan, China

International Advisory Board

Chairs

Joey George   Iowa State University, USA
Robert Kauffman   Copenhagen Business School, Denmark
J. Christopher Westland   University of Illinois at Chicago, USA

Pacific Asian

Patrick Chau   Beijing Normal University-Hong Kong Baptist
                                    University United International College (UIC),
                                    China
Guoqing Chen   Tsinghua University, China
Wei Kwok Kee   National University of Singapore, Singapore
Feicheng Ma   Wuhan University, China
Jiye Mao   Renmin University, China
Michael D. Myers   University of Auckland, New Zealand
Bernard Tan   National University of Singapore, Singapore
Kanliang Wang   Renmin University, China
Nilmini Wickramasinghe   Deakin University, Australia
Kang Xie   Sun Yat-sen University, China
Qiang Ye   University of Science and Technology of China,
                                    China
J. Leon Zhao   City University of Hong Kong, China

North American

Bob Carasik	Wells Fargo Bank, USA
Yili (Kevin) Hong	University of Miami, USA
Zhangxi Lin	Texas Tech University, USA
Ning Nan	University of British Columbia, Canada
Paul A. Pavlou	University of Houston, USA
Arun Rai	Georgia State University, USA
Xinlin Tang	Florida State University, USA
Richard Watson	University of Georgia, USA
Christopher Yang	Drexel University, USA
Han Zhang	Georgia Institute of Technology, USA
Zhongju Zhang	University of Arizona, USA

European

David Avison	ESSEC, France
Niels Bjørn-Andersen	Copenhagen Business School, Denmark
John Qi Dong	Nanyang Technological University, Singapore
Reima Suomi	Turku School of Economics, Finland
Yao-Hua Tan	Vrije Universiteit Amsterdam, The Netherlands
Hans-Dieter Zimmermann	FHS St. Gallen, University of Applied Sciences, Switzerland

Editorial Board of the Proceedings

Yiliu (Paul) Tu (Editor)	University of Calgary, Canada
Maomao Chi (Editor)	China University of Geosciences, China

Advancing Digital Education: Innovations, Challenges, and Opportunities

Xing Wan	Nanjing University of Finance and Economics, China
Jiangnan Qiu	Dalian University of Technology, China
Lin Jia	Beijing Institute of Technology, China

Artificial Intelligence and IoT (AIoT) Enabled Business Innovation

Yaobin Lu	Huazhong University of Science & Technology, China
Ling Zhao	Huazhong University of Science & Technology, China
Jiang Wu	Wuhan University, China

Artificial Intelligence and New Ways of Working

Yi Wang	Southwestern University of Finance and Economics, China
Yuan Sun	Zhejiang Gongshang University, China
Si Shi	Southwestern University of Finance and Economics, China
Jindi Fu	Hangzhou Dianzi University, China

Computing and Complexity in Digital Platforms

Guoyin Jiang	University of Electronic Science and Technology of China
Xiaodong Feng	Sun Yat-sen University, China
Wenping Liu	Hubei University of Economics, China

Data Science and Smart Social Governance

Dongxiao Gu	Hefei University of Technology, China
Jia Li	East China University of Science and Technology, China
Yiming Zhao	Wuhan University, China
Ying Yang	Hefei University of Technology, China
Shuping Zhao	Hefei University of Technology, China
Xiaoyu Wang	First Affiliated Hospital of Anhui University of Chinese Medicine, China

Digital Enablement and Digital Governance

Zhongyun (Phil) Zhou   Tongji University, China
Yongqiang Sun   Wuhan University, China
Xiao-Ling Jin   Shanghai University, China
Zhenya "Robin" Tang   University of Northern Colorado, USA
Qun Zhao   Ningbo University, China
Wei Hu   Tongji University, China

Digital Innovation and Social Impact

Xiaobo (Bob) Xu   Xi'an Jiaotong-Liverpool University, China
Weiyong Zhang   Old Dominion University, USA
Fei Ma   Chang'an University, China

Disruptive Technologies and Digital Transformation

Ping Wang   Central China Normal University, China
Xiuyan Shao   Southeast University, China
Cong Cao   Zhejiang University of Technology, China
Peter Shi   Macquarie University, Australia
Yiran Li   Zhejiang University of Technology, China

E-Business Strategy and Online Marketing

Xiaoling Li   Chongqing University, China
Lu Wang   Zhongnan University of Economics and Law,
                              China
Qing Huang   Chongqing Technology and Business University,
                              China

Emerging E-Commerce Initiatives Enabled by Advanced Technologies

Rong Du   Xidian University, China
Hongpeng Wang   Lanzhou University, China
Peng Wang   Northwestern Polytechnical University, China

Emerging Technologies and Social Commerce

Shaobo Wei   Hefei University of Technology, China
Xiayu Chen   Hefei University of Technology, China
Hua Liu   Anhui University, China
Jinmei Yin   Nanjing University of Aeronautics and
                          Astronautics, China

Engaging Technologies

Nannan Xi   Tampere University, Finland
Hongxiu Li   Tampere University, Finland
Juho Hamari   Tampere University, Finland
Juan Chen   Anhui University of Finance and Economics,
                          China

Healthcare Service and IT Management

Zhaohua Deng   Huazhong University of Science & Technology,
                          China
Tailai Wu   Huazhong University of Science & Technology,
                          China
Jia Li   East China University of Science and Technology,
                          China

Human-Computer/AI Interactions

Haichao Zheng   Southwestern University of Finance and
                          Economics, China
Yuxiang Zhao   Nanjing University of Science and Technology,
                          China
Bin Zhu   Oregon State University, China
Bo Xu   Fudan University, China
Kai Li   Nankai University, China

Information Systems and Operations Management

Hefu Liu	University of Science and Technology of China, China
Meng Chen	Soochow University, China
Zhao Cai	University of Nottingham Ningbo, China
Yuting Wang	Shanghai University, China
Liangqing Zhang	Chongqing University, China
Yao Chen	Jiangsu University of Science and Technology, China

Transformative Digital Innovations: Education, Sports, and Entertainment

Zhao Du	Beijing Sport University, China
Ruoxin Zhou	University of International Business and Economics, China
Shan Wang	University of Saskatchewan, Canada
Fang Wang	Wilfrid Laurier University, Canada

Best Paper Award and Journal Publication Committee

Chairs

Yiliu (Paul) Tu	University of Calgary, Canada
Maomao Chi	China University of Geosciences, China

Members

Alain Chong	University of Nottingham Ningbo China, China
Chris Yang	Drexel University, USA
Chris Westland	University of Illinois at Chicago, USA
Doug Vogel	Harbin Institute of Technology, China
Patrick Chau	Beijing Normal University-Hong Kong Baptist University United International College (UIC), China
Jun Wei	University of West Florida, USA
John Qi Dong	Nanyang Technological University, Singapore

Weiguo (Patrick) Fan   University of Iowa, USA
Wen-Lung Shiau   Chang Gung University, Taiwan RoC

Sponsoring Journals (alphabetical order)

Electronic Commerce Research
Electronic Commerce Research and Applications
Electronic Markets-The International Journal on Networked Business
Internet Research
Journal of Database Management
Journal of Organizational and End User Computing
International Journal of Networking and Virtual Organizations
Journal of Systems and Information Technology

Contents – Part II

Analyzing Influence of Epidemic Policy Adjustment on Public Concerns and Emotional Feedback Using the ABSA Approach

Wei Zhang[1], Nian-xi Yang[1], Chen-guang Li[2(✉)], and Jing Li[3]

[1] School of Information, Central University of Finance and Economics, Beijing 100081, China
[2] School of Insurance, Central University of Finance and Economics, Beijing 100081, China
kddzw@163.com
[3] Business School, Beijing Normal University, Beijing 100875, China

Abstract. Based on the aspect-based sentiment analysis (ABSA), this paper proposed a topic clustering extension method that integrated LDA topic information and BERT context information, constructed the topics and their keyword sequences of microblog comments related to the epidemic policy, and obtained different emotional polarity of those comments on different aspects. Then, based on the Smith policy implementation process model, an empirical model was built to explore the mechanism of different factors in the process of epidemic policy implementation on public emotion. The results turned out that: (1) With the adjustment and optimization of the epidemic policy, the public emotional feedback showed a temporary peak of positive emotion first, followed by a gradual disappearance or a stronger peak of negative emotion; (2) At different stages of epidemic policy, the public concerns were different, but the negative emotion was overwhelming; (3) In the process of the epidemic policy implementation, the construction of medical resources environment was of great significance. The low accessibility of epidemic prevention resources could significantly weaken the performance of personal health protection self-efficacy and indirectly trigger negative emotion; (4) The comprehensive effectiveness of information content and the timely accuracy of information quality could indirectly promote positive emotional feedback by enhancing the self-efficacy for health protection of target groups and improving the government image.

Keywords: Aspect-based Sentiment Analysis · Epidemic Policy · Public Emotion · Public Health Emergencies

1 Introduction

As a major public health emergency in recent years, the COVID-19 epidemic has had a great impact on human society, economy, and life. The joint effect of the high uncertainty of the COVID-19 pandemic, continuous adjustment of the epidemic policy, and fast spreading of negative emotion has increased the complexity and difficulty of emergency management. Further, the adjustment and promulgation of epidemic policies have stimulated corresponding emotional feedback (He & Zhang, 2023), which has been directly

© The Author(s), under exclusive license to Springer Nature Switzerland AG 2024
Y. P. Tu and M. Chi (Eds.): WHICEB 2024, LNBIP 516, pp. 1–13, 2024.
https://doi.org/10.1007/978-3-031-60260-3_1

related to people's willingness to comply with these measures (Liang et al., 2021) and thus affected the implementation of epidemic policies. Therefore, the analysis of the public emotional feedback under different policies plays a key role in guiding the continuous refinement of policy formulation, and ultimately ensuring the efficient implementation of policies. However, most of the existing studies on public emotion in health emergency scenarios have only focused on the impact of the crisis events themselves on public emotion, and few studies have considered the impact of the related policy formulation on emotion adjustment (Sukhwal & Kankanhalli, 2022; Wen & Zheng, 2022).

Therefore, this paper takes the policies of the Chinese government related to the COVID-19 epidemic as the object, adopts the aspect-based sentiment analysis (ABSA), constructs the public concerns and aspect terms, and insights the characteristics of the public emotional feedback in different concern aspects at different stages. Then, based on the Smith policy implementation process model, an empirical model is constructed from the interaction between the implementation object, the target group and the policy environment to explore the impact of epidemic policy adjustment on public emotion.

2 Related Work

2.1 Aspect-Based Sentiment Analysis

The main difference between the generic sentiment classification methods and ABSA is that the latter emphasizes aspect-specific sentiment judgments using contextual contexts associated with aspects (Brauwers & Frasincar, 2022). Although the recurrent neural network-based classification algorithms for automatic extraction of semantic information have achieved good results in aspect-level sentiment classification tasks in recent years, both the discrete vector represented by one-hot and the distributed vector represented by word2vec belong to the static word embedding methods and thus suffer from certain disadvantages, including the inability to achieve multiple meaning disambiguation (Jian et al., 2020). To this end, many studies have proposed post-training methods that use the domain knowledge obtained using the BERT model in the MLM (masked language modeling) and NSP (next sentence prediction) tasks to construct a domain-adapted BERT model (Wu & Ong, 2021). Further, the study in (Hu et al., 2023) constructed an aspect-level sentiment classification task using a single-sentence classification by constructing auxiliary sentences in a sentence-pair classification task; the experimental results showed that the classification performance was significantly improved.

2.2 Public Emotion During COVID-19

In the face of the COVID-19 epidemic, most related researches conducted only the topic analysis without measuring the public emotion in different aspects. Given that, several studies have constructed the LSTM-RNN models and used the fine-grained sentiment calculation models to improve the classification performance (Jangid et al., 2018). However, there has still been an assumption that a single text expresses a single sentiment on a single topic, which will cause the loss of emotion information and bias in the sentiment classification (Brauwers & Frasincar, 2022). The study in (Jang et al., 2021) conducted the LDA topic extraction and manual review by domain experts and then conducted the aspect-level sentiment analysis using the ABSA method. Based on their work, Dutta et al. clustered the text using the K-means algorithm and then used the MCDM technique to identify aspect terms based on different features of each cluster.

These literatures provide a theoretical reference for our work, but are deficient in the following: (1) the two types of tasks, emotion classification and topic identification, were isolated, making it difficult to analyze the causes of emotion triggering and transmission, and to effectively improve and refine current prevention policies based on the development of emotions and topics. (2) Most of the current studies focused on the emotional impact of the crisis events themselves on the public and its feedback characteristics, while, there was a paucity of research on the role of government policy in influencing public emotional feedback during epidemic events (Sukhwal & Kankanhalli, 2022). Therefore, we attempt to integrate deep learning models with ABSA algorithms to enhance the classification effectiveness and improve the rationality and accuracy of epidemic policy formulation.

3　Construction of Aspect-Word Lexicon for Microblog Comments

We propose a BERT word vector model that contains deep bidirectional contextual information and designs a scheme for building an aspect-word lexicon that incorporates LDA topic information, BERT semantic extension, and K-means clustering. Our proposed model includes six key steps:

(1) Extract topic information from the original corpus using the LDA model and obtain the topic probability distribution vector v_lda as follows:

$$v\_lda_i = [t_{i1}, t_{i2}, \ldots \ldots, t_{ik}] \tag{1}$$

where t_{ij} denotes the probability that the text i is the topic j and k is the number of topics.

(2) Obtain the sentence representation vector containing contextual information of the original corpus through the BERT pre-training model.

$$v\_bert_i = [w_{i1}, w_{i2}, \ldots \ldots, w_{im}] \tag{2}$$

where v_bert_i is the pooler_output of the BERT's pre-trained model, which is usually used to represent the sentence vector of the whole sentence, and m is the number of hidden layers.

(3) The v_lda and v_bert are weighted and spliced to obtain $v\_ldabert$; Based on the LDA topic information, the context semantic information in BERT is fused to realize semantic extension.

$$v\_ldabert_i = \lambda \cdot v\_lda_i \oplus v\_bert_i \tag{3}$$

where λ is used to adjust the weight of topic information and context information.

(4) Input the splicing vector into the *AutoEncoder* to achieve dimensionality reduction and obtain a low-dimensional latent space representation z, such that $x = v\_ldabert$.

$$z = f(W^{(1)}x + b^{(1)}) \tag{4}$$

$$\hat{x} = f(W^{(2)}x + b^{(2)}) \tag{5}$$

$$MinimizeLoss = dist(x, \hat{x}) \tag{6}$$

where $W^{(*)}$, $b^{(*)}$ are the learning parameters, x is the high-dimensional input vector, z is the low-dimensional hidden variable, and $\hat{x}$ is the reduced output variable; by minimizing the loss function, the model keeps learning so that $\hat{x}$ reconstructed by the low-dimensional hidden variable z is infinitely close to the initial input variable x.

(5) Input the low-dimensional hidden variable z into the K-Means algorithm to cluster the topic words and obtain corresponding keywords under the topic.

(6) Finally, by crawling local epidemic policy and the comments on the official microblogs, the aspect words and corresponding keyword lists are obtained by manual screening, merging or stratification according to the idea of progressive refinement.

Using the above algorithm, we obtained 7 topics, 12 aspects and related keywords for the "Dynamic Zero-COVID" stage (in Table 1), and obtained 8 topics, 13 aspects and keywords for the "Orderly-Release" stage.

Table 1. Aspect-word lexicon of "Dynamic Zero-COVID" stage (partial)

Topic	Aspect	Keywords
0: Anti-epidemic policies	Anti-epidemic policies	Anti-epidemic policy; Sealing; Silence;…
	Government work	Government leadership; Epidemiological survey; Screening; Delivery…
	Grassroots management	Community; Sub-district; Property management; Stay-at-home…
	Containment scope	Area; End lockdown; Extension; Cross-zone; Risk zone division; Low risk…
1: Nucleic acid policies	Necessity of nucleic acid testing	Swab; Cancel; Test; Mass nucleic acid test; Invalid; Negative nucleic acid results…
	Convenience of nucleic acid testing	Nucleic acid sites; Time limit; Test results…
2: Health code policies	Health code policies	Pop-ups; Sweeping Code; Assignment Code; Transfer Code; Place Code…

(continued)

Table 1. (*continued*)

Topic	Aspect	Keywords
3: Isolation policies	Isolation policies	Quarantine; Residence; Square cabin; Negative; Entry; Red code; Isolation…
4: Information disclosure	Information content	Social side; Tracks chain; Details Explanation causes; Risk sites; Zero-covid…
	Information quality	Update time; Delay; Underreporting; Notification; Number of cases; Rumor; …
5: Livelihood guarantee	Livelihood guarantee	Delivery service; Recovery; Life support; Dispatch; Public transport…
6: Vaccination	Vaccination	Vaccine; Infection inhalation; Virus…

The aspect-word lexicon showed that the two stages had commonalities and differences in terms of the concerns of the public. In terms of commonality, public concerns were consistently expressed during the epidemic management process, such as feedback on anti-epidemic policies, government work, livelihood guarantee, necessity and convenience of nucleic acid testing, health code policies, information content and quality, and vaccination. In terms of differences, aspects related to specific control measures occurred in the public concerns in the control phase, such as grassroots management, containment scope, and isolation policies. However, these aspects were no longer widely considered and discussed in the liberalization stage. Instead, aspects more relevant to the new anti-epidemic situation occurred, such as drug guarantee, medical care guarantee, personal health protection, and health protection of special populations.

4   Emotion Analysis of Aspect-Level Microblog Comments

This study uses the BERT-pair-ABSA model with auxiliary sentence semantic extension to construct auxiliary sentences. In addition, by using keyword sequences to extend the semantics of auxiliary sentences, this study introduces more context-specific prior knowledge into the BERT model, which assists the pre-trained BERT model to focus on specific aspects of a text more comprehensively and precisely.

As shown in Fig. 1, the model contains three modules: sentence-pair conversion module, downstream fine-tuning module of the BERT model, and prediction module that uses the fine-tuned model.

Given a certain microblog comment, the BERT-pair-ABSA model could extract the aspects mentioned in the comment, judge the corresponding sentiment polarity, and compute the probability prediction values of different emotions. Based on this result, first, this paper sets the positive sentiment polarity judgment to 1, the negative to -1, and

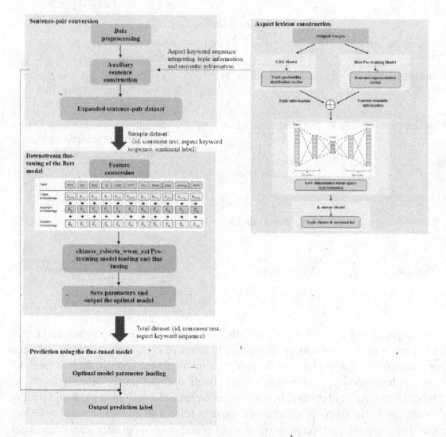

Fig. 1. Flowchart of BERT-pair-ABSA model with semantic expansion of auxiliary sentences

the neutral to 0. Second, we argue that the greater the sentiment prediction probability, the stronger the sentiment of the comment on the aspect can be represented to some extent, so it is: the emotion value of the comment on the aspect = sentiment polarity judgment*the corresponding sentiment prediction probability. This gives us the emotion score.

In addition, the range of the emotion value is $(-1, 1)$, the larger the emotion value, the higher the positive sentiment of the comment on the aspect, the higher the public satisfaction with it; the smaller the emotion value, the higher the negative sentiment of the comment on the aspect, the lower the public satisfaction with it.

5 Theoretical Model and Hypotheses

5.1 Theoretical Model

Smith was the first to construct the policy-implementing-process framework, which included four core variables, namely, idealized policy, implementing organization, target group and environmental factors (Smith, 1973). He argued that policy implementation was a process in which these four factors interacted, and the resulting public feedback on the policy, and especially the conflicts or tensions it generated, drove policy formulation for further optimization and refinement. Inspired by Smith's work, focusing on the implementation of epidemic policies, our research framework (in Fig. 2) was proposed to investigate the specific relationships between the implementation object, the target group and the policy environment, and public emotion, and to reveal the impact mechanism of different factors on public emotional feedback.

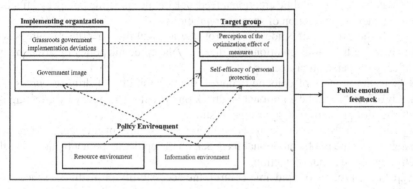

Fig. 2. Theoretical model framework

5.2 Model Hypotheses

Impact of Epidemic Policy Implementation Deviations on Public Emotion. Flores (2017) argued that the symbolic and mechanical implementation by the grassroots government will cause the target group's perception of the implementation effect of policy measures to deviate from the expected goal of the policy, thus causing the negative public emotional feedback. In the process of responding to the COVID-19 epidemic, the deviations of policy implementation by grassroots implementation entities will also affect the public perception of the optimization effect of the closure and control scope in the prevention and control management area. Based on this, this paper puts forward the following hypothesis:

H_0: In the process of epidemic control, the deviations of the epidemic policy implementation by the grass-roots management will cause the negative emotional feedback of the public on the epidemic policy by destroying the target group's perception of the optimization effect of the "containment scope".

Impact of Individual Self-efficacy on Public Emotion. Self-efficacy refers to an individual's presumed judgment or confidence in his or her ability to accomplish a behavior, and is also a core indicator of an individual's self-management ability (Tri Sakti et al., 2021). This paper argues that the self-efficacy of target groups for personal protection and special populations protection in the context of the epidemic will influence the public emotional feedback on the epidemic policy. In addition, self-efficacy depends on the difficulty of the task, the level of effort exerted, the amount of outside assistance received, and the situational conditions for achievement. Based on this, this paper argues that the basic livelihood security and adequate accessible medical resources are the foundation for individuals to carry out health protection work. Therefore, this paper puts forward these following hypotheses:

H_{1a}: In the process of epidemic control, the completeness of basic livelihood security will ultimately affect the public emotional feedback on the epidemic policy by affecting the self-efficacy for personal protection.

H_{1b}: In the process of epidemic control, the completeness of basic livelihood security will ultimately affect the public emotional feedback on the epidemic policy by affecting the self-efficacy for protection of special populations.

H_{2a}: In the process of epidemic control, the accessibility of drug resources will ultimately affect the public emotional feedback on the epidemic policy by affecting the self-efficacy for personal protection.

H_{2b}: In the process of epidemic control, the accessibility of drug resources will ultimately affect the public emotional feedback on the epidemic policy by affecting the self-efficacy for protection of special populations.

H_{2c}: In the process of epidemic control, the accessibility of medical services will ultimately affect the public emotional feedback on the epidemic policy by affecting the self-efficacy for personal protection.

H_{2d}: In the process of epidemic control, the accessibility of medical services will ultimately affect the public emotional feedback on the epidemic policy by affecting the self-efficacy for protection of special populations.

H_{2e}: In the process of epidemic control, the accessibility of vaccination will ultimately affect the public emotional feedback on the epidemic policy by affecting the self-efficacy for personal protection.

H_{2f}: In the process of epidemic control, the accessibility of vaccination will ultimately affect the public emotional feedback on the epidemic policy by affecting the self-efficacy for protection of special populations.

At the same time, the increase of online drug purchase has made the logistics and transportation in livelihood security more closely related to drug security, therefore, this paper proposes the following hypotheses:

H_{2g}: In the process of epidemic control, the completeness of basic livelihood security will affect the self-efficacy for personal protection by affecting the accessibility of drug resources, and ultimately affect the public emotional feedback on the epidemic policy.

H_{2h}: In the process of epidemic control, the completeness of basic livelihood security will affect the self-efficacy for protection of special populations by affecting the accessibility of drug resources, and ultimately affect the public emotional feedback on the epidemic policy.

Impact of Information Notification on Public Emotion. Emotional cognitive information theory suggests that information is an important trigger for emotion generation. Comprehensive and effective information content and timely and accurate information quality provide people with the necessary information to better judge the epidemic situation and risk perception. Therefore, this paper proposes the following hypotheses:

H_{3a}: In the process of epidemic control, the effectiveness of the content of the information notification will ultimately affect the public emotional feedback on the epidemic policy by affecting the self-efficacy for personal protection.

H$_{3b}$: In the process of epidemic control, the effectiveness of the content of the information notification will ultimately affect the public emotional feedback on the epidemic policy by affecting the self-efficacy for protection of special populations.

H$_{3c}$: In the process of epidemic control, the timely and accurate quality of information notification will ultimately affect the public emotional feedback on the epidemic policy by affecting the self-efficacy for personal protection.

H$_{3d}$: In the process of epidemic control, the timely and accurate quality of information notification will ultimately affect the public emotional feedback on the epidemic policy by affecting the self-efficacy for protection of special populations.

The government can establish a good image of itself by timely releasing information related to crisis events to share crisis information with the public (Nimmi et al., 2022). We think that the more comprehensive and effective the information content released by the government and the timelier and more accurate the quality of information communication under the epidemic, the more it helps shaping a good government image, which ultimately affects the public policy emotion. Therefore, this paper proposes the following hypotheses:

H$_{4a}$: In the process of epidemic control, the effectiveness of the content of the information notification will ultimately affect the public emotional feedback on the epidemic policy by influencing the image of the government.

H$_{4b}$: In the process of epidemic control, the timely and accurate quality of information notification will ultimately affect the public emotional feedback on the epidemic policy by influencing the image of the government.

The conceptual model is shown in Fig. 3.

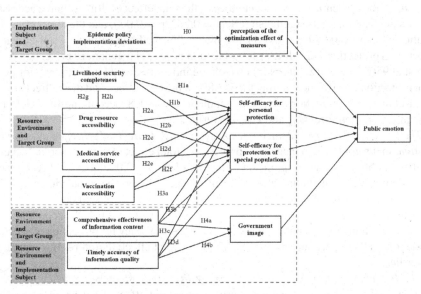

Fig. 3. Research model

5.3 Empirical Analysis

This paper uses the sequential test and Bootstrap test to test the mediating effects, and the empirical results are as follows.

Impact Mechanism of Epidemic Policy Implementation Deviation on Public Emotion. The total effect of *epidemic policy implementation deviation* on *public emotion* is not significant (*effect* $= -0.097, p = 0.090$) and the direct effect is not significant (*effect* $= -0.031, p = 0.588$); however, the mediating effect of *the perception of the effect of measure optimization* passes the test at the 95% confidence interval, and the indirect effect value is 0.066, which suggests that *the perceived effect of measure optimization* plays a full mediating role in the path of the effect of *epidemic policy implementation deviation* on *public emotion*. H_0 is verified.

Impact Mechanism of Individual Self-efficacy on Public Emotion. *The Influence Path of Livelihood Security Completeness - Individual Self-efficacy - Public Emotion.* In the epidemic management process, the total effect of livelihood security completeness on public emotion is significant (effect $= 0.355$, p $= 0.000$) and the direct effect is significant (effect $= 0.265$, p $= 0.000$); meanwhile, the mediating effects of self-efficacy for personal protection and self-efficacy for protection of special populations pass the test at 95% confidence interval, in which the indirect effect value of self-efficacy for personal protection is 0.085, accounting for 23.94% of the total effect; the indirect effect value of self-efficacy for protection of special populations is 0.005, accounting for 1.41% of the total effect; therefore, H_{1a} and H_{1b} are verified.

The Influence Path of Drug Resource Accessibility - Individual Self-efficacy - Public Emotion. In the epidemic management process, the total effect of drug resource accessibility on public emotion is significant (effect $= 0.202$, p $= 0.000$) and the direct effect is significant (effect $= 0.089$, p $= 0.001$); meanwhile, the mediating effects of self-efficacy for personal protection, self-efficacy for protection of special populations protection pass the test at 95% confidence interval, in which the indirect effect of self-efficacy for personal protection is 0.105, accounting for 51.98% of the total effect, and the indirect effect of self-efficacy for protection of special populations is 0.008, accounting for 3.96% of the total effect; therefore, H_{2a} and H_{2b} are verified.

The Influence Path of Medical Service Accessibility - Individual Self-efficacy - Public Emotion. In the epidemic management process, the total effect of medical service accessibility on public emotion is significant (effect $= 0.195$, p $= 0.000$), but the direct effect is not significant; the mediating effects of self-efficacy for personal protection and self-efficacy for protection of special populations pass the test at 95% confidence intervals, where the indirect effect of self-efficacy for personal protection is 0.128, accounting for 65.64% of the total effect, and the indirect effect of self-efficacy for protection of special populations is 0.069, accounting for 35.38% of the total effect; therefore, H_{2c} and H_{2d} are verified.

The Influence Path of Vaccination Accessibility - Individual Self-efficacy - Public Emotion. In the epidemic management process, the total effect of vaccination accessibility on public emotion is significant (effect $= 0.303$, p $= 0.000$) and the direct effect is significant (effect $= 0.175$, p $= 0.001$); meanwhile, the indirect effects of self-efficacy for personal protection and self-efficacy for protection of special populations pass the test at 95% confidence interval, in which the indirect effect value of self-efficacy for personal protection is 0.109, accounting for 35.97% of the total effect; the indirect effect value of self-efficacy for protection of special populations is 0.019, accounting for 6.27% of the total effect; therefore, H_{2e} and H_{2f} are verified.

The Influence Path of Livelihood Security Completeness - Drug Resource Accessibility - Individual Self-efficacy - Public Emotion. Based on the above mediation models, this paper further verifies the influence paths of livelihood security completeness - drug resource accessibility - *individual self-efficacy* - public emotion through the chain mediation model using the sequential test and Bootstrap test. Therefore, H_{2g} and H_{2h} are verified.

Impact Mechanism of Information Notification on Public Emotion. *The Influence Path of Information Content - Public Emotion.* The total effect of comprehensive effectiveness of information content on public emotion is significant (effect $= 0.365$, p $= 0.000$), but the direct effect is not significant (effect $= 0.045$, p $= 0.143$); meanwhile, the mediating effects of self-efficacy for personal protection and government image pass the test at 95% confidence interval, in which the indirect effect value of self-efficacy for personal protection is 0.063, accounting for 17.26% of the total effect; the indirect effect value of government image is 0.259, accounting for 70.96% of the total effect; while the mediating effect of self-efficacy for protection of special populations doesn't pass the test, so H_{3a} and H_{4a} are verified, and H_{3b} is not verified, and the self-efficacy for personal protection and government image play a full mediating role in the mechanism of the influence of information content on public emotion.

The Influence Path of Information Quality - Public Emotion. The total effect of *timely accuracy of information quality* on *public emotion* is significant (*effect $= 0.391$, p $= 0.000$*) and the direct effect is significant (*effect $= 0.363$, p $= 0.000$*); meanwhile, the mediating effects of *self-efficacy for personal protection* and *government image* pass the test at 95% confidence interval, in which the indirect effect value of *self-efficacy for personal protection* is 0.02, accounting for 5.12% of the total effect; the indirect effect value of *government image* is 0.165, accounting for 42.20% of the total effect; and the mediating effect of *self-efficacy for protection of special populations* doesn't pass the test, so H_{3c} and H_{4b} are verified, and H_{3d} is not verified.

The empirical results showed that the deviations in the implementation of the epidemic policy could cause public negative emotion on the epidemic policy by destroying the target group's perception of the effectiveness of the measures, the basic reason of which was the imperfect incentive system under existing management patterns. Therefore, to change the tendency of government employees to avoid responsibility, prevention and control should reasonably be part of the performance evaluation system of local governments. As for the environmental factor, it was found that the completeness of basic livelihood security, the accessibility of drug resources, medical services and vaccination were of vital importance in the process of epidemic control. Therefore, the government should pay more attention to the construction of medical resources environment to improve the self-efficacy for personal health protection and arouse positive public emotion. For the information environment, we verified the significant impact of information communication on public emotion. To form a good government image and arouse positive public emotion, the government should form a rational information releasing strategy and continuously strengthen the ability to communicate with the public.

6 Conclusion

This paper transformed the ABSA task into a BERT sentence pair task with auxiliary sentence semantic extension; based on the aspect word lexicon, a BERT-pair-ABSA model was constructed to analyze the changes of public concerns on different aspects of the epidemic policy in the phases of "Dynamic Zero-COVID" and "Orderly-Release". Empirical results showed that at the "Dynamic Zero-COVID" stage, the public mainly concerned about the control and management measures such as grassroots management and the scope of closure, and the negative emotion feedback was overwhelming; at the "Orderly-Release" stage, drug safety, medical consultation accessibility, personal protection, and protection of special populations were the public concerns, and the negative emotion always dominated, while personal protection showed a brief positive peak and then turned into negative emotion. At the level of information environment, information content and information quality can indirectly promote the positive feedback of the public by enhancing the self-efficacy for personal health protection of target groups and improving the image of the government.

Our study provides an empirical basis for further improving the precision, intelligence, and timeliness of the management of major public health emergencies.

Acknowledgement. This work was supported by National Natural Science Foundation of China under Grant 71874215, 72061147005, National Social Science Foundation of China under Grant 21BZZ108, and Political Education Special Fund in Central University of Finance and Economics under Grant SZJ2208.

References

Brauwers, G., Frasincar, F.: A survey on aspect-based sentiment classification. ACM Comput. Surv. **55**(4), 1–37 (2022)

Dutta, R., Das, N., Majumder, M., Jana, B.: Aspect based sentiment analysis using multi-criteria decision-making and deep learning under COVID-19 pandemic in India. CAAI Trans. Intell. Technol. **8**(1), 219–234 (2023)

Flores, R.D.: Do anti-immigrant laws shape public emotion? A study of Arizona's SB 1070 using Twitter data. Am. J. Sociol. **123**(2), 333–384 (2017)

He, J., Zhang, Y.: Urban epidemic governance: an event system analysis of the outbreak and control of COVID-19 in Wuhan. China. Urban Studies **60**(9), 1707–1729 (2023)

Hu, Z., Wang, Z., Wang, Y., Tan, A.H.: MSRL-Net: a multi-level semantic relation-enhanced learning network for aspect-based sentiment analysis. Expert Syst. Appl. **217**, 119492 (2023)

Jang, H., Rempel, E., Roth, D., Carenini, G., Janjua, N.Z.: Tracking COVID-19 discourse on twitter in North America: Infodemiology study using topic modeling and aspect-based sentiment analysis. J. Med. Internet Res. **23**(2), e25431 (2021)

Jangid, H., Singhal, S., Shah, R.R., Zimmermann, R. Aspect-based financial sentiment analysis using deep learning. In: Proceedings of the Web Conference, pp. 1961–1966 (2018)

Jian, Z., Li, J., Wu, Q., Yao, J.: Retrieval contrastive learning for aspect-level sentiment classification. Inf. Process. Manage. **61**(1), 103539 (2024)

Liang, G., Zhao, J., Lau, H.Y.P., Leung, C.W.K.: Using social media to analyze public concerns and policy responses to COVID-19 in Hong Kong. ACM Trans. Manag. Inf. Syst. **12**(4), 1–20 (2021)

Nimmi, K., Janet, B., Selvan, A.K., Sivakumaran, N.: Pre-trained ensemble model for identification of emotion during COVID-19 based on emergency response support system dataset. Appl. Soft Comput. **122**, 108842 (2022)

Smith, T.B.: The policy implementation process. Policy. Sci. **4**(2), 197–209 (1973)

Sukhwal, P.C., Kankanhalli, A.: Determining containment policy impacts on public emotion during the pandemic using social media data. Proc. Natl. Acad. Sci. **119**(19), e2117292119 (2022)

Tri Sakti, A.M., Mohamad, E., Azlan, A.A.: Mining of opinions on COVID-19 large-scale social restrictions in Indonesia: public emotion and emotion analysis on online media. J. Med. Internet Res. **23**(8), e28249 (2021)

Wen, H., Zheng, J.: On Differences about public emotion feedback of public policies making in major public health emergencies. J. Beijing Univ. Technol. **22**(06), 49–66 (2022). (Social Sciences Edition)

Wu, Z., Ong, D.C.: Context-guided BERT for targeted aspect-based sentiment analysis. In: Proceedings of the AAAI Conference on Artificial Intelligence, pp. 14094–14102 (2021)

Research on Hybrid Teaching Model of Strategic Management from the Ecological Perspective

Haiyan Ma, Maomao Chi[(✉)], and Fei Yang

China University of Geosciences, Wuhan, Hubei, China
chimaomao111@sina.com

Abstract. The rapid development of digital technology has made the hybrid teaching mode combining online learning and face-to-face teaching a new learning paradigm. In this paper, we firstly sort out the background of the hybrid teaching mode of strategic management. Then from the ecological view, it constructs a hybrid teaching model dominated by the concept of student-centered value co-creation with digital technology as the soft foundation and teachers' professionalism as the hard foundation. Thirdly, the paper takes strategic management course for undergraduate students in context of digital transformation of Chinese education as an example to analyze the course organization of hybrid teaching model. It provides reference for the implementation of hybrid teaching of strategic management and related business courses.

Keywords: Hybrid Courses · Strategic Management · Teaching Model · Ecological Perspective · Value Co-creation

1 Background

Digital technologies have transformed the nature and scope of education [1] and have impacted dramatically on educational philosophies, pedagogical models and teaching methods in higher education. At the same time, versatile and disruptive technological innovations and software applications have opened up new opportunities for advancing teaching and learning. Digital transformation has become a top priority for institutions of higher education [2], and education must adapt to social change and accelerate change to cultivate new generations who will adapt to the future society [3]. The use of digital technology in education has been accelerated during the COVID-19 pandemic in recent years, and in-depth pedagogical reforms are imminent. In the digital age, teaching places, tools, resources, means and forms are diversified, and online learning methods allow teaching behavior to completely escape from the constraints of limited time (teaching hours), cramped space (classroom space), and a single relationship (teacher-student relationship) of traditional offline lectures [4]. However, the natural shortcomings of online education, such as the lack of effective interaction between teachers and students, have also been exposed. The hybrid teaching mode, which integrates the two teaching modes of traditional face-to-face teaching and online learning, has developed rapidly in recent

Y. P. Tu and M. Chi (Eds.): WHICEB 2024, LNBIP 516, pp. 14–24, 2024.
https://doi.org/10.1007/978-3-031-60260-3_2

years and has become a new paradigm and an important development direction for college course teaching [5]. As online teaching is still in the primary stage of development, actively attracting students to participate in online content is an important challenge [6], and effectively integrating multiple resources, organically combining online and offline approaches, and comprehensively applying them to the whole process of teaching poses a challenge to the change of teaching modes in different subject areas.

The analysis of hybrid learning in strategic management courses in this paper focuses on undergraduate students because it represents a greater challenge for hybrid learning at the undergraduate level relative to doctoral and master's students [7]. The construction of a hybrid teaching model is a complex and continuous process, which not only requires the efforts of teachers as the main actors in the construction, but also requires that the various participating subjects involved in the space of the educational field improve their level of digitalization capabilities, supporting the establishment of the necessary culture, policies, and infrastructures to support the effective integration of technology and teaching [8]. Therefore, this paper digs deeper from the perspective of ecosystem to find out how teachers, as one of the subjects, can orchestrate multi-channel and diversified resources with the power of the ecosystem in the context of digital economy in order to better enhance the effectiveness of teaching in the course.

2 Literature Review of Hybrid Teaching Models for Strategic Management

Strategic management is a core, high-end course in business administration. In China, the United States, Europe, Japan and other countries, it is generally listed as the main course of business administration undergraduate teaching. This course is the most comprehensive cross-functional management course in the field of business administration, which centers on the basic problem of how to win the sustainable competitive advantage in the dynamic environment, and trains the students to integrate the knowledge of the three layers of the professional "basic layer, business layer and functional layer", and to creatively solve the problems of overall development of the enterprise, which is a "strategic layer" in the core course system of the profession. It is in the top position of "strategic layer" in the professional core curriculum system, which is of great value to promote the quality of talents and the level of discipline in business administration.

In recent years, the use of technology to empower the teaching of strategic management courses has become a focus of attention in research on the teaching of strategic management courses. The introduction of digital technology will significantly change the traditional way of teaching strategic management courses, provide powerful resource support for "learning-centered" teaching activities, and stimulate students' interest and initiative to actively participate in the whole process of course teaching [9]. Information technologies such as smart devices, Internet, Internet of Things (IoT), Artificial Intelligence (AI), Augmented Reality (AR) and Virtual Reality (VR), Blockchain, etc. enhance creativity, interactivity, collaboration and personalization of teaching and learning in business courses, which helps to improve teaching effectiveness [10].

There are relatively few studies on the construction of hybrid teaching mode of strategic management, and most of them are limited to the micro-environment of course construction. Some studies focus on the value of the hybrid teaching model of strategic management, for example, this model is more able to stimulate students' active thinking and growth, reflecting the initiative, motivation and creativity of students as the main body of the learning process, thus effectively enhancing the depth of students' learning in the strategic management course [11]. Some scholars explore the specific methods of the hybrid teaching mode of the course, such as adopting the teaching method of flipped classroom, combining the online teaching resources of micro-assisted teaching, and implementing online and offline hybrid teaching [12]. Some focus on the design of strategic management hybrid teaching mode, such as reference [13] explored the full-case teaching mode in hybrid teaching and took the case seminar course design of Strategic Management course as an example to explore the possibility of a full-case teaching approach for undergraduate students majoring in business administration. It also establishes a teacher-student and student-student learning community through integrated case teaching methods such as flipped teaching, case analysis, case seminar and inquiry learning. There are also some studies that focus on the effectiveness and factors of online and offline teaching in strategic management course. Other literature discusses the application of specific online platforms in the hybrid teaching mode of the course, such as using MOOC as an online platform, using it as a tool for pre-course basic knowledge learning and homework testing, and combining it with traditional classroom teaching [14]. However, the comprehensive use of online platforms and software, the organization and coordination of the process, and the interactive process are missing. Since the construction of China's MOOC in 2013, a number of online platforms and teaching APPs have been formed such as Tencent Classroom, Tencent Conference, Nail, Superstar Learning Pass, Cloud Classroom, Vocational Education Cloud, Ai Classroom, Rain Classroom, and Mucous University, which provide a wealth of options for hybrid teaching courses. Other literature has analyzed how to organize online teaching modules for strategic management [7], which is valuable for how to organize online teaching in hybrid learning, but it lacks the discussion of how to connect traditional face-to-face teaching with online teaching.

For the time being, the current research is worth pursuing in the following two aspects. First, the relevant studies are less concerned with social and school factors. When societies and schools are inexperienced and digitization capacities are low, this will lead to widening gaps, inequalities and learning losses. Reference [1] shows at the school level that the level of digital technology in a school does not only affect the academic performance of students, but also other aspects related to the school and its stakeholders. Socially relevant factors also affect the use of digital technology in education. These factors are interrelated and play a crucial role in the digital transformation of education. Second, there is an overall lack of theoretical support and pedagogical model construction that guides technology-enabled hybrid teaching of strategic management. There is an urgent need to explore in depth the theoretical framework that reflects the interaction between learners and the technological environment to enhance the effectiveness of the hybrid teaching model of strategic management, and to construct a hybrid teaching model that can give full play to the advantages of multiple subjects and integrate the "before-during-after-class" and the "on-line and off-line".

3 The Construction of a Hybrid Teaching Model for Strategic Management

3.1 The Concept of Value Co-creation in the Teaching Ecosystem

Ecosystem is a synthesis of various environment and other elements, refers to the unity of interaction and interdependence between living and non-living components in a certain time and space, through the continuous cycle of material, energy flow and information transfer. It can also be interpreted as a synthesis between biological communities and their living environment, and is also the combination of the living system and the environment in a specific space combination [15].

The strategic thinking of enterprises in the digital era is "standing in the future and looking at the present", and the teaching of strategic management is characterized by complexity, dynamism, personalization, interactivity and cooperation. The ecological perspective can explain the dynamic development process of strategic management under the technological environment, explore the interaction between learners and the teaching ecosystem environment under the technological support, better reveal the role of the technological environment in the development of strategic management capability, and provide a theoretical framework for the exploration of strategic management teaching and learning in the deep integration of technology and teaching in the digital era.

The teaching ecosystem is student-centered and geared towards student development. In the hybrid teaching model, students' learning gains greater rights in the online environment, while the actual binding force of teachers' teaching decreases. Face-to-face teaching is often based on teachers' involvement in supervision, guidance, and management, aiming to familiarize students with basic knowledge and cognitive patterns. While online learning is built on the basis of students' independent operation of network equipment, resources, platforms, etc., it is a kind of self-awareness-led learning behavior. Therefore, the teaching ecosystem should fully reflect the idea of student-centeredness. The teaching subject serves as the touching factor to promote the smooth operation of the whole teaching ecosystem. The operation and evolution of the teaching ecosystem is a process of value co-creation by the participants society, school, teachers and students. The construction of the teaching ecosystem should be based on the concept of value co-creation, which incorporates the teaching stakeholders such as teachers, students, schools and society into the same ecosystem, so that resources are shared and value is created among the teaching subjects. Specifically, for the strategic management course, this value is reflected in the effective enhancement of students' strategic management knowledge mastery, practical application and innovation ability, as well as the self-cultivation of independent thinking, systematic grasp, and future-oriented development of the big picture.

3.2 Composition and Functioning of the Teaching Ecosystem

From the ecological perspective, the ecology of hybrid teaching needs to focus on the connection between the central subjects in the ecosystem (teachers and students) and the ecological environment of teaching. The ecological environment consists of three parts:

the social macro-environment, the university meso-environment, and the course micro-environment. The hybrid teaching model needs the support of the digital technology environment and the educational environment in the ecological environment, and the soft and hard foundations in the three levels of environment interact with each other (as shown in Fig. 1). This pedagogical model emphasizes the interaction of ecological subjects and the learning actions taken by utilizing dynamic perception and absorbing the ecological givens in the environment. Among the technological givens involved in online teaching are online resource platforms such as catechisms, networks, APPs, and communication software such as emails, WeChat, and Tencent meetings. The learning effect of students will be improved through the combined effect of social environment, universities and courses. The existing teaching environment affects the overall level of the teaching ecology of a course to a greater extent, and strategic management courses are no exception.

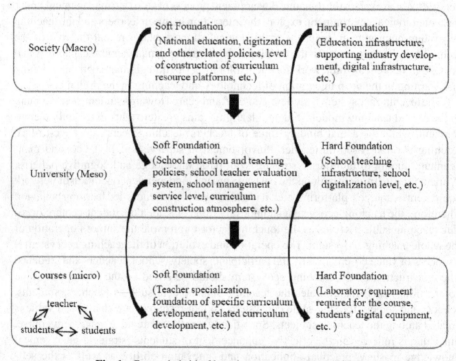

Fig. 1. Course hybrid of learning ecosystem composition

A healthy pedagogical ecology requires the realization of at least three functions. The first is the sharing function. It can realize sharing on a larger scale, especially macro and meso institution building and resource building, such as sharing of educational and teaching resources among universities in the same region, institutions of the same type or programs of the same type, so as to promote common development. The second is the enabling function. The stronger the enabling capacity of the teaching ecology, the greater the functional value of the teaching ecology. This empowerment is reflected in the resource empowerment, institutional empowerment, and structural empowerment of educational subjects by society, schools, and teachers in the educational environment, as well as the mutual empowerment between levels and the empowerment of students' dynamic activism to the activation of the whole teaching ecology. The third is the digitalization function. On the one hand, the teaching platform through the digital network responds to teaching needs in a timely manner, realizes real-time communication, timely feedback, improves the convenience of interaction, prompts the teaching process to be more efficient, and also adds interest to classroom teaching and improves the teaching effect. On the other hand, based on the on-line teaching data, it analyzes the learning situation and the teaching situation, assists teachers in discovering the problems, and finds the pain points, so as to provide a basis for reflection and improvement in teaching.

3.3   General Idea of Hybrid Teaching Model of Strategic Management

"Hybrid" in teaching model originates from the technical level, but it will trigger an overall change in the teaching system, such as the integration of independent learning and cooperative learning, the integration of knowledge content of different disciplines, and the integration of online assessment and offline paper-and-pencil tests. Teachers are required to reform the original traditional face-to-face teaching, based on the regular classroom situation, and introduce networked elements appropriately, at the right time and in the right amount. This kind of change is systematic and requires simultaneous adjustments in a number of areas, such as teaching philosophy, teaching arrangements, and teaching evaluation.

Combined with the existing hybrid teaching research and course characteristics, the following ideas are adopted for the hybrid teaching model of strategic management. In terms of teaching concepts, it is necessary to fully realize that online teaching in hybrid teaching is not an auxiliary or icing on the cake of the whole teaching activities, but a necessary activity to enhance the depth of teaching. Offline teaching is not a copy of traditional classroom teaching activities, but a more in-depth teaching activity based on online first exploration. Teaching arrangements are designed according to social and school conditions, while taking advantage of students' online learning and group classes, and their teaching organization is more flexible and versatile. Teaching is individualized and there is no single solution for how to teach strategic management or other subjects [7]. If the teaching model is built on a timeline, it can be roughly divided into three phases: pioneering exploration, collaborative workshop, and expansion and consolidation [16]. The first and third stages belong to the online virtual classroom, and the middle stage is the real classroom. In the assessment and evaluation of students' course learning, hybrid teaching will strip away the previous identity of the teacher as the sole evaluator and incorporate online learning performance. Online grades are directly generated by the system, and students automatically obtain the identity of "self-evaluator" when they receive their course grades. Figure 2 shows the overall concept of hybrid teaching model of strategic management course.

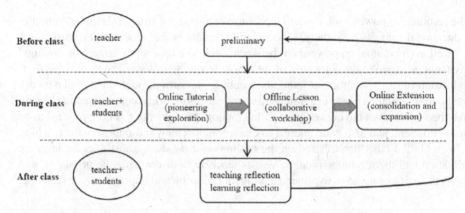

Fig. 2. Overall concept of hybrid teaching model of strategic management course

4   Organizational Practices of the Hybrid Teaching Model of Strategic Management

4.1   Pre-preparation

The preparatory work before the start of the course is mainly the responsibility of the course instructor (or course team). This includes choosing an online teaching platform (or self-built resource platform) and an interactive platform, assigning online and offline tasks, preparing offline course lesson plans, organizing students to complete online preparations before the class, and clarifying the online and offline proportion and standards of students' course assessment.

First, the course instructor needs to understand the course-related online resources currently accessible, including the quantity, quality, content composition covered and their respective characteristics. If the online resources related to the strategic management course are abundant, the course is required to determine the appropriate online teaching resources, such as MOOC, SPOC, etc., according to the characteristics of the student-centeredness and the syllabus arrangement of the strategic management course. If there are no suitable resources, you can choose live broadcast, recorded broadcast or self-built online course platform.

Then, aiming at the teaching objectives and teaching content, according to the teaching arrangement and the degree of difficulty of the knowledge points, determine the online and offline learning tasks of the students as well as the tasks of the teacher's explanations, including the learning objectives and learning content, homework and tests, and so on. For the preparation of online self-tests, according to the availability of online resources and the compatibility with the arrangement of this course, it is clear whether to choose the guided test questions of the existing platform or to create new test questions in addition, with the help of other software such as Rain Classroom and Super Star Learning Channel.

Finally, with the help of the interactive platform to import the course students' information, organize students to do the preliminary preparation for the online course. Teachers can register a course group through WeChat or QQ, and organize students to join the group and divide into groups. Guide students to complete the registration of the online learning platform, and get ready to enter the course. Share the syllabus, teaching calendar and requirements for students of the strategic management course with the course group, so that students know the teaching arrangement of the course.

4.2   Online Guided Learning

This session completes the course introduction through online learning and is set before each offline course. It moves the traditional basic knowledge content taught through classroom lectures forward through online learning, so that students have better knowledge preparation before the teacher's classroom lectures, which contributes to the fun, interactivity and flexibility of the course and improves the quality of classroom teaching. The session is mainly completed by students on their own under the guidance and supervision of the course instructor.

Teachers and students need to cooperate with each other to complete the following three types of activities. First, release guided learning tasks and upload prepared teaching resources to the online teaching platform. Students explore independently and complete the learning tasks within the time limit set by the teacher. Second, organize online discussions and answer questions selectively. Students can take the initiative to raise questions or participate in teacher-initiated question discussions. Third, students complete online self-tests or publish their own comments according to the requirements, and the teacher follows up the learning situation to understand the learning progress and learning status.

In terms of specific steps, we make the following attempts. First, the teacher releases introductory materials on the online learning platform in accordance with the teaching plan, including textual reading materials, video materials and case materials, and requires students to complete the reading of the relevant textbooks and materials, video viewing and case analysis in accordance with the prescribed schedule. Then, the teacher guides the positive feedback of students' online situation through various ways. For example, with the help of online learning platforms and course groups to interact with classmates, guiding the sharing of their own learning gains, discussing the process of watching the video and answering each other's questions about doubts encountered during the pre-course practice. On this basis, the instructor uses the online learning platform to check the students' learning situation, combines the discussion and interaction, organizes the important and difficult points in the online learning of this part of the course, and improves the preparation of classroom lectures and the teaching program in a timely manner in order to achieve better teaching results.

4.3   Offline Lectures

Offline learning should give full play to the face-to-face advantages of the offline classroom, and be accomplished through the interaction between the classroom teachers and students. This part is still student-centered and problem-oriented, and electronic whiteboards, multimedia courseware and micro-course videos are introduced appropriately, at the right time and in the right amount for exploratory and collaborative learning, to enhance the interactive effect, guide students to think and grow on their own initiative, improve students' ability to learn independently, and realize the high-level, innovative and challenging course content.

Offline learning mainly consists of the following activities: (i) feedback from teachers on the status of online guided content and help students with targeted error correction; (ii) explain the key difficulties and easy points to help students improve the depth of understanding; (iii) explore higher-order content through interaction; (iv) summarize course content and assign post-course tasks.

There are various ways of doing this in concrete practice, three of which are given as examples. The first is "students speak and students evaluate" and "students speak and teacher evaluates". Students (or groups of students) report on the results of the online guided learning stage, the main course content for logical sorting, put forward doubts and difficulties as well as the solutions that have been tried and the extent to which they have been solved. The teacher explains the evaluation requirements in advance and guides the students to evaluate each other in terms of learning outcomes and depth of learning. Teachers commented on the results of the students according to the display, explaining the key points. The second is seminar debate. The teacher chooses the discussion material that helps students understand the course content and puts forward the debate topic. Students (or groups of students) decide on the arguments and thesis, and start the discussion and debate. The teacher will comment and explain further according to the course content and students' discussion and debate. The third is case study. According to the characteristics of the strategic management course, the teacher provides enterprise-related cases, guides students to analyze the cases step by step, and allows students to create practical opportunities for how to apply what they have learned in the simulated situation, in order to deepen students' mastery and application of the course knowledge and improve students' ability to analyze and solve problems. All of the above methods involve student discussions, in which the teacher plays the role of organizer, question-answerer, corrector and summarizer. For complex problems, teachers can divide them into several interrelated problems to improve the depth and effectiveness of group discussions.

4.4 Post-course Extensions

The aim of this session is to overcome forgetfulness, consolidate and sublimate what has been learned, and enhance the ability to transfer knowledge. It is mainly guided by the teacher and completed by students on their own. Learning resources such as videos, texts and PPTs on the web platform can be reused indefinitely, which is conducive to students' review of incompletely mastered and forgotten content to strengthen their cognition. Teachers release extended inquiry tasks and post-class practice assignments through the online platform, which can be used to formatively assess students' learning effects [16].

The main content covered includes teachers issuing post-class study tasks and test questions, organizing discussions and Q&A sessions if necessary, and collecting and analyzing learning feedback. Correspondingly, students complete the materials on the online platform or independent study, complete self-tests, find solutions to problems they have doubts about, and improve their study plans.

4.5 Reflection on Teaching and Learning

The instructor or course team analyzes the effectiveness of the hybrid teaching model, and reacquaints and rethinks the various aspects of the hybrid teaching model to improve the design of a new round of instruction. The college often provides a template for this type of teaching reflection, which needs to be filled out and submitted for filing. Students summarize their learning reflections in text or video through course performance, course grades and course gains, and upload them to the online course teaching platform.

5 Conclusion

In the process of digitization of education, hybrid teaching is the mainstream mode of future school curriculum implementation in colleges and universities. Compared with traditional classroom teaching, hybrid teaching has strong complexity, uncertainty and non-linear characteristics, and has higher requirements for both hard and soft environments. From the ecological perspective, this paper emphasizes the necessity and importance of the hybrid teaching model of strategic management, builds a student-centered value co-creative concept dominant, and analyzes the organization and practice of the hybrid teaching mode of strategic management on the basis of the comprehensive consideration of the influencing factors of the teaching ecosystem of the three levels of the society, the university and the curriculum, so as to provide reference for the implementation of the hybrid teaching of the strategic management and the related business courses.

Acknowledgement. We am particularly thankful to the editor and anonymous reviewers for their constructive comments and suggestions. We are grateful for funding support from the China University of Geosciences (Wuhan) Undergraduate Teaching Reform Research Program (2021G56) and Hubei Provincial Teaching Research Project (2021146).

References

1. Timotheou, S., Miliou, O., Dimitriadis, Y., et al.: Impacts of digital technologies on education and factors influencing schools' digital capacity and transformation: a literature review. Educ. Inf. Technol. **28**, 6695–6726 (2023)
2. Kuzu, Ö.H.: Digital transformation in higher education: a case study on strategic plans. High. Educ. Russia **29**(3), 9–23 (2020)
3. Ma, L.T.: Accelerating the digitization of education to build a strong education nation. China Education News (2022). (in Chinese)
4. Liu, X., Li, C.W., Jiang, X.: Research on blended teaching mode of college courses based on network environment. Yanshan University Press, Hebei (2021). (in Chinese)
5. Hu, F.L.: Application of TBL pedagogy in a blended online and offline teaching and learning arena in higher education. Jiangsu Sci. Technol. Inf. **22**, 74–77 (2023). (in Chinese)
6. Green, R., Whitburn, L., Zacharias, A., et al.: The relationship between student engagement with online content and achievement in a blended learning anatomy course. Anat. Sci. Educ. **11**(5), 471–477 (2018)

7. King, D.R., Sizemore, A.: Strategic management in online and hybrid courses. In: Teaching Strategic Management. Sabine Bauman (ed). Edward Elgar: Chettenham: UK, UK (2020)
8. Costa, P., Castaño-Muñoz, J., Kampylis, P.: Capturing schools' digital capacity: psychometric analyses of the SELFIE self-refection tool. Comput. Educ. **162**(3), 1–15 (2021)
9. Jiang, Y., Zhu, Q.: An exploration of teaching methods in digital technology-enabled strategic management courses. J. Educ. Modernization **11**(89), 32–35 (2021). (in Chinese)
10. Liu, W.W., Zhang, J., Hou, N.: Exploring the construction and development of teaching ecological resilience of graduate courses under the new coronavirus epidemic--Taking the course of "Strategic Management of Enterprises" as an Example. Forestry Education in China (S01), 10–14 (2020). (in Chinese)
11. Wang, T.N.: Research on blended teaching mode of "online-offline + flipped classroom"– taking enterprise strategic management course as an example. J. High. Educ. **28**, 114–117 (2022). (in Chinese)
12. Xue, J.G.: Reform and practice of blended first-class curriculum based on OBE concept-taking "Strategic Management" course as an example. Educ. Teach. Forum **23**, 145–148 (2023). (in Chinese)
13. Zhao, Z.X., Chen, J.: Design of a full case teaching mode based on online and offline blended teaching - an example of a case seminar in strategic management course. Educ. Modernization **6**(92), 196–198 (2019). (in Chinese)
14. Li, Y.Y.: Study on promoting the hybrid teaching of "Enterprise Strategy Management" by MOOC. Jiangsu Sci. Technol. Inf. **3**, 49–51 (2021). (in Chinese)
15. Begon, M., Colin, R.T., Harper, J.L.: Ecology-From Individuals to Ecosystems. 4nd edn. Higher Education Press, Beijing (2016)
16. Zhu, X.M.: Blended learning, a new model for the future organization of teaching in schools. China Education News (2019). (in Chinese)

Investigating the Impact of Cultural Tourism NFTs' Perceived Value and Experiential Evaluation on WOM of a Tourism Destination: A Generational Difference Moderation Approach

Yuchen Zhao and Yihong Zhan[✉]

National Research Center of Cultural Industries, Central China Normal University, Wuhan 430079, China
zyh@ccnu.edu.cn

Abstract. As an emerging thing, Non-Fungible Token (NFT) has been used in the tourism sector to attract new customers and promote destinations. However, there is a challenge in how cultural tourism NFT's perceived value influences the experiential evaluation of customers, and induces their WOM on the destination. Additionally, the attitude of generational differences on cultural tourism NFT is unknown. Therefore, this study aims to identify the effects of cultural tourism NFTs' perceived value on destination WOM. Drawing on S-O-R framework, a conceptual model has been proposed to examine the perceived value of cultural tourism NFT (functional, monetary, social, and emotional) on destination WOM through experiential evaluation. The generational difference was assumed as a moderator (i.e., Millennials and Generation Z). The model was tested by data collected from Dunhuang NFT users (N = 383). The results indicate that perceived functional, monetary, and emotional value could improve destination WOM through experiential evaluation, while perceived social value of cultural tourism NFT has no significant impact on experiential evaluation. Meanwhile, the findings reveal that Millennials show more positive destination WOM than Generation Z after they experience cultural tourism NFTs. This study provides valuable insights into the relationships between cultural tourism NFTs and destination WOM.

Keywords: Non-Fungible Token Marketing · Cultural Tourism · Perceived Value · Generational Difference

1 Introduction

The transformative impact of technology on e-commerce and online marketing, specifically through blockchain and the Metaverse, has been monumental. Among the cutting-edge applications in this technological revolution, Non-Fungible Tokens (NFTs) emerge as the most mature innovations [1].

© The Author(s), under exclusive license to Springer Nature Switzerland AG 2024
Y. P. Tu and M. Chi (Eds.): WHICEB 2024, LNBIP 516, pp. 25–36, 2024.
https://doi.org/10.1007/978-3-031-60260-3_3

In the cultural tourism sector, these tokens, empowered by blockchain, serve as a certification of authenticity and ownership for digital content like virtual tours, artwork, historical artifacts, and cultural experiences. Beyond merely contributing to the digital economy of destinations, cultural tourism NFTs can serve as creative showcases, establishing and strengthening connections with visitors. For instance, Xi'an's Datang Everbright City successfully leveraged NFTs in its Metaverse project, releasing 3D models based on the rich history and culture of the Tang Dynasty. These NFTs were well-received and sold out in seconds.

While the literature on NFT marketing has seen substantial growth, there exists a gap regarding cultural tourism NFTs. NFTs are widely used in cultural tourism scenarios and scholars have focused on the promise of NFTs for destination marketing. However, current research findings are limited to narrative outlooks and speculations and lack empirical evidence. Furthermore, unlike general branded NFTs, such as those from Nike or Coca-Cola [2], cultural tourism NFTs intricately intertwine with a destination's cultural significance, featuring creatively designed elements based on local legends, symbols, and art. This distinction implies variations in marketing values compared to other NFT types.

Moreover, the current literature lacks emphasis on the potential bias of NFT marketing effectiveness across generations. As emerging blockchain-based products, NFTs may be interpreted differently based on individuals' varied growth backgrounds. Consequently, there is a need for more literature to explore the influence of generational differences on NFT marketing.

To address these gaps, this study constructs a theoretical model incorporating the Stimulus-Organism-Response (SOR) model, perceived value theory, and generational theory. Employing Dunhuang NFTs as an illustrative example, the study aims to unravel how the perceived value of cultural tourism NFTs contributes to positive destination Word-of-Mouth and whether generational differences act as a potential moderator. The research not only contributes novel insights to the NFT marketing literature but also provides valuable scientific guidance for destination marketers.

2 Literature Review

2.1 NFT Marketing

NFT marketing refers to any form of marketing practice in which a brand utilizes NFTs to cultivate and strengthen brand-customer relationships [3]. This emerging trend has prompted scholars to explore the correlation between the values and attributes of NFTs and their impact on brand marketing outcomes. Lee et al. discovered that the scarcity, financial value, uniqueness, and reputation attributes of NFTs can enhance consumer's brand commitment by influencing brand attitude [2]. Sung et al. pointed out that for luxury brand NFTs, the social value, economic value, authenticity, and scarcity of NFTs contribute to promoting luxury goods purchases, whether in the metaverse or reality [4]. Xie et al. considered the informational value, entertainment value, uniqueness value, and expressive value of NFTs. Using three fashion brand NFTs as the research context, they found a positive association between these values and brand WOM [5].

Regarding the identification of values and attributes of NFTs, the theoretical approaches in relevant literature vary, primarily based on results from text mining, Ducoffe's advertising model, and discussions within specific contexts. The current state of research encourages us to explore the value of NFTs based on additional theoretical frameworks and to integrate these frameworks comprehensively within the studied contexts.

Regarding the context of NFT marketing, the current literature covers various consumer goods industries, including the fashion and luxury sectors. However, this suggests a lack of attention in the literature towards NFTs within the service industry, particularly in the cultural tourism sector. Some scholars have proposed the significant role of NFT in building tourist loyalty to destinations, but empirical testing of this assertion is still pending [6]. Based on this research gap, we try to explore the role of NFTs for destination WOM in cultural tourism.

In addition, it is noted that moderating variables have to some extent received limited attention in the literature. Some scholars have focused on the fact that NFTs may be more appealing to young people [5], yet no in-depth research has been conducted on the mechanisms of user behavior from the perspective of generational differences. Therefore, we intend to study the differences in NFTs-related behaviors between Generation Z and Millennials.

2.2 SOR Model

The SOR model, rooted in environmental psychology, conceptualizes the environment as consisting of stimuli (S) capable of influencing and modifying individuals' internal or organismic states (O). Subsequently, these internal states activate either approach or avoidance responses (R) from individuals [7].

In the realm of information systems, SOR offers a valuable framework for understanding how stimuli in the digital environment influence users' internal states and subsequently shape their responses, providing insights into user behaviors, adoption patterns, and system usability [8].

In the context of tourism management, the SOR model proves instrumental in examining the interplay between environmental stimuli within tourist destinations, the internal states of tourists, and their subsequent behavioral responses. This application allows researchers and practitioners to explore factors influencing tourist satisfaction, loyalty, and engagement, offering a comprehensive perspective on the dynamics that drive success in the tourism industry [9].

In our context, NFTs are characterized as both information products and tourist stimuli. After experiencing NFTs, consumers form an integrated evaluation of the NFTs and the destination and develop subsequent loyalty behaviors, which validate the organism and the response. Therefore, the SOR model is well suited for our analysis to explore how NFTs stimulate interest and influence internal states, thus providing insights into their potential impact on tourism experience and behavior.

2.3 Perceived Value Theory

Perceived value is the overall utility value of a product or service as perceived by the customer. In the marketing literature, perceived value is a multidimensional concept that can be relative and contextual, as well as cognitive and affective.

Regarding the dimensioning of perceived value, widely applied in the tourism domain is the research framework by Sweeney and Soutar, commonly known as PERVAL [10]. Its original version included quality value, price value, emotional value, and social value. Scholars normally modify the PERVAL framework to better align with the evolving nature of their research subjects. This adaptability showcases the framework's versatility in accommodating diverse contexts.

In the current study, the selection of the PERVAL framework to examine perceived value is deliberate, as it comprehensively encompasses various characteristics inherent to cultural tourism NFTs. These features include investment characteristics, entertainment characteristics (i.e., design aesthetics and cultural interaction), social tools, and the function introduced by blockchain technology. Moreover, PERVAL's allowance for partial revision of values ensures a holistic exploration of the multiple dimensions of the perceived value of cultural tourism NFTs.

3 Hypotheses Development

The conceptual model of the study is shown in Fig. 1. First, using the modified PERVAL framework, we identified four perceived values as the stimulus (S) that cultural tourism NFTs generate for consumers. Second, experiential evaluation was identified as an organismic variable (O) because it responds to the consumer's internal state of the destination. Third, consumers' WOM intention toward the destination was used as a response (R). In addition, we considered the potential impact of generational differences on the marketing effectiveness of NFTs.

3.1 Perceived Value of Cultural Tourism NFT

Cultural tourism NFTs are digital credentials generated based on blockchain technology corresponding to the cultural works, artworks, and scenic resources of a specific cultural tourism destination, which can fully demonstrate the cultural connotation and creative value of the destination. According to the PERVAL framework, we modified it to better fit the scenarios of cultural and tourism NFTs. Functional, emotional, and social value are retained, while price value is replaced with financial value. This is due to the consideration that many people engage in NFTs to take advantage of investment opportunities rather than to consume them as reasonably priced products.

Functional value is defined as the utility derived from the perceived performance and quality of a product [10]. In the case of NFTs, functional value may include attributes such as decentralized features, ownership of unique tokens, security, and smart contracts [11]. Furthermore, especially for cultural tourism NFTs, they can be linked with e-tickets, membership benefits, and points exchange, thus generating greater practical utility.

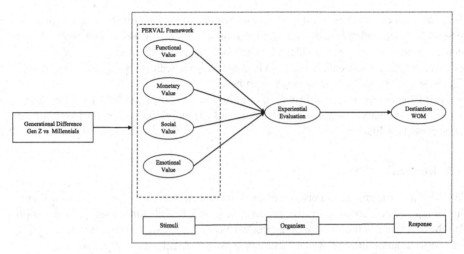

Fig. 1. Research model

Monetary value implies the utility of the exchangeable currency and a worthwhile investment opportunity [2]. The pricing and secondary market of NFTs have been of interest to scholars in the field of finance. Existing evidence suggests that market prices of NFTs issued by highly reputable agents are more promising [12]. For cultural tourism NFTs, their distributors are usually well-known tourist attractions or destinations, ensuring that NFTs can provide incentives to purchasers steadily.

Social value can be defined as the relational value of a product in the form of social acceptance and recognition by and of others [10]. Owners of cultural tourism NFTs can not only communicate with and show off their NFTs to the NFT community but also display their treasured NFTs to friends and fellow travelers of a particular destination.

Emotional value is the utility derived from the various emotional states that arise when interacting with goods and services [10]. The aesthetic value of cultural tourism NFT collections, their specific artistic, cultural, and other relevant characteristics are examples of features that can influence the emotional value. It may also come from a perception of novelty or uniqueness, which is often valued by consumers.

3.2 Experiential Evaluation

Experiential evaluation can be defined as the evaluation of interactions with a brand, including contact with brand representatives, products and services, exposure to brand advertising, product reviews, and branded content marketing [13]. As distinct from satisfaction, this evaluation is based on a variety of consumer experiences related to the product or service, which go beyond direct purchase and use [14]. It can be argued that any experience that is pleasurable, engaging, and memorable is likely to promote positive experience evaluation.

In terms of NFT marketing, NFTs can connect consumers' online and offline experiences to enhance their overall experience of the destination. Xie et al. have demonstrated that perceived exclusivity and perceived financial benefits of fashion brand NFTs can facilitate experience evaluation [13]. In the current study, functional value can provide people with the understanding that destinations value security and visitor rights. Monetary, social, and emotional values can provide people with physical benefits and a positive psychological state, which can lead to favorable feelings toward the destination. Therefore, we propose the following hypotheses:

H1: Consumers' perceived value of cultural tourism NFTs, including (a) functional value, (b) monetary value, (c) social value, and (d) emotional value, positively affect experiential evaluation.

3.3 Destination WOM

WOM is a communication between one person and another in which one person shares his or her opinion about a service, product, or brand. In the tourism sector, destination WOM is defined in the same way as product WOM. It is used to describe the tendency of people to share their views and feelings about a particular destination with others.

Prior literature has demonstrated that consumer values and emotional experiences have an impact on people's willingness to engage in WOM. For instance, Xie et al. found that consumers' evaluations of NFTs as informative, entertaining, and unique promote brand WOM behavior [5]. Nieves-Pavón et al. found a significant positive association between people's positive emotions about smart destinations and their WOM intention about the destination [15]. Hence, experiential evaluation, a concept that reflects people's value judgments and emotional feelings, may have a similar effect on destination WOM:

H2: Experiential evaluation positively affects people's participation in destination WOM.

3.4 Generational Differences

Generational theory emphasizes that both personal and social factors during a person's formative years have an impact on his or her decisions today. Generation Z (Gen Z) has been the most intriguing research subject for scholars in recent years due to their novel decision-making processes and behavioral styles. Gen Z is generally considered to have been born in the 1997–2012 period and acquires knowledge primarily through the Internet and quick information searches [16].

The literature suggests that Gen Z has more positive acceptance and engagement behaviors with new technologies compared to Millennials [17]. Scholarly investigations have highlighted that Gen Z exhibits a markedly different orientation towards technology compared to preceding generations, notably the Millennials. Unlike Millennials, who witnessed the advent of digital technology and adapted to it, Gen Z individuals have been immersed in digital environments from a very young age, leading to a naturalized integration of technology into their daily lives. Consequently, they display heightened comfort, proficiency, and enthusiasm in engaging with novel technological innovations. As an emerging technology, NFTs have spawned a host of unique and innovative products that may appeal to Gen Z. Therefore, we hypothesize that:

H3: Gen Z will respond more positively to cultural tourism NFT marketing compared to Millennials.

4   Methodology

4.1   Data Collection

Dunhuang, selected for research, is a prominent player in China's NFT market, consistently unveiling sought-after NFTs since 2021 in public service projects, digital collections, and NFT tickets. This positions Dunhuang as an ideal case to explore how NFTs can enhance destination WOM.

We conducted an online survey targeting Chinese NFT users through social media platforms like Weibo and WeChat. A pilot study with 54 participants tested the reliability, clarity and consistency of the Chinese translation. The formal survey, conducted in October 2023, consisted of three parts. After a brief study overview and obtaining consent, respondents were presented with the definition of cultural tourism NFTs and four Dunhuang NFT examples with concise introductions from actual campaigns. Attention-check questions ensured respondent focus. The second part involved answering items aligned with research hypotheses based on experiences with these NFTs. The final part gathered demographic information, familiarity with Dunhuang, NFT experience, and primary NFT-following channels. Finally, a total of 383 valid responses were used for the analysis.

4.2   Measurement

All measures of constructs were adapted from existing research to fit the context of NFTs, and a 7-point Likert scale was employed.

The four perceived values relied on Sweeney & Soutar's PERVAL scale and were modified according to the practical characteristics of cultural tourism NFTs and the results of text mining for NFT values by Yilmaz et al. [11]. Experiential evaluation was measured by three items, based on the study by Xie et al. [13]. Destination WOM was measured by three items, adapted from Xie and Muralidharan's study on brand WOM [5].

4.3   Data Analysis

Due to the relatively small size of our sample, PLS-SEM was employed to perform measurement model tests, structural model test, and multigroup analysis.

In terms of the common method bias (CMB), Harman's single-factor test indicated that the percentage of variance extracted from a single factor was 41.32%, which is below the critical value of 50%. In addition, the VIF for all items was below the critical value of 3.3. Therefore, CMB was not a concern.

To justify the reliability of the data, Cronbach's α values of all items were above 0.7. To test for convergent validity, the outer loadings of all items exceeded 0.7, and the composite reliability (CR) and average variance extracted (AVE) exceeded the thresholds of 0.7 and 0.5, respectively (see Table 1). For discriminant validity, our data adopted the Fornell-Larcker criterion and the square root of AVE for each construct was greater than the inter-construct correlations. Moreover, the HTMT values of the data were in the range of 0.494 to 0.770, which is below the critical value of 0.9 by the HTMT method. It can be suggested that our data have good reliability and validity.

Table 1. The results of the data's reliability and validity.

Construct	Items	Loading	Cronbach's α	CR	AVE
Functional value	FV1	0.789	0.810	0.875	0.636
	FV2	0.800			
	FV3	0.778			
	FV4	0.822			
Monetary value	MV1	0.865	0.811	0.888	0.725
	MV2	0.837			
	MV3	0.852			
Social value	SV1	0.811	0.819	0.881	0.648
	SV2	0.824			
	SV3	0.799			
	SV4	0.786			
Emotional value	EV1	0.766	0.821	0.882	0.651
	EV2	0.815			
	EV3	0.809			
	EV4	0.836			
Experiential evaluation	EE1	0.828	0.792	0.878	0.706
	EE2	0.829			
	EE3	0.863			
Destination WOM	WOM1	0.851	0.768	0.866	0.684
	WOM2	0.800			
	WOM3	0.828			

5 Result

5.1 Structural Model

Including age, gender, education, income, NFTs experience, and destination familiarity as control variables, we tested the structural model through 5000 bootstrap cases. The results (see Table 2) revealed that H1a ($\beta = 0.206$, p = 0.009), H1b ($\beta = 0.309$, p = 0.000), H1d ($\beta = 0.342$, p = 0.000) and H2 ($\beta = 0.271$, p = 0.001) were supported. For H1c, the effect of social value on experiential evaluation was not significant ($\beta = -0.026$, p = 0.600). Of the control variables, only destination familiarity ($\beta = 0.303$, p = 0.000) had a significant positive effect on destination WOM.

The R-square of 0.507 for experiential evaluation and 0.266 for destination WOM implies a good explanatory strength of the model. The Q-square for experiential evaluation and destination WOM was 0.485 and 0.268, respectively, which indicates good predictive ability.

Table 2. The results of structural model.

Path	β	p-value	Result
H1a: Functional value → Experiential evaluation	0.206	0.009	Support
H1b: Monetary value → Experiential evaluation	0.309	0.000	Support
H1c: Social value → Experiential evaluation	−0.026	0.600	Not support
H1d: Emotional value → Experiential evaluation	0.342	0.000	Support
H2: Experiential evaluation → Destination WOM	0.271	0.001	Support

5.2 Multigroup Analysis

To validate the impact of generational differences on NFT marketing, we divided the data into Gen Z (N = 145) and Millennials (N = 229) based on age.

Following Matthews's procedure, a three-step measurement invariance of the composite model (MICOM) was first analyzed with permutation multigroup analysis [18]. In the first step, configural invariance was confirmed by using identical indicators, data treatment, and algorithm settings. In the second step, compositional invariance was verified, requiring that the original correlation be greater than or equal to the 5% quantile. The results showed that all the constructs except functional value were recognized to have no compositional differences. In the third step, partial measurement invariance was established for one of the two above (mean or variance original difference) falls between the 2.5% and 97.5% boundaries. Hence, our model met the criteria for further multigroup analysis.

β-diff indicated the difference in path coefficients for the group Gen Z - Millennials (see Table 3). For H1a-H1d, we did not observe significant differences between the two groups, suggesting that Gen Z and Millennials are similar in terms of perceived value. However, for H2, the impact of experiential evaluation on destination WOM is significantly weaker for Gen Z than for Millennials (β-diff = −0.283, p = 0.033). This finding provides evidence to the contrary for H3, suggesting that Millennials tend to respond more positively to NFT marketing compared to Gen Z.

Table 3. The results of multigroup analysis.

Path	β-diff	p-value	Result
H1a: Functional value → Experiential evaluation	−0.023	0.840	Not support
H1b: Monetary value → Experiential evaluation	−0.011	0.926	Not support
H1c: Social value → Experiential evaluation	0.008	0.934	Not support
H1d: Emotional value → Experiential evaluation	0.103	0.478	Not support
H2:Experiential evaluation → Destination WOM	−0.283	0.033	Support

6   Discussion and Conclusion

6.1 Discussion

With the basis of the SOR model, we investigated how the perceived value of cultural tourism NFTs contributes to people's intention to engage in WOM about the destinations and reached some interesting insights.

First, we identified that emotional value has the strongest effect on user experience. This echoes previous literature on NFTs, emphasizing that people's perception and consumption of NFTs are emotionally driven [5, 11]. The prominence of emotional value underscores the profound impact that affective factors hold in shaping users' overall engagement and satisfaction with NFTs.

Second, we indicated that functional value and monetary value are important drivers in experiential evaluation. These values correspond to extensively researched aspects of NFTs, specifically, the financial attributes of NFTs and the underlying blockchain technology. Our study further suggests that the marketing function of NFTs is also closely tied to these fundamental attributes of NFTs.

Third, our study revealed a surprising finding: the social value of cultural tourism NFTs did not exert a significant influence on experiential evaluation. This is a deviation from the results of previous studies [13], especially for the fashion brand NFTs [5, 13]. This outcome may be attributed to the nature of cultural tourism NFTs. Unlike fashion brand NFTs, the value of cultural tourism NFTs could be rooted more in their intrinsic cultural and historical significance, rather than their social status or recognition within the community.

Fourth, the results demonstrate a significant relationship between experiential evaluation and destination WOM. This outcome highlights the role of experiential aspects in influencing individuals to share their impressions, recommendations, and opinions about a destination [19]. The experience with cultural tourism NFTs can be viewed as a virtual connection to the destination. Consequently, a positive and enriching experience tends to foster a greater inclination for individuals to exhibit loyal behavior towards that destination.

Finally, contrary to our initial expectations, the results revealed that Millennials are more inclined to form destination WOM than Gen Z after experiencing NFTs. Millennials, having experienced the transition from traditional forms of tourism to the emerging trend of enhanced experiences, may attribute higher value to these novel encounters.

This heightened perceived value could motivate them to share their experiences more extensively, fostering destination WOM. Generation Z, having been exposed to NFTs as part of their digital landscape, might not perceive the same level of novelty or uniqueness in these experiences, potentially affecting their motivation to engage in destination WOM. Moreover, existing literature designates Millennials as the most frequent visitors to cultural consumption destinations. Their WOM tendencies and previous loyalty behaviors may offer an explanation for their more favorable response to cultural tourism NFT experiences [20].

6.2 Theoretical and Managerial Implications

Integrating the SOR model, NFT marketing, perceived value theory, and generational theory, the current study makes several contributions. First, it extends the application of SOR by showcasing its adaptability for investigating user behavior in metaverse marketing. The linkage of perceived value, experiential evaluation, and WOM offers a comprehensive explanation of the impact of online marketing on real-world user behavior. Second, the study enriches the NFT marketing literature by examining the perceived value of cultural and tourism NFTs, a specific NFT subtype. We reveal that social value may not be a critical aspect of NFT marketing that must provide. Third, the study introduced generational theory into NFT marketing. We focused on the differences between Millennials and Gen Z and revealed that Millennials are more likely to develop destination WOM during NFT experiences. This discovery encourages further research on the interplay between NFT marketing and generational, gender, social, and cultural factors.

Based on our findings, we recommend that destinations adopting NFT marketing strategies prioritize the development of aesthetic and cultural connotations in NFTs to heighten their emotional value for users. Moreover, we advocate for interactive design elements, such as the incorporation of augmented reality (AR) and virtual reality (VR), enabling users to engage with destination attractions through NFTs. Finally, our study highlights that Millennials are more likely to respond positively to cultural tourism NFT marketing. Hence, destination marketers should, in addition to younger groups, consider establishing NFT marketing channels tailored specifically for middle-aged and younger groups such as Millennials. Focusing on their preferences could be a significant opportunity for NFT marketing success.

Acknowledgement. This research was supported by the National Social Science Fund of China under Grant 22CH188.

References

1. Lin, K.J., Ye, H., Law, R.: Understanding the development of blockchain-empowered metaverse tourism: an institutional perspective. Inf. Technol. Tourism **25**(4), 1–19 (2023)
2. Lee, C.T., Ho, T.-Y., Xie, H.-H.: Building brand engagement in metaverse commerce: the role of branded non-fungible tokens (BNFTs). Electron. Commer. Res. Appl. **58**, 101248 (2023)
3. Chohan, R., Paschen, J.: NFT marketing: how marketers can use nonfungible tokens in their campaigns. Bus. Horiz. **66**(1), 43–50 (2023)

4. Sung, E., Kwon, O., Sohn, K.: NFT luxury brand marketing in the metaverse: Leveraging blockchain-certified NFTs to drive consumer behavior. Psychol. Mark. **40**(11), 2306–2325 (2023)
5. Xie, Q., Muralidharan, S., Edwards, S.M.: Who will buy the idea of non-fungible token (NFT) marketing? Understanding consumers' psychological tendencies and value perceptions of branded NFTs. Int. J. Advertising 1–29 (2023)
6. Ioannidis, S., Kontis, A.-P.: Metaverse for tourists and tourism destinations. Inf. Technol. Tourism **25**(4), 1–24 (2023)
7. Mehrabian, A., Russell, J.A.: An Approach to Environmental Psychology. The MIT Press (1974)
8. Chen, C.-C., Yao, J.-Y.: What drives impulse buying behaviors in a mobile auction? The perspective of the Stimulus-Organism-Response model. Telematics Inform. **35**(5), 1249–1262 (2018)
9. Nieves-Pavón, S., López-Mosquera, N., Jiménez-Naranjo, H.: The factors influencing STD through SOR theory. J. Retail. Consum. Serv. **75**, 103533 (2023)
10. Sweeney, J.C., Soutar, G.N.: Consumer perceived value: the development of a multiple item scale. J. Retail. **77**(2), 203–220 (2001)
11. Yilmaz, T., Sagfossen, S., Velasco, C.: What makes NFTs valuable to consumers? Perceived value drivers associated with NFTs liking, purchasing, and holding. J. Bus. Res. **165**, 114056 (2023)
12. Vasan, K., Janosov, M., Barabási, A.-L.: Quantifying NFT-driven networks in crypto art. Sci. Rep. **12**(1), 2769 (2022)
13. Xie, Q., Muralidharan, S.: It's a comparison game! The roles of social comparison, perceived exclusivity and perceived financial benefits in non-fungible token marketing. J. Res. Interact. Mark. **18**(2), 294–314 (2023). (ahead-of-print)
14. Wu, H.-C., Cheng, C.-C.: Relationships between experiential risk, experiential benefits, experiential evaluation, experiential co-creation, experiential relationship quality, and future experiential intentions to travel with pets. J. Vacat. Mark. **26**(1), 108–129 (2020)
15. Nieves-Pavón, S., López-Mosquera, N., Jiménez-Naranjo, H.: The role emotions play in loyalty and WOM intention in a smart tourism destination management. Cities **145**, 104681 (2024)
16. Szymkowiak, A., et al.: Information technology and Gen Z: the role of teachers, the internet, and technology in the education of young people. Technol. Soc. **65**, 101565 (2021)
17. Pichler, S., Kohli, C., Granitz, N.: DITTO for Gen Z: a framework for leveraging the uniqueness of the new generation. Bus. Horiz. **64**(5), 599–610 (2021)
18. Matthews, L.: Applying multigroup analysis in PLS-SEM: A step-by-step process. In: Latan, H., Noonan, R. (eds.) Partial least squares path modeling, pp. 219–243. Springer, Cham (2017). https://doi.org/10.1007/978-3-319-64069-3_10
19. Bastos, W., Moore, S.G.: Making word-of-mouth impactful: why consumers react more to WOM about experiential than material purchases. J. Bus. Res. **130**, 110–123 (2021)
20. Kim, D.-Y., Park, S.: Rethinking millennials: how are they shaping the tourism industry? Asia Pac. J. Tourism Res. **25**(1), 1–2 (2020)

Study on the Path of Enhancing Agricultural Insurance Consumption in the Context of Digital Innovation Through fsQCA Method

Shuhang Guo and Jiapeng Yang[✉]

School of Information, Central University of Finance and Economics, Beijing 102200, China
y2585321336@163.com

Abstract. The current demand for agricultural insurance is insufficient and of low quality. And in the current context of digital innovation, a new market ecology has been created, alleviating the original problems of information asymmetry, low financial availability and high transaction costs. It provides new opportunities to increase consumption of agricultural insurance. To address the question of what combination of conditions can increase agricultural insurance consumption, we focus on six influencing factors of agricultural insurance consumption. The fuzzy set qualitative comparative analysis method is used to identify the group state paths that promote the increase of agricultural insurance consumption in the context of digital innovation. Through configuration analysis, we derive three paths to increase agricultural insurance consumption: autonomy-driven, internally and externally driven, and externally technology-assisted. On this basis, we then put forward relevant policy recommendations with a view to protecting the healthy development of the agricultural economy by increasing agricultural insurance consumption.

Keywords: Digital Innovation · Agricultural Insurance Consumption · Configuration Analysis

1 Introduction

As a large agricultural country, China's primary industry is the backbone of its national economy. The development of the agricultural economy is not only crucial to the smooth operation of the national economy, but also of great significance to the social stability of China. Most activities of agricultural production relying on natural resources such as sunlight and water, agriculture is a high-risk and vulnerable industry. The existence of agricultural insurance can effectively diversify the risk of natural disasters for farmers, to a certain extent, reducing the economic losses of agricultural production.

At present, the development of agricultural insurance in China covers many aspects and has developed into the largest agricultural insurance market in the world [1]. However, the development of agricultural insurance mainly relies on national policy subsidies and support, facing the serious problem of insufficient demand and low development quality. The willingness of farmers to take out insurance and the participation rate in all regions are at a low level, which to a certain extent limits the high-quality development of agricultural insurance. While in the current context of digital innovation, Internet finance, big data technology, e-commerce supply chain finance and other innovations are developing rapidly, which alleviates the previous problems of low financial accessibility and information asymmetry. This enables agricultural insurance to circulate in a wider market, providing new opportunities to promote the development of agricultural insurance consumption.

To summarize, we carry out research on the question of what combination of conditions can increase agricultural insurance consumption. Referring to existing research on digital finance and agricultural insurance consumption and other related topics, we focus on six influencing factors of agricultural insurance consumption (development of digital finance, scale of agricultural production, agricultural insurance compensation expenditure, disposable income of farmers, government support for agriculture, and vigor of digital innovation). We use panel data from 31 provinces across China from 2011–2020 and apply the fuzzy set qualitative comparative analysis (i.e., fsQCA) method to identify the grouping paths that contribute to the increase in agricultural insurance consumption. We hope to reveal the development and change paths of agricultural insurance consumption in the context of digital innovation, and promote the improvement of agricultural insurance consumption and the development of agricultural economy.

2 Literature Review

The current research on the influencing factors of agricultural insurance involves many aspects and is relatively complex. Summarizing the theoretical research on agricultural insurance consumption by scholars at home and abroad, we can classify its influencing factors into four dimensions: external environment dimension, individual farmer dimension, agricultural production dimension and insurance company dimension. The most discussed factors are as follows.

2.1 Digital Finance and Agricultural Insurance Consumption

The development of digital finance will play a contributing role in the improvement of agricultural insurance consumption [2]. The popularization of the Internet enables farmers to access more insurance information and knowledge. It enhances farmers' awareness of risk management while increasing financial availability. At the same time, the development of digital finance makes it possible to solve the problem of information asymmetry in the agricultural insurance market [3]. Higher level of agricultural insurance cognition and wind management awareness with more accurate information delivery improves farmers' consumption of agricultural insurance. Digital finance drives the development of rural e-commerce, digital agriculture and other new models in rural areas, effectively alleviating the borrowing constraints of low-income groups, which plays an important role in promoting rural economic growth [4] and improving the consumption of financial services. In addition, the development of digital finance relying on digital technology, which significantly saves labor costs. It changes the past insurance products can only rely on telephone, door-to-door and other channels to sell the situation, reducing the price of insurance products and improving the availability of insurance products and services [5]. Therefore, digital finance can improve agricultural insurance consumption.

2.2 Production Scale and Agricultural Insurance Consumption

The development of digital technologies such as the Internet of Things, big data and artificial intelligence technology can help agricultural enterprises achieve large-scale production and management and improve the level of agricultural industrialization. Changes in the scale of agricultural production are directly related to food security and stable social and economic development [6]. And the expansion of the scale of agricultural production means that the losses borne by farmers will be correspondingly greater in the event of a natural disaster. Therefore, it will indirectly increase the consumption and demand of farmers for agricultural insurance. U.S. agricultural production practice shows that for most farmers, larger regional agricultural yield insurance is more effective in resisting yield fluctuations than individual farm yield insurance [7]. The larger the scale of agricultural production, the relatively greater the risks faced by farmers. Large-scale agricultural production requires more capital and resources to be invested. The losses will be more serious if they are hit by natural disasters, diseases or other unforeseen events. As a result, large-scale farmers pay more attention to agricultural insurance to reduce risks and protect their investments [8]. Therefore, the expansion of agricultural production scale helps to increase agricultural insurance consumption.

2.3 Claims Expenditure and Agricultural Insurance Consumption

Agricultural insurance claims expenditure refers to the amount of claims paid by insurance companies to farmers or agricultural producers in the agricultural insurance business, which directly reflects the insurance company's ability and capacity to pay claims in the field of agricultural insurance. The larger the claims expenditure of agricultural insurance, the higher the claim payment ability and reliability of the insurance company. Farmers' trust in the insurance company will also increase, believing that the insurance company is able to pay out losses in a timely and comprehensive manner [9]. Therefore, they are more willing to buy agricultural insurance to get support and protection from the insurance company. With digital innovations in rural areas, farmers have improved their ability to access information on financial services as well as related policies. Combined with the herd mentality of farmers purchasing agricultural insurance and the peer effect [10], high payout expenditures for agricultural insurance strengthen farmers' confidence in taking out agricultural insurance and in insurance companies, thus increasing the level of agricultural insurance consumption. Conversely, if insurance payout expenditures are low, farmers may have little knowledge of the existence and effects of agricultural insurance, and thus have a lower willingness to insure. Therefore, an increase in agricultural insurance payout expenditure helps to increase agricultural insurance consumption.

2.4 Disposable Income and Agricultural Insurance Consumption

The disposable income of farmers may have an impact on agricultural insurance consumption in terms of both risk tolerance and willingness to insure. The larger the disposable income, the relatively stronger the economic strength and risk tolerance of farmers

[11]. They are therefore more able to afford agricultural insurance and are willing to purchase insurance to protect themselves against agricultural business risks. The disposable income of farmers is derived from agricultural income. Existing studies divided the types of farm households according to the different share of agricultural income and found that the higher the share of agricultural income, the higher the consumption expenditure of farm households for agricultural insurance [12]. In addition to this, an increase in disposable income may mean that farmers have more money to invest in agricultural production. The higher the disposable income, the more farmers are concerned about the long-term stability and sustainability of agricultural operations, and therefore are more willing to purchase agricultural insurance to protect their investment. Therefore, the increase in disposable income can increase the consumption of agricultural insurance.

2.5 Government Support and Agricultural Insurance Consumption

Agricultural support provided by the government, such as agricultural subsidies, disaster relief, agricultural publicity, can improve the risk tolerance of farmers. Therefore, these incentives can promote the purchase of agricultural insurance by farmers. Current scholars point out that the government's policy subsidies for agricultural insurance can significantly increase the willingness to take out agricultural insurance [13]. And the increase in agricultural insurance consumption and the level of premiums borne by the government are positively correlated. Existing studies have also pointed out that the higher the government subsidies for agricultural insurance premiums, the higher the willingness of farmers to insure [14]. In addition, the government can pass the information of agricultural insurance to farmers through various channels to improve farmers' knowledge and understanding of agricultural insurance. Therefore, the increase in government support for agriculture has a promoting effect on the increase of agricultural insurance consumption.

2.6 Technological Innovation and Agricultural Insurance Consumption

In contrast to the development of digital finance, technological innovation refers to the introduction of new technologies or methods in products, production processes or services to increase efficiency and reduce costs. Technological innovation can provide more accurate risk assessment, more insurance products and lower insurance costs. First, the application of digital technology reduces the cost of farmers' access to information. This can provide more comprehensive data and information and help farmers better assess agricultural risks [15]. In addition, technological innovation can promote the innovation and development of agricultural insurance products and provide diversified insurance products to meet different insurance needs. Third, technological innovation can reduce the cost of agricultural insurance and improve the efficiency and quality of services, for example, by simplifying the claims process to improve service efficiency [16]. Therefore, the more active the technological market innovation, the higher the consumption level of farmers for agricultural insurance.

3   Data Sources and Selection of Variables

3.1   Data Sources

The data used in this paper are obtained from public data sources such as China Rural Statistical Yearbook, Peking University's Digital Finance Research Center, China Insurance Regulatory Commission, National Bureau of Statistics, and relevant statistical reports. To ensure data availability, we select data from 31 provinces during the period 2011–2020 as samples for the study of group effects, excluding Hong Kong, Macao and Taiwan.

3.2   Selection of Variables

Antecedent Variables

Development of Digital Finance. This variable measures the development speed, development trend and development status of digital finance in China. Drawing on the research of existing scholars, we select the Digital Inclusive Finance Index to measure the degree of development of digital finance. The index is a threetier standard system that can completely and accurately measure the level of development of digital finance, established by the Digital Finance Research Center of Peking University in cooperation with Ant Group. It is based on the data about digital finance and mobile payment in the Alipay system.

Scale of Agricultural Production. The area of agricultural land is greatly influenced by geographic environment and policy factors, and the size of the area occupied by each province largely restricts the development of the area of agricultural land. Therefore, we choose the per capita gross agricultural output value of each province as a measure of the size of agricultural production.

Agricultural Insurance Claims Expenditure. We select the data on agricultural insurance claims expenditures in each province released by the China Banking and Insurance Regulatory Commission as the measure of the variable payout expenditures.

Disposable Income. The income of rural residents can be divided into four types according to the source, such as net income from family business, property income and so on. We choose the sum of the four types of income as the measure of this variable.

Government Support for Agriculture. We select the local agriculture, forestry and water affairs expenditure data obtained from the Wind database as well as the provincial finance departments to measure the strength of agricultural policy support in each province.

Technological Innovation. The turnover of the technology market epitomizes China's science and technology-supported economy. Compared to digital financial development, a vibrant technology market constantly spawns IT innovations and promotes the level of informatization in villages. We select the technology market turnover in the China Statistical Yearbook as a measure of technological innovation vitality.

Outcome Variable   Agricultural insurance premium data can visualize the consumption of agricultural insurance by farmers. Because of the different population densities and significant demographic differences among provinces, we calculate the per capita agricultural insurance premiums of farm households by making a ratio between the agricultural insurance premiums published in the website of the China Insurance Regulatory Commission and the total rural population of that year recorded in the China Rural Statistical Yearbook, which serves as a measure of the consumption of agricultural insurance.

Reliability and Validity Analysis In summary, the description of each variable and the descriptive statistical analysis are shown in Table 1 below

Table 1. Descriptive statistical analysis of variables

Variable type	Variable name	Code	Variable measurement	Unit	Mean	Standard deviation	Minimum	Maximum
Outcome variable	Agricultural insurance consumption	AIC	Agricultural insurance premiums	Yuan per person	1.05	3.15	0.01	7.02
Antecedent variables	Development of digital finance	DF	Digital financial inclusion index	–	2.16	0.97	0.16	4.32
	Scale of agricultural production	SA	Agricultural output per capita	Thousand yuan per person	9.81	4.58	1.63	36.92
	Agricultural insurance claims expenditure	CE	Agricultural insurance compensation expenditure	Hundred million yuan	9.44	10.10	0.13	68.03
	Disposable income	DI	Per capita disposable income	Ten thousand yuan per person	12.49	5.49	3.90	34.91
	Government support for agriculture	GS	Government expenditure on agricultural affairs	Trillion yuan per person	5.39	2.72	0.92	13.39
	Technological innovation	TI	Technology market turnover	Ten billion yuan per person	4.03	8.08	0.04	63.17

The reliability and validity tests of all antecedent and outcome variables are shown in Table 2 below. The minimum value of Alpha coefficient of each variable is 0.859. Combined reliability reflects the internal consistency of the indicator, and the minimum value of combined reliability CR is 0.842, which indicates that the reliability of the indicator is good. Minimum value of KMO is 0.875 and minimum factor loading of each variable is more than 0.5. Cumulative variance contribution ratio is more than 70%. Minimum AVE value is 0.553, indicating that the validity of the indicator is good.

Table 2. Reliability and validity analysis

Variables	Alpha	CR	KMO	Cumulative variance contribution	Minimum factor loading	AVE
AIC	0.877	0.890	0.893	71.33%	0.516	0.579
DF	0.929	0.842	0.875	72.51%	0.623	0.590
SA	0.912	0.885	0.932	80.01%	0.562	0.553
CE	0.870	0.921	0.901	78.24%	0.590	0.612
DI	0.859	0.963	0.881	79.09%	0.602	0.674
GS	0.862	0.913	0.905	70.30%	0.634	0.595
TI	0.924	0.877	0.899	82.13%	0.612	0.603

Variable Calibration. Variable calibration transforms the data to the extent that they fit a certain description (full affiliation, intersection, full non-affiliation). There are two types of variable calibration in fsQCA studies, direct and indirect calibration methods. The direct calibration method is usually used for calibration. We selected the anchors for data calibration as 5% quartile, 50% quartile, and 95% quartile, respectively. The variable calibration data are shown in Table 3.

Table 3. Variable skewness, kurtosis and calibration

Variables	Anchor point		
	Full affiliation	Intersection	Full non-affiliation
AIC	0.147	0.670	3.117
DF	0.335	2.235	3.595
SA	3.837	8.867	18.538
CE	0.643	5.755	28.429
DI	5.530	11.626	24.217
GS	1.491	5.014	10.151
TI	0.027	1.078	17.76

4 Configuration Analysis Results

4.1 Necessity Test

Configuration theory needs to consider both necessary and sufficient conditions. In order to explore whether the single factor meets the necessity condition of the outcome variable, we refer to the existing literature and choose the size of the consistency threshold as 0.9

[17]. The test results are shown in Table 4 below. The consistency of all antecedent variables is below 0.9, so there is no necessity condition. The path of increasing agricultural insurance consumption is affected by the combined effect of multiple conditions.

Table 4. Results of necessity test

Variables	High AIC		Low AIC		Variables	High AIC		Low AIC	
	Consistency	Coverage	Consistency	Coverage		Consistency	Coverage	Consistency	Coverage
DF	0.729	0.830	0.508	0.475	~ DF	0.540	0.572	0.819	0.713
SA	0.736	0.788	0.613	0.539	~ SA	0.569	0.642	0.758	0.703
CE	0.786	0.803	0.576	0.484	~ CE	0.495	0.587	0.765	0.746
DI	0.784	0.799	0.602	0.505	~ DI	0.515	0.612	0.761	0.743
GS	0.645	0.699	0.618	0.549	~ GS	0.584	0.650	0.661	0.605
TI	0.770	0.727	0.700	0.543	~ TI	0.515	0.676	0.648	0.698

4.2 Conditional Configuration Analysis

In order to obtain the influencing factor grouping of agricultural insurance consumption enhancement paths, we set the original consistency threshold to 0.8 [18], the minimum coverage sample size to 3, and the PRI consistency threshold to 0.6 [19]. This allows for the screening of condition combinations with strong explanatory power and representativeness. The results of fsQCA analysis are shown in Table 5, which shows that there are three different growth paths for agricultural insurance consumption.

Path 1 is autonomously driven by digital finance, high rural incomes and technological innovation. Path 2 is externally driven by digital finance and government support and internally driven by large-scale agricultural production. Path 3 is mainly externally driven by high compensation expenditures and government support, assisted by digital finance and technological innovation. The consistency of the three paths is 0.962, 0.934, and 0.937. And the consistency of the overall solution is 0.907. All consistencies are higher than 0.9, which constitutes a sufficiently explanatory condition for promoting higher consumption of agricultural insurance.

In path 1, higher consumption of agricultural insurance is driven by a combination of digital financial development, high rural incomes and active technology markets. The development of digital finance and technology markets represents an active capital and technology market that promotes informatization and urbanization in rural areas. Higher incomes of rural residents, on the other hand, directly reflect an increase in economic levels and also allow residents to have more capital to allocate to agricultural insurance. Under the combined effect of changes in the economic environment and market conditions, the increase in agricultural insurance consumption is significantly promoted. Hebei Province has vigorously developed digital countryside construction to empower smart agriculture, with an urbanization rate of more than 65%. Rural per capita disposable income in Hebei Province has been growing at an average annual rate of about 9%. Together, this has contributed to a 10% average annual increase in the consumption level of agricultural insurance.

Table 5. Configuration analysis results

	Path 1	Path 2	Path 3
DF	●	●	•
SA		●	
CE	⊗	⊗	●
DI	●		⊗
GS	⊗	●	●
TI	●		•
Consistency	0.962	0.934	0.937
Raw coverage	0.282	0.221	0.223
Unique coverage	0.065	0.015	0.015
Consistency of solution		0.907	
Coverage of solution		0.610	

Note: Sign ● indicates that the core condition exists. Sign ⊗ indicates that the core condition is missing. Sign • indicates a marginal condition exists. Sign ⊗ indicates that a marginal condition is missing. A blank space indicates that the condition may or may not be present.

In path 2, despite the relative lack of spending on agricultural insurance claims, the consumption of agricultural insurance is still increased by the popularization of digital finance and the relatively concentrated scale of production, combined with adequate government policy support for agriculture. The expansion of the scale of agricultural production leads to a greater concentration of risk for farmers, boosting demand. Digital financial inclusion as well as government policy subsidies can increase the availability of agricultural insurance. The province where this path is represented in practice is Jiangxi Province, where the average expenditure on agricultural insurance claims over a decade was only 560 million yuan. However, the average government expenditure on agricultural affairs in Jiangxi is as high as 53 billion yuan. On top of that, Jiangxi Province has experienced high growth in both per capita agricultural output and the Digital Finance Index, driving the average annual growth in agricultural insurance consumption to over 15 percent.

In path 3, the guidance of external policies and the support of insurance companies play the main pulling role while digital finance and digital innovation play a supporting role, which jointly promote the increase of agricultural insurance consumption. The increase in compensation expenditure and favorable policies to support agriculture boost farmers' confidence and stimulate their willingness to insure. The popularization of emerging information technology solves the problem of information asymmetry and helps to promote farmers' consumption of agricultural insurance. The representative province of this path in practice is Hunan Province. The average expenditure on agricultural insurance claims in Hunan Province in the past ten years is nearly 1.7 billion and the average government expenditure is nearly 70 billion, both at a high level. And technology market turnover as well as the urbanization rate have grown steadily. With gross agricultural output growing at only 3%, it has driven up average annual consumption of agricultural insurance by 13%.

4.3 Robustness Test

We first increase the minimum number of coverage cases from 3 to 4 by adjusting the threshold setting, generating essentially the same configuration results. Then we set the PRI consistency to 0.7, which generates essentially the same configuration results. Finally, the quartiles used for data calibration are changed from 5%, 50%, and 95% to 25%, 50%, and 75%, and the resultant paths are essentially the same. In summary, the robustness is favorable.

5 Conclusions and Recommendations

5.1 Main Conclusions

Based on the panel data of 31 provinces in China for the period of 2011–2020, we explore the path of improving agricultural insurance consumption composed of six conditions, including digital finance, through the fsQCA fuzzy set comparative analysis method. The main conclusions drawn are as follows.

Through configuration analysis, we have come up with three paths to increase agricultural insurance consumption and given typical case provinces. Path 1 is autonomously driven by digital finance, high rural incomes and technological innovation with Hebei being the typical province. Path 2 is externally driven by digital finance and government support and internally driven by large-scale agricultural production with Jiangxi being the typical province. Path 3 is mainly externally driven by high compensation expenditures and government support, assisted by digital finance and technological innovation with Hunan being the typical province. Through this section, we find that government support is often accompanied by support from other external factors. Path 2 and Path 3 provide additional explanations for the positive correlation [14] of government support on agricultural insurance consumption.

5.2 Policy Recommendations

The findings of this paper can provide a reference for the growth path of provinces with a poor level of agricultural insurance development. The three growth paths can help provinces rationally utilize their resource endowments and promote the effectiveness of agricultural insurance as a risk management tool. Based on the above findings, we propose the following policy recommendations.

Firstly, for areas where the scale of agricultural production is limited and the development of rural financial institutions is slow, efforts to build rural information technology should be increased. Farmers should be encouraged to use the Internet technologies for insurance purchases and claims operations. At the same time, local residents can improve the income level of rural residents through measures such as agricultural science and technology innovation, agricultural product processing and rural industrial restructuring.

Secondly, for regions with superior conditions for agricultural production and small agricultural insurance coverage, the government should fully support the development of agricultural production on a large scale under the conditions of digital inclusive finance. Local residents can improve the scale of agricultural production through agricultural industry clusters and agricultural cooperatives. In addition, the government should accelerate the construction of an agricultural risk management system to reduce agricultural production risks and costs.

Finally, for regions that hope to jointly pull agricultural insurance through the dimensions of the government and insurance companies, the government should further improve agricultural insurance policies and increase the strength and scope of insurance subsidies, which can reduce the cost of insurance purchase. At the same time, the publicity of agricultural insurance should be increased to raise the awareness of farmers to take out agricultural insurance and popularize the relevant knowledge and operational skills of agricultural insurance. Insurance companies, on the other hand, should strengthen the innovation of agricultural insurance products, promote the application of insurance technologies and enhance the consumption of agricultural insurance with digital innovation as the core.

References

1. Wei, H.: Insurance policy and poverty reduction in china: experiences, dilemmas and path optimization. Manag. World **35**(1), 135–150 (2019)
2. Fu, Q., Huang, Y.: Digital finance's heterogeneous effects on rural financial demand: evidence from china household finance survey and inclusive digital finance index in Chinese. J. Financ. Res. (11), 68–84 (2018)
3. Donghao, Z., Zhichao, Y.: Financial inclusion, risk coping and rural household poverty vulnerability in Chinese. Chin. Rural Econ. (4), 54–73 (2018)
4. Jiaxing, P., Ningfei, W., Xue, L., Xiang, L., Huiyu, W., Xingpeng, C.: Impact of economic development level and agricultural water use on agricultural production scale in China in Chinese. Int. J. Environ. Res. Public Health (17), 18 (2021)
5. Mario, J.M.: Area-yield crop insurance reconsidered. Am. J. Agric. Econ. (2), 73 (1991)
6. Jaap, S., Rossi, B.J., Peter, S., Icek, A.: Farmer behaviour as reasoned action: a critical review of research with the theory of planned behaviour. J. Agric. Econ. (2), 72 (2020)
7. Bao, X., Zhang, F., Guo, S., Deng, X., Song, J., Xu, D.: Peer effects on farmers' purchases of policy-based planting farming agricultural insurance: evidence from Sichuan province, China in Chinese. Int. J. Environ. Res. Public Health (12), 19 (2022)
8. Fan, Y.: Study on the relevance of large-scale agricultural operations and agricultural insurance in Chinese. Finance Econ. (2), 62–63 (2011)
9. Zhichkin, A.K., Nosov, V.V., Zhichkina, N.L..: Agricultural insurance, risk management and sustainable development. Agriculture **13**(7), 1317 (2023)

10. Guan, W., Zheng, S., Ma, J.: On government support, product and system innovation in agricultural insurance in Chinese. Manag. World (6), 155–156 (2005)
11. Caifeng, T., Jianping, T., Lan, Y., et al.: Dynamic relationship between agricultural technology progress, agricultural insurance and farmers' income in Chinese. Agriculture 12(9), 1331 (2022)
12. Hou, Y., Zhang, Q.: Comprehensive analysis on influencing factors of smallholder's willingness to purchase agricultural insurance in Chinese. Chin. J. Agric. Resour. Reg. Plann. 40(4), 210–216 (2019)
13. Du, Y., Jia, L.: Group perspective and qualitative comparative analysis (QCA): a new path for management research. Manage. World 6, 155–167 (2017)
14. Ragin, C.C., Fiss, P.C.: Net effects analysis versus configurational analysis: an empirical demonstration. Redesigning Soc. Inq. Fuzzy Sets Beyond 240, 190–212 (2008)
15. Shijie, J., Lilin, W., Feiyun, X.: The effect of agriculture insurance on agricultural carbon emissions in China: the mediation role of low-carbon technology innovation. Sustainability 15(5), 4431 (2023)
16. Jiaduo, E., Kibria, G.M., Aspy, N.N.: The impact of agricultural employment and technological innovation on the environment: evidence from BRICS nations considering a novel environmental sustainability indicator. Sustainability 15(20), 15083 (2023)
17. Fu, M., Qi, C.: Factor endowments, technological progress bias and total factor productivity growth in agriculture: a comparative analysis based on 28 countries. Chin. Rural Econ. (12), 76–90 (2016)
18. Cheng, C, Liang, D.J.: Research on the driving pattern of China's enterprise cross-border M&as: a qualitative comparative analysis. Nankai Bus. Rev. 19(6), 113–121 (2016)
19. Greckhamer, T.: CEO compensation in relation to worker compensation across countries: the configurational impact of country-level institutions. Strateg. Manag. J. 37(4), 793–815 (2016)

Backers' Preferences in Crowdfunding Projects: Field Experiments Based on Project Characteristics

Ziyi Tian and Nianxin Wang[✉]

Jiangsu University of Science and Technology, Zhenjiang 212100, China
nianxin.wang@gmail.com

Abstract. How to attract backers in the process of crowdfunding has always been a research hotspot. However, the existing research ignores that the key to solve this problem is to clarify the preference type of backers, and lacks discussion on the influence mechanism of backers' preferences. Therefore, this paper takes backers' preferences as the research object and combines the existing literature to propose hypotheses on the relationship between risk level, innovation type and backers' preferences. Inter-group experimental design was adopted to explore the difference of backers' preferences and influencing factors among different crowdfunding projects through field experiments. The results show that risk level and innovation type have significant influence on backers' preferences. The effects of two types of characteristics can be reflected in investing, following and forwarding intention. The interaction effect between two types of characteristics only exists in forwarding intention. The research results reveal the reasons for the difference in backers' preferences, which supplementing and improving the understanding of the hidden connection between backers' preferences and project characteristics. Moreover, these results help creator adjust their projects to meet backers' preferences and reduce the cost of time and money for backers.

Keywords: Crowdfunding · Backers' preferences · Risk level · Innovation type

1 Introduction

Crowdfunding refers to an emerging financing method that supports entrepreneurs to complete specific purposes in the form of donations, returns or voting rights through Internet platforms [1]. In recent years, the global crowdfunding market has doubled in size every year. However, at present, it has shown a slow growth or even decline trend. In order to explore the reasons for this trend, scholars have conducted a large number of qualitative and quantitative studies. However, these scholars gave too much consideration to the participation motivation of backers and the key factors that contribute to project success, ignored that backers often decide whether to support projects based on their own preferences rather than objective data. This way of thinking greatly increases the uncertainty of decision-making, thus affecting the financing performance of crowdfunding projects. Therefore, clear the type and degree of backers' preferences is the most

© The Author(s), under exclusive license to Springer Nature Switzerland AG 2024
Y. P. Tu and M. Chi (Eds.): WHICEB 2024, LNBIP 516, pp. 49–61, 2024.
https://doi.org/10.1007/978-3-031-60260-3_5

important to solve the market decline. At present, some scholars have carried out research on this aspect. The first kind is to help projects improve financing performance by quantifying backers' preferences. For example, a recommendation method was designed to help projects attract financial support at different stages after considering backers' preferences [2]. And some researchers [3] integrated backers' preferences into decisions and built a recommendation system that significantly improve the search efficiency. The second kind starts with project characteristics to explore its impact on backers' preferences. Such as adding products with decoy prices in the project could transfer backers' preferences for low-priced products to high-priced products [4]. In addition, studies have shown that the public tends to support projects with small target financing amount emotionally, while adopting a conservative or avoidance attitude towards projects with large target financing amount [5]. However, the above studies still have shortcomings. In the first kind, the calculation method of backers' preferences is not designed enough, because it is not realized that the difference of preference is caused by the difference of characteristics between projects. Although the second kind has associated the two, the project characteristics involved are relatively single. So, in order to make up for these shortcomings, this paper firstly combines the existing literature to theoretically analyze the two most important project characteristics of crowdfunding projects. Subsequently, the data are collected through field experiments to verify the degree of influence and existence conditions on backers' preferences, and to further clarify whether there are interactive effects between two characteristics, which is of great practical significance for both backers and creators.

2 Theoretical Background

The creators of crowdfunding projects are often innovative entrepreneurial enterprises, and the rewards used to return backers are mostly innovative products with strong uncertainty. This forces backers to take a higher risk of failure, but also makes them have a higher demand for product innovation. In addition, most of backers are the general public without professional financial knowledge, so their support intention is more likely to be affected by project quality signals and their own past experience. And compared with traditional backers, the behavior of crowdfunding backers has been proved to be driven by a wider range of motives [6]. Combining the two points, it is concluded that there are obvious preference differences between backers. Therefore, this part will discuss the relevant research progress from three aspects: risk characteristic, innovation characteristic and backers' preferences.

In terms of risk characteristic, a large number of scholars have conducted in-depth research on the premise of avoiding or reducing risks. For example, project creator can alleviate the risk concerns of backers on project's quality and information credibility through platform publicity [7]. Only a few scholars have studied different decision-making behaviors of backers in the face of dynamic risks. Like Acar [8] found that backers generally prefer to support crowdfunding projects, but for projects in high-risk stage, backers believe that the crowdfunding model lacks sufficient professionalism to reduce risks, so they will reverse their preferences. And in terms of innovation characteristic, it has been proved that when a project achieves radical innovation (RI) at the core level, backers will change their views on this type of project, which will directly lower the evaluation of other similar projects [9]. However, some researchers believe that the challenges associated with progress due to product complexity in RI projects can undermine backers' crowdfunding intentions, while incremental innovation (II) products do not have the similar problem [10]. Finally, most of the research on backers' preferences is based on two key characteristics of the project, and studies how this information will affect the psychological activities of backers. Such as the project quality certification launched by platform can help backers judge project risks and identify high-quality projects [11]. And higher level of uniqueness leads to better crowdfunding performance, that is, backers tend to support projects that provide more freshness [12].

Summarizing the above studies, it can be found that first of all, there are few studies that explore the influence of dynamic changes in risk level on backers' preferences. Although some studies used the project stage to reflect risk level, their lack of uniform criteria for dividing results in an inability to integrate similar conclusions. Secondly, the advantages and disadvantages of two types of innovation have been analyzed in detail, but it is not clear which type of innovation is more attractive to backers. In addition, most studies on backers' preferences pay too much attention to the preference differences caused by a single project characteristic and verify it, lacking the comprehensive impact of the two characteristics. Finally, most studies take backer's investing intention (INVI) as the only standard to measure the difference in backers' preferences, ignoring that with the rapid development of Internet technology, backers are no longer mere buyers of products or services, but also followers and forwarders of information on network platforms [13]. They will voluntarily log on to various media to obtain all kinds of project information, and then spread it on social platforms that affect others' buying habits. Therefore, it is crucial to clarify whether backer's following intention (FI) and forwarding intention (FWI) for are also affected by the characteristics of projects and the changes after the impact.

3 Research Model and Hypotheses

This paper takes backers' preferences as research object, uses risk level and innovation type as influencing factors, and three types of intention as measurement index to analyze the influence of two types of characteristics on the backers' preferences, the specific degree of these influences under different conditions, and whether there is an interaction effect between two types of characteristics. The research model is shown in Fig. 1. Control variables include number of project updates, number of comments, amount raised, target amount, number of backers, remaining days, etc.

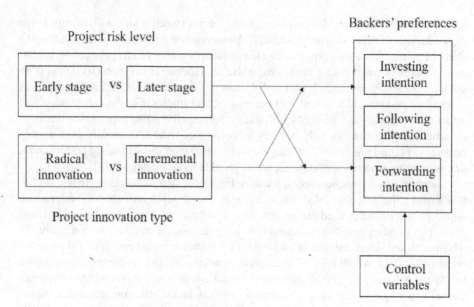

Fig. 1. Research model

3.1 The Influence of Risk Level

In the traditional financing process, economists generally assume that backers are completely rational, will invest according to the maximum utility theory and all have the trait of risk aversion. Therefore, projects with high returns and low-risk are more favored by backers. At the same time, the literature mentioned above has also confirmed the existence of similar conclusions in crowdfunding but still have shortcomings caused by different evaluation criteria of risk level. In order to perfect this conclusion, firstly the project stage is divided into "concept", "prototype", "production" and "shipping" stages according to the criteria of Indiegogo crowdfunding platform. Both the "production" and "shipping" stages represent the high degree of product completion and close to the success of crowdfunding. And "concept" and "prototype" stages all represent that the project is still in the state of ideation and the crowdfunding risk is high. Therefore, this paper integrates four stages into the "early stage" (ES) and the "later stage" (LS) to clearly and accurately represent two types of risk level so as to explore the impact of dynamic changes in project risk level on backers' preferences. This paper proposes the following hypotheses:

H1a. The risk level of project has a significant impact on backer's INVI. Compared with high-risk projects, backers prefer to invest low-risk projects.

H1b. The risk level of project has a significant impact on backer's FI. Compared with high-risk projects, backers prefer to follow low-risk projects.

H1c. The risk level of project has a significant impact on backer's FWI. Compared with high-risk projects, backers prefer to forward low-risk projects.

3.2 The Influence of Innovation Type

Most of the backers of technological and innovation crowdfunding projects are not satisfied with the existing technical system. They are eager to obtain new products, and have unique or even strict requirements for the technical functions, service experience and use value of the project. So, it's clear that II doesn't satisfy these people. In addition, in online marketing, enterprises let consumers perceive a significant increase in their own benefits and a significant reduction in payment costs, thus making them more willing to support a series of innovative activities at the psychological level [14]. Coincidentally, RI projects adopt emerging technologies to greatly improve perceived benefits of backers, and thus have a more positive impact on backer's intention to support than II projects, leading to significant preference differences between the two types of innovation projects. Based on the above analysis, this paper proposes the following hypotheses:

H2a. The innovation type of project has a significant impact on backer's INVI. Compared with II projects, backers prefer to invest RI projects.

H2b. The innovation type of project has a significant impact on backer's FI. Compared with II projects, backers prefer to follow RI projects.

H2c. The innovation type of project has a significant impact on backer's FWI. Compared with II projects, backers prefer to forward RI projects.

3.3 Interaction Effect

After studying the direct and indirect effects of the innovativeness and perceived risk of new products on consumers' purchase intention, some researchers [15] concluded that perceived risk and purchase intention were negatively correlated, and the innovativeness indirectly affected this connection. Specifically, a high level of innovativeness can significantly reduce a consumer's perceived risk of that product, thereby increasing their purchase intention. In addition, current research [16] showed that consumers search for more and more information when perceived risk is high. And under high perceived risk conditions, the information about the innovation dimension of the enterprise is more diagnostic for consumer's purchase decision. But under low perceived risk conditions, consumers are more concerned about product's specific attributes and benefits, and less concerned about enterprise innovation.

There is a common point that in online investment, there is an interaction effect between risk level and innovation type, which jointly affects consumer. But does this common point also apply to crowdfunding, a particular form of online financing, and can backers' preference also be affected by interaction effect between two types of project's characteristics? Therefore, this paper proposes the following hypothesis:

H3a. At the aspect of backers' investing preferences, there is an interaction effect between risk level and innovation type.

H3b. At the aspect of backers' following preferences, there is an interaction effect between risk level and innovation type.

H3c. At the aspect of backers' forwarding preferences, there is an interaction effect between risk level and innovation type.

4 Methods: Field Experiment

4.1 Experimental Designs

A 2 (Risk level: high-risk vs low-risk) × 2 (Innovation type: RI vs II) intergroup experimental design was used. The demographic characteristics of graduate students are relatively consistent, and they have a certain ability to distinguish the risk level and innovation type of crowdfunding projects, so they are selected as experimental sample. In order to better simulate the real online crowdfunding situation, this paper designed the pictures of stimulus objects with reference to the Indiegogo official website that Chinese backers are not familiar with. The specific approach is select two different types of innovation projects based on their functionality, patents and innovative vocabulary, and then adjust projects' current stage to produce eight web screenshots. The eight screenshots contain the same control variables and correspond to the eight experimental groups one by one. The specific groups are shown in Table 1. In the course of the experiment, the risk level and innovation type perceptions of subjects are evaluated, and INVI, FI, FWI are also measured. All use the 5-point Likert scale, with 1 representing "Strongly disagree/reluctant" and 5 representing "Strongly agree/willing".

Table 1. Experimental group design

Group number	Project characteristics	Project stage	Project category
1	Low-risk, II	Shipping	Food and beverages
2	Low-risk, II	Production	Food and beverages
3	High-risk, II	Prototype	Food and beverages
4	High-risk, II	Concept	Food and beverages
5	Low-risk, RI	Shipping	Audio
6	Low-risk, RI	Production	Audio
7	High-risk, RI	Prototype	Audio
8	High-risk, RI	Concept	Audio

4.2 Formal Experiment

The field experiment lasted for four days, a total of 160 students participated in the experiment, and 157 effective samples. There were 80 males (50.96%) and 77 females (49.04%). Among them, 97 (61.78%) were 20–25 years old, 46 (29.30%) were 26–30 years old, and 14 (8.92%) were over 30 years old. The 160 students were divided into eight groups, and each group was assigned to one of the experimental groups. Before the experiment began, the basic concepts of crowdfunding were briefly explained to the subjects. Then the subjects began to browse pictures and fill in the information and score according to the questionnaire content. Part of the project screenshot is shown in Fig. 2. The left side of Fig. 2 is the "prototype" stage and RI project, and the right side is the "production" stage and II project.

Fig. 2. Sample screenshots of some projects

5 Results

5.1 Manipulation Test

In this paper, the reliability tests of two types of characteristics were using existing scales [10, 17, 18] and adjusted according to Chinese semantics. The risk level test includes eight items ($\alpha = 0.854$), such as "Due to the high expected performance level of this project, I would consider supporting this project" and "I think this project has a high potential investment risk". The innovation type test also includes eight items ($\alpha = 0.872$), like "The project creator is good at implementing existing ideas" and "The project creator offers a whole new way to use it". About the validity test, the perceived score of risk level decreases significantly with the progress of the project, and the perceived score of the RI group is significantly higher than that of the II group. This indicates that the experiment is successful in controlling the risk level and innovation type. Subsequently, the risk and innovation scores of the projects were pairwise tested by independent sample T-test. All results meet the requirements of experiment. It is not shown here due to space limitations.

5.2 Hypothesis Test

5.2.1 Main Effect Test

A 2×2 ANOVA analysis of variance was performed on the obtained data, and the results are shown in Table 2.

Table 2. Differences in the influence of risk level and innovation type on backers' preferences

Source	DV	SSE (3)	df	MS	F	P
Corrected Model	INVI	102.216[a]	3	34.072	38.672	0.000
	FI	61.283[b]	3	20.428	27.080	0.000
	FWI	102.165[c]	3	34.055	52.681	0.000
Intercept	INVI	1276.423	1	1276.423	1448.731	0.000
	FI	1307.107	1	1307.107	1732.734	0.000
	FWI	896.905	1	896.905	1387.460	0.000
Risk level	INVI	82.936	1	82.936	94.131	0.000
	FI	40.985	1	40.985	54.331	0.000
	FWI	66.953	1	66.953	103.572	0.000
Innovation type	INVI	17.667	1	17.667	20.052	0.000
	FI	19.137	1	19.137	25.368	0.000
	FWI	29.037	1	29.037	44.918	0.000
Risk level* Innovation type	INVI	1.148	1	1.148	1.303	0.255
	FI	0.864	1	0.864	1.146	0.286
	FWI	5.824	1	5.824	9.010	0.003
Error	INVI	134.803	153	0.881		
	FI	115.417	153	0.754		
	FWI	98.905	153	0.646		
Total	INVI	1504.000	157			
	FI	1478.000	157			
	FWI	1092.000	157			
Corrected Total	INVI	237.019	156			
	FI	176.701	156			
	FWI	201.070	156			

Notes [a] $R^2 = 0.431$(adjusted $R^2 = 0.420$)

[b] $R^2 = 0.347$(adjusted $R^2 = 0.334$)

[c] $R^2 = 0.508$(adjusted $R^2 = 0.498$)

Table 2 shows that the main effect of risk level on the three types of intention is significant (M $_{ES, INVI}$ = 2.125 < M $_{LS, INVI}$ = 3.584; M $_{ES, FI}$ = 2.375 < M $_{LS, FI}$ = 3.403; M $_{ES, FWI}$ = 1.975 < M $_{LS, FWI}$ = 3.667). That is, compared with high-risk projects, backers prefer to invest, follow and forward low-risk projects, assuming that H1a, H1b and H1c are initially established. The main effect of innovation type on the three types of intention is also significant (M $_{II, INVI}$ = 2.500 < M $_{RI, INVI}$ = 3.177; M $_{II, FI}$ = 2.526 < M $_{RI, FI}$ = 3.228; M $_{II, FWI}$ = 1.949 < M $_{RI, FWI}$ = 2.810). That is, compared with II projects, backers prefer to invest, follow and forward RI projects, assuming that H2a, H2b and H2c are initially established.

5.2.2 Paired Test

In order to further verify whether H1 and H2 are valid under different conditions, three types of intention data are paired for ANOVA, and the results are shown in Table 3 and Table 4.

Table 3. Paired analysis of backers' preferences differences (divided according to risk level)

DV	IT	RL	CRL	MD	SSE (3)	df	MS	F	P
INVI	II	ES	LS	1.283	32.072	1	32.072	49.314	0.000
	RI	ES	LS	1.625	52.144	1	52.144	47.029	0.000
FI	II	ES	LS	0.874	14.875	1	14.875	24.273	0.000
	RI	ES	LS	1.171	27.055	1	27.055	30.261	0.000
FWI	II	ES	LS	0.921	16.531	1	16.531	40.188	0.000
	RI	ES	LS	1.692	56.510	1	56.510	64.329	0.000

Notes IT: Innovation type, RL: Risk level, CRL: Control's risk level

Table 3 shows that there is a significant gap in the three types of intention data between the two types of risk level projects, regardless of whether they are both II projects or RI projects. So, under the condition of the same innovation type, backers prefer to invest, follow and forward low-risk projects. So, H1a, H1b and H1c are all valid.

Table 4. Paired analysis of backers' preferences differences (divided according to innovation type)

DV	RL	IT	CIT	MD	SSE (3)	df	MS	F	P
INVI	ES	II	RI	0.500	5.000	1	5.000	4.345	0.040
	LS	II	RI	0.842	13.649	1	13.649	22.721	0.000
FI	ES	II	RI	0.550	6.050	1	6.050	7.293	0.008
	LS	II	RI	0.847	13.802	1	13.802	20.411	0.000
FWI	ES	II	RI	0.475	4.513	1	4.513	5.968	0.017
	LS	II	RI	1.246	29.862	1	29.862	56.090	0.000

Note CIT: Control's innovation type

Table 4 shows that there is a significant gap in the three types of intention data between the two types of innovation projects, regardless of whether they are both ES projects or LS projects. So, under the condition of the same risk level, backers prefer to invest, follow and forward RI projects. So, H2a, H2b and H2c are all valid.

5.2.3 Interaction Effect Test

There is no interaction between risk level and innovation type at the aspect of INVI and FI (F_{INVI} (1,153) = 1.303, p_{INVI} = 0.255; F_{FI} (1,153) = 1.146, p_{FI} = 0.286), but there is a significant interaction in FWI (F (1,153) = 9.010, p = 0.003). Taking risk level as the simple main effect, the greater the degree of innovation (RI), the greater the impact of risk level on FWI (β_{RI} = 1.692, β_{II} = 0.921); Taking innovation type as the simple main effect, the greater the risk level, the greater the impact of innovation degree on FWI (β_{LS} = 1.246, β_{ES} = 0.475). So, H3a and H3b are not valid, H3c is valid.

6 Conclusion

This paper shows that there are significant differences in the influence of two types of project characteristics on backers' preferences in different situations. Table 5 summarizes the results of hypothesis test.

First, on the whole, compared with high-risk projects, backers prefer to invest, follow and forward low-risk projects, which is in line with the general law of economics. Second, overall, backers are more likely to invest, follow, and forward RI projects than II projects, which is consistent with the conclusion of recent research. Third, regarding the interaction effect between risk level and innovation type, this paper concludes that there is no interaction effect in INVI and FI, but only exists in FWI. For this result, this paper holds that the preference psychology of backers in decision-making process may not be the pursuit of project perfection, that is, when one of the characteristics has met their preferences, backers will reduce their requirements for another characteristic. Therefore, backers lack the interactive consideration of two types of characteristics when making investing and following decisions. When deciding whether to forward, backers

Table 5. Summary of results

Hypothesis		Result
H1a	The risk level of project has a significant impact on backer's INVI. Compared with high-risk projects, backers prefer to invest low-risk projects	Valid
H1b	The risk level of project has a significant impact on backer's FI. Compared with high-risk projects, backers prefer to follow low-risk projects	Valid
H1c	The risk level of project has a significant impact on backer's FWI. Compared with high-risk projects, backers prefer to forward low-risk projects	Valid
H2a	The innovation type of project has a significant impact on backer's INVI. Compared with II projects, backers prefer to invest RI projects	Valid
H2b	The innovation type of project has a significant impact on backer's FI. Compared with II projects, backers prefer to follow RI projects	Valid
H2c	The innovation type of project has a significant impact on backer's FWI. Compared with II projects, backers prefer to forward RI projects	Valid
H3a	At the aspect of backers' investing preferences, there is an interaction effect between risk level and innovation type	Not Valid
H3b	At the aspect of backers' following preferences, there is an interaction effect between risk level and innovation type	Not Valid
H3c	At the aspect of backers' forwarding preferences, there is an interaction effect between risk level and innovation type	Valid

need to consider if others have the same needs and evaluation criteria, so as to have a deeper comprehensive consideration of the two types of characteristics. Therefore, the interaction effect of two types of characteristics only exists in FWI.

6.1 Research Implications

First, the theoretical implications, this paper does not discuss how to avoid risks to make the project crowdfunding successful, but studies the impact of dynamic changes in risk level on the backers' preferences, so as to help backers better understand risks. At the same time, this paper unifies different but similar stage division standards in different literatures, so as to draw conclusions that are in line with the research status but more universal and accurate. Secondly, existing studies have been arguing about "which type of innovation projects are more supported by backers". Through field experiments, this paper not only obtains the most real and natural data, but also skips the complex decision-making analysis process and conducts analysis directly on the basis of the data, providing new evidence for the positive backer reaction of radical innovation. Then, this paper does not ignore the project characteristics or pay too much attention to a single characteristic like existing literature, but combines two types of characteristics to explore the specific degree of the two types of effects under different conditions and whether there is interaction. Also, different from the existing literature that only uses investing intention to measure preference differentiation, this paper considers the different identities of backers on the network platform, and concludes that the following and forwarding data also reflect the preference degree of backers to a certain extent. Finally, the practical implication is that project creators can make use of the two characteristics of their projects to cater to the backers' preference for RI projects and low-risk projects to the maximum extent so as to obtain more support. And according to the analysis results, backers can not only make decisions quickly to save time cost, but also get rewards in kind with high probability when facing a wide variety of crowdfunding projects.

6.2 Limitations and Future Research

There are still some problems in this paper, which deserve further discussion. First, this paper selected two projects of different innovation types as experimental materials for experiments. However, these two projects are not the same category, which may cause unnecessary error. So, the same category of products should be selected for research in the future. Second, this paper selected university graduate students as experimental objects, and the scope is relatively single, so the conclusion may not be universal and applicable. In the future, the experimental scope can be expanded to obtain more diverse experimental sample data.

Acknowledgement. This research was supported by the National Natural Science Foundation of China under Grant 72272066.

References

1. Schwienbacher, A., Larralde, B.: Crowdfunding of small entrepreneurial ventures. SSRN Electron. J. **1578175**, 1–23 (2010)
2. Li, Y.-M., Liou, J.-H., Li, Y.-W.: A social recommendation approach for reward-based crowdfunding campaigns. Inform. Manage. **57**(7), 103246 (2020)
3. Li, Y.-M., Hsieh, C.-Y., Zeng, W.-Z.: A social discovery mechanism for endorsing investors in equity crowdfunding. Decis. Support. Syst. **176**, 114049 (2024)
4. Weinmann, M., Mishra, A.N., Kaiser, L.F., et al.: The attraction effect in crowdfunding. Inf. Syst. Res. **34**(3), 1276–1295 (2023)
5. Ahlers, G.K., Cumming, D., Günther, C., Schweizer, D.: Signaling in equity crowdfunding. Entrep. Theory Pract. **39**(4), 955–980 (2015)
6. Nielsen, K.R., Binder, J.K.: I am what i pledge: the importance of value alignment for mobilizing backers in reward-based crowdfunding. Entrep. Theory Pract. **45**(3), 531–561 (2021)

7. Courtney, C., Dutta, S., Li, Y.: Resolving information asymmetry: signaling, endorsement, and crowdfunding success. Entrep. Theory Pract. **41**(2), 265–290 (2017)
8. Acar, O.A., Dahl, D.W., Fuchs, C., Schreier, M.: The signal value of crowdfunded products. J. Mark. Res. **58**(4), 644–661 (2021)
9. Bagga, C.K., Noseworthy, T.J., Dawar, N.: Asymmetric consequences of radical innovations on category representations of competing brands. J. Consum. Psychol. **26**(1), 29–39 (2015)
10. Chan, C.S.R., Parhankangas, A.: Crowdfunding innovative ideas: how incremental and radical innovativeness influence funding outcome. Entrep. Theory Pract. **41**(2), 237–263 (2016)
11. Yu, J., Xiao, S.: Project certification and screening in the reward-based crowdfunding market. J. Bus. Res. **165**, 114004 (2023)
12. Taeuscher, K., Bouncken, R., Pesch, R.: Gaining legitimacy by being different: optimal distinctiveness in crowdfunding platforms. Acad. Manag. J. **64**(1), 149–179 (2021)
13. Pai, P., Tsai, H.-T.: Reciprocity norms and information-sharing behavior in online consumption communities: an empirical investigation of antecedents and moderators. Inform. Manage. **53**(1), 38–52 (2016)
14. Blut, M., Kulikovskaja, V., Hubert, M., Grewal, D.: Effectiveness of engagement initiatives across engagement platforms: a meta-analysis. J. Acad. Mark. Sci. **51**(5), 941–965 (2023)
15. Cowart, K.O., Fox, G.L., Wilson, A.E.: A structural look at consumer innovativeness and self-congruence in new product purchases. Psychol. Mark. **25**(12), 1111–1130 (2008)
16. Gürhan-Canli, Z., Batra, R.: When corporate image affects product evaluations: the moderating role of perceived risk. J. Mark. Res. **41**(2), 197–205 (2004)
17. Grewal, D., Gotlieb, J., Marmorstein, H.: The moderating effects of message framing and source credibility on the price-perceived risk relationship. J. Consum. Res. **21**(1), 145–153 (1994)
18. Featherman, M.S., Pavlou, P.A.: Predicting e-services adoption: a perceived risk facets perspective. Int. J. Hum. Comput. Stud.Comput. Stud. **59**(4), 451–474 (2003)

Backer Preference Modeling and Prediction of Crowdfunding Campaign Success

Sijia Feng, Nianxin Wang[✉], and Yan Qiu

Jiangsu University of Science and Technology, Zhenjiang 212100, China
nianxin.wang@gmail.com

Abstract. Crowdfunding market has witnessed rapid growth; however, the overall success rate remains relatively low. Therefore, predicting crowdfunding success has garnered significant attention, offering benefits for backers, platforms, and campaign creators in terms of risk reduction and optimized resource allocation. Departing from the traditional campaign-centric perspective, we proposed a novel backer-centric approach for predicting crowdfunding success: Modeling backer preference based on their pledge history and aggregating preference of active backers within categories for predicting crowdfunding success. To validate the performance of this approach, we identified backers who participated in the discussion of recently popular campaigns on Indiegogo platform. A total of 7895 backers were captured along with the 91299 campaigns they either followed or contributed to. Additionally, we gathered 73581 campaigns for training and testing predictive models. Results indicate that considering backer preferences significantly enhances that accuracy of crowdfunding success prediction models. Further, we observed that modeling backer preferences based on higher activity level can further enhance the performance of the predictive model.

Keywords: Crowdfunding · Backers' Preference · Success Prediction

1 Introduction

The crowdfunding mechanism has proven to be a practical way which raise a small amount of money from a large number of individuals to back different campaigns and goals through the internet [1]. As an open market, creators on crowdfunding platforms face intense competition to achieve fundraising success. They must distinguish their campaigns and align with backer preferences to attract and retain backers [2]. For instance, on Kickstarter, the world's largest crowdfunding platform with over 3000 real-time active campaigns across 15 categories, the average success rate is less than 40%. Numerous studies have considered a range of campaign-related factors, attempting to analyze their impact on fundraising performance and leaning towards predicting crowdfunding success from the perspective of campaigns [3].

These studies are based on a common assumption: that a campaign appeals to every backer at the same way and the same level. Backers, as a key determinant of whether a campaign can achieve its fundraising goals or not haven't been fully studied. Backers are one of the key decision-makers in crowdfunding campaigns, and their support and investment directly impact the ultimate outcome of the campaign. Understanding and catering to the preferences of backers can increase the popularity of a project and enhance its chances of success. By comprehending the likes and preferences of backers, it is possible to more accurately predict the level of appeal and potential success of a campaign, thereby providing investors and platforms with a more reliable basis for decision-making. In fact, due to the difference in age, backgrounds, experience and favourite, the campaigns which the backers pay attention to are also different. That is to say, a campaign attracts different backers' attention to different degrees. Therefore, when predicting the success of a campaign, it is crucial to consider the preference of backers. When the campaign features are close to or in line with the preferences of backers, they are more likely to pledge to the campaign. Our research hopes to jump out of the campaign-centric perspective by delving into backer preference, opening the black box of the backers' decision-making process. We propose a backer-centric predictive model based on backer preferences, seeking to match campaign characteristics with backer preferences and further validating the performance of this backer-centric model.

Investigating all the potential backers on the platform is impractical. Fortunately, backers' pledge history serves as strong evidence of their attention to specific campaigns, showcasing their preferences perfectly. By observing backers' behaviors, such as following and funding, we model their preferences, analyzing overall backer preference within categories. This enabled the prediction of crowdfunding success based on campaign features and collective backer preferences.

2 Literature Review

2.1 Influencing Factors of Crowdfunding Performance

Over the past decade, the crowdfunding market has witnessed strong growth.in 2022, the global crowdfunding market reached a size of $88.7 billion, maintaining a double-digit compound annual growth rate since 2014. Despite the substantial market size, the overall success rate of the campaigns remains less optimistic. This indicates the need for further research into the key factors influencing crowdfunding success and predicting campaign success to mitigate risks. The previous researches mainly focus campaign information and creator information.

When backers make funding decisions, the primary consideration is the quality of the campaign. Many researches point to a number of factors such as the campaign's pledge goal [4], duration [5], campaign category [6], rewards offered [6], comprehensive campaign description [7], language style [8], campaign updates, and even strategies [9]. These studies indicate that campaign information features significantly impact backers' funding decisions, consequently influencing crowdfunding success.

Most existing prediction models for crowdfunding success typically incorporate various factors, including campaign characteristics, creator characteristics, and social network. From the perspective of campaign-centric view, machine learning algorithms such as regression analysis, decision trees, and neural networks are employed to analyze these factors and attempt to predict whether a campaign will successfully achieve its funding goal. While these models can provide references, they do not guarantee the accuracy of predicted results but rather aim to identify key factors that influence crowdfunding outcomes.

Backers' decisions are not only influenced by multifaceted campaign features but also affected by characteristics of campaign creators, including gender [10], passion [11], professional expertise, social connections [12, 13], and historical experience. Specifically, backers tend to believe that the campaigns initiated by individuals with successful experiences are more likely to succeed.

In this research, existing factors influencing crowdfunding success will be leveraged to model backer preferences, investigating the significance of backers' pledge history in predicting crowdfunding success.

2.2 Backer Preferences

Preference is defined as an individual's inclination toward different options, choices, or outcomes, reflecting personal degree of liking. Behind preferences, there is typically an implicit ranking or evaluation based on an individual's experience, value, needs, cultural background, or other factors, and the ultimate decision-making behavior reflects the combined influence of real preferences and decision errors. Preferences are crucial factors in the decision-making process, influencing behavior when facing different choices [14].

When making funding decisions, preferences can influence whether the backer support a particular campaign and how to support it. Backers are more inclined to fund campaigns that align with their interest, values, or needs [15]. As crucial decision-maker for fundraising, studying backer preferences is essential for understanding the factors influencing crowdfunding success, backer behaviors on the platform, and individual decision- making processes. We need to move beyond the previous perspective of treating all backers equally and give due consideration to each unique backer to aid in predicting and assessing the likelihood of success for specific campaigns.

3 Research Methodology

The proposed method comprises three key steps. First, we collected factors that have been widely shown to have a significantly impact on crowdfunding success. Based on it, we represented campaign features. Second, we gathered all the campaigns previously supported by backers, representing them as pledge history matrix and calculate into backer preferences. Finally, we employed machine learning algorithms to assign weights to active backers to quantify their significance in the predictive model and mathematically aggregated backer preferences to derive collective preferences within categories.

Based on literature review, we selected a set of factors that have been empirically proven to significantly impact crowdfunding success, including campaign information and creator information. The foundational information for campaigns includes campaign category [6], pledge goal [4], duration of fundraising [5], number of images, number of videos, updates count, and comment count [16]. Creator historical experience information includes the number of campaigns the creator was on, funded, succeed, and the success rate among the initiated campaigns [9]. The variables and definitions are outlined in Table 1.

Table 1. Variable and definition.

Variable	Definition
Dependent Variable	
Success (Success)	The dummy variable takes the value of 1 if the campaign was successfully funded and 0 otherwise
Campaign Basic Feature (BF)	
Pledge goal (PG)	Target pledge goal set by campaign creator
Campaign Category (CG)	A category assigned to a campaign in platform, including TECH & INNOVATION, CREATIVE WORKS, COMMUNITY PROJECTS
Subcategory (SCG)	The Indiegogo platform contains a total of 28 subcategories under three broad categories
Duration (DU)	Number of days the campaign is open for funding
Videos (VI)	Number of videos in campaign description
Picture (PIC)	Number of pictures in campaign description
Comments from backers (CB)	Number of comments on the campaign during the funding period
Update (UP)	Number of updates about the campaign during the funding period
Creator Feature (CF)	
HistoryOn (HO)	Number of campaigns initiated by this creator
HistoryFunded (HF)	The number of campaigns that the creator has ever supported
HistorySuccess (HS)	The number of campaigns that the creator has ever succeeded
SuccessRate (SR)	The success rate of campaigns initiated by this creator

Utilizing these influencing factors as features to represent the campaign, representing all variables related to a campaign in a row vector, and integrating the backer's pledge history, we constructed the backer's preference matrix. By calculating the average value of each feature across all funded campaigns, we derived the backer's preference vector, comprehensively reflecting the backer's preferences in various aspects. When predicting the likelihood of campaign fundraising success, considering the preferences of an individual backer alone is far from sufficient. It is crucial to take into account the preferences of the majority of active backers within the category. The data features a high dimensionality with numerous features, necessitating prevention of overfitting. Hence, the selection of a machine learning model that excels in these aspects is paramount. Therefore, employing three classical machine learning algorithms (Support Vector Machine – SVM, Convolutional Neural Network – CNN, and Random Forest – RF), we allocated weights to active backers within the category to quantify their importance in the prediction model. The mathematical aggregation of backer preferences, combined with weights, yields the collective preferences within the category. This collective preference, along with campaign features, is employed to predict crowdfunding success. The training and prediction processes are illustrated in Fig. 1.

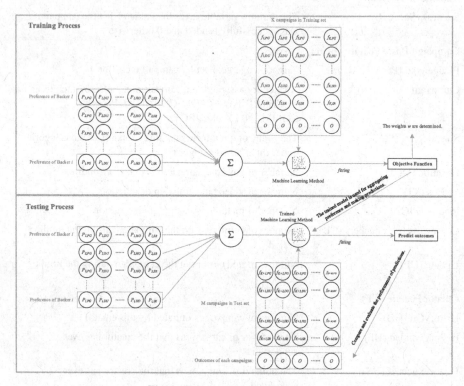

Fig. 1. Training and testing process.

From the dataset, it was observed that many backers on the platform exhibited low level of activity, supporting only a few campaigns. These backers might have been introduced to support specific campaign by friends and might not continue to engage with other campaigns or provide additional support. Such silent backers can impact the accurate calculation of collective preferences among category backers. Hence, this research also excluded backers who have funded only one or two campaigns, focusing on active backers to set another model for comparison.

In this research, we concentrated on comparing the performance of several models in terms of prediction effectiveness, using it as a basis for evaluating the practical application of the models. To verify whether the proposed backer-centric method outperforms the campaign-centric method in prediction performance, we also established a campaign-centric model, selecting the same variables, employing the same algorithms, and only controlling for the change in the central perspective. This ensures that any differences in model performance are attributed to the change in model design perspective. An overview of the model is provided in Table 2. These model designs aim to compare prediction models built from different starting points, thereby assessing their effectiveness and applicability in crowdfunding success prediction. By contrasting these models, we can better understand the influence of model design perspective and the backer activity on the predictive model performance.

Table 2. Model and description.

Model	Description
Baseline (Campaign-centric)	Conventional crowdfunding success prediction methods, this model is campaign-centric. It regards all backers as homogeneous, and predict the crowdfunding success from the characteristics of campaign and creator, ignoring the influence of individual backer selection
Model 1 (Backer-centric) (Funded campaigns > 0)	Backer-centric foundation model, considers all the backers' preferences who have funded at least one campaign, using the campaign and creator information
Model 2 (Backer-centric) (Funded campaigns > 2)	In this backer-centric model, in addition to considering the backers' preference for campaign and creator information, the active degree of backers is taken into consideration. The inactive backers who have only supported one or two campaigns in the dataset are excluded

4 Data

We collected data from campaigns released on Indiegogo before September 2023. Due to the platform policy prohibiting the disclosure of backer list for each campaign, we accessed information on backer homepages, which included details about their following and funding campaigns. Some backers were also campaign creators, and their homepages including information about the campaigns they initiated. We started the data collection process by entering the discussion section of each campaign. We identified backers who had posted at least one comment on the platform, ensuring that these backers had participated in campaign discussions and were potential contributors. The collected data consisted of two parts.

The first part comprised backer behavior data, including basic information about backers and their interactions, such as campaigns they followed, funded and initiated. Each campaign's information included its main category, subcategory, pledge goal, fundraising duration, number of images, videos, comments, updates, and the creator's historical experience, including the campaigns initiated, successfully initiated, and the number of campaigns the creator had funded. This backer behavior information was used to determine backer preferences. A total of 7,895 backer profiles were collected, corresponding to 91,299 campaigns. The second part comprised campaign information used to train and test the model's prediction accuracy. This part includes details from 75258 campaigns.

To ensure that the backer data used to determine preferences only included backers who had actually made contributions, we filtered out backers who only followed campaigns without making any contributions from the collected data. For the data to train and test prediction model, we excluded campaigns with empty titles, insufficient information, campaigns that failed to raise any funds, as well as ongoing, canceled, and campaigns that are no longer publicly displayed to ensure dataset quality. In the final dataset, there were 2459 backers who had made actual contributions. The second part of the campaign information included 73581 campaigns.

5 Results

Three common metrics for evaluating classification model performance and their corresponding standard deviation were selected, including F-1 score, and AUC (Area Under the ROC Curve). Accuracy measures the proportion of correctly predicted samples to the total number of samples, i.e., the number of correctly predicted campaigns divided by all campaigns, providing the most intuitive measure of model performance. The F-1 score considers the precision and recall of the model, where precision measures how many successful campaigns predicted are actually successful, and recall measures how many actually successful campaigns are correctly predicted as successful. The F-1 score is the integrated mean of these two, offering a comprehensive evaluation of the model's overall performance in predicting crowdfunding success. The AUC is the area under the Receiver Operating Characteristic (ROC) curve, describing the relationship between the true positive rate and the false positive rate at different thresholds. AUC is used to evaluate the model's ability to distinguish between successful and unsuccessful campaigns, with a higher AUC indicating better discrimination. Simultaneously, standard deviations are used to measure the dispersion of these metrics, assessing the stability of the model on these metrics.

The results are shown in Table 3. In the campaign-centric model, the SVM algorithm achieves the highest accuracy, reaching 72.10%, while the CNN achieves the lowest accuracy at 69.20%. The F-1 score and AUC are also optimal for SVM algorithms, with the value of 71.79% and 74.92%, respectively. These results indicate that the SVM demonstrates better classification capabilities in the campaign-centric prediction model.

In the backer-centric model, the Backer-centric-1 model, which considers all the backers' preferences who have funded at least one campaign, showing a significant improvement in performance compared to the campaign-centric model. Taking SVM as an example, the accuracy, F-1 score, and AUC improve by 18.50%, 20.59%, and 18.95%, respectively. The model performance comparison is illustrated in Fig. 2. This strongly demonstrates the importance of considering backers' preferences when predicting crowdfunding success, highlighting the multi-dimensional understanding of backers' preferences in enhancing model performance.

Table 3. Comparison of model performance.

Method	Model	Accuracy, Avg.	Accuracy, SD	F-1, Avg.	F-1, SD	AUC, Avg.	AUC, SD
SVM	Baseline Campaign-centric	0.7210	0.0001	0.7179	0.0001	0.7492	0.0001
	Backer-centric-1 (Campaign $\geq$ 1)	0.9060*	$2.2204e^{-16}$	0.9238*	0.0001	0.9389*	$3.3306e^{-16}$
	Backer-centric-2 (Campaign $\geq$ 3)	0.9209*	$3.3306e^{-16}$	0.9321*	0.0001	0.9582*	0.0001
CNN	Campaign-centric	0.6810	0.0001	0.6379	0.0001	0.7729	0.0001
	Backer-centric-1 (Campaign $\geq$ 1)	0.9059*	0.0035	0.9237*	0.0033	0.9389*	0.0004
	Backer-centric-2 (Campaign $\geq$ 3)	0.9207*	0.0027	0.9320*	0.0023	0.9582*	0.0009
RF	Campaign-centric	0.6989	0.0037	0.7009	0.0038	0.7720	0.0017
	Backer-centric-1 (Campaign $\geq$ 1)	0.9059*	0.0038	0.9237*	0.0034	0.9339*	0.0005
	Backer-centric-2 (Campaign $\geq$ 3)	0.9209*	0.0037	0.9319*	0.0050	0.9580*	0.0033

* Means the *p-value* is < .001.

In the promotion process of crowdfunding campaigns, there exists the phenomenon of "word-of-mouth marketing" or "social influence marketing." Word-of-mouth marketing refers to the spread of information, campaign recommendations, or services through social circles and personal connections by backers or creators. For example, backers may rally friends to support a campaign through social networks. Some backers become one-time silent users during this promotional process, supporting only a single campaign and not continuing to follow other campaigns on the platform. Such backers cannot be considered as active backers. Therefore, we excluded the backers who have only supported one or two campaigns in the dataset. The results show that the Backer-centric-2 model (supporting campaigns $\geq$ 3) outperforms the Backer-centric-2 model (supporting campaigns $\geq$ 1) by 1.49%, 0.83%, and 1.93% on the three metrics, respectively. This result confirms that our consideration of one-time backers brought in by word-of-mouth marketing (supporting only one campaign) is correct. Excluding inactive backers further enhances the accuracy of the backer-centric prediction model, indicating the contribution of active backers to model performance.

During the model validation process, CNN and RF algorithms were also employed in addition to the SVM algorithm. Although these algorithms showed slight differences in evaluation metrics during the validation process, overall fluctuations were small, indicating relatively stable performance. These minor differences did not significantly impact the predictive effectiveness of the models. This result demonstrates the robustness and consistency of the models. Therefore, the ultimate determinant of crowdfunding success prediction model performance is the model design approach, once again emphasizing the importance of backers' preferences as the crucial determinants of crowdfunding success. Additionally, we also conducted t-tests to assess the significance of the model evaluation metrics. The results indicate that our proposed backer-centric prediction method based on backers' preferences outperforms the campaign-centric approach.

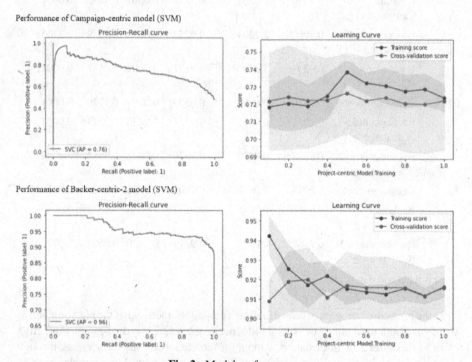

Fig. 2. Model performance.

6 Conclusion and Discussion

Backers, as crucial decision-makers in the fundraising process, play a pivotal role in predicting campaign crowdfunding success. Due to variations in backgrounds, cultures, interests, and experiences, backers' preferences are diverse and unique, and treating all backers as homogeneous has limitations. When using preferences for success prediction, it is essential to thoroughly and comprehensively consider backers' unique preferences. Our research results demonstrate that transitioning the predictive model from a campaign-centric perspective to a backer-centric perspective improves accuracy, F-1 score, and AUC by 8.70%, 12.73%, and 13.58%, respectively. Additionally, excluding less active backers when calculating collective preferences within categories further enhances the model's predictive performance. These findings confirm the effectiveness of predicting campaign success based on backers' preferences and validate that the backer-centric approach can enhance existing campaign-centric methods. Therefore, our research makes significant contributions both theoretically and practically.

Our study contributes to crowdfunding theoretical research by spotlighting the importance of individual backer preferences. It introduces a novel approach and perspective for studying crowdfunding platforms. Through the analysis of backer preferences to forecast campaign success, we deepen our understanding of backers' behaviors and decision-making processes. This insight sheds light on backers' inclinations toward campaign concepts, products, and perceived risks behind campaigns, as well as the factors influencing their funding decisions.

In practical terms, our findings offer valuable insights for crowdfunding platforms. By predicting campaign success more accurately, platforms can enhance their ability to evaluate the likelihood of a campaign's success. This, in turn, enables platforms to offer targeted support and guidance to campaigns, thereby improving their chances of securing funding and boosting overall success rates. Furthermore, by identifying which campaigns are more likely to succeed, both backers and platforms can allocate resources more efficiently, maximizing returns while minimizing risks. Moreover, the ability to predict campaign success provides entrepreneurs and creators with essential market insights. It helps them formulate future business strategies and decisions based on prevailing market dynamics and trends, allowing for more informed and effective decision-making. By understanding market demand and trends, entrepreneurs and creators can adapt their approaches to align with backer preferences, thereby increasing their likelihood of success in the crowdfunding landscape.

Several limitations of this paper should be notices. This study selected a set of factors that have been proven to significantly influence crowdfunding success to represent campaigns and backer preferences, but it may not be a complete representation. In future research, more factors could be incorporated to capture preferences from different perspectives. Second, this study employed recently active backers on the platform to model and predict, which may not necessarily represent the preferences of all backers. Obtaining a comprehensive dataset of backer information could potentially further enhance predictive accuracy.

Acknowledgement. This research was supported by the National Natural Science Foundation of China under Grant 72272066.

References

1. Belleflamme, P., Lambert, T., Schwienbacher, A.: Crowdfunding: tapping the right crowd. J. Bus. Ventur. **29**(5), 585–609 (2014)
2. Li, Y., Cabano, F., Li, P.: How to attract low prosocial funders in crowdfunding? matching among funders, project descriptions, and platform types. Inform. Manage. **60**(7), 103840 (2023)
3. Lukkarinen, A., Teich, J., Wallenius, H., Wallenius, J.: Success drivers of online equity crowdfunding campaigns. Decis. Support. Syst. **87**, 26–38 (2016)
4. Kuppuswamy, V., Bayus, B.L.: Does my contribution to your crowdfunding project matter? J. Bus. Ventur. **32**(1), 72–89 (2017)
5. Chen, Y., Zhou, S., Jin, W., Chen, S.: Investigating the determinants of medical crowdfunding performance: a signaling theory perspective. Internet Res. **33**(3), 1134–1156 (2023)

6. Ba, Z., Zhao, Y., Zhou, L., Song, S.: Exploring the donation allocation of online charitable crowdfunding based on topical and spatial analysis: evidence from the Tencent GongYi. Inf. Process. Manage. **57**(6), 102322 (2020)
7. Gerber, E.M., Hui, J.: Crowdfunding: Motivations and deterrents for participation. ACM Trans. Comput.-Human Interact. (TOCHI) **20**(6), 1–32 (2013)
8. Du, Q., Li, J., Du, Y., Wang, G.A., Fan, W.: Predicting crowdfunding project success based on backers' language preferences. J. Am. Soc. Inf. Sci. **72**(12), 1558–1574 (2021)
9. Lee, C.H., Chiravuri, A.: Dealing with initial success versus failure in crowdfunding market: serial crowdfunding, changing strategies, and funding performance. Internet Res. **29**(5), 1190–1212 (2019)
10. Chaganti, R., DeCarolis, D., Deeds, D.: Predictors of capital structure in small ventures. Entrep. Theory Pract. **20**(2), 7–18 (1996)
11. Li, J.J., Chen, X.-P., Kotha, S., Fisher, G.: Catching fire and spreading it: a glimpse into displayed entrepreneurial passion in crowdfunding campaigns. J. Appl. Psychol. **102**(7), 1075 (2017)
12. Yang, S., Ke, X., Cheng, C., Bian, Y.: A matter of life and death: the power of personal networks for medical crowdfunding performance. Soc Sci Med **329**, 115968 (2023)
13. Gupta, J.P., Li, H., Kärkkäinen, H., Mukkamala, R.R.: The role of project owners' and potential backers' implicit social ties in crowdfunding project success. Internet Res. **34**(7), 1–23 (2023)
14. Li, Y.M., Liou, Y.M., Li, Y.W.: A social recommendation approach for reward-based crowdfunding campaigns. Inform. Manage. **57**(7), 103246 (2020)
15. Jiménez-Jiménez, F., Alba-Fernández, M.V., Martínez-Gómez, C.: Attracting the right crowd under asymmetric information: a game theory application to rewards-based crowdfunding. Mathematics **9**(21), 2757 (2021)
16. Ba, Z., Zhao, Y.C., Song, S., Zhu, Q.: Understanding the determinants of online medical crowdfunding project success in China. Inf. Process. Manage. **58**(2), 102465 (2021)

A Text-Based Analysis of Crowdfunding Innovation

Lei Liu and Nianxin Wang[✉]

Jiangsu University of Science and Technology, Zhenjiang 212100, China
nianxin.wang@gmail.com

Abstract. Innovation plays a crucial role in enabling crowdfunding campaigns to establish distinctive competitive advantages and in enabling backers to assess the investment potential of the campaign. The alignment of potential backers' innovation preferences with the innovation of micro-campaigns will significantly impact their investment decisions and, consequently, the performance of crowdfunding. However, assessing the degree of innovation as an implicit evaluation factor is more challenging compared to explicit evaluation factors such as titles, comments, and pictures directly presented on the platform. Furthermore, corporate innovation measurement methods based on patents, R&D expenditures, and new product indicators are not applicable to micro-campaigns within the crowdfunding domain. Consequently, the accurate measurement of innovation in micro-campaigns within crowdfunding presents an urgent issue to be addressed in the examination of backers' innovation preferences and the campaign innovation mechanism. We present a novel approach for measuring innovation by integrating topic modeling and word embedding to assess text similarity. The study involved analyzing the textual content of 15,761 crowdfunding campaigns on Indiegogo. The findings indicate that the text-based innovation measurement method is capable of capturing a wide range of innovations, including those that fall within the scope of patent disclosure and innovation description. The study suggests that text-based innovation proxy indicators are effective and outperform traditional innovation indicators in comprehensively capturing innovation practices in crowdfunding campaigns. Furthermore, this study identified an empirical "inverted U"-shaped correlation between innovation and crowdfunding performance. This article presents concepts and criteria for investigating innovation mechanisms and influential factors in the realm of crowdfunding, focusing on methods for measuring innovation.

Keywords: Crowdfunding · Innovation · Text Analysis · Topic Modeling · Indiegogo · Campaign Story

1 Introduction

Crowdfunding provides a low-threshold, high-efficiency, and diverse means of commercial financing for showcasing, promoting, and executing creative ideas and innovative campaigns via online platforms on the Internet [1]. The global crowdfunding market is projected to reach US$1.41 billion in 2023, with a sustained growth rate of over 10%.

© The Author(s), under exclusive license to Springer Nature Switzerland AG 2024
Y. P. Tu and M. Chi (Eds.): WHICEB 2024, LNBIP 516, pp. 73–83, 2024.
https://doi.org/10.1007/978-3-031-60260-3_7

Nevertheless, the global crowdfunding activities exhibit an average success rate of only 23.7%, and many innovative campaigns encounter challenges in securing the anticipated funds. Research on the factors influencing crowdfunding performance has been crucial. Existing studies have examined the effects on performance and offered expert advice based on the fundamental aspects of the campaign, the behavioral motivations and experiences of creators, and the preferences of backers [2].

"Indiegogo is where new launches." is the core concept of the mainstream crowdfunding platform Indiegogo [3]. Crowdfunding involves individuals or organizations presenting new products, models, or processes to the public in order to secure financial backing. The core of its model lies in securing financial support by promoting innovation to raise funds. The extent to which the backers' subconscious expectations for innovation align with the actual innovation of the initiating campaign is a crucial determinant of whether the campaign will receive funding. Consequently, research on innovation has a significant influence on the innovation preferences of backers, funding decisions, and crowdfunding performance. Conducting research on influential factors is of paramount importance. Nevertheless, there is limited scholarly attention directed towards the innovation of crowdfunding micro-campaigns. The primary rationale is that innovation, as an implicit factor, presents greater challenges and costs in comparison to explicit evaluation factors such as platform titles and comments. The precision of innovation measurement is impacted by a range of factors, such as the diversity of innovation dimensions, the complexity of the business environment, and the variety of potential customers. Previous studies typically employ input-output innovation indicators in corporate settings, such as patents, R&D investments, new product features, and talent acquisition, to assess innovation [4]. The focus of their attention is typically on product and technology dimensions, while neglecting the multi-dimensional innovations such as market channels and organizational forms [5]. They also exhibit less consistency with crowdfunding micro-campaigns in terms of measurement dimensions and data content. Additionally, it is important to note that applying for a patent does not necessarily indicate high innovation, and the absence of patent disclosure may also be a form of self-protection for innovative campaigns. As a result, conventional indicators are inadequate for fully and effectively representing the innovation of micro-campaigns in the realm of crowdfunding.

Unstructured text analysis using natural language processing (NLP) provides a novel approach to measuring innovation in terms of objectivity, comprehensiveness, and cost-effectiveness. This paper presents the integration of the Word2Vec and LDA fusion model in the context of crowdfunding innovation research. It serves as a fundamental element in the development of a text-based measurement method for crowdfunding innovation. It leverages latent semantic information from textual descriptions to develop innovation measurement indicators, addressing the challenge of innovation measurement. We elucidated the benefits of utilizing crowdfunding for campaign texts, outlined the design principles of the method, and detailed the construction process of the fusion model that is based on topic and word embeddings. Furthermore, we performed a comparative analysis between the text-based crowdfunding innovation measurement method and traditional innovation indicators, demonstrating the effectiveness and advantages of the design methods presented in this article. The study also identified an inverted U-shaped relationship between innovation and crowdfunding performance.

This study presents a text vectorization approach that combines LDA and Word2Vec models to create an easily interpretable and modelable method. It calculates the load of crowdfunding campaign text and standard innovation vectors to derive text-based crowdfunding innovation indicators. The method offers a comprehensive innovation measurement approach based on objective data, capable of capturing innovation beyond traditional indicators such as patent disclosure and innovation description. The study broadens the utilization of NLP and text analysis techniques within the realm of crowdfunding, while also establishing the foundational requirements for future investigations into the internal mechanisms and performance correlations of crowdfunding innovation.

2   Literature Review

2.1   Innovation in Crowdfunding

Crowdfunding research primarily encompasses four main entities: campaigns, backers, creators and platforms, focuses on the factors affecting performance through the examination of attribute characteristics, behavioral motivations and preferences, and platform mechanisms. Innovation serves as the fundamental rationale and primary impetus for the advancement of the crowdfunding industry. Research on innovation in the field of crowdfunding primarily emphasizes the macro level. The majority of the research is centered on examining the influence of crowdfunding as an emerging business model on macro-level innovation within social, industrial, and corporate contexts [1, 6]. It is hard to offer specific guidance on business behaviors and decisions. The alignment between campaign innovation and the innovation preferences of backers is a crucial factor at the micro level, which has the potential to influence funding decisions and crowdfunding performance. Nevertheless, there is a paucity of research on innovation in micro campaigns. The primary challenge lies in the difficulty and cost associated with measuring campaign innovation.

The process of innovation involves the recombination of various production factors, including products, technology, personnel, and markets, making its measurement a complex undertaking [5]. The predominant approach to measuring enterprise innovation typically involves using patents, R&D, and new products as primary indicators. However, this method may not be suitable for assessing innovation in micro-campaigns on online platforms. Based on the comprehensiveness of innovation, several studies have expanded upon traditional innovation measurement methods by considering data acquisition from two main dimensions: subjective data obtained from real experiments and questionnaires, and objective data derived from text descriptions. Chan and Parhankangas employed empirical methods to assess incremental innovation and crucial innovation in the context of crowdfunding, and examined the influence of different innovation types on funding outcomes [7]. Other researchers utilized questionnaire surveys to investigate the correlation between firms and their competitors in terms of product innovation performance, as well as variances in innovation performance across market, management, and other dimensions. The assessment outcomes based on subjective evaluation can be significantly influenced by the immediate condition and psychological predisposition of the participants, resulting in relatively low objectivity and scalability, as well as high associated costs. Utilizing objective textual data from sources such as corporate annual reports, company reports, and project descriptions, it ensures the comprehensiveness, objectivity, and cost-effectiveness of innovation practice characteristics. Additionally, it offers novel insights for measuring innovation in micro-campaigns. For instance, Bellstam developed a model based on the S&P 500 corporate reports' text. The new proxy indicator for innovation effectively forecasts the company's innovation performance and identifies opportunities for improvement over the next four years [8].

2.2 Text Analysis and Topic Modeling

As an interdisciplinary subject in linguistics and computer science, text analysis has attracted much attention in academic, business, and social contexts. It has evolved from early rule matching to the current use of machine learning and deep learning techniques. The topic model is a traditional method of text analysis. The process involves the conversion of documents into word frequency vectors, transforming intricate textual data into easily modelled digital information, and serving a crucial function in tasks such as topic extraction and sentiment analysis.

Crowdfunding operates as an intermediary business model that relies on user-generated content (UGC). Creators disseminate information on the platform in various forms such as text, comments, and pictures. Accurately analyzing both structured and unstructured data is essential for research in crowdfunding and innovation. Text analysis is predominantly utilized in crowdfunding research to examine the influence of textual information characteristics on campaign performance and to forecast success [9]. The topic model is primarily utilized for identifying the principal themes of a campaign, including the creator's intent, campaign innovation, and for conducting dynamic evolution analysis of textual topics [10]. Jiang's team utilized text analysis methods and LDA topic models to analyze the campaign's description text. They extracted campaign topics and backers' emotions as soft information in order to investigate their relationship with financing performance [11]. Text analysis methods and classic topic models play an important role in crowdfunding influence mechanisms, prediction recommendations, and measuring corporate innovation. Nevertheless, there is a scarcity of studies that measure and apply innovation based on textual and topical analysis. The primary rationale is that the majority of the aforementioned research emphasizes the characteristics of the method. The LDA model specifically concentrates on elucidating and tracing the development of topics. This article aims to propose a novel approach for evaluating innovation in crowdfunding campaigns by leveraging the comprehensiveness and objectivity of textual features, as well as the ease of modeling and interpretability offered by the LDA topic model.

3 Data

3.1 Data Sources

The data presented in this article originates from the incentive crowdfunding platform Indiegogo [3]. Python was utilized to collect fundamental data from 16,789 campaigns categorized under TECH & INNOVATION, which included detailed descriptive text (referred to as the STORY section) for each campaign. The data was subjected to several processing steps: removal of invalid project samples (test samples, outliers, and those with missing values), elimination of duplicate samples, exclusion of samples in languages other than English. To ensure the stability and accuracy of text vectorization and topic extraction results during the training process of the LDA and Word2Vec fusion model, and to scientifically capture the overall structure and features of the text, campaign samples with detailed descriptions containing fewer than 50 words (the 3rd percentile of word count distribution) are excluded. Subsequently, 15,764 campaign observation samples were obtained for the design and application of the innovation measurement model.

3.2 Innovation Textbook

Text-based innovation measurement requires authoritative innovation textbook as a benchmark. After conducting thorough literature research, we have chosen "MANAGING INNOVATION-INTEGRATING TECHNOLOGICAL, MARKET AND ORGANIZATIONAL CHANGE" ("MANAGING INNOVATION") by JOE TIDD & JOHN BESSANT as the primary source for the innovation standard text [8]. This book addresses various dimensions of innovation, including management innovation, new product development, market and organizational change. It includes numerous real case studies, illustrative examples, and problem discussions. The text is rich in semantic content and objective authenticity. Furthermore, it offers a evidence-based innovation management methodology that is underpinned by the latest academic research and real-world management practice. To mitigate forward-looking bias, we opted to use the 2018 sixth edition of "MANAGING INNOVATION" as the reference point for the innovation in crowdfunding campaigns from 2014 to 2018 [12].

4 Text-Based Measure of Innovation in Crowdfunding

4.1 Informativeness of Crowdfunding's Story Text

The information asymmetry present in crowdfunding platforms may influence backers' perceptions of the creator's capacity to fulfill commitments, leading to the emergence of a "trust gap." In order to secure optimal financing, creators will utilize the platform to showcase a comprehensive array of campaign advantages and innovative value information, with the aim of proactively mitigating risks and fostering trust. The detailed description section of a crowdfunding campaign, such as Indiegogo's STORY section, is where the largest proportion of information is displayed. It represents the creator's best effort to qualitatively describe the value of the campaign. Indiegogo was established to empower innovation. In the detailed description of the campaign, the creator will disclose the basic information and emphasize the core value of innovation to enhance trust from backers. The STORY module on Indiegogo encompasses campaign introduction, technical details, innovative features, user value, funding and return plans, partnerships, and more. Consequently, the detailed description section serves as a high-quality data source for comprehensively and objectively capturing and measuring innovation. The detailed description section serves as fundamental data for the design of innovation measurement methods.

4.2 Measurement Method Design

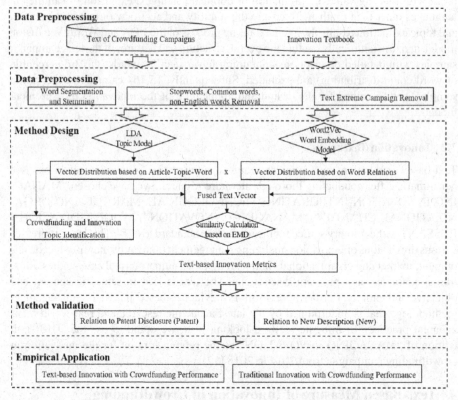

Fig. 1. Design and Application of Innovation Measure Method

The text-based innovation measurement model calculates the load of the campaign description on the innovation criterion by measuring the textual similarity between the description and "MANAGING INNOVATION", which represents the degree of innovation. First, the integration of the LDA topic model and the Word2Vec word embedding model is employed to transform the two sets of texts into vectors that encapsulate topic-level relationships and vocabulary-level relationships. Secondly, the distinction between the description and the standard innovation is determined by computing the similarity index EMD (Earth Mover's Distance) between the two vectors. Finally, the difference indicators are standardized in order to derive innovation proxy indicators. The measurement method incorporates NLP technology to comprehensively capture the semantic and correlation features between texts. It combines the topic model and word embedding model, while also considering the semantic relationship between "document-topic-vocabulary" and "vocabulary-vocabulary". This enhances the comprehensiveness, accuracy, and interpretability of the measurement. The campaign description's innovation is ultimately assessed through precise similarity calculations. This method provides support for assessing innovation in extensive samples (Fig. 1).

The "bag of words" model based on unordered sets - the LDA topic model cannot represent vocabulary-level contextual semantic relationships in vectors. Consequently, we capture vocabulary-level contextual semantic information by merging the Word2Vec word embedding model. The text vector is computed to represent the comprehensive semantic content of the document, based on the fusion of LDA and Word2Vec models [13]. The process of model fusion involves several steps. Firstly, the LDA model is utilized to acquire the topic distribution of the document. Secondly, the Word2Vec model is employed to map each word into a low-dimensional vector space. Finally, the overall vector representation of the document is obtained through weighted summation. The formula is presented as follows:

$$D = \sum_{t=1}^{i} P(t|d) \times (\sum_{k=1}^{j} P(w_k|t) \times V_{w_k})$$

D represents the vector representation of the document.

$P(t|d)$ is the probability distribution of topic t in document d in the LDA model.

$P(w_k|t)$ is the probability distribution of word w_k in topic t in the LDA model.

V_{w_k} is the vector representation of word w_k in the Word2Vec model.

4.3 Crowdfunding Innovation Topics

See Table 1.

Table 1. Crowdfunding innovation campaigns text topic word cloud

Number	Topic	Topic Words (Top 15)
Topic 0	Product Development and Design	product device design battery power phone light bike production work campaign smart charge quality case
Topic 1	Sustainable and Green	water food product coffee energy people plant new local beer bottle campaign clean project world
Topic 2	Education & Community Support	school student community child people project program support education campaign world fund family goal work
Topic 3	Innovation and Technological Development	new innovation business development technology project product people user service system work company data market
Topic 4	Humanities and Family Health	people campaign world goal family support new share health perk work product money woman book

The study identified the ideal number of topics in LDA as K = 5 by evaluating perplexity, coherence, and pyLDAvis visualization. It also extracted and summarized the topics related to crowdfunding innovation campaigns, specifically focusing on five scenarios: product development and design, sustainability and environmental protection, education and community support, humanities and family health, and innovation and technological development. The textual content of each campaign exhibits a distinct distribution across the five topics, thereby facilitating the elucidation of the campaign's innovative significance. The degree of campaign innovation is determined by assessing the disparity in content between the crowdfunding campaign text and the standard text on innovation for each topic.

4.4   Comparison with Traditional Metrics

The disclosure of patents and the description of innovation are commonly used as proxy indicators for measuring innovation [14]. This study validates the efficacy and advantages of text-based innovation indicators through an examination of the relationship between text-based innovation indicators and patent disclosure, innovation description. The non-parametric Mann-Whitney test was employed to compare the distribution of patent disclosures and innovation descriptions in terms of text-based innovation. The results were visually represented using box plots to display the quartiles. The findings revealed that the degree of innovation in the presence of patent disclosure and innovation description was 0.0374 and 0.0332 higher, respectively, compared to the absence of patent disclosure and innovation description. This suggests a significant positive association between text-based innovation and patent disclosure, innovation description. The new indicator has the capability to capture the innovation represented by patent disclosure and innovation description (Table 2).

Table 2. Mann-Whitney Non-parametric Test Results of Sample Grouping

Variable	All	Patents > 0	Patents = 0	(2) − (3)	New > 0	New = 0	(5) − (6)
	(1)	(2)	(3)	(4)	(5)	(6)	(7)
Text-Based Innovation	0.4268	0.4611	0.4237	0.0374***	0.4322	0.3990	0.0332***
Patents	0	1	0	1***	0	0	0
New	3	4	3	1***	3	0	3***

Note: * p < 0.10; ** p < 0.05; *** p < 0.01

Furthermore, according to the results of the Mann-Whitney non-parametric test and the box plot distribution presented above, it is evident that there is a substantial degree of overlap in the distribution of text-based innovation indicators between the sample groups with and without patent disclosure, as well as between the sample groups with and without innovation description. The statement implies that text-based innovation measurement methods may be able to capture project innovation practices that go beyond patent disclosures and innovation descriptions. Consequently, the research chose three projects, each with and without patent disclosure, from the top 30% of innovative projects to qualitatively assess whether the text-based innovation measurement method accurately identifies campaign innovation in the absence of patent disclosure (Fig. 2).

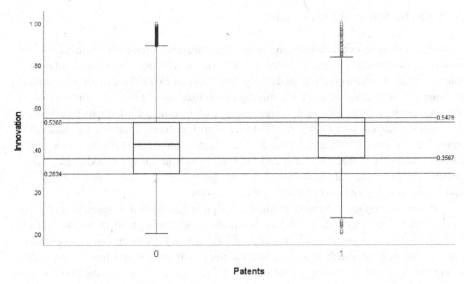

Fig. 2. Distribution of Text-Based Innovation on Patents

Three campaigns that chose not to disclose patent are:

1. "The Controls: Control your Appliances from Anywhere", which employed Wi-Fi timing and web remote control for IoT monitoring and smart controllers, was initiated in 2015.
2. The "Mooz: Industrial Grade Transformable 3D Printer", introducing an industrial-grade 3D printer capable of converting between laser engraving and CNC engraving at will.
3. The "HiGame PC - Affordable High-Performance Mini PC", which was initiated in 2018, showcases a mini processor that achieves high-performance integration at a size 15 times smaller than that of a traditional PC.

At that time, Internet of Things technology, 3D printing technology, and mini processor integration technology were all emerging technologies, exerting significant influence and disruptive effects in their respective fields. Although the patent status of the campaigns is not disclosed in their descriptions, the advanced integrated technologies and achieved product features suggest a high level of advancement and innovation. This highlights the capacity of the text-based innovation measurement method to encompass innovation beyond patent metrics. Similarly, the qualitative comparison method was utilized to validate the capability of our approach to capture innovation that extends beyond the mere description of innovation. The study concludes that the effectiveness and superiority of the text-based innovation measurement method were confirmed through a combination of quantitative and qualitative perspectives.

5   Conclusion and Discussion

Crowdfunding empowers innovation, and the accurate measurement of campaign innovation is a fundamental aspect in the examination of innovation mechanisms and performance impact mechanisms. The study integrated LDA and Word2vec models to conduct a comprehensive analysis and topic mining of the text content available on Indiegogo. This approach facilitated the vector representation of document-topic-word-level semantics, and employed a similarity model to develop text-based methods for measuring innovation in design and development. The comparison with traditional proxy indicators demonstrates that the text-based innovation measurement method is capable of capturing a wide range of innovation practices, encompassing not only patent disclosure and innovation description but also other dimensions.

The innovation measurement method's design is based on the integration of topic models and word embedding models. Innovation indicators are derived through the computation of standard innovation loads, offering a novel approach to measuring innovation. The new approach is appropriate for micro campaigns and has the capability to encompass multidimensional innovation, including innovation represented by conventional indicators like innovation description and patent disclosure. It addresses the limitations of current research in measuring innovation in micro-campaigns and can also be applied to assess innovation in other macro- and micro-research contexts.

Based on this premise, the measurement and application of crowdfunding campaign innovation can analyze the innovation mechanism and its impact value at the micro project level. Furthermore, it can offer insights for macro-level innovation research and facilitate the development of more objective and comprehensive corporate strategies or micro project implementations. In comparison to "A Text-Based Analysis of Corporate Innovation" by Gustaf Bellstam et al. in the 2021 issue of "Management Science" [8], our research centers on micro-projects within the realm of crowdfunding and achieves micro-level insights in the emerging domain of innovation measurement techniques. In the application, the measurement model was designed using a fusion model of Word2Vec and LDA to address the limitations of the disordered set characteristics of separate LDA. An objective comparative analysis of the four indicators KL, JS, COS, and EMD was conducted during the distance calculation stage. The process of indicators selection made the approach design more scientific.

Nevertheless, this study is still subject to certain limitations. From a data perspective, it is important to consider not only the detailed description text, but also the brief text in the title and "TAG" when measuring innovation. Furthermore, instances exist in which pictures are utilized for the purpose of conveying information in the campaign description. The text within the pictures needs to be identified, extracted, and analyzed consistently to ensure the comprehensiveness and scientific rigor of the data.

Subsequently, an inverted U-shaped relationship between campaign innovation and crowdfunding performance was identified, using the results of innovation measurement. Backers tend to favor moderately innovative campaigns, and excessively low or high levels of innovation are not conducive to the success of campaign fundraising. This statement confirms the presence of the "innovation maximization fallacy" from a consumer perspective [15].

Acknowledgement. This research was supported by the National Natural Science Foundation of China under Grant 72272066.

References

1. Mollick, E.: The Dynamics of Crowdfunding: An Exploratory Study. J. Bus. Ventur. **29**(1), 1–16 (2014)
2. Wang, N.X., Li, Q.X., Liang, H.G., Ye, T.F., Ge, S.L.: Understanding the im-portance of interaction between creators and backers in crowdfunding success. Electron. Commer. Res. Appl. **27**, 106–117 (2018)
3. Crowdfund Innovation & Support Entrepreneurs | Indiegogo, https://www.indiegogo.com
4. Andries, P., Faems, D.: Patenting Activities and Firm Performance: Does Firm Size Matter?: Patenting Activities and Firm Performance. Journal of Product Innovation Man-agement **30**(6), 1089–1098 (2013)
5. Schumpeter, J.A.: The Theory of Economic Development: An Inquiry Into Profits, Capital. Interest, and the Business Cycle. Economics Third World studies Transaction Books, Credit (1983)
6. Brem, A., Bilgram, V., Marchuk, A.: How crowdfunding platforms change the nature of user innovation – from problem solving to entrepreneurship. Technol. Forecast. Soc. Chang. **144**, 348–360 (2019)
7. Chan, C.S., Parhankangas, A.: Crowdfunding Innovative Ideas: How Incremental and Radical Innovativeness Influence Funding Outcomes. Entrep. Theory Pract. **41**(2), 237–263 (2017)
8. Bellstam, G., Bhagat, S., Cookson, J.: A Text-Based Analysis of Corporate Innovation. Manage. Sci. **67**(7), 4004–4031 (2020)
9. Chen, Y., Zhou, S., Jin, W., Chen, S.: Investigating the determinants of medical crowd-funding performance: a signaling theory perspective. Internet Res. **33**(3), 1134–1156 (2023)
10. Shafqat, W., Byun, Y.: Topic Predictions and Optimized Recommendation Mechanism Based on Integrated Topic Modeling and Deep Neural Networks in Crowdfunding Plat-forms. Appl. Sci. **9**(24), 5496 (2019)
11. Jiang, C., Han, R., Xu, Q., Liu, Y.: The impact of soft information extracted from de-scriptive text on crowdfunding performance. Electronic Commerce Research and Applica-tions **43**, 101002 (2020)
12. Tidd, J., Bessant, J.R.: Managing Innovation: Integrating Technological. Wiley, Market and Organizational Change (2018)
13. Moody, C.: Mixing Dirichlet Topic Models and Word Embeddings to Make lda2vec. (2016)
14. Seigner, B., Milanov, H., McKenny, A.: Who can claim innovation and benefit from it? Gender and expectancy violations in reward-based crowdfunding. Strategic Entrepreneur-ship Journal **16**(2), 381–422 (2022)
15. Parhankangas, A., Renko, M.: Linguistic style and crowdfunding success among social and commercial entrepreneurs. J. Bus. Ventur. **32**(2), 215–236 (2017)

Why Does Perceived Humanness Predict AI Use Intention? The Mediating Roles of Perceived Values and Perceived Risk

Tian Xia[1(✉)], Xiangyin Kong[2], Qiang Mai[1], Huijing Guo[3], and Xiaoxiao Liu[4,5]

[1] School of Management, Harbin Institute of Technology, Harbin 150001, China
xiatian2009726@163.com
[2] School of Management, Harbin Engineering University, Harbin 150001, China
[3] School of Economics and Management, China University of Mining and Technology, Xuzhou 221116, China
[4] School of Management, Xi'an Jiaotong University, Xi'an 710049, China
[5] China Institute of Hospital Development and Reform, Xi'an Jiaotong University, Xi'an 710049, China

Abstract. Nowadays artificial intelligence (AI) has been widely used in the healthcare industry. AI can provide improved healthcare services by advancing technologies and individuals expect AI's human-like responses. This study aims to understand how the perceived humanness of AI influences individuals' use intention of AI in health consultations. In view of the influencing mechanism model, this study carries out an in-depth study. This study develops a model to explore the relationship among perceived humanness, AI use intention, perceived values (utilitarian value and hedonic value), and perceived risk (PR). Meanwhile, it tests the mediating roles of perceived values and perceived risk on the relationship between perceived humanness and AI use intention. 275 university students were involved in this study. Results show that perceived utilitarian value and perceived hedonic value fully mediate the relationship, while perceived risk could not show a significant effect. This study shows evidence of why designing AI with perceived humanness increases users' intention in health consultations.

Keywords: AI · Perceived Humanness · Perceived Values · Perceived Risk

1 Introduction

The term artificial intelligence (AI) was coined in the 1950s. And the application of AI in the healthcare industry is gradually becoming popular. There are multiple subdomains in the healthcare domain where AI-based services are utilized, like nursing assistants, health consultation, treatment design, medication management, and so on [1]· In this study, we focus on the application of AI in health consultations and carry out the following research.

Chat Generative Pre-trained Transformer (ChatGPT) is a public tool with a pre-trained AI model designed to engage in natural language conversations. Meanwhile, it creates responses to user prompts like humans and it could respond to a wide range of

Y. P. Tu and M. Chi (Eds.): WHICEB 2024, LNBIP 516, pp. 84–94, 2024.
https://doi.org/10.1007/978-3-031-60260-3_8

health topics. In this study, we use ChatGPT as the research tool to investigate people's AI use intention.

In the process of AI use, other than simply receiving responses with similar output every time, people expect more. A human-like feeling is needed in a conversational interaction. During the interaction with AI, users will feel to be heard if they receive the responses that AI understands them, facilitating further interactions [2]. The perceived humanness of AI does increase the willingness of AI to be used, but few research tried to understand the mechanism that how perceived humanness influence AI use intention.

This study tries to fill this research gap. To achieve our research objectives, we try to understand how the perceived humanness of AI influences individuals' use intention of AI in health consultations. This study develops a model to explore the relationship among perceived humanness, AI use intention, perceived values, and perceived risk. Meanwhile, it tests the mediating roles of perceived values and perceived risk on the relationship between perceived humanness and AI use intention.

2 Literature Review and Hypotheses Development

Based on existing literature and discussion, we propose ten hypotheses. A research model is developed to explore the relationship among perceived humanness, AI use intention, perceived values,.and perceived risk (PR). Meanwhile, we try to understand the mediating roles of perceived values and perceived risk between perceived humanness with AI use intention.

2.1 Perceived Humanness and AI Use Intention

Conversations can take place not just between humans but also between humans and other people who are perceived to have awareness. In computer science, AI is the study of the "automation of intelligent behavior". AI technology allows machines to be trained to "think", or at least appear to think. It has taken decades for humans to develop AI that can mimic human intelligence or the human mind [3]. The goal of AI development has been to make it look more human.

AI systems are becoming more and more integrated into people's daily lives and work environments. The use of AI in the healthcare industry has risen rapidly in various areas, including mobile health, virtual patient education, intelligent medical robots, and human body monitoring and processing systems, and previous studies highlight the importance of AI in healthcare. Meanwhile, AI is able to provide improved healthcare services by advancing technologies.

Perceived humanness refers to the degree to which a person believes that AI might be human. Previous research confirms that users expect AI to behave in a human-like manner [4]. Users are attracted to human-like AI [5] and the perceived humanness of AI would increase the intention to use AI [6]. Then we propose the hypothesis below:

H1: Perceived humanness of AI has a positive impact on AI use intention for health consultation.

2.2 Mediating Role of Perceived Values

Perceived value can be categorized into utilitarian value, hedonic value, and symbolic value. When individuals engage in AI-enabled health consultations, they tend to prioritize the usefulness of the AI's health advice, rather than aspects unrelated to health. Therefore, we specifically focus on utilitarian value and hedonic value.

In AI-enabled health consultations, the utilitarian value represents the pursuit of usefulness in health outcomes [7], including factors like time savings, effectiveness, and access to better health information. Perceived humanness of AI positively influences the characteristics of service value expectations especially utilitarian value expectations [8]. Because during the cognitive process of expectations, underlying satisfaction is closely related to assessments of utilitarian value [9]. Then we propose the hypothesis below:

H2a: Perceived humanness of AI has a positive impact on users' perceived utilitarian value.

Prior research demonstrates the disparities between utilitarian and hedonic value's respective influences on online behavioral intention and that utilitarian value has a stronger correlation with intention than hedonic value [10]. People's online behavioral intention is driven more by utilitarian value, meaning that individual health consultation choice patterns are influenced by their perceived utilitarian value [11]. Then we propose the hypothesis below:

H2b: Perceived utilitarian value has a positive impact on AI use intention for health consultation.

Before using AI to conduct health consulting behavior, users will evaluate the perceived utilitarian value. It can be inferred that the evaluation of perceived utilitarian value will mediate the relationship between the perceived humanness of AI and AI use intention. Based on the hypothesis analysis of H2a and H2b, we propose the hypothesis below:

H2c: Perceived utilitarian value mediates the interaction between perceived humanness and AI use intention for health consultation.

Perceived hedonic value, different from perceived utilitarian value, also influences consumers' responses toward products or services. Taking the context of AI-based health consultation environments into account, hedonic value emphasizes the subjective experience of using artificial intelligence for health consultations, such as deriving enjoyment from the process [12].

When using AI for health consultation, users expect to have a more enjoyable experience during the process. AI responses to health queries often have anthropomorphic features, and the more human-like the AI replies are, the more they can stimulate user interest. Compared to mechanized AI services, highly anthropomorphic AI interaction forms can provide users with a more intriguing diagnostic experience [13]. Based on this analysis, we propose the following hypothesis.

H3a: Perceived humanness of AI has a positive impact on users' perceived hedonic value.

With the perceived hedonic value of AI health consultation, users are more likely to engage in further actions. Perceived hedonic value aligns better with people's psychological expectations of using AI to solve health issues. When users have a high perceived hedonic value, they are guided by this psychological cognition to develop more positive intentions [14], ultimately manifested as the intention to use AI for health consultation. Therefore, based on this analysis, we propose the following hypothesis.

H3b: Perceived hedonic value has a positive impact on AI use intention for health consultation.

Previous research has shown that users emphasize their interest in the usage process when considering whether to use AI [15]. Therefore, it can be inferred that perceived hedonic value plays a mediating role between perceived humanness and AI use intention. Based on the hypothesis analysis of H3a and H3b, we propose the hypothesis below:

H3c: Perceived hedonic value mediates the interaction between perceived humanness and AI use intention for health consultation.

2.3 Mediating Role of Perceived Risk

The definition of PR is that person becomes 'paralyzed' into a state of cognitive dissonance driven by their uncertainty and concern for losses [16]. In the context of health counseling, despite AI's human-like features in responding to health queries, users still perceive uncertainty and potential risks in the health services provided by AI. The higher the perceived uncertainty, the greater the perceived risks. Like online doctor consultations, the human-like characteristics of AI consultations can reduce users' perception of uncertainty. Therefore, based on this analysis, we propose the following hypothesis:

H4a: Perceived humanness of AI negatively impacts users' perceived risk.

Previous studies have found that people's perception of risk can affect their behavioral intention to use [17]. Users compare AI responses with medical advice and common knowledge. When users perceive higher uncertainty in AI responses, they are more likely to consider potential risks in using AI for health counseling, resulting in a lower likelihood of continued usage. This ultimately leads to a refusal to use AI for health counseling. Therefore, based on this analysis, we propose the following hypothesis:

H4b: Perceived risk negatively impacts users' AI use intention for health consultation.

The perception of risks by users often affects their use of AI [18]. Therefore, it can be inferred that perceived risk plays a mediating role between perceived humanness and AI use intention. Based on the hypothesis analysis of H4a and H4b, we propose the hypothesis below:

H4c: Perceived risk mediates the interaction between perceived humanness and AI use intention for health consultation.

2.4 Research Model

Based on existing literature and discussion, we developed a research model to understand the mediating roles of perceived value and perceived risk between perceived humanness with AI use intention. Specifically, we considered perceived humanness as the antecedent, utilitarian value, hedonic value, and perceived risk as the mediating variables of the research model, and AI use intention as the outcome to construct a research model. We built a research model like Fig. 1.

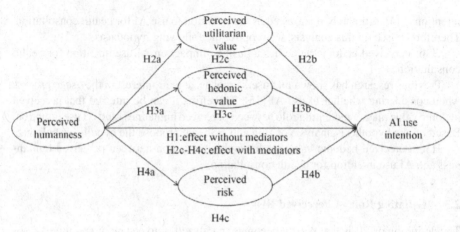

Fig. 1. Research model.

3 Methodology

3.1 Data Collection and Measures

To test the variables in this study, we adopted and developed the measurement items from previous studies (see Table 1). Before administering the formal questionnaire, we conducted preliminary tests by seeking guidance from experts in the fields of health care and AI. Their invaluable insights and recommendations played a significant role in refining our measurement items. Based on the above support and the background of this study, we translated the questionnaire into Chinese and made it more suitable for answering. Building upon this foundation, we designed and administered the questionnaires to collect data for our subsequent research.

Data for this study was collected using a paid sample service provided by an online questionnaire platform called Wenjuanxing. We conducted an online survey targeting university students, including undergraduates, masters, and doctoral students. To ensure that respondents had a clear understanding of using AI for health consultation, we presented and explained screenshots of the web pages using ChatGPT like Fig. 2. This approach helped enhance participants' comprehension of AI implementation in health consultations.

Initially, a total of 308 participants were involved in our study. To ensure the quality of the data, a systematic and manual screening process was implemented during the distribution of the questionnaire. Excluding 33 participants who did not meet the criteria of having sought AI-based consultations for health issues before completing the questionnaire, we deemed 275 responses suitable for further research. The demographic breakdown of the participants is presented in Table 2.

Table 1. Measurement scales.

Constructs	Items	
Behavioral intention	BI1	I intend to use the Chatbot for health consultations in the next three months
	BI2	I predict I would use the Chatbot for health consultation in the next three months
	BI3	I plan to use the Chatbot for health consultation in the next three months
Perceived humanness	PH	My chat partner was: 'definitely computer,' 'probably computer,' 'not sure, but guess computer,' 'not sure, but guess human,' 'probably human,' and 'definitely human'
Constructs	Items	
Perceived utilitarian value	UTV1	Health consultation services provided through Chatbot seem genuine to me
	UTV2	Health consultation services provided through Chatbot appear to be authentic
	UTV3	The way health consultations provided by Chatbot helps me to understand the details of the health-related problems
	UTV4	I am able to easily understand the health problems as it appears on Chatbot
	UTV5	I feel that I can ask Chatbot to find the health solutions I want
Perceived hedonic value	HDV1	Asking health questions through Chatbot is entertaining
	HDV2	I enjoy asking health-related questions through Chatbot
	HDV3	While asking health-related questions through Chatbot, I feel a sense of adventure
	HDV4	Asking health-related questions through Chatbot is a way of relieving stress
	HDV5	Asking health-related questions through Chatbot is a thrill for me
	HDV6	I enjoy getting a great deal when I ask health-related questions through Chatbot
	HDV7	Health consultations on Chatbot get me excited
Perceived risk	PR1	I'm worried that using Chatbot may cause me financial loss
	PR2	I worry that using Chatbot will waste me a long time
	PR3	I am worried that using Chatbot can cause information leakage and other security problems

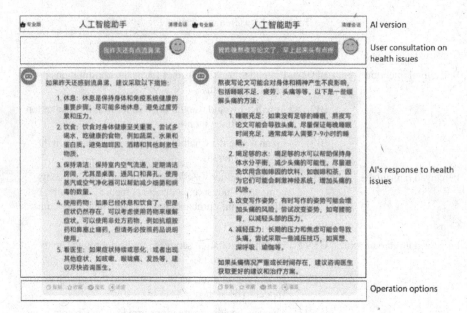

Fig. 2. Sample pictures shown to the investigator.

Table 2. Demographic statistics.

	Characteristics	Number	Percentage
Gender	Male	111	40.4%
	Female	164	59.6%
Education	Undergraduate	255	92.7%
	Postgraduate	20	7.3%
Have at least one doctor among relatives or friends	YES NO	91 184	33.1% 66.9%

3.2 Data Analysis

This study begins by assessing the reliability and validity of the constructs through the examination of item loading, average variance extracted (AVE), composite reliability (CR), and Cronbach's alpha (CA). The results are summarized in Table 3, which demonstrates that the AVE ranged from 0.569 to 1, surpassing the threshold of 0.5, and the CR ranged from 0.816 to 1, surpassing the threshold of 0.7. Additionally, all item loadings exceeded 0.7, indicating strong reliability and convergence validity of the scales. To evaluate the discriminant validity of the constructs and concepts, Table 4 presents the results, which indicate satisfactory discriminant validity of the measurements.

Further, we analyzed to examine the impact of perceived humanness on behavioral intention. The findings indicate that direct effects were supported ($\beta = 0.263$, t $= 7.126$ p < 0.001). Furthermore, the results demonstrate that both hedonic value and utilitarian

Table 3. Testing of reliability and convergent validity.

	Item	Item loading	Cronbach's alpha (CA)	Composite reliability (CR)	Average variance extracted (AVE)
Perceived humanness	PH	1	1	1	1
Behavioral intention	BI1	0.883	0.885	0.885	0.813
	BI2	0.918			
	BI3	0.903			
Hedonic value	HDV1	0.716	0.883	0.889	0.587
	HDV2	0.766			
	HDV3	0.723			
	HDV4	0.779			
	HDV5	0.758			
	HDV6	0.814			
	HDV7	0.803			
Perceived risk	PR1	0.711	0.727	0.837	0.634
	PR2	0.770			
	PR3	0.896			
Utilitarian value	UTV1	0.725	0.811	0.816	0.569
	UTV2	0.802			
	UTV3	0.728			
	UTV4	0.739			
	UTV5	0.775			

Table 4. Cross Loadings.

	Behavioral intention	Hedonic value	Perceived humanness	Perceived risk	Utilitarian value
BI1	0.883	0.539	0.28	−0.197	0.524
BI2	0.918	0.549	0.283	−0.105	0.499
BI3	0.903	0.556	0.298	−0.167	0.494
HDV1	0.369	0.716	0.343	−0.121	0.435
HDV2	0.502	0.766	0.28	−0.125	0.579
HDV3	0.331	0.723	0.228	−0.039	0.356

(continued)

Table 4. (*continued*)

	Behavioral intention	Hedonic value	Perceived humanness	Perceived risk	Utilitarian value
HDV4	0.485	0.779	0.302	−0.098	0.364
HDV5	0.499	0.758	0.253	−0.13	0.494
HDV6	0.509	0.814	0.324	−0.135	0.576
HDV7	0.52	0.803	0.388	−0.089	0.456
PH	0.318	0.399	1	−0.142	0.296
PR1	−0.066	−0.015	−0.07	0.711	0.034
PR2	−0.114	−0.082	−0.112	0.77	−0.094
PR3	−0.193	−0.177	−0.138	0.896	−0.166
UTV1	0.39	0.373	0.234	−0.129	0.725
UTV2	0.484	0.455	0.228	−0.092	0.802
UTV3	0.393	0.464	0.219	−0.115	0.728
UTV4	0.367	0.47	0.214	−0.121	0.739
UTV5	0.467	0.546	0.224	−0.032	0.775

value play significant mediating roles in the relationship between perceived humanness and behavioral intention ($t = 4.848$, $p < 0.001$; $t = 2.980$, $p < 0.01$). However, the perceived risk does not play a significant mediating role in the relationship between perceived humanness and behavioral intention ($t = 1.146$, $p > 0.05$). The remaining results are listed in Table 5.

Table 5. Partial least squares results.

	Original sample	Sample mean	Standard deviation	Tstatistics	Pvalues	Results
PH - > BI	0.263	0.264	0.037	7.126	0.000	Supported
PH- > UTV	0.296	0.297	0.051	5.801	0.000	Supported
UTV- > BI	0.293	0.296	0.076	3.871	0.000	Supported
PH- > UTV - > BI	0.087	0.088	0.029	2.980	0.003	Supported
PH- > HDV	0.399	0.399	0.047	8.406	0.000	Supported
HDV - > BI	0.415	0.413	0.072	5.79	0.000	Supported

(*continued*)

Table 5. (*continued*)

	Original sample	Sample mean	Standard deviation	Tstatistics	Pvalues	Results
PH- > HDV - > BI	0.166	0.165	0.034	4.848	0.000	Supported
PH - > PR	−0.142	−0.147	0.068	2.078	0.038	Supported
PR - > BI	−0.074	−0.078	0.049	1.498	0.134	Unsupported
PH- > PR- > BI	0.010	0.011	0.009	1.146	0.252	Unsupported

4 Discussion and Conclusion

4.1 Discussion

Our research findings suggest that the perceived humanness of AI can significantly influence individuals' behavioral intention to use it for a health consultation. To investigate this process further, this study introduces three psychological perceptions: hedonic value, utilitarian value, and perceived risk. Our study demonstrates that both hedonic value and utilitarian value act as mediators in the relationship between perceived humanness and AI use intention. However, we found that perceived risk does not play a mediating role in this relationship. This finding suggests that individuals may prioritize the positive aspects of utilizing AI, potentially overlooking the associated risks to some extent.

4.2 Conclusion

This study reveals the mechanisms of the relationship between perceived humanness and AI use intention by testing the mediating roles of hedonic and utilitarian value. The results of this research can contribute to the AI industry's understanding of why designing AI with perceived humanness increases users' intention to consult on health. For individuals, using AI to consult on health issues can enhance their ability to manage health and cope with various diseases. However, it is important to acknowledge the limitations of this study, which require further investigation in the future, such as considering the different mediating variables to study this mechanism.

References

1. Väänänen, A., Haataja, K., Vehviläinen-Julkunen, K., Toivanen, P.: AI in healthcare: a narrative review. F1000Research **10**, 6 (2021). https://doi.org/10.12688/f1000research.269 97.1
2. Rietz, T., Benke, I., Maedche, A.: The impact of anthropomorphic and functional Chatbot design features in enterprise collaboration systems on user acceptance. International Conference on Wirtschafts informatik, pp. 1642–1656. Siegen, Germany (2019)
3. Westerman, D., Edwards, A.P., Edwards, C., Luo, Z., Spence, P.R.: I-it, I-thou, I-robot: the perceived humanness of AI in human-machine communication. Commun. Stud. **71**(3), 393–408 (2020)

4. Zamora, J.: I'm sorry, dave, i'm afraid i can't do that: Chatbot perception and expectations. In: Proceedings of the 5th International Conference on Human Agent Interaction, pp. 253–260 (2017)

5. Ahmad, N.A., Che, M.H., Zainal, A., Abd Rauf, M.F., Adnan, Z.: Review of Chatbots design techniques. Int. J. Comput. Appl. **181**(8), 7–10 (2018)

6. Svenningsson, N., Faraon, M.: Artificial intelligence in conversational agents: a study of factors related to perceived humanness in chatbots. In: Proceedings of the 2019 2nd Artificial Intelligence and Cloud Computing Conference, pp. 151–161 (2019)

7. Babin, B.J., Darden, W.R., Griffin, M.: Work and/or fun: measuring hedonic and utilitarian shopping value. J. Consum. Res. **20**(4), 644–656 (1994)

8. Belanche, D., Casaló, L.V., Schepers, J., Flavián, C.: Examining the effects of robots' physical appearance, warmth, and competence in frontline services: the humanness-value-loyalty model. Psychol. Mark. **38**(12), 2357–2376 (2021)

9. Jones, M.A., Reynolds, K.E., Arnold, M.J.: Hedonic and utilitarian shopping value: Investigating differential effects on retail outcomes. J. Bus. Res. **59**(9), 974–981 (2006)

10. Wang, E.S.T.: Internet usage purposes and gender differences in the effects of perceived utilitarian and hedonic value. Cyberpsychol. Behav. Soc. Netw. **13**(2), 179–183 (2010)

11. Chiu, C.M., Wang, E.T., Fang, Y.H., Huang, H.Y.: Understanding customers' repeat purchase intentions in B2C e-commerce: the roles of utilitarian value, hedonic value and perceived risk. Inf. Syst. J. **24**(1), 85–114 (2014)

12. Fiore, A.M., Jin, H.J., Kim, J.: For fun and profit: hedonic value from image interactivity and responses toward an online store. Psychol. Mark. **22**(8), 669–694 (2005)

13. Chi, N.T.K., Hoang, V., N.: Investigating the customer trust in artificial intelligence: the role of anthropomorphism, empathy response, and interaction. CAAI Trans. Intell. Technol. **8**(1), 260–273 (2023)

14. Akdim, K., Casaló, L.V., Flavián, C.: The role of utilitarian and hedonic aspects in the continuance intention to use social mobile apps. J. Retail. Consum. Serv. **66**, 102888 (2022)

15. Kumar, V., Rajan, B., Venkatesan, R., Lecinski, J.: Understanding the role of artificial intelligence in personalized engagement marketing. Calif. Manage. Rev. **61**(4), 135–155 (2019)

16. Gemünden, H.G.: Perceived risk and information search. a systematic meta-analysis of the empirical evidence. Int. J. Res. Mark. **2**(2), 79–100 (1985). https://doi.org/10.1016/0167-8116(85)90026-6

17. Wu, J.H., Wang, S.: What drives mobile commerce?: an empirical evaluation of the revised technology acceptance model. Inf. Manage. **42**(5), 719–729 (2005)

18. Rohden, S.F., Zeferino, D.G.: Recommendation agents: an analysis of consumers' risk perceptions toward artificial intelligence. Electron. Commer. Res. **23**(4), 2035–2050 (2023)

An Empirical Study of E-commerce Promoting Rural Industrial Structure Optimization: Evidence from China

Yameng Wang and Luning Liu[✉]

Harbin Institute of Technology, Harbin 150001, China
liuluning@hit.edu.cn

Abstract. There is increasing interest in understanding how e-commerce can promote rural development in developing countries. This study uses a dynamic panel data set of 225 prefecture-level cities in China to empirically investigate the effect of e-commerce on the quality of rural economic development in developing countries. The results show that e-commerce makes a positive contribution to the optimization of rural industrial structure, especially the promotion of industrial structure supererogation, mainly by influencing the development of the tertiary industry. The effect of e-commerce on the optimization of rural industrial structure is modulated by the local economic base and time factors. Our research emphasizes the importance of e-commerce for rural development. The research results show that e-commerce can be part of an effective strategy to break the bottleneck of rural economic development and address the structural contradictions of economic development in developing countries.

Keywords: E-commerce · Industrial Structure · Rural area · Developing Country

1 Introduction

Rural residents, especially in developing countries, live in poverty with limited access to education, health care, and economic opportunity. Thus, rural development is an urgent priority for many countries, especially developing countries [1]. Since the 1990s, ICT has been recognized as a way to bring about economic change in rural areas and transform the lives of rural people. The use of ICT to modernize agriculture and industry can increase farmers' income and promote agriculture. ICT can narrow the gaps between urban and rural areas, industry and agriculture for coordinated development and common urban and rural economic prosperity. ICT includes the infrastructure and components that enable modern computing, and e-commerce is a kind of ICT with significant coverage. With growing use of ICT in rural areas, governments of all countries, particularly developing countries, aim to promote the development of e-commerce in rural areas to promote rural economic development [2].

The development of e-commerce is occurring in rural areas around the world, and there is significant interest in understanding the effects on rural development. Underlying the worldwide expansion of support for e-commerce is optimism that investment in rural e-commerce will have a positive impact on development [3]. E-commerce has been shown to have the potential to boost rural economic development and improve farmers' well-being. Although recent research has studied the impact of e-commerce on the rural economy, most studies have focused on the role of e-commerce in improving farmers' lives and promoting rural economic growth, with few studies exploring the impact of e-commerce on the quality of economic development, especially industrial effects. Further, no work has been done to determine the internal logic between the development of e-commerce and the optimization of rural industrial structure.

With the development of economy and the weakening of demographic dividend, the main contradiction in the economic development of developing countries has changed from the quantity contradiction to the quality contradiction. That is, the economic structure has become an important starting point to improve the quality and resilience of economic development. The rural economic development may be limited by long-term development conditions and natural conditions, and rural industrial structures face greater challenges than their urban counterparts [4]. Because the powerful ubiquitous connection ability of e-commerce can enhance the ability of cooperation between industries, it can give birth to a new industrial model for rural areas. E-commerce can effectively improve market efficiency and production efficiency, and then promote the formation of higher quality association cooperation and cross-border integration between industries. Therefore, e-commerce may become an important way to optimize the rural industrial structure.

The overall purpose of our study was to empirically examine the influence of e-commerce on the optimization of rural industrial structure in developing countries. The three basic research questions of this work are: (1) Does rural e-commerce effectively promote the optimization of rural industrial structure and what are the impacts on industrial structure supererogation and industrial structure rationalization? (2) What is the influence mechanism of e-commerce on the optimization of rural industrial structure? (3) What factors influence the role of e-commerce in the optimization of industrial structure? The answers to the above questions will help to enrich the existing literature on the impact of e-commerce on the optimization of rural industrial structure, especially in developing countries.

The contributions of this work are as follows. This is the first study to explore the relationship between rural e-commerce and industrial structure optimization with empirical methods. Additionally, the results of this study provide insight into the factors influencing the optimization and upgrading of rural industrial structure in developing countries. Finally, our empirical study considers the dynamic and progressive optimization of industrial structure, as well as the influence of time on industrial structure. Overall, this study provides a new perspective of the economic effects of rural e-commerce.

2   Literature Review and Theoretical Hypothesis

2.1   E-commerce for Development

As an important application form of ICT, e-commerce has profoundly affected the production and life of residents. With advantages of low threshold, small technical difficulty, and low initial capital demand, e-commerce has become one of the main ways for many people to participate in market competition. For farmers with insufficient funds and limited traditional sales channels, e-commerce can break regional restrictions of traditional agricultural sales, enabling the sales of agricultural products throughout the whole country or even overseas. In some rural areas, e-commerce has developed into an important part of the local economy and an important means to promote development [5].

Previous work on rural e-commerce has focused on its economic effects, mainly from the perspective of promoting industrial integration, increasing farmers' income and consumption, and promoting rural economic growth [6]. The development of rural e-commerce allows an increase in the numbers of individuals or companies engaged in e-commerce in a given location. The goods or services provided by these e-commerce practitioners are usually clustered in the same or relatively similar industries, which can improve the efficiency of local economic cooperation, adjust the industrial structure, and promote the upgrading of traditional industries. Previous studies found that rural e-commerce can significantly increase the income of rural households by increasing non-agricultural employment, improving the level of entrepreneurship, and improving the land transfer rate. By deeply integrating ICT and rural development, e-commerce can maximize the utilization of rural resources, thus enhancing the resilience of rural development to cope with social risks and challenges.

Although there have been abundant studies on the economic effects of rural e-commerce, there have been no studies of the impact of rural e-commerce on the optimization of rural industrial structure or investigated the logical relationship from the perspective of industrial structure supererogation and rationalization.

2.2 Industrial Structure Optimization

Industrial structure optimization (ISO) refers to the allocation of production factors among different industries to change the output value ratio among them. Industrial structure optimization requires both the supererogation changes in the industrial proportions, and rationalization of industrial structure, as well as their interrelationships and influence [7].

Industrial structure supererogation (ISS) refers to a change in industrial proportion [7]. Using this measure, it is possible to distinguish between a service-oriented economic structure and an industrial structure that is developing in a more advanced manner. We measure industrial structure superposition by dividing the output value of the tertiary industry by the output value of the secondary industry, as shown below. ISS indicates the index of industrial structure supererogation, Y indicates the output value, Y_2 indicates the output value of the secondary industry, and Y_3 indicates the output value of the tertiary industry. An increasing ISS value indicates that the economy is moving in a service-oriented direction and that the industrial structure is undergoing a transformation.

$$ISS = Y_2/Y_3 \tag{1}$$

Industrial structure rationalization (ISR) refers to the connections or degree of aggregation between industries, and also includes the effective utilization of resources, such as labor [7]. Thus, this term is a measure of how closely input structure and output structure factors are coupled, and represents the degree of coupling between different industries in a region. The following formula is used to measure the rationalization of industrial structure based on the deviation of the industrial structure. ISR represents the industrial structure rationalization index, Y represents the output value, L represents employment, i represents the industry, and n represents the total number of industrial sectors. L_i/L represents productivity, and Y_i/Y represents output structure. The larger the ISR value, the more balanced the economy and the more reasonable the industrial structure.

$$ISR = 1 - \frac{1}{3}\sum_{i=1}^{n}\left|\frac{Y_i}{Y} - \frac{L_i}{L}\right| \tag{2}$$

2.3 Theoretical Hypothesis

In terms of general operation modes, e-commerce is both fundamental and innovative. Through the scale effect and competition effect, ICT can not only promote the development of high-tech industries, but also upgrade traditional industries. With powerful ubiquitous connectivity, e-commerce promotes the diffusion, application, and innovation of industrial technology and encourages cross-industry and cross-field data sharing, information interaction, and knowledge coding. Optimizing the traditional industrial production mode, management mode, and value chain can enhance the overall operational efficiency of industrial enterprises.

By affecting production and marketing, rural e-commerce promotes the innovation and upgrading of regional agricultural product brands. As e-commerce reduces information asymmetry, and transaction cost advantages decrease, farmers can obtain market information more easily, change the status of previous price takers. Additionally, e-commerce can facilitate the matching of information across time and space constraints and significantly expand market opportunities [8]. Thus, e-commerce can promote the development of local related industries, resulting in greater supply-side economies of scale effect to enhance the optimization and upgrading of rural industrial structure. Overall, e-commerce is considered an effective way to develop rural economies and promote industrial structure supererogation [9]. Therefore,

- H1: Rural E-commerce can promote the optimization of rural industrial structure.

The optimization of rural industrial structure can be measured as the change in the proportion between industries and the increase in labor productivity. The development of e-commerce can enhance the proportion advantage of rural tertiary industry, and optimize the original industrial structure of rural primary industries. Job opportunities are created in response to e-commerce transaction activities, expanding the employment scope of rural labor so more farmers can join the entrepreneurial world of employment for enhanced labor productivity, which can promote the rationalization of rural industries [10]. We can propose,

- H2: Rural E-commerce promotes the optimization of rural industrial structure by driving the development of tertiary industry.

To further develop e-commerce, better infrastructure is necessary. Rural areas with relatively developed economies have reasonable resource allocation, basic industries in place to support e-commerce, and sufficient ICT facilities and logistics service systems that facilitate the robust development of e-commerce in these areas. Second, obtaining the equipment, knowledge, and channels necessary to participate in e-commerce is an important prerequisite for farmers to participate in e-commerce. Many farmers, particularly those who reside in economically underdeveloped areas, may not be highly educated, do not understand the benefits of e-commerce, have limited information, and cannot take risks, thus limiting e-commerce adoption [11].

E-commerce development has a certain threshold due to the requirements of infrastructure and professional quality, thus, the development of rural e-commerce may present great challenges for poor areas. Only when rural e-commerce has developed to a certain level and scale can it affect the optimization of industrial structure. It may be difficult to make a significant contribution in a short period to the optimization of industrial structure. The development conditions of the relatively superior rural areas, easy to have the objective conditions for the development of e-commerce needs, e-commerce once entered, can be more obvious and significantly promote the optimization and upgrading of industrial structure. Based on this, we propose,

- H3: The effect of e-commerce on the optimization of rural industrial structure is affected by the local economic foundation, and the weak infrastructure will limit the effect of e-commerce in the optimization of industrial structure.

3 Identification Strategy

3.1 Identification Strategy and Econometric Model

China is a developing country that has successfully promoted the construction of rural e-commerce, with effects on construction and development. E-commerce has become an important component of the rural economy in China. Therefore, it is reasonable to study China's rural e-commerce development to explore the impact of e-commerce on the optimization of rural industrial structure.

To improve the rural economy, the Chinese government has implemented the "Comprehensive Demonstration Plan for E-commerce in Rural Areas" since 2014 and selected some counties each year for e-commerce construction. The comprehensive demonstration of e-commerce in rural areas included 1,231 counties in China in 2019. The Chinese government evaluates the performance of rural e-commerce policies annually to supervise and stimulate the development of rural e-commerce. This is the most comprehensive and influential e-commerce policy in China, which can directly determine the level of rural e-commerce development and construction [12]. Using data from the "Comprehensive Demonstration Plan for E-commerce in Rural Areas", we selected 2010 to 2019 as the research period to build a panel data model.

A base model was set up to verify the role of e-commerce in rural industrial structure optimization and test the theoretical hypotheses.

$$ISO_{it} = \alpha_0 + \alpha_1 Ecommerce_{it} + \beta_n X_{it}^n + \gamma_n P_{it}^n + \mu_i + \varepsilon_{it} \tag{3}$$

where the subscript i represents the city and t represents the year. ISO is the explained variable, namely, the optimization level of the rural industrial structure. E-commerce is the main explanatory variable, and indicates the development level of rural e-commerce. We focus on the coefficient of α1, which represents the net impact of e-commerce on rural industrial structure. X^n is the control variable. P^n is other factors control variable, which is used to control other policy effects. γ, β, and α represent the coefficient terms, μ represents the non-observed regional fixed effect, and ε represents the random error term.

As the industrial structure optimization is a dynamic and gradual process with development inertia, the current industrial structure depends on the past level. However, the traditional static panel data model cannot represent the change of explained variables over time, which may cause estimation errors. We used the strategy of Arellano and Bond and used a dynamic panel data model, which adds the lag period of the industrial structure as an explanatory variable, indicating that the explained variable of an individual partly depends on the value of the previous period. The dynamic panel data model is appropriate to study the impact of e-commerce on the optimization of rural industrial structure. The model is shown as follows. Where, ISO_{it-1} represents the lag of the industrial structure.

$$ISO_{it} = \alpha_0 + \varphi IS_{it-1} + \alpha_1 Ecommerce_{it} + \beta_n X_{it}^n + \gamma_n P_{it}^n + \mu_i + \varepsilon_{it} \qquad (4)$$

3.2 Variable Selection and Description

This study selects industrial structure optimization (*ISO*) as the explained variable. We establish two indexes, industrial structure supererogation (*ISS*) and industrial structure rationalization (*ISR*), to measure the optimization of industrial structures.

$$ISO = ISS/2 + ISR/2 \qquad (5)$$

The key explanatory variable of this study is the development level of rural e-commerce (*Ecommerce*). We selected e-commerce demonstration counties to represent the development level of rural e-commerce. We construct a core variable based on the proportion of demonstration counties to the total number of prefecture-level cities' county-level administrative units to quantify the development level of rural e-commerce for each prefecture-level city.

To more comprehensively investigate the relationship between the e-commerce into rural and industrial structure, we also add a series of control variables (X_{it}^n) into the model. If there are other relevant policies are implemented at the same time, the estimated results of this model may wrongly capture other effects, so a control variable (P_{it}^n) for other factors can be introduced. They are shown in Table 1.

Table 1. Variable definitions and descriptive statistics.

Variable	Variable definition	Obs	Mean	S.D.	Min	Max
Explained variables						
ISO	Industrial structure optimization index	2250	0.86	0.30	0.39	6.32
ISS	Industrial structure supererogation index	2250	0.89	0.58	0.15	11.69
ISR	Industrial structure rationalization index	2250	0.83	0.08	0.51	0.99
Key explanatory variable						
Ecommerce	The development level of rural e-commerce	2250	0.14	0.22	0.00	1.00
Control variables						
Poverty	National poverty alleviation and development work	2250	0.15	0.24	0.00	1.00
City	National-level e-commerce demonstration city	2250	0.12	0.32	0.00	1.00
Economy	The logarithm of rural per capita GDP	2250	10.36	0.57	8.54	12.89
ICT	The logarithm of the number of broadband Internet access users	2250	3.98	0.88	0	6.66
Finance	The proportion of the balance of rural loans to GDP	2250	0.66	0.79	−3.04	16.88
Manpower	The logarithm of rural population density	2250	5.36	0.95	0.70	7.54
Consumption	The logarithm of the total retail sales of consumer goods in rural society	2250	14.64	1.03	4.96	17.56
Government	The logarithm of fiscal expenditure of rural government	2250	14.20	0.75	7.70	16.63

3.3 Data and Descriptive Analysis

Data from Chinese prefecture-level cities from 2010 to 2019 are used in this analysis. Several cities are removed due to incomplete data availability, and finally, data from 225 prefecture-level cities are selected as our sample. Relevant data on *ISO, ISS, ISR, Economy, ICT, Finance, Manpower, Consumption,* and *Government* are obtained from China Urban Statistical Yearbook. The list of rural comprehensive demonstration counties for e-commerce from 2014 to 2019 and the list of national demonstration cities for e-commerce are obtained from the government website, and the identification of counties with poverty is performed based on a list published by the government in 2012. Table 1 provides the descriptive statistics for each variable.

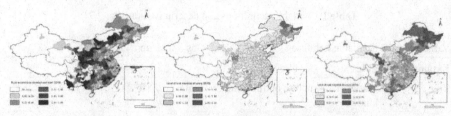

Fig. 1. China's e-commerce development in rural areas in 2019.

Fig. 2. China's industrial structure in rural areas in 2010.

Fig. 3. China's industrial structure in rural areas in 2019. (Note: This map is made based on the standard base map of the standard map service system of the State Bureau of Surveying and Mapping of China (No.: GS (2022)1873) without modification.)

Figure 1 depicts the project implementation level of e-commerce into rural areas in China's prefecture-level cities as of 2019. Figure 2 and Fig. 3 illustrate the optimization of the rural industrial structure by region in China in 2010 and 2019, respectively. The rural industrial structure of each region is significantly optimized and upgraded in 2019 compared with 2010. In particular, the degree of supererogation and rationalization of rural industrial structure is relatively high in the central and northeast regions, which is consistent with the implementation level of rural e-commerce development in these regions.

4 Results and Mechanism Testing

4.1 Basic Regression Results

We use Stata16.0 for regression analysis. We preliminarily test the influence of rural e-commerce on the rural industrial structure optimization according to model (1). The results are listed in columns (1), (3), and (5) in Table 2. Rural e-commerce shows a significant positive impact in all results at a level of at least 1%. Thus, the results show that rural e-commerce has a significant positive impact on the optimization of the industrial structure after controlling for regional fixed effects. This indicates that the introduction of e-commerce into rural areas can significantly contribute to the supererogation and rationalization of rural industrial structure, and promote the optimization of rural industrial structure. This preliminarily supports hypothesis H1. Furthermore, the significance level and coefficient of the impact of rural e-commerce on industrial structure rationalization are lower than those for industrial structure supererogation. This finding indicates that the rural e-commerce has a greater impact on the supererogation of industrial structures than the rationalization of industrial structures.

In order to control the influence of the past industrial structure on the current period, we then use the dynamic panel data Model (2) for estimation. This type of model, whether fixed effect or random effect, has lag-dependent variables that are related to disturbance terms, causing some estimators to be inconsistent. Explanatory variables may also have endogeneity problems. It is possible to obtain unbiased and consistent estimators using the instrumental variable method or a generalized moment estimation method (GMM). However, it is difficult to select appropriate instrumental variables using instrumental variable methods, weakening the econometric model. As a result, we estimate Model (2) using GMM. To consider the dynamic nature of industrial structure optimization, the serial correlation of common models, and the validity of estimation results, we will use SYS-GMM to estimate the impact of rural e-commerce on industrial structure optimization [13]. The autocorrelation test (AR) shows that there is no second-order autocorrelation of error terms, and the Hansen overidentification test indicates that the null hypothesis of the validity of instrumental variables could not be rejected.

The SYS-GMM results are presented in columns (2), (4), and (6) in Table 2. The results from SYS-GMM are generally consistent with those obtained from fixed effect regression. This further supports hypothesis H1. And e-commerce has a greater impact on rural industrial structure supererogation than structure rationalization. It may because that e-commerce can transfer farmers from direct agricultural production and processing to high-efficiency sectors, driving the overall efficiency of rural industry. E-commerce can also promote the development of advanced industries such as information industry, sales industry and logistics industry, and play a significant role in the rural industrial structure supererogation. Second, a certain level of development is required to create employment opportunities, and e-commerce is still at an early stage in most rural areas with a limited labor force [14]. Thus, it may be too early to see significant effects to improve labor productivity, leading to limited rationalization of the industrial structure.

4.2 Test of Influence Mechanism

4.2.1 Mediating Effect of the Tertiary Industry Development

Based on Model (2), we conducted a mediating effect test to test how the rural e-commerce affects the optimization of economic structure. *T_industry* is a mediating variable, representing the proportion of tertiary industry output to GDP.

Table 3 presents the results of the test. As shown in column (1), e-commerce has a significant positive effect when *T_industry* is the dependent variable. This finding is consistent with the conclusions of a recent study that the development of e-commerce promotes the output of rural tertiary industries. When *ISO* is taken as dependent variables, *T_industry* is still significant in the regression results and the coefficient is positive, while e-commerce is not, as shown in column (3). This indicates that tertiary industry output plays a complete intermediary effect. This result verifies that in H2, rural e-commerce promotes the optimization of rural industrial structure by driving the development of tertiary industry.

4.2.2 Moderating Effect of the Poverty Degree

In 2016, the Chinese government placed an increasing emphasis on the role of e-commerce in poverty alleviation, with more e-commerce projects initiated in rural areas. To investigate the influence of local economic base on the promotion of e-commerce to

Table 2. Effects of e-commerce on rural industrial structure optimization.

Variables	(1)	(2)	(3)	(4)	(5)	(6)
	ISO		ISS		ISR	
Ecommerce$_{it}$	0.293***	0.122***	0.565***	0.255***	0.0210**	−0.001
	(10.14)	(3.97)	(10.01)	(4.19)	(3.23)	(−0.31)
Constant	1.692***	0.088	3.241***	0.237	0.143	−0.042
	(4.77)	(0.26)	(4.68)	(0.37)	(1.79)	(−0.72)
X^n	Yes	Yes	Yes	Yes	Yes	Yes
P^n	Yes	Yes	Yes	Yes	Yes	Yes
City FE	Yes	Yes	Yes	Yes	Yes	Yes
Observations	2250	2025	2250	2025	2250	2025
Individuals		225		225		225
Adj-R2	0.215		0.196		0.092	
AR (2) p-value		0.614		0.630		0.171
Hansen p-value		0.222		0.204		0.219

Notes: * $p < 0.05$, ** $p < 0.01$, *** $p < 0.001$

the optimization of rural industrial structure, an interaction term between the development level of rural e-commerce and the poverty level, which represents the development basis of local economy, can be added as an explanatory variable.

The results of GMM regression are shown in columns (4) (5) (6) of Table 3. According to columns (4), the interaction *Ecommerce*Poverty* has a significantly negative impact on economic structure optimization, suggesting that the promotion effect of e-commerce varies according to the local economic base. There is a greater role of e-commerce in optimizing rural industrial structure in areas with a better economic base and a weaker role in areas with a poor economic base. Hypothesis H3 is confirmed.

The GMM regression with industrial structure supererogation as the dependent variable shows significant interaction between rural e-commerce and local economic base. In the regression with industrial structure rationalization as the dependent variable, the interaction between the development of rural e-commerce and local economic base is not in GMM regression. This shows that the moderating effect of local economic base is mainly affecting the supererogation of rural industrial structure. We find that the weak economic foundation plays a limiting role in optimizing the rural industrial structure of e-commerce. There will be weaker effect of e-commerce on industrial upgrading in rural areas with weak economic foundation than that in economically developed areas.

4.3 Test of Influence Mechanism

To verify the reliability of the conclusions, a series of robustness tests are conducted. (1) A robustness test is conducted using one-step system GMM (One-GMM) and DIF-GMM methods. The One-GMM and DIF-GMM results are not significantly different

Table 3. Mediating effect of tertiary industry and moderating effect of poverty level.

Variables	(1)	(2)	(3)	(4)	(5)	(6)
	T_industry	ISO		ISO	ISS	ISR
Ecommerce^{it}	0.041***	0.122***	0.027	0.267***	0.538***	0.005
	(7.37)	(3.97)	(1.21)	(4.68)	(4.68)	(0.46)
T_industry$_{it}$			1.553***			
			(5.41)			
Ecommerce$_{it}$ × Poverty$_{it}$				−0.344**	−0.683**	−0.015
				(−2.84)	(−2.76)	(−0.73)
Constant	−0.146*	0.088	0.904*	0.274	0.569	−0.0347
	(−2.09)	(0.26)	(2.27)	(0.81)	(0.89)	(−0.57)
X^n	Yes	Yes	Yes	Yes	Yes	Yes
P^n	Yes	Yes	Yes	Yes	Yes	Yes
City FE	Yes	Yes	Yes	Yes	Yes	Yes
Observations	2025	2025	2025	2025	2025	2025
Individuals	225	225	225	225	225	225
AR (2) p-value	0.128	0.614	0.697	0.585	0.606	0.168
Hansen p-value	0.194	0.222	0.250	0.172	0.180	0.229

Notes: * $p < 0.05$, ** $p < 0.01$, *** $p < 0.001$

from the two-step GMM regression results, demonstrating the robustness of the results. (2) We then consider the possibility of estimation bias due to the short development time of rural e-commerce in some areas. We remove the samples of the counties selected in 2018 and 2019 before calculating the regression coefficients with no significant change. (3) Extreme values may affect analysis. We conduct 1%, 2%, 5%, and 10% indentation of explanatory variables and explained variables to eliminate bias caused by extreme values in regression analysis. The results are robust.

5   Discussion and Conclusions

As an important tool of ICT for development, rural e-commerce has advantages such as low cost, convenience and high efficiency, and can be a technological catalyst to change the local industrial structure and employment pattern [15]. With the wide application of ICT, developing countries represented by China are vigorously developing e-commerce to promote local economic development and improve people's living standards.

First, our research shows that e-commerce can promote the optimization of rural industrial structure. We find that the industrial optimization effect of rural e-commerce is more significant in industrial structure supererogation. This makes sense because industrial structure rationalization is mainly affected by rural labor productivity. However, at present, e-commerce in most rural areas is still in the development stage, absorbing limited labor force and low labor efficiency, so the improvement of productivity may not be obvious.

Second, we find that rural e-commerce mainly promotes the optimization of rural industrial structure by driving the development of tertiary industry. As a technological innovation, e-commerce can lead to changes in the input structure of various rural industries, increasing resource allocation to tertiary industry with higher output efficiency.

Additionally, the effect of e-commerce on the optimization of rural industrial structure depends on the local economic base, where a weak economic foundation will limit the effect of e-commerce on the optimization of industrial structure. Finally, there is growing awareness of the need to consider time factor when evaluating impact. Our results show that e-commerce has a sustained effect on the optimization of rural industrial structure, and this becomes stronger over time.

Acknowledgement. This research was supported by the National Natural Science Foundation of China (#72034001, #71974044), Heilongjiang Provincial Natural Science Foundation of China (#YQ2020G004) and the Fundamental Research Funds for the Central Universities (Grant No. HIT.OCEF.2022054 and HIT.HSS.DZ201905).

References

1. Njihia, J.M., Merali, Y.: The broader context for ICT4D projects: a morphogenetic analysis. Mis Quart. **37**, 881–905 (2013)
2. Roberts, E., Anderson, B.A., Skerratt, S., Farrington, J.: A review of the rural-digital policy agenda from a community resilience perspective. J. Rural. Stud. **54**, 372–385 (2017)
3. Li, X., Guo, H., Jin, S., Ma, W., Zeng, Y.: Do farmers gain internet dividends from E-commerce adoption? Evidence from China. Food Policy **101**, 102024 (2021)
4. Müller, J.M., Kiel, D., Voigt, K.-I.J.S.: What drives the implementation of Industry 4.0? The role of opportunities and challenges in the context of sustainability **10**(1), 247 (2018)
5. Couture, V., Faber, B., Gu, Y., Liu, L.: Connecting the countryside via e-commerce: evidence from China. Am. Econ. Rev. Insights **3**(1), 35–50 (2021)
6. Karine, H.: E-commerce development in rural and remote areas of BRICS countries. J. Integr. Agric. **20**(4), 979–997 (2021)
7. Tu, S., Long, H.J.J.O.G.S.: Rural restructuring in China: theory, approaches and research prospect **27**, 1169–1184 (2017)
8. Leong, C., Pan, S.L., Newell, S., Cui, L.: The emergence of self-organizing E-commerce ecosystems in remote villages of China. MIS Q. **40**(2), 475–484 (2016)
9. Venkatesh, V., Sykes, T., Zhang, X.: ICT for development in rural India: a longitudinal study of women's health outcomes. MIS Q. **44**(2), 605–629 (2020)
10. Zhang, Y., Long, H., Ma, L., Tu, S., Li, Y., Ge, D.: Analysis of rural economic restructuring driven by e-commerce based on the space of flows: the case of Xiaying village in central China. J. Rural. Stud. **93**, 196–209 (2022)
11. Choshin, M., Ghaffari, A.J.C.I.H.B.: An investigation of the impact of effective factors on the success of e-commerce in small-and medium-sized companies **66**, 67–74 (2017)
12. Chao, P., Biao, M., Chen, Z.: Poverty alleviation through e-commerce: village involvement and demonstration policies in rural China. J. Integr. Agric. **20**(4), 998–1011 (2021)

13. Roodman, D.: How to do xtabond2: an introduction to difference and system GMM in Stata. Stand. Genomic Sci. **9**(1), 86–136 (2009)
14. Liu, M., Zhang, Q., Gao, S., Huang, J.: The spatial aggregation of rural e-commerce in China: an empirical investigation into Taobao Villages. J. Rural Stud. **80**, 403–417 (2020)
15. Li, G., Qin, J.: Income effect of rural E-commerce: empirical evidence from Taobao villages in China. J. Rural. Stud. **96**, 129–140 (2022)

Theme Mining and Evolutionary Analysis of Artificial Intelligence Integration in Higher Education Research

Jiajun Hou[1] and Jiangping Wan[2(✉)]

[1] Guangzhou City University of Technology, Guangzhou 510800, China
[2] South China University of Technology, Guangzhou 510640, China
13763342117@163.com

Abstract. This study conducted thematic mining and evolutionary analysis of research outcomes on the integration of artificial intelligence into higher education. A total of 418 core journal articles published between 2018 and 2023 from the CNKI and Web of Science databases were selected. The LDA+Word2vec topic model was used for thematic mining, and cosine similarity was calculated to explore the similarity between topics. Finally, a Sankey diagram was created to illustrate the evolutionary relationships between different themes. The results indicate that research on the integration of artificial intelligence into higher education can be divided into three time periods with six themes. These themes include intelligent medical education talent cultivation, research on intelligent online education platforms/systems, intelligent disciplinary major construction, transformation of personalized teaching modes through human-machine collaboration, digitized higher education talent cultivation, the application and impact of generative artificial intelligence, as well as two thematic evolutionary paths: intelligent medical education talent cultivation and research on intelligent online education platforms—intelligent disciplinary major construction—digitized higher education talent cultivation, research on intelligent online education platforms—transformation of personalized teaching modes through human-machine collaboration—application and impact of generative artificial intelligence. The purpose is to provide insights into research on the integration of artificial intelligence into higher education.

Keywords: Artificial Intelligence · Higher Education · Topic Mining · Topic Evolution · LDA+Word2Vec

1 Introduction

Artificial intelligence is a strategic technology leading a new round of technological revolution, industrial transformation, and social change, with the government placing high importance on the cultivation of AI talents. In 2019, the U.S. Department of Education released the "Artificial Intelligence for Future Learning Report," outlining principles and guidelines for the application of AI in education. In 2020, the Chinese Ministry of

Education issued the "Opinions on Promoting Subject Integration in Double First-Class Universities to Accelerate Graduate Education in the Field of Artificial Intelligence," emphasizing the establishment of a training system that focuses on both foundational theoretical talents and compound talents in "AI+X." In recent years, there have been numerous theoretical achievements in academia regarding the integration of artificial intelligence into higher education. For example, Zhang, YB et al. proposed the Artificial Intelligence-assisted Interactive Intelligent Education Framework (AIISE) to enhance student interaction in higher education [1]. Allen, B et al. conducted surveys among university lecturers and students to explore best practices in higher education under the backdrop of artificial intelligence [2]. Zhou, C relied on experimental design to investigate the impact of integrating AI technologies into personalized learning platforms on improving the education system [3]. This study utilizes the LDA+Word2vec topic model to analyze core journal articles on the research of integrating artificial intelligence into higher education over the past six years, identifying researchers' themes and examining the evolution of these themes.

The organization of this paper is as follows: Sect. 2 presents the research methods and design, Sect. 3 discusses data collection and preprocessing, Sect. 4 presents the LDA+Word2Vec topic modeling analysis, Sect. 5 focuses on topic evolution analysis, and Sect. 6 concludes with findings and inspiration.

2 Research Methods and Design

2.1 Research Methods

This paper employs the LDA+Word2vec topic model to explore the topics related to the integration of artificial intelligence in higher education research, as well as to analyze the evolution of these topics. The LDA+Word2vec model is a hybrid model that combines the LDA topic model and the word2vec model to capture semantic information in text. It is commonly used in the fields of text mining and natural language processing. Compared to using the LDA topic model alone, the LDA+Word2vec model can better capture the semantic relationships between words and the correlations between topics, thereby improving the efficiency and accuracy of the topic model. Below are brief introductions to the LDA topic model and word2vec.

The LDA (Latent Dirichlet Allocation) topic model is a probabilistic generative model based on Bayesian distribution [4]. It is also known as a three-level Bayesian probability model, consisting of word, topic, and document layers. LDA is an unsupervised generative model that assumes each word in a document is generated through a process of "selecting a topic with a certain probability and then selecting a word from that topic with another probability." The LDA topic model has been widely applied in various fields such as text classification, sentiment analysis, advertising recommendation, social media analysis, cross-lingual research, and bioinformatics research. The graphical representation of the LDA probabilistic model is shown in Fig. 1.

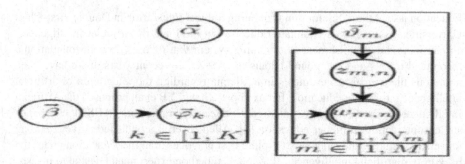

Fig. 1. LDA probability graph model

The meanings of various parameters in LDA topic model are as follows: K denotes the number of topics, M denotes the total number of documents, Nm denotes the total number of words in the m-th document, Zm,n denotes the topic of the n-th word in the m-th document, Wm,n denotes the n-th word in the m-th document, α and β denote their prior parameters, θm denotes the topic distribution of the m-th document, and φk denotes the word distribution under the k-th topic. The joint distribution function of LDA is shown in formula (1).

$$p(\vec{z}, \vec{w}|\vec{\alpha}, \vec{\beta}) = p(\vec{z}|\vec{\alpha})p(\vec{w}|\vec{z}, \vec{\beta})$$

$$= \prod_{m=1}^{M} \frac{\Delta(\vec{\alpha} + \vec{n}_m)}{\Delta(\vec{\alpha})} \prod_{k=1}^{K} \frac{\Delta(\vec{\beta} + \vec{n}_k)}{\Delta(\vec{\beta})} \qquad (1)$$

The limitation of the LDA model lies in its use of the bag-of-words model for text vectorization. The bag-of-words model only considers the frequency of words and ignores their order and context, which can lead to a loss of semantic information and limit the ability of the model to capture the underlying meaning of the text.

Word2vec is a model used to generate word embeddings and can be trained on large amounts of text data. This model uses a shallow two-layer neural network during training and leverages the relationship between input words and context words to predict the context of a given word, thereby learning the vector representation of the word and obtaining a vector value for each word. Word2vec is divided into two models: continuous bag-of-words (CBOW) and skip-gram. The CBOW model predicts the target word given the context, while the Skip-Gram model predicts the context words given the target word. Word2vec has two efficient training methods: negative sampling and hierarchical softmax [5].

The formula 2 represents the calculation process of combining the research topics derived from the LDA topic model in embedding AI into higher education with the text word vectors obtained from Word2vec training to obtain a fused topic vector that incorporates semantic information. In formula 2, each topic ti (assuming there are N topics {t1, t2,..., tn}) is represented as a vector by multiplying the word vectors of the top h topic words with their corresponding weights and then summing them up.

Ultimately, this process yields the topic vectors for each of the ti topics [4].

$$v(t_i) = \sum_{n=1}^{h} w_{i_n} v(t_{i_n})$$ (2)

Formula 3 represents the calculation process for computing the cosine similarity, which is used to measure the similarity between different topics in order to identify topic evolution paths for topic evolution analysis in adjacent time periods. In this study, cosine similarity is calculated to determine the similarity between different topics. Formula 3 calculates the cosine similarity by considering the coordinate values of each word vector in a document, where n represents the number of word vectors in the document [4].

$$\cos(\theta) = \frac{\sum_{i=1}^{n}(x_i \times y_i)}{\sqrt{\sum_{i=1}^{n}(x_i)^2 \times \sum_{i=1}^{n}(y_i)^2}}$$ (3)

2.2 Research Design

To investigate the research topics and topic evolution relationship of embedding artificial intelligence in higher education, this study conducted a literature search in the CNKI and Web of Science databases to identify relevant articles on this topic. The literature data underwent preprocessing steps such as stop word removal, text tokenization, and bag-of-words construction. The LDA+word2vec topic model was then employed to extract topics from the literature and calculate textual word vectors. Subsequently, topic vectors and cosine similarity were computed to derive the evolution paths of these topics, enabling visualization and analysis of the topic evolution process. The research framework of this study is illustrated in Fig. 1.

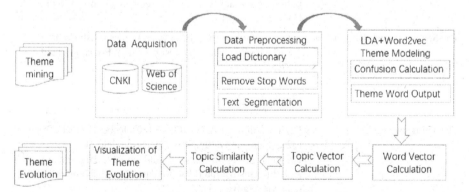

Fig. 2. Research Framework

3 Data Collection and Preprocessing

This study conducted a precise search on the theme of "Artificial Intelligence in Higher Education" in the CNKI and Web of Science d This study conducted a precise search on the theme of "Artificial Intelligence in Higher Education" in the CNKI and Web of Science databases, selecting core journal articles (including PKU Core, CSSCI, CSCD, SCI, SSCI) from the period of 2018 to 2023. Currently, research on the integration of artificial intelligence into higher education is still in the developmental stage, with a limited number of publications. A total of 489 relevant articles were retrieved initially. After manual screening, 418 articles that closely matched the theme were selected. The titles and abstracts of these articles were used as the research dataset, which was divided into three sub-datasets based on time periods (each spanning two years). These three sub-datasets are as follows: Sub-dataset 1 covering the years 2018–2019 with 55 articles, Sub-dataset 2 covering the years 2020–2021 with 116 articles, and Sub-dataset 3 covering the years 2022–2023 with 247 articles.

The research dataset can be imported into Python programming software for processing. First, load the vocabulary lists for education and artificial intelligence, as well as the Harbin Institute of Technology stop words list. Then, use the jieba word segmentation method in Python to tokenize each subset of the dataset corresponding to the three stages. After tokenization, remove numbers and English words, and limit the token length to be greater than 2. Finally, calculate the keyword frequency and obtain the top 15 high-frequency keywords for each stage of the subset. The results can be displayed in Table 1 as follows:

Table 1. Top 15 High-Frequency keywords in Each Stage

stage	High-Frequency keywords (word frequency)
The First stage (2018–2019)	Talent cultivation (63), Big Data (16), Intelligence (11), Blockchain (10), MOOC (7), new generation (6), education (6), large-scale (6), personalization (6), MOOCs (6), radiology (6), liquidity (6), biomedical (5), Infrastructure (5), radiology (5)
The Second stage (2020–2021)	Talent cultivation (69), Personalization (35), Blockchain (18), College teachers (17), Robots (16), Education field (15), Intelligence (14), Teaching mode (12), Combination (11), Mental health (11), Possibility (11), Uncertainty (11), Virtual reality (9), Ecosystem (9), Discipline construction (9)
The Third stage (2022–2023)	Digitalization (115), ChatGPT (110), Robots (91), Learners (52), Talent cultivation (45), Education field (41), Personalization (38), College students (37), High-quality (30), Informatization (29), Big data (29), Teaching methods (27), Generative (24), Postgraduates (23), Teaching quality (22)

According to Table 1, it can be observed that the high-frequency keywords in the three stages are interconnected yet distinct from each other. The research in the three stages primarily focuses on the application of blockchain technology, generative AI technology, virtual reality technology, etc., in the field of education. Additionally, there is a significant emphasis on personalized talent development for undergraduate and graduate students, as well as collaboration between university teachers and robots in teaching.

4   LDA+Word2vec Theme Modeling Analysis

Based on the segmentation results of three-stage sub-datasets, the LDA+Word2Vec topic model is used for modeling. The key step in LDA+Word2Vec topic modeling is determining the number of research topics. In this study, the optimal number of topics for the three-stage sub-datasets is determined using perplexity. Figure 2 below shows the trend of topic perplexity for each stage.

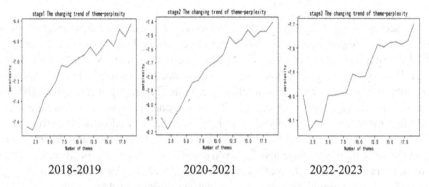

| 2018-2019 | 2020-2021 | 2022-2023 |

Fig. 3. The changing trend of theme perplexity

According to Fig. 2, it can be observed that the topic perplexity for all three stages reaches its lowest point when the number of topics is set to 2. Considering the limited number of literature in each stage, this study defines 2 topics for each stage. Table 2 below displays the number of topics obtained through LDA+Word2Vec topic modeling for each stage, along with the customized topic names.

This paper defines the first stage as the initial phase of integrating artificial intelligence into higher education, focusing on the application of AI technology in medical education, particularly in the fields of biomedical science and radiology, where AI plays a significant role in medical imaging. Scholars in this stage have also explored the development of Massive Open Online Course platforms (MOOCs platforms) integrated with AI technology. These AI-enhanced MOOC platforms can better guide learners in their studies, with intelligent recommendations, interactions, and assessments enhancing the learning experience. Murray, Jo-Anne introduced the current application of MOOCs in the field of biomedical science and the future potential of artificial intelligence in providing virtual classroom assistants [6].

Table 2. Number of themes and theme names

stage	Number of themes	theme names
The First stage (2018–2019)	2	Theme 0:Intelligent Medical Education Talent Cultivation Theme1: Research on Intelligent Online Education Platform/System
The Second stage (2020–2021)	2	Theme0:Intelligent Discipline Major Construction Theme1:Transformation of Personalized Teaching Mode with Human-Computer Collaboration
The Third stage (2022–2023)	2	Theme0:Digitalization of Higher Education Talent Cultivation Theme1:Applications and Impacts of Generative Artificial Intelligence

The second stage is defined as the developmental stage of incorporating artificial intelligence into higher education. During this stage, some scholars proposed the integration of "artificial intelligence+disciplinary construction" in a cross-disciplinary fusion model. Wang Guoyin and Qu Zhong suggested the need to consolidate the disciplinary foundation in the field of artificial intelligence while integrating it into other advantageous disciplines [7]. Tian Xianpeng and Tian Liangchen proposed breaking the structured thinking of disciplinary specialization and continuously adjusting the structure of disciplinary specialization and talent cultivation to adapt to changes in market demand [8]. At the same time, this stage also involved discussions on the role positioning of university teachers and the transformation of teaching methods. Bucea-Manea-Tonis, R et al. proposed new educational methods that emphasize morality, values, problem-solving, and daily activities [9]. Zhang Xilin put forward three roles that today's university teachers should possess: mature technology users, research-oriented knowledge sharers, and emotionally interactive individuals [10]. In the era of artificial intelligence, university teachers need to enhance their information literacy, learn to utilize AI technology to assist in teaching, establish a human-machine collaborative teaching system, accurately predict students' academic performance, learning ability, psychological well-being, etc., identify at-risk students, and provide more personalized teaching models. Personalized teaching models can greatly improve the success rate and reduce the dropout rate of university students.

The third stage can be defined as the emerging phase of integrating artificial intelligence into higher education, with topics like generative AI and educational digital transformation being the focal points of research. Since 2022, generative AI represented by ChatGPT has shown significant potential in teaching. Teachers can leverage ChatGPT to design more challenging tasks, while students can use ChatGPT to autonomously solve problems. However, ChatGPT is also a double-edged sword. The academic community has provided numerous insights into the application scenarios of generative AI like

ChatGPT in universities and the opportunities and challenges they may face. Dai Xiang and Guo Lijun pointed out that ChatGPT will greatly affect students' learning methods, university education methods, and evaluation methods [11]. Li Huichun pointed out that ChatGPT increases the operational risk of university courses, makes the teacher-student relationship more complex, and may lead to academic ethical risks [12]. Killian, CM et al. proposed that prediction technologies such as ChatGPT may make mistakes, and we need to maintain a critical social viewpoint and use ChatGPT appropriately [13]. Taking corresponding measures to deal with risks and challenges is also one of the tasks for implementing digital transformation of education in China over the past two years. The digital transformation of education proposed in this stage aims to cultivate high-quality talents, empower education with digital technology, reform and innovate from various aspects such as students, teachers, teaching resources, infrastructure, and teaching environment, and form a digital education ecosystem.

5 Theme Evolution Analysis

Based on the topics and word vectors obtained from LDA+word2vec topic modeling, we calculate the vector values for each topic in each stage. We then use the topic vector values of adjacent time periods to calculate the cosine similarity between them. By drawing a Sankey diagram, we can visualize the evolution path of topics across the three time periods. Following the practices of relevant scholars, this study sets the similarity threshold at 0.3 [14]. If the cosine similarity between adjacent time period topics is greater than 0.3, it indicates high similarity and can be analyzed for evolutionary patterns. Conversely, if the cosine similarity is below 0.3, we filter out the topic pairs with lower similarity. This study employs a Sankey diagram to conduct the analysis of topic evolution.

A Sankey diagram is a special type of flow chart that visually represents the flow direction and quantity of elements. It can be used to analyze the flow of various stages in a business process or the interaction volume among users in a social network. In the context of topic evolution analysis, a Sankey diagram can be used to illustrate the evolutionary path of topics across adjacent time periods. In a Sankey diagram, each stage's topic is represented by a node. The length of the nodes indicates the strength of the topic's evolutionary ability, with longer nodes representing stronger evolution. The colored edges between nodes represent the connections between topics. The width of the colored edges reflects the strength of the associations between topics, with wider edges indicating stronger connections. Below is Fig. 3, which illustrates the evolutionary path of topics across adjacent time periods using a Sankey diagram (Fig. 4).

From Fig. 3, we can observe that there are certain differences in the evolutionary abilities of each topic in each time period. Specifically, in the initial stage, Topic 1 (Research on Intelligent Online Education Platforms) exhibits a stronger evolutionary capability compared to Topic 0 (Intelligent Medical Education Talent Cultivation). In the developmental stage, Topic 0 (Intelligent Discipline Construction) demonstrates a significantly stronger evolutionary ability than Topic 1 (Transformation of Personalized Teaching Models with Human-Machine Collaboration). In the upward stage, Topic 0 (Digitized Higher Education Talent Cultivation) displays a noticeably stronger evolutionary ability than Topic 1 (Application and Impact of Generative Artificial Intelligence).

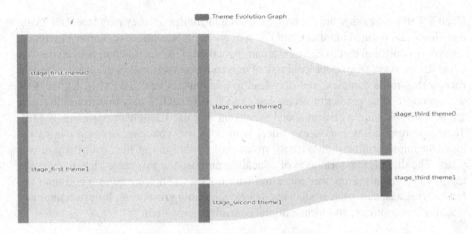

Fig. 4. Evolutionary Path of Themes

The topic evolution can be divided into two paths: the first path consists of Intelligent Medical Education Talent Cultivation, Research on Intelligent Online Education Platforms—Intelligent Discipline Construction—Digitized Higher Education Talent Cultivation. The second path includes Research on Intelligent Online Education Platforms—Transformation of Personalized Teaching Models with Human-Machine Collaboration—Application and Impact of Generative Artificial Intelligence.

The first path of topic evolution indicates the gradual exploration of talent cultivation in the era of artificial intelligence. In the initial stage, the focus is on intelligent medical education talent cultivation and research on intelligent online education platforms. In the development stage, the focus shifts to the construction of intelligent disciplines. In the ascending stage, the focus is on digitized higher education talent cultivation. The emergence of massive open online courses (MOOCs) in the early stages and their application in certain cutting-edge disciplines, such as medical education, have drawn attention to online educational resources. The global outbreak of the COVID-19 pandemic has highlighted the importance of online education, leading to reforms in various disciplinary majors, with a combination of online and offline teaching becoming the norm. With the exponential growth of online teaching data and the emergence of new technologies such as cloud computing, blockchain, the Internet of Things, and artificial intelligence, disciplinary majors face new challenges, and information technology will play a significant role in their development.

In 2018, the Ministry of Education proposed the concepts of New Liberal Arts and New Engineering, emphasizing interdisciplinary integration. The focus was on the fusion of social sciences with technology and the vigorous development of emerging disciplines such as artificial intelligence, intelligent manufacturing, and robotics. In 2020, the Ministry of Education announced plans to establish 20 to 30 Future Technology Institutes nationwide within the next four years, with a focus on key areas like aerospace, artificial intelligence, and quantum information science. Responding to national policies, as of December 2023, there were 513 universities in China offering majors in artificial intelligence. Scholars have concentrated their research on the construction of academic disciplines, emphasizing reforms on the supply side of disciplinary majors. They have emphasized the deep integration of artificial intelligence with other disciplines, the logical pathway of AI's assistance in constructing New Liberal Arts, and highlighted the weak faculty strength in AI discipline construction. The ultimate goal of disciplinary major construction is talent cultivation, evolving from the intelligent discipline construction to the digitized higher education talent cultivation is a highly reasonable thematic evolution path. Since 2022, the government has introduced several policies aimed at educational digital transformation and fostering high-quality talents. There have been 45 documents related to digital higher education talent cultivation, with academia discussing pathways for cultivating digital higher education talents, the use of digital tools, methods for constructing digital education ecosystems, and strategies for addressing digital risks.

The evolution path of the second theme indicates scholars' attention to the specific application of artificial intelligence technology in higher education teaching. In the initial stage, the focus was on research into intelligent online education platforms, while in the development stage, attention shifted to the transformation of personalized teaching modes through human-machine collaborative models. In the advanced stage, the focus turned to the application and impact of generative artificial intelligence. The academic community's research on online education platforms started early, with most studies exploring how these platforms can promote student learning and make the educational process more effective. Initially, the technology used in online education platforms was simple, and the functionality was limited. Over time, research on online education platforms has shifted towards "artificial intelligence+online education platforms." Research findings indicate that online education platforms empowered by AI, known as "AI education platforms," can significantly enhance students' learning motivation compared to traditional online education platforms, making the learning process more interesting and engaging.

Against this backdrop, scholars have proposed the concept of human-machine collaborative teaching to provide personalized learning experiences for students. The role and tasks of university teachers are transforming, with teachers responsible for knowledge dissemination while AI education platforms collect, analyze, and provide feedback on a large amount of student learning data. By utilizing advanced algorithms, these platforms assist teachers in gaining a clear understanding of each student's learning progress and tailor personalized teaching methods accordingly. However, scholars also point out that the current concept of human-machine collaborative teaching is not yet widely implemented in domestic universities, and there are still many difficulties and challenges. For example, universities may lack the financial resources and technological capabilities to establish AI education platforms, teachers may not possess the necessary digital literacy, and there may be constraints from traditional thinking among university leaders. Consequently, when generative artificial intelligence models like ChatGPT were introduced, they entered universities with unstoppable momentum. Since its release in 2022, ChatGPT has continuously updated and iterated, offering diverse functionalities. Its powerful natural language processing capabilities can assist teachers in teaching and research, as well as facilitate independent learning for students. However, improper use of ChatGPT can also pose risks, such as excessive student reliance leading to a reduction in critical thinking and innovation, an inability to engage in deep learning, and issues like academic plagiarism and cheating among teachers. ChatGPT also has its limitations, such as its inability to participate in moral education within higher education institutions. In recent years, the academic community has been exploring various risk mitigation strategies, solution measures, and additional application scenarios, with ongoing research expected in the future.

6 Conclusion and Inspiration

The application of artificial intelligence in the field of education has been a research hotspot in recent years, especially in higher education. One of the most important tasks for universities currently is how to cultivate high-quality and highly skilled talents with artificial intelligence expertise across various disciplines. Current research focuses on the specific applications of artificial intelligence technology in educational settings, employing research methods such as questionnaire surveys, case studies, and interviews. This paper systematically reviews the research topics and their evolving relationships in the integration of artificial intelligence into higher education over the past six years from a macro perspective. The research methodology employed in this paper is the LDA+Word2vec topic modeling, which is an innovative empirical research method not yet widely used in the field of education research.

This paper collected research literature on the integration of artificial intelligence into higher education from the CNKI and Web of Science databases for the years 2018 to 2023. The LDA+Word2vec topic modeling technique was utilized to identify research topics, resulting in six major themes across three time periods. Cosine similarity was calculated to explore the similarities between these topics, revealing two evolutionary paths. The findings of this study are closely related to the content published by scholars, and with the increasing number of subsequent literature, this paper can continue to conduct research and obtain more abundant results, providing valuable insights for future research on the application of artificial intelligence in higher education and the cultivation of AI professionals in universities.

In the future, the application of artificial intelligence in higher education has unlimited possibilities and is an irreversible trend. With the continuous development of AI technology, the use of human-machine collaborative teaching will become increasingly widespread, leading to a fundamental transformation in the modes of teaching and learning. Students will be able to have more immersive, interactive, and dynamic learning experiences. The existing risks and challenges will also find reasonable solutions. Universities will break boundaries and become places for lifelong learning and creative living. Governments, universities, and businesses will collaborate to cultivate highly skilled and innovative talents. There will be significant changes in job demands and the criteria used to assess talent in society. Future research will continue to focus on optimizing AI technology in personalized learning and fostering collaboration across different disciplines.

References

1. Zhang, Y.B., Qin, G.: Interactive smart educational system using AI for students in the higher education platform. J. Multiple-Valued Logic Soft Comput. **36**(1–3), 83–98 (2021)
2. Allen, B., McGough, A.S., Devlin, M.: Toward a framework for teaching artificial intelligence to a higher education audience. ACM Trans. Comput. Educ. **22**(2), 1–29 (2022)
3. Zhou, C.: Integration of modern technologies in higher education on the example of artificial intelligence use. Educ. Inf. Technol. **28**(4), 3893–3910 (2023)
4. Hu, Z., Han, Y., Wang, M.: Topic evolution and hot topic recognition in machine learning research in the field of library and information technology based on LDA-Word2vec. J. Mod. Inf. (in Chinese). https://link.cnki.net/urlid/22.1182.G3.20231206.1646.006
5. Xi, X., Guo, Y., Song, X., et al.: Research on visualization of technical similarity based on Word2vec and LDA topic models. J. Intell. **40**(09), 974–983 (2021). (in Chinese)
6. Murray, J.-A.: Massive open online courses: current and future trends in biomedical sciences. Biomed. Visualisation **4**, 47–53 (2019)
7. Wang, G., Qu, Z., Zhao, X.: Exploration and practice of interdisciplinary construction of "artificial intelligence+." Comput. Sci. **47**(04), 1–5 (2020). (in Chinese)
8. Tian, X., Tian, L.: The structural transformation of disciplinary and professional talent training in universities in the era of artificial intelligence: from the perspective of market supply and demand structure. J. Educ. Sci. Hunan Normal Univ. **19**(04), 63–70 (2020). (in Chinese)
9. Bucea-Manea-Tonis, R., Kuleto, V., Gudei, S.C.D.: Artificial intelligence potential in higher education institutions enhanced learning environment in Romania and Serbia. Sustainability **14**(10), 25–37 (2022)
10. Zhang, X.: The identity crisis and reshaping of university teachers in the era of intelligence. Mod. Educ. Technol. **30**(11), 5–11 (2020). (in Chinese)
11. Dai, X., Guo, L.: ChatGPT's intervention in higher education: ways, risks, and response strategies. Explor. High. Educ. **5**, 12–17 (2023). (in Chinese)
12. Li, H.: The smart generation characteristics of ChatGPT and its challenges to higher education. Jiangsu High. Educ. **8**, 1–12 (2023). (in Chinese)
13. Killian, C.M., Marttinen, R., Howley, D.: "Knock, Knock … Who's There?" ChatGPT and artificial intelligence-powered large language models: reflections on potential impacts within health and physical education teacher education. J. Teach. Phys. Educ. **42**(3), 385–389 (2023)
14. Zhang, L., Yun, C., Yin, S., et al.: Comparative analysis of China's research integrity policy and the evolution of literature themes. J. Mod. Inf. **43**(6), 108–120 (2023). (in Chinese)
15. Ivanov, S.: The dark side of artificial intelligence in higher education. Serv. Ind. J. **43**(15), 1055–1082 (2023)

Does Online Review Inconsistency Matter? The Effect of Inconsistency on Product Sales

Yao Lu, Yu Jia[✉], Nianxin Wang, and Shilun Ge

School of Economics and Management, Jiangsu University of Science and Technology,
Zhenjiang 212003, Jiangsu, China
jiayu@just.edu.cn

Abstract. Online reviews play pivotal roles in the dissemination of information and provide essential mechanisms for consumers to express opinions and make purchasing decisions. In recent years, review inconsistency as a peculiar phenomenon has triggered several challenges, including consumer confusion, the spread of misinformation, and a decline in market competitiveness, etc. To mitigate these effects of inconsistency, we investigate review inconsistency in two aspects, rating sentiment inconsistency and rating dispersion, and examine the different effects on product sales. In this paper, we employ the theoretical framework of HSM to develop an empirical model and collect 94,843 reviews from JD.com. The findings indicate that rating sentiment inconsistency exerts a negative impact on product sales. Conversely, rating dispersion has a positive effect on sales. Furthermore, rating dispersion and timeliness act as moderators, mitigating the negative impact of sentiment inconsistency on sales, while review richness intensifies this negative impact.

Keywords: Review Inconsistency · Rating Sentiment Inconsistency · Rating Dispersion · Product Sales · Heuristic Systematic Model

1 Introduction

Online reviews provide consumers with the convenience of sharing their opinions on products or services from anywhere, anytime. A recent consumer survey in 2023 revealed that 98% of consumers consult ratings and reviews before making a purchase decision [1]. Online reviews play pivotal roles in reducing information asymmetry and aiding potential consumers in making informed decisions. Prior studies indicated that online reviews written by previous customers have significant impacts on product sales [2]. Earlier studies have examined various aspects of online reviews, including their usefulness, authenticity, valence, volume, quality, and linguistic style, leading to numerous findings. Recently, scholars have also begun to investigate online review inconsistency, a topic that has gained interest in the field of online review research. Review inconsistency occurs when the information presented in different parts of a review or across multiple reviews evaluating the same product or service is inconsistent or conflicting [3].

Y. P. Tu and M. Chi (Eds.): WHICEB 2024, LNBIP 516, pp. 120–132, 2024.
https://doi.org/10.1007/978-3-031-60260-3_11

When consumers read online reviews, they typically consider both the rating and the review content [3]. However, there are instances where the rating and the accompanying textual review content are noticeably inconsistent. Consumers often fear that negative reviews may prompt retaliation from sellers, leading them to favor positive reviews. According to communication persuasion theory [4], conflicting environmental stimuli are less effective in shaping a person's behavior. Consequently, inconsistent reviews have a diminished impact on consumers' perceptions, diminishing their perceived usefulness and willingness to purchase the product [5]. Similarly, inconsistencies within a message can undermine the recipient's assessment of its credibility [6].

Although prior studies have examined review inconsistency, little consideration has been given to the impact on product sales. In literature, some studies suggest that inconsistency has a negative impact, others indicate that it can promote product sales growth. Others still found no significant effect [6]. Therefore, we aim to investigate the relationship between rating sentiment inconsistency and product sales based on the HSM model, further examining the moderating effects of rating dispersion, review richness, and timeliness on this relationship.

2 Literature Review

2.1 Review Inconsistency

Prior studies have explored the phenomenon of review inconsistency across different review factors, such as rating inconsistency [7] and language inconsistency [3]. Specifically, rating inconsistency was defined as the disparity between individual review ratings and the average rating, and has garnered significant academic attention [7, 8] due to its close correlation with various rating correlates. According to Yin et al. [8], rating inconsistency can undermine the helpfulness of online reviews [8]. Conversely, Aghakhani et al. [9] observed that as rating inconsistency increases, online reviews receive more helpful votes.

While numerous studies have primarily focused on the impact of review inconsistency on review usefulness, relatively little has addressed its impact on product sales, which is a critical outcome for merchants. For instance, Aghakhani et al. [9] investigated the moderating effect of rating inconsistency on the relationship between review consistency and review usefulness. Therefore, the present study aims to explore the relationship between rating sentiment inconsistency and product sales across various rating dispersion scenarios.

2.2 Online Reviews and Product Sales

Online reviews have become an essential source of information for online shoppers seeking to evaluate product quality. These reviews effectively bridge the information gap between online merchants and customers, ultimately shaping consumers' purchasing decisions. While the impact of online reviews on product sales is widely recognized, prior studies have primarily focused on the overall characteristics of these reviews, such as their volume and sentiment, rather than their specific content.

Numerous studies have delved into the diverse effects of online reviews on sales. Eslami et al. [10] highlighted the unique importance of review positivity and review score consistency in driving sales for low-engagement and high-engagement products. Wang et al. [6] examined the moderating role of perceived review credibility on the relationship between review sentiment and product sales. Hang et al. [11] demonstrated that reviews incorporating videos or follow-up reviews have a positive impact on sales. Overall, these findings underscore the complex nature of online review effects on product sales, highlighting the need for further research into the specific content and characteristics of these reviews.

2.3 Heuristic Systematic Model

The Heuristic System Model (HSM) is a pivotal component of the dual-process persuasion theory [12], encapsulating both heuristic and systematic processing [13]. Heuristic processing represents a rapid, intuitive mode of thought that relies on personal experience and intuition to shape decisions. Conversely, systematic processing involves a slower, more deliberative mode of thinking where individuals engage in in-depth analysis of information to arrive at more rational and objective decisions [13]. When evaluating information through heuristic processing, individuals rely on easily accessible cues, such as the length of information, or make judgments based on sparse non-content clues. The theory posits that individuals with sufficient motivation, ability, and cognitive resources will choose to process systematically.

The HSM has been widely employed in the area of online reviews [6, 10]. Wang et al. [6] employed the HSM to examine the perceived credibility of online reviews, thereby modulating the impact of review sentiment on product sales. The HSM posits that consumers utilize the principles of least effort and sufficiency in making decisions, seamlessly integrating heuristic and systematic processing. These principles have been used to explain information service and information-seeking behavior, as well as the utilization of online review information.

3   Hypotheses Development

3.1 Effect of Rating Sentiment Inconsistency

Online reviews encompass various elements, for instance, star ratings, text content, pictures, etc. These elements are perceived by review readers as distinct information sources [14]. In this study, we define rating sentiment inconsistency as the extent to which the rating and review content conflict [3]. Information consistency is defined as the degree to which the current information aligns with the available information. As information consistency increases, so does credibility. Information credibility refers to the extent to which individuals perceive the information they consume as credible [6].

Additionally, according to the theory of communicative persuasion [4], exposure to contradictory messages diminishes their persuasive power on reader behavior. Similarly, rating sentiment inconsistency within a message can impact a user's evaluation of its credibility. Consequently, reviews with inconsistencies may be viewed as less credible.

We posit that this inconsistency can have a negative impact on product sales. Therefore, we propose the following hypothesis:

H1. Rating sentiment inconsistency is negatively related to product sales.

3.2 Effect of Rating Dispersion

The least effort principle and the sufficiency principle guide consumers in their decision-making processes, allowing them to use either heuristic or systematic processing methods [15]. The sufficiency principle encourages consumers to engage in more systematic processing when making informed and reliable decisions. When consumers have a strong motivation to make informed decisions, they may deviate from the least effort principle and invest more cognitive effort into their decision-making processes [15].

These two principles can well explain how the processing of online review information changes based on rating dispersion. A low dispersion of ratings suggests that the reviews provide consistent assessments, indicating a high level of confidence in the overall ratings. According to the principle of least effort, consumers may not process all available source cues or assign equal cognitive weight to the given information [7]. Therefore, when there is low dispersion, individuals are less likely to rely on individual reviews to evaluate a product. On the other hand, a high dispersion of ratings suggests that the overall rating does not accurately reflect the true quality of the review. A high degree of dispersion in review scores can undermine the credibility of online reviews, which can adversely impact consumers' perceptions of product quality [7]. In this case, consumers may lose confidence in the overall rating and instead focus on individual reviews and ratings due to the sufficiency principle. Therefore, we hypothesize that:

H2. Review dispersion is negatively related to product sales.

H3. Review dispersion can moderate the relationship between rating sentiment inconsistency and product sales.

3.3 Moderating Effects of Review Richness and Timeliness

We also consider review richness as a systematic factor. A higher level of review richness suggests that consumers have access to more detailed information about specific product attributes, thereby reducing uncertainty about the product [11] and ultimately boosting product sales. However, when presented with an overabundance of information, consumers may experience cognitive overload due to their limited processing capabilities [11]. According to information processing theory, individuals require high-quality information to address uncertainty and make optimal decisions [11]. Therefore, within an optimal informational scope, consumers can learn more about a product from reviews with higher richness. Excessive detail in the review content, however, can have a negative impact [16]. It may diminish consumers' perception of the review's credibility and lead to a decline in product sales. Hence, we hypothesize that:

H4. Review richness intensifies the negative impact of rating sentiment inconsistency on product sales.

In the context of online reviews, timeliness serves as a valuable heuristic cue for consumers, aiding them in promptly assessing the value of a review. Timeliness is a pivotal aspect of review information quality, providing an up-to-date evaluation of the product [17]. The timeliness of online product review information refers to the number of days between a consumer's purchase and the writing of a review. A longer interval between purchase and review results in lower timeliness. Typically, higher timeliness translates to a more accurate representation of the product's quality or the consumer's perception of it [17]. This enhances the review's utility as a reference for other consumers. Nevertheless, if the rating and content are inconsistent, it can erode consumer trust and increase cognitive costs [9]. Therefore, timely reviews may mitigate the negative impact of inconsistent reviews on product sales. Hence, we propose the following hypothesis:

H5. Timeliness mitigates the negative impact of rating sentiment inconsistency on product sales.

The research model is illustrated in Fig. 1.

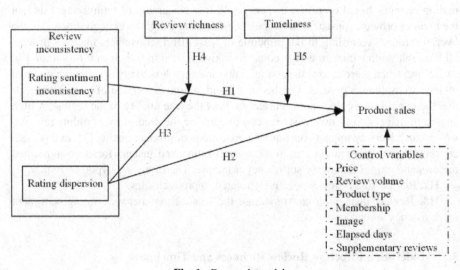

Fig. 1. Research model

4 Methodology

4.1 Data Collection

To examine the relationship between review inconsistency and product sales, we collected 99,065 reviews across 26 products sourced from JD (www.jd.com), the leading E-commerce platform in China. During the data processing phase, we refined the raw data by removing missing values, duplicate reviews, and those with default values. Moreover, reviews with fewer than 5 words were also excluded from the analysis. To gain a deeper understanding of the impact of product characteristics on review inconsistency, we categorized the 26 products into search-based and experience-based categories. Finally, we obtained a dataset containing 94,843 online reviews.

4.2 Definition of Variables

Product Sales. In empirical analysis, we consider product sales as the dependent variable. To determine product sales, we consider the number of newly added reviews a product receives within seven days of an online review. To ensure data accuracy, we used the raw review

Rating Sentiment Inconsistency. The primary independent variable rating sentiment inconsistency was measured as the absolute difference between the sentiment conveyed in the review content and the star rating assigned to the same review. The specific formula is as follows:

$$rating\_senti\_incon^j = \left| z\_rating^j - z\_senti^j \right| \tag{1}$$

$$z\_rating^j = \frac{rating^j - \overline{rating}}{\sigma_{rating}} \tag{2}$$

$$z\_senti^j = \frac{senti^j - \overline{senti}}{\sigma_{senti}} \tag{3}$$

The rating $rating\_senti\_incon^j$ represents the rating sentiment inconsistency of the jth review; z_rating^j and z_senti^j represent the z-scores of the rating and sentiment of the jth review, respectively; $\overline{rating}$ and $\overline{senti}$ denote the mean values of ratings and sentiments of reviews of the same products, respectively; $rating^j$ and $senti^j$ indicate the rating and sentiment of the jth review, respectively; and σ_{rating} and σ_{senti} denote the standard deviations of ratings and sentiment scores for a group of reviews, respectively. In other words, both sentiment and rating were normalized using z-scores.

Sentiment refers to the score assigned to a review text that indicates a positive or negative attitude. The sentiment scores of the review texts were computed using the SnowNLP library for Python, which was utilized in conjunction with Jieba. The sentiment score obtained from this analysis ranges from 0 to 1. A score closer to 1 indicates a more positive effect, while a score closer to 0 indicates a more negative effect.

Rating Dispersion. The rating dispersion was operationalized as the absolute difference between the star rating of a review and the overall rating of the corresponding product. The specific formula is as follows:

$$indivi\_overall\_incon^j = \left| indivi\_rating^j - overall\_rating \right| \tag{4}$$

$$indivi\_rating^j = \frac{star\_rating^j}{5} \tag{5}$$

The rating $rating\_dispersion^j$ represents the rating dispersion of the jth review; $indivi\_rating^j$ stands for the scaled value of the star rating of jth review, which ranges between [0, 1]. $overall\_rating$ denotes the overall rating of the product.

Moderator. The moderating variable considered was rating dispersion, alongside time-liness and review richness. To calculate review richness, we utilized the Gensim open-source toolkit to develop an LDA (Latent Dirichlet Allocation) model for classifying all reviews. The optimal number of categories was determined through the perplexity method. Subsequently, we extracted 15 high-frequency words from each topic and combined them with commonly used functional attributes and experiential words to create a dictionary. This dictionary was then utilized to calculate the richness of a review. This evaluation was only performed if the review content included an attribute or experience word.

Control Variables. Following prior studies [13, 16], we incorporated several control variables, including image, price, review volume, product type, membership, elapsed days, and supplementary review. Table 1 provides a comprehensive overview of all variable names and their corresponding descriptions.

Table 1. Description of variables

Variable	Description	Sources
Product sales	The number of new reviews in 7 days since a review is written	-
Rating sentiment inconsistency	The extent to which star ratings are inconsistent with content sentiment in the same review	Shan et al. [3]
Rating dispersion	The absolute value of the difference between an average of reviews' rating and the rating of a review	Lee et al. [7]
Timeliness	The number of days that subtract from the review date to the purchase date	Fu et al. [17]
Review richness	The review contains the attribute word count for the product or platform attributes	–
Price	Product price	Wang et al. [2]
Review volume	Number of reviews of a product	Wang et al. [2]
Product type	Classification of products based on different characteristics, 0 = search products, 1 = experience products	Yin et al. [11]

(continued)

Table 1. (*continued*)

Variable	Description	Sources
Membership	Whether the reviewer is a Plus member of JD.com, 0 = not member, 1 = member	Wang et al. [16]
Image	Whether the review contains a photo image or not, 0 = not image, 1 = image	Lee et al. [7]
Supplementary review	Whether the review contains a supplementary review or not, 0 = not supplementary review, 1 = supplementary review	Yin et al. [11]
Elapsed days	Take the number of days that are subtracted from the crawling date to review the date	Aghakhani et al. [14]

5 Results

5.1 Main Results

Table 2 presents the descriptive statistics of the variables, while Table 3 provides a correlation matrix. Table 4 presents the estimation results of the proposed model. In Model 1, we only included control variables. Model 2 examines the impact of independent variables on product sales, along with the moderating effect of rating dispersion. Model 3 and Model 4 further investigate the moderating effects of review richness and timeliness, respectively, by incorporating their interaction terms with rating sentiment inconsistency. To mitigate multicollinearity, we mean-centered and standardized the independent and moderating variables. The variance inflation factor (VIF) checks have confirmed that the issue of multicollinearity is not significant.

Model 4 reveals that the coefficient of rating sentiment inconsistency is negative and significant (coefficient = -0.030, $p < 0.001$), thus supporting H1. This suggests that lower rating sentiment inconsistency leads to higher product sales. Furthermore, rating dispersion exerts a positive impact on product sales (coefficient = 0.500, $p < 0.001$), indicating that greater rating dispersion is associated with higher product sales. Therefore, H2 is not supported. This finding might be explained by the fact that when ratings are highly dispersed, some consumers perceive the product as unique or distinctive, fostering a desire to purchase and ultimately boosting product sales.

To explore the moderating impact of rating dispersion on the relationship between rating sentiment inconsistency and product sales, we included an interaction term in the model. The results indicate a significant positive influence of this interaction term on product sales (coefficient = 0.114, $p < 0.001$). This suggests that as rating dispersion increases, the effect of rating sentiment inconsistency on product sales diminishes. Therefore, H3 is supported.

Table 2. Descriptive statistics

Variable	Obs	Min	Max	Mean	SD
P	94843	39	8299	2956.66	2901.93
RV	94843	20000	3000000	514419.83	783301.56
PT	94843	0	1	0.43	0.50
M	94843	0	1	0.57	0.49
T	94843	0	114	14.81	16.28
I	94843	0	1	0.61	0.49
SR	94843	0	1	0.04	0.21
RD	94843	0.02	0.78	0.24	0.30
RR	94843	0	20	2.52	2.72
ED	94843	0	4124	232.87	360.41
RSI	94843	0.00002	2.55	0.27	0.45
PS	94843	0	3975	1042.73	794.37

Note: P: Price, M: Membership, T: Timeliness, I: Image, RV: Review volume, PT: Product type, SR: Supplementary reviews, RD: Rating dispersion, RR: Review richness, ED: Elapsed days, RSI: Rating sentiment inconsistency, PS: Product sales

Model 4 reveals a negative and significant coefficient for the interaction between rating sentiment inconsistency and review richness (coefficient $= -0.026$, $p < 0.001$). This finding suggests that as review content becomes richer, the negative impact of rating sentiment inconsistency on product sales intensifies. Consequently, H4 is supported. Similarly, Model 4 also indicates that the interaction term between rating sentiment inconsistency and timeliness significantly buffers the relationship between rating sentiment inconsistency and product sales (coefficient $= 0.040$, $p < 0.001$). Timeliness, therefore, acts as a positive moderator of the negative impact of rating sentiment inconsistency on product sales. This supports H5.

5.2 Robustness Checking

To enhance the reliability of our empirical findings, we conducted additional regression analyses with variable substitution. We evaluated the stability of our outcomes with respect to the number of new reviews (as a proxy for product sales) across various time intervals. These supplementary analyses indicate that our primary results are consistent across different time periods, thus affirming the robustness of our findings.

Table 3. Correlation matrix

Variables	1	2	3	4	5	6	7	8	9	10	11	12
PT	1											
M	0.064**	1										
I	-0.111**	0.238**	1									
SR	-0.082**	-0.077**	-0.060**	1								
RD	-0.045**	-0.370**	-0.477**	0.153**	1							
RSI	0.014**	-0.163**	-0.250**	0.052**	0.266**	1						
RR	-0.215**	0.188**	0.395**	-0.041**	-0.411**	-0.280**	1					
LNT	0.017**	0.104**	-0.088**	-0.035**	-0.020**	-0.009**	-0.017**	1				
LNP	-0.807**	-0.080**	0.055**	0.083**	0.057**	0	0.157**	-0.032**	1			
LNRV	-0.054**	-0.073**	-0.091**	-0.004	0.202**	0.105**	-0.043**	-0.013**	-0.022**	1		
LNED	0.258**	-0.099**	-0.110**	0.049**	0.318**	0.119**	-0.129**	-0.061**	-0.202**	-0.042**	1	
LNPS	-0.085**	-0.146**	-0.038**	0.077**	0.309**	0.094**	-0.002	-0.134**	0.070**	0.186**	0.569**	1

Note: ** $p < 0.01$. PT: Product type, M: Membership, I: Image, SR: Supplementary reviews, RD: Rating dispersion, RSI: Rating sentiment inconsistency, RR: Review richness, LNT: Ln (Timeliness + 1), LNP: Ln (Price), LNRV: Ln (Review volume), LNED: Ln (Elapsed days + 1), LNPS: Ln (Product sales + 1)

Table 4. Regression results

Variables	Model 1	Model 2	Model 3	Model 4
RSI		−0.030*** (0.008)	−0.031** (0.010)	−0.030** (0.010)
RD		0.390*** (0.015)	0.503*** (0.016)	0.500*** (0.015)
LNP	0.025*** (0.004)	0.024*** (0.004)	0.024*** (0.004)	0.020*** (0.004)
LNRV	0.238*** (0.003)	0.223*** (0.003)	0.219*** (0.003)	0.217*** (0.003)
M	−0.171*** (0.007)	−0.122*** (0.007)	−0.126*** (0.007)	−0.099*** (0.007)
PT	−0.564*** (0.012)	−0.537*** (0.012)	−0.495*** (0.012)	−0.502*** (0.012)
I	0.119*** (0.007)	0.207*** (0.008)	0.171*** (0.008)	0.142*** (0.008)
LNED	0.557*** (0.002)	0.535*** (0.002)	0.531*** (0.002)	0.527*** (0.002)
SR	0.169*** (0.017)	0.124*** (0.017)	0.120*** (0.017)	0.107*** (0.017)
RR			0.032*** (0.002)	0.032*** (0.002)
LNT				−0.101*** (0.003)
RD × RSI		0.188*** (0.027)	0.113*** (0.027)	0.114*** (0.027)
RR × RSI			−0.028*** (0.005)	−0.026*** (0.004)
LNT × RSI				0.040*** (0.007)
N	94843	94843	94843	94843
R^2	0.426	0.431	0.434	0.441
F	10058.139***	7172.145***	6068.174***	5333.928***

Note: The higher the value for review timeliness, the lower the timeliness. *** $p < 0.001$, ** $p < 0.01$, * $p < 0.05$. RSI: Rating sentiment inconsistency, RD: Rating dispersion, LNP: Ln (Price), LNRV: Ln (Review volume), M: Membership, PT: Product type, I: Image, LNED: Ln (Elapsed days + 1), SR: Supplementary reviews, RR: Review richness, LNT: Ln (Timeliness + 1)

6 Discussion and Conclusion

Online reviews play pivotal roles in enabling consumers to make informed purchasing decisions. However, the impact of inconsistent reviews on product sales remains under-examined. This study sought to investigate the influence of online reviews on sales, considering both rating sentiment inconsistency and rating dispersion based on the HSM model. The findings indicate that rating sentiment inconsistency exerts a negative impact on sales. Conversely, rating dispersion has a positive effect on sales. Furthermore, rating dispersion and timeliness mitigates the negative impact of sentiment inconsistency on sales, while review richness intensifies this negative impact.

This study has several theoretical implications. First, while exploring the intricate impact of two distinct types of review inconsistency on sales, this paper also examines the variation in the effect of rating sentiment inconsistency on sales at different levels of rating dispersion. In prior academic studies, review inconsistency has often been treated as a singular construct [7, 9]. However, we posit that a more thorough exploration of review inconsistency is warranted. Additionally, the impact of review inconsistency on sales is further validated. Prior studies have often overlooked the impact of inconsistent reviews on sales. It is crucial for online merchants to gain a comprehensive understanding of the impact of inconsistent reviews on product sales in order to effectively market their products and enhance customer satisfaction.

The study also carries practical implications. By implementing an alert system that alerts reviewers to inconsistencies within their reviews, along with a policy of limiting the richness of reviews, we can minimize consumer confusion and potentially boost product sales.

It is important to acknowledge the limitations of this study. Firstly, in this investigation, we examined the moderating effect of rating dispersion without considering its directional impact. Therefore, further exploration is warranted. Secondly, this study focused solely on review data from JD.com, and therefore the findings may not be generalized to other countries or platforms. Future research could use data from various countries and platforms to assess the generalizability of these results.

Acknowledgement. This research is partly supported by the National Natural Science Foundation of China [72272066, 71971101, 72372060, and 71972090], General Project of Philosophy and Social Science Research in Universities in Jiangsu Province [2022SJYB2238], Jiangsu University of Science and Technology Youth Science and Technology Innovation Project [1042922212].

References

1. PowerReviews: the complete guide to ratings & reviews (2023 Edition). https://www.powerr eviews.com/insights/complete-guide-ratings-reviews-2023/
2. Wang, Q., Zhang, W., Li, J., et al.: Benefits or harms? The effect of online review manipulation on sales. Electron. Commer. Res. Appl. **57**, 101224 (2023)
3. Shan, G., Zhou, L., Zhang, D.: From conflicts and confusion to doubts: examining review in-consistency for fake review detection. Decis. Support. Syst. **144**, 113513 (2021)
4. Leventhal, H.: Findings and theory in the study of fear communications. Adv. Exp. Soc. Psychol. **5**, 119–186 (1970)

5. Lakhiwal, A., Bala, H., Léger, P.-M.: Ambivalence is better than indifference: a behavioral and neurophysiological assessment of ambivalence in online environments. MIS Q. **47**, 705–732 (2023)
6. Wang, Q., Zhang, W., Li, J., et al.: Effect of online review sentiment on product sales: the moderating role of review credibility perception. Comput. Hum. Behav. **133**, 107272 (2022)
7. Lee, S., Lee, S., Baek, H.: Does the dispersion of online review ratings affect review helpfulness? Comput. Hum. Behav. **117**, 106670 (2021)
8. Yin, D., Mitra, S., Zhang, H.: When do consumers value positive vs. negative reviews? An empirical investigation of confirmation bias in online word of mouth. Inf. Syst. Res. **27**(1), 131–144 (2016)
9. Aghakhani, N., Oh, O., Gregg, D.G., et al.: Online review consistency matters: an elaboration likelihood model perspective. Inf. Syst. Front. **23**(5), 1287–1301 (2021)
10. Eslami, S.P., Ghasemaghaei, M.: Effects of online review positiveness and review score inconsistency on sales: a comparison by product involvement. J. Retail. Consum. Serv. **45**, 74–80 (2018)
11. Hang, Y., Shuang, Z., William, Y., et al.: How online review richness impacts sales: an attribute substitution perspective. J. Assoc. Inf. Sci. Technol. **72**(7), 901–917 (2021)
12. Chaiken, S., Trope, Y.: Dual-Process Theories in Social Psychology. The Guilford Press, New York (1999)
13. Choi, J., Yoo, S.H., Lee, H.: Two faces of review inconsistency: the respective effects of internal and external inconsistencies on job review helpfulness. Comput. Hum. Behav. **140**, 107570 (2023)
14. Aghakhani, N., Oh, O., Gregg, D., et al.: How review quality and source credibility interacts to affect review usefulness: an expansion of the elaboration likelihood model. Inf. Syst. Front. **25**(4), 1513–1531 (2023)
15. Zhang, K.Z.K., Zhao, S.J., Cheung, C.M.K., et al.: Examining the influence of online reviews on consumers' decision-making: a heuristic–systematic model. Decis. Support. Syst. **67**, 78–89 (2014)
16. Wang, Y., Ngai, E.W.T., Li, K.: The effect of review content richness on product review helpfulness: the moderating role of rating inconsistency. Electron. Commer. Res. Appl. **61**, 101290 (2023)
17. Xiaorong, F., Zhang, B., Xie, Q., et al.: Impact of quantity and timeliness of EWOM Information on consumer's online purchase intention under C2C environment. Asian J. Bus. Res. **1**(2), 37–48 (2011)

The Impact of Empowering Leadership on Employees' Deviant Innovation Behavior from the Perspective of Planned Behavior

Yinyu Gu, Fengqin Diao$^{(\boxtimes)}$, and Xianqiu Cao$^{(\boxtimes)}$

School of Economics and Management, China University of Geosciences (Wuhan), Wuhan, Hubei, China
xianqiu_cao5988@163.com

Abstract. Based on the Theory of Planned Behavior, this study constructed a multiple mediation model of empowering leadership affecting employees' deviant innovation behavior. The analysis results show that the higher the level of empowering leadership, the more likely employees are to have deviant innovation behavior. Psychological security, organizational innovation climate and creative self-efficacy play a significant mediating role in the process of empowering leadership to stimulate employees' deviant innovation behavior. The results of this study provide new theoretical support for the subsequent research on deviant innovation behavior, and provide decision-making basis for enterprise managers to promote employees' deviant innovation behavior and improve enterprise innovation performance.

Keywords: Empowering Leadership · Psychological Security · Organizational Innovation Climate · Creative Self-efficacy · Deviant Innovation

1 Introduction

Innovation is the soul of enterprise survival and development. However, the traditional centralized leadership style not only fails to meet the power needs of employees, but also inhibits their creativity. Therefore, the importance of inspiring employees' innovative behavior through leadership authorization has become increasingly prominent. Based on this, in order to gain competitive advantages and achieve long-term sustainable development, enterprises have introduced policies and taken measures to encourage and support internal employee innovation. However, due to the shortage of resources and the Riskiness of innovation, not all ideas can be recognized and supported as formal innovation projects. When employees forecast or already know that their ideas cannot be supported, these innovators may continue to seek innovation in informal ways for the long-term interests of the organization, that is, deviant innovation. It has been found that deviant innovation behavior is common in organizations, and a certain degree of deviant innovation can activate organizational creativity and improve enterprise innovation performance. Therefore, deviant innovation behavior has been favored by researchers in recent years.

Y. P. Tu and M. Chi (Eds.): WHICEB 2024, LNBIP 516, pp. 133–146, 2024.
https://doi.org/10.1007/978-3-031-60260-3_12

According to the existing research, the significant impact of leadership factors on the behavior has been demonstrated by scholars. However, there are few studies on the relationship between empowering leadership and deviant innovation, and existing studies have only demonstrated that empowering leadership can positively influence deviant innovation by influencing employees work autonomy [1] and psychological availability [2]. Other mechanisms of empowering leadership on deviant innovation require further research. In addition, some scholars use different theories to explore the mechanism of deviant innovation from different perspectives, which ignore the initiative and planning of employees' deviant innovation behavior from the perspective of employees' subjectivity [3]. The Theory of Planned Behavior can start from the behavior result itself and assume that all external factors affect behavior through attitude, subjective norms and perceived behavior control as well as the relative weights of the three factors. It can well explain planned behavior [4] in various behavioral fields, especially in the study of behaviors with intentional characteristics. In addition, scholars have tried to construct a theoretical model of planned behavior to explain constructive deviance. Therefore, based on the Theory of Planned Behavior, this paper has an exploratory value to study the influence mechanism of empowering leadership on deviant innovation.

Based on the above analysis, this study builds a triple mediation model based on the Theory of Planned Behavior, and aims to explore how empowering leaders influence employees' deviant innovation behavior through three mediating variables: psychological security (attitude), organizational innovation climate (subjective norms) and creative self-efficacy (perceived control). In the process of transitioning to an independent innovation country, it is significant for leaders to adjust management behaviors to stimulate the innovation vitality of employees and guide their innovation practices. Therefore, this study hopes to provide guidance for enterprise managers from a new perspective.

2 Theoretical Foundations and Research Hypothesis

2.1 The Theory of Planned Behavior

Since its inception, the Theory of Planned Behavior has been widely used in various fields [4], and it has become a universal theory for behavioral explanation and prediction research, as it integrates factors such as individual psychological state, organizational scenario and work characteristics. Studies have proved that the theory has good reliability and validity, and can explain and predict the emergence of individual behavior and intention more comprehensively. Deviant innovation has a high behavioral cost, the actors need to spend time and resources on careful thinking and planning. So only when employees fully consider the potential risks, the attitudes of others and their own capabilities will they choose deviant innovation. It can be seen that deviant innovation is a rational and planned behavior. Based on the above analysis, the Theory of Planned Behavior can provide a new theoretical perspective to reveal the process of employees' deviant innovation behavior occurring.

2.2 The Influence of Empowering Leadership on Deviant Innovation

Scholars interpret "empowerment" mainly from two aspects: situational empowerment and psychological empowerment [5]. This study believes that empowering leadership changes employees' psychological perception and experience by granting power and assigning responsibilities, and guides them to change their behavior and attitude. Deviant innovation is a kind of conscious and voluntary behavior with dual properties of purpose legitimacy and behavior illegality [6]. The generation of behavior is related closely to not only the innovator's intrinsic motivation level, but also the space for private innovation. Therefore, employees with stronger innovation motivation and higher autonomy are more inclined to produce deviant innovation.

Empowering leadership can provide a strong explanation for the occurrence of deviant innovation behavior. Job autonomy is a prerequisite for private innovation. Leadership empowerment can help employees eliminate the boundary between roles and tasks [7], provide employees with a relatively free working environment and sufficient space for development. Employees can arrange their time, energy and resources independently and devote themselves to out-of-role innovation practices. It provides action space for deviant innovation behavior. On the one hand, leaders encourage teamwork and information sharing. The employees can freely express their thoughts and fully stimulate creativity in the collision with others' thinking. High creativity is an important driving factor for deviant innovation [8], so they have stronger intrinsic motivation to implement deviant innovation. On the other hand, empowering leaders participate in the employees' work goals setting, provide information resource support, care about employees' psychological feelings and provide emotional encouragement. Under the traditional cultural background of advocating "gratitude for gratitude", employees transform the leadership's support and care into a sense of belonging and responsibility, then generate emotional connection beyond duty [9], increasing the level of extrinsic motivation to return to the organization and the leaders. If employees realize that their creativity can bring great benefits to the enterprise, they are more willing to repay the organization by making efforts to innovate, which may lead to more deviant innovation behaviors. In summary, this study puts forward the hypothesis:

H1: Empowering leadership positively affects employees' deviant innovation.

2.3 The Mediating Role of Psychological Security

According to the Expected Value Theory, employees' attitude towards deviant innovation behavior is affected by the behavior result and the evaluation of the behavior result [4]. Obviously, deviant innovation behavior has a negative impact on employees. Therefore, employees' attitude toward deviant innovation mainly depends on the subjective evaluation of the behavior results, that is, the safety judgment of implementation of deviant innovation. Psychological security, as employees' perception of being able to show themselves without worrying about the negative consequences of self-image or career, can truly reflect employees' positive or negative evaluation of deviant innovation. Therefore, this study chooses psychological security as employees' attitude towards deviant innovation.

Empowering leadership can improve employees' psychological security. First of all, delegating power and participating in decision-making shown by empowering leadership break the routine, which enables employees to form the cognition that leaders allow behaviors that violate organization rules. Employees will not be afraid of violating the rules and worry too much about their own words and deeds, which can effectively promote the emergence of a high level of psychological security for employees. Secondly, leaders break the hierarchy to eliminate communication barriers, encourage teamwork to promote free communication, which will promote internal staff to produce positive psychological experience of the organizational atmosphere. When the organizational environment and values are agreed and recognized by employees, they will gradually transform their trust in external colleagues into enhancement of the psychological security [10]. Finally, leaders provide employees with sufficient decision-making power to improve their perceived insider status, and their psychological security perception level will be higher. Summarizing the above analysis, this study proposes the following hypothesis:

H2a: Empowering leadership positively affects employees' psychological security.

Psychological security can effectively reduce individual risk perception. When a high level of psychological security is generated, employees will think that deviant innovative behavior is safe for themselves. They may not avoid innovation for fear of negative impact on their interpersonal relationship and career, and even increase their willingness to implement deviant innovative behavior in return for the psychological security provided by leaders and organizations. Empowering leadership helps to build interpersonal relationships full of trust and care within the organization. Employees in such a friendly and supportive organizational environment can reduce their sense of alienation from each other and the risk perception of being isolated and excluded for breaking organizational rules and carrying out deviant innovation [11]. When they perceive that the external threat to themselves is reduced, in the face of innovation obstacles, employees are more inclined to maintain a positive attitude. According to the Theory of Planned Behavior, the more positive an employee's attitude toward deviant innovation, the more likely the behavior is to occur. Based on the above analysis, this study proposes the following hypothesis:

H2b: Psychological security positively affects employees' deviant innovation.

H2: Psychological security plays a significant mediating role between empowering leadership and employees' deviant innovation.

2.4   The Mediating Role of Organizational Innovation Climate

Subjective norm refers to the environmental pressure that an individual feels when making the decisions, which reflects the degree of influence of important persons or groups on individual behavior [4]. Organizational climate has an informational implication on employee behavior. When employees decide whether to adopt deviant innovation behavior, the subjective norms they perceive are mainly derived from the pressure of leaders' innovation expectations and the demonstration of colleagues' innovative behavior. Organizational innovation climate can well reflect the influence of organizational environment that employees perceive when making decisions about deviant innovation behavior. Strong innovation atmosphere means the organization's recognition and support for innovation activities [12]. The greater the perceived support from important others, the more inclined employees are to implement deviant innovation behaviors. Therefore, this paper takes organizational innovation climate as the representative variable of subjective norms.

It has been pointed out that empowering leadership style and its dimensions can promote the construction of organizational innovation climate [13], but there is a lack of specific demonstration. This paper summarizes previous studies and believes that empowering leadership affects organizational innovation climate mainly through three ways. First of all, organizations that adopt the empowering leadership style are more flexible and open, and tend to have flatter structures due to fewer management levels, which will speed up the rate of information transfer and facilitate the formation of organizational innovation atmosphere. Secondly, empowering leadership encourages teamwork and information sharing, which promotes the formation of a harmonious communication atmosphere. Candid communication and cooperation among members can stimulate more innovative ideas and create a higher innovation climate. Finally, leaders grant their subordinates greater autonomy based on trust, they give fair and supportive evaluation to employees' suggestions and provides a broad platform for employees to display their new ideas and viewpoints. All these enhance employees' sense of innovation support and thus affect their perceived level of innovation climate. Based on the above analysis, this study proposes the following hypothesis:

H3a: Empowering leadership positively affects organizational innovation climate.

To a certain extent, the organizational innovation climate can increase the "compliance" of deviant innovation. On the one hand, the strong organizational innovation climate will make employees realize that the organization values and expects employees to innovate. The success of innovation will bring benefits for company and career promotion for themselves. Even if fails, leaders will give objective evaluation, which further stimulates employees' enthusiasm for innovation. On the other hand, the tension of resources will be amplified [14]. The structure of the organization with a higher level of innovation atmosphere is often more flexible, and can tolerate a certain degree of behavior beyond the organizational norms. Therefore, employees are more inclined to take perverse ways to complete their work in the face of obstacles. In addition, innovation climate can promote team communication and knowledge sharing. Employees can not only feel the innovation support from organization, but also enhance their knowledge acquisition ability and creativity. Employees with high creativity have stronger motivation to implement deviant innovation [14]. Based on the above analysis, this study proposes the following hypothesis:

H3b: Organizational innovation climate positively affects employees' deviant innovation.

H3: Organizational innovation climate plays a significant mediating role between empowering leadership and deviant innovation.

2.5   The Mediating Role of Creative Self-efficacy

Perceived behavioral control refers to the degree of control over resources, opportunities and abilities [4], which reflects individual's perception of the difficulty of performing a specific behavior and the confidence in successfully completing the target behavior [15]. This meaning is close to self-efficacy. Employees with high sense of creative self-efficacy are more confident in their own innovation resources and ability, have a stronger sense of control over the implementation of deviant innovation behavior, and are more inclined to produce deviant innovation behavior when confronted with environmental resistance. Therefore, this study takes creative self-efficacy as the concrete variable of perceived behavior control.

Creative self-efficacy is the belief that individuals perceive whether they can achieve innovative results, which reflects the degree of confidence. By summarizing previous studies, this study believes that empowering leadership affects employees' creative self-efficacy mainly by perception of autonomy and job competence. First of all, empowering leadership creates a loose and free environment by decentralization, which effectively enhances employees' perception of resource availability and behavior controllability [16]. Employees are less bound by rules and have higher behavioral autonomy, and the obstacles of deviant innovation are reduced, which will help strengthen their confidence in the execution of deviant innovation. Secondly, empowering leadership not only encourages employees to exert their potential to learn knowledge and solve problems independently, but also proactively provides more skills training and work guidance, which makes employees feel the support and assistance to improve their confidence [17]. On the other hand, leaders empower subordinates and encourage them to participate in decision-making, making employees feel valued and appreciated by the organization. The awareness of value and competence greatly enhances their creative self-efficacy. Based on the above analysis, this study proposes the following hypothesis:

H4a: Empowering leadership positively affects employees' creative self-efficacy.

Employees with high creative self-efficacy are full of confidence in their own innovation ability and have stronger challenge spirit. They believe that they have greater advantages in knowledge acquisition and skill learning, and believe that their own ability can successfully innovate and bring benefits to the enterprise. Even in the face of innovation resistance, they are more likely to break through constraints and actively integrate internal and external resources to seek innovation. Empowering leadership gives employees more authorization, attention, skill training, work resources and fewer regulations, which improves employees' actual work ability and confidence. When employees have a higher creative self-efficacy, they have a stronger sense of control over deviant innovation behavior. According to the Theory of Planned Behavior, the stronger the sense of control is, the greater the tendency of employees to engage in the behavior. Based on the above analysis, this study proposes the following hypothesis:

H4b: Creative self-efficacy positively affects employees' deviant innovation.

H4: Creative self-efficacy plays a significant mediating role between empowering leadership and deviant innovation.

Based on the above analysis, the research model of this paper is shown in Fig. 1.

Fig. 1. Research model

3   Research Design

This study adopts questionnaire survey method to collect data. Drawing on previous studies, this survey selected gender, age, educational level, years of working in the current organization and position as population control variables. The other variables were measured with reference to the maturity scale widely used at home and abroad, which has high reliability and validity. Human resource management professors and English teachers were invited to carry out semantic translation and adjustment, so as to enhance the applicability and validity in the Chinese organizational context. All scales use the Liket-5 point scale ("1" to "5" represents "completely disagree", "disagree", "general", "agree", "fully agree", respectively).

Deviant innovation was measured using the single-dimension scale developed by Criscuolo et al., which consisted of 5 items. Empowering leadership was measured using the four-dimension scale compiled by Ahearne et al., which included 12 items. The scale revised by Li Ning and Yan Jin based on Chinese context was adopted in this study to measure psychological security, which included 5 items. The organizational innovation climate scale was modified by Liu Yun et al. based on the KEYS Scale, which included 12 questions from three dimensions of colleagues, leaders and organizations. The scale compiled by Carmeli et al. was adopted in this study to measure creative self-efficacy, which included 8 items.

The samples are from first-tier cities and new first-tier cities. A small-scale pre-survey was conducted before the formal investigation, and the questionnaire item settings were adjusted based on the feedback results. A total of 349 questionnaires were collected in this survey, and 301 valid questionnaires were obtained after deleting those with incomplete data, consistent options and inconsistencies. According to the final collected data, 48.50% of the respondents were females and 51.50% were males; In terms of age, 25.91% are under 25 years old, 34.55% are between 26 and 30 years old, 26.91% are between 36 and 45 years old, and 12.63% are over 46 years old; 21.59% have a college degree or below, 48.17% have a bachelor's degree, 24.58% have a master's degree, and 5.65% have a doctoral degree; In terms of work experience, 21.93% of people work for 1 year or less, 33.55% work for 1–3 years, 18.27% work for 4–6 years, 15.61% work for

7–10 years, and 10.63% work for more than 10 years; In terms of job rank, 67.11% are ordinary employees, 21.93% are grassroots managers, 8.97% are middle-level managers, and 1.99% are senior managers.

4 Data Analysis and Hypothesis Testing

4.1 Reliability Analysis

This study collected data at different time points to reduce the impact of homology bias; Exploratory factor analysis of the study variables obtained a KMO value of 0.950, and the result of Bartlett's Test of Sphericity approximated 0, indicating that the data in this study were suitable for factor analysis. The results of unrotated factor analysis showed that the maximum factor variance explained was 26.95% < 40%, so this study didn't not have serious homoscedasticity bias problems, and the results of the study were reliable.

The study used AMOS 24 to test the structural validity and discriminative validity of each variable in the model. The model fitting indexes all reached the critical value standard generally recognized by the academic community: CMIN/DF = 1.326 < 3, RMSEA = 0.038 < 0.05, and GFI, AGFI, CFI, IFI and TLI values were all > 0.9. In addition, the fitting indexes of the hypothesized model are obviously superior to those of the other factor models. It can be seen that the model in this study has good structural validity and discriminative validity. The study also conducted a path analysis to test the degree of convergence of each factor on the variables to which it belongs. Results of the analysis shows the factor loadings are all >0.7, the AVE values of each variable are all > 0.5, and CR values are all > 0.7, indicating that the model has a good degree of convergence validity.

4.2 Correlation Analysis

The means, standard deviation and correlation coefficient of study variables are shown in Table 1. Empowering leadership is significantly correlated with psychological security (r = 0.539, p < 0.01), organizational innovation climate (r = 0.333, p < 0.01), creative self-efficacy (r = 472, p < 0.01) and deviant innovation (r = 0.580, p < 0.01). Deviant innovation is significantly correlated with psychological security (r = 0.687, P < 0.01), organizational innovation climate (r = 0.475, p < 0.01), and creative self-efficacy (r = 0.525, p < 0.01). The above results provide preliminary support for further exploration of the relationship between variables.

4.3 Hypothesis Test

This paper uses SPSS 26.0 and hierarchical regression method to test the main effect and intermediate effect, and the results are shown in Table 2. Test results of main effect and intermediate effect. Among them, M1 and M2 are regression models of psychological security, M3 and M4 are regression models of organizational innovation climate, M5 and M6 are regression models of creative self-efficacy, and M7-M11 are regression models of deviant innovation.

Table 1. Correlation analysis

Variables	Mean	Standard Deviation	1	2	3	4	5
1. Empower Leadership	3.616	0.802	1				
2. Psychological Security	3.247	0.832	0.539**	1			
3. Organizational Innovation Climate	3.317	0.899	0.333**	0.104*	1		
4. Creative Self-efficacy	3.335	0.859	0.472**	0.081*	0.187*	1	
5. Deviant Innovation	2.939	0.900	0.580**	0.687**	0.475**	0.525**	1

Note: ** $p<0.01$,* $p<0.05$

The first is the effect test of the empowering leadership on the mediator variables: According to M2, M4 and M6, empowering leadership has significant positive effects on psychological security ($\beta = 0.758$, $p < 0.001$), organizational innovation climate ($\beta = 0.860$, $p < 0.001$) and creative self-efficacy ($\beta = 0.862$, $p < 0.001$). Therefore, hypotheses H2a, H3a and H4a are all valid.

In the regression results on deviant innovation, it can be seen from M8 that there is a significant positive effect of empowering leadership on deviant innovation ($\beta = 0.691$, $p < 0.001$), and hypotheses H1 is valid. On this basis, M9, M10 and M11 added the mediating variables psychological security, organizational innovation climate and creative self-efficacy, respectively. Psychological security ($\beta = 0.302$, $p < 0.001$), organizational innovation climate ($\beta = 0.248$, $p < 0.01$) and creative self-efficacy ($\beta = 0.509$, $p < 0.001$) had significant effect values on deviant innovation, which suggests hypotheses H2b, H3b and H4b are valid. After adding the mediating variables, the effect of empowering leadership on deviant innovation decreased from 0.691 to 0.462 ($p < 0.001$), 0.478 ($p < 0.001$) and 0.253 ($p < 0.01$). The addition of intermediary variables weakened the influence of independent variables on dependent variables, suggesting that psychological security, organizational innovation climate and creative self-efficacy all played a partial mediating role between empowering leadership and deviant innovation. Hypotheses H2, H3 and H4 are valid.

EL: empowering leadership; PS: psychological security; OIC: organizational innovation climate; CS: creative self-efficacy; DI: deviant innovation.

In order to further verify the hypothesis, this paper also performs Bootstrap test, and the results are shown in Table 3. Results of Bootstrap path test. As can be seen from Table 3: The 95% confidence interval for the path "empowering leadership → psychological security → deviant innovation" is [0.038, 0.257], not including 0. The 95% confidence interval for the path "empowering leadership → organizational innovation climate → deviant innovation" is [0.016, 0.161], not including 0, and for the path "empowering leadership → creative self-efficacy → deviant innovation" is [0.125, 0.457], not including 0. Thus, hypotheses H2, H3, and H4 are further supported, there are significant mediating effects of psychological security, organizational innovation climate and creative self-efficacy.

Table 2. Test results of main effect and intermediate effect

Variables	PS		OIC		CS		DI				
	M1	M2	M3	M4	M5	M6	M7	M8	M9	M10	M11
Constant	3.148	0.861	3.228	0.378	3.091	-0.149	2.721	0.280	-0.025	0.180	-0.398
1. Gender	0.011	0.019	0.044	0.054	0.000	0.009	0.078	0.086*	0.080	0.073	0.081*
2. Age	0.160	0.035	0.259**	0.117*	0.296**	0.153**	0.242**	0.128	0.117*	0.099	0.050
3. Education	-0.019	-0.058	-0.024	-0.069	0.001	-0.043	0.079	0.043	0.061	0.061	0.065
4. Years	-0.096	-0.021	-0.164	-0.079	-0.140	-0.055	-1.111	-0.042	-0.036	-0.023	-0.014
5. Posion	0.113	0.003	0.060	-0.065*	0.032	-0.093*	-0.002	-0.102*	-0.103*	-0.086*	-0.055
6. EL		0.758***		0.860***		0.862***		0.691***	0.462***	0.478***	0.253**
7. PS									0.302***		
8. OIC										0.248**	
9. CS											0.509***
R square	0.006	0.568	0.015	0.739	0.027	0.755	0.022	0.488	0.526	0.503	0.550
ΔR square	-	0.562	-	0.724	-	0.728	-	0.466	0.038	0.015	0.062
F	1.363	66.755	1.928	142.788	2.679	154.837	2.330	48.697	48.564	44.294	53.407

Note: *** p<0.001, ** p<0.01, * p<0.05

Table 3. Results of Bootstrap path test

Paths	Effect	Boot-Standard Deviation	95% Confidence Interval		Effect Percentage (%)
			LL	UL	
Total Effect	0.761	0.047	0.669	0.852	–
Direct Effects	0.230	0.091	0.051	0.410	30.28
EL → PS → DI	0.147	0.057	0.038	0.257	19.32
EL → OIC → DI	0.090	0.094	0.016	0.161	11.81
EL → CS → DI	0.294	0.093	0.125	0.457	38.59

5 Research Conclusions and Implications

5.1 Research Conclusions

Based on the Theory of Planned Behavior, this study constructs a triple mediation model, and studies the influence mechanism of empowering leadership on employees' deviant innovation behavior. The following conclusions are drawn:

First, empowering leadership has a positive impact on employees' deviant innovation behavior. Empowering leadership can strengthen employees' motivation for innovation, provide the space for deviant implementation, which makes employees produce more deviant innovative behaviors.

Second, psychological security, organizational innovation climate and creative self-efficacy all mediate between empowering leadership and employees' deviant innovation behavior. Firstly, empowering leadership can improve employees' psychological security level by providing work autonomy, caring for subordinates, and strengthening interpersonal trust. The higher the level of psychological security, the more positively employees evaluate the results of risky behavior decisions, and the more inclined they are to implement deviant innovation behaviors. Secondly, by accelerating information transmission, optimizing the communication process and providing innovation support, empowering leadership can make employees perceive a stronger organizational innovation climate. In innovative organizations, employees will have the cognition of "compliance" with the deviant innovation behavior, thereby increasing the possibility of implementing deviant innovation behavior. Finally, empowering leadership can positively affect employees' sense of creative self-efficacy by enhancing their sense of autonomy and competence. The higher the level of employees' sense of creative self-efficacy, the more confident they are in their own innovation ability, the stronger their sense of control over the deviant innovation behavior, and thus produce more deviant innovation behavior.

5.2 Theoretical Contributions

This study has the following theoretical contributions: First, this paper introduces and verifies the applicability of the Theory of Planned Behavior in the field of deviant innovative behavior, deepens the theoretical connection between empowering leadership and deviant innovation, provides new theoretical support for subsequent relevant research, and broadens the application scope of the Theory of Planned Behavior. Second, the research proposed and confirmed the intermediary mechanism of empowering leadership to stimulate employees' deviant innovation behavior, strengthened the attitude, subjective norms and perceived behavioral control advantages of psychological security, organizational innovation climate and innovation self-efficacy in stimulating deviant innovation behavior, which helps to deepen the understanding of the mechanism of deviant innovation behavior, and enriched the research on deviant innovation antecedent variables.

5.3 Practical Implication

The research conclusion of this paper answers the organizational challenge of how to effectively stimulate and control employees' deviant innovation behavior to promote the improvement of enterprise innovation performance, and has the following implications for enterprise management practice:

First, enterprise managers should be aware of the importance of empowering leadership style. Empowering leadership can effectively influence employees' deviant innovation behavior through various ways, and deviant innovation, as an important supplement to the conventional innovation, is the key to cultivate employees' innovation potential, enhance organizational innovation vitality and improve enterprise innovation performance. Therefore, for organizations and departments with high innovation demand, they should cultivate and guide the empowering leadership style actively. On the one hand, when recruiting and selecting leaders, an effective evaluation system can be established to evaluate candidates' ability level in delegation, so as to effectively identify managers with empowering leadership style; On the other hand, the organization should improve the internal communication and feedback channels, so that managers can timely reach the feedback information of employees, so as to actively adjust and guide leaders to form an empowering leadership style.

Second, leaders should pay attention to cultivating employees' perception of psychological safety, organizational innovation climate and creative self-efficacy in the organization. First of all, empowering leadership can enhance employees' work autonomy on the premise of completing of work results, and build a mutual assistance, trust and inclusive organizational atmosphere to enhance employees' psychological security. Secondly, enterprise managers should actively build an organizational atmosphere that encourages and supports innovation, optimize organizational structure design, reduce unnecessary hierarchical restrictions, establish an efficient communication mechanism, accelerate the efficiency of information transmission, and promote information and resource sharing among members. Enterprises can rely on the existing structure to add a dedicated department for reviewing innovative projects to understand employees' creativity timely and give professional feedback on the basis of feasibility analysis. For some of the strong feasibility and high value of the creative, companies can provide effective resources and policy support. Finally, leaders should enhance employees' confidence in their own knowledge and skills through daily practice. On the one hand, they should grant employees greater autonomy in their work within the scope of their responsibilities to enhance their perception of work autonomy; On the other hand, leaders should encourage employees to think positively about work issues and express their ideas, give timely feedback on employees' suggestions, and provide more skills training and work guidance. However, leaders also need to improve the risk control mechanism of enterprises to reduce the risks brought by informal innovation while promoting deviant innovation through authorization behaviors, so that guide deviant innovation to develop in a controllable direction, and help the innovative development of enterprises.

5.4 Lack of Research and Future Prospects

This paper has the following shortcomings: (1) Although the two-stage data collection was adopted, and relevant analysis indicators proved that homology bias had little impact on the research results, the research data were all derived from employees' subjective self-evaluation, and there would still be some bias. In the future, the leader-employee pairing method could be adopted to collect required data to further reduce the bias and improve the scientificity. (2) The research receipts mainly come from high-tech enterprises, and the applicability of the research conclusions to other enterprises needs to be tested. Therefore, the research samples can be expanded in the future to improve the universality of the research conclusions. (3) The concrete variables selected in this study, psychological security, organizational innovation climate and creative self-efficacy, only cover one aspect of attitude, subjective norms and perceived behavior control in the Theory of Planned Behavior. In the future, appropriate variables can be selected from other perspectives to study the mechanism of deviant innovation behavior.

References

1. Wang, Y., Wang, J., Liu, Y.: Empowering leadership and bootleg innovation: the moderating role of the leader-member exchange relationship. In: Proceedings of the 17th (2022) China Annual Management Conference, pp. 417–433. (2022). (in Chinese)
2. Ding, W., Zhang, L., Yan, L.: Research on the influence of empowering leadership on employees' deviant innovative behavior: a moderated mediation model. China Circ. Econ. **17**, 70–76 (2022). (in Chinese)
3. Lyu, R., Feng, Y., Zhang, Y., Hao, L.: A Literature review and prospects of employees' deviant innovation. Sci. Technol. Progress Policy. **39**(23), 151–160 (2022). (in Chinese)
4. Duan, W., Jiang, G.: A review of the theory of planned behavior. Adv. Psychol. Sci. **16**(2), 315–320 (2008). (in Chinese)
5. Srivastava, A., Bartol, K.M., Locke, E.A.: Empowering leadership in management teams: effects on knowledge sharing, efficacy, and performance. Acad. Manag. J. **49**(6), 1239–1251 (2006)
6. Criscuolo, P., Salter, A., Ter Wal, A.L.: Going underground: bootlegging and individual innovative performance. Organ. Sci. **25**(5), 1287–1305 (2014)
7. Li, N., Chiaburu, D.S., Kirkman, B.L.: Cross-level influences of empowering leadership on citizenship behavior: organizational support climate as a double-edged sword. J. Manag. **43**(4), 1076–1102 (2017)
8. Yang, G., Song, J., Ji, P.: Employee creativity and creative deviance: based on the research of psychological entitlement and moral disengagement. Sci. Technol. Progress Policy. **36**(07), 115–122 (2019). (in Chinese)

9. Lin, L., Li, P.P., Roelfsema, H.: The traditional Chinese philosophies in inter-cultural leadership: the case of Chinese expatriate managers in the Dutch context. Cross Cult. Strateg. Manage. **25**(2), 299–336 (2018)

10. Shi, Q., Guo, Y., Wang, H., Zhang, H.: Research on the deviant innovation behavior path of new generation employees from the perspective of differential order pattern. Modernization Manage. **42**(1), 94–102 (2022). (in Chinese)

11. Hou, M., Wang, Q., Zhang, P.: Research on the influence mechanism of entrepreneurship on deviant innovation behavior: based on the social influence theory perspective. J. Harbin Univ. Commer. **01**, 54–63 (2022). (in Chinese)

12. Gumusluoğlu, L., Ilsev, A.: Transformational leadership and organizational innovation: the roles of internal and external support for innovation. J. Prod. Innov. Manag. **26**(3), 264–277 (2009)

13. Konczak, L.J., Stelly, D.J., Trusty, M.L.: Defining and measuring empowering leader behaviors: development of an upward feedback instrument. Educ. Psychol. Measur. **60**(2), 301–313 (2000)

14. Wang, H., Cui, Z., Zou, C., Yu, J., Zhao, D.: Loyal or rebel? Employee bootleg innovation in Chinese context. Adv. Psychol. Sci. **27**(06), 975–989 (2019). (in Chinese)

15. Norman, P., Hoyle, S.: The theory of planned behavior and breast self-examination: distinguishing between perceived control and self-efficacy. J. Appl. Soc. Psychol. **34**(4), 694–708 (2004)

16. Li, S., He, W., Yam, K.C.: When and why empowering leadership increases followers' taking charge: a multilevel examination in China. Asia Pacific J. Manage. **32**, 645–670 (2015)

17. Tierney, P., Farmer, S. M.: Creative self-efficacy: its potential antecedents and relationship to creative performance. Acad. Manage. J., 1137–1148 (2002)

Research on Digital Maturity Evaluation Model of Public Hospitals

Benhai Yu and Zishan Wang[✉]

School of Economics and Management, Shanghai University of Applied Sciences,
Shanghai 200235, China
18621873679@163.com

Abstract. Building an evaluation model of digital maturity in public hospitals, combining the data management maturity model with the digital maturity model, evaluating the research progress of digital transformation in public hospitals, and interpreting the meaning of digital maturity are all based on the systematic review of the body of literature that has already been published. The model will then be put into practice. It is discovered that public hospitals are still developing digital transformation, and there are gaps in the implementation of digital technology, data quality, and human resources. The well-established approach for evaluating digital maturity offers tools for assessments as well as insightful analysis and recommendations for the digital transformation of public hospitals.

Keyword: Public Hospitals · Digital Transformation · Digital Maturity Evaluation Model

1 Introduction

The digital transformation of public hospitals is rapidly coming with the implementation of policies like "Internet + medical," "smart hospitals," and "high-quality development of public hospitals." The digital transformation of public hospitals has not yet been realized; "the degree of transformation and how to do" refers to the digital transformation of the significant issues faced. China's public hospital informatization and digital construction have made some progress, but they still fall far short of the true meaning of digital health care. The majority of the hospital's current study on digital transformation focuses on path research and influencing variables; there is a dearth of professional evaluation model application practice, and the assessment process is subjective. Thus, this paper builds a public hospital digital maturity evaluation model using a mathematical approach that combines fuzzy and gray theories, all based on the data management perspective. This approach not only adds to the body of knowledge on the digital transformation of public hospitals but also serves as a guide for hospital digital transformation practices.

Y. P. Tu and M. Chi (Eds.): WHICEB 2024, LNBIP 516, pp. 147–163, 2024.
https://doi.org/10.1007/978-3-031-60260-3_13

2 Literature Review

2.1 Research on Digital Maturity of Public Hospitals

Digital maturity is a measure of an organization's current level of digital transformation that attempts to show how far along the process is. The Digital transformation in healthcare refers to the process of change whereby healthcare organizations employ digital technologies as the main engine to reorganize their core business [1], improve service models [2], and enhance the patient experience [2]. There isn't a single scholarly definition for digital maturity at the moment; nevertheless, Duncan et al. [2] define it as the degree to which healthcare providers use digital technologies to give high-quality care that enhances service delivery.The right degree of health information technology (IT) services to meet the demands of patients and regulators for effective and efficient health service delivery is known as digital maturity, according to Mettler and Pinto [3]. The majority of the time, researchers describe digital maturity as the extent to which a technology is used [4], neglecting to consider the usefulness of applying data across systems [5]. In light of this, this paper makes the case that digital maturity in public hospitals refers to a state attained through digital transformation strategies that emphasize the value of data standardization and integration services, data quality, and governance principles, use data as the primary engine, and disrupt business segments through the use of digital technologies.

2.2 Research on Maturity Modeling

Data Management Maturity Model. In 2014, a number of data management maturity models were published. The Data Management Maturity Model (DMM) was released by the Carnegie Mellon University-affiliated CMMI Institute. The Data Management Capability Assessment Model (DCAM) was released by the Enterprise Data Management Association in North America. The DCMM, China's first official data center service capability evaluation standard, was unveiled in 2016, as shown in Table 1. A closer examination finds that each data management maturity model has elements related to the four primary areas of data strategy, data governance, data quality, and platform and architecture, even though the evaluation dimensions vary between the models.

Digital Maturity Model. This paper conducts a keyword search for "digital maturity" in China Knowledge, Wanfang, Wipro, and other well-known domestic databases. The results indicate that there is a dearth of academic literature on the topic of hospital digital maturity in relation to comparable research findings, and that the majority of the country's digital maturity model is focused on enterprise and government digitalization. This work ultimately chooses five typical maturity models as the primary reference basis, as shown in Table 2, based on the compilation of international literature and associated research reports. The strategy, culture, people, technology, and significant elements of corporate operations are the main focuses of the five maturity models.

Table 1. Data management maturity model.

Maturity Model	Evaluation Dimension	Maturity Level
CMMI DMM	data management strategy, data governance, data quality, data operations, data platforms and architecture, support processes	Level 5
EDM DCAM	data management strategy and business case, data management programs and funding models, business and data architecture, data and technology architecture, data quality management, data governance, data control environment	Level 6
China DCMM	data strategy, data governance, data architecture, data standards, data quality, data security, data applications, data lifecycle management	Level 5

Table 2. Digital maturity model.

Researcher	Evaluation Dimension	Maturity Level
Kubricki	human resources, technology resources, data strategy, content strategy, channel strategy and social business strategy	Level 4
Rhona Duncan	gvernace and management, ITcapability, people skills and behaviors, Inter-operability, strategy, data analytics, patient-centered care	——
Jahn and Pfeiffer	strategy and vision, digital leadership, governance, organizational culture, products and services, value creation process, customer interaction	Level 3
Company McKinsey	strategy, IT capabilities, culture, organization and people	Level 5
Leino et al	strategy, business model, customer impact, organization and processes, people and culture, IT	Level 4

2.3 Research on Digital Maturity Evaluation Model of Public Hospitals

Fewer academics have studied the digital capabilities of public hospitals using maturity models; most utilize them to assist enterprises in clarifying their digital capabilities in terms of evaluation criteria including digital readiness, digital intensity, and digital contribution [6, 7]. Previous research indicates that public hospital digital maturity models are not only poorly researched but also have gaps and ambiguities in the assessment aspects. In this work, data modification is added based on the four common elements from Table 1 that serve as evaluation dimensions.

When it comes to evaluation techniques, the majority of academics employ the Delphi method, hierarchical analysis [8], multi-criteria decision-making [9], and other techniques to determine weights and comprehensive scores. However, these approaches ignore the interdependence between the elements [10] and call for a substantial volume of data, which is insufficient to facilitate decision-making in situations where there is little data. In order to calculate the weights of the indicators, we have chosen in this paper to combine the decision-making test and evaluation laboratory method with the network hierarchical analysis method, also known as the DANP [11] method. The evaluation value is then calculated using the gray fuzzy comprehensive evaluation method, which is a reasonable and scientific solution to the problem of the system's grayness and fuzziness.

3 Evaluation Model Construction of Digital Maturity of Public Hospitals

3.1 Evaluation Index System Construction

This paper builds on the DAMA Guide to Data Management Knowledge System and the digital maturity model in Table 2, combining the features of public hospitals to create an evaluation index system with five primary indicators, 14 secondary indicators, and 35 tertiary indicators, as indicated in Table 3. The evaluation index system is based on the five dimensions of data strategy, data governance, data quality, data operation, and platform and architecture derived from the previous paper.

3.2 DANP Gray Fuzzy Comprehensive Evaluation Method

Use DANP to Calculate Indicator Weights. The questionnaire was administered to each of the m experts to create a direct impact matrix between the indicators A_m.

Solve for the average direct impact matrix B.

$$B = \frac{1}{m} \sum_{m=1}^{m} A_m = (b_{ij})_{n \times n} \tag{1}$$

Calculate the normative impact matrix M. The direct impact matrix is normalized by Eq. (2) to obtain the canonical impact matrix M.

$$M = \frac{b_{ij}}{\max(\sum_{j=1}^{n} b_{ij})} \tag{2}$$

Calculate the integrated impact matrix T. The integrated impact matrix T is obtained through Eq. (3).

$$T = (t_{ij})_{n \times n} = M + M^2 + M^3 + \ldots = \sum_{l=1}^{\infty} M^l = M(I - M)^{-1} \tag{3}$$

Table 3. Digital maturity evaluation index system for public hospitals.

Level 1 Indicators	Secondary Indicators	Tertiary Indicators	Interpretation	References
data strategy	data management strategy	robust data management system	Includes stakeholders, a roadmap for implementation, the vision, goals, and scope of data management	[12]
		data managers trained on a regular basis	Current level of data managers' expertise and understanding	[12]
	data management responsibilities	sectoral division of labor and degree of coordination	Mechanisms of communication, both internal and external	[13]
		data management awareness for leaders	Support from leaders and agreement on data management	[13]
		data literacy for healthcare professionals	Demonstrates how knowledgeable healthcare professionals are about data management.	[13]
data governance	data governance organization	data literacy for healthcare professionals	Information and data management departments and personnel, authority and responsibility distribution, and management decision-making procedures	[12]

(continued)

Table 3. (*continued*)

Level 1 Indicators	Secondary Indicators	Tertiary Indicators	Interpretation	References
		data governance organizational processes	Organizational procedures like self-service information services, quality assessment organizations, and automated data gathering and storage	[13]
	data standard	a comprehensive glossary of business terms	Maintain company-wide business jargon appropriately; application data repositories make reference to it	[14]
		compliance with the Electronic Medical Record Basic Data Set Standard	Using business jargon correctly	[14]
		conforms to the Electronic Medical Record Shared Documentation Standard	Using business jargon correctly	[14]
	metadata management	metadata management normality	Adhere to a metadata management procedure	[4]
		consistency of basic data	Data that has been cached matches the original data	[4]
data quality	data analysis	satistical analysis using data	Applying technologies for data analysis to managerial decision-making	[4]

(*continued*)

Table 3. (*continued*)

Level 1 Indicators	Secondary Indicators	Tertiary Indicators	Interpretation	References
		data analysis of human resources match	Human resources for technical expertise acquisition or training	[4]
	data cleaning	platform data uniqueness	Sites are able to filter out redundant info	[15]
		The platform allowed data to be corrected for errors, harmonized specifications and correction logic	Data conversion to ensure adherence to domain regulations and data standards	[15]
	data quality improvement	diversity of data sources	Gathering and preserving data from various sources	[12]
		multi-source heterogeneous data classification and fusion	Artificial intelligence, blockchain, federated learning, data lakes, data warehouses, and other techniques	[12]
		integrity of diagnosis and health data collection	Keeping an eye on the accuracy of electronic health records, electronic medical records, and other crucial data	[12]
		timeliness of treatment and health data updates	Monitoring of data delay and data disorder	[12]

(*continued*)

Table 3. (*continued*)

Level 1 Indicators	Secondary Indicators	Tertiary Indicators	Interpretation	References
		healthcare data porivacy protection	Techniques for data sharing, hierarchical data management, and encrypting critical hospital data and sensitive patient information	[12]
	data quality assessment	regular data validation	Data evaluation and screening	[12]
		specialized assessment tools and techniques	Big data analytics, machine learning, connected sharing and integration technologies, and other techniques	[12]
		regular publication of data quality results and reports	Comprises SLA metrics, data quality issue management, data quality scorecards, data quality trends, and more	[12]
data manipulation	definition of data requirements	data requirements definition meets business objectives	Addressing the requirements of external organizational interconnection, internal and external control, and organizational applications	[12]
		data requirement definitions follow approved standards	For the purposes of organizational management, specifications for the creation and administration of data models were created	[12]

(*continued*)

Table 3. (*continued*)

Level 1 Indicators	Secondary Indicators	Tertiary Indicators	Interpretation	References
	data lifecycle managemen	data design and development	Data state stability and complete alignment with business goals	[12]
		data operations and Maintenance	Execute a range of tasks, including istalling database software, optimizing configurations, choosing and implementing backup strategies, recovering and migrating data, doing fault dispensing preventative inspections, and more	[12]
		data decommissioning	The design, execution, and tracking of data decommissioning	[12]
platform and architecture	data management platform	dedicated data management platform in place	For example, data middle offices, operational data centers, clinical data centers, research data centers, huge data centers, etc	[12]
		support various forms of data exchange and interface calls	Make that the interfaces and scope align with the business data model	[12]
	data integration	effective data consolidation in case of data redundancy	Transfer or combine data between two or more apps	[15]

(*continued*)

Table 3. (*continued*)

Level 1 Indicators	Secondary Indicators	Tertiary Indicators	Interpretation	References
		data from each application can be mapped to standard data	The source data to be extracted along with the rules identifying the extracted data, the target to be loaded with the rules indicating the target rows to be updated, and any transformation or computation rules to be performed	[15]
	archiving of historical data	integrity of historical data	To ensure the integrity of data that has been archived, employ monitored archiving strategies	[12]
		archived historical data is retrieved and integrated in the · same way as current data	The data warehouse meets the demands of the company	[12]

Compute the unweighted supermatrix U.

$$U = T \tag{4}$$

Compute the weighted supermatrix $\overline{U}$.

$$\overline{U} = \begin{bmatrix} U_{11}/\sum_{i=1}^{n} U_{i1} & U_{12}/\sum_{i=1}^{n} U_{i2} & \cdots & U_{1n}/\sum_{i=1}^{n} U_{in} \\ U_{21}/\sum_{i=1}^{n} U_{i1} & U_{22}/\sum_{i=1}^{n} U_{i2} & \cdots & U_{2n}/\sum_{i=1}^{n} U_{in} \\ \vdots & \vdots & \vdots & \vdots \\ U_{n1}/\sum_{i=1}^{n} U_{i1} & U_{n2}/\sum_{i=1}^{n} U_{i2} & \cdots & U_{nn}/\sum_{i=1}^{n} U_{in} \end{bmatrix} \tag{5}$$

Compute the limit supermatrix U^*. Indicator weights were calculated according to Eq. (6).

$$U^* = \lim_{k \to \infty} \overline{U}^* \tag{6}$$

The DANP Method Calculates Indicator Weights. Clarifying the gray class level and the whitening weight function is essential to improving the evaluation gray class's effectiveness and the model's correctness. Assuming a small number of experts on the three-level index score, this study builds the whitening weight function (Table 4) and the maturity evaluation value (Table 5).

Table 4. Gray class, threshold, gray number and whitening weight function.

Ggray Class	Threshold	Gray Number	Whitening Weight Function
$e = 1$	0.1	$V_1 \in [0, 0.1, 0.3]$	$f_{ijk}^1(s_{ijkh}) = \begin{cases} 0, s_{ijkh} \notin (0 \, 0.3) \\ 1, s_{ijkh} \in [0, 0.1] \\ \frac{0.3 - s_{ijkh}}{0.3 - 0.1}, s_{ijkh} \in (0.1, 0.3] \end{cases}$
$e = 2$	0.3	$V_2 \in [0.1, 0.3, 0.5]$	$f_{ijk}^2(s_{ijkh}) = \begin{cases} 0, s_{ijkh} \notin (0.1, 0.5) \\ \frac{s_{ijkh} - 0.1}{0.3 - 0.1}, s_{ijkh} \in [0.1, 0.3] \\ \frac{0.5 - s_{ijkh}}{0.5 - 0.3}, s_{ijkh} \in (0.3, 0.5] \end{cases}$
$e = 3$	0.5	$V_3 \in [0.3, 0.5, 0.7]$	$f_{ijk}^3(s_{ijkh}) = \begin{cases} 0, s_{ijkh} \notin (0.3, 0.7) \\ \frac{s_{ijkh} - 0.3}{0.5 - 0.3}, s_{ijkh} \in [0.3, 0.5] \\ \frac{0.7 - s_{ijkh}}{0.7 - 0.5}, s_{ijkh} \in (0.5, 0.7] \end{cases}$
$e = 4$	0.7	$V_4 \in [0.5, 0.7, 0.9]$	$f_{ijk}^4(s_{ijkh}) = \begin{cases} 0, s_{ijkh} \notin (0.5 \, 0.9) \\ \frac{s_{ijkh} - 0.5}{0.7 - 0.5}, s_{ijkh} \in [0.5, 0.7] \\ \frac{0.9 - s_{ijkh}}{0.9 - 0.7}, s_{ijkh} \in (0.7, 0.9] \end{cases}$
$e = 5$	0.9	$V_5 \in [0.7, 0.9, 1.0]$	$f_{ijk}^5(s_{ijkh}) = \begin{cases} 0, s_{ijkh} \notin (0.7, 1.0) \\ \frac{s_{ijkh} - 0.7}{0.9 - 0.7}, s_{ijkh} \in [0.7, 0.9] \\ 1, s_{ijkh} \in (0.9, 1.0] \end{cases}$

Table 5. Gray fuzzy evaluation matrix and maturity rating values.

Target	Gray Evaluation Weight Vector	Gray Fuzzy Evaluation Matrix	Maturity Rating
Tertiary Indicators	$r_{ijk} = \left(r_{ijk}^1, r_{ijk}^2, r_{ijk}^3, r_{ijk}^4, r_{ijk}^5 \right)$	$R_{ij} = \begin{bmatrix} r_{ij1} \\ r_{ij2} \\ \vdots \\ r_{ijk} \end{bmatrix} = $ $\begin{bmatrix} r_{ij1}^1 & r_{ij1}^2 & \cdots & r_{ij1}^5 \\ r_{ij2}^1 & r_{ij2}^2 & \cdots & r_{ij2}^5 \\ \vdots & \vdots & \cdots & \vdots \\ r_{ijk}^1 & r_{ijk}^2 & \cdots & r_{ijk}^5 \end{bmatrix}$	$Z_{ijk} = r_{ijk}V^T$
Secondary Indicators	$l_{ij} = W_{ij}R_{ij} = (l_{ij1}, l_{ij2}, l_{ij3}, l_{ij4}, l_{ij5})$	$L_i = \begin{bmatrix} l_{i1} \\ l_{i2} \\ \vdots \\ l_{ij} \end{bmatrix} = $ $\begin{bmatrix} l_{i11} & l_{i12} & l_{i13} & l_{i14} & l_{i15} \\ l_{i21} & l_{i22} & l_{i23} & l_{i24} & l_{i25} \\ \vdots & \vdots & \vdots & \vdots & \vdots \\ l_{ij1} & l_{ij2} & l_{ij3} & l_{ij4} & l_{ij5} \end{bmatrix}$	$Z_{ij} = l_{ij}V^T$
Level 1 Indicators	$p_i = W_i L_i = (p_{i1}, p_{i2}, p_{i3}, p_{i4}, p_{i5})$	$P = \begin{bmatrix} p_1 \\ p_2 \\ \vdots \\ p_i \end{bmatrix} = $ $\begin{bmatrix} p_{11} & p_{12} & p_{13} & p_{14} & p_{15} \\ p_{21} & p_{22} & p_{23} & p_{24} & p_{25} \\ \vdots & \vdots & \vdots & \vdots & \vdots \\ p_{i1} & p_{i2} & p_{i3} & p_{i4} & p_{i5} \end{bmatrix}$	$Z_i = p_i V^T$
Overall Target	$q = WP = (q_{i1}, q_{i2}, q_{i3}, q_{i4}, q_{i5})$		$Z = qV^T$

4   Model Application Study

In this study, a survey questionnaire consisting of 35 tertiary indicators is constructed. Hospital practitioners who participate in the survey are asked to rate the 35 questions on a scale of 0 to 1, taking into account the hospital's level of digitalization. Following the collection of 786 questionnaires, it was discovered that the survey participants were primarily located in four hospitals. This article evaluates the degree of digital transformation in four hospitals using them as examples. The weighting results were determined using the DANP approach, and ten experts were requested to build the direct influence matrix between the indicators (refer to Table 6).

Table 6. Public Hospital Digital Maturity Model Evaluation Indicator System Weights.

Level 1 Indicators	Weights	Secondary Indicators	Weights	Tertiary Indicators	Weights
G_1	0.1015	G_{11}	0.0536	G_{111}	0.0341
				G_{112}	0.0194
		G_{12}	0.0480	G_{121}	0.0096
				G_{122}	0.0277
				G_{123}	0.0107
G_2	0.2130	G_{21}	0.0594	G_{211}	0.0284
				G_{212}	0.0310
		G_{22}	0.0690	G_{221}	0.0206
				G_{222}	0.0243
				G_{223}	0.0242
		G_{23}	0.0847	G_{231}	0.0427
				G_{232}	0.0420
G_3	0.3213	G_{31}	0.0574	G_{311}	0.0191
				G_{312}	0.0383
		G_{32}	0.0324	G_{321}	0.0162
				G_{322}	0.0162
		G_{33}	0.1370	G_{331}	0.0394
				G_{332}	0.0235
				G_{333}	0.0273
				G_{334}	0.0273
				G_{335}	0.0195

(*continued*)

Table 6. (*continued*)

Level 1 Indicators	Weights	Secondary Indicators	Weights	Tertiary Indicators	Weights
		G_{34}	0.0944	G_{341}	0.0314
				G_{342}	0.0355
				G_{343}	0.0276
G_4	0.1655	G_{41}	0.0562	G_{411}	0.0225
				G_{412}	0.0337
		G_{42}	0.1093	G_{421}	0.0362
				G_{422}	0.0384
				G_{423}	0.0347
G_5	0.1987	G_{51}	0.0972	G_{511}	0.0441
				G_{512}	0.0531
		G_{52}	0.0549	G_{521}	0.0256
				G_{522}	0.0293
		G_{53}	0.0466	G_{531}	0.0238
				G_{532}	0.0227

4.1 Analysis of Results

Table 7 displays the four hospitals' respective levels of digital maturity, with Hospital A having the highest level of digitization and Hospital D having the lowest. The leadership's awareness of data management (G_{122}) and the protection of healthcare data privacy (G_{335}) was found to be the primary reason for Hospital A's high degree of digitization, based on the scores of the three-level indicators in Fig. 1. However, there were some weaknesses, such as the data standard (G_{22}) that did not fully comply with the Shared Documentation Standard for Electronic Medical Records (G_{223}) and the application data's inability to map to the standard data (G_{522}) in the data integration (G_{52}) mapping. Hospital B gained the most from leaders' knowledge of organizational procedures related to data governance (G_{212}) and data management (G_{122}). However, professional assessment tools and methodologies were lacking (G_{342}), and the data management platform (G_{51}) did not facilitate interface calls or data interchange (G_{512}). In terms of departmental division of labor and cooperation, Hospital C received the greatest score (G_{121}). However, it also received the top ratings in terms of organizational processes related to data governance (G_{212}), matching human resources for data analysis (G_{312}), and specialized evaluation tools and techniques (G_{342}). All of the metrics showed weak signs for Hospital D, with platform and architecture (G_5) and data quality (G_3) having the lowest indicators.

Table 7. Maturity rating.

Hospitals	Maturity Rating
A	0.7222
B	0.5454
C	0.4252
D	0.3673

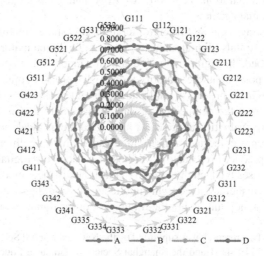

Fig. 1. Tertiary indicator maturity rating values

5 Discussion

Public hospitals are still in the continuous development stage of digital transformation and exhibit shortcomings in digital technology, data quality, and human resources, according to the evaluation results of the four hospitals. Consequently, three enhancement strategies are suggested in this research.

High-value data mining and digital technology advancements should be prioritized by public hospitals. In order to support data mining, this includes tools and technologies for assessing the quality of data, sharing and integrating connections, big data analysis, data privacy protection, natural language processing, medical visualization, machine learning, etc.

To achieve high-quality, high-standard, high-availability, and high-integration data-driven systems, improve medical data management. To standardize data collection, extraction, and interaction processes, build a full-process data governance system, enhance organizational structure, define data standards and meanings, preserve consistency and standardization of the data model, establish the guidelines for data quality verification, and build information systems like data centers, integration platforms, and automated data quality verification.

Raise the bar for labor division and human resources to support the long-term growth of the information management industry. Improve the training and communication between medical staff and data management workers, make rights and responsibilities clear, and create business synergy and cross-departmental process optimization.

6 Conclusions

Public hospitals will soon undergo a digital makeover, and part of that change will involve improving data administration, therefore it's important to evaluate those facilities' current state of data management.

First, by contrasting local and foreign literature, this study creatively suggests the meaning of public hospitals' digital maturity. Second, the digital maturity index system is thoroughly described, the digital maturity evaluation model that is applicable to public hospitals is first proposed, and the maturity theory is rigorously applied to analyze the significant indicators in the process of public hospitals undergoing digital transformation. All of this is done from the perspective of data management. Lastly, the DANP gray fuzzy comprehensive evaluation approach is applied to the medical industry and a new measuring method is presented and refined. Three transformation paths are outlined when the model is used in practice to evaluate public hospitals' degree of digital transformation.

This paper addresses the lack of a digital maturity assessment model in the medical industry and offers a resource for assessing public hospitals' digital transformation from a data management standpoint within the framework of the digital economy.

Acknowledgement. This research was supported by the National Natural Science Foundation of China under Grant No.71974131 and the Shanghai Society of Graduate Education under Grant No.ShsgeY202213.

References

1. Budd, J., Miller, B.S., Manning, E.M.: Digital technologies in the public-health response to COVID-19. Nat. Med. **26**(8), 1183–1192 (2020)
2. Duncan, R., Eden, R., Woods, L.: Synthesizing dimensions of digital maturity in hospitals: systematic review. J. Med. Internet Res. **24**(3), 1–11 (2022)
3. Mettler, T., Pinto, R.: Evolutionary paths and influencing factors towards digital maturity: an analysis of the status quo in Swiss hospitals. Technol. Forecast. Soc. Chang. **133**, 104–117 (2018)
4. Wang, Y.G., Wang, L.L., Li, X.: An iterative transformation study from digital search to digital ecology - A case study based on Schneider Electric's digital transformation. Manage. World **39**(8), 91–114 (2023)
5. Kang, J., Chen, K.H.: Digital innovation development economic system: framework, evolution and value-added effects. Res. Manage. **42**(4), 1–10 (2021)
6. Wang, H.C., Wang, S.W., Liu, R.H.: Research on enterprise digital maturity model. Manage. Rev. **33**(12), 152–162 (2021). (in Chinese)
7. Wu, J., Chen, T., Gong, Y.W., et al.: Theoretical framework and research outlook of enterprise digital transformation. J. Manage. **18**(12), 1871–1880 (2021). (in Chinese)

8. Gao, L., Ji, M., Yang, J.H.: Intelligent manufacturing capability maturity model for small and medium-sized enterprises. Sci. Technol. Manage. Res. **42**(6), 36–42 (2022). (in Chinese)
9. Brodny, J., Tutak, M.: Assessing the level of digital maturity of enterprises in the Central and Eastern European countries using the MCDM and Shannon's entropy methods. Plos one **16**(7), e0253965 (2021)
10. Li, H., Wen, S.B., Jiao, R.: DANP variable-weight financial early warning model based on earnings quality. Syst. Eng. Theory Pract. **39**(7), 1651–1668 (2019). (in Chinese)
11. Cui, Q., Wu, C.Y., Kuang, H.B.: Application of BP-DEMATEL in the identification of factors influencing the competitiveness of airports. Syst. Eng. Theory Pract. **33**(6), 471–1478 (2013). (in Chinese)
12. Data Management Association (DAMA International): DAMA Guide to the Data Management Body of Knowledge. Machinery Industry Press, Beijing (2020)
13. Wang, C., Yi, X.W., Zhang, Z.X.: A new paradigm for management research in the era of big data: the case of CEO termination. J. Manage. Sci. **26**(5), 200–213 (2023)
14. Zhang, G.Q., Li, Y.X., Wang, Z.F.: New challenges and trends in the development of biomedical big data. Proc. Chin. Acad. Sci. **33**(8), 853–860 (2018)
15. Yang, D.P.: Research on the mechanism and countermeasures of data open sharing: an empirical analysis based on Zhejiang. China Soft Sci. **S1**, 392–398 (2021)

How Platform Companies Achieve Value Co-creation: A Dual-Case Study Based on Resource Orchestration Perspective

Xueyan Dong[1], Fuying Li[1(✉)], and Tienan Wang[2]

[1] Northwestern Polytechnical University, Xi'an 710072, China
15731952078@mail.nwpu.edu.cn
[2] Harbin Institute of Technology, Harbin 150001, China

Abstract. With the widespread use of information technology, such as big data and the Internet of Things, traditional companies generally show the strategic direction of platform transformation to create value. However, few studies have explored the challenging issue of how to achieve value co-creation in platform companies. This dual-case study constructs a framework that explores the value co-creation mechanism of platform companies based on the resource orchestration perspective. By dividing platform companies into two categories (organizational-oriented and individual-oriented), this study clarified the resource bases, resource orchestration actions, and advantage results of value co-creation in each type of platform companies. At the same time, we followed the logic of "elements-actions-results". Then two primary paths were advanced respectively trying to outline the realization mechanism of value co-creation in platform companies. This research contributes to revealing the "black box" of how to achieve value co-creation in platform companies theoretically and enriching the interpretation boundary of resource orchestration practically.

Keywords: Platform companies · Value co-creation · Resource orchestration · Resource bases · Value advantage

1 Introduction

The new generation of information technologies has given rise to platform companies (PCs), which have become an emerging crucial organizational form to optimize resource allocation and facilitate the matching of supply and demand. Although there exist successful PCs that have enhanced their strengths and become industry leaders through platformization (e.g., Alibaba, Amazon, TikTok, DiDi), there are still many examples in practice that have suffered collapse due to the lack of effective resources management. Therefore, for PCs (including sharing economy platforms, online e-commerce platforms, business incubation parks, etc.), the key to maintaining continuing development is to achieve value co-creation [1], which enables them to achieve outstanding performance that cannot be achieved by themselves alone and contributes favorably to the stakeholders [2].

© The Author(s), under exclusive license to Springer Nature Switzerland AG 2024
Y. P. Tu and M. Chi (Eds.): WHICEB 2024, LNBIP 516, pp. 164–177, 2024.
https://doi.org/10.1007/978-3-031-60260-3_14

The existing literature notes that value co-creation has always been defined as joint activities which require direct interaction between companies and stakeholders [2]. Prior studies have examined the importance of value co-creation, such as enhancing the loyalty and repurchase intention of consumers [3], empowering companies and their stakeholders [1], improving customers' well-being [4]. However, more attention are required to gain insight into the approaches to achieving value co-creation [1].

Prior studies propose the integrating heterogeneous resources can be of the most significance for value co-creation [5]. Emphasizing the structuring, bundling, and leveraging of resources are the key actions to companies to gain competitive advantages, the resource orchestration theory (ROT) provides the framework to open the "black box" that how to understand the process from resources possessing to value achieving, which is a useful tool to investigate the value creation process [6]. While some studies tried to explore the competitive advantages of PCs using ROT, however, there still has been limited focus on how to establish the specific mechanisms of value co-creation in PCs from the perspective of ROT.

To explore the mechanism of achieving value co-creation in PCs, this research follows the logical line of "elements-actions-results" to classify the preconditions, actions, and advantages of value co-creation for PCs. Resource elements are the preconditions for PCs to achieve value co-creation through resource orchestration actions. Resource orchestration actions are the critical actions to reduce costs and increase efficiency as well as they can be dynamically adjusted according to the difference of the resource elements. The results of the value co-creation can mainly be considered as a kind of value advantage that PCs have formed through resource orchestration actions.

Taking two PCs-Shi Wai Tao Yuan and Yong Xin Tuan-as the objects, this case study analyses the specific processes of integrating heterogeneous resources of PCs based on the resource orchestration perspective and reveals the validating value co-creation mechanisms of PCs in detail. By doing so, we try to articulate the realization paths of the two primary types of PCs, organizational-oriented PCs and individual-oriented PCs.

This study tries to make three key contributions to future research on the scope of value co-creation. First, we expanded the application context and interpretation boundary of resource orchestration. Second, we revealed how PCs integrate resources by identifying the resource bases, resource orchestration actions, and value advantages and further clarifying the mechanism among them. Third, we provided two paths for two types of PCs to achieve value co-creation.

2 Theoretical Background

2.1 PCs and Platform Ecosystem

Platforms can provide services or products for suppliers, users and other participants, facilitate economic transactions and information interactions [7], and satisfy the needs of multilateral users so as to realize value creation [1]. On the one hand, it is difficult for a single company to have all the resources to realize value creation in the context of digital economy. On the other hand, digital platforms make it possible for multiple

companies to share heterogeneous resources. Therefore, the platformization of companies has gradually been a trend in recent years, which formed a new business model [8].
PCs have also become the core of multilateral market research [9].

Platform ecosystem is an important organizational form for enterprises value co-creation [8]. As ecosystems develop, there are more and more challenges in management, and PCs need to promote the maturation of partnerships through co-operation [10]. PCs integrate heterogeneous resources and synergize participants by building an information platform, and gradually form a platform ecosystem centered on its own product technology and complemented by participating entities.

Existing studies have examined that co-creating value with platform participants is the basis of long term development of PCs, because users prefer platforms that offer value for them. However, we still have a limited understanding of the mechanism of value co-creation in PCs.

2.2 The Realization Path of Value Co-creation

In recent years, the Internet technology (big data, Internet of Things, artificial intelligence, etc.) closely links companies and consumers, providing the technological basis for consumers to participate in the value creation together with companies. It has led to the increasing application and expansion of value co-creation in recent studies, especially in the study of PCs.

Some scholars have divided the concept of value co-creation in the field of management into two branches, value co-creation based on consumer experience [11] and value co-creation based on service-dominant logic [12]. Both of these perspectives emphasise the key role of resource integration in the process of value co-creation.

However, the topic of how PCs integrate resources to achieve value co-creation is still insufficiently explained. Furthermore, prior research focus on the value co-creation between companies and customers, but other value co-creators still need to be taken attention to.

2.3 Resource Orchestration in PCs

The resource-based view (RBV) has long been widely used by scholars [13]. As theory and practice developed, scholars began to realize the fact that it is difficult to result in good economic benefits by possessing resources only. A firm's ability to manage its resources is at least as important as having those resources [6]. The resource orchestration theory (ROT) is derived from the resource management model and the asset orchestration model [14]. Drawing on the prior studies, the resource orchestration can be regarded as ability or action. In this research, resource orchestration as action is more desirable because we are trying to explore the specific actions of resource integration to achieve value co-creation.

Existing studies proposed using resource orchestration theory to open the "black box" from resources to the competitive advantage in platform enterprises. However, they did not isolate the specific types of resources and lacked the further analysis of the resource orchestration process mechanism of PCs. Furthermore, value advantage, as the result of value co-creation and the centralized reflection of competition advantage, has long been ignored and requires further exploration.

3   Methodology

3.1   Research Method

The core question addressed in this study is "How can PCs achieve value co-creation", which requires revealing the process and mechanism of achieving value co-creation in PCs, and case study are suitable for this type of "HOW" and "WHY" research questions [15].

Considering the research context of this research, we adopt the dual-case study method for the following reasons: 1) Compared with single-case study, the dual-case study can form a complementary relationship between the two cases, which makes the theoretical model of this research more persuasive and has higher external validity; 2) The dual-case study has both Enrichment and complementary, which can help us to conclude different paths for different companies [15]; 3) The emergence of PCs is not an extreme phenomenon in business practice, but is gradually becoming more and more common. The dual-case study weakens the requirement of the case's extremity, and can make up for the defects of the lack of the extremity of the cases.

3.2   Case Selection

In case selection, we use theoretical sampling method and select two companies, *Ningxia Shi Wai Tao Yuan commercial management company (Shi Wai Tao Yuan)* and *Shaanxi Yong Xin Tuan trading company (Yong Xin Tuan)*, as research objects based on the principles of revelation, matching research questions, and accessibility [15]. It is worth mentioning that the development cases of the two companies have been selected into the case database of China Management Case-sharing Centre, which shows that both of them deserve the scientific study. We refer to *Shi Wai Tao Yuan* as an "organizational-oriented PC" and *Yong Xin Tuan* as an "individual-oriented PC".

3.3   Data Collection

In the data collection stage, we followed the principle of triangular validation [16] to obtain data to avoid common methodological bias and to improve the reliability and validity of this study. Our data are mainly based on in-depth interview records and internal information, complemented by field observation records, web-based information such as the company's official website and the media, and government projects information. The corporate information of *Shi Wai Tao Yuan* and *Yong Xin Tuan* are shown in Tables 1 and 2.

Table 1. Corporate information of *Shi Wai Tao Yuan*

No.	Access to information	Sources	Topic	Frequency of interviews: times/person	Interview length: minutes/person
1	In-depth interviews with senior and middle managers	Founder (Mr. Wang)	evolution and innovation of enterprise business model; empowerment model; value co-creation mechanism; future business model planning, etc.	3	180
2		executive director(Mr. Zhang)	basic overview of the enterprise, the current situation of community services, types of product business, and the design of profitability models, etc.	3	120
3		operations director(Mr. Li)	operation status of company community service platform, general idea, construction process of value chain system	3	120
4		marketing director(Mr. Li, et al.)	practical issues in the operation of community service platforms, platform participation	2	90

(*continued*)

Table 1. (*continued*)

No.	Access to information	Sources	Topic	Frequency of interviews: times/person	Interview length: minutes/person
5	Intra-corporate textual information	provided with the assistance of company executives	《Company Operations Manual》, 《Merchandising Manual》, 《Client Orientation Manual》, minutes of meetings and other textual information, totaling 330 pages		
6	Coverage of media and government	provided with the assistance of the company's brand managers	A total of 19 related graphic report materials on different types of media in video, audio, press, social media and company-owned media platforms		
7	Research notes from the research team	internal collation of interview recordings	A total of 8 interview themes, nearly 2G audio recordings and nearly 80,000 words of interview text material		

Table 2. Corporate information of *Yong Xin Tuan*

Access to information	Sources	statistical data
interview	general manager (Duna)	follow-up interviews for three years
	agent (Li)	
observation	chat records of workgroup	three years of continuous observation with over 10G materials
second-hand information	online shopping platform(WeChat applet)	*Yong Xin Tuan* enjoying
	official media presentation	more than 4,000 words
	super talk in microblogging, notes in small red book and other online materials	more than 90,000 words
	materials from China Management Case-sharing Centre	more than 30,000 words

3.4 Data Analysis

We adopted the structured data processing method proposed by Gioia [17]. After continuous iteration, we extracted the constructs from the numerous data and established the connections between the constructs, so as to form a theoretical model.

The data analysis specifically includes the following three steps. Firstly, the research team organizes the voices, videos, pictures and other documents into textual information, and categorizes the collected qualitative data for quick finding and iterative checking.

Secondly, back-to-back coding was conducted simultaneously by multiple researchers in the team. Finally, first-level concepts are refined in a continuous iterative process of data and theory. Then, we summarize the first-level concepts into second-level themes, and then integrate the second-level themes into aggregated dimensions. Theoretical saturation is reached when the emergence of new data no longer has an impact on the theory, thus presenting the theoretical model of this paper.

The data structure of this research is shown in Fig. 1.

4   Findings and Development of Propositions

In the following sub-sections, we explain the "elements-actions-results" framework in detail, including the interpretations of resources basis, resource orchestration actions, value advantages and the interrelationships of these concepts (P1, P2), which are show in Table 3.

4.1   The Precondition of Value Co-creation

Resources are the foundation of PCs' continuous innovation and their construction of business ecosystems. Our evidence showed that *Shi Wai Tao Yuan* has a richer access to resources than *Yong Xin Tuan*, mainly from the organizations with which it cooperates. That is, the resource basis of *Shi Wai Tao Yuan* is more externally dependent, while that of *Yong Xin Tuan* is more internally dependent. Therefore, we comparatively analyzed *Shi Wai Tao Yuan* and *Yong Xin Tuan* to identify two types of social capital resources (SCRs) as precondition of value co-creation, externally dependent social capital resources and internally dependent social capital resources [18].

4.2   Resource Orchestration Actions of PCs Extending ROT

Resource orchestration actions provides PCs a specific insight of achieving value co-creation with stakeholders, thus dealing with the problem "how PCs integrate heterogeneous resources to achieve value co-creation".

Resource Structuring.   Resource structuring in organizational-oriented PCs is achieved by combining, activating, and divesting. First, PCs combine the resources that are valuable to them in the environment. Secondly, *Shi Wai Tao Yuan* activates resources in investment institutions with common philosophy, so as to help promote its own chain business model. Thirdly, with the development of the company, *Shi Wai Tao Yuan* has experienced the phenomenon of excess resources and needs to divest old business and expand new business timely. Resource structuring in individual-oriented PCs is achieved by identifying, generating, and seeking. Relatively, *Yong Xin Tuan* is able to identify resources such as civilianization centre in the community and establish cooperation with such special consumers, thus bringing value to the company. For the benefit of the business, *Yong Xin Tuan* needs to seek sources of goods and suppliers in the beginning of entrepreneurship. Furthermore, the way *Yong Xin Tuan* acquires new resources is mainly through resource generation.

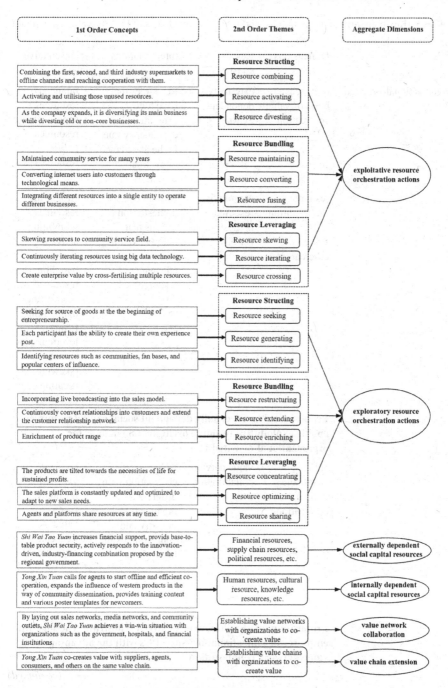

Fig. 1. Data structure

Table 3. Key constructs, interpretations, and representative labels of PCs for value co-creation

PCs	Dimensions	Key constructs	Interpretations	representative labels
organizational-oriented PCs	resources basis of value co-creation	externally dependent SCRs	Resources that have high external dependency due to the abundance of external resources	• financial resources • supply chain resources • political resources
	resource orchestration of PCs for value co-creation	exploitative resource orchestration actions	Resource orchestration actions that mainly exploit the existing adequate resources	• structuring resources (combining, activating, divesting) • bundling resources (converting, maintaining, fusing) • leveraging resources (skewing, iterating, crossing)
	Proposition 1A: Externally dependent social capital resources enable exploitative resource orchestration actions for organizational-oriented PCs			
	value advantage of value co-creation	value network collaboration	Achieve value co-creation with different organizational industry and conforming value network	• co-create value with hospitals • co-create value financial institutions • co-create value local government agencies
	Proposition 2A: Exploitative resource orchestration actions will empower organizational-oriented PCs with the advantage of value network collaboration			

(*continued*)

Table 3. (*continued*)

PCs	Dimensions	Key constructs	Interpretations	representative labels
individual-oriented PCs	resources basis of value co-creation	internally dependent SCRs	Resources that have high internal dependency due to the limitation of external resources	• human resources • cultural resource • knowledge resources
	resource orchestration of PCs for value co-creation	exploratory resource orchestration actions	Resource orchestration actions that mainly explore inadequate resources	• structuring resources (identifying, generating, seeking) • bundling resources (extending, enriching, restructuring) • leveraging resources (concentrating, optimizing, sharing)

Proposition 1B: Internally dependent social capital resources enable exploratory resource orchestration actions for individual-oriented PCs

| | value advantage of value co-creation | value chain extension | Achieve value co-creation with different individuals and conforming value chain | • co-create value with agents
• co-create value financial consumers |

Proposition 2B: Exploratory resource orchestration actions will empower individual-oriented PCs with the advantage of value chain extension

Resource Bundling. Resource bundling in organizational-oriented PCs is achieved by converting, maintaining, fusing. *Shi Wai Tao Yuan* has been committed to community service business for many years, and can obtain more support from the government. It is also good at fusing different resources into the same entity to carry out different businesses.

By pushing the news of community business to Internet users, it can convert online Internet users into its own customers and obtain high-quality customer resources. Resource bundling in individual-oriented PCs is achieved by extending, enriching, restructuring. As the participants are mostly individuals with low resourcefulness, *Yong Xin Tuan* needs to enrich its resources so as to improve its business capacity. Resource reconstruction is also an important way for individual -oriented PCs to bundle resources to form capabilities. In addition, *Yong Xin Tuan* has also extended its resources, transforming interpersonal relationships into customers and extending its customer relationship network.

Resources Leveraging. Resources leveraging in organizational-oriented PCs is achieved by skewing, iterating, crossing. *Shi Wai Tao Yuan* skews its resources to the community service level, and actively carries out a series of ecological structures with the service of the families and communities. In order to adapt to new digital business needs, *Shi Wai Tao Yuan* uses big data technology to continuously iterate its resources. *Shi Wai Tao Yuan* has formed a new community business model of "cross-border combined operation" by organically integrating consumers' needs and enterprise services through intelligent interconnection. Resources leveraging in individual-oriented PCs is achieved by concentrating, optimizing, sharing. *Yong Xin Tuan* has concentrated its product business on necessities in order to sustain profits. Compared to products with a long repurchase time, such as home appliances, necessities of life can generate continuous demand from customers. *Yong Xin Tuan* also uses software technology to continuously update and optimize its sales system and platform to adapt to changing sales needs. In addition, *Yong Xin Tuan* enterprises and agents can share high-quality customer resources and promotional materials to achieve resource sharing.

Therefore, we can obtain the following propositions.

Proposition 1A: Externally dependent social capital resources enable exploitative resource orchestration actions for organizational-oriented PCs.

Proposition 1B: Internally dependent social capital resources enable exploratory resource orchestration actions for individual-oriented PCs.

4.3 Value Advantages of PCs and Two Paths for Value Co-creation

Value Network Collaboration. *Shi Wai Tao Yuan* has a wide range of business operations, including e-commerce, government projects, community service projects, landscaping projects and agricultural production and operation. Therefore, *Shi Wai Tao Yuan*'s business involves multiple value chains. The result of *Shi Wai Tao Yuan*'s value cocreation is the organic synergy of these value chains, thus forming a value chain network and maintaining the stability of its ecosystem.

Value Chain Extension. For *Yong Xin Tuan*, it has only one main business, which is online e-commerce. As an individual-oriented platform company, it's online platform only provides online e-commerce related services, including displaying product information, reaching transactions, and after-sales services. Therefore, we suggest that *Yong Xin Tuan* has mainly one value chain, which is also limited by the enterprise's resources.

The resources of individuals are often more limited than those of organizations. Therefore, for individual-oriented PCs with smaller scale, if they can operate a single value chain well, it is enough to generate good economic benefits.

Therefore, we can conclude two paths to achieve value co-creation: exploitative path for organizational-oriented PCs and exploratory path for individual-oriented PCs. In summary, we can obtain the following propositions.

Proposition 2A: Exploitative resource orchestration actions will empower organizational-oriented PCs with the advantage of value network collaboration.

Proposition 2B: Exploratory resource orchestration actions will empower individual-oriented PCs with the advantage of value chain extension.

4.4 A Value Co-creation Model in PCs Extending Resource Orchestration

The model of value co-creation in PCs under the perspective of resource orchestration is shown in Fig. 2.

5 Discussion

In this study, we are aiming to make three main theoretical contributions. Firstly, this study reveal how PCs integrate resources drawing on the perspective of resource orchestration, thus opening the black box from resources to value co-creation in PCs.

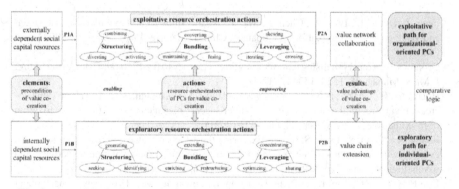

Fig. 2. A model of value co-creation in PCs under the perspective of resource orchestration

Secondly, this study expand the application context and interpretation boundary of resource orchestration, and use resource orchestration perspective to explain the value co-creation realization mechanism of PCs. Thirdly, this study provides two paths for PCs to achieve value co-creation, from the precondition, the specific actions and the advantage of value co-creation.

This study provides several practical suggestions for PCs. Firstly, richness of resources should be taken into consideration when companies develop strategic decisions. Secondly, PCs should focus on the efficient orchestration of resources, which is the key action of achieving value co-creation. Thirdly, more attention should be paid to the stakeholders on the same value chain or value network, which is exactly the difference between value co-creation and value creation. We concluded the exploitative path and the exploratory path separately for organizational-oriented PCs and individual-oriented PCs, considering the forms of stakeholders and the richness of resources. By doing so, this research can make up for the gap that prior research is limited in the achievement mechanism of value co-creation.

Inevitably, there are some limitations to this study which provide opportunities for future research. First, this study compares and analyses the differences in the mechanisms for achieving value co-creation between the two types of companies, but just takes consumers as a kind of resources. Future studies may pay more attention to the interactive actions between companies and consumers. In addition, this research classifies PCs into organizational-oriented PCs and individual -oriented PCs based on the difference of participating subjects, but perhaps there exists a more reasonable way of division. Finally, the theoretical model proposed in this research is only derived from the comparative analyses of Shi Wai Tao Yuan and Yong Xin Tuan, and it still needs to be tested and constantly revised by more PCs in practice.

Acknowledgement. This work was supported by the grants from the National Natural Science Foundation of China [grant numbers: 72272122, 71902158, 72172043, 71972061].

References

1. Feng, J., Dong, X., Luo, W., Chen, J., Ma, Y.: A case study of collaborative empowerment and value co-creation in platform companies. Chin. J. Manage. **19**(07), 965–975 (2022). (in Chinese)
2. Grönroos, C.: Conceptualising value co-creation: a journey to the 1970s and back to the future. J. Mark. Manag. **28**, 1520–1534 (2012)
3. Hochstein, B., Chaker, N.N., Rangarajan, D., Nagel, D., Hartmann, N.N.: Proactive value co-creation via structural ambidexterity: customer success management and the modularization of frontline roles. J. Serv. Res. **24**, 601–621 (2021)
4. Zhang, X., Singh, S., Li, J., Shao, X.: Exploring the effects of value co-creation strategies in event services on attendees' citizenship behaviors: the roles of customer empowerment and psychological ownership. J. Retail. Consum. Serv. **76**, 103619 (2024)
5. Liu, H., Chung, L., Tan, K.H., Peng, B.: I want to view it my way! How viewer engagement shapes the value co-creation on sports live streaming platform. J. Bus. Res. **170**, 114331 (2024)
6. Sirmon, D.G., Hitt, M.A., Ireland, R.D.: Managing firm resources in dynamic environments to create value: looking inside the black box. Acad. Manage. Rev. **32**(1), 273–292 (2007). https://doi.org/10.5465/amr.2007.23466005
7. Dougherty, D., Dunne, D.D.: Organizing ecologies of complex innovation. Organ. Sci. **22**, 1214–1223 (2011)
8. Moore, J.F.: The Death of Competition: Leadership and Strategy in the Age of Business Ecosystems (1996)
9. McIntyre, D.P., Srinivasan, A.: Networks, platforms, and strategy: emerging views and next steps. Strateg. Manag. J. **38**, 141–160 (2017)

10. Daymond, J., Knight, E., Rumyantseva, M., Maguire, S.: Managing ecosystem emergence and evolution: strategies for ecosystem architects. Strateg. Manag. J. **44**, O1–O27 (2023)
11. Prahalad, C.K., Ramaswamy, V.: Co-creation experiences: the next practice in value creation. J. Interact. Mark. **18**, 5–14 (2004)
12. Vargo, S.L., Lusch, R.F.: Evolving to a new dominant logic for marketing. J. Mark. **68**, 1–17 (2004)
13. Wernerfelt, B.: A resource-based view of the firm. Strateg. Manag. J. **5**, 171–180 (1984)
14. Sirmon, D.G., Hitt, M.A., Ireland, R.D., Gilbert, B.A.: Resource orchestration to create competitive advantage: breadth, depth, and life cycle effects. J. Manag. **37**, 1390–1412 (2011)
15. Eisenhardt, K.M.: Building theories from case study research. AMR **14**, 532–550 (1989)
16. Glaser, B.G., Strauss, A.L.: The Discovery of Grounded Theory. Aldine de Gruyter (1967)
17. Gioia, D.A., Corley, K.G., Hamilton, A.L.: Seeking qualitative rigor in inductive research: notes on the gioia methodology. Organ. Res. Methods **16**(1), 15–31 (2013). https://doi.org/10.1177/1094428112452151
18. Bhandari, H., Yasunobu, K.: What is social capital? A comprehensive review of the concept. Asian J. Soc. Sci. **37**, 480–510 (2009)

Some Considerations on Metaverse Empowering Business Innovation

Jiangping Wan$^{(\boxtimes)}$, Yuge Wang$^{(\boxtimes)}$, and Lianzheng Zhou

School of Business Administration, South China University of Technology, Guangzhou 510640, China

csjpwan@scut.edu.cn, frost_leaf@163.com

Abstract. Today, the development of the metaverse is on the rise. This paper uses work program of complexity to analyze the metaverse, which empowers business innovation. Four major parts are included: description, diagnosis, design and implementation. The focus is on the value empowerment of the metaverse to the business model, the mechanism and measures for enterprises to integrate into the metaverse era from the perspective of innovation, and how the metaverse reintroduces the three business elements of "user, production and scene" to reach the value re-creation, value re-transmission and value re-realization of the retail industry, so as to improve the operational efficiency and business performances as well as realize business innovation. As the metaverse continues to evolve, a new business landscape is on the horizon. we also need to pay attention to its market challenges, innovative applications, industrial policies, and governance structures.

Keywords: Business Innovation · Metaverse · User-Production-Scene · Retail · The Work Program of Complexity

1 Introduction

In 2021, Facebook changed its name to Meta, making the concept of the metaverse burst into a commercial hot spot. The development of emerging digital technologies and the online transformation of the epidemic have promoted the metaverse industry into the public perspective and ushered in outstanding growth. Fudan University believes that accelerating digital transformation with the help of metaverse-related concepts and technologies is the main innovation direction for China to initially explore the metaverse at present. In the future, the metaverse industrial chain will be further strengthened, the consumption scene will be further improved, and the metaverse will further empower the real economy to achieve the coexistence of virtual and real [1].

The emerging virtual world is the driving force behind the evolution of consumption, and as the revolutionized system generation of the Internet, we believe that the metaverse has a certain complexity for how to empower business. The work program of complexity proposed by the famous scholar professor Warfield is the main result of complexity science, which includes two main parts: (1) Discovering complexity (insight); (2) Resolution complexity (action). It can be subdivided into four sub-processes: description process, diagnosis process, design process and implementation process. The description and diagnosis constitute the discovery part, and the design and implementation constitute the solution part [2]. This paper attempts to apply work program of complexity to interpret the digital business transformation of retail industry in the metaverse era.

This paper is organized as follows: Sect. 2 (description process) summarizes the concept and connotation of the metaverse from the perspective of its technical support basis, empowered business model and commercial enterprise application, aiming to provide a foothold for the possibility of the integration of metaverse and business. Section 3 (diagnosis process) discusses the key digital capabilities of retail enterprises in the metaverse, that is, when the event of metaverse enabling commerce has sufficient possibilities, it discusses the capabilities that retail enterprises should have to enter the metaverse. Section 4 (design process) proposes the metaverse empowerment mode based on the user-production-scene theory,aiming to put forward the business logic under the metaverse scenario and hope that the retail enterprises can grasp the essential key of this composite system when developing the metaverse. Section 5 (implementation process) discusses the commercial innovation of retail enterprises in the metaverse so as to demonstrate the commercial metaverse really explored by retail giants in practice. Section 6 gives enlightenment to the management of retail enterprises under the situation of the metaverse, with the purpose of guiding the necessary actions for retail enterprises to tap the value of the metaverse.

2 Concept and Connotation of Metaverse (Description)

The metaverse is considered the next revolution of the Internet, yet there is no clear conclusion about its definition and the ultimate form in all walks of life. In the study by Harrisson-Boudreau et al., 29% of respondents said that retail was the reason for entering the metaverse [3]. At present, the views of all circles on the retail metaverse basically focus on the stimulation of consumers by sensory new experience brought by technology upgrading, which then has an impact on brand building (Table 1). This paper argues that marketing experience and brand upgrading are only one aspect of the impact of the metaverse on the retail industry. The power of the metaverse should go far beyond that level but drive the holistic digital business transformation of retail companies.

From the perspective of retail companies, this paper defines the metaverse as a decentralized digital space-time ecosystem constructed by integrating virtual images, virtual products and virtual scenes based on the technical support of intelligent connection of everything, super intelligent computing and artificial intelligence, which can have a fundamental impact on the internal organizational structure and external business model of enterprises.

Table 1. Key views of various sectors on the retail metaverse

Focused perspective	Authors	Definitions and perceptions
Sensory experience	Jill Standish 2022 [4]	The metaverse is a continuous, immersive experience. In many ways, it may resemble the early days of online or mobile commerce. Now, the challenge for retailers is to create, shape, and market products, services, and experiences that can move between the physical and virtual worlds. They need to do this while coordinating networks of experts, skills, and technologies to help make this happen
	Harrisson-Boudreau et al. 2022 [3]	As consumer preferences evolve, the primary purpose of metaverse retail is to provide customers with memorable and engaging experiences throughout their shopping journey
	Yoo et al. 2023 [5]	One of the key areas where the metaverse is expected to have an impact is retail, where consumers can navigate through virtual environments that are designed to replicate the real-world shopping experience but with added interaction and immersion
Brand building	Barbara E. Kahn 2023 [6]	The importance of sensory mobilization is central to the definition of the metaverse, especially in the context of retail entering the metaverse. The metaverse enhances the retail sector's interaction with customers, thereby boosting brand loyalty
	Belk et al. 2022 [7]	Just as in the physical world, brands, branded products, and branded environments will significantly influence how consumers behave in the metaverse
Channel of distribution	Bruni et al. 2023 [8]	The Metaverse can act both as an alternative and a complement to physical spaces such as hyper-specialized shops, supermarkets, and niche markets. As such, integrating the Metaverse into the omnichannel marketing strategy is essential

Intelligent connection of everything refers to using Internet of things, blockchain and other technologies to create a complete operation and link to the real world of interactive perception system in the metaverse. Super-intelligent computing refers to the computing power support for the productivity of the metaverse, which is the basis for its simulation modeling, interaction and realtime linking. Artificial intelligence includes two main fields: machine learning and content generation. Internal machine learning can realize human learning behavior through computer simulation, constantly acquire new knowledge and skills, reorganize the existing knowledge structure and improve the performance of the metaverse. External generative AI tools can reshape the knowledge-based work of enterprises with full functions in the whole industry, boost job transformation and performance improvement in key fields such as marketing and sales, customer operation and software development [9].

3   Key Capabilities in the Metaverse (Diagnosis)

Consumption and retail have been identified as one of the industries which are most likely to be affected by the metaverse. In McKinsey's 2023 Metaverse Consumer survey, it was found that many metaverse initiatives are pushing technological boundaries but missing consumer goals, which means they failed to empower core value products through the metaverse. The metaverse wins by providing consumers with value-added products and services they can use today alone or in combination with the physical world. Even in the virtual world, the key to driving metaverse product adoption and value creation is to engage target consumers in the use cases they are most interested in [10]. This is also consistent with the underlying logic of the key elements of digital start-ups, that is, the consumer-centered operation based on the Internet is the fundamental difference between digital start-ups and traditional enterprises [11].

Therefore, we can see that the metaverse practice of most enterprises is still in the construction stage, and the real metaverse form has not yet formed. PWC believes that at present, the seeds of the metaverse exist in independent experiences, and assets and values cannot be interacted or exchanged [12]. The main reason why the metaverse has not yet evolved is the lack of underlying technical support. Existing computing power, headsets, software protocols and network capacity are not ready to support a truly immersive and shared virtual world, which leads to imperfect industry applications. The elements of the early stage are not fully light up, and user participation is low, so it is impossible to enter the next stage. However, the metaverse is a process of development and evolution. Although it is still in the initial stage, there have been many segmentation tracks. Enterprises should seize the era to participate in the change.

How can retail companies navigate a virtual world that is still taking shape? From the perspective of progressive cognition, exploration and application, we believe that the key capabilities of the metaverse (Table 2) should include three levels of strategy, driving and execution, as well as specific eight capabilities and key actions. From top-level design to opening channels and terminal applications, the essences of key capabilities in the metaverse should be: (1) Identifying available resources; (2) Building a winning model; (3) Forming differential value.

Table 2. Key capabilities of the metaverse

	Category	Key Action	Essence
Metaverse Strategic Capability (cognition)	Demand positioning capability (external)	Collect, analyze, introduce, validate and promote	Identify available resources in the metaverse
	Core advantage positioning capability (internal)	Analyze internal and external advantages and disadvantages to create differentiated competitiveness	
Metaverse Driving Capability (exploration)	Business driving capability	Create a business collaboration ecosystem with the Internet of everything	Build a winning model for the metaverse
	Technology driving capability	Construct data-driven intelligence for digital thinking	
	Channel driving capability	Establish a channel partner alliance	
Metaverse Execution Capability (application)	Product and service innovation capability	Provide metaverse experience and value empowerment for products and services	Form differentiated value in the metaverse
	Organizational structure change capability	Build a flexible management model and a metaverse talent team	
	Operational system efficiency capability	Form an intelligent scenario-based operation system to achieve all-round improvement of efficiency	

4   Metaverse Business Empowerment (Design)

The essence of business is to explore the relationship among users, products and scenes. Guanhua Liu et al. proposed that the key to the three points is to rebuild users' cognition, to re-recognize product innovation and continuous dynamic operation respectively. Accordingly, the upgrading of three business concepts was brought: product personalization, value-added sustainability and scene socialization [13]. Corresponding to "users, products and scenes" are cognition, relationship and transaction, forming a spiraling business closed loop. From bystanders to consumers, members, fans, fans and partners, with the upgrading of the relationship, the unit price of trading customers will change from low to high, and the product experience and service experience after the transaction will further strengthen user cognition [14]. Accordingly, we propose that the business logic in the metaverse situation is community relationship trust, IP cognitive proactiveness and scene transaction immersion. Furthermore, it refers to the reliability of the key opinion consumers (KOCs) and key opinion leaders (KOLs) in the community for users' cognitive guidance, product IP innovation which occupies the commanding heights of users first, and sensory experience of scene immersion and upgrading which stimulates purchase decisions (Table 3). The essence of metaverse business is to make deeper connections between users and users as well as between users and products with the support of intelligent hardware and various technologies, then use users and products to create a scene ecosystem, which empowers business.

Table 3. The users, products and scenes in the metaverse

	Core	Business Idea	Underlying Logic in the Metaverse
User	Rebuild users' cognition	Product personalization	Community relationship trust
Product	Re-recognize product innovation	Value-added sustainability	IP cognitive proactiveness
Scene	Continuous dynamic operation	Scene socialization	Scene transaction immersion

Jon Radoff, the founder of Bearable, summarized the seven layers of value chain in the metaverse, which are: (1) Experience layer; (2) Discovery layer; (3) Creator economy; (4) Spatial computing; (5) Decentralization; (6) Human-computer interaction; (7) Hardware devices. Shenghui Cheng further explained its internal meaning [15], combined with the theory of user-production-scene, we can look at the metaverse value chain (Table 4):

Table 4. Value chain of user-production-scene in the metaverse

	Value Chain Level	Connotation	User-production-scene Value
User	Experience Layer	Reflecting real-World Life Scenes	Expand the possibility of consumer consumption field
	Discovery Layer	A key area of content consumption	Build an economic ecosystem for creators
Product	Creator Economy	Sharing and co-creation	Dual identities encourage participation and new product creation

(continued)

Table 4. (*continued*)

	Value Chain Level	Connotation	User-production-scene Value
Scene	Spatial Computing	A key technology to achieve boundless	Break down the barriers between reality and virtuality
	Decentralization	The core of the ecosystem in the metaverse era	Ensure the growth of creator economy
	Human-computer Interaction	The technical core of high immersion	Ensure the upgrade of consumer sensory experience
	Hardware Devices	Infrastructure in the metaverse	Technically support the Internet of everything

5   Metaverse Business Innovation (Implementation)

Festa et al. proposed in 2022 that the metaverse not only contributes to the theoretical level, that is, the scientific possibility of using the concept of the meta world, but also provides great opportunities for the business world in terms of innovation management opportunities at the practical level [16]. In practical application, the metaverse provides virtual digital images for the participation of "users", transforms goods into virtual assets to meet the needs of "products", builds twin Spaces to replicate the real world or opens new three-dimensional fields to create "scenes" experience. The metaverse allows customers to further personalize and customize their virtual identities by creating digital images, enabling further sensory experiences of behavior; build virtual trials and fittings for goods to provide a better buying experience, and create new digital collections and digital assets to diversify the economic system; by expanding the spatiotemporal experience of commercial scenes as well as the integration of online and offline, the high efficiency and low cost of the digital world are connected with the experience and timeliness of offline scenes in the same scene, so that the traditional two-dimensional commercial space operation is upgraded to multi-dimensional operation of digital space, and the operation efficiency is continuously improved. The metaverse links the business environment with new technological innovation, building a new enterprise business model to follow the evolution of the digital age.

For the retail industry, marketing is considered as the key behavior to convert products into value and carry out acquisition. Benny proposed that when using metaverse marketing, visual components are one of the most important aspects to maintain users' interest in the virtual world of the metaverse, immersing them and promoting sales. Sales of physical and digital goods in the metaverse will benefit from visual appeal [17]. Traditional brand content presents static and flat characteristics, which makes it difficult to achieve close and all-round interaction with consumers. Afkar et al. found in their study that compared with the role of perceived consumer experience and gamification, the role of perceived brand engagement has a greater impact on the intention to use, and specifically stronger brand engagement will make the intention to use the metaverse stronger as well [18]. At present, the widely adopted measures are using AR and VR visualization technology and innovative metaverse gameplay to attract consumers, enhance consumers' perception and emotional connection to the brand, carry out deeper user mental penetration, and combine the characteristics and value of the brand (Table 5).

Table 5. Commercial innovation of the metaverse in the retail industry

	Category	Action	Case
User	Virtual Idol	Collaborate with existing virtual idols	Mac, Shiseido, Moody and other brands cooperated with AYAYI, the first hyperrealistic digital person in China, for brand promotion
		Create own virtual idols	NAXUE creates a virtual idol called NAYUKI, announcing the entry of new tea drinking metaverse era. Incremental points buried by IP have prepared for grafting of new stories and new surroundings
	Virtual Character	Generate user-specific avatars	QQ Music launched the Music Zone function, but the experience of the virtual image needs to be further deepened
Product	Digital Collection	Sell digital art and digital mystery boxes	Budweiser has entered a long-term partnership with NFT media store VaynerNFT, using NFT to convert tickets and merchandise into NFT, providing new experiences in sports, entertainment and music In November 2021, YHKT ENTERTAINMENT, the producer of *Incarnation* officially released the world's first AR series digital blind box, which not only attracted a lot of attention in the NFT trading market, but also created a transaction record of 120,000 yuan in the Yongle auction digital collection

(continued)

Table 5. (continued)

	Category	Action	Case
	Improvement of Sensory Experience	Innovate the sensory experience of product use	Poison has established the industry's largest trend commodity model database and created a 360-degree 3D platform for product display. Customers can try on shoes through AR, which is convenient for details to be viewed for authenticity inspection, and helps consumers personalize their favorite products
Scene	Thematic Economy	Build own long-term virtual platform	NetEase Yaotai allows users to freely hold a variety of meta-cosmic activities, such as virtual concerts, online exhibitions, etc., and even build their own meta-cosmic museums and scenic spots to experience unprecedented immersive interaction. The emergence of NetEase Yaotai not only provides users with a new entertainment and social platform, but also a bold prediction and exploration of the future lifestyle
		Cooperate with existing platforms to create space	Nike entered the 3D sandbox creative community Roblox and acquired the blockchain startup RTFKT to obtain the core technology for making virtual sneakers. Then came the immersive Nikeland
		The media set up a platform and brands participate in the exhibition	Tmall holds the Double 11 space art exhibition

6   Management Enlightenment of Metaverse Business

We believe that the necessary actions for retail enterprises to tap the value of the metaverse are as follows: (1) Formulate the strategy centered on consumer value, reconstruct the core competitiveness of enterprises in the metaverse context and create product value; (2) To introduce, test, learn and apply. Monitor the operation results of the metaverse to make adjustments. Use measures such as project management and performance monitoring to ensure the effective implementation of the metaverse plan; (3) Keep pace with the development of the metaverse, tap metaverse talents and technology applications, and embed them into business strategies and business models.

As the comprehensive transformation of production mode, metaverse not only affects the external business model of retail enterprises, but also affects the function of internal organizational structure, such as the recruitment and training of human resources, financial assets and currency, and of course, the marketing mentioned above. Although the future of the metaverse is not yet clear, senior managers need to start learning and experimenting now. Rui Chen, Bilibili's chief executive, thinks that if anyone hears the concept of the metaverse and decides to get into the business, it may be too late. It is an important opportunity for the development of metaverse retail enterprises to quickly enter the metaverse and seize the leading position in the segmentation track for transformation.

In addition, the risks of the metaverse include external bubble risks and internal mechanism risks. Although the underlying technology has been developing for years, the metaverse has suddenly become a hot topic only in the last few years. Similar to the early days of the Internet, this innovative concept and application may involve speculation, excessive valuation, and some unwise investments. Furthermore, privacy security and protection may become the most concerned preventive guarantee due to its decentralized nature. Even if the metaverse users have the ownership of their own data, there is still a risk that the individual data will be exploited in the case of imperfect supervision in the early stage. In a sense, building or introducing a strong privacy barrier may be more of an action to attract consumers than marketing. Entering the game at an early stage when the mechanism is being formed also helps companies to become one of the makers of new retail rules.

References

1. Fanhai International School of Finance, Fudan University: Metaverse report: 2022 review and 2023 outlook. https://fisf.fudan.edu.cn/show-79-4475.html. Accessed 12 Jan 2024. (in Chinese)
2. Wan, J., Yang, J.: Some considerations on interactive management. J. Syst. Dialect. **12**(1), 70–74 (2004). (in Chinese)
3. Harrisson-Boudreau, J.P., Bellemare, J., Bacher, N., Bartosiak, M.: Adoption potentials of metaverse omnichannel retailing and its impact on mass customization approaches. In: Galizia, F.G., Bortolini, M. (eds.) Production Processes and Product Evolution in the Age of Disruption. CARV 2023. LNME. Springer, Cham (2023). https://doi.org/10.1007/978-3-031-34821-1_13
4. Forbes: Consumer are Ready to Shop In The Metaverse This Holiday Season. https://www.forbes.com/sites/jenniferhicks/2022/11/29/consumer-are-ready-to-shop-in-the-metaverse-this-holiday-season/?sh=146bb50bbaf0. Accessed 12 Jan 2024
5. Yoo, K., Welden, R., Hewett, K., Haenlein, M.: The merchants of meta: a research agenda to understand the future of retailing in the metaverse. J. Retail. **99**, 173–192 (2023)
6. Wharton School of the University of Pennsylvania: Doing Business in the Metaverse: Leveraging Innovations in Immersive Technology. https://mackinstitute.wharton.upenn.edu/2023/doing-business-in-the-metaverse-leveraging-innovations-in-immersive-technology/. Accessed 12 Jan 2024

7. Belk, R., Humayun, M., Brouard, M.: Money, possessions, and ownership in the Metaverse: NFTs, cryptocurrencies, Web3 and wild markets. J. Bus. Res. **153**, 198–205 (2022)

8. Bruni, R., Colamatteo, A., Mladenović, D.: How the metaverse influences marketing and competitive advantage of retailers: predictions and key marketing research priorities. Electron. Commer. Res. (2023)

9. McKinsey: Generative AI in China: $2 trillion economic value. https://www.mckinsey.com.cn/生成式ai在中国:2万亿美元的经济价值/. Accessed 12 Jan 2024. (in Chinese)

10. McKinsey: Unlocking commerce in the metaverse. https://www.mckinsey.com/capabilities/growth-marketing-and-sales/our-insights/unlocking-commerce-in-the-metaverse. Accessed 12 Jan 2024

11. Fang, S., An, X., Mao, J.: Innovations and trends in China's digital economy. Commun. ACM **64**(11), 44–47 (2021)

12. PWC: Uncovering the Meta-Universe: Business leaders need to know and do. https://www.pwccn.com/zh/industries/telecommunications-media-and-technology/publications/uncover-the-meta-universe-mar2022.html. Accessed 12 Jan 2024. (in Chinese)

13. Liu, G., Liang, L., Ai, Y.: The Theory of User, Production and Scene: New Business Upgrading Methodology. China Machine Press, Beijing (2017). (in Chinese)

14. Lu, Y.: The three axes of meta-universe marketing: reconstructing users, products and scenes. https://www.imspm.com/shichangyunying/163217.html. Accessed 12 Jan 2024. (in Chinese)

15. Cheng, S.: Metaverse. In: Cheng, S. (ed.) Metaverse: Concept, Content and Context. Springer, Cham (2023)

16. Festa, G., Melanthiou, Y., Meriano, P.: Engineering the metaverse for innovating the electronic business: a socio-technological perspective. In: Thrassou, A., Vrontis, D., Efthymiou, L., Weber, Y., Shams, S.M.R., Tsoukatos, E. (eds.) Business Advancement through Technology Volume II. Palgrave Studies in Cross-disciplinary Business Research, In Association with EuroMed Academy of Business. Palgrave Macmillan, Cham (2022)

17. Benny, T.: Demystifying metaverse in business: a conceptual study. In: El Khoury, R., Alareeni, B. (eds) How the Metaverse Will Reshape Business and Sustainability. Contributions to Environmental Sciences & Innovative Business Technology. Springer, Singapore (2023). https://doi.org/10.1007/978-981-99-5126-0_1

18. Afkar, E., Hamsal, M., Kartono R., Furinto, A.: Prediction of perceived consumer experience, perceived brand engagement, and gamification towards the intention to use metaverse: an extended TAM approach. In: 2022 6th International Conference on Information Technology, Information Systems and Electrical Engineering (ICITISEE), Yogyakarta, Indonesia, pp. 239–244 (2022)

The Research on the Multi-stage Influence Mechanism of New User Behavior During the Implementation of Digital Transformation Systems

RuTao Ma, Jun Yin[(⊠)], and YanHong Peng

School of Economics and Management, Jiangsu University of Science and Technology, Zhenjiang 212100, China
bamhill@163.com

Abstract. Leveraging insights from Adaptive Structuration Theory and Structural Hole Theory, this study elaborates on the relationship between task diversity and system complexity, and new user behavior across different implementation phases of digital transformation in manufacturing enterprises. This study elaborates on the relationship between task diversity and system complexity, and new user behavior across different implementation phases of digital transformation in manufacturing enterprises. It particularly examines the moderating effect of structural holes in various stages on the relationship between task diversity, system complexity, and new user behavior. The analysis is based on 1,370,389 usage log data collected over six years from a typical domestic manufacturing enterprise undergoing digital transformation. The findings indicate that in the initial rapid response phase, high task diversity and system complexity inhibit new user behavior, with task network structural holes intensifying this negative impact. In the early stable adjustment phase, increased task diversity shifts to facilitate new user behavior, while high system complexity continues to restrain user usage. In the later stages, high task diversity positively affects new user behavior, with task network structural holes playing a positive moderating role, and the adverse effect of high system complexity on new user usage diminishes.

Keywords: Digital Transformation · New User · System Usage behavior

1 Introduction

Digital transformation endows enterprises with enhanced capabilities to adapt to rapidly changing market demands and technological advancements [1]. Among the critical elements of digital transformation, the implementation of systems occupies an essential position [2]. Given the multifaceted and multivariate changes during the system implementation process, a phased study of the digital transformation implementation becomes imperative.

Previous research has indicated that digital transformation exhibits distinct characteristics in various implementation phases. Throughout this process, the continuous addition of new users injects more vitality into an enterprise's digital transformation but also brings a series of challenges. Firstly, compared to experienced users, new users are relatively unfamiliar with the system, making it difficult for them to rely on the system to complete digital work tasks, which can lead to negative emotions [3]. Secondly, new users often exhibit unpredictable behavior due to their lack of operational experience [4]. Therefore, paying attention to the multi-stage changes in new users' system usage behavior and its influencing mechanisms during different phases of digital transformation system implementation is key to effectively realizing enterprise digital transformation.

Previous studies have extensively investigated the traits and behavioral patterns of new users. Initially, their lack of proficiency impacts how they use the system [5]. Difficulties with system features can hinder its full effectiveness for new users. Furthermore, the complex process of becoming accustomed to the system also influences their usage behavior. This difficult adjustment can make new users question the system's worth, leading to resistance [6]. On the positive side, once new users appreciate the system's benefits, they tend to adopt it for task completion, unlike seasoned users who might rely on established routines. Additionally, new users are more influenced by peer support [7]. They can improve their system use by watching and mimicking their colleagues' use of the system.

During the complex process of system implementation in enterprise digital transformation, existing research still exhibits the following deficiencies: 1) Literature on new users' system usage predominantly focuses on analyzing their characteristics, with relatively insufficient exploration of the multifaceted mechanisms impacting their usage behavior. 2) Current research primarily concentrates on the behavior of new users in a single phase of information system implementation, lacking investigation into the dynamic changes in users' system usage across various phases. 3) Regarding data sources, most researchers obtain data through surveys and interviews, with fewer studies utilizing large-scale, real-world enterprise data. To address the aforementioned research gaps, this paper primarily focuses on the following research questions:

(1) How does the impact on new user system usage behavior vary across different stages of the implementation of digital transformation systems?
(2) During the implementation process of digital transformation systems, how does the interaction between new users and the task environment influence the usage behavior of new users?

Building upon this, the current paper starts from the Adaptive Structuration Theory and Structural Hole Theory to analyze how task factors, system factors, and task environment factors influence new users' behavior at various stages of digital transformation system implementation. Drawing on previous literature, this study selected task diversity, system complexity, and task network structural holes as representative variables for these factors. Using actual data from various stages of the digital transformation system implementation of a typical domestic shipbuilding enterprise, this study examines the impact of these factors on new user behavior through empirical analysis, providing an empirical foundation and behavioral insights for the digital transformation of manufacturing enterprises.

2 Theoretical Foundation and Research Hypothesis

2.1 Theoretical Foundation

Adaptive Structuration Theory (AST) provides a framework for understanding how users adapt to new information technologies within organizations, emphasizing the importance of the interplay between tasks, the system, and the organizational environment for effective system usage. It suggests that modern information systems initiate an adaptation process in users, influencing their behavior [8]. However, AST does not fully address the role of user interconnectedness.

Structural Hole Theory complements AST by focusing on the network positions of users, particularly how occupying 'structural holes'—positions connecting otherwise unconnected network segments—provides access to diverse information and advantages in information control. This position enhances the user's capabilities and influences others' usage behavior in information systems.

Integrating AST with Structural Hole Theory allows for a more comprehensive analysis by considering both the process of user adaptation to technology (AST) and the significance of users' positions within social networks (Structural Hole Theory). This combination can more thoroughly explain new users' system usage behaviors during digital transformation by examining task diversity, system complexity, and users' network positions, highlighting the importance of both technological adaptation and network advantages in influencing system usage.

2.2 Research Model

This study introduces a model to investigate how task, system, and task environmental factors differentially affect new user behavior in the various stages of digital transformation system implementation, as shown in Fig. 1. The focus is on the evolving system usage behavior of new users, gauged by their feature usage frequency at each stage of digital transformation. Key independent variables include task diversity and system complexity. The role of structural holes as a moderating factor is explored, along with control variables like job title, gender, age, and department, which potentially influence user behavior during digital transformation.

2.3 Task Diversity and New User System Usage Behavior

Task diversity in digital transformation changes with each phase. During the SRP phase, new users, especially those less skilled, struggle with diverse tasks due to unfamiliarity with new systems and workflows [5], leading to potential resistance and usage issues. In the SAP phase, interacting with more stable task modules helps new users appreciate the system's value, increasing their enthusiasm and willingness to learn and use its functionalities.

By the LP phase, as the information system better aligns with tasks, new users rely more on the system. High task diversity makes work more engaging and motivating [9], prompting users to learn the system more actively, improve their skills, explore various functionalities, and use them more effectively for task completion. Therefore, this paper proposes the following hypothesis:

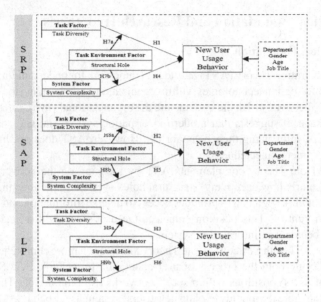

Fig. 1. Research Model

H1: High task diversity negatively impacts new user system usage in the SRP phase of digital transformation.

H2: High task diversity positively impacts new user system usage in the SAP phase of digital transformation.

H3: High task diversity positively impacts new user system usage in the LP phase of digital transformation.

2.4 System Complexity and New User System Usage Behavior

During digital transformation, system complexity evolves with updates, impacting user interaction. In the early SRP phase, higher complexity deters new users due to uncertainty about the system's efficacy, reducing their usage of advanced functionalities [10]. In the SAP phase, complexity increases with module adjustments, heightening the risk of errors and potentially causing data inaccuracies, leading new users to limit their use of complex features. By the LP phase, challenges are largely overcome, encouraging new users to explore additional functionalities and seek assistance, enhancing their understanding and usage of the system. Therefore, the following hypothesis is proposed:

H4: High system complexity negatively influences new user system usage in the SRP phase of digital transformation.

H5: High system complexity negatively influences new user system usage in the SAP phase of digital transformation.

H6: High system complexity positively influences new user system usage in the LP phase of digital transformation.

2.5 Moderation of Structural Holes

As digital transformation systems progress through multi-stage implementation, the task environment for new users changes with each phase, influenced by the moderating effects of structural holes.

In the SRP phase, new users facing high task diversity can effectively use structural holes for control and knowledge connection opportunities, improving their system module usage [11]. Those in structural holes may act as information intermediaries, easing the adverse effects of task diversity on new user behavior. However, for new users grappling with high system complexity, the diverse information within structural holes could compound their challenges [12], exacerbating the complexity's negative impact on their system usage. Therefore, the following hypothesis is proposed:

H7a: Users in structural holes negatively moderate the relationship between task diversity and new user system usage in the SRP phase of digital transformation.

H7b: Users in structural holes positively moderate the relationship between system complexity and new user system usage in the SRP phase of digital transformation.

In the SAP phase, with system usage stabilizing, new users engage more frequently with others. Occupying structural holes, they gain access to diverse, rich information, enhancing system usage. These users, bridging connections across the network, accrue varied work experiences and minimize redundant information, bolstering their system engagement. Despite escalating complexity in information systems, those in structural holes can aid new users in acquiring skills and knowledge, thereby reducing the negative effects of system complexity on new users' usage. Hence, the following hypothesis is proposed:

H8a: Users in structural holes positively moderate the relationship between task diversity and new user system usage in the SAP phase of digital transformation.

H8b: Users in structural holes negatively moderate the relationship between system complexity and new user system usage in the SAP phase of digital transformation.

In the LP phase, task integration into system functionalities leads to user interactions across departmental boundaries. New users with high task diversity, positioned in structural holes, enhance their work experience by engaging with various colleagues and utilizing multiple modules. These users, by gaining extensive information and processing experience, navigate complex systems more adeptly, positively influencing their system usage and augmenting the beneficial effects of system complexity on their usage. Hence, the following hypothesis is proposed:

H9a: Users in structural holes positively moderate the relationship between task diversity and new user system usage in the LP phase of digital transformation.

H9b: Users in structural holes positively moderate the relationship between system complexity and new user system usage in the LP phase of digital transformation.

3   Research Design

3.1   Sample Selection and Data Collection

Sample Selection. The criteria for sample selection were as follows: ① Enterprises typical of digital transformation; ② More than four years of digital transformation system implementation; ③ Users reliant on the system for work completion. After screening, a typical domestic shipbuilding manufacturing enterprise was selected as the subject of study, having undergone a comprehensive digital transformation. Empirical research was conducted by analyzing system usage logs, features, and operation data from the company's ERP system.

Data Collection. This study analyzed data from an ERP system covering the period from November 2011 to October 2016 for 1,370,389 new user logs and system operational data. New users were defined as those with less than a year's experience with the system. In the first year of the task network, only connections between new users were considered, and from November 2012 onwards, some users started to transition to old users. After removing anomalies, the final dataset consisted of 371 new users and 1,311,063 log entries. The study used a monthly aggregation method to combine individual users' monthly usage (including types of modules used, login/logout frequency, and user demographics) into a single log entry per user per month.

Drawing on prior scholars' research, the construction of task networks is primarily based on user logs, extracting new users and their operational functional modules to form a bipartite network. A triad is represented as: $G = \langle U, F, e \rangle$, where U denotes user nodes, F represents functional nodes, and e signifies the edges connecting users to functions. Then, focusing on user nodes, the bipartite network is projected into a "task network" with users as vertices.

3.2   Variable Selection and Calculation

Dependent Variable: In this study, the dependent variable is the new user system usage behavior, indicating how extensively users utilize the information system. Following established metrics like usage frequency and duration [13], new users' system usage is measured by the frequency of functionality use in each phase.

Independent Variables: Task diversity and system complexity are identified as independent variables. Task diversity, as per Liang et al. [10], is the extent of user engagement in various tasks, measured by the number of different functionalities used by new users across phases. System complexity pertains to the ease of understanding and using the enterprise system, quantified using data complexity, which includes the complexity of data structures and data volume calculated via information entropy and complex space theory.

Moderating Variable: Structural holes in this study represent non-redundant relationships between network nodes, with constraint used as the measurement, following Burt [14]. Higher constraint means fewer structural holes available to a user.

Control Variables: Demographic factors are included as control variables due to their potential impact on research outcomes. Differences in age can lead to varied perceptions of work methods, gender differences might result in different attitudes and solutions, job titles indicate diverse job contents and knowledge capabilities, and different departments signify varying work natures and information resources. These factors - age, gender, job title, and department - are considered to potentially influence new users' behavior. Table 1 lists the measurement formulas for these variables.

Table 1. Variables and formulas

Variable	Formula
Task diversity	$F = \frac{n}{T}$
System complexity	$|W|_E = \sum_{i=1}^{n} |S_{ki} - S_{k(i-1)}|$
System usage	$f = \frac{x}{365 \times y}$
Structural holes	$ci = \sum_j \left(p_{ij} + \sum_{q,q \neq i, q \neq j} p_{iq} p_{qj} \right) p_{ij} = \frac{a_{ij} + a_{ji}}{\sum_k (a_{ik} + a_{ki})}$

Notes: x represents user visits; y is the user count; n denotes functions of the information system adopted over time; T is the total functions count; $\|W\|_E$ measures the entropy of tensors; $\|S_i\|$ symbolizes the unified management information energy in tensor form; p_{ij} shows the connection strength between i and j; a_{ij} indicates the edge weight between i and j.

4 Data Analysis and Results

4.1 Data Analysis

The data for this study come from enterprise information systems undergoing digital transformation. In order to resolve potential multicollinearity, the correlation coefficient analysis in Table 2 shows that the absolute value of the variable coefficient is lower than 0.5, indicating that the correlation is weak and multicollinearity can be preliminarily excluded. Furthermore, the variance inflation factor analysis in Table 3 shows that the VIF value does not exceed 2 and remains below the multicollinearity concern threshold of 10, confirming that multicollinearity is not a significant issue in this study.

Table 2. Pearson Correlation Coefficient Matrix for Variables Across Different Phases

Phase	Variable	System Usage	Department	Gender	Job Title	Age	Task Diversity	System Complexity	Structural Hole
SRP	System Usage	1							
	Department	0.164**	1						
	Gender	0.189**	0.362**	1					

(*continued*)

Table 2. (*continued*)

Phase	Variable	System Usage	Department	Gender	Job Title	Age	Task Diversity	System Complexity	Structural Hole
	Job Title	−0.011	−0.039**	0.044	1				
	Age	0.199**	0.087**	−0.077	−0.046	1			
	Task Diversity	0.462**	−0.124**	0.182**	−0.095**	0.134**	1		
	System Complexity	0.134**	−0.181**	0.215**	−0.002*	−0.013	0.009**	1	
	Structural Hole	0.283**	−0.066*	0.152**	0.023	−0.009	0.024	0.045	1
SAP	System Usage	1							
	Department	0.199**	1						
	Gender	0.095**	0.069*	1					
	Job Title	0.071*	0.125**	−0.055	1				
	Age	0.095**	−0.144**	−0.033	0.014	1			
	Task Diversity	0.381**	0.341**	0.229**	0.121**	0.098**	1		
	System Complexity	−0.018	−0.070*	0.196**	−0.077*	−0.042	0.158**	1	
	Structural Hole	−0.046	0.136**	−0.010*	−0.012	−0.020	0.013	0.276**	1
LP	System Usage	1							
	Department	−0.029	1						
	Gender	0.265**	0.249**	1					
	Job Title	−0.132	0.034	−0.172*	1				
	Age	−0.015	0.189**	0.086	−0.071	1			
	Task Diversity	0.432**	0.462**	0.335**	−0.097	0.089	1		
	System Complexity	0.074	0.164*	−0.061	0.163*	0.075	0.198*	1	
	Structural Hole	0.143**	0.246**	−0.006	−0.071	0.241**	0.068	0.059	1

Note: * $P < 0.05$, ** $P < 0.01$, *** $P < 0.001$

To test the research hypotheses, linear regression analysis with SPSS software was utilized. Data was categorized into three groups corresponding to different implementation phases. The regression model included control and main variables, assessing the principal effects of task diversity and system complexity, along with their interaction effects. To mitigate multicollinearity, standardization was applied to all variables. Interaction terms were formed by combining structural holes with independent variables, namely, Structural Holes × Task Diversity and Structural Holes × System Complexity. The results of this moderation analysis are depicted in Fig. 2.

Table 3. Multicollinearity Test

Variable	SRP		SAP		LP	
Metrics	VIF	1/VIF	VIF	1/VIF	VIF	1/VIF
Department	1.200	0.833	1.253	0.798	1.444	0.693
Gender	1.268	0.789	1.110	0.901	1.220	0.820
Job Title	1.020	0.980	1.059	0.944	1.114	0.898
Age	1.047	0.955	1.061	0.943	1.153	0.867
Task Diversity	1.550	0.645	1.334	0.750	1.481	0.675
System Complexity	1.087	0.920	2.105	0.475	1.108	0.903
Structural Hole	1.025	0.975	1.128	0.887	1.130	0.885

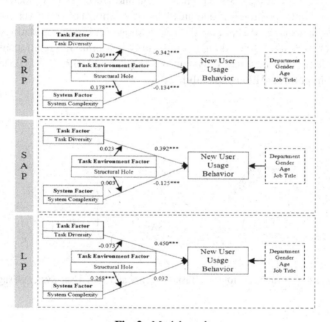

Fig. 2. Model results

The regression analysis for the SRP phase showed a negative correlation between task diversity and new users' system usage ($\beta = -0.342$, $P < 0.001$), and a similar negative impact of system complexity on their system usage ($\beta = -0.134$, $P < 0.05$).Therefore, hypotheses H1 and H4 are validated. In the SAP phase, there is a significant positive correlation between task diversity and new users' system usage ($\beta = 0.392$, $P < 0.001$), and a significant negative correlation exists between system complexity and new users' system usage ($\beta = -0.125$, $P < 0.01$). Hence, hypotheses H2 and H5 are validated. In the LP phase, task diversity significantly influences new users' system usage ($\beta = 0.450$, $P < 0.001$), validating hypothesis H3. System complexity does not significantly impact new users' system usage ($\beta = 0.032$, $P > 0.05$); therefore, hypothesis H6 is not validated.

This paper, by introducing the moderating variable of structural holes, describes the impact of task diversity and system complexity on new users' system usage under the moderation of structural holes. In the SRP phase, if new users occupy structural hole positions, they significantly positively moderate the relationship between task diversity and system usage ($\beta = 0.240$, $P < 0.001$), as shown in Fig. 3. Hence, hypothesis H7a is not validated. The interaction between system complexity and structural holes has a significant positive impact on new users' system usage ($\beta = 0.178$, $P < 0.001$), as depicted in Fig. 4, validating hypothesis H7b. In the SAP phase, structural holes do not moderate the relationship between task diversity and system usage for new users ($\beta = 0.003$, $P > 0.05$), as illustrated in Fig. 3. Structural holes do not significantly influence the relationship between system complexity and system usage for new users ($\beta = 0.023$, $P > 0.05$), as shown in Fig. 4, so hypotheses H8a and H8b are not validated. In the LP phase, structural holes positively moderate the positive impact of task diversity on system usage for new users ($\beta = 0.268$, $P < 0.001$), as shown in Fig. 3, validating hypothesis H9a. However, structural holes do not significantly moderate the relationship between system complexity and new users' system usage ($\beta = -0.073$, $P > 0.05$), as seen in Fig. 4, hence hypothesis H9b is not validated.

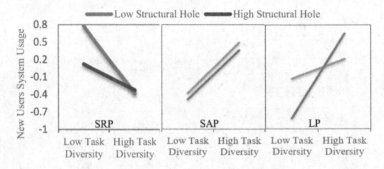

Fig. 3. Impact of Structural Holes on Task Diversity and New User System Usage Chart

4.2 Robustness Test

To ensure the reliability of the findings, a robustness test focusing on sample selection was conducted. By analyzing 50% of the sample data through regression analysis, consistency was observed in the regression coefficients for both independent variables and interaction terms, mirroring the initial results. This consistency in significance levels confirms the robustness and reliability of the regression outcomes, effectively addressing any autocorrelation issues.

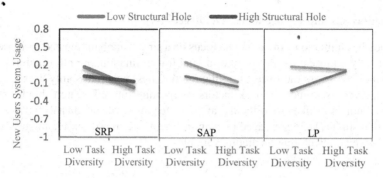

Fig. 4. Impact of Structural Holes on System Complexity and New User System Usage Chart

5   Research Conclusions and Discussion

5.1   Research Conclusions and Significance

In the initial SRP phase of digital transformation, high task diversity significantly challenges new users, leading to decreased system functionality usage. As the process advances into the SAP and LP phases, this diversity becomes more manageable, positively affecting new users' engagement and integrating system use into their daily activities. Furthermore, system complexity varies across these phases; it initially deters user exploration due to uncertainties in the SRP phase and demands increased cognitive effort during the SAP phase because of module adjustments. However, in the LP phase, as digital transformation stabilizes, the adverse effects of system complexity on user engagement lessen, facilitated by fewer updates and a more cohesive task network.

In the SRP phase of digital transformation, structural holes can exacerbate the challenges new users face due to task diversity and system complexity, leading to reduced system interaction [15]. This is due to the stress caused by diverse and heterogeneous information. However, a lower presence of structural holes can foster trust and collaboration within the network, simplifying the learning process for new users. In the SAP phase, the influence of structural holes diminishes, as the effect of task diversity on system usage depends more on individual user efforts. In contrast, during the LP phase, structural holes beneficially moderate the link between task diversity and system usage, facilitating knowledge transfer and adaptation to the system. Since system complexity is less impactful in this phase, structural holes have a limited moderating effect on system usage.

This study illuminates the complexities of digital transformation, highlighting the interplay between task diversity, system complexity, and structural holes across different stages, thereby enriching Adaptive Structuration Theory with insights into social and technological dynamics. For practitioners, it offers guidance on tailoring support and training to navigate these challenges, promoting effective user adaptation and system utilization. Recognizing the impact of structural holes can help managers foster networks that enhance knowledge sharing and collaboration, facilitating a smoother digital transformation process.

5.2 Limitations and Future Research Directions

This study has limitations, including its focus on a single shipbuilding enterprise, which may not fully represent the diversity of digital transformation and information system implementation across industries, limiting the findings' generalizability. It exclusively uses task diversity to measure task factors, suggesting future research should include additional indicators like task difficulty and type for a more detailed analysis. Additionally, further studies are encouraged to examine the deeper reasons affecting new users' system usage by integrating mediating variables.

References

1. Fernandez-Vidal, J., Antonio Perotti, F., Gonzalez, R., Gasco, J.: Managing digital transformation: the view from the top. J. Bus. Res. **152**, 29–41 (2022)
2. Elbanna, A., Newman, M.: The bright side and the dark side of top management support in Digital Transformation –a hermeneutical reading. Technol. Forecast. Soc. Chang. **175**, 121411 (2022)
3. Azanza, M., Irastorza, A., Medeiros, R., Díaz, O.: Onboarding in software product Lines: concept maps as welcome guides. Subjects: Software Engineering, Cite as: arXiv:2103.03829 (2021)
4. Aanestad, M., Jensen, T.B.: Collective mindfulness in post-implementation IS adaptation processes. Inf. Organ. **26**(1–2), 13–27 (2016)
5. Ross, J.W., Vitale, M.R.: The ERP revolution: surviving vs thriving. Inf. Syst. Front. **2**(2), 233–241 (2000)
6. Goh, J.M., Gao, G., Agarwal, R.: Evolving work routines: adaptive routinization of information technology in healthcare. Inf. Syst. Res. **22**(3), 565–585 (2011)
7. Karimikia, H., Safari, N., Singh, H.: Being useful: how information systems professionals influence the use of information systems in enterprises. Inf. Syst. Front. **22**(2), 429–453 (2020)
8. Desanctis, G., Poole, M.S.: Capturing the complexity in advanced technology use: adaptive structuration theory. Organ. Sci. **5**(2), 121–147 (1994)
9. Weiss-Cohen, L., Konstantinidis, E., Speekenbrink, M., Harvey, N.: Task complexity moderates the influence of descriptions in decisions from experience. Cognition **2018**(170), 209–227 (2018)
10. Liang, H., Peng, Z., Xue, Y., Guo, X., Wang, N.: Employees' exploration of complex systems: an integrative view. J. Manag. Inf. Syst. **32**(1), 322–357 (2015)
11. Lauterbach, J., Mueller, B., Ḳahrau, F., Macedche, A.: Achieving effective use when digitalizing work: the role of representational complexity. MIS Q. **44**(3), 1023–1048 (2020)
12. Raman, R., Grover, V.: Studying the multilevel impact of cohesion versus structural holes in knowledge networks on adaptation to IT-enabled patient-care practices. Inf. Syst. J. **30**(1), 6–47 (2019)
13. Venkatesh, V., Windeler, J.B., Bartol, K.M., Williamson, I.O.: Person-Organization and person-job fit perceptions of new it employees: work outcomes and gender differences. MIS Q. **41**(2), 525–558 (2017)
14. Burt, R.S., Jannotta, J.E., Mahoney, J.T.: Personality correlates of structural holes. Social Networks **20**(1), 63–87 (1998)
15. Grosser, T.J., Obstfeld, D., Choi, E.W., Woehler, M., Borgatti, S.P.: A sociopolitical perspective on employee innovativeness and job performance: the role of political skill and network structure. Organ. Sci. **29**(4), 612–632 (2018)

Does Overconfident CEO Matter? An Empirical Examination of CEO Overconfidence and Digital Transformation

Yanlin Zhang, Xuwei Zhang, and Hongting Tang[✉]

Guangdong University of Technology, Guangzhou 510520, Guangdong, China
ht_tang@gdut.edu.cn

Abstract. Although previous studies have emphasized the importance of CEO in IT performance, there is little literature exploring how CEO overconfidence affects digital transformation. We propose a research model that suggests that CEO overconfidence can positively impact digital transformation. In addition, we identified three moderating factors that can enhance the positive relationship between CEO overconfidence and digital transformation: the presence of Chief Information Officer (CIO), the board of directors with IT expertise, and industry competitiveness. By using the panel data of Chinese listed companies from 2011–2021 to test our model, the results will support our research hypothesis. This article expands the relevant research on CEO overconfidence and further reveals how the psychological factors of CEOs affect IT-related activities in enterprises by discovering the positive relationship between CEO overconfidence and digital transformation, as well as the moderating mechanisms that influence CEO overconfidence. Our analysis results also provide theoretical guidance and practical inspiration for CEOs and businesses on how to successfully achieve digital transformation.

Keywords: CEO overconfidence · digital transformation · CIO · board of directors · industry competitiveness

1 Introduction

Digital transformation empowers enterprises to swiftly identify and respond to market risks and opportunities, overhaul business processes, instigate organizational change, and yield enhanced financial performance and competitive advantage [1, 3]. Despite corporate executives acknowledging the substantial strategic significance of digital transformation and increasing their investments in digital technologies [6], numerous enterprises have faltered in achieving their objectives or outright failed in their transformation endeavors [25]. Consequently, the successful execution of digital transformation by enterprises has emerged as an urgent concern [6].

As the top decision-maker of an organization, the CEO bears the responsibility of spearheading its digital transformation [1, 3]. Although previous IS research emphasizes the significant impact of CEO support or involvement on enhancing IT performance [7, 12], there has been limited attention to CEO overconfidence, a psychological attribute

© The Author(s), under exclusive license to Springer Nature Switzerland AG 2024
Y. P. Tu and M. Chi (Eds.): WHICEB 2024, LNBIP 516, pp. 201–212, 2024.
https://doi.org/10.1007/978-3-031-60260-3_17

that has attracted considerable scholarly attention. Although prior studies predominantly focused on the negative effects of CEO overconfidence [18, 21, 23], recent research indicates its strong association with enhancing positive outcomes such as R&D investment and firm innovation [7, 12]. Despite the numerous empirical evidence on the innovative role of CEO overconfidence, there still remains unclear that whether CEO overconfidence positively influences digital transformation, which is associated with the continuous digital investment [1, 3, 13] and potential risks [4, 9]. Consequently, we propose two research questions: firstly, does CEO overconfidence positively influence digital transformation? Secondly, if the former answer is affirmative, are there other factors that moderate the relationship between CEO overconfidence and digital transformation?

To address the aforementioned questions, we present a research model. Firstly, we posit that CEO overconfidence positively influences corporate digital transformation. Secondly, we delineate three moderating factors. At the internal organizational level, CIOs and boards of directors with IT expertise can effectively moderate the relationship between CEO overconfidence and digital transformation. At the external environmental level, we propose that industry competitiveness strengthens the positive impact of CEO overconfidence on digital transformation. We employ the panel data from Chinese listed firms from 2011–2021 as our sample to empirically test our proposed model. The results provide stronger support for our hypothesis.

This paper contributes to the literature in several ways. Firstly, it extends research on CEO overconfidence by establishing a positive association between CEO overconfidence and digital transformation. Secondly, this paper adds to the IS literature on CEO support for IT performance by observing the positive impact of CEO overconfidence on digital transformation. Lastly, by identifying moderators from both internal and external organizational environments, we illuminate the contextual factors shaping the positive impact of CEO overconfidence. Our findings offer theoretical guidance and practical insights into facilitating successful digital transformation for CEOs and organizations.

2 Literature Review

Upper Echelons Theory (UET) suggests that CEO cognitive characteristics can influence a company's strategic decision-making and performance [2, 11]. In particular, CEO overconfidence has recently garnered scholarly attention, particularly in finance, accounting, and strategic management. CEO overconfidence is defined as CEOs' overly optimistic and erroneous assessments of their own abilities and knowledge [2, 21]. While prior research has primarily explored the negative implications of overconfidence, like overinvestment and M&A premium [18, 21, 22], recent studies have also revealed its positive effects. For instance, Hirshleifer et al. (2012) and demonstrated that overconfident CEOs exhibit greater innovativeness [12]. Similarly, Galasso and Simcoe (2011) established a positive correlation between CEO overconfidence and R&D investment performance [7]. Additionally, Burkhard et al. (2022) observed that overconfident CEOs tend to take higher risks in their firms [2].

Previous IS literature has consistently highlighted the significance of top management support for IT performance [6, 20]. As the most influential decision-maker in the top management team, the CEO may play a crucial role in determining the success or failure of enterprise digital transformation. Recent studies have investigated the positive impact of CEO on organizational IT performance and digital outcomes, including CEO tenure [1], and IT-related or digital-related human capital [4, 5, 10]. However, it remains unclear whether CEO overconfidence, as an important cognitive characteristic, impacts digital transformation. Previous research has shown that overconfident CEOs are better innovators [7, 12] and risk-takers [2]. Given that digital transformation is a business activity that involves innovation and risk [1, 3, 4, 9], this article aims to explore the impact of CEO overconfidence on digital transformation.

Furthermore, according to UET, the CEO's decision-making process is influenced by both organizational and environmental factors [2]. At the organizational level, some CEOs may make imprudent decisions due to overconfidence, overvaluing digital technologies and overlooking potential risks [21]. This mandates firms to mitigate financial losses through a rational governance framework. The roles of Chief Information Officers (CIOs) and boards of directors with IT expertise in guiding over-confident CEOs are crucial. CIOs, with their expertise in digital technologies and strategic planning, can provide CEOs with prudent counsel on digital investments [1]. Boards of directors can oversee CEOs while leveraging their IT acumen to craft effective digital strategic blueprints [5, 19]. At the environmental level, it is argued that industry competition significantly influences the decision-making of overconfident CEOs. Previous research suggests that highly competitive industry landscapes foster overconfidence among CEOs [7]. In conclusion, Fig. 1 illustrates our research model.

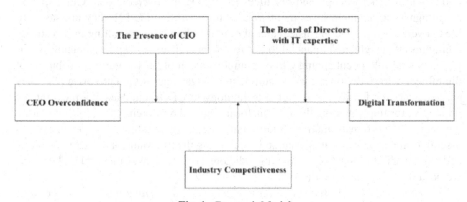

Fig. 1. Research Model

3 Hypotheses Development

3.1 CEO Overconfidence and Digital Transformation

Firstly, overconfident CEOs exhibit greater optimism regarding digital transformation. The extended payback period associated with digital transformation typically offers uncertain and delayed benefits, providing limited contributions to short-term performance improvement. Overconfident CEOs harbor optimistic views on the success likelihood of their digital technology investments [7, 21], fostering higher expectations for long-term digital returns and, consequently, a greater willingness to support digital transformation. Secondly, overconfident CEOs demonstrate a willingness to embrace the risks inherent in the digital transformation process and exhibit a readiness to allocate more substantial investments. While digital transformation necessitates continuous investments in technical resources and capital, it also accompanies inherent high risks, including data leakage and cyberattacks [9], which are challenging to mitigate. Overconfident CEOs tend to underestimate the likelihood of risks materializing [2], demonstrating a greater readiness to overestimate the potential advantages and expected returns of digital transformation. Additionally, overconfident CEOs are perceived as radical innovators, and empirical evidence indicates their greater inclination, compared to rational CEOs, to augment innovation-related investments [7, 12]. Consequently, CEO overconfidence propels firms to consistently augment their digital investments. Based on the aforementioned arguments, we posit the following hypothesis:

Hypothesis 1: CEO overconfidence is positively associated with digital transformation.

3.2 The Moderating Effects of the Presence of CIO

Chief Information Officers (CIOs) typically possess IT expertise, business knowledge, and strategic comprehension, enabling them to assist companies in surveilling the external technological landscape for emerging opportunities in digital technology and assimilating pertinent knowledge and resources [3, 19]. While overconfident CEOs exhibit a willingness to augment investments related to innovation [7, 12], they are susceptible to overestimating the intrinsic value of digital technologies, resulting in investment premiums and heightened financial losses for the organization [21]. Strategically, CIOs play a pivotal role in enhancing CEOs' comprehension of the potential contribution of digital technology to bolstering the competitive advantage of the enterprise [1]. They can elucidate the feasibility of digital technology to CEOs, emphasizing the strategic imperative for implementing digital transformation and reinforcing the CEO's enduring confidence in this transformation. Additionally, regarding investments, CIOs function as essential gatekeepers, adept at accurately appraising the true value of digital technology and guiding CEOs effectively in making judicious IT-related investments [1]. Therefore, we posit the following hypothesis:

Hypothesis 2: The presence of CIO will enhance the positive relationship between CEO overconfidence and digital transformation.

3.3 The Moderating Effects of the Board of Directors with IT Expertise

The board of directors typically serves as a source of strategic counsel and resource backing for CEOs [5]. Consequently, the extent to which the board endorses the CEO's digital decisions can significantly impact digital transformation. Moreover, an excessively confident CEO may subject the company to losses due to bold investment choices [21], necessitating vigilant supervision and guidance by the board of directors. Particularly, a board with substantial IT experience is better positioned to comprehend the advantages of supporting digital technology and assess strategic issues related to digital initiatives

[5, 19]. Regular engagements with CEOs, offering pertinent advice on digital investments and development strategies, can effectively steer overly confident CEOs toward sound digital decisions. In summary, board members with IT-related expertise leverage their experience to furnish valuable investment counsel to the CEO, gain a deeper understanding of the trajectory of digital technology development, and thereby contribute to guiding enterprises through digital transformation. Grounded in this rationale, we posit the following hypothesis:

Hypothesis 3: The board of directors with IT expertise will promote the positive impact of CEO overconfidence on digital transformation.

3.4   The Moderating Effects of Industry Competitiveness

In highly competitive industries, CEO overconfidence in IT investment has a more substantial impact on company performance. Unlike a low-competition environment, high competitive intensity renders enterprises acutely attuned to maintaining a competitive edge, thereby amplifying the consequences of any advantage or disadvantage on company performances [13]. An overconfident CEO fosters an optimistic outlook on long-term digital returns, guiding executives and employees to concentrate on establishing enduring advantages through digital transformation [7]. Hence, CEO overconfidence assumes heightened importance in highly competitive environments, exerting a more pronounced impact on digital transformation. Formulated on this premise, we posit the following hypothesis:

Hypothesis 4: The industry competitiveness will positively moderate the relationship between CEO overconfidence and digital transformation.

4   Research Method

4.1   Sample and Data

The research samples for this study consisted of Chinese listed firms from 2011 to 2021. All statistics were obtained from the China Securities Market and Accounting Research Database (CSMAR). To ensure data availability, we followed a two-step process. Firstly, we excluded the annual sample of companies with missing severe financial data. Secondly, we excluded annual samples of listed financial companies. (3) Excluded from the study were all annual Special Treatment/Property Treatment (ST/PT) category enterprises. (4) We only included listed companies from Shanghai and Shenzhen A-shares. (5) To ensure data accuracy, all continuous variables were winzorized at the 1% and 99% levels. The final valid sample consisted of 13,277 firm-year observations.

4.2   The Definition and Measurement of Variables

Dependent Variable: Digital Transformation (*DT_Index*)
We use the Digital Transformation Index from the CSMAR database to measure the digital transformation of enterprises [17]. CSMAR extracts data from multiple data sources to construct a comprehensive Digital Transformation Index. Due to space constraints, the

construction of the Digital Transformation Index can be found in CSMAR's description of the use of enterprise digital transformation databases[1]. In addition, we also selected the frequency of words related to digitalization (*DT_Num*) in the management discussion and analysis section of listed companies' annual reports as an alternative proxy for digital transformation for robustness testing [15].

Independent Variable: CEO Overconfidence (*OC*)

The main indicator of CEO overconfidence is the measure of the change in their stock holdings. As suggested by Malmendier et al. (2005), a risk-averse CEO may minimize their holdings of company stock to divest themselves of idiosyncratic risk [21]. However, CEOs who are overconfident tend to overestimate the future returns of their investment projects and believe that the stock prices of their companies will continue to rise under their leadership more than they should expect objectively [21, 22]. Therefore, if a CEO purchases additional company stock despite already having a high exposure to company risk, they can be identified as an overconfident CEO [21]. If the CEO does not reduce their stock holdings when the firm's stock return falls in the current year, they are considered overconfident. This is coded as 1 if they are overconfident and 0 otherwise [21]. Additionally, we will use other measures as a robustness test of CEO overconfidence.

Moderating Variables

The Presence of CIO (CIO). Information about CIOs was obtained from the CSMAR database of executive titles. CIO job titles vary across organizations, including 'CIO,' 'chief information officer,' 'senior IT executive,' and others. Following previous literature [19], executives with these titles were identified as CIOs during the collection process. To ensure the validity of the CIO data, we manually identified and validated each collected executive's title and role description. After validation and organization, we coded the CIO data as binary variables. The CIO position was coded as 1 if it existed in the firm and 0 otherwise.

Board of Directors with IT Expertise (IT_Board). Board of directors is considered to have IT expertise when its members possess IT-related educational or practitioner experience [5, 10]. IT educational background refers to a professional background in computer science, information management, and related fields. IT experience refers to work experience in IT-related industries. The educational background and work experience of executives were organized and coded as binary variables based on the information provided by the CSMAR database. *IT_Board* was coded as 1 if the board of directors had IT educational background or experience, and 0 otherwise.

Industry Competitiveness (HHI_Dum). Consistent with previous literature [24], industry competition is measured by the Herfindahl Index (*HHI*), which indicates lower competition intensity as the *HHI* increases. We use a binary variable called *HHI_Dum*, where the firm's annual *HHI* is compared to the sample's *HHI* median for each year (*HHI_Med*). If the firm's annual *HHI* is lower than *HHI_Med*, *HHI_Dum* is coded as 1, indicating a high level of competition in the industry, and 0 otherwise.

---

[1] https://data.csmar.com.

Control Variables

We also include several control variables [5, 6]. At the CEO level, we control for four control variables: age (*Age*), gender (*Gender*), education level (*Degree*) and whether the CEO is duality (Duality). At the firm level, we selected the control variables of firm size (*Size*), firm's listed years (*ListedYear*), ROA, asset liability ratio (*AssetLiabilityRatio*), book-to-market ratio (*BookToMarketRatio*), firm growth (*Growth*), property nature (*PropertyNature*), and number of employees (*Employees*). At the board level, we control for number of board of directors (*BoardSize*) and the percentage of independent directors (*IndDirectorRatio*). In addition, we also control for industry fixed effects and year fixed effects. The industries of listed companies are classified according to the 2012 CSRC industry classification standards.

5 Empirical Analysis

5.1 Descriptive Statistic

Table 1 reports the descriptive statistics of the variables. Due to space constraints, the correlation matrix between the variables is not shown for the time being. In order to prevent the problem of multicollinearity, we performed a variance inflation factor (VIF) test. We found that the largest of these VIFs is 2.96, which is much smaller than the threshold of 10, and thus it can be determined that multicollinearity will not be a concern in this paper.

Table 1. Descriptive statisitcs

	Mean	SD	Min	Median	Max
DT_Index	36.73	9.862	23.47	34.43	64.94
OC	0.30	0.459	0	0	1
CIO	0.01	0.074	0	0	1
IT_Board	0.53	0.499	0	1	1
HHI_Dum	0.51	0.500	0	1	1
Age	49.63	6.685	26	50	81
Gender	0.93	0.251	0	1	1
Degree	3.66	1.250	1	4	7
Duality	0.26	0.438	0	0	1
Size	22.25	1.242	16.16	22.12	28.02
ListedYear	11.71	7.017	−1	11	31
ROA	0.04	0.948	−3.60	0.03	108.37
AssetLiabilityRatio	0.43	0.250	−0.19	0.42	8.26

(*continued*)

Table 1. (*continued*)

	Mean	SD	Min	Median	Max
BookToMarketRatio	0.34	0.168	−0.75	0.32	1.29
Growth	5.96	518.491	−11.68	0.12	59411.55
PropertyNature	0.37	0.483	0	0	1
BoardSize	8.63	1.690	4	9	18
IndDirectorRatio	37.33	5.555	16.67	33.33	75
Employees	7.75	1.172	2.30	7.72	12.57

5.2 Hypotheses Testing

The main model's regression results are presented in Table 2. Both Model 1 and Model 2 exhibit a consistently significant positive correlation between CEO overconfidence and enterprise digital transformation, irrespective of the inclusion of control variables. Additionally, we employ digital-related word frequency as an alternative dependent proxy in Model 3 and Model 4. The outcomes also reveal that CEO overconfidence continues to exert a significantly positive impact on corporate digital transformation.

Table 2. The results of main effects

	DT_Index		DT_Num	
	(1)	(2)	(3)	(4)
OC	1.887***	1.429***	0.407***	0.308***
	(0.172)	(0.196)	(0.052)	(0.059)
Controls	NO	YES	NO	YES
Constant	36.159***	31.271***	1.813***	0.326
	(0.090)	(40.039)	(0.025)	(0.656)
Observations	13,277	10,163	13,277	10,163
R-squared	0.225	0.279	0.244	0.281
Industry FE	YES	YES	YES	YES
Year FE	YES	YES	YES	YES

Note: Robust standard errors in parentheses. Symbol ***$p < 0.01$, **$p < 0.05$, *$p < 0.1$

The regression analyses for the three moderating variables are presented in Table 3. Model 5 and Model 6 depict the moderating influence of the CIO. The outcomes reveal a significantly positive coefficient for the interaction term between OC and CIO. In Model 7 and Model 8, the board of directors with an IT background exhibits a significantly positive moderating effect. These results indicate that the presence of CIO and IT-savvy boards enhances their ability to bolster the catalyzing impact of CEO overconfidence in propelling digital initiatives. Model 9 and Model 10 investigate the moderating impact of industry competitiveness on the relationship between CEO overconfidence and digital transformation. The findings suggest that the amplifying effect of CEO overconfidence on digital transformation is more pronounced in highly competitive industries.

Table 3. The results of moderating effects

	(5)	(6)	(7)	(8)	(9)	(10)
OC	1.841***	1.399***	0.913***	0.487**	2.200***	1.737***
	(0.172)	(0.196)	(0.213)	(0.239)	(0.252)	(0.278)
CIO	5.064***	3.187**				
	(1.169)	(1.411)				
OC*CIO	4.715**	4.729*				
	(2.090)	(2.572)				
IT_Board			4.554***	4.505***		
			(0.172)	(0.195)		
OC*IT_Board			1.389***	1.501***		
			(0.318)	(0.345)		
HHI_Dum					−0.461**	−0.483**
					(0.186)	(0.211)
OC*HHI_Dum					−0.709**	−0.700*
					(0.338)	(0.370)
Controls	NO	YES	NO	YES	NO	YES
Constant	36.137***	31.124***	33.775***	28.349***	36.393***	31.150***
	(0.090)	(2.230)	(0.108)	(2.149)	(0.137)	(2.229)
N	13,277	10,163	13,277	10,163	13,277	10,163
R^2	0.228	0.280	0.286	0.337	0.226	0.280
Industry FE	YES	YES	YES	YES	YES	YES
Year FE	YES	YES	YES	YES	YES	YES

Note: Robust standard errors in parentheses. Symbol ***$p < 0.01$, **$p < 0.05$, *$p < 0.1$

5.3 Robustness Check and Endogeneity Concerns

Alternative Measures. We substituted the CEO overconfidence measure for robustness testing. We employed three successively utilized measures: investment-based [23], earnings forecast-based [18], and composite indicator [23]. Nevertheless, the regression coefficients for CEO overconfidence consistently exhibit significant positivity across all measurement methods, affirming the robustness of our regression results.

Reverse Causation. Firms might intentionally appoint overconfident CEOs [8] due to their effectiveness in fostering firm innovation [7, 12], ultimately driving digital transformation. To mitigate endogeneity concerns, we lag the CEO's overconfidence and control variables by one period. The estimated coefficient remains significantly positive at the 1% level, indicating that CEO overconfidence propels firms to enhance their digital transformation. Therefore, even after addressing the endogeneity of reverse causality, the findings of this paper maintain their robustness.

Propensity Score Matching (PSM). PSM is employed to mitigate sample selection bias. Utilizing control variables, industry, and year dummies as characteristics, we perform logit regression to calculate propensity score values. Subsequently, we construct matched samples via 1:1 matching, 1:3 nearest-neighbor matching, radius matching, and kernel matching. After matching, the outcomes reveal that the average treatment effect on the treated (ATT) is significantly positive at the 1% level across all matching techniques, affirming the robustness of the paper's conclusions.

6 Discussion

This article investigates the influence of overconfident CEOs on enterprise digital transformation and the moderating role of organizational and environmental factors. Empirical analysis of data from Chinese listed companies indicates that CEO overconfidence actively facilitates the digital transformation of the enterprise. Additionally, CIOs and boards with IT backgrounds play crucial roles in moderating the impact of CEO overconfidence on digital transformation. Lastly, in a highly competitive environment, an overconfident CEO proves advantageous for the enterprise, effectively promoting digital transformation.

6.1 Theoretical Contributions

We have made several theoretical contributions. First, we extended our exploration of CEO overconfidence. Despite prior literature predominantly emphasizing the negative effects of CEO overconfidence [14, 16, 18, 21, 22], some scholars argue for its positive impact, especially concerning enhanced corporate innovation performance [7, 12] and risk-taking level [2]. Our analysis reinforces this 'bright side' of CEO overconfidence by revealing a positive correlation between CEO overconfidence and digital transformation.

Second, we advance the UET and contribute to the IS literature on CEO support for IT performance by observing the positive impact of CEO overconfidence on digital transformation. Based on the previous research highlighting the vital role of CEO attributes in the IT performance [1, 4–6, 10], our research focuses on how CEO cognitive characteristics affect IT performance. By investigating CEO overconfidence and uncovering its promoting effect on digital transformation, we further shed light on the importance of CEO support for IT-related activities.

Finally, we explore more moderating mechanisms of CEO overconfidence on digital transformation. Based on the previous literature showing the crucial roles of CIOs and boards in influencing and guiding digital activities effectively [1, 3, 5, 19], we further reveal their amplifying effects on the positive impact of CEO overconfidence on digital transformation. In addition, existing literature suggests that high industry competition can foster overconfidence and increase investment in corporate innovation [7]. We further discover that CEOs who are overconfident in a highly competitive environment can boost digital investment to drive digital transformation.

6.2 Practical Implications

Our research findings have practical implications. Firstly, companies should recognize the potentially positive role of overconfident CEOs, particularly in the current digital environment. Although digital transformation may involve prolonged challenges and substantial costs, enterprises that undergo this process often achieve significant success. Overconfident CEOs, with their enduring optimism toward corporate innovation [7, 12] and digital transformation, are willing to increase digital investment even in fiercely competitive industry environments. They can actively influence the organization's perception of digital technology and foster an innovative atmosphere, facilitating successful digital transformation.

Secondly, CIOs and boards should guide overconfident CEOs in making sound digital investments. An overly confident CEO's optimistic assessment of digital technology may lead to erroneous judgments, resulting in substantial economic losses for the company [14, 21]. The CIO and the board, heading IT functions and corporate strategy decision-making, respectively, should leverage their professional IT experience to offer valuable digital investment advice to the CEO [1, 5, 19], steering overconfident CEOs toward more effective digital transformation strategies.

6.3 Limitations and the Future of Research

This article acknowledges certain limitations that merit further investigation. Firstly, although we empirically analyzed data from Chinese listed companies to illustrate the positive impact of CEO overconfidence on digital transformation, we aim to enhance the robustness of this conclusion by collecting data from diverse countries and non-listed companies in future studies. Secondly, despite establishing a direct relationship between CEO overconfidence and digital transformation, the mediating mechanism remains unclear and requires in-depth exploration in subsequent research. Lastly, we plan to investigate the impact of additional psychological or personality factors, such as narcissism and humility in CEOs, on digital transformation. Furthermore, we intend to identify more contextual factors, such as CEO power, industry IT intensity, and so on.

Acknowledgement. This research was supported by the National Natural Science Foundation of China under Grants [72272039, 72101060]. We also sincerely appreciate the three anonymous reviewers for their critical and valuable review comments that greatly helped us improve this paper.

References

1. Bendig, D., Wagner, R., Piening, E.P., Foege, J.N.: Attention to digital innovation: exploring the impact of a chief information officer in the top management team. MIS Q. **47**(4), 1487–1516 (2023)

2. Burkhard, B., Sirén, C., van Essen, M., Grichnik, D., Shepherd, D.A.: Nothing ventured, nothing gained: a meta-analysis of CEO overconfidence, strategic risk taking, and performance. J. Manag., 84175202 (2022)
3. Chen, D.Q., Zhang, Y., Xiao, J., Xie, K.: Making digital innovation happen: a chief information officer issue selling perspective. Inf. Syst. Res. 32(3), 987–1008 (2021)
4. Choi, I., Chung, S., Han, K., Pinsonneault, A.: CEO risk-taking incentives and IT innovation: the moderating role of a CEO's IT-related human capital. MIS Q. 45(4), 2175–2192 (2021)
5. Filatotchev, I., Lanzolla, G., Syrigos, E.: Impact of CEO's digital technology orientation and board characteristics on firm value: a signaling perspective. J. Manage. (2023)
6. Firk, S., Gehrke, Y., Hanelt, A., Wolff, M.: Top management team characteristics and digital innovation: exploring digital knowledge and TMT interfaces. Long Range Plann. 55(3), 102166 (2022)
7. Galasso, A., Simcoe, T.S.: CEO overconfidence and innovation. Manage. Sci. 57(8), 1469–1484 (2011)
8. Goel, A.M., Thakor, A.V.: Overconfidence, CEO selection, and corporate governance. J. Financ. 63(6), 2737–2784 (2008)
9. Haislip, J., Lim, J., Pinsker, R.: The impact of executives' IT expertise on reported data security breaches. Inf. Syst. Res. 32(2), 318–334 (2021)
10. Haislip, J.Z., Richardson, V.J.: The effect of CEO IT expertise on the information environment: evidence from earnings forecasts and announcements. J. Inf. Syst. 32(2), 71–94 (2018)
11. Hambrick, D.C., Mason, P.A.: Upper echelons: the organization as a reflection of its top managers. Acad. Manag. Rev. 9(2), 193–206 (1984)
12. Hirshleifer, D., Low, A., Teoh, S.H.: Are overconfident CEOs better innovators? J. Financ. 67(4), 1457–1498 (2012)
13. Ho, J.L.Y., Wu, A., Xu, S.X.: Corporate governance and returns on information technology investment: evidence from an emerging market. Strateg. Manag. J. 32(6), 595–623 (2011)
14. Ho, P., Huang, C., Lin, C., Yen, J.: CEO overconfidence and financial crisis: evidence from bank lending and leverage. J. Financ. Econ. 120(1), 194–209 (2016)
15. Hu, Y., Che, D., Wu, F., Chang, X.: Corporate maturity mismatch and enterprise digital transformation: evidence from China. Financ. Res. Lett. 53, 103677 (2023)
16. Kim, J.B., Wang, Z., Zhang, L.: CEO overconfidence and stock price crash risk. Contemp. Account. Res. 33(4), 1720–1749 (2016)
17. Kong, D., Liu, B., Zhu, L.: Stem CEOs and firm digitalization. Financ. Res. Lett. 58, 104573 (2023)
18. Lee, J.M., Park, J.C., Chen, G.: A cognitive perspective on real options investment: CEO overconfidence. Strateg. Manag. J. 44(4), 1084–1110 (2023)
19. Li, J., Li, M., Wang, X., Bennett Thatcher, J.: Strategic directions for AI: the role of CIOs and boards of directors. MIS Q. 45(3), 1603–1644 (2021)
20. Liang, H., Saraf, N., Hu, Q., Xue, Y.: Assimilation of enterprise systems: the effect of institutional pressures and the mediating role of top management. MIS Q. 31(1), 59–87 (2007)
21. Malmendier, U., Tate, G.: CEO overconfidence and corporate investment. J. Financ. 60(6), 2661–2700 (2005)
22. Malmendier, U., Tate, G.: Who makes acquisitions? CEO overconfidence and the market's reaction. J. Financ. Econ. 89(1), 20–43 (2008)
23. Schrand, C.M., Zechman, S.L.C.: Executive overconfidence and the slippery slope to financial misreporting. J. Account. Econ. 53(1–2), 311–329 (2012)
24. Tang, Y., Li, J., Yang, H.: What i see, what i do: how executive hubris affects firm innovation. J. Manag. 41(6), 1698–1723 (2015)
25. Wade, M., Shan, J.: Covid-19 has accelerated digital transformation, but may have made it harder not easier. MIS Q. Executive 19, 213–220 (2020)

The Impact of Live Broadcast Content Inconsistency on Consumer Forgiveness Behavior

Zhao Chao[✉] and Yuqing Qi

Shenyang University of Technology, Shenyang 110870, China
zhaochao@sut.edu.cn

Abstract. In the context of Live streaming eCommerce, false publicity problems occur frequently. However, in the face of merchant fraud, some consumers will choose to forgive the merchant. The underlying mechanisms that generate this forgiving behavior when the content of the live broadcast does not match the actual product have not been fully explored. The focus of this study is on informational content inconsistency in Live streaming eCommerce context-product attributes content inconsistency and price promotion content inconsistency. Based on the Rational Behavior Theory (TRA) model, we propose a conceptual framework to understand whether, how, and when live broadcast content inconsistency affects consumer forgiveness behavior. Among them, the higher the degree of inconsistency of live broadcast content, the less forgiving consumers will be, and this effect is realized through the chain mediation of satisfaction and tolerance. In addition, these effects vary by product type. We discuss the theoretical and practical implications of these findings and identify several aspects for future research.

Keywords: Consumer Forgiveness Behavior · Live Broadcast Content · Inconsistency · Product Type · Product Attributes · Price Promotions

1 Introduction

With the development of digital technology, live streaming e-commerce has become a new format to stimulate consumption. According to data from CNNIC (2023), as of June 2023, the number of e-commerce live broadcast users in my country reached 562 million, an increase of 11.94 million from December 2022, accounting for 48.8% of the total Internet users. Traditional e-commerce only provides relevant information about product attributes. On this basis, live e-commerce integrates offline marketing scenarios into online channels. The anchor can display and introduce recommendations to remotely participating consumers in real time through immersive marketing products, and engage in emotional and product interactions with the audience [1]. However, live broadcast e-commerce also faces problems such as false propaganda, induced consumption, and dishonest operations by merchants. In order to deal with the increasingly serious problems of false propaganda and induced consumption, domestic and foreign scholars conduct research from different perspectives. Some scholars believe that consumers' corresponding behaviors when purchasing products that do not conform to expectations can also solve problems such as the false publicity of Live streaming eCommerce, such as consumers' turn complaint behavior and rights protection behavior, which will make merchants change from dishonest strategy to honest strategy to a certain extent.

But when consumers are deceived by merchants, unexpected consumer behavior— forgiving behavior may occur. Forgiveness behavior refers to a consumer's willingness to give up retaliation, alienation, and other destructive behaviors and respond in a constructive manner following an organizational breach of trust and related recovery efforts [2]. The reason why consumer forgiveness behavior attracts attention is that obtaining forgiveness is an important goal of all companies, and consumer forgiveness will affect consumer satisfaction, repurchase intention, word-of-mouth, etc. Among them, research shows that consumer forgiveness will have a negative effect on avoidance and retaliation behaviors [3]. Therefore, understanding consumers' forgiveness behavior has theoretical and practical significance for governing merchant fraud. Previous research has shown that the content in e-commerce live broadcasts mainly contains information-based content [4]. This raises a question: In the context of live broadcast e-commerce, does the inconsistency between information-based live broadcast content and the actual product situation (hereinafter referred to as live broadcast content inconsistency) have an impact on consumer forgiveness behavior?

In the traditional consumer behavior research of e-commerce, the research on forgiveness behavior mostly focuses on how remedial measures affect consumer forgiveness in online shopping failure situations [5]. There are few studies on the factors that influence consumer forgiveness behavior as merchants remedy and apologize for their online shopping failure. In studies of service failure in other traditional industries, it has been demonstrated whether service failure affects consumer forgiveness. Service failure negatively affects forgiving behavior, but this effect can be amplified or attenuated [6]. More importantly, service failures may have different effects in traditional eCommerce industries than they do in Live streaming eCommerce because the consumer-merchant relationship in the two scenarios is different, which affects how consumers handle and respond to merchant service failures. Live streaming eCommerce creates more social interaction environments for consumers and merchants than traditional eCommerce and traditional industries, where online relationships between consumers and service providers may be personal and friendly [7], which may make consumer forgiveness for service failures more likely to occur based on the blind effect of love [8]. But the consumer-merchant relationship can also hinder consumer forgiveness, as loyal consumers feel more betrayed after service violations than disloyal consumers [9]. Our study aims to gain a deeper understanding of consumer forgiveness behavior by examining the role of informational content inconsistency on consumer forgiveness in a live broadcast context. Although merchant fraud involving inconsistent live streaming content is currently widespread, little is known about whether, how, and when live streaming content inconsistency affects consumers' forgiving behavior. In this article, we mainly answer the following three questions.

First, does the inconsistency of live broadcast content affect consumers' forgiving behavior? Although studies of product service failures have shown that product attributes information inconsistent with advertising has a negative impact on consumer forgiveness behavior [10], whether the inconsistency of live broadcast content will negatively affect the forgiveness behavior of consumers is still a question to be studied. Because the quality of the relationship between consumers and merchants in the live broadcast situation is stronger than that in the traditional e-commerce situation, so it is very important to study whether the service failure in the live broadcast situation will trigger the blind effect of love or the love-hate effect.

In summary, we examine whether, how, and when live broadcast content inconsistency affects consumer forgiveness behavior. Our work adds to the research on consumer forgiveness behavior and, more broadly, the impact of service failure on consumer forgiveness behavior in the field of live streaming e-commerce. Our research also provides practical implications for live streaming e-commerce players, including live streaming platforms, and consumers.

2 Theoretical Development and Hypotheses

Our research model is based on TRA, which has been widely used by researchers in the field of consumer behavior. TRA believes that subjective norms and attitudes towards behavior influence consumer behavior through behavioral intentions. Attitudes toward a behavior are people's positive or negative emotional reactions to a behavior; subjective norms are a person's perception that most people important to him or her think he or she should or should not perform the behavior [11]. Current research on consumer forgiveness behavior is mostly based on the theoretical perspective of the ABC attitude model, which focuses on the role of emotional factors. Researchers believe that consumers' negative emotions after service failure are an important factor affecting forgiveness, especially anger. In contrast, the impact of attitudes on forgiving behavior has received less attention. Therefore, TRA provides a new theoretical perspective for understanding the role of content inconsistency on forgiveness behavior in live broadcast situations.

2.1 Live Broadcast Content Inconsistency and Consumer Forgiveness Behavior

In this paper, we explore the impact of live broadcast content inconsistency on consumer forgiveness behavior. According to the definition of comment consistency, we define live broadcast content inconsistency as the degree of difference between the informational content of live advertising and the product itself.

In the context of Live streaming eCommerce, due to the high interactivity of Live streaming eCommerce, consumers and live merchants may develop quasi-romantic relationships, which will drive individuals to have higher levels of expectations for anchors [12]. After generating high levels of expectation, consumers' love for live merchants tends to turn into hatred if they are cheated by live merchants [13]. At the same time, consumer forgiveness behavior is related to the degree of service failure. When the perceived severity of failure is low, consumers tend to control the emotion caused by discomfort, thus producing more positive evaluation and behavior intention; when the perceived severity of failure is high, consumers tend to make negative judgments. The more severe the failure, the harder it is for consumers to forgive [14]. Therefore, we speculate that in the situation of Live streaming eCommerce, when the purchased products do not conform to the public, consumers will avoid and retaliate against the merchants, and the higher the degree of non-conformity, the more negative attitudes consumers will stimulate. Thus, choosing not to forgive the live broadcast merchants.

H1: The inconsistency of live broadcast content has a negative impact on consumers' forgiveness behavior, and the lower the degree of inconsistency, the more likely consumers are to forgive the merchant.

2.2 The Mediating Role of Satisfaction and Tolerance

We believe that the inconsistency of live broadcast content affects consumer tolerance by affecting consumer satisfaction, and ultimately has an impact on consumer forgiveness behavior. Satisfaction refers to a consumer's perception of whether the product or service paid and received during the purchase process is appropriate. Tolerance refers to the degree of tolerance and acquiescence of people towards certain things or phenomena. The definition of tolerance in this article mainly refers to the degree of acquiescence and tolerance of consumers for the differences between the purchased goods and the goods promoted during the live broadcast.

The reason why we focus on these two mediating variables is that previous literature usually treats consumer satisfaction and tolerance as outcome variables [15], but satisfaction is also a key antecedent variable in the consumer decision-making process [16]. At present, there are few studies on the impact of tolerance on behavior, and most of them focus on uncertainty tolerance and corruption tolerance.

First, based on cognitive dissonance theory, we proposed that inconsistency in live broadcast content negatively affects consumer satisfaction. Cognitive dissonance refers to an uncomfortable or tense psychological state caused by factors such as conflicting information in the environment, inconsistency between one's own beliefs and actions, or new information [17]. Because individuals have difficulty processing contradictory information, the presence of live broadcast content inconsistencies—direct contradictions between what is shown and promoted on the live broadcast and what is actually happening—increases cognitive dissonance. Increased cognitive dissonance has a negative impact on consumer satisfaction. According to cognitive dissonance theory, when consumers' expectations are inconsistent with reality, a state of dissonance will occur, in which case they adopt a series of strategies to reduce dissonance, thereby adversely affecting their attitudes. Benlian observed this effect in a study of information systems usage, whereby the higher the perceived congruence between IS professionals and IS users, the higher the user satisfaction [18]. At the same time, this state of dissonance usually varies according to the severity of the problem and the degree of inconsistency [19]. Generally, the higher the perceived inconsistency, the higher the psychological discomfort felt. We believe this also applies to situations where consumers are dissatisfied with live broadcast promotions when purchasing products from live streaming e-commerce. From this, we derive the following hypothesis:

H2: Inconsistency in live broadcast content has a negative impact on consumer satisfaction, and the higher the degree of inconsistency, the lower consumer satisfaction.

Satisfaction has an important impact on consumer tolerance. Tolerance appeared earlier in the field of venture capital and has now been widely used in the fields of finance, political science, and management. We believe that consumer satisfaction positively affects tolerance. Recent positive psychology research suggests that higher levels of satisfaction produce positive cognitive and affective states. And people who feel positive emotions exhibit more tolerant attitudes than people who feel negative [20]. Therefore, high-satisfaction consumers will be more tolerant than low-satisfaction consumers.

H3: Consumer satisfaction has a positive impact on tolerance.

Tolerance, in turn, influences consumers' forgiving behavior. Consumer tolerance represents the consumer's acceptance of product defects in attributes or other aspects, which may cause anxiety or uneasiness. Because people don't like to be in a dissonant state, they use different strategies to recover from such negative mental states. Rationalization is one such strategy [21], through which consumers can reduce negative emotions. When consumers feel more threatened, they engage in a greater number of rationalizing behaviors. Therefore, the higher consumers' tolerance for inconsistency in live broadcast content, the stronger their rationalization psychology. Chen, J (2022) found that the stronger the rationalization psychology of consumers, the more they will actively avoid adverse information in the purchasing process, thereby making their purchasing and consumption activities reasonable. In the research context of this article, we believe that consumers with higher levels of tolerance are more likely to engage in forgiving behavior. When high-tolerance consumers purchase products that are falsely advertised, they will rationalize the inconsistency and forgive the merchant.

H4: Tolerance has a positive impact on consumer tolerance behavior.

2.3   The Moderating Effect of Product Type

Informational content can be divided into product attribute content and price promotion content [22], so the live broadcast content inconsistency in this paper includes product attribute content inconsistency and price promotion content inconsistency. Product attribute content inconsistency refers to the degree of difference between the main attributes (i.e. features or functions) of the product and the corresponding attributes advertised in the live broadcast, while price promotion content inconsistency refers to the degree of difference between the price paid by the product when purchasing the product and the price when the live broadcast is advertised.

Next, we focus on the moderating effect of product type. Products can be divided into practical products and hedonic products based on consumers' motivations for purchasing products and services. Hedonic products refer to goods whose consumption is mainly characterized by emotional and sensory experiences of aesthetic or sensory pleasure, fantasy, and fun, while the consumption of practical products is more cognitively driven, instrumental, goal-oriented, and completion-oriented. Functional or practical tasks [23]. Previous research has shown that there are differences in the information that consumers pay attention to when purchasing these two types of products. Compared with utilitarian products, consumers pay more attention to the price of hedonic products. When hedonic products are provided at free prices, people's relative preference for hedonic products will be disproportionately enhanced [24]; consumers are more willing to pay a premium for practical products than for hedonic products [25]; consumers mainly improve their satisfaction in life areas by frequently consuming hedonic products at low prices. Therefore, when consumers purchase hedonic products, consumers are less able to accept deception at the price level than deception at the product attribute level. Faced with deception at the product price level, consumers will choose to avoid or retaliate to a greater extent than the merchant. On the contrary, when consumers purchase practical products, consumers are more inclined to capture attribute information such as product features and functions. When faced with differences between the attributes of the actual purchased product and the advertised attributes, it may be difficult for consumers to reconcile Conflicting opinions make it more likely that you will be unwilling to forgive the merchant for deception. Based on the above discussion, we propose the following hypotheses:

H5: Product type will moderate the impact of two types of live broadcast content inconsistency - product attributes content inconsistency and price promotion content inconsistency on consumer forgiveness behavior.

H5a: When purchasing practical products, consumers are more likely to forgive inconsistencies in price promotion content than inconsistencies in product attribute content.

H5b: When purchasing hedonic products, consumers are more likely to forgive inconsistencies in product attribute content than inconsistencies in price promotion content.

3 Study1

3.1 Experimental Design and Participants

Experiment 1 was designed with one-factor two-level between-subject design. We recruited 72 registered users of Credamo to participate in the experiment. They were randomly assigned to one of two scenarios: high or low live broadcast content inconsistency.

3.2 Experimental Stimuli and Pretests

For attributes content inconsistency, we create a scenario where the primary attributes of the digital camera purchased by the consumer do not match the primary attributes advertised. This scenario describes two main attributes of the advertised product in the live broadcast room and the actual experience of consumers with these two attributes, among which the main attributes are the autofocus function and ease of operation of the camera. First, we manipulate the degree of inconsistency in the content of product attributes by varying the amount to which the primary attributes of digital cameras differ from the primary attributes experienced by consumers. Specifically, in the context of low attributes content inconsistency, live broadcast merchants claim that the digital camera has an autofocus function and is easy to operate, but in fact consumers find that the digital camera is convenient to operate after experience, but the autofocus function is inconsistent with the live broadcast promotional content. In the context of high attributes content inconsistency, both attributes experienced by consumers are inconsistent with live advertising content. We recruited 70 participants, randomly assigned to one of four scenarios, to test the validity of these manipulations, culling the invalid samples to yield 68 valid samples. In the pre-experiment, participants' perceptions of inconsistency between product attributes and price promotion content were measured with reference to the Huang Minxue et al. (2018) scale (Cronbach's α live broadcast content inconsistency = 0.865). The pre-experiment results showed that perceived inconsistency was significantly higher in the high attribute content inconsistency scenario than in the low attribute content inconsistency scenario (M high live broadcast content inconsistency = 5.67, SD high live broadcast content inconsistency = 1.42; M low live broadcast content inconsistency = 4.70, SD low live broadcast content inconsistency = 1.44; t (66) = − 2.763, p < 0.05).

3.3 Procedure and Measures

After reading the instructions, participants were asked to imagine that they wanted to buy a digital camera, happened to see the anchor introducing a new brand of digital camera in the live broadcast room, and made the purchase after seeing the camera attributes described by the attribute, and then showed the actual attributes of the camera after purchase. After reading the material, as a manipulation test, we measured the extent to which consumers perceived inconsistencies in the live broadcast content, and then the participants rated the consumer's forgiveness behavior according to their own feelings.

All measurements were scored on a 7-point Likert scale (1 = "strongly disagree", 7 = "strongly agree"). Consumer forgiveness behavior was adapted according to McCullough et al. (1998) Interpersonal Aggression Motivation Scale and combined with Live streaming eCommerce situation, and was measured from two dimensions: revenge intention and avoidance intention. The degree of inconsistency of live broadcast content is based on Huang Minxue et al. (2018) scale. Finally, participants filled in basic personal information.

4 Study2

4.1 Experimental Design, Participants and Pretests

Experiment 2 was also done online, and we recruited participants from Credamo. They were randomly assigned to one of eight scenarios in a 2 (live broadcast content inconsistency: product attributes content inconsistency vs. price promotion content inconsistency) × 2 (degree: high vs. low) × 2 (product type: utility vs. pleasure) between-subjects design.

We used the same stimulus as in study 1, manipulating the degree of attribute content inconsistency by changing the number of main attributes. For price promotion content inconsistency, we created a situation in which the anchor advertised that the price of the product was historically low in the broadcast room. This scenario describes the price of a product purchased by a consumer in a live broadcast room and the price of the product in the same live broadcast room at different times. We manipulate the inconsistency of price promotion content by changing the deviation between the two prices. Price deviation is set to 5% in case of low price promotion inconsistency and 15% in case of high price promotion inconsistency.

The purpose of the pre-experiment is to select suitable utility products and enjoyment products and determine the main attributes of the products. By combing the relevant literature, we select U disk, detergent, calculator, shampoo as practical products; perfume, jewelery, yogurt, chocolate as enjoyment products. In the pilot experiment (n = 116), we first explained the definitions of utility and pleasure products to participants and showed them pictures of each product. Then each participant was asked to judge eight product types. We used the method of Dhar et al. (2010) to judge the type of product. Specifically, the researcher rated the subject score greater than 4 as a hedonistic product and less than 4 as a practical product. The experimental results show that the detergent has the lowest mean value, less than 4, and has strong practical product attributes. (M = 1.56, SD = 1.182), whereas jewelry has the highest mean value, and more than 4, with strong hedonistic product attributes (M = 5.87, SD = 1.748). Paired sample T test showed that there was a significant difference between the two products in product type (T = −23.499, p < 0.001). Therefore, in study 2, we chose detergent as the experimental stimulus of practical products and jewelry as the experimental stimulus of hedonic products. Next, we climbed the comments on detergent and jewelry from JD.com, classified and integrated the evaluations of the two types of products, and confirmed the product attributes that often appeared. A questionnaire was formed by randomly coding. Participants (n = 30) were asked to rank product attributes according to their importance, choosing three important attributes for two types of products based on how often they chose attributes. The results showed that important attributes of detergent included cleaning power (n = 28), composition (n = 25) and smell (n = 21), and important attributes of jew included style (n = 28), quality (n = 27) and documentation (n = 23).

4.2 Procedure and Measures

The experiment flow is the same as study 1. After the beginning of the experiment, we show the situational materials to each group, and only add the experimental manipulation of product type after the situational display. In this paper, we use the single-item Likert seven-point scale of Dhar et al. (2000) to measure the manipulation of product type. The procedure for manipulating the degree of inconsistency of live broadcast content was similar to that of study 1. Next, the subjects were asked to fill out a measurement item of consumer forgiveness behavior, which was measured using the same scale as the previous study, consisting of seven items such as "I will make this live merchant pay". Finally, we complete the statistics of the demographic information of the subjects.

5 Study3

5.1 Method

A 2 (live broadcast content inconsistency: product attributes content inconsistency vs. price promotion content inconsistency) × 2 (degree: high vs. low) × 2 (product type: practical vs. hedonic) between-subjects design was used in this experiment.

According to the results and criteria of the pre-experiment in study 2, the USB flash drive with a lower score was selected as the practical product (M = 1.66, SD = 1.244), and the perfume with a higher score was selected as the enjoyment product (M = 5.42, SD = 2.907). The previous test (n = 116) confirmed that there was a significant difference between USB flash drive and perfume in product type (T = −18.260, p < 0.001). In order to determine the important attributes of USB flash drives and perfumes, we followed the steps of the second pre-experiment, crawling random brand USB flash drives and perfumes from JD.com, integrating the reviews, and identifying the frequently appearing product attributes. A questionnaire was formed by randomly coding. Participants (n = 30) were asked to rank product attributes according to their importance, choosing three important attributes for two types of products based on how often they chose attributes. The results showed that important attributes of USB stick included capacity (n = 25), portability (n = 21) and durability (n = 18), and important attributes of perfume included odor (n = 29), durability (n = 29) and appearance (n = 15).

We used the same scenarios and stimuli as in study 1 to create experimental scenarios. After reading the situational material, participants were asked to answer questions that measured the degree of inconsistency in the live broadcast content. After explaining to them the meaning of practical products and hedonic products, the participants were asked to judge the product types of the material using the same scale as in the previous study. After all the manipulations were completed, the subjects were asked to fill out the satisfaction, tolerance and forgiveness measures. According to Oliver et al. (1980), Mano et al. (1993) and live broadcast situation, the measurement of consumer forgiveness behavior is composed of 5 items, such as "I am very satisfied with this purchase decision"; Tolerance refers to the measurement item of tolerance for false advertising in Bae S et al. (2022), and combines with the actual determination of the item of this study, which consists of two items: "I can accept the behavior of live broadcast merchants to publish deceptive publicity content". Likert 7-point scale was used for all the above scales, with 1 being complete disagreement and 7 being complete agreement.

6 Discussion

6.1 Theoretical Implications

As more and more attention is paid to forgiving behavior, there is a considerable amount of research exploring the factors that influence forgiving behavior. Our study expands on this research in the following ways.

First, previous studies focused on service failure situations such as product mismatching or product quality problems. Our study considered not only the impact of product attributes content inconsistency on customer forgiveness, but also the impact of promotion failure on customer forgiveness. Our research shows that live broadcast content inconsistency has a negative impact on consumer forgiveness behavior, and the higher the degree of inconsistency, the less consumers choose to forgive merchants. Second, unlike previous studies, which only considered the mechanism of service failure on consumer forgiveness from the emotional point of view, our results show that service failure can affect forgiveness behavior through consumer attitudes, at least for live broadcast content inconsistency. The findings advance our understanding of how false advertising on Live streaming eCommerce affects consumer behavior. Third, our findings also contribute significantly to the mediating role of satisfaction and tolerance. Early studies focused on exploring the antecedents of tolerance, and few studies discussed the impact of tolerance on consumer behavior. Our research confirms that consumer satisfaction affects tolerance, and makes a theoretical contribution to tolerance research. Finally, we found differences in the impact of live broadcast content inconsistency on consumer forgiveness behavior. We also found that consumers tend to forgive inconsistencies in price promotion content if they buy utility products, and they are more likely to forgive inconsistencies in product attributes content if they buy hedonistic products. In the existing research on traditional e-commerce service failure, the role of product attributes in consumer forgiveness behavior has been ignored. We supplemented this gap in the context of Live streaming eCommerce, and our findings highlight the importance of understanding the impact of live broadcast content inconsistency on consumer forgiveness behavior from a product perspective.

6.2 Practical Implications

Our research also provides inspiration for Live streaming eCommerce platforms and consumers. We find that the lower the degree of inconsistency of live broadcast content, the more forgiving consumers will be, and the higher the degree of inconsistency, the less forgiving consumers will be. Therefore, in order to reduce consumers' forgiveness behavior and promote merchants' integrity propaganda, the platform should take measures to encourage consumers who buy goods with low inconsistency to return goods, complain or take punitive measures against merchants. For example, the platform can focus on monitoring the publicity of the main attributes of the product by the anchor in the live broadcast. When it is found that the publicity of one of the attributes is inconsistent with the actual situation, it will issue a warning to the merchant and take corresponding punishment measures. Consumers in this situation should also improve the awareness of rights protection, and do not fear trouble and not return goods, do not protect rights. Our study also highlights the moderating role of product type. When buying hedonistic products, people tend to pay more attention to the consistency of price promotion content and ignore the difference in product attributes; when they buy practical products, they tend to pay more attention to the consistency of product attribute content and ignore the difference in price promotion. Therefore, the platform should disclose information according to different products. For example, the platform should disclose the price fluctuation of the product in the past week on the interface of the practical product, while the interface of the hedonic product should provide the relevant attribute information of the product, so as to ensure that consumers have some understanding of the price of the practical product and the attributes of the hedonic product.

6.3 Limitations and Future Research

Our research has certain limitations, and future research can be improved in the following aspects. First, this article is only theoretical deduction, research conclusions need to be tested. In the following research, we can use online experiments to verify the hypothesis of this paper. Second, in Live streaming eCommerce platform, platform policies and merchant services may also have an impact on consumer forgiveness behavior. Future research can explore the role of different platform strategies and merchant strategies in the impact of live content inconsistency on forgiving behavior.

References

1. Chen, X.Y., Shen, J.Y., Wei, S.B.: What reduces product uncertainty in live streaming e-commerce? From a signal consistency perspective. J. Retail. Consum. Serv. **74**, 103441 (2023)
2. Xie, Y., Peng, S.Q.: How to repair customer trust after negative publicity: the roles of competence, integrity, benevolence, and forgiveness. Psychol. Mark. **26**(7), 572–589 (2009)
3. Rasouli, N., Rasoolimanesh, S.M., Rahmani, A.K., et al.: Effects of customer forgiveness on brand betrayal and brand hate in restaurant service failures: does apology letter matter? J. Hosp. Market. Manag. **31**(6), 662–687 (2022)
4. Kumar, A., Bezawada, R., Rishika, R., et al.: From social to sale: the effects of firm generated content in social media on customer behavior. J. Market. **80**, 7–25 (2016)
5. Wei, J., Wang, Z., Hou, Z., et al.: The influence of empathy and consumer forgiveness on the service recovery effect of online shopping. Front. Psychol. **13** (2022)
6. Alnawas, I., Al Khateeb, A., Abu Farha, A., et al.: The effect of service failure severity on brand forgiveness: the moderating role of interpersonal attachment styles and thinking styles. Int. J. Contemp. Hosp. Manage. **35**(5), 1691–1712 (2023)
7. Fu, X., Pang, J., Gursoy, D.: Effects of online commercial friendships on customer revenge following a service failure. J. Bus. Res. **153**, 102–114 (2022)
8. Kordrostami, M., Kordrostami, E.: Secure or fearful, who will be more resentful? Investigating the interaction between regulatory focus and attachment style. J. Prod. Brand Manag. **28**(5), 671–683 (2019)
9. Wolter, J.S., Bacile, T.J., Smith, J.S., et al.: The entitlement/forgiveness conflict of self-relevant and self-neutral relationships during service failure and recovery. J. Bus. Res. **104**(C), 233–246 (2019)
10. Kim, A., Dennis, A.R.: Says who? The effects of presentation format and source rating on fake news in social media. MIS Q. **43**(3), 1025–1039 (2019)
11. Fishbein, M.A., Ajzen, I.: Belief, attitude, intention and behaviour: an introduction to theory and research (1975)
12. Fehr, E., Gächter, S.: Fairness and retaliation: the economics of reciprocity. J. Econ. Perspect. **14**(3), 159–181 (2000)
13. Grégoire, Y., Tripp, T.M., Legoux, R.: When customer love turns into lasting hate: the effects of relationship strength and time on customer revenge and avoidance. J. Mark. **73**(6), 18–32 (2009)
14. Riek, B.M., Mania, E.W.: The antecedents and consequences of interpersonal forgiveness: a meta-analytic review. Pers. Relat. **19**(2), 304–325 (2011)
15. Alexander, D., Boone, C., Lynn, M.: The effects of tip recommendations on customer tipping, satisfaction, repatronage, and spending. Manage. Sci. **67**(1), 146–165 (2021)
16. Wang, S., Chen, T., Wang, C., et al.: The effect of customer satisfaction on floral product purchase behavior, evidence from Shanghai, China. Sci. Rep. **13**(1), 7945 (2023)
17. Leon, F.: A Theory of Cognitive Dissonance. Stanford University Press, Stanford (2020)
18. Alexander, B.: Effect mechanisms of perceptual congruence between information systems professionals and users on satisfaction with service. J. Manag. Inf. Syst. **29**(4), 63–96 (2014)
19. Szajna, B., Scamell, R.W.: The effects of information system user expectations on their performance and perceptions. MIS Q. **17**(4), 493–516 (1993)
20. Tenenbaum, H.R., Capelos, T., Lorimer, J., et al.: Positive thinking elevates tolerance: experimental effects of happiness on adolescents' attitudes toward asylum seekers. Clin. Child Psychol. Psychiat. **23**(2), 346–357 (2018)

21. Quilty-Dunn, J.: Rationalization is irrational and self-serving, but useful. Behav. Brain Sci. **43** (2020)

22. Choi, B., Lee, I.: Trust in open versus closed social media: the relative influence of user- and marketer-generated content in social network services on customer trust. Telemat. Inform. **34**(5), 550–559 (2017)

23. Dhar, R., Wertenbroch, K.: Consumer choice between hedonic and utilitarian goods. J. Mark. Res. **37**(1), 60–71 (2000)

24. Hossain, M.T., Saini, R.: Free indulgences: enhanced zero-price effect for hedonic options. Int. J. Res. Mark. **32**(4), 457–460 (2015)

25. Wei, Q., Lv, D., Lin, Y.X., et al.: Influence of utilitarian and hedonic attributes on willingness to pay green product premiums and neural mechanisms in China: an ERP study. Sustainability **15**(3), 2403 (2023)

Research on the Influence Mechanism of Blind Box Product Characteristics on Consumers' Purchase Intention

Linmei Zhan and Ying Xiong[⊠]

Economics and Management College, China University of Geosciences, Wuhan, China
thamansa@126.com

Abstract. In recent years, blind boxes have won the favor of consumers by virtue of their mysterious and uncertain features as well as their delicate and lovely shapes, and have become a social bond between young consumer groups. Based on the SOR model, this paper introduces consumer sentiment and product involvement as mediating and moderating variables to construct a theoretical model for the study of the influence mechanism of blind box product characteristics on consumer purchase intention. The results show that the uncertainty, sociality, aesthetics and interestingness of the blind box have a positive effect on consumer purchase intention, and the two dimensions of consumer emotions (pleasure and arousal) play a mediating role. The product involvement negatively moderates the effect of the sociality, aesthetics and interestingness of the blind box on consumers' purchase intention, but its moderating effect is not significant in the effect of the uncertainty of the blind box on consumer purchase intention.

Keywords: Blind box · Purchase intention · Consumer sentiment · Product involvement

1 Introduction

With the development of economy and culture, consumers will pay extra attention to the spiritual consumption experience that the goods can bring while pursuing the practicality of the goods, and this consumption pattern can be called self-consumption. As a representative of self-consumption, "blind box" has gradually become a "star" product with high attention. Blind Boxes refers to commodities being sold in a closed, opaque box, and consumers do not know the specific style of the purchased goods before opening the box. Since 2017, with the hot rise of Bubble Mart, the blind box has become a common economic phenomenon. Since then, stationery blind boxes, beauty blind boxes, and airline ticket blind boxes have sprung up, and various industries have begun to draw on the marketing model of blind boxes to sell their products [1]. According to the *"2020 Blind Box Economic Insight Report"* released by Mob Research Institute, the market size of China's blind box industry is expected to grow from 7.4 billion yuan in 2019 to 30 billion yuan in 2024. However, behind the "blind box heat", it has also caused the phenomenon of consumers' lack of rationality and blind consumption, and the social criticism of the blind box industry has gradually increased. Therefore, in order to understand the reasons behind the "blind box fever", to help the design and marketing of blind box enterprises to provide theoretical guidance, to allow consumers to set up the correct consumption concepts, and to allow society to guide the healthy development of the blind box industry, it is of great practical significance to study the factors affecting the consumer willingness of blind box products.

Previous studies on blind box mostly focused on product design or marketing strategy, or based on perceived value and customer experience to study the influencing factors of blind box consumption behavior. However, there are relatively few researches on the influence of blind box product features on consumers' purchase intention. Based on SOR theory, this paper introduces consumer emotion as an intermediary variable to study the influence mechanism of blind box product characteristics on consumers' purchase intention. Since consumers with different levels of involvement react and deal with products in different ways, this paper takes product involvement as a regulating variable to reveal that different product involvement degrees will affect the relationship between the characteristics of blind box products and consumers' purchase intention.

2 Literature Review and Research Hypothesis

2.1 S-O-R Theory

SOR theory was first proposed by Mehrabian and Russell. It is mainly used to explain how external stimuli in the physical environment affect individuals' internal affective and cognitive states and thus influence their behavioral responses. It consists of three main elements: stimulus (S), which refers to a certain attribute in the physical environment, such as product features, promotion, price, layout, etc.; organism (O), which refers to the intermediate emotional and cognitive states produced by the individual when interacting with the stimulus; and response (R), which refers to the behavioral reaction shown by the individual after being stimulated by the physical environment [2]. The model provides a new idea and research framework for subsequent scholars to study consumer behavior. Therefore, this study chose the SOR theory as the research framework to build the model, using the blind box characteristics as the stimulus, which can make consumers produce emotional and cognitive responses, and then trigger the corresponding purchase behavior.

2.2 Blind Box Product Characteristics and Purchase Intention

The concept of "blind box" originated from the "lucky bag" promotion method in Japan. Wang et al. [3] proposed in their study of blind box consumption that blind boxes have the attributes of unknown, aesthetic, collectability and socialization. Gao et al. [4] combined with the characteristics of apparel products to classify the attributes of apparel blind boxes into five dimensions, which are aesthetics, socialization, uncertainty, symbolic, and innovativeness. Zhang [5] argued that the "blindness" of the blind box is interesting and anonymous in his study of blind box product packaging. To summarize, this paper classifies the characteristics of blind boxes into uncertainty, sociality, aesthetics and interestingness based on previous studies.

Blind boxes are the embodiment of young people's pursuit of life experience and subjective happiness, behind which lies the kernel of emotional consumption. Under the blind box economy, merchants will reveal the "rules of the game" to consumers and hide the product information in an appropriate amount, so as to stimulate the curiosity of consumers about the specific style of the product in the blind box, and make consumers generate consumption motivation. In today's social media era, blind box enthusiasts will share their shopping experiences through close social interactions with groups of people who share common interests and values through social platforms. If the products consumers buy or share can bring them added value such as identity or praise from others in social situations, it will lead to a stronger willingness to buy. Usually, the modeling of blind box products is usually based on the style elements that young groups like, which is in line with the trend and can bring consumers a good visual feeling and aesthetic experience. The good visual effect will affect consumers' evaluation of the product and their desire to own it. At the same time, compared with traditional goods, consumers buying blind box goods can bring more fun and sense of anticipation, from recognizing the blind box to purchasing the goods to the anticipation of the goods, and finally opening the box to unveil the "mystery", the process is easy, enjoyable, and attractive. Therefore, this study proposes the following hypothesis:

H1a: The uncertainty of blind box has positive effect on consumer purchase intention.
H1b: The sociality of blind box has positive effect on consumer purchase intention.
H1c: The aesthetics of blind box has positive effect on consumers purchase intention.
H1d: The interestingness of blind box has positive effect on consumer purchase intention.

2.3 Blind Box Characteristics and Consumer Emotion

Oliver [6] introduced emotions into the field of marketing earlier and defined consumer emotions as a set of emotional responses resulting from an individual's perception of the performance and attributes of a product or service. Subsequently, Mehrabian and Russell [7] proposed a two-dimensional model of PA, which categorized emotions into two dimensions: pleasure and arousal, where pleasure refers to the degree to which an individual feels happy or satisfied, and arousal refers to the degree to which an individual is stimulated by the environment.

The generation of consumer emotions usually has a close relationship with its surrounding environment. In addition, some scholars have also pointed out that product attributes also affect consumer emotions, which in turn affects consumer purchasing behavior [8]. For the blind box, what consumers want more is the thrill of shopping and the joy that comes from unwrapping the box and seeing the goods. Shen et al. [9] believe that uncertainty can be a source of positive experience, which can increase consumer pleasure and satisfaction. Blind box belongs to a kind of probability products, consumers have to draw their favorite style by luck. Consumers will make guesses and inferences about the specific style of the product in the box during the process of "unboxing", which will give them unlimited fantasies, forming an instantaneous hedonic experience for them and instantly increasing their positive emotions when their initial guesses are verified. From picking a blind box to opening the box to verify the guess, the whole process is full of entertainment and fun, and this fun will evoke continuous pleasure and excitement in consumers. In addition, the blind box, whether it is the outer packaging or the specific product inside the box, has the aesthetic characteristics of delicacy, cuteness, and colorfulness, so consumers will be visually attracted by the appearance of the product displayed on the product's outer packaging or on the promotional pictures to attract their attention and generate positive emotions such as surprise [10]. Consumers gradually form network interest groups on social media, using the blind box as a link to establish network identity and gain social benefits such as recognition from others. This can bring consumers a sense of belonging and identity and satisfy their needs for emotional comfort and flexible socialization. Therefore, this study proposes the following hypothesis:

H2a: The uncertainty of the blind box has positive effect on pleasure emotion.
H2b: The sociality of the blind box has positive effect on pleasure emotion.
H2c: The aesthetics of the blind box has positive effect on pleasure emotion.
H2d: The interestingness of the blind box has positive effect on pleasure emotion.
H3a: The uncertainty of the blind box has positive effect on arousal emotion.
H3b: The sociality of the blind box has positive effect on arousal emotion.
H3c: The aesthetics of the blind box has positive effect on arousal emotion.
H3d: The interestingness of the blind box has positive effect on arousal emotion.

2.4   Consumer Emotion and Purchase Intention

Consumers' purchase intention will be affected by consumer sentiment, no matter whether this consumer sentiment comes from consumers themselves or consumers' consumption experience. Consumers' purchase intention will be affected by consumer sentiment, no matter whether this consumer sentiment comes from consumers themselves or consumers' consumption experience. Consumer emotional responses triggered by product attributes are directly related to consumers' purchase intention, satisfaction evaluation and reputation [8]. When consumers trigger positive emotions due to stimuli, they will take a series of behaviors to affect the occurrence and expression of emotions, such as the desire to own products. Blind box is essentially a hedonic product, which can bring users a sense of beauty or pleasure, such as feelings, fun, emotions, etc. The continuous positive emotional response of consumers will gradually cause their desire to buy, which may make consumers exceed the original purchase plan. Therefore, the following hypothesis is proposed in this study:

H4a: Pleasure emotion has positive effect on consumer purchase intention.
H4b: Arousal emotion has positive effect on consumer purchase intention.

2.5   The Mediating Role of Consumer Emotion

In existing research, scholars have conducted in-depth studies on consumer emotions and the mediating role they play between consumer cognition and behavior. According to the SOR theory, it is known that external factor stimuli will cause consumers to produce internal psychological changes such as emotions and cognition, thus producing a series of behaviors. Based on the SOR theory, He [11] took online reviews as an external stimulus and found that the quality of online reviews positively affects impulse shopping intention through arousing emotions, and the number of online reviews positively affects impulse shopping intention through pleasurable emotions. Some scholars believe that the stimulus that causes an individual to produce an emotional response may come from the environment or the product itself, and it will also cause an individual to have a strong desire to buy. Blind box is a gamified, emotional and artistic product. Consumers can experience pleasure and excitement in the process of interacting with blind box lovers, and its cute, pious, delicate and rounded design can also bring positive emotional experience to players, arouse consumers' sense of arousal and stimulate pleasant emotions, thus promoting purchase intention and behavior. Therefore, this study proposes the following hypothesis:

H5a: Pleasure emotion mediate the relationship between the uncertainty of blind box and consumer purchase intention.
H5b: Pleasure emotion mediate the relationship between the sociality of blind box and consumer purchase intention.
H5c: Pleasure emotion mediate the relationship between the aesthetics of blind box and consumer purchase intention.
H5d: Pleasure emotion mediate the relationship between the interestingness of blind box and consumer purchase intention.
H6a: Arousal emotion mediate the relationship between the uncertainty of blind box and consumer purchase intention.
H6b: Arousal emotion mediate the relationship between the sociality of blind box and consumer purchase intention.
H6c: Arousal emotion mediate the relationship between the aesthetics of blind box and consumer purchase intention.
H6d: Arousal emotion mediate the relationship between the interestingness of blind box and consumer purchase intention.

2.6 The Moderating Role of Product Involvement

The concept of involvement was first proposed by Sheth and Howard in 1953, and then Krugman cited the concept of involvement to the field of consumer behavior, which was used to study the important factors influencing the effectiveness of advertising. Zaichkowsky [12] categorized involvement into three aspects according to different objects: advertising involvement, product involvement and purchase decision involvement, where product involvement refers to the degree to which consumers perceive a certain product as important. Past research has shown that product involvement is the connection between consumers and brand products, and under the influence of different levels of product involvement, consumers will go through different purchase decision-making processes and produce different psychology and behavior. Consumers with high involvement will have great interest and attention to the product, and will not only collect information about the product from various channels, but also go to the physical store to feel it in person [13]. They have stronger judgment and more experience in processing the huge and complex information they receive, and their product-related knowledge reserves are also richer. Consumers will make decisions based on various considerations and trade-offs, so the purchase decision will be more complex. In contrast, low-involvement consumers have a higher level of risk acceptance, do not conduct detailed information gathering and brand evaluation, and consider fewer factors when purchasing. Therefore, this study proposes the following hypothesis:

H7a: Product involvement negatively moderates the relationship between the uncertainty of blind box and consumer purchase intention;

H7b: Product involvement negatively moderates the relationship between the sociality of blind box and consumer purchase intention;

H7c: Product involvement negatively moderates the relationship between the aesthetics of blind box and consumer purchase intention;

H7d: Product involvement negatively moderates the relationship between the interestingness of blind box and consumer purchase intention.

Based on the above literature review and research hypotheses, the theoretical model shown in Fig. 1 is proposed:

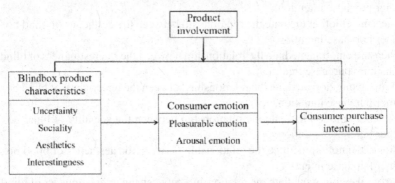

Fig. 1. Study model

3   Empirical Evidence and Analysis of Results

3.1   Questionnaire Design and Collection

The scales in the study were developed by drawing on well-established scales from existing studies with modifications based on blind box characteristics. Among them, uncertainty referred to the scale developed by Shen [9], sociality referred to the well-established scale by Preece, aesthetics referred to the scale developed by Homburg [14], interestingness referred to the scale by Kim & Moon [15], consumer emotions referred to the scale developed by Mehrabian [7], and the emotions was categorized into two dimensions: pleasure and arousal, purchase intention referred to the maturity scale developed by Dodds [16], and product involvement referred to the scale by Liu [17]. The analysis of all variables measurement included 8 variables and a total of 24 question items were designed. The questionnaire was based on a five-point Likert scale, in which "1" means "strongly disagree" and "5" means "strongly agree ". This study utilized an online questionnaire, which was forwarded and disseminated through WeChat, QQ, Weibo, circles of friends and other online channels to collect data and ensure sample diversity. A total of 309 questionnaires and 234 valid questionnaires were obtained, and the effective recovery rate was 75.73%.

3.2 Reliability and Validity Analysis

SPSS 23.0 was used for the reliability and validity tests in this study. The results showed that the overall Cronbach's α coefficient of the scale was 0.877, and the Cronbach's α coefficients of each variable were between 0.841 and 0.9, which indicated that the scale had good construct reliability. Exploratory factor analysis results showed that the KMO value of the overall scale was 0.829, the approximate chi-square value of the Bartlett's Sphericity Test was 2459.379 and significant, and the KMO values of the variables in the scale were all greater than 0.7, which indicated that the scale items in this study were eligible for factor analysis. In addition, exploratory factor analysis showed that the factor loadings of all items in the scale were greater than 0.7, the AVE values of all variables were greater than 0.5, the CR values were greater than 0.7, and the square root of the AVE value of each variable was greater than the correlation coefficients between that variable and the others, which suggests that there is a good convergent validity and discriminant validity among the variables.

3.3 Hypothesis Testing

Main Effect Test. Hierarchical regression analysis was conducted to analyze the relevant hypotheses using SPSS23.0. First, the four dimensional characteristics of the blind box were used as independent variables, consumer purchase intention was used as the dependent variable, and consumers' gender, age, education, income, and occupation were used as control variables in the regression model, and the results are shown in Table 1. Model 1 has tested the effect of control variables on consumer purchase intention, Models 2–5 tested the effect of each of the four dimensions of blind box characteristics on consumer purchase intention. The results showed that uncertainty ($\beta = 0.456, P < 0.001$), sociality ($\beta = 0.332, P < 0.001$), aesthetics ($\beta = 0.346, P < 0.001$), and interestingness ($\beta = 0.322, P < 0.001$) have a significant positive effect on consumer purchase intention, therefore, hypotheses H1a, H1b, H1c and H1d are supported. Model 6–7 examined the effects of consumers' pleasure emotion and arousal emotion on purchase intention by taking pleasure emotion and arousal emotion as independent variables and consumers' purchase intention as dependent variables, respectively. The results demonstrated that pleasure emotion has a significant positive effect on consumer purchase intention ($\beta = 0.436$, p < 0.001) and arousal emotions has a significant positive effect on consumer purchase intention ($\beta = 0.44$, p < 0.001), therefore, hypotheses H4a and H4b are supported.

The four dimensions of blind box product characteristics were used as independent variables, and the consumer's pleasure emotion and arousal emotion were used as dependent variables for linear regression analysis, respectively, and the results are shown in Table 2. As can be seen from Models 2–5, after controlling for gender, age, education, income, and occupation, the uncertainty ($\beta = 0.432, P < 0.001$), sociality ($\beta = 0.306$, P < 0.01), aesthetics ($\beta = 0.334$, P < 0.01), and interestingness ($\beta = 0.263, P < 0.001$) of the blind box have a significant positive influence on consumer pleasure emotion, therefore, hypotheses H2a, H2b, H2c, and H2d are all verified. From Models 7–10, after controlling for gender, age, education, income, and occupation, the uncertainty of the blind box ($\beta = 0.389$, P < 0.01), the sociality ($\beta = 0.287$, P < 0.01), aesthetics ($\beta = 0.321$, P < 0.001), and the interestingness ($\beta = 0.298, P < 0.001$) all have a significant

Table 1. Analysis of the influence of blind box characteristics on consumer sentiment and consumer purchase intention.

Variable	Consumer purchase intention						
	Model 1	Model 2	Model 3	Model 4	Model 5	Model 6	Model 7
Gender	0.018	0.034	0.009	0.003	0.027	0.029	0.019
Age	-0.031	-0.023	0.004	-0.009	-0.018	0.02	-0.023
Education	-0.12	-0.121	-0.104	-0.098	-0.132	-0.139	-0.101
Income	-0.092	-0.032	-0.086	-0.084	-0.064	0.00	-0.043
Occupation	0.016	0.003	0.012	0.043	-0.007	0.003	0.017
Uncertainty		0.456***					
Sociality			0.332***				
Aesthetics				0.346***			
Interestingness					0.322***		
Pleasure						0.436***	
Arousal							0.44***
R2	0.031	0.236	0.139	0.147	0.134	0.208	0.221
Adjusted R2	0.01	0.216	0.116	0.125	0.111	0.187	0.200
F value	1.452	11.704***	6.103***	6.53***	5.858***	9.938***	10.711***

Note: ** represents P<0.01, *** represents P<0.001.

positive effect on consumers' arousal emotion, therefore, hypotheses H3a, H3b, H3c, and H3d are tested.

Table 2. Analysis of the Impact of Blind Box Product Characteristics on Consumer Sentiment.

Variable	Pleasure					Arousal				
	Model 1	Model 2	Model 3	Model 4	Model 5	Model 6	Model 7	Model 8	Model 9	Model 10
Gender	-0.026	-0.01	-0.034	-0.04	-0.018	-0.003	0.011	-0.01	-0.017	0.006
Age	-0.117	-0.11	-0.086	-0.097	-0.107	-0.018	-0.011	0.012	0.002	-0.006
Education	0.044	0.042	0.058	0.064	0.034	-0.042	-0.044	-0.029	-0.022	-0.053
Income	-0.211*	-0.154	-0.205*	-0.203*	-0.188*	-0.112	-0.06	-0.106	-0.104	-0.086
Occupation	0.03	0.017	0.026	0.056	0.011	-0.003	-0.015	-0.006	0.022	-0.025
Uncertainty		0.432***				0.389**				
Sociality			0.306**				0.287**			
Aesthetics				0.334**				0.321***		
Interestingness					0.263***					0.298***
R2	0.068	0.252	0.16	0.176	0.136	0.018	0.167	0.099	0.118	0.106
Adjusted R2	0.048	0.232	0.138	0.154	0.114	-0.003	0.145	0.075	0.095	0.083
F value	3.329**	12.737***	7.205***	8.093***	5.979***	0.841	7.612***	4.166**	5.077***	4.509***

Note: * represents P<0.05, ** represents P<0.01, *** represents P<0.001.

Mediating Effect Test. This study tested the mediating effect of consumer emotions, and the results are shown in Table 3. First of all, uncertainty, sociality, aesthetics, interestingness and pleasure emotion were introduced simultaneously on the basis of putting in control variables. Models 1–4 show that there is a significant positive effect of pleasure emotion on consumer purchase intention, while uncertainty ($\beta = 0.334$, $P < 0.001$), sociality ($\beta = 0.22$, $P < 0.001$), aesthetics ($\beta = 0.227$, $P < 0.001$), and interestingness ($\beta = 0.224$, $P < 0.001$) also have a significant positive effect on consumer purchase intention. A comparison with the models in Tables 1 and 2 reveals that the regression coefficients have all decreased. This suggests that pleasure emotion all play a partially mediating role in the effects of uncertainty, sociality, aesthetics and interestingness of blind box on consumer purchase intention, and hypotheses H5a, H5b, H5c, and H5d are supported. Secondly, uncertainty, sociality, aesthetics, interestingness and arousal emotion are added simultaneously with the introduction of control variables, and as shown in Models 5–8. Arousal emotion has a significant positive effect on consumer purchase intention, while uncertainty ($\beta = 0.336$, $P < 0.001$), sociality ($\beta = 0.224$, $P < 0.001$), aesthetics ($\beta = 0.228$, $P < 0.001$), and interestingness ($\beta = 0.21$, $P < 0.01$) also have a significant positive effect on consumer purchase intention. By comparing with the models in Tables 1 and 3, it was found that the regression coefficients have decreased. It can be seen that arousal emotion plays a partial mediating role in the effect of uncertainty, sociality, aesthetics, and interestingness of blind box on consumer purchase intention, and hypotheses H6a, H6b, H6c, and H6d are supported.

Table 3. Results of mediation effect tests

Variable	Consumer purchase intention							
	Model 1	Model 2	Model 3	Model 4	Model 5	Model 6	Model 7	Model 8
Gender	0.037	0.021	0.017	0.034	0.031	0.013	0.009	0.025
Age	0.008	0.035	0.025	0.022	-0.019	-0.001	-0.01	-0.016
Education	-0.133	-0.125	-0.121	-0.144	-0.108	-0.093	-0.09	-0.111
Income	0.012	-0.011	-0.011	0.006	-0.013	-0.046	-0.046	-0.031
Occupation	-0.002	0.003	0.023	-0.011	0.007	0.015	0.035	0.002
Uncertainty	0.334***				0.336***			
Sociality		0.22***				0.224***		
Aesthetics			0.227***				0.228***	
Interestingness				0.224***				0.21**
Pleasure	0.283***	0.365***	0.357***	0.373***				
Arousal					0.308***	0.375***	0.367***	0.376***
R2	0.296	0.251	0.252	0.254	0.315	0.266	0.266	0.261
Adjusted R2	0.275	0.228	0.229	0.231	0.294	0.243	0.243	0.238
F value	13.599***	10.813***	10.891***	11.015***	14.868**	11.688***	11.703***	11.377***

Note: * represents P<0.05, ** represents P<0.01, *** represents P<0.001.

Moderating Effect Test. The moderating effect of product involvement was tested in this study. In order to avoid the problem of multicollinearity, the independent variables and the moderating variables were firstly centered to present the interaction terms, and then regression analysis was performed. The test results are shown in Table 4. Model 2 shows that the interaction term between uncertainty and product involvement ($\beta = -0.029$, $P > 0.5$) has no significant effect on consumer purchase intention, which indicates that product involvement does not play a moderating role in the effect of blind-box uncertainty on consumer purchase intention, and hypothesis H7a is not valid. Models 4, 6, and 8 show that the interaction terms of sociality and product involvement ($\beta = -0.166$, $P < 0.01$), aesthetics and product involvement ($\beta = -0.15$, $P < 0.05$), and interestingness and product involvement ($\beta = -0.15$, $P < 0.05$) have a significant effect on consumer purchase intention. Therefore, product involvement negatively moderates the effect of sociality, aesthetics, and interestingness on consumer purchase intention, and hypothesis H7b, H7c, and H7d hold.

Table 4. Moderating effect test results

Variable	Consumer purchase intention							
	Model 1	Model 2	Model 3	Model 4	Model 5	Model 6	Model 7	Model 8
Gender	0.032	0.032	0.005	0.006	0.00	-0.013	0.025	0.031
Age	-0.025	-0.025	0.00	0.021	-0.013	0.006	-0.021	-0.018
Education	-0.112	-0.114	-0.090	-0.086	-0.085	-0.092	-0.123	-0.134
Income	-0.036	-0.039	-0.092	-0.104	-0.089	-0.104	-0.068	-0.082
Occupation	0.013	0.013	0.028	0.035	0.058	0.064	0.003	-0.008
Uncertainty	0.451***	0.446***						
Sociality			0.333***	0.33***				
Aesthetics					0.345***	0.343***		
Interestingness							0.314***	0.316***
Product involvement	0.070	0.068	0.108	0.125*	0.101	0.128*	0.064	0.049
Uncertainty * product involvement		-0.029						
Sociality *Product involvement				-0.166**				
Aesthetics *Product involvement						-0.15*		
Interestingness*Product involvement								-0.15*
R2	0.241	0.242	0.15	0.177	0.157	0.178	0.138	0.16
Adjusted R2	0.217	0.215	0.124	0.148	0.131	0.149	0.111	0.13
F value	10.252***	8.971***	5.708***	6.051***	6.021***	6.102***	5.172***	5.349***

Note: * represents P<0.05, ** represents P<0.01, *** represents P<0.001.

4 Research Conclusion and Insight

4.1 Research Conclusion

The rise of blind box economy provides an emerging marketing method for enterprises. This study is based on previous studies on the subject, the characteristics of blind box products were categorized into four dimensions: uncertainty, sociality, aesthetics, and interestingness, and the effects of different characteristics on consumers' purchase intention were investigated, and consumer emotion and product involvement were introduced to examine their mediating and moderating roles, respectively. The results of the empirical analysis are as follows: (1) The uncertainty, sociality, aesthetics and interestingness of the blind box positively affect consumers' pleasure and arousal emotions and their purchase intention, of which uncertainty has the greatest influence; (2) Consumers' emotions (pleasure and arousal) have a significant positive effect on their purchase intention, and the pleasure and arousal play a positive and partially intermediary role in the process of influencing consumers' purchase intention by the characteristics of the blind box products. (3) The degree of product involvement negatively moderates the relationship between the sociality, aesthetic and interestingness of the blind box and consumer purchase intention, but the moderating effect in the relationship between uncertainty and consumer purchase intention is not significant.

4.2 Marketing Inspiration

First, in the future, companies can learn from blind box marketing, using uncertainty to bring positive emotions to consumers and increase their curiosity and desire to buy the product. Innovative marketing content according to brand personality, bring consumers unpredictable and unique experience. Second, make full use of social media to build a communication platform to promote communication and sharing between designers and consumers. While understanding consumers' feedback on product evaluations and preferences, it increases the stickiness between consumers and brands. Enterprises can also encourage consumers to share, comment and like by releasing interesting promotional advertisements and other ways. Third, innovate blind box packaging and product appearance design to eliminate consumers' aesthetic fatigue. In the future, enterprises can learn from Bubble Mart's way of giving IP stories to blind box products to increase the entertainment of the products. Set up interesting and diversified creative games to provide consumers with a constant stream of consumer surprises. Fourth, adopt personalized and diversified promotional methods to push different contents to customers with different product engagement.

4.3 Research Shortcoming and Prospect

There are still some shortcomings in this study. First of all, while blind boxes bring consumers a sense of surprise and excitement, they also bring certain risks, especially for the youth group, which is prone to gambling psychology and addictive behavior. This paper only investigates the positive impact of blind box product features on consumers, and future research can further incorporate risk factors into the research scope. Secondly, this paper only investigates the moderating role of product involvement in the influence of blind box product features on consumers' purchase intention, and future research can introduce other moderating variables, such as brand trust and consumer attitude, to further enrich the research model.

References

1. Wang, T.Y., Bi, S.M.: The marketing model of the "blind box" of trendy toys. Mod. Bus. **23**, 15–17 (2021). (in Chinese)
2. Chen, Z.G., Pan, F.: Research on the influencing factors of short game videos on players' intention to purchase virtual props based on the SOR model. Manage. Adm. (3), 67–75 (2023). (in Chinese)
3. Wang, D.Z., Zhou, C.C.: Blind box consumption: a new phenomenon in contemporary youth consumption lifestyle. Gansu Soc. Sci. **2**, 120–126 (2021). (in Chinese)

4. Gao, T.H., Li, P.: The effect of blind boxes for clothing on consumers' impulsive purchase intentions. J. Beijing Inst. Fashion Technol. (Nat. Sci. Ed.) **42**(4), 66–73+82 (2022). (in Chinese)
5. Zhang, Z.Z.: Research on packaging design of blind box products under the "Blind Box Economy" model. Packag. Eng. **42**(8), 227–233+275 (2021). (in Chinese)
6. Oliver, R.L.: Conceptual issues in the structural analysis of consumption emotion, satisfaction, and quality: evidence in a service setting. In: ACR North American Advances (1994)
7. Mehrabian, A., Russell, J.A.: A verbal measure of information rate for studies in environmental psychology. Environ. Behav. **6**(2), 233 (1974)
8. Westbrook, R.A., Oliver, R.L.: The dimensionality of consumption emotion patterns and consumer satisfaction. J. Consum. Res. **18**(1), 84 (1991)
9. Shen, L., Fishbach, A., Hsee, C.K.: The motivating-uncertainty effect: uncertainty increases resource investment in the process of reward pursuit. J. Consum. Res. **41**(5), 1301–1315 (2015)
10. Hoegg, J., Alba, J.W.: Seeing is Believing (Too Much): the influence of product form on perceptions of functional performance. J. Prod. Innov. Manag. **28**(3), 346–359 (2011)
11. He, J.H., Du, S.R., Li, Z.X.: The impact of the effect of online reviews on impulsive mobile shopping intentions. Contemp. Econ. Manage. **41**(5), 25–31 (2019). (in Chinese)
12. Zaichkowsky, J.L.: Conceptualizing involvement. J. Advert. **15**(2), 4–34 (1986)
13. Rothschild, M.L.: Perspectives on involvement: current problems and future directions. In: ACR North American Advances (1984)
14. Homburg, C., Schwemmle, M., Kuehnl, C.: New product design: concept, measurement, and consequences. J. Mark. **79**(3), 41–56 (2015)
15. Moon, J.-W., Kim, Y.-G.: Extending the TAM for a World-Wide-Web context. Inf. Manage. **38**(4), 217–230 (2001)
16. Dodds, W.B., Monroe, K.B., Grewal, D.: Effects of price, brand, and store information on buyers' product evaluations. J. Mark. Res. **28**(3), 307–319 (1991)
17. Liu, X.Y., Xu, J.N.: Influence of live shopping contextual factors on users' purchase intention under the mindstream perspective - moderating effect based on product involvement. J. Jilin Bus. Technol. Coll. **38**(6), 41–49 (2022). (in Chinese)

Understanding the Effects of the Multidimensional Content of Streamers' Live Speech on Consumer Purchase Behavior in Livestreaming E-commerce: Empirical Evidence from TikTok

Ting Chen[1] , Jiang Wu[1,2(✉)] , Xi Chen[3] , Honghao Ding[1] ,
and Jingxuan Cai[4]

[1] School of Information Management, Wuhan University, Wuhan 430072, China
jiangw@whu.edu.cn
[2] E-Commerce Research and Development Center, Wuhan University, Wuhan 430072, China
[3] State Key Laboratory of Information Engineering in Surveying, Mapping and Remote Sensing, Wuhan University, Wuhan 430072, China
[4] Research Center for Smarter Supply Chain, Dongwu Business School, Soochow University, Suzhou 215031, China

Abstract. Livestreaming e-commerce has emerged as an effective way of facilitating consumer purchase decisions. Moreover, streamers play a crucial role in promoting product sales through live speech. Existing research has focused primarily on the effects of streamers' competencies, linguistic characteristics, and social interaction-oriented content on purchase decisions by analyzing streamers' conversation content, ignoring the differential impact of multidimensional content. Therefore, this study identifies and examines how the multidimensional content of streamers' live speech influences consumer purchase behavior in livestreaming e-commerce, with a particular focus on the moderating role of streamer influence. By analyzing a fine-grained dataset comprising 1,030 livestreaming events of 582 streamers from TikTok and matching them with actual sales transactions, a negative binominal regression model is used to estimate the research model, and the results show that product and social information contained in streamer conversation content has an inverted U-shaped relationship with consumer purchase behavior, while emotional information has a negative linear relationship with consumer purchase behavior. Furthermore, streamer influence significantly and positively moderates the effects of streamers' conversation content (product, social and emotional information) on consumer purchase behavior. This research establishes the paramount role of streamers' multidimensional conversation content in customer purchase behavior, lending credence to the epistemological applicability of persuasion theory in the context of livestreaming e-commerce. The study's findings offer some practical implications for developing conversation content in the context of livestreaming e-commerce.

Keywords: Livestreaming e-commerce · Conversation content · Purchase behavior · Video analysis · TikTok

Y. P. Tu and M. Chi (Eds.): WHICEB 2024, LNBIP 516, pp. 237–249, 2024.
https://doi.org/10.1007/978-3-031-60260-3_20

1   Introduction

With livestreaming becoming increasingly popular, many vendors in China have adopted livestreaming as a tool to promote consumers' purchase decisions and enhance firms' economic benefits. Based on innovative livestreaming technologies, live streaming e-commerce has transformed product displays from textual and graphical descriptions to real-time videos. It provides customers with more detailed information and reduces the perceived risk of online shopping [1].

Livestreaming, as a new phenomenon, has received rapidly growing research attention. Existing studies have reported a series of antecedents of consumer purchase decisions from the perspective of streamers, platforms, consumers, and information content [2–5]. Moreover, it has been acknowledged that the streamers' conversation content, such as social interaction-oriented content, plays an important role in viewers' consumption behaviors [6]. However, these studies ignore the differential impact of other content, such as product and emotional information contained in streamers' conversation content. Given that there are multiple customers' motivations to purchase products in live streaming e-commerce [7], it is epistemologically significant and pragmatically relevant to explore the impact of the multidimensional content of streamers' live speech on consumer purchase decisions. Another theoretical gap is that it is unclear how the effects of streamers' conversation content depend on streamer attributes such as streamer influence. Existing research indicates that streamers are one of the critical antecedents that impact consumer purchase decisions in livestreaming e-commerce [2, 8, 9]. However, no studies have explored whether there is any possible interaction effect between the streamers' conversation content and streamer influence.

Motivated by these research gaps, this research aims to address two questions: (1) How does streamers' multidimensional conversation content affect consumer purchase behavior? (2) Can streamer influence moderate the effect of streamers' multidimensional conversation content on consumer purchase behavior?

2   Theoretical Background, Proposed Research Model, and Hypothesis Development

2.1   Livestreaming E-commerce

Livestreaming e-commerce is a novel e-commerce model that provides a more immersive and interactive virtual shopping experience [10]. The literature on livestreaming e-commerce has investigated the antecedents of consumer engagement and purchase decisions from the perspectives of streamers, platforms, consumers, and information content. From the perspective of streamers, scholars have reported on factors such as competencies and linguistic characteristics that impact consumer purchase decisions. For example, Liao et al. (2023) reported that streamers' cognitive, emotional, and social competencies significantly influence sales performance [8]. Liu et al. (2023) proposed that streamers' linguistic styles could promote sales performance [9]. In terms of platforms, studies have shown that technical and social attributes are crucial determinants of consumer behavior. For instance, Li et al. (2021) demonstrated that technical attributes and social attributes could affect user stickiness behavior via emotional attachments to streamers and platform attachment [3]. The consumer perspective research indicates that motivation, trust, and perceived value are crucial for encouraging purchase decisions. For example, Ma et al. (2021) reported that motivations such as enjoyment and self-presentation promote customer engagement [4]. Wongkitrungrueng and Assarut (2020) indicated that perceived value has a close relationship with consumer trust building, thereby impacting purchase intention [7]. In regard to information content, studies have focused on exploring the effects of streamer and consumer information content on consumer purchase decisions. For instance, Yang et al. (2023) proved that social interaction-oriented content in streamers' live speech and purchase behavior share an inverted U-shaped relationship [6].

Although the studies above have made considerable efforts to investigate the determinants of consumer engagement and purchasing, these studies have mainly used scenario-based experiments and questionnaires to investigate individual behaviors. Additionally, prior studies have investigated information content from streamer and consumers' perspectives, but they have not revealed the multidimensional nature of streamers' conversation content.

2.2 Streamers' Conversation Content in Livestreaming

The conversation content of streamers is the main information that persuades customers to purchase products in livestreaming rooms [6]. To create utilitarian, social, and hedonic value for customers, streamers usually convey product, social, and emotional information through their live speech. Product information refers to the product attribute information contained in streamers' live speech to help customers assess the products. Social information can be defined as social interaction information contained in streamers' live speech to build harmonious relationships with consumers, while emotional information reflects streamers' tendency to convey emotions, which can modify consumers' emotions and thus make purchase decisions in livestreaming rooms.

Although there have been some studies on streamers' conversation content in the context of livestreaming e-commerce, these studies have focused on single-dimensional conversation content. For instance, Yang et al. (2023) explored the impact of social interaction-oriented content contained in streamers' live speech [6]. Wang et al. (2023) examined the influence of streamers' conversational emotions on consumers' instant order cancellation via group emotions [11].

2.3 The Proposed Research Model and Hypothesis Development

Based on persuasion theory, we propose our research model. Persuasion theory argues that persuasion information can directly impact the behavior of a persuasion object, and persuader influence can potentially moderate the relationship between persuasion information and persuasion object behavior. In the context of livestreaming e-commerce, we propose that streamers' multidimensional conversation content has a direct impact on consumer purchase behavior. Moreover, we explore the moderating effect of streamer influence to shed light on their impact on the relationship between streamers' conversation content and consumer purchase behavior. Figure 1 depicts our research model.

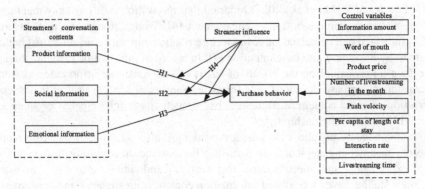

Fig. 1. Research model

2.3.1 The Relationship Between Product Information and Purchase Behavior

Previous research has investigated product information in online contexts and has shown that this kind of information impacts customers' information processing and purchase intention [12]. In livestreaming e-commerce, product information delivered by streamers through live speech greatly reduces customers' perception of uncertainty and their efforts in product search and assessment [5], thus benefiting consumers' purchasing decisions [8, 13]. However, according to information overload theory, beyond a certain threshold, more information leads to a person's perception of being overwhelmed by incoming information that exceeds his/her cognitive capacity, thus causing a worse subjective state toward purchasing decisions [14]. Therefore, when product information in streamers' conversation content exceeds the optimal level, customers could be less likely to make purchase decisions. Accordingly,

  H1: Product information contained in streamers' conversation content and consumer purchase behavior exhibit an inverted U-shaped relationship.

2.3.2 The Relationship Between Social Information and Purchase Behavior

Previous studies have indicated that social information is a key factor that impacts consumer purchase behavior in online contexts. In the context of livestreaming e-commerce, the flow of social information enables sellers and buyers to build stable and strong relationships, which is beneficial for consumer purchase behavior [8]. Related research on attention theory has suggested that when customers pay more attention to a product, their purchasing probability increases, and when consumers are distracted from a product, they are less likely to purchase that product [6]. Therefore, when social information in streamers' conversation attention exceeds a certain threshold, consumers could focus more on interactions with streamers and be distracted from promoted products since social and product information must compete for scarce attention resources. Furthermore, this eclipsing effect leads customers to ignore product information, which disrupts consumer purchase behavior [15]. Thus,

H2: Social information contained in streamers' conversation content and consumer purchase behavior exhibit an inverted U-shaped relationship.

2.3.3 The Relationship Between Emotional Information and Purchase Behavior

According to emotional contagion theory, environmental emotions can be contagious, modifying or shaping individuals' emotions and subsequently determining their behaviors [11]. Therefore, streamers usually display strong positive emotions when introducing products, which subsequently triggers customers' emotional responses and boosts product sales. Furthermore, customers expect salespeople to express an emotional state during interactions and encounters [16]. Streamers who deliver more emotional information through live speech can effectively meet consumer expectations and impact consumer purchase behavior. Therefore,

H3: Emotional information contained in streamers' conversation content is positively related to consumer purchase behavior.

2.3.4 The Moderating Effect of Streamer Influence on the Impact of Streamers' Conversation Content on Purchase Behavior

Streamer influence is related to the level of popularity and source credibility [17]. Existing research has indicated that high-credibility sources are more persuasive than sources with no or little credibility [8]. In other words, the persuasiveness of high-influence streamers' conversation content is more pronounced than that of low-influence streamers' conversation content, and such persuasion power can motivate consumer purchase behavior. Thus,

H4: The effect of streamers' conversation content (product, social, and emotional information) on consumer purchase behavior will be positively moderated by streamer influence.

3 Research Design and Methodology

3.1 Data Collection and Preprocessing

This study focuses on the online platform TikTok as the research context. This platform is one of China's largest livestreaming e-commerce platforms, with more than 600 million daily active users. Our dataset included live video and sales data. First, we recorded 1,030 livestreaming events involving 582 streamers from TikTok. We collected sales data from Huitun.com after the livestreaming events. Next, we conducted data preprocessing, including data transformation and data integration. In the data transformation stage, voice recognition technology was used to convert the streamer audio speech into text data for each minute. In the data integration stage, the minute-level text data were matched with the sales data. Finally, the dataset included more than 36 million words of text data and 114,871 min of real-time dynamic structured data.

3.2 Variables and Measures

Dependent Variable. The dependent variable is consumer purchase behavior. Consistent with the measurement of Yang et al. (2023), we measured consumer purchase behavior by the increase in sales during each minute [6].

Independent Variables. Product information is measured by the frequency of product words in the streamers' conversation content. We first build the product dictionary based on product titles provided by sellers, and the e-commerce dictionary. Next, based on the product dictionary, the frequency of product words in the streamers' conversation content is calculated. Social information is measured by the frequency of social words in the streamers' conversation content, which is calculated based on the social dictionary in linguistic inquiry and word count (LIWC). Emotional information is measured by the emotional score of the streamers' conversation content, which is analyzed through the Baidu Cloud Chinese Semantic Sentiment Analysis System.

Moderator Variable. Since the number of followers is an effective indicator for evaluating the influence and popularity of celebrities [13], we measured streamer influence by the number of followers.

Control Variables. To address concerns about the potential endogeneity, we controlled for several variables in this research model. Specifically, we controlled for information amount, word of mouth, product price, the number of livestreaming in the month, push velocity of the platform, per capita length of stay, interaction rate and livestreaming time (morning, afternoon, evening, late night, weekend). The descriptive statistics are summarized in Table 1.

Table 1. Results of the descriptive statistics

Variable full name	Variable acronym or abbreviation	Mean	SD	Min	Max
Purchase behavior	PurBeh	11.716	91.177	0	7,673
Product information	ProInf	20.119	9.077	0	75
Social information	SocInf	18.824	8.964	0	82
Emotional information	EmoInf	0.529	0.404	0	1
Streamer influence	StrInf	1,532,021.950	4,572,221.956	11,000	60,520,000
Information amount	InfAmo	198.141	53.940	0	372

(*continued*)

Table 1. (*continued*)

Variable full name	Variable acronym or abbreviation	Mean	SD	Min	Max
Word of mouth	WOM	4.741	0.222	3.2	5
Product price	ProPrice	117.149	331.984	0.652	9,611.744
Number of livestreaming in the month	LivNum	37.434	26.555	1	215
Push velocity	PushVel	819.503	1,935.922	0	45,759.333
Length of stay	StayLen	77.891	63.145	9	529
Interaction rate	IntRate	1.035	3.672	0	110
Morning	Morning	0.113	0.317	0	1
Afternoon	Afternoon	0.423	0.494	0	1
Evening	Evening	0.447	0.497	0	1
LateNight	LateNight	0.017	0.131	0	1
Weekend	Weekend	0.214	0.410	0	1

3.3 Estimation Models

Formula (1) is used to test the influence of conversation content on consumer purchase behavior and examine how streamer influence moderates the relationship between conversation content and consumer purchase behavior.

$$
\begin{aligned}
PurBeh_{i,t} =& \beta_0 + \beta_1 ProInf_{i,t} + \beta_2 SocInf_{i,t} + \beta_3 EmoInf_{i,t} \\
& + \beta_4 ProInf_{i,t} * Ln(StrInf)_i + \beta_5 SocInf_{i,t} * Ln(StrInf)_i \\
& + \beta_6 EmoInf_{i,t} * Ln(StrInf)_i + \beta_7 InfAmo_{i,t} + \beta_8 WOM_i \\
& + \beta_9 Ln(ProPrice)_{i,t} + \beta_{10} LivNum_{i,t} + \beta_{11} Ln(PushVel)_{i,t} \\
& + \beta_{12} StayLen_{i,t} + \beta_{13} Ln(IntRate)_{i,t} + \beta_{14} Morning_{i,t} \\
& + \beta_{15} Afternoon_{i,t} + \beta_{16} Evening_{i,t} + \beta_{17} LateNight_{i,t} \\
& + \beta_{18} Weekend_{i,t} + \varepsilon_{i,t}
\end{aligned}
\tag{1}
$$

Consumer purchase behavior is a non-negative count variable, and the variable variance (8313.25) is much greater than its mean (11.72), representing the nature of overdispersion. Thus, we used a negative binominal regression model to estimate our research model.

4 Results and Analysis

4.1 Main Models

The results are reported in Table 2. Model 1 includes only the control variables, and the results indicate that information amount, word of mouth, product price, the number of livestreaming in the month, push velocity of the platform, interaction rate and livestreaming in the afternoon affect consumer purchase behavior. The results of Model 2 reveal that the beta parameter for product information was positive and significant ($\beta = 0.0309, p < 0.001$), and the parameter for the squared term of product information was negative and significant ($\beta = -0.0007, p < 0.001$), implying that the relationship between product information and purchase behavior was shaped like an inverted U. Moreover, the parameter for social information was positive and significant ($\beta = 0.0128, p < 0.001$), and the parameter for the squared term of product information was negative and significant ($\beta = -0.0004, p < 0.001$), implying that the relationship between social information and purchase behavior was shaped like an inverted U. However, emotional information ($\beta = -0.1970, p < 0.001$) negatively impacted purchase behavior. Therefore, H1 and H2 were supported, while H3 was rejected.

We then added the moderating variable to Model 3. The results of Model 3 show that the interaction effect between streamer influence and product information was negative and significant ($\beta = -0.0074, p < 0.001$), and the interaction effect between streamer influence and product information squared term was positive and significant ($\beta = 0.0002, p < 0.001$), implying that high-influence streamers increased the range of the positive impact of product information on purchase behavior. Moreover, the interaction effect between streamer influence and social information was negative and significant ($\beta = -0.0174, p < 0.001$), and the interaction effect between streamer influence and social information squared term was positive and significant ($\beta = 0.0003, p < 0.001$), indicating that high-influence streamers increased the range of the positive impact of social information on purchase behavior. Furthermore, the interaction effect between streamer influence and emotional information was positive and significant ($\beta = 0.0992, p < 0.001$). Thus, H4 was supported.

Table 2. Results of the main models' estimations

Variables	Model 1	Model 2	Model 3
InfAmount	0.0054***	0.0053***	0.0053***
	(0.0002)	(0.0002)	(0.0002)
WOM	0.5354***	0.5336***	0.2602***
	(0.0346)	(0.0348)	(0.0387)
Ln (ProPrice)	−0.1855***	−0.1869***	−0.1988***
	(0.0080)	(0.0080)	(0.0080)
MonthLivNum	−0.0068***	−0.0067***	−0.0072***
	(0.0003)	(0.0003)	(0.0003)

(continued)

Table 2. (*continued*)

Variables	Model 1	Model 2	Model 3
Ln (PushVelocity)	0.9159*** (0.0056)	0.9116*** (0.0056)	0.8480*** (0.0066)
StayLength	0.0002 (0.0001)	0.0002 (0.0001)	0.0004** (0.0001)
Ln (IntRate)	0.0801*** (0.0074)	0.0814*** (0.0074)	0.0607*** (0.0074)
Morning	0.0991 (0.0616)	0.0625 (0.0617)	0.1360** (0.0620)
Afternoon	−0.1137* (0.0589)	−0.1344** (0.0590)	−0.0910 (0.0592)
Evening	−0.0265 (0.0590)	−0.0407 (0.0590)	0.0329 (0.0592)
LateNight	/	/	/
Weekend	−0.0130 (0.0175)	−0.0107 (0.0175)	0.0222 (0.0176)
ProInformation		0.0309*** (0.0031)	0.1311*** (0.0268)
ProInformation^2		−0.0007*** (0.0001)	−0.0031*** (0.0006)
SocInformation		0.0128*** (0.0031)	0.2428*** (0.0268)
SocInformation^2		−0.0004*** (0.0001)	−0.0048*** (0.0006)
EmoInformation		−0.1970*** (0.0186)	−1.5200*** (0.1740)
Ln (StrInfluence)			0.3022*** (0.0250)
ProInformation * Ln (StrInfluence)			−0.0074*** (0.0020)
ProInformation^2* Ln (StrInfluence)			0.0002*** (0.0000)
SocInformation * Ln (StrInfluence)			−0.0174*** (0.0020)
SocInformation^2* Ln (StrInfluence)			0.0003*** (0.0000)

(*continued*)

Table 2. (*continued*)

Variables	Model 1	Model 2	Model 3
EmoInformation * Ln (StrInfluence)			0.0992***
			(0.0131)
Constant	−6.0538***	−6.2302***	−8.6293***
	(0.1828)	(0.1846)	(0.3567)
Log likelihood	−250471.76	−250327.54	−250080.89
Pseudo R^2	0.0557	0.0563	0.0572
χ^2	29564.30***	29852.74***	30346.03***
AIC	500969.5	500691.1	500209.8
BIC	501094.7	500864.4	500440.9
N	112,451	112,451	112,451

Note: * $p < 0.05$, ** $p < 0.01$, *** $p < 0.001$

4.2 Robustness Checks

We conducted additional two additional robustness checks to ensure the robustness of our results. First, we checked whether the inverted U-shaped relationship between the dependent and independent variables existed within the dataset's scope. For instance, the slope must be adequately steep at both ends of the data range and possess opposite signs, and the turning point must be situated well within the data range [6]. Our further inverted U-shaped relationship test results indicated that less product information (slope = 0.0309, $p < 0.001$) and less social information (slope = 0.0128, $p < 0.001$) positively and significantly affected purchase behavior. Moreover, more product information (slope = −0.0706, $p < 0.001$) and social information (slope = −0.0529, $p < 0.001$) negatively and significantly affect purchase behavior. Moreover, the turning points for product information (turning point = 22.8525) and social information (turning point = 15.9852) were within the limits of the dataset. These results confirmed that the relationships between product information and purchase behavior and between social information and purchase behavior were inverted U-shaped. Second, since the transmission of streamers' conversation content is real-time, dynamic and continuous, the influence of product information, social information, and emotional information on purchase behavior may exist within a few minutes after the transmission of conversation content. Therefore, to test the lag influence of conversation content on purchase behavior, we set the t minute product information, social information, and emotional information as independent variables, and set the $t + 1$ min sales as the dependent variable to conduct the regression analysis again. The results further supported the findings of our research model. Due to space limitations, we do not show the robustness test results.

5   Discussions and Conclusions

This study found that product information has an inverted U-shaped relationship with purchase behavior. Specifically, product information is positively related to purchase behavior within the optimal range of streamers' conversation content, and it could decrease consumer uncertainty [5], thus promoting purchase behavior. When product information exceeds the threshold, it could cause consumer cognitive overload, thus negatively impacting purchase behavior. Moreover, there is also an inverted U-shaped relationship between social information and purchase behavior. Specifically, social information positively influences purchase behavior within the optimal range of streamers' conversation content, and it could narrow the distance between streamers and consumers and improve consumers' attachment, trust and sense of belonging to steamers, which further promote consumer purchase behavior. When social information exceeds this threshold, consumers may pay too much attention to steamers and ignore products [6], thus negatively affecting purchase behavior. However, unlike existing research emphasizing the role of steamers' emotions in livestreaming e-commerce [11], we found that emotional information negatively influences purchase behavior. This result can be explained by the findings of Liao et al. (2023), who reported that consumers regard streamers' positive emotions as a signal that streamers profit at their expense in negotiations [8]. Therefore, consumers will doubt the ability and credibility of streamers, and then reduce their purchase activities. Further analysis revealed the moderating role of streamer influence. Specifically, streamer influence expands the scope of product information and social information positively affecting purchase behavior and increase the impact of emotional information on purchase behavior. Previous research has suggested that high-influence streamers can prompt followers to irrationally transfer their emotions and focus on streamers to products, resulting in herd behavior. Therefore, when high-influence streamers convey product information, social information, and emotional information in their conversation content, consumers will express their support for streamers by purchasing products in livestreaming rooms.

This study makes significant theoretical contributions to the literature on livestreaming e-commerce. First, previous studies on the influence of streamers' conversation content on consumer behavior have focused on single-dimensional conversation content such as social or emotional information. Therefore, we offer insights into the differential influence of product, social, and emotional information on consumer purchase behavior in livestreaming e-commerce. Second, this study investigates the moderating effect of streamer influence on the relationship between conversation content and purchase behavior. The findings expand the analytical perspective and boundary conditions for the studies of livestreaming conservation persuasion strategies. Third, prior research on livestreaming e-commerce generally depends on scenario-based experiments and questionnaires to investigate consumer purchase intentions. Our study is among the first to adopt text mining methods to measure product, social, and emotional information in streamers' conversation content by gathering real-world livestreaming data, offering an additional viable research approach that complements survey questionnaires in studying livestreaming e-commerce.

The findings offer valuable insights for marketers, particularly steamers and firms involved in livestreaming e-commerce. First, these insights can guide firms in effectively training and screening streamers. For example, they could conduct systematic training on product-related knowledge and social interaction, thus improving the professional and social ability of streamers. Furthermore, they can cooperate with streamers with a large number of followers, so as to expand the scope of product and social information to positively impact purchase behavior. Second, streamers should show their product expertise and social interaction ability in the process of livestreaming. For instance, they could use more technical terms and accurate numbers to show the performance and quality of products. Moreover, streamers should skillfully interact with consumers and encourage them to express needs or concerns. However, streamers should be aware that excessive amounts of product and social information in their conversation content negatively impact consumer purchase behavior. Thus, they should take measures to balance product and social information to achieve the best product sales. Moreover, streamers should avoid emotional and exaggerated expressions when introducing products. For example, they could use neutral language expressions to promote consumer purchase behavior. Furthermore, high-influence streamers can convey more product and social information in their language, thus reducing consumer uncertainty about products and establishing a harmonious atmosphere in livestreaming rooms.

The limitations of this study provide insights for future research. First, the data were gathered from only one Chinese livestreaming e-commerce platform. Future research may consider using data from other livestreaming e-commerce platforms with different cultural orientations. Second, we used the frequency of product and social words in streamers' conversation content to measure product and social information. Although this approach has been widely used in the text analysis literature, future studies could consider employing machine learning algorithms to analyze streamers' conversation content, in order to develop more comprehensive metrics for measuring conversation content. Third, our study focused solely on the influence of streamers' conversation content on consumer purchase behavior. We recognize that product, social, and emotional information on bullet screens may also play an important role in impacting purchase behavior during livestreaming. Future research could encompass a more comprehensive test of information and investigate its holistic impact on consumer behavior in live streaming environments.

Acknowledgement. This research was supported by the Key Project of National Natural Science Foundation of China under Grant 72232006.

References

1. Sun, Y., Shao, X., Li, X., et al.: How live streaming influences purchase intentions in social commerce: an IT affordance perspective. Electron. Commer. Res. Appl. **37**, 100886 (2019)
2. He, W., Jin, C.: A study on the influence of the characteristics of key opinion leaders on consumers' purchase intention in live streaming commerce: based on dual-systems theory. Electron. Commer. Res. (2022)
3. Li, Y., Li, X., Cai, J.: How attachment affects user stickiness on live streaming platforms: a socio-technical approach perspective. J. Retail. Consum. Serv. **60**, 102478 (2021)

4. Ma, Y.: To shop or not: Understanding Chinese consumers' live-stream shopping intentions from the perspectives of uses and gratifications, perceived network size, perceptions of digital celebrities, and shopping orientations. Telematics Inform. **59**, 101562 (2021)
5. Xiao, L., Lin, X., Mi, C., et al.: The effect of dynamic information cues on sales performance in live streaming e-commerce: an IFT and ELM perspective. Electron. Commer. Res. (2023)
6. Yang, Q., Huo, J., Li, H., et al.: Can social interaction-oriented content trigger viewers' purchasing and gift-giving behaviors? Evidence from live-streaming commerce. Internet Res. **33**(7), 46–71 (2023)
7. Wongkitrungrueng, A., Assarut, N.: The role of live streaming in building consumer trust and engagement with social commerce sellers. J. Bus. Res. **117**, 543–556 (2020)
8. Liao, M., Fang, J., Han, L., et al.: Boosting eCommerce sales with livestreaming in B2B marketplace: a perspective on live streamers' competencies. J. Bus. Res. **167**, 114167 (2023)
9. Liu, L., Fang, J., Yang, L., et al.: The power of talk: exploring the effects of streamers' linguistic styles on sales performance in B2B livestreaming commerce. Inf. Process. Manage. **60**(3), 103259 (2023)
10. Zhang, M., Liu, Y., Wang, Y., et al.: How to retain customers: understanding the role of trust in live streaming commerce with a socio-technical perspective. Comput. Hum. Behav. **127**, 107052 (2022)
11. Wang, Z., Luo, C., Luo, X., et al.: Understanding the effect of group emotions on consumer instant order cancellation behavior in livestreaming E-commerce: empirical evidence from TikTok. Decis. Support Syst. **179**, 114147 (2023)
12. Fan, L., Wang, Y., Mou, J.: Enjoy to read and enjoy to shop: an investigation on the impact of product information presentation on purchase intention in digital content marketing. J. Retail. Consum. Serv. **76**, 103594 (2024)
13. Guo, Y., Zhang, K., Wang, C.: Way to success: understanding top streamer's popularity and influence from the perspective of source characteristics. J. Retail. Consum. Serv. **64**, 102786 (2022)
14. Chen, Y.C., Shang, R.-A., Kao, C.Y.: The effects of information overload on consumers' subjective state towards buying decision in the internet shopping environment. Electron. Commer. Res. Appl. **8**(1), 48–58 (2009)
15. Ilicic, J., Webster, C.M.: Eclipsing: when celebrities overshadow the brand. Psychol. Mark. **31**(11), 1040–1050 (2014)
16. Hennig-Thurau, T., Groth, M., Paul, M., et al.: Are all smiles created equal? How emotional contagion and emotional labor affect service relationships. J. Mark. Am. Mark. Assoc. ISSN **70**, 58–73 (2006)
17. Dong, L., Zhang, J., Huang, L., et al.: Social influence on endorsement in social Q&A community: moderating effects of temporal and spatial factors. Int. J. Inf. Manage. **61**, 102396 (2021)

A Quantitative Study on Digital Health and Wellness Policies from the Combination Perspective of "Subject-Theme-Tool"

Jiang Wu[1,2], Yiyuan Liu[1], Haodong Chen[1(✉)], Xiao Huang[3], and Yufan Wang[1]

[1] School of Information Management, Wuhan University, Wuhan 430072, China
ghauxtungc@whu.edu.cn
[2] Center for E-Commerce Research and Development, Wuhan University, Wuhan 430072, China
[3] School of Information Management, Central China Normal University, Wuhan 430079, China

Abstract. [Purpose/Significance] The health and wellness sector comprises various domains, including healthcare, eldercare, medical services, and tourism. It has garnered significant public attention. In recent years, the rapid growth of digital technology has presented opportunities for enhancing the health and wellness industry. A systematic analysis of China's digital health and wellness policies and strategies is necessary to assess if current policies align with industry needs. This assessment aims to genuinely promote the digital empowerment of the health and wellness sector, align with China's national health strategy, thus offer fresh insights and directions for the adjustment of China's digital health and wellness industry. [Method/Process] To accomplish this, policy documents pertaining to digital health and wellness in China were retrieved from the Peking University's legal and regulatory database and the State Council Policy Document Library. Employing a "subject-theme-tool" framework, a comprehensive analysis of 160 central policy documents was conducted utilizing text econometrics, social network analysis, LDA theme modeling, and content analysis tools. [Results/Conclusion] The research findings reveal shortcomings in China's digital health policies, characterized by a lack of depth in the implementation of healthcare services. In addition, there appears an uneven distribution of policy instruments and a pressing need for enhanced coordination among policy stakeholders. Recommendations include a focus on the digital transformation and deployment of high-quality healthcare services, the promotion of policy tool optimization and equilibrium, the enhancement of a multi-party collaborative policy framework, and the formation of policy synergies across different domains.

Keywords: digital health and wellness · digital empowerment · industrial policy · policy content analysis

1 Introduction

The health and wellness industry represents an emerging sector in China's economic development landscape. It constitutes a comprehensive service industry originated from the healthcare sector, with the overarching objective of enhancing public health and delivering health-related services across various domains, including healthcare, elder-care, medical services, and tourism, etc. [1–3] The report of the 20th National Congress of the Communist Party of China explicitly highlights the strategic importance of prioritizing public health and shifting the focus from disease treatment-centric approaches to people-centered health initiatives. Presently, capital entities such as medical institutions, financial firms, tech enterprises, and internet companies have taken proactive steps in entering the healthcare market [4, 5]. This marks a significant strategic move towards the development of China's digital healthcare industry, where information technology plays a critical role in building a national health information system. The advancement of the digital health and wellness sector closely related to national policy formulation, offering fresh perspectives and future developmental pathways. This article delves into the efficient categorization of core digital health and wellness industry policies, the reasonableness of current policy instruments, and the directions for future policy enhancements. Considering this context, this article adopts a "subject-theme-tool" perspective to quantitatively assess the content of central government policy documents pertaining to the digital health and wellness industry. Thereafter, it puts forward policy recommendations grounded in the derived conclusions.

2   Related Research

An analysis of existing literature reveals that research on digital health and wellness policies predominantly concentrates on the domains of smart elderly care and telemedicine. From a qualitative standpoint, Hung J evaluates the gaps in existing elderly care technologies and policy formulation [6]. Meanwhile, Mao et al. delve into application policies in robotic healthcare [7]. In terms of quantitative analysis, researchers primarily employ quantitative methods to analyze factors such as policy release dates and publication topics. One commonly utilized approach for policy text analysis involves coding policy clauses in policy documents according to specific rules, employing frameworks such as "policy tools policy objectives policy effectiveness," "hierarchy of elderly needs policy tools," and "health and medical big data value chain policy tools" for multidimensional analysis [8, 9]. Another approach involves constructing a keyword co-occurrence network using text mining methods and evaluating and comparing policies based on PMC index [10]. In summary, while the aforementioned research systematically categorizes and analyzes policies in key health sectors in China, the public's focus on the health industry has expanded beyond medical treatment and elderly care with economic development. Presently, there is limited literature on the field of national health informatization. Most existing research analyses are relatively one-dimensional, with research scope limitations. There is a dearth of exploration into the adaptability of policy structures from a comprehensive perspective.

Therefore, this article introduces a three-dimensional analytical framework including "subject, theme, and tool." By analyzing the adaptability between subjects, themes, and tools, this framework aims to elucidate the operational logic and intrinsic connections in digital health and wellness policies, promoting the informatization transformation of national health in China.

3 Data Acquisition and Technical Roadmap

3.1 Data Sources

To enhance the reliability and validity of the policy, this article formulates the initial search criteria based on thematic characteristics and performs comprehensive text searches utilizing keywords such as "smart elderly care," "health informatization," "digital health care," "smart health," and "health digitization" in the policy document repositories of the State Council and Peking University's legal and regulatory database. Following review and content filling, a total of 160 policy documents were finally collected, forming the foundational dataset for policy text analysis.

3.2 Technology Roadmap

This article employs a comprehensive array of text econometric methods, social network analysis, LDA topic models, and content analysis tools to construct a three-dimensional analytical framework incorporating external attributes, thematic elements, and policy instruments. It focuses on assessing the adaptability of "subject-theme," "subject-tool," and "theme-tool" from a combined perspective.

(1) External policy characteristics
This article conducts an analysis of key aspects in digital health and wellness policy, including the timing of policy releases and their focal subjects. By analyzing the timing of policy releases, one can gain an intuitive understanding of policy evolution and make predictions regarding the future developmental direction of digital health and wellness policies. Examining policy subjects allows us to identify the primary policy makers and understand the communication and collaborative relationships among various departments, as determined through social network analysis.

(2) Policy themes
The LDA topic model, a classical bag of words model, represents documents using word vectors and generates both "document-subject distribution" and "topic-word distribution." To optimize the effectiveness of the analysis, this article first employs the 'jieba' tool to segment policy texts, eliminating words devoid of substantive meaning. The distribution probability of each topic in each document is then calculated. On an annual basis, this article determines the evolution of theme intensity for each theme in a unit of time.

(3) Policy tools
Policy tools serve as the government's means to translate policy objectives into specific implementation methods [11]. Currently, the academic community lacks a consensus on the classification of policy tools. The most established approach involves categorizing policy tools into three categories based on their differing effects on industrial development: supply-oriented, demand-oriented, and environmental-oriented. This categorization proves suitable for policy analysis pertaining to industrial innovation and aligns well with contemporary research on digital health and wellness industry policies in China (Table 1).

Table 1. Name, connotation, and definition of policy tools

Type	Name	definition
Supply-oriented	infrastructure construction	Improve the various supporting basic equipment required for digital health and wellness
	public services	Building public service platforms and other service carriers to provide support for the construction of digital health and wellness systems
	talent cultivation	Provide talent guarantee for the development of digital health and wellness industry
	capital investment	The government provides financial support in the form of financial appropriations, special funds, research and development funds, etc.
	technology investment	The government provides technical support for the digital health and wellness industry by supporting high-tech research and development such as information technology
	education and training	Carry out health education promotion and skill training activities to enhance the digital health management level of residents
	policy support	The government encourages preferential policies such as industrial land use and management fee income incentives to support the development of the digital health and wellness industry
Environment-oriented	standardization construction	Develop digital health and wellness standards for relevant sub sectors to promote standardized development
	financial support	By improving tax preferential policies, providing subsidies for related expenses, to optimize health management measures
	regulatory safeguards	The government ensures the healthy development of the digital health industry by formulating a series of regulations, systems, and other supervision measures

(*continued*)

Table 1. (*continued*)

Type	Name	definition
	evaluation mechanisms	Use evaluation mechanisms to objectively evaluate the development of the digital health and wellness industry
	goal planning	Propose specific goals and tasks around the requirements for digital upgrading throughout the entire lifecycle health
	policy promotion	Clearly propose to do a good job in policy promotion and strengthen public opinion guidance
Demand-oriented	Industry Convergence	Develop industry chain alliances and optimize the innovative value chain of the digital health and wellness industry
	Cooperation	Encourage the integration of overseas governments, universities, and technology enterprises to accelerate the transformation of digital health and wellness research achievements
	Service system	Build and improve the digital health and wellness industry service system, and shape a distinctive health and wellness market
	Pilot demonstration	Encourage the construction of pilot cities and play a demonstrative and leading role
	Achievement transformation	Improve the mechanism for transforming achievements and encourage digital empowerment of the digital health and wellness industry

4 Analysis of the Structure of Digital Health and Wellness Policies Based on a Three-Dimensional Analysis Framework

4.1 External Policy Characteristics

4.1.1 Policy Releasing Time

Since 2013, China's digital health and wellness policies have exhibited an overall fluctuating upward trend. Based on the changes in policy introductions, this article categorizes the evolution of digital health and wellness policies into three stages: the embryonic stage (2013–2016), marked by relatively few policy releases, all of which remain below 10; the exploration and development stage (2016–2020), characterized by a continued increase in policy releases, with an average annual publication volume of nearly 10 articles; and the deepening and improvement stage (2020–2023). In the backdrop of the COVID-19 pandemic, the government's attention to digital health and wellness has surged. While some fluctuations persist, the overall level remains high, and it is expected that the number of policies will continue to exhibit a high level in the future (Fig. 1).

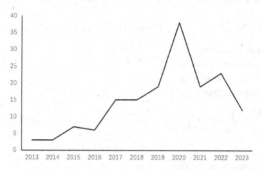

Fig. 1. Changes in the number of publications

4.1.2 Policy Issuing Subject

(1) Issuing subject

The study comprises a total of 54 government departments, illustrating the diversity of subjects covered by digital health and wellness policies. Among these, the National Health Commission emerges as the central driving force behind the promotion of digital healthcare, boasting the highest number of independent publications. From the perspective of collaborative publications, most departments have issued policy documents through cooperative efforts. This collaborative approach is primarily driven by the recognition that digital health and wellness constitute a comprehensive industry, necessitating the collective participation of various entities to effectively leverage the potential of digital empowerment, considering the current state of the industry (Table 2).

(2) Collaboration network

The findings reveal that the National Health Commission serves as the core department in the formulation body, demonstrating the closest connections with the National Administration of Traditional Chinese Medicine, the Ministry of Industry and Information Technology, the National Medical Security Bureau, the Ministry of Civil Affairs, the Ministry of Education, and the Ministry of Finance. These departments oversee matters closely related to national health and digital transformation, often necessitating collaborative efforts, thereby reflecting the central focus of China's digital health policy (Fig. 2).

Table 2. Issuing frequency (part)

Subject	Frequency	Separate publication	Joint publication
National Health Commission	34	74	108
State Administration of Traditional Chinese Medicine	5	49	54
Ministry of Finance	0	33	33
National Development and Reform Commission (including former National Development and Planning Commission and former National Planning Commission)	1	32	33
Ministry of Civil Affairs	3	30	33
National Medical Security Administration	0	31	31
Ministry of Education	0	24	24
Ministry of Human Resources and Social Security	0	19	19
Ministry of Industry and Information Technology	0	17	17
National Health and Family Planning Commission (revoked)	6	7	13

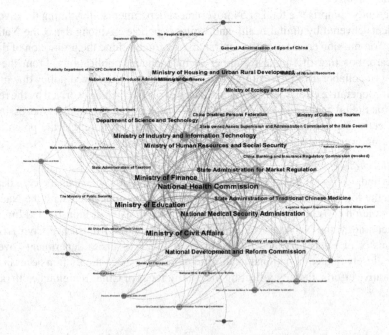

Fig. 2. Cooperation network diagram

4.2 Analysis of Policy Text Content

(1) Policy Theme Mining

Firstly, digital security and standardization. The frequent occurrence of characteristic words such as "standards," "data," "information," and "norms" in this theme indicates that policies under this category primarily aim to establish a robust legal and policy framework for digital health [12]. Secondly, the national health information system. The prevalence of characteristic words such as "electronics," "platforms," "data," and "sharing" in this theme highlights policies' objectives to utilize information technology for health information collection, enable cross-departmental data sharing, and create a strong foundation for real-time monitoring and analysis of public health. Thirdly, digital transformation of health institutions. In this context, characteristic terms such as "Internet," "medical," "medical institutions," and "diagnosis and treatment" are frequently encountered [13, 14]. Finally, digital health and wellness services. The recurring presence of characteristic terms such as "elderly care," "smart," "intelligent," and "product" emphasizes that elderly care and medical care are the primary application scenarios for digital healthcare in China (Table 3).

Table 3. Classification of Digital Health and wellness Policy Themes

Topic	Topic Type	Keyword
0	digital security and standardization	health, data, standards, medical treatment, information, systems, traditional Chinese medicine, hygiene, informatization, norm
1	national health information system	health, information, electronics, platforms, hygiene, residents, data, internet, informatization, national
2	digital transformation of health institutions	medical treatment, internet, remote, medical institutions, hospitals, diagnosis and treatment, health, patients, grassroots, institutions
3	digital health services	health, elderly care, intelligence, traditional Chinese medicine, elderly people, traditional Chinese medicine, products, technology, community

(2) Analysis of Policy Intensity Evolution

To begin, the level of awareness regarding data security and standardization appears relatively subdued. Attention towards data security standards has consistently remained at a low ebb, but there has been a notable growth trend in the past two years. Secondly, the health information system assumes a critical role in the broader landscape of national healthcare. Thirdly, there is growing recognition of the digital transformation in healthcare institutions. In recent years, healthcare institutions have leveraged online consultations to extend medical services to rural and home-based settings. Notably, in 2020, amidst the COVID-19 outbreak, telemedicine emerged as a critical tool for healthcare delivery across China. Fourthly, the development of digital health and wellness applications is progressing steadily. China has employed information technology to broaden elderly care and medical access, including models such as community-based elderly care and home-based elderly care. While there have been some fluctuations in attention towards digital health and elderly care services since 2017, the overall trend indicates growth compared to previous years (Fig. 3).

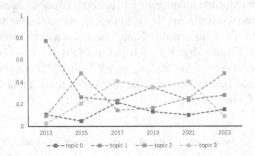

Fig. 3. Evolution process of theme intensity in different years

4.3 Quantitative Analysis of Policy Texts

All three primary policy tool categories and their sub-items are covered. However, there exists a significant imbalance in their utilization: supply-oriented policy tools constitute the highest share at 43.87%, followed by environmental-oriented policies at 35.20%, with demand-oriented policies having the lowest share at 20.93% in supply-oriented policy tools (Table 4).

Table 4. Distribution Table of Basic Policy Tools

Category	Tool Name	Number	Internal proportion	Overall proportion	Total
Supply-oriented	Infrastructure construction	47	11.33%	4.97%	415
	public services	292	70.36%	30.87%	
	talent cultivation	18	4.34%	1.90%	
	capital investment	5	1.20%	0.53%	

(continued)

Table 4. (*continued*)

Category	Tool Name	Number	Internal proportion	Overall proportion	Total
	technology investment	19	4.58%	2.01%	
	education and training	23	5.54%	2.43%	
	policy support	11	2.65%	1.16%	
Environment-oriented	standardization construction	128	38.44%	13.53%	333
	financial support	4	1.20%	0.42%	
	regulatory safeguards	79	23.72%	8.35%	
	evaluation mechanisms	28	8.41%	2.96%	
	goal planning	66	19.82%	6.98%	
	policy promotion	28	8.41%	2.96%	
Demand-oriented	Industry Convergence	29	14.65%	3.07%	298
	Cooperation	18	9.09%	1.90%	
	Service system	114	57.58%	12.05%	
	Pilot demonstration	36	18.18%	3.81%	
	Achievement transformation	1	0.51%	0.11%	

4.4 "Subject-Tool" Combination Analysis

This article selects the utilization of policy tools by the top 10 core institutions with the highest number of publications (Table 5). It is evident that most core institutions exhibit a balanced selection of policy tools in their publications, effectively addressing the roles of supply, environmental, and demand policy tools in advancing digital health and wellness. Comparatively, these core institutions exhibit a greater focus on supply-oriented policy tools to drive the growth of the digital health and wellness industry. However, it is notable that the National Health and Planning Commission displays a noticeable deficiency in the utilization of demand-oriented policy tools, potentially overlooking the market-driven factors influencing industrial development.

Table 5. "Subject-Tool" Combination Analysis

Subject	supply-oriented	environmental-oriented	demand-oriented
National Health Commission	252	196	148
State Administration of Traditional Chinese Medicine	160	105	72
Ministry of Finance	32	18	22
National Development and Reform Commission (including former National Development and Planning Commission and former National Planning Commission)	27	17	18
Ministry of Civil Affairs	52	31	40
National Medical Security Administration	45	24	23
Ministry of Education	30	10	15
Ministry of Human Resources and Social Security	19	13	13
Ministry of Industry and Information Technology	51	26	40
National Health and Family Planning Commission (revoked)	46	42	6

4.5 "Subject-Theme" Combination Analysis

This article selects the top 10 institutions with the highest number of publications to analyze their thematic tendencies (Table 6). It was observed that due to the unique roles played by various institutions, there exist significant differences in the focus of their research topics. The National Health Commission and the State Administration of Traditional Chinese Medicine emerge as critical entities in the establishment of the national health information system. The Ministry of Civil Affairs, being the primary institution responsible for civil affairs in China, relies on community and other civil affairs service institutions to support the national health information system. The enactment of policies related to digital healthcare services correlates directly with elderly care and other business sectors, resulting in a higher number of publications under these two themes. The Ministry of Finance's policy issuance pattern reflects China's robust financial support for the health service system, which is relatively lacking in other thematic areas. The Ministry of Industry and Information Technology places significant emphasis on the development of the national health information system and digital healthcare services, demonstrating its active involvement in health informatization initiatives.

Table 6. "Subject-theme" Combination Analysis

Subject	topic 0	topic 1	topic 2	topic 3
National Health Commission	104	213	193	86
State Administration of Traditional Chinese Medicine	50	139	110	38
Ministry of Finance	2	27	32	141
National Development and Reform Commission (including former National Development and Planning Commission and former National Planning Commission)	2	17	29	14
Ministry of Civil Affairs	7	33	17	66
National Medical Security Administration	2	32	47	11
Ministry of Education	2	20	24	9
Ministry of Human Resources and Social Security	1	12	25	7
Ministry of Industry and Information Technology	5	28	35	49
National Health and Family Planning Commission (revoked)	19	44	28	3

4.6 "Tool-Theme" Combination Analysis

Data security and regulation are established by government departments to define industry standards and laws; therefore, they are predominantly influenced by environment-oriented policy instruments. The national health information system aims to aggregate extensive data on national health through platforms, with communities, hospitals, and medical institutions at its core. Therefore, supply-oriented policy tools are widely employed, focusing on infrastructure and public services. Simultaneously, environment-oriented policy instruments are actively utilized in this context to promote and standardize extensive public health data and to bolster the concept of public health information. The theme of digital transformation in healthcare institutions demands attention to the development of foundational information systems. Utilizing information technology to establish online data platforms and expanding service models to deliver accurate and efficient healthcare services through remote medical care, online consultations, and similar means is essential. This taps into the burgeoning market demand to drive the digital transformation of healthcare institutions. Policy tools employed in digital health and wellness services are relatively balanced, with a significantly higher proportion of demand-oriented policy tools compared to other themes. Digital health and wellness services aim to cater to the health and wellness needs of the entire population using a variety of health products and service models. As a result, the primary focus in this theme revolves around exploring the implementation and application of health and wellness services through service systems and pilot demonstrations (Fig. 4).

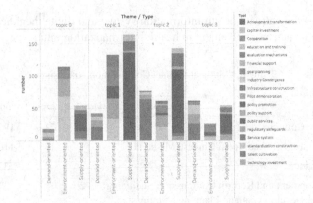

Fig. 4. "Tool-theme" Combination Analysis

5   Policy Recommendations for the Digital Health and Wellness Industry

This article analyzes the content structure of digital health and wellness policy documents, revealing the characteristics of these policies from the perspective of the "subject-theme-tool" combination. It also identifies areas of weakness to aid in enhancing the current digital health and wellness work system.

(1) Insufficient richness of health service applications
In an era characterized by evolving and diverse social demands, the concept of health has transcended traditional physical well-being to consist of holistic health, including physical, psychological, spiritual, environmental, and other facets. However, the government's current focus on digitalizing the health and wellness industry primarily revolves around healthcare and elderly care sectors. This limited attention to higher-level health needs, such as monitoring personal living conditions, addressing mental stress, and promoting social engagement, leaves it ill-prepared to adapt to the continually emerging digital healthcare scenarios.

(2) Imbalance in the application structure of policy tools
Considering that China's digital health and wellness industry is still in its early stages, the government primarily focuses on bolstering the supply aspect, including infrastructure and public services, to provide internal impetus for the advancement of the digital health and wellness sector. However, due to the absence of external factors such as communication and cooperation, industrial integration, and achievement transformation, there exists a deficiency in industrial coordination and collaboration among multiple stakeholders. Therefore, this hinders the effective establishment of an open and shared social health and wellness industry, thus limiting the integrated development of the digital health and wellness sector.

(3) The coordination and cooperation among policy entities need to be strengthened
China has progressively established a decision-making body circle comprising core entities such as the National Health Commission, the National Administration of Traditional

Chinese Medicine, the Ministry of Industry and Information Technology, the National Medical Security Bureau, the Ministry of Civil Affairs. While the current policy-making bodies are reasonably structured, the complex scope of digital healthcare groups and scenarios necessitates enhanced cooperation among key stakeholders throughout the entire national health industry process.

To sum up, our country should make precise efforts in the following three aspects. Firstly, focusing on the digital transformation and implementation of high-level health services. Secondly, promote the optimization and balance of policy tools, and improve the adaptability between policy tools and themes. Thirdly, improve the policy system of multi-party collaboration, and form policy synergy for different themes.

Acknowledgement. This research was supported by Major Research Project on Philosophy and Social Sciences of The Ministry of Education 20JZD024.

References

1. Fang, H., Zhang, X.: Health care industry: concept definition and theory construction. J. Sichuan Univ. Sci. Eng. **35**(04), 1–20 (2020). (in Chinese)
2. Rajesh, P., et al.: Role of the personal KinetiGraph in the routine clinical assessment of Parkinson's disease: recommendations from an expert panel. Expert Rev. Neurother. **18**(8), 669–680 (2018)
3. Swarthout, M., Bishop, M.A.: Population health management: review of concepts and definitions. Am. J. Health Syst. Pharm. **74**(18), 1405–1411 (2017)
4. Singh, B., Davis, L.S.: An analysis of scale invariance in object detection-SNIP. In: Proceedings of IEEE Conference on Computer Vision and Pattern Recognition, pp. 3578–3587 (2018)
5. Nowak, D.J., Crane, D.E., Stevens, J.C.: Air pollution removal by urban trees and shrubs in the United States. Urban Forestry Urban Greening **4**(3), 115–123 (2006)
6. Hung, J.: Smart elderly care services in China: challenges, progress, and policy development. Sustainability **15**(1), 178 (2022)
7. Mao, Z., Liu, Z., et al.: Research on the application policy in medical and health robots from the perspective of international comparison. Sci. Technol. Manage. Res. **41**(10), 49–59 (2021). (in Chinese)
8. Yang, L., Hu, K., et al.: China's smart elderly care policy based on content analysis. J. Shanghai Univ. **38**(04), 118–127 (2021). (in Chinese)
9. Hu, Y., Liu, X., et al.: Quantitative study of China's policies on smart elderly care industry: based on a three-dimensional analytical framework. J. Beijing Univ. Aeronaut. Astronaut. **36**(02), 67–77 (2023). (in Chinese)
10. Zhai, Y., Guo, L., et al.: Evaluation of telemedicine policies base on PMC index model. J. Inf. Resour. Manage. **12**(02), 112–122+137 (2022). (in Chinese)
11. Rothwell, R., Zegveld, W.: Reindustrialization and Technology, pp. 113–130. Longman, M. E. Sharpe (1985)
12. Azaria, A., Ekblaw, A., Vieira, T., et al.: Using blockchain for medical data access and permission management. In: 2nd International Conference on Open and Big Data (OBD) (Vienna, 2016), pp. 1–2 (2016)
13. Vayena, E., Haeusermann, T., Adjekum, A., et al.: Digital health: meeting the ethical and policy challenges. Swiss Med. Wkly. **148**, w14571 (2018)
14. Bates, D.W., Saria, S., Ohno-Machado, L., et al.: Big data in health care: using analytics to identify and manage high-risk and high-cost patients. Health Aff. **33**(7), 1123–1131 (2014)

Selling in Prompt Marketplace: An Empirical Study on the Joint Effects of Linguistic and Demonstration Signals on Prompt Sales

Cuicui Cao[1], Ling Zhao[2(✉)], Yuni Li[1], and Chongyang Xie[3]

[1] Hubei University of Economics, Wuhan 430205, China
[2] Huazhong University of Science and Technology, Wuhan 430074, China
lingzhao@mail.hust.edu.cn
[3] China University of Geosciences (Wuhan), Wuhan 430074, China

Abstract. The proliferation of generative artificial intelligence (GAI) spawns a new type of freelance digital platform: prompt marketplace, on which prompt engineers upload their prompts and sell them to potential buyers. As only freelancers themselves know about the prompt in detail and they can only provide limited textual information, great information asymmetry exists that may hinder exchange. Besides, one distinct feature of prompt marketplace is that prompt engineers can display part of their prompt to potential buyers. Thus, drawing on the signaling theory, this study investigates the joint effects of linguistic and demonstration signals on prompt sales. Data from 16,890 prompts were collected and analyzed. Results show that linguistic signals and their interaction with demonstration signals significantly influence prompt sales. Interestingly, we found the negative direct influence of demonstration signals on prompt sales. Our study has theoretical contributions to freelance digital platform literature and extends signaling theory to prompt marketplace. This study can also provide practical suggestions to platforms and freelancers alike.

Keywords: Prompt Engineering · Prompt Sales · Informational Signal · Affective Signal · Demonstration Signal

1 Introduction

Recent years has witnessed the astonishing progress in generative artificial intelligence (GAI). Currently, typical GAI models include text-generation AI like ChatGPT and image-generation AIs like DALL-E and Midjourney. Different from prior AI assistants (e.g., Siri), GAI is capable of generating novel content similar to that created by humans, and has the potential to fundamentally disrupt how content is produced [6]. GAI has and will become increasingly integrated into organizational and individual task performing and decision-making[14]. Therefore, effective usage of GAI is critical, which means that users should know how to write appropriate prompt to obtain high-quality output. Despite prompts appearing as simple text sentences, some individuals may find it challenging to effectively communicate with GAI models and convey their

Y. P. Tu and M. Chi (Eds.): WHICEB 2024, LNBIP 516, pp. 264–275, 2024.
https://doi.org/10.1007/978-3-031-60260-3_22

desired output [11]. Accordingly, specialized prompt marketplaces have emerged, such as PromptBase, PromptSea and TipStore, on which prompt engineers can create and sell high-quality prompts [11]. These prompt engineers are mostly freelancers, who are interested in prompt engineering. Their sales performance is of great significance to the long-term prosperity of prompt marketplaces. The reason is that if their prompt cannot be sold to potential buyers, then these engineers may quit and switch to other platforms. Thus, understanding the contributing factors of the prompt's sales performance is very important.

Based on prior research, prompt marketplace can be regarded as a kind of high-skill and location-independent freelance platform [5, 8]. These platforms such as Upwork and Fiverr mostly adopt the form of crowd work. That is, buyers post gigs or short-term service projects aiming to initiate interested freelance workers to submit bids to offer their services [5, 8]. However, in prompt marketplace, freelancers create prompts they are good at and submit them to the platform. Then, the platform validates the effectiveness of these prompts and they can be sold to the potential buyers. Meanwhile, the platform provides payment services and trust building mechanisms [5]. Despite the above differences, these platforms suffer great information asymmetry, because they rely on text-based messages [8], which may create uncertainty and hinder the exchange. Take the prompt marketplace for instance, the prompt is not a standard product and only the prompt engineer knows about the details. Thus, they provide prompt descriptions to tell something about the prompt to the potential buyers. However, the role of prompt descriptions on prompt sales is unclear.

Besides, in prior freelance market, the final delivered product or service is invisible to potential buyers before the final transaction [8]. However, on prompt marketplace, freelancers can display part of their prompt to potential buyers. For instance, ChatGPT prompt engineers can display example input and output of the corresponding prompt, which is something like a free sample [10]. This kind of display may transfer additional information about the free-lancer and the prompt. Currently, this example display is a must on many prompt marketplaces [10] and different engineers' display varies greatly. Thus, having a deep understanding of the role of this example display on prompt sales is quite important for platforms and prompt engineers.

Further, considering the information asymmetry between potential buyers and prompt engineer in our context, we apply linguistic signal (i.e., how a prompt engineer communicates with potential consumers through the linguistic descriptions of prompt) [13] to capture prompt descriptions and demonstration signal (i.e., actions taken by the service provider from which outsiders can experience certain unobservable aspects about the provider and product) to capture example display of prompt [15]. Accordingly, our study intends to address the following research questions: How do linguistic signals of prompt descriptions interact with demonstration signals to influence prompt sales?

To solve the above research questions, we applied signaling theory to build our theoretical model and proposed the joint effect of linguistic and demonstration signal on prompt sales. Then, we collected 16,890 pieces of prompt information from PromptBase to validate the theoretical model. Our results verify the significant in-fluence of linguistic signals and their interaction with demonstration signals.

2 Theoretical Background

2.1 Prompt Marketplace as a Digital Freelance Platform

This study regards prompt marketplace as a special kind of digital freelance platform considering its similarity and uniqueness. Specifically, as a type of digital freelance platform, prompt marketplace is similar with traditional digital freelance platform in terms of flexibility, actors, and information asymmetry. Firstly, freelancers' work on the platform is flexible and is not limited by time and space [5]. They depend on this platform to provide their services. Secondly, the prompt marketplace is a matchmaker that not only brings together prompt engineers and recipients of prompts but also provides payment services and trust building mechanisms [5]. There are three main actors, including sellers (i.e., prompt engineers), buyers and intermediary platform. Finally, great information asymmetry exists between freelancers and potential buyers [8]. Only freelancers themselves know about their product in detail. On prompt marketplace, only textual descriptions of prompt and prompt examples are provided.

However, prompt marketplace is different from traditional digital freelance plat-form in in terms of task type, workflow and the visibility of the final delivery product. Firstly, different from the various task types on previous freelance platform, task type on prompt marketplace is single. That is, freelancers' task is to create high-quality prompt. Secondly, the workflow on prompt marketplace is different and accordingly the main actors' role differs. Specifically, prompt engineers usually create prompts by themselves and then post them to the prompt marketplace. Then, the platform checks the effectiveness of the prompt and the prompt can appear on the marketplace. Finally, when potential buyers need relevant prompt, they may search for prompts by themselves and then make the final purchase. Finally, opposed to the invisibility on prior freelance platform, on prompt marketplace, freelancers usually provide examples of the final delivery product before transaction.

These above-mentioned differences make conclusions from prior freelance market in current literature not be applicable to prompt marketplace. For instance, in prior freelance market, as buyers needs to describe a gig and then multiple freelancers apply by formulating bids that describe themselves, freelancers' success depends not only on their own descriptions but on their mimicry of the buyers [8]. Besides, as the final delivery product before transaction in current literature is mostly invisible and accordingly the role of prompt example has not been considered. Thus, the current study aims to investigate the role of prompt descriptions and prompt example on prompt sales performance, which is an indicator of freelancer success.

2.2 Signaling Theory

As mentioned, higher information asymmetry exists between freelancers and buyers in prompt marketplace. To improve this asymmetry, prompt descriptions and prompt example are provided to potential buyers, which aligns with the goal of signaling theory. Signaling theory was proposed to analyze how individuals with information advantage in the market can credibly transmit information to individuals with information disadvantage through "signal transmission" to achieve efficient market equilibrium [12]. In information systems research, this theory has been used to investigate online healthcare market [15], live streaming e-commerce [3] and crowd sourcing [13], all of which are characterized by information asymmetry. Therefore, it is suitable to apply this theory to investigate the role of prompt descriptions and example on sales performance.

Based on prior studies, signals can be classified into many types according to different dimensions [13]. Contextualized in the current study, we classify signals into description signal and demonstration signal [15]. Description signals are provided to outsiders by way of descriptions about a provider and their products. Specifically, we regard prompt description as a kind of linguistic description signals and classify them into informational and affective linguistic description signals [13]. Besides, demonstration signals refer to actions taken by the service provider from which outsiders can experience certain un-observable aspects about the provider and product [15]. In the current study, we mainly focus on prompt input style, which implies the engineers' refinement, expertise and effort, as the demonstration signal [1]. The next section will discussion the detailed conceptualization and its influence on prompt sales.

3   Research Model and Hypotheses

Based on the previous discussion, we display our research model in, Firstly, we hypoth-esize the direct influence of two kinds of linguistic signals on prompt sales, namely, informational and affective signals. Then, we hypothesize the direct influence of demon-stration signals (i.e., prompt input style) on prompt sales. Finally, we hypothesize the joint effects of linguistic and demonstration signals on prompt sales. We will expound these research hypotheses in the following sections (Fig. 1).

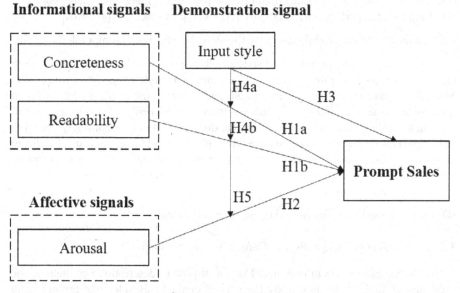

Fig. 1. Research Model

3.1 Direct Influence of Linguistic and Demonstration Signals

Firstly, we consider the influence of informational linguistic signals of prompt descriptions, which can improve the comprehensibility of signals sent by the prompt engineer [13]. Specifically, we focus on the concreteness and readability of the prompt descriptions [2, 13]. On the one hand, concreteness describes the extent to which a word pertains to an actual, tangible, or "real" entity, describing objects and actions in a way that is more concrete, familiar, and easily perceived [13]. Thus, the concreteness level of the prompt description can enhance potential buyers' comprehension of the functions of the prompt, thereby increasing their likelihood to buy this prompt. On the other hand, readability refers to the ease or difficulty of reading caused by the usage of words in written texts[2]. Thus, the more readable prompt descriptions enable potential buyers to grasp the purposes of the prompt effortlessly. Meanwhile, concreteness and readability also indicate the prompt engineers' effort in crafting the description, which can also persuade potential consumers. Thus, we propose the following hypotheses:

H1a: The concreteness of the prompt description positively influences prompt sales.
H1b: The readability of the prompt description positively influences prompt sales.

Secondly, we analyze the influence of affective linguistic signals in prompt descriptions, which can influence evaluation and judgement of attitude objects [13], such as products. Specifically, we focus on the emotional arousal conveyed by prompt descriptions, which indicates the emotional intensity in prompt descriptions and level of activation exhibited by the actor [4]. Based on prior studies, higher level of arousal in text can be perceived as a stronger reflection of the actor's subjective opinion, signaling irrationality [4]. Consequently, in the context of prompt descriptions, potential buyers may perceive the arousal as an exaggeration by the prompt engineer, potentially impeding the prompt's sales performance. Thus, we propose the following hypothesis:

H2: The arousal of the prompt description negatively influences prompt sales.

Finally, we consider prompt input style as a demonstration signal pertaining to both the prompt engineer and the prompt itself. Prompt input style is important for refining prompts to match user expectations and are added during the creation process [1]. It necessitates persistent efforts by prompt engineers to repeatedly refine the specifics of the concrete prompt and ultimately extract the distinctive styles. Accordingly, the input style indicates a time-consuming and resource-intensive endeavor that takes significant effort, thus serving as a high-credibility demonstration signal in prompt marketplace [15]. Thus, potential buyers are likely to view a prompt with input style as exhibiting expertise and effort and we propose the following hypothesis:

H3: Prompt input style positively influences prompt sales.

3.2 Joint Effect of Linguistic and Demonstration Signals

As mentioned earlier, the informational signal of prompt description can improve the understandability of signals sent by the prompt engineer. Besides, the prompt input style as a demonstration signal implies expertise and effort. It is more diagnostic and can provide additional evidence to the potential buyers to directly observe the prompt engineer's ability to write high-quality prompts as well as their effort [15]. Thus, exposure to this kind of demonstration signal will further strengthen the positive influence of informational signals [15]. Meanwhile, the potential buyers will also perceive the arousal that signals irrationality differently when being exposed to this demonstration signal. That is, when an engineer of high expertise says something irrational about the prompt, it will be more easily accepted. Thus, we propose the following hypothesis:

H4a: Input style strengthens the positive influence of concreteness on prompt sales.
H4b: Input style strengthens the positive influence of readability on prompt sales.
H5: Input style weakens the negative influence of arousal on prompt sales.

4   Research Method

4.1   Data Collection and Preprocessing

To test our research hypotheses, we crawled data from PromptBase (https://promptbase. com/), one of the earliest and largest prompt marketplaces. We programmed a web crawler to obtain information regarding ChatGPT prompt, including title, tips, author name, description, and prompt details. Figure 2 displayed an example of our dataset. We collected 16,890 pieces of ChatGPT prompt information in total.

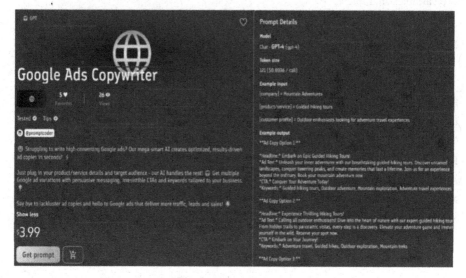

Fig. 2. Example dataset

4.2   Variable Description

Prompt Sales (PS): This variable measured the sales performance of each prompt.

Concreteness (CR): This variable measured the concreteness of prompt descriptions. Based on prior research [13], we applied Linguistic Inquiry and Word Count (LIWC) 2015 software to obtain word frequency of articles, prepositions and quantifiers and finally summed them up.

Readability (RD): This variable measured the readability of prompt descriptions. Based on prior research, we operationalized it as the number of words per sentence (WPS), which can be obtained from LIWC 2015 [2].

Arousal (AR): This variable measured the emotional intensity of prompt descriptions [4]. Based on prior research, we used the dictionary developed by Mohammad who quantified arousal scores for nearly 20,000 English words [9]. The arousal level of a prompt description is calculated by the total arousal scores of matched words.

Input Style (IS): This variable measured the input style of example prompt input. We operationalized it as 1 if it disclosed key parameters, such as the "[company]" in Fig. 2; or else, we would operationalize it as 0 [1].

Control Variables: We also controlled the effect of following variables on prompt sales: Tip, which is measured by whether the prompt provided tips; Price (PR), which is measured by the price of the prompt; Rating (RA), which is measured by the review rating displayed on the prompt page; Cost, which is measured by the monetary amount per call; Author_sold (AS), which is measured by the history sales of the author displayed on the profile page. We displayed the descriptive statistics and correlations among these core variables in Table 1.

Table 1. Correlations and descriptive statistics

	PS	IS	CR	RD	AR
PS	1				
IS	−0.034	1			
CR	0.014	−0.017	1		
RD	0.010	0.028	0.148	1	
AR	−0.013	−0.003	−0.182	−0.098	1
Mean	2.160	0.333	21.088	16.716	0.469
Std	20.179	0.471	6.433	7.793	0.0494

4.3 Hypothesis Testing Results

As the dependent variable (prompt sales) in the current study is over-dispersed (i.e., the standard deviation value is far greater than its mean) [7], we applied negative binomial regression (NBR) model in Stata 15 to test our hypothesis. The results are shown in Table 2. Model 1 only contained control variables, model 2 added core variables of the current study and model 3 added the interaction terms. As can be seen from Table 2, concreteness and readability had a significantly positive effect on prompt sales, thus supporting H1a and H1b; arousal had a significantly negative effect on prompt sales, thus supporting H2; input style negatively influenced prompt sales, thus not supporting H3. The interaction effect for readability and input style was significantly positive and the result indicates that input style strengthened the positive effect of readability on prompt sales, thus supporting H4b. Besides, the interaction effect for arousal and input style was significantly positive and the result indicates that input style weakened the negative effect of arousal on prompt sales, thus supporting H5. However, the interaction effect for concreteness and input style was insignificant and H4a was not supported.

Table 2. NBR results

Variable	Model 1	Model 2	Model 3
Tip	0.241*** (0.0571)	0.236***(0.0569)	0.239***(0.0571)
PR	0.0321**(0.00969)	0.0336**(0.00928)	0.0345**(0.00921)
RA	0.603***(0.0176)	0.588***(0.0171)	0.587***(0.0169)
Cost	9.961***(2.721)	9.122**(2.719)	9.129**(2.698)
AS	0.649***(0.0475)	0.623***(0.0465)	0.628***(0.0468)
IS		−0.353***(0.0393)	-0.358***(0.0393)
CR		0.00892**(0.00295)	0.00632(0.00369)
RD		0.00613**(0.00226)	0.00164(0.00273)
AR		−2.802***(0.366)	−3.369***(0.449)
CR*IS			0.00886 (0.00613)
RD*IS			0.0130**(0.00481)
AR*IS			1.907**(0.769)
Obs	16,890	16,890	16,890
Pseudo R^2	0.0871	0.0917	0.0920

Notes: * $p < 0.05$, ** $p < 0.01$, *** $p < 0.001$; robust errors in parentheses. We divided author_sold by 1000 during the regression

4.4 Robustness Check

To ensure the robustness of our results, we also performed a series of robustness check (Table 3). Firstly, we chose prompt sales of the lagged 2 months to reanalyze our model and the empirical results (Model 4 and Model 5) remained similar, demonstrating the robustness of our results. Secondly, as arousal and concreteness were summed up by specific category words in prompt descriptions, shorter prompt descriptions might have extreme values and influence the empirical results. As a result, we removed prompt descriptions shorter than 10 words (Model 6 and Model 7). The empirical results still remained similar and this indicated the robustness of our results.

Table 3. Robustness check

Variable	Model 4	Model 5	Model 6	Model 7
Tip	0.203*** (0.0543)	0.205*** (0.0545)	0.260*** (0.0588)	0.262*** (0.0590)
PR	0.0353*** (0.00915)	0.0361*** (0.00909)	0.0342*** (0.00928)	0.0353*** (0.00922)
RA	0.585*** (0.0167)	0.583*** (0.0167)	0.588*** (0.0172)	0.586*** (0.0172)
Cost	8.947*** (2.653)	8.948*** (2.636)	8.635*** (2.794)	8.582*** (2.763)
AS	0.611*** (0.0456)	0.615*** (0.0459)	0.619*** (0.0465)	0.624*** (0.0469)
IS	−0.337*** (0.0384)	−0.340*** (0.0384)	−0.357*** (0.0400)	−0.367*** (0.0399)
CR	0.00779** (0.00289)	−0.00540 (0.00363)	0.0113*** (0.00319)	0.00747 (0.00395)
RD	0.00564** (0.00219)	0.00185 (0.00266)	0.00656** (0.00232)	0.00178 (0.00279)
AR	−2.735*** (0.358)	−3.274*** (0.439)	−2.881** (0.393)	−3.502*** (0.481)
CR*IS		0.00812 (0.00603)		0.0131* (0.00659)
RD*IS		0.0109** (0.00466)		0.0140** (0.00495)
AR*IS		1.808** (0.756)		2.113** (0.814)
Obs	16,890	16,890	16,088	16,088
Pseudo R^2	0.0911	0.0914	0.0923	0.0927

5 Discussion

5.1 Summary of Findings

First, we found the significant influence of linguistic signals (i.e., concreteness and readability) on prompt sales. Specifically, informational signals including concrete-ness and readability positively influence prompt sales. This finding is consistent with prior research, indicating that informational signals are helpful for potential buyers to under-stand the details of the prompt [13]. Meanwhile, we found that affective signals in terms of arousal of the prompt description negatively influenced prompt sales, further validating the irrationality effect of linguistic arousal [4].

. Second and most interestingly, it is found that the demonstration signal (i.e., prompt input style) negatively influences prompt sales, which does not support our hypothesis.

This finding is also inconsistent with prior research, which states that demonstration signals are very important predictor of market demand [15]. We suppose the reason lies in the characteristics of prompt itself. That is, when key parameters of prompt input are disclosed, some potential buyers can infer the main content of the prompt, which decreases their likelihood to buy the prompt.

Finally, and most importantly, we found that prompt input style significantly moderates the influence of readability and arousal on prompt sales. Specifically, it strengthened the positive influence of readability on prompt sales and weakens the negative influence of arousal on prompt sales. This further validates the demonstration signals' potential to provide additional evidence for potential consumers to observe the expertise and effort of the prompt engineer [15].

5.2 Theoretical Implications

Our study has the following theoretical implications. Firstly, this study extends re-search on digital freelance platform by investigating the role of linguistic signals in prompt descriptions. In traditional digital freelance platform, freelancers' success depends not only on their own descriptions but on their mimicry of the buyers [8]. However, the workflow of prompt marketplace is different and the buyer's role is attenuated. Thus, our study emphasizes the significant role of freelancers' own description of prompt.

Secondly, this study extends research on digital freelance platform by investigating the role of demonstration signals on prompt sales. In traditional digital freelance platform, the final delivery product before transaction is completely invisible. However, in prompt marketplace, freelancers can provide an example input and output. Specifically, we examined the prompt input style and found its negative influence. Thus, our study emphasizes the significant role of demonstration signals.

Finally, this study extends research on digital freelance platform by investigating the joint effects of linguistic and demonstration signals on prompt sales. As recent studies emphasize the joint signaling effect [15], our study is timely to provide empirical evidence in our unique context.

5.3 Practical Implications

Our study also has some implications for platforms and prompt engineers. Firstly, our study found the significant role of linguistic signals on prompt sales. Specifically, informational signals including concreteness and readability positively and affective signals (i.e., arousal) negatively influence prompt sales. On the one hand, prompt marketplace can remind prompt engineers regarding how to write prompt descriptions (e.g., more concrete and readable). On the other hand, prompt engineers themselves should invest great effort to write their prompt descriptions as they are helpful to their sales performance.

Secondly, our study found the significant joint effects of linguistic and demonstration signals on prompt sales. Specifically, it strengthened the positive influence of readability on prompt sales and weakens the negative influence of arousal on prompt sales. This means that both platform and prompt engineers should provide additional signals that can demonstrate their expertise, effort and quality of prompt.

Finally, our study found the negative influence of prompt input style on prompt sales. This means that both platform and prompt engineers should take great caution when providing additional demonstration signals. That is, they may provide demonstration signals that do not disclose content of prompt itself.

5.4 Limitations and Future Research Directions

Despite the above-mentioned implications, our study also suffers from the following limitations. Firstly, our study mainly considers informational and affective linguistic signals in terms of prompt descriptions. Future research is encouraged to adopt other perspectives such as the speech act theory. Secondly, we only collect data from Prompt-Base, which is one of the earliest and largest prompt marketplaces. Future research is encouraged to compare the empirical results with other platforms, such as Tipstore in China. Finally, our study only considers prompt input style as a kind of demonstration signal. Future research is encouraged to investigate other demonstration signals, such as the example output quality of the corresponding prompt.

6 Conclusions

The proliferation of GAI models give birth to the prompt marketplace. As a new form of digital freelance platform, conclusions from prior studies cannot be applied directly to it. By considering its uniqueness, this study applies signaling theory to investigate the joint effects of linguistic and demonstration signals on prompt sales. Empirical results show that informational signals (i.e., concreteness and readability) positively and affective signals (i.e., arousal) negatively influence prompt sales. Besides, demonstration signals (i.e., prompt input style) exert significantly negative influence on prompt sales. Further, it strengthened the positive influence of readability on prompt sales and weakens the negative influence of arousal on prompt sales. This study offers practical suggestions for prompt marketplace and prompt engineers regarding how to describe prompt and display prompt example.

Acknowledgement. This research was supported by the Youth Research Fund of Hubei University of Economics under Grant XJYB202307.

References

1. Braun, M., et al.: Can (A) I have a word with you? A taxonomy on the design dimensions of AI prompts. In: Proceedings of the 57th Hawaii International Conference on System Sciences, pp. 559–568 (2024)
2. Chen, L., et al.: A linguistic signaling model of social support exchange in online health communities. Decis. Support Syst. **130**(December 2019), 113233 (2020)
3. Chen, X., et al.: What reduces product uncertainty in live streaming e-commerce? From a signal consistency perspective. J. Retail. Consum. Serv. **74**, 103441 (2023)
4. Chou, Y.C.: How much is too much? The nonlinear link between emotional arousal and review helpfulness. Decis. Support Syst. **175**(September 2022), 114035 (2023)

5. Dunn, M., et al.: Dynamics of flexible work and digital platforms: task and spatial flexibility in the platform economy. Digit. Bus. **3**(1), 100052 (2023)
6. Dwivedi, Y.K., et al.: "So what if ChatGPT wrote it?" Multidisciplinary perspectives on opportunities, challenges and implications of generative conversational AI for research, practice and policy. Int. J. Inf. Manag. **71**, 102642 (2023)
7. Li, Y., Zhao, L.: Collaborating with bounty hunters: how to encourage white hat hackers' participation in vulnerability crowdsourcing programs through formal and relational governance. Inf. Manag. **59**(4), 103648 (2022)
8. Ludwig, S., et al.: Communication in the gig economy: buying and selling in online freelance marketplaces. J. Mark. **86**(4), 141–161 (2022)
9. Mohammad, S.M.: Obtaining reliable human ratings of valence, arousal, and dominance for 20, 000 English words. In: Proceedings of the 56th Annual Meeting of the Association for Computational Linguistics, pp. 174–184 (2018)
10. PromptBase: Prompt details. https://promptbase.com/sell
11. Sparkes, M.: The rise of AI prompt engineers. New Sci. **259**(3454), 17 (2023)
12. Spence, M.: Job market signaling. Q. J. Econ. **87**(3), 355–374 (1973)
13. Wu, S., et al.: Attracting solvers' participation in crowdsourcing contests: the role of linguistic signals in task descriptions. Inf. Syst. J. **34**(1), 6–38 (2024)
14. Yang, B., et al.: Understanding the antecedents of user satisfaction with AI-generated content from a cognitive fit perspective. In: Proceedings of the 57th Hawaii International Conference on System Sciences, pp. 411–420 (2024)
15. Zhou, J., et al.: Description and demonstration signals as complements and substitutes in an online market for mental health care. MIS Q. **46**(4), 2055–2084 (2022)

Enhancing Doctor Performance on Online Health Platforms: The Role of Service Diversity and Differentiation in Patient Choice

Zixuan Wang, Zhaohua Deng, and Guorui Fan[✉]

School of Management, Huazhong University of Science and Technology, Wuhan 430074, China
guoruifan@hust.edu.cn

Abstract. Amidst growing competition on evolving online health platforms, enhancing patient choice and doctor performance is increasingly crucial. This paper aims to explore the influence of service diversity and differentiation in doctor services on patient choice. After collecting data from the platform "HaoDF" and processing the data to screen for outliers, negative binomial regression was utilized for stepwise regression analysis, in which the moderating effects of the degrees of internal and external competition are also considered. The results show that service diversity, service differentiation and their interaction term all have a significant effect on patient's choice positively, with the degrees of internal and external competition enhancing their impacts. This study highlights that for doctors on online platforms, diversifying and differentiating services is key to attracting patients and outperforming in competitive settings, providing an important practical reference for doctors and online health platforms to attract more patients and maximize economic benefits.

Keywords: service diversity · service differentiation · patient choice · online medical services · competition

1 Problem Statement

With the rapid advancement of technology, Online Health Platforms (OHP) have become an integral part of the contemporary healthcare service system. These platforms transcend the boundaries of geography, time, hospital departments, offering a convenient channel for patient-doctor interaction, thereby enhancing the accessibility, continuity, and personalization of medical services. They also provide social and economic returns for healthcare professionals [1]. In OHPs, doctors have the autonomy to determine the pricing and types of their services, a stark contrast to the more regulated environment of offline medical institutions, where doctors have to follow the protocol set by their working places. This autonomy affords doctors greater flexibility and personalized space, simultaneously offering patients a more diverse range of choices. Such diversity and differentiation in service models not only meet the personalized demands of modern consumers but also foster healthy competition in the medical services market. In this competitive landscape, understanding how to enhance online patient selection intentions

© The Author(s), under exclusive license to Springer Nature Switzerland AG 2024
Y. P. Tu and M. Chi (Eds.): WHICEB 2024, LNBIP 516, pp. 276–287, 2024.
https://doi.org/10.1007/978-3-031-60260-3_23

and improve doctor performance has become a key issue in fully realizing the potential value of OHPs and in elevating doctors' income and status.

Current research primarily focuses on the impact of online trust [2, 3], doctor effort [4, 5], and doctor online reputation and word-of-mouth [6] on patient choice behavior. While these studies provide significant insights for maximizing the potential value of OHPs, they have not yet explored the impact of service diversity and differentiation on patient choice. In a competitive environment, service diversity helps attract a broader patient base, and service differentiation helps establish deeper connections within specific patient groups. With diversity expanding patient coverage and differentiation increasing patient loyalty, the combination of these two factors may potentially create an interactive effect. Thus, this study aims to explore how service diversity and differentiation affect doctor performance and how competition between doctors moderates the relationship between service diversity, differentiation, and doctor performance. This exploration is crucial for understanding how doctors can improve their performance on platforms and provides practical guidance for maximizing benefits.

2 Literature Review and Research Hypotheses

2.1 Diversity and Differentiation of Physician Services in Online Health Platforms

Service diversity in the context of Online Health Platforms (OHP) refers to the provision of a range of different types of services by doctors, such as online consultation and team-based approaches, to meet the diverse needs of various patient groups. Differentiation, on the other hand, emphasizes the uniqueness in the degree of specialization or methodology of the services provided, aiming to fulfill patient needs more profoundly. By offering diversified and differentiated services, doctors are able to cater to a broader patient base and establish deeper trust relationships. This not only better satisfies current patients but also facilitates wider and more rapid dissemination of their reputation. While the domain of online doctor services has matured with extensive research focusing on doctor behavior [5, 7] and patient feedback [8] regarding patient choice, only a minority of studies have concentrated on the impacts of diversity, analyzed the impact of service diversity [9] and doctor team diversity [10] on doctor service performance. However, existing research has not yet fully addressed the influence of service differentiation on patient choice and its interactive effect with diversity, thus warranting further investigation into its impact on patient choice.

2.2 Competition Among Doctors in Online Health Platforms

Online Health Platforms offer a transparent and public environment, significantly facilitating patients' ability to compare doctors across the platform in terms of response speed, satisfaction, and professional level. This has introduced a level of competition that is more intense than traditional offline channels. Existing research primarily focuses on the direct impacts of competition, examining how competition among healthcare providers impacts service quality and evaluations [11, 12]. While a few studies have focused on the moderating role of competition, analyzing its moderating effect on the impacts of service quality signals on doctor selection [13], there is a notable gap in exploring how competition moderates the impact on service diversity and differentiation. This area warrants further discussion.

2.3 Research Model and Hypotheses

Based on the above analysis, the theoretical model is established as shown in Fig. 1.

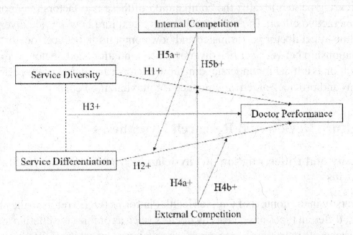

Fig. 1. Model diagram of the theoretical framework of this study

Effect of Service Diversity

In the field of healthcare services, the diversity of services provided by a doctor is positively correlated with the time and effort required. This diversity not only enhances the doctor's ability to attract patients but also meets the needs of a varied patient base more comprehensively. Doctors with a high level of service diversity attract a more diverse patient population, thereby establishing a broader patient social network. Through this network, the doctor's reputation is more widely disseminated, gaining increased exposure and recognition within patient communities, which in turn attracts more new patients. Therefore, the following hypothesis is proposed.

H1: Doctor performance is positively correlated with service diversity, with greater service diversity leading to an increase in the number of new patients acquired by doctors.

Effect of Service Differentiation

Greater differentiation in the services provided by healthcare providers often suggests a requirement for higher professional competencies. Such differentiation may not only strengthen patients' trust in the doctors, leading to a greater likelihood of patients choosing these doctors, but also due to the enhanced trust, make it easier for patients to recommend these doctors within their social networks. Therefore, the following hypothesis is proposed.

H2: Doctor performance is positively correlated with service differentiation, with greater service differentiation leading to an increase in the number of new patients acquired by doctors.

Interactive Effect between Service Diversity and Service Differentiation

Service diversity and differentiation, when aligned, could potentially amplify each other's benefits. For instance, a variety of services (diversity) that are distinct in their execution (differentiation) can cater to a broader spectrum of patient needs and preferences, thereby enhancing a doctor's appeal and marketability and potentially leading to higher patient satisfaction and increased patient referrals. Therefore, the following hypothesis is proposed.

H3: Doctor performance is positively associated with the interactivity between service diversity and service differentiation.

Moderating Effect of External Competition Level

In a highly competitive environment, practitioners in the healthcare sector, especially doctors from various hospitals, are inclined to form cooperative networks for sharing the latest medical technologies and knowledge. This sharing of resources not only aids in enhancing the diversity and distinctiveness of doctors' services but also improves the overall quality of medical care. Additionally, in a competitive milieu, the emphasis that doctors place on their personal reputation markedly increases. Existing academic research indicates that a doctor's reputation significantly influences patient choice. Therefore, the following hypothesis is proposed.

H4a: The degree of external competition has a positive moderating effect between service diversity and doctor performance.
H4b: The degree of external competition has a positive moderating effect between service differentiation and doctor performance.

Moderating Effect of Internal Competition Level

Existing research has shown that internal competition positively influences the enhancement of medical service quality [11]. This improved quality, particularly in terms of better understanding and responding to patient needs, aids in the effective implementation of diversified and differentiated services, thereby more efficiently meeting individual patient requirements. Therefore, the following hypothesis is proposed.

H5a: The degree of internal competition has a positive moderating effect between service differentiation and doctor performance.
H5b: The degree of internal competition has a positive moderating effect between service diversity and doctor performance.

3 Research Methods

3.1 Background and Data Sources for the Study

The data for this study were sourced from the online medical community "HaoDF", covering the period from March 23, 2023, to July 23, 2023, spanning four months. During this time, systematic data collection and analysis were conducted monthly on approximately 70,000 doctors, encompassing their basic personal information, service status, and affiliated hospital information. All incomplete records were removed to ensure the reliability of the results. After removing invalid observations, we obtained a sample of 47,206 users.

3.2 Variables Measurement

Dependent Variable

The dependent variable in this study is the individual performance of doctors, reflected in the change in the total number of patients served. While existing research often measures doctor performance on online health platforms through patient satisfaction (service quality) [14] and the number of new patients (service quantity) [5], this study focuses on patient choice behavior from the patients' perspective, a pre-service behavior unrelated to satisfaction. Hence, patient growth is chosen as the indicator of doctor performance.

Independent Variables

The independent variables in this study are the number of services offered by doctors and the price difference between these services, representing service diversity and service differentiation, respectively. The price difference is defined as the gap between the highest and lowest priced services offered by the doctor. Existing research in marketing has established a link between service differentiation and pricing strategies [15], highlighting that pricing strategies are influenced by service differentiation. On the selected research platform, 'HaoDF', doctors set their own service prices, which reflects the perceived effort for specific services and is impacted by the level of service differentiation. Therefore, a larger price difference signifies greater service differentiation.

Moderator Variables

In this study, the moderating variables of internal and external competition are quantified through specific ratios. specifically, the degree of internal competition is measured by the ratio of the total number of doctors to patients within the same department and hospital on an online health platform. This ratio reflects the intensity of competition for scarce resources—patients—within the same medical environment. Given the similarity in professional roles and service scopes among doctors in the same department and hospital, they form direct competitors in vying for patient resources. Conversely, the degree of external competition is defined by the ratio of the total number of doctors to patients from different hospitals but in the same department on the platform. This ratio reveals the intensity of competition among doctors from different institutions vying for the same patient resources in a competition environment that transcends traditional geographical boundaries. The advent of online health platforms allows doctors from different hospitals to share the same pool of patients, thereby creating a more extensive competitive network within the same department.

Control Variables

In considering doctor performance, several control variables are incorporated to ensure the accuracy of causal inferences. The number of science popularization articles reflects the doctor's effort, as more active engagement in public education typically signi-fies greater professional dedication. Post-treatment reports, warm-hearted gifts, post-treatment evaluations, and satisfaction directly represent patient feedback and satisfac-tion, which can influence future patient choices. Additionally, a doctor's academic title, position, and the tier of the hospital they practice at might influence initial patient selec-tion, as these factors are often perceived as indicators of professional competence and reputation (Table 1).

Table 1. Variable Description

Dimension	Name	Symbol	Definition
Dependent Variable	Patient Increase	Patients	Amount of change in the total number of patients served over a 1-month period
Independent Variable	Service Diversity	Services_num	Number of services provided by doctors
	Service Differentiation	ln_diff_price	Logarithm of the maximum price difference for services provided by doctors
Moderating Variable	Degree of Internal Competitiveness	Internal	Number of doctors in the same department and hospital / number of patients in the same department and hospital
	Degree of External Competitiveness	External	Number of doctors in the same department across different hospitals / Number of patients in the same department across different hospitals
Control Variable	Doctor Title	Doctitle	Divided into 3 levels (2 = Chief physician; 1 = Associate chief physician; 0 = else)
	Hospital Level	Hoslevel	Divided into 2 levels (1 = tertiary hospital; 0 = else)
	Total Hits	ln_hits	Logarithm of total hits

(*continued*)

Table 1. (*continued*)

Dimension	Name	Symbol	Definition
Control Variable	Amount of Science articles	ln_articles	Logarithm of the amount of science articles a doctor posts
	Post-diagnosis check-in	ln_check-in	Logarithm of the total amount of patients who check-in after diagnosis
	Post-diagnosis Review	ln_review	Logarithm of the amount of reviews a doctor got
	Warmhearted Gift	ln_gift	Logarithm of warmhearted gift a doctor got
	Satisfaction	Satisfaction	Between 0 and 1, doctor's satisfaction rating

3.3 Empirical Model

Considering that the dependent variable in this study is a count-based integer continuous variable, a negative binomial regression is utilized to investigate the impact of the explanatory variables:

$$
\begin{aligned}
Patients = {} & \beta_0 + \beta_1 Services\_num + \beta_2\ ln\_diff\_price + \beta_3 Internal + \beta_4 External \\
& + \beta_5 Doctitle + \beta_6 Hoslevel + \beta_7\ ln\_hits + \beta_8\ ln\_articles + \beta_9\ ln\_check-in \\
& + \beta_{10}\ ln\_review + \beta_{11}\ ln\_gift + \beta_{12} Satisfaction + \beta_{13} Service\_num \times ln\_diff\_price \\
& + \beta_{14} Service\_num \times Internal + \beta_{15}\ ln\_diff\_price \times Internal \\
& + \beta_{16} Service\_num \times External + \beta_{17}\ ln\_diff\_price \times External + \epsilon
\end{aligned}
$$

$$(1)$$

β_1 to β_{17} are the regression coefficients, β_0 is the constant term and ϵ is the residual term.

4 Research Findings

Given the high degree of dispersion in the collected data, this study employed a negative binomial regression model for parameter estimation. This model is appropriate for addressing the issue of over-dispersion in count data and provides a more accurate fit to the distribution of the data. The level of statistical significance for all tests was set at $p < .05$. All data were processed and analyzed using STATA. Descriptive statistics and correlation analysis are as follows (Table 2).

4.1 Descriptive Statistics

Table 2. Descriptive statistics for variables

Variable	Obs	Mean	Std.Dev.	Min	Max
Patients	179054	9.743195	32.11451	0	2063
Services_num	179054	2.639612	.8454532	1	5
ln_diff_price	179054	3.362912	1.321584	0	9.21934
Internal	179054	1.057756	2.152093	.0018484	28
External	179054	.4196164	1.213756	.0018692	70
Doctitle	179054	1.117909	.8066699	0	2
Hoslevel	179054	.9507132	.2164668	0	1
ln_hits	179054	11.55173	2.161382	0	18.9283
ln_articles	179054	1.272414	1.508519	0	9.094817
ln_check-in	179054	3.36524	2.730373	0	1.83072
ln_review	179054	2.174709	1.670155	0	8.61722
ln_gift	179054	.6328503	1.124105	0	8.598957
Satisfaction	179054	.2626214	.4371267	0	1

4.2 Empirical Results

The results of the stepwise negative binomial regression are shown in Table 3.

Table 3. Stepwise negative binomial regression results (N = 179054)

Variable	Model 1		Model 2		Model 3		Model 4	
Patients	Coef	S.E.	Coef.	S.E.	Coef.	S.E.	Coef.	S.E.
Serv ~ num	.682***	.013	.619.***	.014	.645***	.014	.612***	.014
ln_dif ~ price	.102***	.009	.098***	.010	.093***	.009	.163***	.004
Doctitle	.229***	.007	.247***	.007	.224***	.007	.245***	.007
Hoslevel	.160***	.025	.030	.025	.065***	.026	−.004	.025
ln_hits	.016***	.004	.024***	.005	.019***	.004	.025***	.005
ln_articles	−.026***	.005	−.022***	.005	−.022***	.005	−.021***	.005
ln_check_in	.011***	.004	.010***	.004	.008**	.004	.009**	.004
ln_review	.015**	.007	−.007	.007	.009	.007	−.008	.004
ln_gift	.005	.009	.006	.008	.009	.008	.007	.008
Satisfaction	.047***	.018	.050	.017	.043**	.018	.049***	.017

(continued)

Table 3. (*continued*)

Variable	Model 1		Model 2		Model 3		Model 4	
Patients	Coef	S.E.	Coef.	S.E.	Coef.	S.E.	Coef.	S.E.
Internal			−1.105***	.017			−1.051***	.018
Serv ~ num# ln_dif ~ price	.036***	.003	.027***	.003	.035***	.003	.028***	.003
Serv ~ num #Internal			.192***	.005			.189***	.006
ln_dif ~ price #Internal			.013***	.003			.007***	.003
External					−1.040***	.034	−.303***	.031
Serv ~ num #External					.155***	.009	.023**	.010
ln_dif ~ price #External					.046***	.005	.032***	.005
t								
2	−.041*	.021	−.040**	.020	−.030	.021	−.041**	.020
3	−.361***	.022	−.302***	.021	−.306***	.021	−.292***	.021
4	−.060***	.021	−.050**	.020	−.045**	.021	−.048**	.020
_cons	−1.190***	.058	−.630***	.049	−.874***	.059	−.550***	.058
/lnalpha	1.640	.004	1.475	.004	1.597	.004	1.472	.004
alpha	5.154	.022	4.372	.019	4.940	.021	4.360	.019
Log likelihood	−423871		−414373		−421659		−414178	
Pseudo R2	.0307		.0524		.0357		.0529	

Note:* p < .1, ** p < .05, *** p < .01

From Table 3, it is evident that Hypotheses 1, 2, 3, 4a, 4b, 5a and 5b are supported. A detailed analysis reveals the following insights: In terms of direct effects, both service diversity and service differentiation exhibit a significant positive impact on individual performance among doctors. Moreover, the interaction between service diversity and service differentiation is also found to be significantly positively related to doctor performance. Concerning moderating effects, the degree of internal and external competition interact significantly with both service diversity and service differentiation in influencing individual doctor performance. Hence, it can be inferred that in a highly competitive environment, the enhancement of service diversity and differentiation by doctors significantly contributes to increasing the likelihood of patients opting for their services. This implies that the relationship between service diversity, service differentiation, and individual performance is substantially moderated by both internal and external competitive factors.

Table 4. Robustness test

Variables	Model 1		Model 2	
	Coef.	Std.Err	Coef.	Std.Err.
Services_num	.613***	.014	.613***	.014
ln_diff_price	.093***	.006	.093***	.010
Imteraction	.027***	.003	.027	.003
Doctitle	.244***	.007	.245***	.007
SchoolTitle	.030***	.007		
Hoslevel	−.006	.025	−.005	.025
ln_hits	.019***	.004		
ln_articles	−.020***	.005	−.009**	.004
ln_check-in	.011***	.004		
ln_review	−.008	.007	.022***	.005
ln_gift	.007	.008	.010	.008
Satisfaction	.051***	.017	.038**	.015
Internal	−1.051***	.018	−1.050***	.018
Services_num#Internal	.190***	.006	.190***	.006
ln_diff_price#Internal	.007***	.003	.007**	.003
External	−.300***	.031	−.303***	.031
Services_num#External	.022**	.010	.023***	.010
ln_diff_price#External	.032***	.005	.032***	.005
t				
2	−.042**	.020	−.007	.020
3	−.292***	.021	−.258***	.020
4	−.049**	.020	−.014	.020
_cons	−.509***	.059	−.340***	.036
/lnalpha	1.472	.004	1.472	.004
alpha	4.357	.019	4.360	.019
Log likelihood	−414169		−414201	
Pseudo R^2	.0529		.0528	

Note:*p < .1, **p < .05, ***p < .01

4.3 Robustness Test

The robustness test of this study was conducted in two steps. In the first step, academic rank (labeled as "schoolTitle" and coded as 2 for Professor, 1 for Associate Professor, and 0 for Others) was included as a control variable. In the second step, the previously included control variables of total hits and post-diagnosis check-in were removed. The outcomes of these tests are presented in Table 4. The results indicate that, irrespective of whether considering the independent variables or the moderating variables, the effects of service diversity, service differentiation, degree of internal competition, degree of external competition, and their interactions with the independent variables remained basically the same across both regression analyses. This consistency demonstrates the robustness of the results.

5 Conclusions and Limitations

Using empirical data, this study explores the impact of service diversity and service differentiation by doctors on online health platforms on patient choice. The findings reveal that both service diversity and differentiation positively influence patient selection of doctor services (i.e. doctor performance), as well as their interaction. Furthermore, the levels of internal and external competition enhance the positive effects of service diversity and differentiation on doctor performance. The conclusions of this research offer practical insights for doctors operating on online health platforms: 1) Doctors improving service diversity and differentiation significantly affect patients' choices, and they can adjust these factors to boost their performance, thereby achieving higher social and economic value [1]. They can enhance service diversity by integrating a wider range of specialties or offering unique treatments and consultations not readily available elsewhere. For differentiation, they could focus on developing niche expertise within their field or providing personalized treatment plans based on patient history and preferences; 2) In highly competitive environments, the enhancement of service diversity and differentiation has a more pronounced impact on improving performance. Therefore, the more intense the competition, the more doctors should focus on improving their own skills and enhancing service diversity and differentiation to be more competitive in acquiring limited patient resources. They can adopt advanced medical technologies, such as AI diagnostics and telemedicine to provide accessible and efficient care and employ data analytics to provide more personalized care, aligning services closely with patient needs; 3) Online health platforms should encourage doctors to provide diversified and differentiated services and promote the building of social networks among doctors. They could implement features like 'Doctor Spotlights' that showcase innovative service offerings or unique approaches to care, encouraging other doctors to diversify and specialize. Additionally, fostering a community forum for professional development and sharing of best practices can stimulate service enhancement. These moves help doctors learn and adopt each other's strategies in service diversity and differentiation, further enhancing these aspects and creating a virtuous cycle. Improving doctor performance not only enhances platform benefits but also realizes a win-win scenario; 4) For government bodies, medical institutions and policy makers, there is a need to encourage doctors to innovate in their service delivery by providing technical and financial support. This aids doctors in improving service diversity and differentiation. Concurrently, while fostering healthy competition, it is vital to regulate and ensure a fair and healthy competitive environment on online health platforms, safeguarding the rights and interests of both doctors and patients.

The limitations of this study are manifested in several aspects: Firstly, the conclusions are derived from data analysis based on a single online health platform, hence the generalizability of these findings requires further validation across different platforms. Secondly, the data utilized in this study spans only a four-month period, which may constrain our comprehensive understanding of the long-term trends in doctor service diversity and differentiation. Finally, although the quantitative data analysis provides valuable insights, such methodologies might not fully capture patients' subjective experiences and satisfaction with service quality. Therefore, incorporating qualitative research methods in future studies, such as patient interviews or case studies, would be beneficial for a more in-depth and comprehensive exploration of the findings presented in this study.

References

1. Guo, S., Guo, X., Fang, Y., Vogel, D.: How doctors gain social and economic returns in online health-care communities: a professional capital perspective. J. Manag. Inf. Syst. **34**(2), 487–519 (2017)
2. Xu, Y., Jiang, H., Sun, P.: Research on patients' willingness to conduct online health consultation from the perspective of web trust model. Front. Publ. Health **10**, 963522 (2022)
3. Gong, Y., Wang, H., Xia, Q., Zheng, L., Shi, Y.: Factors that determine a patient's willingness to physician selection in online healthcare communities: a trust theory perspective. Technol. Soc. **64**, 101510 (2021)
4. Qiao, L., Jifeng, L., Zhiyan, W.: The impact of doctor's efforts and reputation on the number of new patients in online health community. Chin. J. Health Policy **10**(10), 63–71 (2017). (in Chinese)
5. Deng, Z., Hong, Z., Zhang, W., Evans, R., Chen, Y.: The effect of online effort and reputation of physicians on patients' choice: 3-wave data analysis of China's good doctor website. J. Med. Internet Res. **21**(3) (2019)
6. Shukla, A.D., Gao, G., Agarwal, R.: How digital word-of-mouth affects consumer decision making: evidence from doctor appointment booking. Manag. Sci. **67**(3), 1546–1568 (2021)
7. Jing, L., Hong, W., Lining, S., Juan, X.: Study on the influence of physicians' gratuitous treatment on patients' choices in online health community. J. Med. Inform. **40**(3), 10–16 (2019)
8. Yang, H., Du, H.S., Shang, W.: Understanding the influence of professional status and service feedback on patients' doctor choice in online healthcare markets. Internet Res. **31**(4), 1236–1261 (2021)
9. Cao, X., Liu, J.: Patient choice decision behavior in online medical community from the perspective of service diversity. J. Syst. Manag. **30**(1), 76–87 (2021). (in Chinese)
10. Si, G., Liu, S., Wu, Y.: Effect of the diversity of physician team on the service performance on online health platform. Chin. J. Manag. **20**(3), 422–431 (2023). (in Chinese)
11. Brosig-Koch, J., Hehenkamp, B., Kokot, J.: Who benefits from quality competition in health care? A theory and a laboratory experiment on the relevance of patient characteristics. Health Econ. **32**(8), 1785–1817 (2023)
12. Brosig-Koch, J., Hehenkamp, B., Kokot, J.: The effects of competition on medical service provision. Health Econ. **26**, 6–20 (2017)
13. Fang, J., Wen, L., Ren, H., Wen, C.: The effect of technical and functional quality on online physician selection: moderation effect of competition intensity. Inf. Process. Manag. **59** (2022)
14. Rider, E.A., Perrin, J.M.: Performance profiles: the influence of patient satisfaction data on physicians' practice. Pediatrics **109**(5), 752–757 (2002)
15. Wang, Z., Zhu, C., Tian, S., Li, P.: Differentiation and pricing power of online retailers. Front. Bus. Res. China **13**, 5 (2019)

Research on the Impact of Digital Finance on the Optimization of the Manufacturing Industry's Structure

Gang Li, Yingjia Xiong, and Shuyun Zhang[✉]

School of Information, Central University of Finance and Economics, Beijing 100098, China
shuyun_zhang@163.com

Abstract. As an important industry in China, the structural upgrading of the manufacturing industry is a key element in promoting China's economic development. In the process of upgrading, digital finance, as an effective supplement to the traditional financial system, can better serve the real economy and help the manufacturing industry achieve transformation and upgrading. This paper selects the relevant data of manufacturing and digital finance industry in 28 provinces in China from 2011 to 2019, and analyzes the development status of manufacturing and digital finance industry from the provincial and regional levels. Firstly, the manufacturing industry is divided according to the elements using the fuzzy C-mean clustering method; secondly, the manufacturing structure advanced index at the provincial and regional levels is constructed using the vector pinch angle measurement method; finally, the constructed manufacturing structure advanced index is used to establish an econometric model to empirically analyze the impact of digital finance on the structural advancement of the manufacturing industry in four regions, namely, East, Central, West and Northeast, by using the constructed digital finance index and the total digital finance indicators, the breadth of coverage, the depth of use, and the digitalization subindexes. East, Central, West, and Northeast, and empirically analyzed the impact of regional digital finance on the advanced manufacturing structure. The results of the study can help each region to identify the effect of digital finance according to the actual situation, and reasonably use digital finance tools.

Keywords: manufacturing structure · digital finance · transformation and upgrading

1 Introduction

With the development of the times, China's economy and society are completing the connotative transformation from high-speed growth to high-quality development, and China is also in a period of attack to optimize its industrial structure and raise the level of economic growth. As a manufacturing powerhouse, China's total production volume currently ranks among the top in the world, however, high volume is not equal to strong quality. The Central Economic Work Conference in 2019–2022 pointed out the urgent task of the transformation and upgrading of China's manufacturing industry, and the structural upgrading of the manufacturing industry, as an important industry in China, is a key element for China to achieve high-quality and efficient economic development. In the upgrading and development of the manufacturing industry, financial means are given the role of a booster. The working report of the fifth national financial work conference in 2017 and the government work report of the two sessions in 2022 both put forward the idea that the starting point and the ending point of financial work are to better provide quality services for the real economy. Digital finance, as an effective supplement to the existing financial system, can alleviate the constraints of enterprise financing, give play to the long-tail effect and knowledge spillover effect, effectively improve the mismatch of information resources in traditional finance, further improve the effectiveness of information resources, and realize the rise of total factor productivity [1–4]. And by supplementing the deficiencies of traditional finance and exploring the impact of digital finance on the transformation and upgrading of the manufacturing industry at this stage, it can better serve the real economy and society and help the manufacturing industry to complete its transformation and upgrading. At the same time, digital finance has shown different development conditions in different regions of China, and the heterogeneity shown comes from the differences in policy guidance direction, resource endowment, economic development level and other aspects [5]. Based on the study of regional heterogeneity, the results of the study can help each region identify the effect of digital finance according to its own actual situation, and reasonably use digital financial tools.

2 Literature Review

The results of previous studies on the impact of finance on the upgrading of the manufacturing industry can be categorized as positively facilitating and conditionally facilitating or inhibiting the development of the manufacturing industry. Martin (2009), Xi et al. (2021) concluded that finance has a facilitating effect on the development of the manufacturing industry from the point of view of the financial industry as a whole [6, 7]. Binh et al. (2006), Daway - Ducanes (2020) disaggregated finance into dimensions such as scale, structure, efficiency, depth, and access mechanism, and concluded that these sub-dimensions of the financial industry have a facilitating effect on the development and upgrading of the manufacturing industry, and the impact effect varies according to the choice of dimension, or the object of the study [8, 9]. While some other scholars believe that financial instruments do not unconditionally promote the development of the manufacturing industry, and even present an inhibitory effect to some extent. For example, Tomasz (2011) suggests that the analysis of industrial structure is an important step in the study of the relationship between the two promotional impacts, and it is difficult to generalize the same points of the impact relationship [10]. Daway-Ducanes (2019) concludes that the financial development can only promote the development of manufacturing industry upgrading when it exceeds the critical value [11].

Digital finance belongs to a type of financial sector. Regarding "digital finance", Peter Gomber et al. (2017) highlights the concept of digitalization of digital finance, where financial products and services are integrated with digitalization, which has grown significantly in the financial sector [12]. Peterson K (2018) argues that digital finance is still based on financial services as a basis, but these services are provided through various types of digital technologies, such as mobile terminals, personal computers, the Internet [13]. There is no official definition of digital finance, and in the literature and information combing, it can be summarized that the essence of digital finance is still anchored in finance, embodied in new financial products and services, new financial business models, new financial forms, etc., and the transformation from traditional finance to digital finance is achieved with the help of a series of digital technologies, such as big data, cloud computing, artificial intelligence, and other digital technologies that can be applied to mobile devices, personal computers and other multi-terminal digital technologies. The most widely used and relatively comprehensive measure in existing research is the "Peking University Digital Financial Inclusion Index" compiled by Feng Gou and others.

Without considering the heterogeneity of industries and regions, Teng (2021) found that digital finance has a significant positive impact on the high-quality development of the national manufacturing industry through empirical research [14]. When considering heterogeneity in terms of industry and region, Wang (2020), using provincial data from 2011–2016 as a sample, finds that digital finance can enhance the complexity of man-ufacturing exports, but the extent of the impact is affected by industry heterogeneity. Capital-intensive industries can obtain more significant support effects of digital finance compared to labor-intensive industries, and technology-intensive industries obtain the lowest support effects [15]. Song et al. (2022) selected China's A-share listed manu-facturing enterprises from 2011 to 2020 as the research object, and found that digital finance can promote the high-quality development of manufacturing enterprises, and there is heterogeneity in this effect in terms of region and property rights [16].

In the existing research on the upgrading and development of the manufacturing industry, only a few scholars have included the consideration of regional heterogeneity. At present, there are relatively few domestic macro-level studies on the upgrading of manufacturing structure based on regional heterogeneity. Based on this, this paper firstly uses the 2011–2019 data to divide the manufacturing industry according to the capital and technology elements using the fuzzy C-mean clustering method; secondly, on the basis of the industry division, the vector angle method is used to construct the index of the advanced manufacturing structure of each province and city; finally, on the basis of the research in the previous two parts, we empirically analyze the impact of digital finance on the advanced manufacturing structure based on regional heterogeneity. The Impact of Digital Finance on the Advanced Manufacturing Structure.

3 Construction of the National Manufacturing Structure Advanced Index

3.1 Classification of Manufacturing Industries by Capital and Technology Factors

Variables and Data Descriptions

Description of Variables. In the classification of manufacturing industries, OECD divides them into four categories according to the technological level: low-end, medium-low-end, medium-high-end and high-end technology. This paper refers to the previous practice and adopts the fuzzy C-mean clustering method to classify the manufacturing industry according to the capital and technology elements, obtains the classification results of the industry, and constructs the index of advanced manufacturing structure based on this.

The construction method of capital and technology production factor indexes used in industry classification is shown in Table 1.

Table 1. Calculation of indicators and required data for the classification of manufacturing types.

Indicator name	Required data	Calculation of indicators
Capital per capita (CPC)	Industry net fixed assets (INFA)	$CPC = \dfrac{INFA - Accumulated\ depreciation}{NOEP}$
	Number of employed persons (NOEP)	
R&D inputs	Number of employed persons in R&D (R&D_NOEP)	$R\&Dinputs = \dfrac{\frac{R\&D\_NOPE}{TEP} + \frac{R\&D\_INVEST}{TIO}}{2}$
	Total employed persons (TEP)	
	R&D investment (R&D_INVEST)	
	Total industry output (TIO)	

Description of Data. According to Table 1, this paper selects relevant data from 2011 to 2019. The geographic scope of the data is the total data for the entire country. Twenty manufacturing sub-industries, such as agri-food processing industry and food manufacturing industry, were selected based on data availability and caliber issues. In terms of data sources, data were collected from the China Industrial Statistical Yearbook, the China Science and Technology Statistical Yearbook, the China Statistical Yearbook, the National Bureau of Statistics and other sources. Some of the missing data were supplemented by means of mean substitution or trend analysis.

Calculation of Indicators. Before using the fuzzy C-mean clustering method to classify industries, it is necessary to first calculate the index values of capital and technology elements. Through the resulting indicators based on the fuzzy C-mean clustering method can be obtained clustering results: manufacturing industry is divided into labor-intensive, capital-intensive and technology-intensive.

Labor-intensive industries include agri-food processing, food manufacturing, textiles, wood processing and wood, bamboo, rattan, palm and grass products, furniture manufacturing, paper and paper products, printing and recording media reproduction, and non-metallic mineral products.

Capital-intensive industries include tobacco products, petroleum processing, coking and nuclear fuel processing, chemical materials and products manufacturing, ferrous metal smelting and rolling, and non-ferrous metal smelting and rolling.

Technology-intensive industries include the pharmaceutical manufacturing industry, the chemical fiber manufacturing industry, the general equipment manufacturing industry, the special equipment manufacturing industry, the electrical machinery and equipment manufacturing industry, and the computer, communications and other electronic equipment manufacturing industry.

3.2 Constructing a National Index of Structural Sophistication in the Manufacturing Sector

Variables and Data Descriptions

Description of Variables. In this section, the vector angle measure is used to calculate the manufacturing structure advanced index of each province and each region, given the availability of data, this paper selects the ratio of manufacturing output value of sub-industries as the indicator value reflecting the development capacity of its industry, Table 2 lists the calculation of the spatial vector indicators used in the construction of the manufacturing structure advanced index, the spatial vector components of the labor-, capital-, and technology-intensive industries are $x\_0,1$, $x\_0,2$, $x\_0,3$, and the three constitute the manufacturing spatial vector X_0.

Table 2. Spatial vector indicators for measuring the index of advanced manufacturing structure

Indicator name	Required data	Calculation of indicators
space vector X_0	Gross manufacturing output per category (GMO_PC)	Space Vector Classification $= \dfrac{GMO\_PC}{GMO}$
	Gross manufacturing output (GMO)	

Description of Data. The data in this section are mainly from the classification of manufacturing industry above and the output data of manufacturing sub-industries. The selected data are from 2011–2019, and the processed data include 28 provinces. At the same time, the output value data of the East, Central, West and Northeast are summarized and summed up to calculate the index of advanced manufacturing structure from the regional dimension.

Calculation of Indicators. When constructing the index of advanced manufacturing structure, the index is calculated at the provincial level and regional level respectively. The results are shown in Tables 3 and 4. From the results, it can be seen that the advanced manufacturing structure of the eastern region is more obvious, the advanced manufacturing structure of the western region also has certain advantages, for the central and northeastern regions, the index of advanced manufacturing structure does not reflect obvious advantages.

Table 3. Index value of advanced manufacturing structure by province and city, 2011–2019

	2011	2012	2013	2014	2015	2016	2017	2018	2019
Beijing	6.6946	6.6530	6.7253	6.7662	6.8319	6.8060	6.8697	6.9564	7.0201
Tianjin	6.1153	6.0604	6.1018	6.0535	5.9858	5.8871	5.8414	5.8038	5.7546
Hebei	5.7476	5.7046	5.6616	5.6200	5.5865	5.5671	5.5340	5.5093	5.4949
Shanxi	6.0685	6.0652	6.0938	6.0716	6.0530	6.0575	6.0687	6.1306	6.1016
Neimenggu	5.5603	5.5566	5.5429	5.5405	5.5062	5.4906	5.7398	5.9952	5.9348
Liaoning	5.6971	5.6142	5.6101	5.6136	5.6435	5.8492	5.8961	5.9107	5.8822
Jilin	5.2382	5.2028	5.2190	5.2488	5.2804	5.3212	5.3189	5.3589	5.4043
Heilongjiang	5.3105	5.2013	5.1411	5.1213	5.0611	5.0412	5.0468	5.1433	5.3340
Shanghai	6.7161	6.6686	6.6434	6.6604	6.7081	6.7148	6.7335	6.7245	6.7031
Jiangsu	6.3572	6.3157	6.2965	6.2891	6.3054	6.3022	6.2998	6.2980	6.2967
Zhejiang	5.8820	5.9018	5.8934	5.9101	5.9442	5.9853	6.0515	6.1053	6.1367
Anhui	5.7427	5.7640	5.7763	5.7988	5.8618	5.8936	5.8823	5.8108	5.8110
Fujian	5.5613	5.5126	5.4998	5.4547	5.4391	5.4353	5.4303	5.4092	5.3913
Jiangxi	5.7021	5.6418	5.6358	5.5856	5.5657	5.5776	5.5697	5.5767	5.5855
Shandong	5.4563	5.4551	5.4798	5.4915	5.4936	5.5030	5.5092	5.5197	5.5321
Henan	5.3399	5.3635	5.3687	5.3947	5.4176	5.4231	5.4231	5.5928	5.6141
Hubei	5.4628	5.3828	5.3603	5.3405	5.3339	5.3302	5.3751	5.4330	5.4158
Hunan	5.6391	5.6537	5.6291	5.6109	5.6069	5.6517	5.6412	5.5231	5.5699
Guangdong	6.4901	6.5417	6.4976	6.5160	6.5604	6.6057	6.6907	6.7639	6.7561
Guangxi	5.4308	5.4303	5.4142	5.4110	5.3924	5.3953	5.4093	5.4267	5.4527
Hainan	5.7496	5.6899	5.6883	5.6889	5.6600	5.6610	5.6566	5.3491	5.6622
Chongqing	5.8816	6.0482	6.1384	6.2254	6.2685	6.3593	6.5023	6.5228	6.5060
Sichuan	5.5975	5.6847	5.7404	5.7605	5.7681	5.7344	5.7682	5.7871	5.7946
Guizhou	5.8525	5.5945	5.5766	5.5860	5.6311	5.4809	5.4987	5.4771	5.5690
Yunnan	6.0311	5.9918	5.9551	5.9143	5.8629	5.7701	5.7913	5.8184	5.8022
Shaanxi	5.8409	5.7947	5.7328	5.6889	5.6648	5.6755	5.6905	5.6506	5.6887
Gansu	6.0769	6.0142	5.9769	5.9432	5.9056	5.8345	5.9729	6.0054	5.9925
Xinjiang	5.9102	6.0983	6.0888	6.1059	6.0599	5.7165	5.7815	5.8451	5.7806

Table 4. Subregional values of the index of advanced manufacturing structure, 2011–2019

	2011	2012	2013	2014	2015	2016	2017	2018	2019
Eastern Region	6.8266	6.7961	6.8693	6.9051	6.9693	6.9579	6.9799	7.0469	7.0960
Central Region	5.5387	5.5267	5.5213	5.5118	5.5188	5.5343	5.5486	5.6156	5.6326
Western Region	5.6451	5.6426	5.6349	5.6313	5.6170	5.5838	5.6298	5.6504	5.6533
North-eastern Region	5.5268	5.4345	5.4320	5.4287	5.3828	5.3670	5.3790	5.4476	5.4870

4   The Impact of Digital Finance on the Structure of Manufacturing

Variables and Data Descriptions

Description of Variables. The research in this chapter is about the impact of digital finance on the advanced manufacturing structure, the explained variable is the index of advanced manufacturing structure, and the explanatory variable is the digital finance index, which is divided into the total index and the three sub-indicators of breadth of coverage, depth of use and degree of digitalization. Meanwhile, in the study, control variables are introduced in order to fully consider the impact of other influencing factors on the explanatory variables. Four control variables were finally selected by synthesizing previous studies: human resources, investment situation, government size, and degree of openness. The variable representation and calculation formula are shown in Table 5:

Table 5. Model variable information

Variable type	Indicator name	Markings	Indicator source or calculation
Explained Variable	Index of advanced manufacturing structure	MNSTRUCT	Calculation of chapter 3.1
Explanatory Variable	Digital Finance Indicators	TO_IND	Overall digital finance indicators
		WIDTH	Digital Finance Breadth of Coverage Index
		DEPTH	Depth of use index for digital finance
		DIGITAL	Degree of digital finance digitization

(continued)

Table 5. (*continued*)

Variable type	Indicator name	Markings	Indicator source or calculation
Control Variable	Human Resources	HUM	Calculated by the years of schooling method
	Investments	INVEST	Logarithm of investment in fixed assets (including domestic and foreign investment)
	Size of Government	GOVER_SCALE	(financial expenditure - Expenditure on education)/gross regional product
	Degree of openness	OPEN	Total exports and imports/gross regional product

Description of Data. The sample interval of the research data in this chapter is 2011–2019, and the research object is the four major regions of the country: east, center, west and northeast. With reference to the results of the latest regional division in 2022[1], as well as the exclusion of Tibet, Qinghai, and Gansu based on the availability of data, the data covered in this section are all panel data. Table 6 shows the basic statistics of the variables.

Table 6. Descriptive statistics results for variables

variable	Max	Min	Mean	Sd
TO_IND	358.510	29.817	201.651	89.037
WIDTH	338.507	20.031	180.715	87.074
DEPTH	361.970	34.987	197.200	86.187
DIGITAL	418.296	40.277	278.880	117.003
HUM	17.989	13.470	14.769	1.082
INVEST	11.934	10.376	11.159	0.494
GOVER_SCALE	0.257	0.113	0.180	0.040
OPEN	0.115	0.015	0.039	0.032

---

[1] Reference to statistical systems and classifications issued by national statistical offices.

4.1 Construction of the Empirical Model

Based on the research questions, two panel data models are finally constructed, which differ in terms of the explanatory variables. The explanatory variable in Model 1 is the total digital finance index, which aims to explore the impact of digital finance as a whole on the structural upgrading of manufacturing in each region. The explanatory variables in Model 2 are the three sub-indices of digital finance: breadth of coverage, depth of use, and degree of digitization.

4.2 Results and Analyses of Model Estimation with Explanatory Variables as Aggregate Indicators of Digital Finance

Model Construction for Panel Data. This part investigates the impact of total digital financial indicators on the advanced manufacturing structure, and constructs the final regression model through model selection as shown in Eq. (1):

$$Mnstruct_{it} = C_{it} + \alpha_{1i}To\_ind_{it} + \beta_{1i}Hum_{it} + \beta_{2i}Invest_{it}$$
$$+ \beta_{3i}Open_{it} + \beta_{4i}Gover\_scale_{it} + \varepsilon_{it} \tag{1}$$

i is the province and t is the year.

Model Estimation. In this section, cross-section weighted estimation method is used for regression to eliminate the effect of cross-section heteroskedasticity and autocorrelation, and the specific regression results are shown in Table 7.

Table 7. Model 1 panel data model regression results

variable	Eastern Region	Central Region	Western Region	North-eastern Region
TO_IND	0.000436 (1.606764)	−8.67E−05 (−0.635816)	−0.000315*** (−3.383474)	−0.000340* (−1.945053)
HUM	−0.010020 (−0.499662)	−0.012491* (−1.815722)	−0.011881** (−2.380266)	0.012768 (1.743144)
OPEN	−0.054307 (−0.019242)	−14.36875*** (−3.303745)	4.101779* (2.164834)	8.331023*** (3.734650)
GOVER_SCALE	4.246931 (0.956354)	2.213769 (1.674329)	3.433739** (2.907142)	1.234201*** (3.155148)
INVEST	0.330199 (1.776027)	0.629747*** (5.937643)	0.376149*** (4.451694)	0.137441 (0.943237)
C	2.552127 (1.181332)	−1.440913 (−1.134275)	0.796038 (0.757972)	3.402576** (2.357870)

Note: p is the probability of t-test, * means $p < 0.1$, ** means $p < 0.05$, *** means $p < 0.01$

Analysis of Results. From Table 7, the following results can be drawn, in the eastern and central regions, the total digital finance indicator does not have a significant effect on the advanced manufacturing structure, but it has a significant negative effect on the advanced manufacturing structure in the west and north-east, and the effect on the north-east is greater than that in the west.

For each control variable, human resources have a negative inhibitory effect on the advanced manufacturing structure in the central and western regions, and a non-significant effect on the eastern and north-eastern regions; the degree of openness has a negative effect on the central region, a positive effect on the western and north-eastern regions, and does not have a significant effect on the eastern region; the size of the government has a positive contribution to the advanced manufacturing structure in the western and north-eastern regions, and a non-significant effect on the eastern and central regions; and the investment situation has a positive effect on the central and western regions, and does not have a significant effect on the eastern and north-eastern regions.

4.3 Results and Analysis of Model Estimation with Explanatory Variables as Sub-indicators of Digital Finance

Model Construction for Panel Data. In order to explore the impact of the components of digital finance on the advanced manufacturing structure, this part of the study of the impact of the three sub-indicators of digital finance coverage breadth, depth of use, and degree of digitization on the advanced manufacturing structure, and construct a regression model through the model selection as shown in Eq. (2):

$$Mnstruct_{it} = C_i + \alpha_1 Width^{\frac{3}{2}}{}_{it} + \alpha_2 Depth_{it} + \alpha_3 Digital_{it}$$
$$+ \beta_1 Hum_{it} + \beta_2 Invest_{it} + \beta_3 Open_{it} + \beta_4 Gover_{scale\,it} + \varepsilon_{it} \tag{2}$$

i is the province and t is the year.

Model Estimation. This section is a variable intercept model, get the depth of digital financial use (DEPTH), human resources (HUM), the size of the government (GOVER_SCALE) three variables of the coefficients are not significant, so the non-significant variables will be excluded and then regression is carried out again, after the exclusion of the non-significant variables, the coefficients of the other variables of the sign of the coefficients did not change, the value of the size of the value of the significant changes did not occur, the specific regression results are shown in Table 8:

Table 8. Model 2 panel data model regression results

variable	Eastern Region	Central Region	Western Region	North-eastern Region
C	2.156496*** (3.417611)			

(continued)

Table 8. (*continued*)

variable	Eastern Region	Central Region	Western Region	North-eastern Region
Fixed Effects (Cross)	1.031679	−0.451979	−0.339055	−0.240645
WIDTH	1.75E−05*** (4.880977)			
DIGITAL	−0.000276*** (−6.452003)			
OPEN	−4.305689*** (−8.330950)			
INVEST	0.352341*** (6.225768)			

Note: p is the probability of t-test, * means $p < 0.1$, ** means $p < 0.05$, *** means $p < 0.01$

Analysis of Results. The final model selected for this part of the study was the variable intercept model based on the F-test, and the heterogeneity in the East, Centre, West and North East is mainly reflected in the intercept term, as can be seen from the results in Table 8:

1. The breadth of digital financial coverage has a significant positive impact on the advanced manufacturing structure in all four regions: East, Central, West and Northeast.
2. The degree of digital finance digitization has a significant negative impact on the structural sophistication of manufacturing.

In Model 2, the depth of use of digital finance does not have a significant effect on the advanced manufacturing structure in each region. For each control variable, human resources and government size do not have a significant effect on the advanced manufacturing structure in the East, Central, West, and Northeast; whereas the degree of openness has a significant negative effect; and the investment situation has a significant positive effect on the advanced manufacturing structure in all four regions.

5 Conclusions and Policy Recommendations

5.1 Main Findings

Based on the above empirical results, the following conclusions can be drawn:

(1) The growth of the advanced manufacturing structure has been achieved in all three parts of the East, the Centre and the West, with a tendency for the North-East to decrease and then increase over the time span under study.

(2) The impact of digital finance overall indicators on the advanced manufacturing structure in the east and central China is not significant, but it has a significant negative impact on the advanced manufacturing structure in the west and northeast, while the results show that the negative impact for the northeast is slightly larger than that for the west.

(3) The breadth of digital financial coverage has a significant positive impact on the advanced manufacturing structure in the four regions of the East, Central, West and Northeast; the depth of digital financial use does not have a significant impact on the advanced manufacturing structure in the East, Central, West and Northeast; and the degree of digital financial digitization has a significant negative impact on the East, Central, West and Northeast.

5.2 Policy Recommendations

In order for digital finance to better contribute to the structural advancement of manufacturing, the following three recommendations are made in this regard:

(1) Control and regulate the development of digital finance in general in the western and north-eastern regions. The western region should enrich digital financial products and strengthen the content of digital financial services. The northeastern region needs to guide the flow of capital in the direction of high-technology, high-value-added industries, strengthen the supervision of digital financial institutions and regulate digital financial services.

(2) Enhance the coverage of digital financial services in the East, Central, West and Northeast. Firstly, the service tentacles can be extended through technical means to break through the space-time barriers with technological capabilities. Second, digital technology and platforms can be used to mine data and integrate information to broaden the coverage of financial services.

(3) Improve the suitability of digitization and financialization in digital finance in the East, Central, West and North East. Further enhance the quality and relevance of digital finance digitization, thereby improving the appropriateness of digitization levels and the financial services themselves, while upgrading the level of technological development in regions with inherent weaknesses in technological advantages.

References

1. Kapoor, A.: Financial inclusion and the future of the Indian economy. Futures **10**, 35–42 (2013)
2. Xie, X., Shen, Y., Zhang, H.X., Feng, G.: Can digital finance promote entrepreneurship? – Evidence from China. Economics (Q.) (4), 1557–1580 (2018). (in Chinese)
3. Huang, Y., Tao, K.: China's digital financial revolution: development, impact and regulatory insights. Int. Econ. Rev. **6**, 24–35 (2019). in Chinese
4. Tang, S., Lai, X., Huang, R.: How FinTech innovation affects total factor productivity: promotion or inhibition? – Theoretical analysis framework and regional practice. China Soft Sci. **7**, 134 (2019). in Chinese

5. Nie, X.: Research on the path and heterogeneity of digital finance to promote technological innovation of small and medium-sized enterprises. Western Forum **30**(04), 37–49 (2020). in Chinese

6. Zagler, M.: Growth, structural change and search economic unemployment. J. Econ. **96**(1), 63 (2009)

7. Xi, M., Li, X., He, B.: Has financial inclusion promoted manufacturing employment? – An empirical study based on county-level panel data. Secur. Mark. Her. **03**, 13–22 (2021). in Chinese

8. Binh, K., Park, S.Y., Shin, B.: financial structure dose matter for industrial growth: direct evidence from OECD countries (11), 16–21 (2006)

9. Daway-Ducanes, S.L.S., Gochoco-Bautista, M.S.: Aspects of financial development and manufacturing and services growth: which matter?. Int. J. Finance Econ. (8), 1–21 (2020)

10. Rachwal, T.: Industrial restructuring in Poland and other European Union states in the era of economic globalization. Procedia Soc. Behav. Sci. **19**, 1–10 (2011)

11. Daway-Ducanes, S.L.S., Gochoco-Bautista, M.S.: Manufacturing and services growth in developing economies: 'too little' finance? **19**(1), 55–82 (2019)

12. Gomber, P., Koch, J.-A., Siering, M.: Digital finance and FinTech: current research and future research directions. J. Bus. Econ. **87**(5) (2017)

13. Ozili, P.K.: Impact of digital finance on financial inclusion and stability. Borsa Istanbul Review (2017)

14. Teng, F.: Research on the impact of regional differences of digital finance on the high-quality development of manufacturing industry. Jiangxi University of Finance and Economics (2021). (in Chinese)

15. Wang, H.: Research on the impact of digital finance on the position of China's manufacturing value chain. South China University of Technology (2020).(in Chinese)

16. Song, J., Zhang, J.: The intrinsic connection and role mechanism of digital finance and high quality development of manufacturing enterprises. Enterp. Econ. **41**(07), 127–138 (2022). in Chinese

Analysis of Scientific Growth Patterns and Citation Distribution Driven by Educational Data Based on ArXiv Database

Yuancai Huang[1], Nannan Sun[1], Fan Wang[1,2(✉)], and Gaogao Dong[1(✉)]

[1] School of Mathematical Sciences, Jiangsu University, Zhenjiang 212013, Jiangsu, China
wwwfanang@gmail.com, gago999@126.com
[2] Department of Physics, Bar-Ilan University, 52900 Ramat-Gan, Israel

Abstract. Research on the number of scientific papers and citations in education data has yielded insights into potential patterns and general laws of scientific growth. We use the arXiv database, encompassing over 1.88 million scientific papers and their citations spanning the years 1991 to 2022. Through an analysis of the growth rate of the number of scientific papers, the findings indicate a gradual slowdown in the scientific growth pattern over different periods. Comparative assessments of growth rates across the disciplines of physics, mathematics and computer science reveal diverse growth patterns in different disciplines. The exploration extends to the analysis of directed citation network constructed by scientific papers, highlighting that only a fewer paper exhibits higher connectivity. This observation emphasizes the significant contributions made by few papers and helps to understand the relationship between collaboration and information dissemination in scientific research. Furthermore, an analysis of the citation distribution and cumulative citation proportion of scientific papers over the preceding ten years. The results show a discernible time decay phenomenon in citation patterns and emphasize the significance of recent research in advancing the scientific process. This find contributes to a deeper understanding of the dynamics of scientific growth, collaboration, and the impact of contemporary research in the academic landscape.

Keywords: Science of Science · Digital Education · Growth Patterns · Data Analysis · Network Analysis · Citation Distribution

1 Introduction

With the rapid advancement of science and technology, the field of education has transitioned into the digital era, presenting unparalleled opportunities and challenges for educational practices [1]. In this era of information explosion, the volume of data generated within the field of education continues to expand [2, 3]. The field of education has amassed a wealth of scientific data, encompassing crucial information such as learning data [4], assessment results [5], and research papers [6]. Science of science offers a novel perspective for delving into and extracting information from the educational growth process embedded within vast scientific datasets [7]. Simultaneously, the analysis of educational data has emerged as a potent tool for comprehending and exploring the practical complexities inherent in the field of science education. This provides an important guarantee for researchers to understand educational progress and scientific processes.

Employing scientific methodologies to transform raw scientific data into substantive scientific knowledge is imperative for uncovering the universal laws that govern the scientific realm [7]. Numerous scholars are actively employing educational data to conduct thorough analyses. Wang et al. proposed quantifying long-term scientific impacts [8]. Martinez discussed the impact of scientific and technological development on employment and education [9]. The application of knowledge graph [9] and network analysis [11] can further enhance the understanding of educational data. Deagen et al. systematically explored the framework of knowledge graphs through the application of customized interactive data graphs [12]. He et al. enhanced the performance of knowledge graphs by proposing a generalized type-enhanced knowledge graph embedding framework, incorporating entity types into embedding learning [13].

It is noteworthy that knowledge undergoes dynamic evolution and fluidity throughout the dissemination process [14]. Numerous researchers integrate the theories and methodologies of network analysis to conduct more in-depth analyses of scientific data [15]. Peel et al. utilize the interconnections between data and theory within network science to augment the amalgamation of theoretical frameworks and practical applications [16]. Citation networks show broad applications in the examination of science communication. Nielsen et al. leveraged global authorship and scientific paper data to observe an intensification in global citation inequality [17]. Pan et al. employed the world citation network and collaborative network to unveil the influence of geographic location in scientific endeavors [18]. Xu et al. quantified the processes of academic impact, knowledge utilization, and knowledge transfer by constructing a PubMed knowledge graph and integrating it with network analysis [19].

To explore potential patterns in education and scientific production, we conduct analysis of education data for general rules. This work fosters the exploration of conceivable patterns within the realm of education and scientific production, contributing to a heightened understanding of the fundamental laws governing the developmental processes of both science and education.

2 Data Resources

The arXiv database (https://arxiv.org/), an extensive compendium that encapsulates a substantial volume of academic literature. This database provides open access to preprint papers and is extensively utilized within the scientific community. The arXiv database stands as a freely accessible and open data resource, fostering scientific collaboration and facilitating the expeditious exchange of scholarly knowledge.

Notably, the arXiv database covers multiple disciplines and serving as a robust source of rich data. This database is an important platform for disseminating papers in multiple disciplines, including physics, mathematics, and computer science. Saier et al. meticulously organized and categorized over 1.88 million scientific papers and over 10 million citations using arXiv data spanning the years 1991 to 2022 [20]. However, this data source only organizes and classifies the arXiv database, lacking further analysis. Based on this database, we analyze the potential patterns of different disciplines in their development process. Noteworthy details encompassed within the arXiv dataset include the title, publication year, abstract, authorship, full-text, and disciplinary classification. Table 1 delineates a categorical representation of the quantity of papers sourced from arXiv data, utilized in this study, spanning diverse disciplines.

Table 1. Number of papers across various disciplines sourced from the arXiv database.

ID	Discipline	Number of papers
1	Physics	1, 036, 313
2	Mathematics	432, 389
3	Computer science	277, 388
4	Statistics	80, 292
5	Electrical Engineering and Systems Science	23, 241
6	Quantitative Biology	20, 503
7	Quantitative Finance	9, 170
8	Economics	2, 051
Total		1, 882, 082

The scientific papers in the database are mainly from physics, mathematics and computer science. These three disciplines account for more than half of all scientific papers. This significantly contributes to fostering scientific productivity and advancing scientific processes. The inclusion of the citation network comprising all scientific papers within the arXiv database ensures a broad and inclusive perspective, enabling a holistic understanding of the interconnections and impact patterns among various scientific disciplines.

3 Methodology

3.1 Scientific Growth Pattern

Considering that scientific papers as important scientific products of science education, studying the growth pattern of scientific papers is indispensable in exploring the process of scientific research. The systematic investigation into scientific growth patterns holds great significance in elucidating the evolutionary trends and knowledge accumulation within the scientific domain. Hence, conducting an effective analysis of the growth patterns in educational science data is imperative.

Analyzing the growth rate of scientific papers serves as a pivotal work in quantifying the intricacies of the scientific research process. Employing the annual growth rate of scientific papers as an effective tool to examine scientific growth patterns. We analyze the overall growth patterns of all scientific papers in the arXiv database to identify and understand the basic laws of the growth patterns of scientific processes. Furthermore, we systematically study the scientific growth pattern of physics, mathematics, and computer science. The number of scientific papers in these three disciplines ranks among the top three among all disciplines (Table 1). By examining growth patterns in three different disciplines helps to elucidate the unique growth characteristics inherent in each discipline.

3.2 Citation Network Analysis in Scientific Papers

The typical representation of citation relationships among papers involves a structured network, often delineated as a directed graph or knowledge graph, known as a citation network [19]. In this framework, individual papers and their respective citations are denoted as nodes and directed edges. Employing network analysis for scrutinizing the developmental patterns within science education is instrumental in unveiling collaborative dynamics within the field and elucidating the fundamental patterns of knowledge dissemination [20].

Here, the arXiv database is employed to construct of a citation network. The citation network comprises nodes representing individual papers, with edges delineated by the interconnection of citation relationships among diverse papers. It is important to highlight that the citations within the articles are arranged in a chronological order, thereby establishing a directed network. The directed network exhibits a distinct orientation, with edges originating from the cited references and pointing towards the papers, encapsulating the dynamic and fluid propagation of knowledge.

Citation networks offer numerous characteristics worthy of study. This section studies the degree distribution of the citation network constructed based on all scientific papers and their citations, involving out-degree distribution and in-degree distribution. The out-degree distribution and in-degree distribution within this directed citation network encapsulate the frequency distribution of each paper being cited by other papers and the frequency distribution of citing other papers, respectively. Furthermore, we also conduct a comprehensive analysis, comparing the disparities in citation network characteristics among the three disciplines: physics, mathematics, and computer science.

3.3 Citation Distribution and Cumulative Citation Proportion

The preceding analysis has underscored the significance of citations in the dissemination of scientific knowledge. However, citations of scientific papers or publications often show inherent inequality, affected by factors such as author citation inequality [16] and national citation differences [17]. To address this, we employ the citation relationships among papers spanning various years to examine the citation distribution for scientific papers in a specific year in comparison to those from preceding years.

We introduce a basic citation distribution model, as depicted in Fig. 1. This model shows the citation distribution of scientific papers from year j and is a directed graph with time series. The number of citations in a given year to publications in the previous i year can be denoted by $C(i, j)$, signifying the number of citations from scientific papers in year j to publications in the i-th year before. This analytical approach enables researchers to quantitatively capture the citation count associated with scholarly works from distinct temporal contexts. By quantifying the citations received by a publication in a given year at a specific point in time, $C(i, j)$ encapsulates the scholarly recognition accorded to previous work within the academic community. In order to improve the validity of the research, we analyzed the citation distribution of scientific papers in the past 10 years, wherein j spans the years from 2013 to 2022.

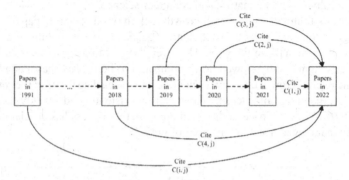

Fig. 1. Citation distribution model. Icons represent scientific papers appearing in each year, while the edges delineate the citation relationships among these scientific papers. $C(i, j)$ is the number of citations of scientific papers in year j to scientific papers in the previous i-th year.

The citation distribution through the application of the cumulative citation proportion $(P(i, j))$ within the realm of scientific literature. $P(i, j)$ can be obtained by dividing the cumulative citations of a specific year in the previous i years by the total citations in a given year.

$$P(i,j) = \frac{\sum_{i}^{max} C(i,j)}{A(j)}, \ (i = 0, 1, 2, 3, \ldots, \ max) \tag{1}$$

where $A(j)$ refers to the total number of citations in year j.

This section focuses on analyzing the citation distribution of all scientific papers and in particular on the citation distribution of physics, mathematics and computer science. In addition, we further analyze the trend of cumulative citation proportion in different disciplines, which helps to obtain the main citation sources cited in a certain year and compare the citation differences in different disciplines. This can help explore academic influence dynamics and changes in the impact of scientific publications over a specified time frame. This indicator illustrates the correlation between the volume of citations garnered by scientific papers within a specific year and the corresponding citations accrued by papers in the preceding i years.

4   Results

4.1   Scientific Growth Pattern

Analyzing the annual growth rate of the number of scientific papers from two aspects is helpful to explore the scientific growth pattern. The study analyzes the overall growth pattern of all scientific papers, and further analyzes the growth pattern of the three disciplines of physics, mathematics, and computer science.

The analysis found that the overall growth pattern of all scientific papers showed a two-stage growth pattern (Fig. 2 (a)). Scientific academic papers exhibited a sustained rapid growth pattern in the initial years. However, the growth pattern of scientific papers after 1998 has significantly slowed down compared to before and has tended to grow steadily. The overall growth rate for all scientific papers reached 0.197 in the early years. Subsequently, the output of scientific papers has consistently and steadily increased at a rate of 0.036. While the pace of the scientific research process has decelerated, it has consistently maintained a stable trajectory of growth.

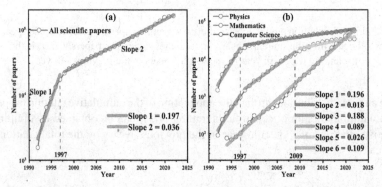

Fig. 2. Scientific growth pattern. (a) Number of all scientific papers. (b) Number of scientific papers in physics, mathematics, computer science. These values are the slopes of the number of papers in different periods.

The discipline of physics provides the largest number of scientific papers compared to other disciplines (Fig. 2 (b)). The discipline of physics provides more than half of the scientific products of the entire scientific database, accounting for approximately 55.08%. The findings show that the research process of the physics discipline maintains a similar research process compared with the research process of all disciplines. The research process slows down gradually and has two stages growth pattern. The initial scientific output of the physics discipline experienced rapid growth at a rate of 0.196, and then the research process slowed down and stabilized. The growth rate in the later period reached 0.018, representing approximately half of the growth observed in the overall scientific growth.

The growth pattern of mathematics shows distinctive characteristics compared with the growth pattern of physics. The growth model of mathematics gradually slows down, and the growth process can be divided into three stages of growth pattern (Fig. 2 (b)). The observation shows that the growth rates of scientific papers in the mathematics discipline in different periods were 0.188, 0.089 and 0.026 respectively. Although the number of scientific papers in computer science is relatively small among the three disciplines, it still shows different growth patterns and characteristics. Computer science has always shown a growth pattern since its birth and continues to maintain a relatively high growth rate. The discipline of computer science has exhibited a remarkable and continuous expansion since its emergence, establishing itself as a thriving field within the scientific domain. Notably, the realm of computer science has witnessed an unwavering upward trajectory, corroborated by the consistent growth rate of 0.109 observed in scientific publications within this domain.

4.2 Citation Network Analysis in Scientific Papers

Constructing directed citation networks through scientific papers and their citations to analyze the general rules of knowledge flow. Firstly, an overall directed citation network was established using all scientific papers available in the arXiv database. Secondly, separate citation networks were established by using scientific papers within three distinct disciplines: physics, mathematics, and computer science. Using citation network analysis can help explore the complex dynamics of knowledge diffusion. Table 2 shows the basic information of four citation networks, including the number of nodes and edges.

Table 2. Basic information about four citation networks.

Network Type	Nodes	Edges
All scientific papers	1, 882, 082	5, 675,730
Physics	1, 036, 313	3, 327, 723
Mathematics	432, 389	680, 130
Computer science	277, 388	779, 375

The analysis shows the out-degree distribution and in-degree distribution of the citation network composed of all scientific papers on arXiv database (Fig. 3 (a)). The study found that large-scale citation networks in the literature exhibit a discernible characteristic in both their out-degree distribution and in-degree distribution. The out-degree distribution and in-degree distribution trends of the citation network always gradually decrease. This observation indicates that the majority of nodes exhibit a relatively low degree, signifying that most articles possess a limited number of connections. Nodes with low degrees predominate within the citation network. There are fewer nodes with higher degrees, which means that only a smaller number of papers have higher connections. The analysis presents instances where the degree value is truncated to 200. Specifically, an unusually high out-degree or in-degree value indicates that an article has received widespread citations.

Moreover, the analysis reveals a distinct intersection point at varying degree values in both the out-degree and in-degree distributions across diverse citation networks. The

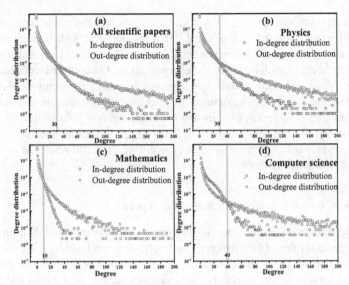

Fig. 3. Out-degree and in-degree distributions of directed citation networks. (a) All scientific papers. (b) Physics. (c) Mathematics. (d) Computer science.

intersection of the in-degree distribution and out-degree distribution occurs where degree = 30. This indicates that scientific papers with either 30 incoming citations or 30 outgoing citations exhibit a propensity for high citation frequency.

This study further analyzes the out-degree distribution and in-degree distribution in three different disciplines: physics (Fig. 3 (b)), mathematics (Fig. 3 (c)), and computer Science (Fig. 3 (d)). The study found that the out-degree distribution and in-degree distribution trends of citation networks in physics, mathematics, and computer science are also gradually decreasing. The in-degree distribution and out-degree distribution of the citation networks of three different disciplines, physics, mathematics and computer science, will also show an intersection at different degree values. The in-degree distribution and out-degree distribution of the citation network in the disciplines of physics, mathematics, and computer science intersect when the degree value is equal to 30, 10, and 40 respectively, showing high frequency citation behavior.

4.3   Citation Distribution and Cumulative Citation Proportion

The study analyzes the citation distribution of scientific papers in a certain year to papers in each previous year, including the analysis results in the past 10 years from 2013 to 2022 (Fig. 4 (a)). The findings reveal a clear time decay phenomenon in citation patterns. The study found that the number of citations of scientific papers in a certain year to scientific papers in previous years gradually decreased as the distance between citation years increased. The study shows that citations to scientific papers each year are mainly concentrated in citations to papers within 3 years, with citations to the previous year being particularly significant and dominating the total number of citations. This work highlights the critical role of recent research in advancing scholarship pursuits, especially the research from the preceding year.

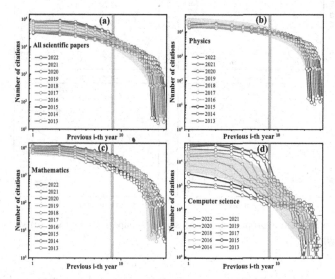

Fig. 4. The citation distribution of scientific papers in a certain year to the previous i-th year. (a) All scientific papers. (b) Physics. (c) Mathematics. (d) Computer science.

Furthermore, we also analyze the citation distribution in the three main disciplines of physics (Fig. 4 (b)), mathematics (Fig. 4 (c)) and computer science (Fig. 4 (d)) in the past 10 years spanning from 2013 to 2022. The observation shows that the citation distribution of these disciplines also has the same time decay phenomenon. As the time distance increases, the citation distribution of a certain year relative to previous years gradually decreases. It is noteworthy that a substantial proportion of scientific papers across diverse disciplines exhibit a reliance on articles published in preceding years. Notably, the concentration of citations was most pronounced in the preceding year.

Subsequently, this study quantified the cumulative citation proportion (Eq. 1) of scientific papers within a specific year. This method involves a statistical analysis of the cumulative citations in a given year to the previous i-th year, divided by the total citations in that specific year. This study unveils the primary origins of citations bestowed upon scientific papers during the same period. The results show that the cumulative citation proportion of all scientific papers in a specific year showed a steady and gradual increase over a certain period of time (Fig. 5. (a)). Specifically, the cumulative citation proportion of scientific papers in a specific year has a slope of approximately 0.66 over the past 8 years, and the citation ratio at this time reaches approximately 0.78, accounting for the dominant position in the total citations in that year. The trend of the cumulative citation proportion beyond 8 years has gradually slowed down, and the number of citations at this time only accounts for a small part of the total number of citations.

Employing the cumulative citation proportion to conduct a more analysis across three diverse disciplines, namely physics (Fig. 5 (b)), mathematics (Fig. 5 (c)), and computer

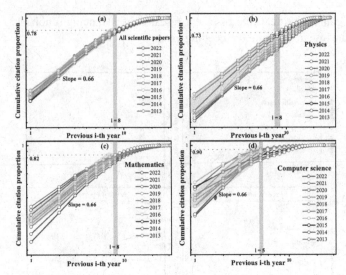

Fig. 5. Cumulative citation proportion. (a) All scientific papers. (b) Physics. (c) Mathematics. (d) Computer science.

science (Fig. 5 (d)). The observations show that the citation distributions within the three aforementioned disciplines in a given year exhibit analogous trends and phenomena to those manifested in the citation distributions across the entire spectrum of scientific papers within the same temporal parameter. The citation ratios within the disciplines of physics and mathematics have demonstrated a stable trajectory over the preceding eight years, characterized by a growth slope of 0.66. Notably, the cumulative citation proportion for physics and mathematics stand at 73% and 82%. The cumulative citation proportion within the field of computer science has undergone a marked and substantive increase. Over the course of a five-year period, the growth rate of the cumulative citation proportion has consistently stood at 0.66. Significantly, the cumulative citation proportion has attained a notable 90%, thereby substantiating its commanding stature in the realm of total citations.

5   Conclusions

This paper analyzes scientific growth patterns and citation behavior using the number of scientific articles and citations in the arXiv database. In addition, this study further analyzes and compares the development process of the three disciplines of physics, mathematics and computer science.

Through an examination of the annual growth rate in the number of papers across all scientific papers, we identify a discernible two-stage pattern in the trajectory of scientific growth. Initial stages witnessed rapid growth, followed by a gradual deceleration and stabilization. Further analysis across various disciplines of physics, mathematics and computer science, revealing the diversity of growth patterns within each discipline. The construction of a directed citation network based on all articles, enables the analysis of fundamental characteristics of the network, such as out-degree distribution and in-degree distribution, revealing the basic rules of information dissemination in the field of scientific research. Moreover, we also analyze the citation distribution of scientific papers for each of the preceding ten years spanning from 2013 to 2022. The findings reveal a discernible time decay phenomenon in citation patterns. The observation shows that the citation distribution of a certain year to previous years gradually decreased as the time distance increased. Furthermore, an analysis of the cumulative citation proportion showed a steady growth trend in the short term, with a slope of approximately 0,66. Especially for the cumulative citations in the previous 8 years, which accounted for approximately 73% of the total citations, underscoring the paramount importance of the latest research as the primary source of citations, and highlighting the significance of the recent scientific contributions in advancing the scientific process.

In conclusion, by analyzing the growth patterns and citation distributions of different disciplines from the arXiv database, we can discover the development trends and popular disciplines of scientific research. This work emphasizes the crucial role of staying abreast of the latest scientific research for scientific researchers, underscoring the importance of timely access to contemporary studies in advancing knowledge in the respective domains. This can help researchers gain valuable insights into scientific research and academic communication, and provide valuable inspiration for academic research.

Acknowledgment. This research was supported by grants from the National Natural Science Foundation of China (Grant No. 62373169), National Statistical Science Research Project (Grant No. 2022LZ03), Special Project of Emergency Management Institute of Jiangsu University (Grant No. KY-A-08) and the Jiangsu Postgraduate Research and Innovation Plan (Grant No. KYCX22_3601).

References

1. Samsul, S.A., Yahaya, N., Abuhassna, H.: Education big data and learning analytics: a bibliometric analysis. Humanities Social Sci. Commun. **10**(1), 1–11 (2023)
2. Bornmann, L., Haunschild, R., Mutz, R.: Growth rates of modern science: a latent piecewise growth curve approach to model publication numbers from established and new literature databases. Humanities Social Sci. Commun. **8**(1), 1–15 (2021)
3. Liu, L., et al.: Data, measurement and empirical methods in the science of science. Nature Human Beh. **7**(7), 1046−1058 (2023)
4. Angrist, N., et al.: Measuring human capital using global learning data. Nature **592**(7854), 403–408 (2021)
5. Chan, J.C., Ahn, D.: Unproctored online exams provide meaningful assessment of student learning. Proc. Natl. Acad. Sci. **120**(31), e2302020120 (2023)
6. Barabási, A.L., Song, C., Wang, D.: Handful of papers dominates citation. Nature **491**(7422), 40–41 (2012)
7. Fortunato, S., et al.: Science of science. Science **359**(6379), eaao0185 (2018)
8. Wang, D., Song, C., Barabási, A.L.: Quantifying long-term scientific impact. Science **342**(6154), 127–132 (2013)
9. Martinez, W.: How science and technology developments impact employment and education. Proc. Natl. Acad. Sci. **115**(50), 12624–12629 (2018)

10. Weis, J.W., Jacobson, J.M.: Learning on knowledge graph dynamics provides an early warning of impactful research. Nat. Biotechnol. **39**(10), 1300–1307 (2021)
11. Neal, Z.P., et al.: Critiques of network analysis of multivariate data in psychological science. Nature Rev. Methods Primers **2**(1), 90 (2022)
12. Deagen, M.E., et al.: FAIR and interactive data graphics from a scientific knowledge graph. Scientific Data **9**(1), 239 (2022)
13. He, P., et al.: A type-augmented knowledge graph embedding framework for knowledge graph completion. Sci. Rep. **13**(1), 12364 (2023)
14. della Briotta Parolo, P., et al.: Tracking the cumulative knowledge spreading in a comprehensive citation network. Phys. Rev. Res. 2(1), 013181 (2020). https://doi.org/10.1103/PhysReVResearch.2.013181
15. Dong, G., et al.: Optimal resilience of modular interacting networks. Proc. Natl. Acad. Sci. **118**(22), e1922831118 (2021)
16. Peel, L., Peixoto, T.P., De Domenico, M.: Statistical inference links data and theory in network science. Nat. Commun. **13**(1), 6794 (2022)
17. Nielsen, M.W., Andersen, J.P.: Global citation inequality is on the rise. Proc. Natl. Acad. Sci. **118**(7), e2012208118 (2021)
18. Pan, R.K., Kaski, K., Fortunato, S.: World citation and collaboration networks: uncovering the role of geography in science. Sci. Rep. **2**(1), 902 (2012)
19. Xu, J., et al.: Building a PubMed knowledge graph. Sci. data **7**(1), 205 (2020)
20. Saier, T., Krause, J., Färber, M.: unarxive 2022: All arxiv publications pre-processed for nlp, including structured full-text and citation network. arXiv preprint arXiv:2303.14957 (2023)

An Empirical Investigation of Consumers' Switching Intention from Traditional E-commerce to Short Video E-commerce from the Perspective of Information Processing

Xinyu Yao[1], Chen Tao[1], Yi Cui[1(✉)], and Jie Li[2]

[1] Communication University of China, Beijing 100024, China
yicui@cuc.edu.cn
[2] Hangzhou Dianzi University Information Engineering College, Hangzhou 311305, Zhejiang, China

Abstract. In recent years, short video e-commerce has rapidly developed due to its characteristics such as vividness, simplicity, and accessibility of information. Many merchants and short video platforms have actively engaged in short video e-commerce. However, there still exists fundamental differences in the information processing dimension between short video e-commerce and traditional e-commerce, which requires in-depth exploration. This study, based on push-pull-mooring theory, explores the factors and mechanisms influencing consumers' switching intention from traditional e-commerce to short video e-commerce from the perspective of information processing. The research results indicate that overload confusion, virtual touch, vicarious learning, and online consumer inertia influence the switching intention by affecting perceived value or customer satisfaction. The findings of this study contribute to a deeper understanding of the motives behind consumer switching for short video platforms and merchants. The understanding assists platforms to optimize e-commerce functions and merchants to implement differentiated operations for different e-commerce channels.

Keywords: Switching Intention · Short Video E-commerce · E-commerce · Push-Pull-Mooring Theory

1 Introduction

In recent years, short video platforms have been recognized as the fastest-growing form of social media. China, in particular, stands out in this regard. According to data released by the China Internet Network Information Center, as of June 2023, the user base of short video applications in China reached 1.026 billion [1]. Short videos are also rapidly becoming an emerging e-commerce model. The growing short video e-commerce sector is swiftly capturing market share from traditional e-commerce platforms. In the current era of information explosion, information processing plays an increasingly important role in consumers' purchasing decisions. There are significant differences in information processing between traditional e-commerce and short video e-commerce. Therefore, it is important to understand the factors that influence consumers' information processing, as well as the mechanisms that promote switching intentions.

Given that short video e-commerce is a relatively recent business model, there is a scarcity of pioneering research in this field. Most existing studies have predominantly used qualitative analysis methods. Moreover, there is a deficiency in research that compares the information processing dimensions between the two types of e-commerce platforms and explores consumer switching intentions. To fill this gap, this study will focus on the following research questions:

RQ1: From the perspective of information processing, what factors influence consumers' switching intention from traditional e-commerce to short video e-commerce?

RQ2: What are the mechanisms through which these factors affect consumers' switching intention?

The Push-Pull-Mooring theory (PPM) is effective in analyzing switching intentions. Therefore, this study adopts PPM to describe the influencing factors on consumers' switching intentions from traditional e-commerce to short video e-commerce. We posit that push factors involve overload confusion experienced by consumers when shopping on traditional e-commerce platforms, mooring factors encompass online consumer inertia, and pull factors include vicarious learning and virtual touch. Through a questionnaire survey and data analysis, this study aims to demonstrate the impact of these factors on customer satisfaction and perceived value, subsequently affecting switching intentions.

This study contributes to literature and practice for both traditional e-commerce and short video e-commerce. Firstly, by integrating the PPM theory, the study analyzes the differential characteristics of the two from the perspective of information processing. It also employs quantitative analysis for the first time to reveal the influencing factors and mechanisms affecting the switching intention between traditional e-commerce and short video e-commerce. Secondly, the inclusion of virtual touch and vicarious learning in the research model adds an innovative dimension. In terms of practical value, the research findings can provide insights for e-commerce practitioners to optimize their operational strategies, enhancing market competitiveness and user satisfaction while adapting to market changes.

2   Literature Review and Theoretical Background

2.1   PPM Theory

PPM provides a unified and clear theoretical framework that significantly helps to understand the competitive factors influencing consumer switching behavior [4]. In the PPM theory, push factors refer to the elements that compel users to abandon their current choices; pull factors refer to the factors that attract and drive users toward new choices; mooring factors reflect the individual, environmental, and situational factors that may hinder or facilitate users' switch from their original choices to new ones. This theory has been extended to the study of consumer switching intention and behavior in various information technology services, such as Bansal et al. study on service switching [2] and Li et al. research on social e-commerce websites [3].

Based on the literature background provided, this study utilizes the PPM theory to examine and classify the factors that influence consumers' intention to switch between traditional e-commerce platforms and short video e-commerce platforms, and investigate the mechanisms behind these influences. When designing the model, the distinctive characteristics of both platforms are considered to determine the push-pull factors, and the personal factor of "online consumer inertia" is introduced as a mooring factor.

2.2 Short Video E-commerce

Short video platforms have social characteristics such as information sharing and interactive communication, which make them social platforms, positioning short video e-commerce as a novel business model within the realm of social commerce. In view of the paucity of literature on short video e-commerce, this study aims to delve into the definition of social commerce and conduct an in-depth exploration of short video e-commerce.

Social commerce is generally regarded as a subset of e-commerce [6]. Yadav et al. define social commerce as "exchange-related activities that occur in, or are influenced by, an individual's social network in computer-mediated social environments, where the activities correspond to the need recognition, pre-purchase, purchase, and post-purchase stages of a focal exchange" [5]. Compared to traditional social commerce, short video e-commerce exhibits stronger personalization.

Due to the social characteristics in short video e-commerce, it exhibits differences in information processing when compared to traditional e-commerce. According to the elaboration likelihood model, audiences choose information processing paths based on the motivation and ability to analyze information. In short video e-commerce, unlike being passive information recipients, users gain information from more diverse and comprehensive sources. User sharing in short video e-commerce is more genuine compared to traditional platforms, as the information comes from friends or acquaintances. Additionally, the video presentation format in short video e-commerce is more vivid compared to the graphic and text format in traditional e-commerce. Consequently, compared to traditional e-commerce, users in short video e-commerce are more willing to engage in information processing, thus influencing purchasing decisions.

In summary, short video e-commerce, as a novel form of social commerce, exhibits differences and advantages in comparison to traditional e-commerce from the perspective of information processing. This paper, rooted in the information processing perspective, analyzed factors influencing consumer switching intentions between traditional e-commerce and short video e-commerce based on differences in information quantity, vividness, and accessibility.

3   Hypothesis Development and Research Model

Given the differences in information processing dimensions between traditional e-commerce and short video e-commerce, we employed the PPM model to analyze the distinct characteristics of the two platforms. Push factors refer to elements that drive consumers away from traditional e-commerce websites. In this study, we set it as overload confusion in consumer confusion, investigating whether this phenomenon becomes a factor pushing consumers away from traditional e-commerce, thus proposing H1a and H1b. Pull factors refer to elements that attract consumers to short video e-commerce. We considered the unique information dissemination features of short video e-commerce, including virtual touch and vicarious learning, reflecting vividness and accessibility of information. These advantages in information processing may positively influence switching intentions. Therefore, we proposed H3a, H3b, H4a, and H4b.

Beyond the differences in information processing dimensions between the platforms, we also took into account users' psychological characteristics, setting mooring factors as online consumer inertia and proposing H2. Additionally, perceived value and customer satisfaction, commonly considered consumer perception-related variables in studies related to switching intentions [7], were included in the variable design as direct factors affecting switching intention. The relationships among these two variables and switching intention were explored, leading to the proposition of H5, H6, and H7.

3.1   Push Factor: Overload Confusion

Consumer confusion refers to the psychological state of uneasiness that consumers experience during the preparation stage of purchase decisions. Overload confusion arises when consumers face information and alternatives beyond their processing capacity. Research by Wathieu et al. suggests that an excess of choices may lead to consumer overload, thereby diminishing their sense of control [8]. Studies have shown that the subjective sense of control over choices has an impact on customer satisfaction and overall happiness. Furthermore, information overload can make consumers feel that service providers have not fulfilled their obligation to handle information, reducing their overall evaluation of service providers and affecting perceived value. In traditional e-commerce, the abundance of content on webpages requires consumers to invest considerable time and effort in browsing. In contrast, short video e-commerce employs personalized recommendations, making product information more targeted. Faced with more choices, consumers may delay making purchasing decisions to seek additional information or explore new alternatives. Based on the above discussion, we propose the following hypotheses:

H1a: Consumers' overload confusion with traditional e-commerce positively influences their perceived value for short video e-commerce.

H1b: Consumers' overload confusion with traditional e-commerce positively influences their customer satisfaction for short video e-commerce.

3.2 Mooring Factor: Online Consumer Inertia

Inertia refers to consumers adopting an attitude of passiveness or inaction when dealing with service providers and tending to maintain the current state [9]. Inertia arises from a lack of motivation or goal orientation. Consequently, these consumers may be unwilling to express positive or negative evaluations of a particular service provider. In this study, online consumer inertia emphasizes the inertia exhibited by consumers in their use of online platforms. Traditional e-commerce has a much longer development history than emerging short video platforms, and thus, the former possesses more inherent users, including those with long usage times and deep involvement. These users may exhibit high inertia. Given their indifference to service providers, this online consumer inertia can diminish consumers' perceived value of e-commerce platforms. Therefore, we propose the hypothesis:

H2: Online consumer inertia of traditional e-commerce users negatively influences their perceived value for short video e-commerce.

3.3 Pull Factor: Virtual Touch

The sense of touch is a direct experiential aspect for consumers in relation to products. Klein et al. argue that although consumers cannot physically touch products when shopping online to assess quality, they can use virtual reality technology to gain a perception of the products, thereby compensating to some extent for the lack of tactile experience [10]. Based on the compilation of relevant literature, the formation of virtual touch can be primarily attributed to two aspects. Firstly, due to the interactive integration function of human senses, well-developed "visual" and "auditory" experiences can compensate for certain tactile perceptions. Secondly, the activation of historical tactile memories through situational perception triggers tactile sensations through association. On short video platforms, content producers reconstruct daily life to create a familiar, authentic shopping atmosphere, thereby offering the scenario-based product information to enhance consumer perceived value. Studies have found that the shopping environment created by short videos, the closer it is to daily life, the more it enhances consumers' satisfaction with the products. It also makes it easier for consumers with a strong sense of virtual touch to "touch" the products through the recreation of short video life scenes. Combining the above discussion, we propose the following hypotheses:

H3a: Virtual touch generated by consumers on short video e-commerce platforms positively influences their perceived value of short video e-commerce.

H3b: Virtual touch generated by consumers on short video e-commerce platforms positively influences customer satisfaction with short video e-commerce.

3.4 Pull Factor: Vicarious Learning

Gioia and Manz introduced the concept of vicarious learning, stating that during the process of vicarious learning, observers learn from the behaviors and outcomes of others rather than from their own actions or experiences [11]. Myers, based on the interactive nature of the learning process, suggests that vicarious learning can be divided into two types: independent vicarious learning and coactive vicarious learning [12]. In short video e-commerce, both independent and coactive vicarious learning coexist. The objects of independent vicarious learning can include short video hosts or video comments, while peers in coactive vicarious learning are mainly others in the media, such as other consumers. This unique information acquisition method in social e-commerce enhances the accessibility of shopping information for consumers, elevating their perceived value and satisfaction with the products. Based on the findings mentioned above, we propose the following hypotheses:

H4a: Consumer vicarious learning behavior on short video e-commerce platforms positively influences their perceived value of short video e-commerce.

H4b: Consumer vicarious learning behavior on short·video e-commerce platforms positively influences customer satisfaction with short video e-commerce.

3.5 Perceived Value

Perceived value refers to consumers' overall evaluation of the utility of a product based on their received and given perceptions [13]. It is suggested that businesses offering services with a high perceived value (providing quality services at reasonable prices) are more likely to meet consumer needs and achieve high customer satisfaction. Additionally, research evidence indicates that consumers who perceive "value for money" are more likely to experience high satisfaction than those who do not perceive that [13]. In other words, the higher the perceived value, the higher the customer satisfaction. Bansal and Taylor's study also suggests that low perceived value is a direct cause of consumer switching [14]. Therefore, we propose the following hypotheses:

H5: Perceived value generated by consumers on short video e-commerce platforms positively influences customer satisfaction with short video e-commerce.

H6: Perceived value generated by consumers on short video e-commerce platforms positively influences consumers' switching intention from traditional e-commerce to short video e-commerce.

3.6 Customer Satisfaction

The study of customer satisfaction can be traced back to 1965 when Cardozo defined customer satisfaction as the evaluation made by consumers after using a product or service, compared to their initial expectations [15]. Studies have demonstrated a causal relationship between customer satisfaction and switching intention. Bansal and Taylor, for instance, found that lower customer satisfaction is associated with a higher likelihood of switching [14]. Hence, we propose the following hypothesis:

H7: Customer satisfaction with short video e-commerce platforms positively influences consumers' switching intention from traditional e-commerce to short video e-commerce.

Figure 1 illustrates the research model of this study.

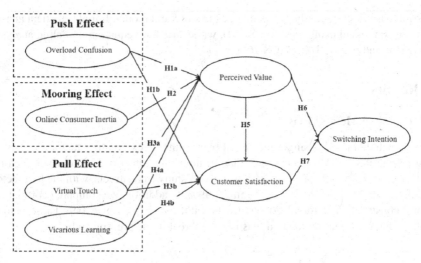

Fig. 1. Research model

4 Methodology

4.1 Measurement Development

Based on existing literature on e-commerce and switching intentions, a scale was developed by integrating mature scales and considering the differences between short video e-commerce and traditional e-commerce in terms of information processing. The research model involves seven variables: overload confusion, online consumer inertia, virtual touch, vicarious learning, perceived value, customer satisfaction, and switching intention. A 5-point Likert scale was employed to assess consumers' usage of traditional e-commerce and short video e-commerce, ranging from 1 (strongly disagree) to 5 (strongly agree). To ensure the clarity and comprehensibility of the questions and enhance data validity, preliminary sampling interviews and pilot tests were conducted, leading to the final survey questionnaire.

4.2 Data Collection

During the data collection phase, we utilized a professional online survey platform (www.wjx.cn) to distribute the questionnaire. The data collection period spanned two weeks, during which we gathered a total of 775 responses. In the data cleaning stage, we removed questionnaires with more than 5 missing values and those with identical responses to all questions. Additionally, we checked respondents' IP addresses to prevent multiple responses from the same individual. Ultimately, we yielded 628 samples with a valid rate of 80.9%.

4.3 Data Analysis

Following the two-step approach recommended by Anderson and Gerbing [16], we initially examined the measurement model to assess the reliability and validity of the questionnaire. Subsequently, we evaluated the structural model. Initial statistical analyses were conducted using IBM SPSS 24.0, while structural equation modeling analysis was performed using IBM AMOS 26.0.

5 Results

5.1 Common Method Bias

We conducted Harman's single-factor test by running an exploratory factor analysis of all the scale items. The result shows that all items are categorized into seven factors. All factors explain 74.86% of the variance in this study's constructs, with the first factor explaining 36.29% and the last explaining 3.99%. In addition, we compared correlation among constructs and found no constructs with correlations over 0.9. These results indicate that the common method bias is not a threat in the present study.

5.2 Measurement Model

To ensure the reliability and validity of the data collected through the survey questionnaire, we conducted a comprehensive assessment of reliability and validity. The Cronbach's alpha values for each variable ranged from 0.780 to 0.886, all surpassing the 0.7 threshold. Additionally, composite reliability (CR) values for each factor loading all surpassed the 0.7 benchmark, confirming structural reliability. Regarding structural validity, we first assessed the average variance extracted (AVE) and standard loading values for each factor loading. All AVE values exceeded 0.5, with the majority of standard loading values surpassing 0.7, which demonstrates good convergent validity. Through a comprehensive assessment of the data, we confirmed that the scales used in this study exhibit high reliability and content validity.

Additionally, we tested discriminant validity by comparing the square root of the AVE with the correlations between variables. According to the data in Table 1, all the square roots of the AVE for each construct are greater than the inter construct correlations, indicating good discriminant validity.

Table 1. Correlations among constructs

Constructs	OC	OCI	VT	VL	PV	CS	SI
OC	**0.763**						
OCI	0.160	**0.738**					
VT	0.504	0.109	**0.804**				
VL	0.446	0.189	0.491	**0.758**			
PV	0.468	0.000	0.564	0.590	**0.802**		
CS	0.542	0.053	0.512	0.475	0.658	**0.814**	

(*continued*)

Table 1. (*continued*)

Constructs	OC	OCI	VT	VL	PV	CS	SI
SI	0.583	0.046	0.450	0.510	0.585	0.710	**0.879**

Note: Diagonal numbers in bold are the square root of the average variance extracted of each construct; Pearson correlations are shown below the diagonal

After verifying the measurement validity and reliability, this study employed the maximum likelihood method for the goodness-of-fit test. All fit indices for model evaluation meet the recommended values, thus confirming the goodness of fit for both the measurement and structural models in this study.

5.3 Structural Model and Hypothesis Testing

The results of the structural model test are presented in Table 2. We depicted the results in Fig. 2.

Table 2. The results of SEM analysis

Path	Coefficient Value	S.E.	C.R.	P-value	Result
H1a: OC → PV	0.196	0.041	3.717	***	Supported
H1b: OC → CS	0.311	0.042	5.565	***	Supported
H2: OCI → PV	−0.125	0.050	−2.601	0.009**	Supported
H3a: VT → PV	0.347	0.057	5.638	***	Supported
H3b: VT → CS	0.026	0.055	0.422	0.673	Not Supported
H4a: VL → PV	0.346	0.054	5.999	***	Supported
H4b: VL → CS	0.157	0.055	2.623	0.009**	Supported
H5: PV → CS	0.430	0.066	6.359	***	Supported
H6: PV → SI	0.226	0.076	3.737	***	Supported
H7: CS → SI	0.545	0.084	8.279	***	Supported

Note: * p < 0.05, ** p < 0.01, *** p < 0.001

6   Discussion and Implications

6.1   Discussion and Findings

This study elucidates the influencing factors and mechanisms underlying consumers' switch from traditional e-commerce to short video e-commerce.

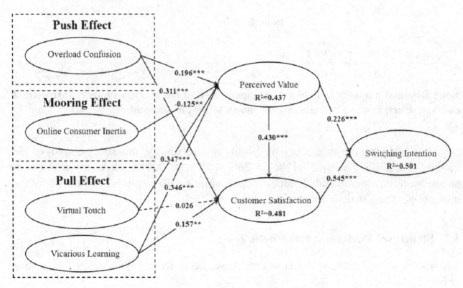

Fig. 2. Results of the research model tests

Firstly, consumer overload confusion on traditional e-commerce platforms will positively influence their perceived value and customer satisfaction with short video e-commerce (H1a, H1b). Overload confusion on traditional e-commerce platforms will prompt consumers to choose the more concise and targeted information presentation of short video e-commerce platforms. The advantage of short video e-commerce platforms in information processing will enhance consumers' perceived value and satisfaction with the platform.

Secondly, virtual touch has a positive impact on perceived value (H3a), and vicarious learning has positive effects on both perceived value and customer satisfaction (H4a, H4b). But virtual touch does not influence customer satisfaction (H3b). We hypothesize that this is primarily due to the varying quality of merchants on short video platforms. A lower level of customer satisfaction will be caused when the actual product does not meet expectations or differs significantly from the displayed product.

Thirdly, perceived value and customer satisfaction both contribute to the generation of switching intention (H6, H7), aligning with findings from previous scholars. However, in comparison to perceived value, customer satisfaction exerts a greater influence on switching intention. This implies that consumers are more likely to develop switching intentions when they are highly satisfied with the shopping platform or when their experience exceeds expectations.

6.2 Theoretical Implication

This article can enhance the theoretical understanding of switching intention in the context of traditional e-commerce and short video e-commerce. Firstly, short video e-commerce is a relatively new research field, thus few studies to date have directly and empirically discussed consumers' switching intention from traditional e-commerce to short video e-commerce. In addition, the use of the PPM theory has not yet been employed for investigating in this field. To address this gap, this paper relies on the PPM theory to empirically investigate which factors influence consumers in switching from traditional e-commerce platforms to short video e-commerce platforms and gain an understanding on how push, pull, and mooring factors shape their switching intention, thus extending the PPM theory and switching research into the field of short video e-commerce.

Secondly, to the best of our knowledge, little research have investigated consumers' switching intention between different online shopping channels from the perspective of information processing. In the era of information explosion, the efficiency of information processing affects consumers' shopping decisions. Therefore, based on the information processing differences between traditional e-commerce and short video e-commerce, this study enriches the PPM theory and switching intention research field by identifying the push factor (i.e. overload confusion) and the pull factors (i.e. virtual touch and vicarious learning), which reveals the significant impact of information processing on consumers' switching intention between online shopping channels.

6.3 Practical Implication

This study, based on the PPM theory and adopting an information processing perspective, explores the factors influencing consumers' switch from traditional e-commerce platforms to short video e-commerce platforms. It holds practical significance. Firstly, short video e-commerce platforms and merchants should take measures to avoid information overload. For instance, when creating videos, showcasing the key features of the product and ensuring a clear storyline with a central focus can help mitigate overload confusion.

Secondly, virtual touch enhances perceived value, while vicarious learning contributes to an increase in both perceived value and customer satisfaction. Merchants can create videos that capture scenes resembling daily life, employing authentic sounds and clear visuals to stimulate virtual touch. Additionally, creating groups to encourage interactions among consumers can foster vicarious learning, assisting consumers in making purchasing decisions.

Thirdly, Short video platforms and merchants should conduct various attention-grabbing marketing activities aligned with consumer needs. By doing so, the perceived value is heightened, mitigating the negative impact of online consumer inertia and fostering the switching intention towards short video e-commerce.

7 Conclusion

In recent years, short video e-commerce has gradually matured with the rapid development of short video platforms. However, consumer behavior differences across different e-commerce platforms and how businesses can conduct differentiated operations on various platforms based on their attributes require further research. This study, based on the PPM theory, analyzes the characteristics of short video e-commerce and traditional e-commerce in the information processing dimension, revealing the factors influencing consumers' switching intention from traditional e-commerce platforms to short video e-commerce platforms. This research aims to fill the gaps in relevant studies in the field of e-commerce and provide practical insights for short video platforms and practitioners in the changing times.

The study findings indicate that overload confusion and vicarious learning positively influence consumers' perceived value and customer satisfaction with short video e-commerce, while virtual touch only positively affects perceived value. Both perceived value and customer satisfaction have positive effects on switching intention, and perceived value also positively influences customer satisfaction. On the other hand, online consumer inertia, as a mooring factor, negatively impacts consumers' perceived value in short video e-commerce.

Acknowledgement. This research was supported by the National Natural Science Foundation of China under Grant 72202219.

References

1. CNNIC: The 52th Statistical Report on Internet Development in China. https://cnnic.cn/n4/2023/0828/c199-10830.html. Accessed 18 Dec 2023
2. Bansal, H.S., Taylor, S.F., St James, Y.: "Migrating" to new service providers: toward a unifying framework of consumers' switching behaviors. J. Acad. Mark. Sci. **33**(1), 96–115 (2005)
3. Li, C.Y., Ku, Y.C.: The power of a thumbs-up: will e-commerce switch to social commerce? Inf. Manage. **55**(3), 340–357 (2017)
4. Hsieh, J.K., Hsieh, Y.C., Chiu, H.C., Feng, Y.C.: Post-adoption switching behavior for online service substitutes: a perspective of the push-pull-mooring framework. Comput. Hum. Behav.. Hum. Behav. **28**(5), 1912–1920 (2012)
5. Yadav, M.S., Valck, K.D., Hennig-Thurau, T., Hoffman, D.L., Spann, M.: Social commerce: a contingency framework for assessing marketing potential. J. Interact. Mark. **27**(4), 311–323 (2013)
6. Curty, R.G., Zhang, P.: Website features that gave rise to social commerce: a historical analysis. Electron. Commer. Res. Appl. **12**(4), 260–279 (2013)
7. Yang, Z., Peterson, R.T.: Customer perceived value, satisfaction, and loyalty: the role of switching costs. Psychol. Mark. **21**(10), 799–822 (2004)
8. Wathieu, L., Brenner, L., Carmon, Z., Chattopadhyay, A., Wertenbroch, K., Drolet, A., et al.: Consumer control and empowerment: a primer. Mark. Lett. **13**(3), 297–305 (2002)
9. Bawa, K.: Modeling inertia and variety seeking tendencies in brand choice behavior. Mark. Sci. **9**(3), 263–278 (1990)
10. Klein, L.R.: Creating virtual product experiences: the role of telepresence. J. Interact. Mark. **17**(1), 41–55 (2003)
11. Gioia, D.A., Manz, C.C.: Linking cognition and behavior: a script processing interpretation of vicarious learning. Acad. Manag. Rev. **10**(3), 527–539 (1985)
12. Myers, C.G.: Coactive vicarious learning: towards a relational theory of vicarious learning in organizations. Acad. Manag. Rev. **43**(4), 610–634 (2018)
13. Zeithaml, V.A.: Consumer perceptions of price, quality, and value: a means-end model and synthesis of evidence. J. Mark. **52**(3), 2–22 (1988)

14. Bansal, H.S., Taylor, S.F.: The Service Provider Switching Model (SPSM): a model of consumer switching behavior in the services industry. J. Serv. Res. **2**(2), 200–218 (1999)
15. Cardozo, R.N.: An experimental study of customer effort, expectation, and satisfaction. J. Mark. Res. **2**(3), 244–249 (1965)
16. Anderson, J.C., Gerbing, D.W.: Structural equation modeling in practice: a review and recommended two-step approach. Psychol. Bull. **103**(3), 411–423 (1988)

Optimal Distinctiveness and Apps' Participation on Mini-programs Platforms

Xing Wan and Yi Li[✉]

School of Business Administration, Nanjing University of Finance and Economics,
Nanjing 210046, China
19852830516@163.com

Abstract. Platforms have become an important meta-organization to orchestrate re-sources and coordinate interests in the digital economy. Market positioning is crucial for value creation and value capture by platform complementors. Based on the theory of Optimal Distinctiveness, this paper examines the relationship between Apps' positioning and their participation in Mini-Program (MP) platform. Unlike traditional digital platforms, APP needs to make decisions on positioning in light of both the platform owner and other apps within the same category on the platform. The paper finds that the more similar the APP is to the MP platform owner, the more inclined it is to participate in the platform, and the more similar it is to the positioning of other APPs within the same category of the MP platform the more inclined it is to participate in the platform. In addition, complementors with high reputation tend to have stronger relationships between positioning similarity and participation decision, complementors with better relationship with the platform owner tend to have weaker relationships between positioning similarity and participation decision. This paper deepens the understanding on the behavior and decision-making by platform complementors, and provides practical implications for complementors to make correct platform selection decisions. Please polish the paragraph.

Keywords: Platform ecosystem · Optimal distinctiveness · Complementors strategy · Mini-Programs

1 Introduction

In the increasingly competitive landscape of the mobile Internet, the growth rate has entered the single-digit era, posing a challenge for the industry to explore new sources of traffic. In this context, Mini-Programs (MPs) emerged and gained immense popularity since the release of WeChat in early 2017, attracting other major players such as Alipay, Baidu, and Douyin [1]. MPs have enriched the functionalities of these super apps, enabling them to build their own ecosystems and develop unique features and strengths [2]. APP developers have seized the opportunity to create MPs for these platforms, collaborating with MP platform owners to generate value. However, they face the dual challenge of leveraging platform resources for capability development [3] and

Y. P. Tu and M. Chi (Eds.): WHICEB 2024, LNBIP 516, pp. 326–338, 2024.
https://doi.org/10.1007/978-3-031-60260-3_27

navigating competition from the platform owner and other complementors within the same category [4]. When participating in MP platforms, APP developers must make two critical positioning decisions. Firstly, they need to identify the commonalities they share with the platform owner, leveraging the platform's strengths and catering to the primary user base to maximize traffic and support from the platform. Secondly, APP developers must consider their own legitimacy and acceptance among other APPs in the same MP category. They must utilize their own resources and strengths to effectively compete with other complementors and seek new avenues for growth while maintaining consistency.

In summary, this paper explores the following questions: First, how does the similarity in positioning with the MP platform owner influence APPs' decisions to participate? Second, how does the similarity in positioning with other APPs within the same category impact APPs' participation decisions? Third, how does APP reputation moderate the relationship between positioning similarity and participation decisions? Fourth, how does the relationship with the MP platform owner moderate the relationship between positioning similarity and participation decisions? Drawing on the Optimal Distinctiveness theory, this paper delves into the decision-making process of APPs when choosing to participate on MP platforms. Its objective is to provide theoretical support and practical guidance for the effective governance of platform ecosystems by shedding light on these intricate dynamics.

2 Theoretical Framework and Hypotheses

2.1 Optimal Distinctiveness Theory and Its Application to Platform Ecosystems

"To be different, or to be the same?" is an enduring strategic choice that enterprises must confront during their growth process. With the continuous development of the platform economy, the theory of Optimal Distinctiveness has gradually found application in the platform market. Research has explored various aspects such as product development strategy in video game platforms [5], product portfolio in catechism platforms [6], product innovation in crowdfunding platforms [7], and strategic positioning in the mobile app market [8]. However, the existing research on complementors' competition and cooperation within platform ecosystems, which possess multilateral architectural features [9] remains fragmented. In this study, we focus on MP platform owners, such as WeChat, Alipay, Baidu, and Douyin, who are APPs of similar scale as their complementors and have their own distinct usage scenarios and established user bases [2]. Consequently, for the complementors of MP platforms, it becomes essential to coordinate with the platform owners to gain better access to platform traffic. Simultaneously, these complementors also face competition from other complementors and must consider whether to follow or differentiate themselves from their counterparts before participating in the platform. Therefore, building an integrated framework to study the participation decisions of complementors based on the theory of Optimal Distinctiveness holds significant value. This paper explores the unique characteristics of MPs platforms, partially unveiling the black box surrounding complementors' participation on MP platforms and filling a gap in the existing literature.

2.2 The Effect of Positioning Similarity Between APP and MP Platform Owner on APP's Participation Decisions

The trend of monopoly in the app market is becoming increasingly evident, with platforms like WeChat, Alipay, Baidu, and Douyin evolving into super-APPs while maintaining their core attributes. These platforms continue to serve users through their respective core functions. As a result, their focus lies in fostering the development of MPs that align with their own positioning, rather than adopting a more innovative platform approach that encourages all complementors, similar to Apple's APP STORE. Furthermore, the potential market size that a platform possesses significantly influences the choices made by complementors regarding which platform to participate in. When complementors decide to join an MP platform, they must consider factors such as the user base and usage scenarios of that platform. This consideration allows them to embed themselves effectively within the MP platform and gain access to the traffic generated by it [10]. The consistent positioning of the platform indicates that its user base is similar to the target audience, and the usage scenarios align with expectations. This alignment facilitates complementors in better penetrating the market. Consequently, each APP makes a decision based on its own interests, thereby realizing its own development through the choice between different MP platforms. Over time, each MP platform has developed its own strengths, leading to a multi-party rivalry. WeChat, with social media as its core, has become a fertile ground for numerous social and entertainment MPs. AliPay's MP ecosystem focuses on providing life services and tools. Baidu's MP ecosystem revolves around search and information flow. Douyin, as a latecomer, has made its mark in the entertainment track by continuously enhancing its entertainment functions through MPs. Therefore, this paper proposes the hypothesis:

H1: The similarity in positioning between an App and the MP platform owner has a positive impact on the App's decision to participate.

2.3 The Effect of Positioning Similarity Between APP and Other APPs Within the Same Category of the MP Platform on APP's Participation Decision

Haunschild and Miner highlight the presence of inter-organizational imitations, which can be both outcome-based and frequency-based [11]. When faced with the decision of which platform to participate in, complementors often observe the actions of other complementors, leading to a herd-like product development strategy. If APPs of the same type choose to participate in a particular platform by developing MPs, other APPs may choose to follow suit, believing that such participation is advantageous for their own development due to low participation thresholds and learning costs. According to institutional scholars, aligning with other products in the market can enhance legitimacy through market recognition [12]. Thus, when selecting an MP platform, APPs also consider whether they can gain legitimacy by associating with similar groups. Otherwise, they risk their product being perceived by MP platform users as an outsider in the existing market, which can hinder users' ability to assess product quality [13]. Therefore, this paper proposes the hypothesis:

H2: The similarity in positioning between an App and other Apps within the same category of the MP platform has a positive impact on the App's decision to participate.

2.4 The Moderating Role of APP's Reputation

Reputation refers to the overall cognitive judgment of groups regarding the past behavior of enterprises [14], in the context of this paper, the reputation of a complementor refers to the recognition of APP users and the quality of the product. It represents the social evaluation and status of the enterprise's product within the specific market segment to which it belongs [15]. Unlike the APP STORE, the MP platform lacks a recommendation mechanism, and users' understanding and usage of MPs are primarily based on their familiarity with and usage of the native app. Therefore, the reputation of the native app has a significant impact on the newly developed MP. The competition effect arises when both the APPs and MP platform owners offer similar products or services and rely on the same market for exchange. The greater the similarity in positioning between APPs and MP platform owners, the stronger the competitive relationship becomes with the platform owner. Consequently, the platform owner may leverage their market power to encroach upon the value of the complementor, such as through product imitation, flow restrictions, or unfair pricing practices [16, 17]. Some apps with low reputation may choose not to participate due to fear of platform suppression. On the other hand, high-reputation complementors can bring more value to the platform, generate their own traffic without concerns about the platform owner's restrictions, and possess a strong bargaining advantage [18]. Therefore, this paper proposes the hypothesis:

H3a: When an App's reputation is high, the positive effect of positioning similarity between the APP and the MP platform owner on the APP's participation decision is strengthened.

Similarly, when complementors are more similar to other complementors within the platform category, they face increased competition. In this scenario, the high reputation of the native app serves as an endorsement for the MP. When MPs have similar positions, users may find it challenging to determine which one is better. However, MPs with a higher reputation are more familiar to users and are more likely to gain their trust. Therefore, this paper proposes the hypothesis:

H3b: When an App's reputation is high, the positive effect of positioning similarity between the APP and other apps within the same category of the MP platform on the APP's participation decision is strengthened.

2.5 The Moderating Role of the Relationship Between APP and MP Platform Owner

Platform business governance must consider whether the platform provides products through self-management or third-party markets [19]. Platforms often choose to develop self-management products to expand their market presence, especially in segments where they lack specialization. This strategy allows platforms to quickly address their own shortcomings, reduce dependence on other complementors, and increase profitability. Consequently, for complementors associated with the platform's self-management or invested products, even if they are not closely aligned with the platform's primary positioning, they are given priority for participation. This prioritization results in lower participation thresholds and access to more platform-provided resources, enhancing their competitive advantage. Self-management is a common practice within MP platforms, as evidenced by Tencent alone, which hosts over 100 MPs on the WeChat platform. Therefore, this paper proposes the hypothesis:

H4a: When an APP has a better relationship with the MP platform owner, the positive effect of positioning similarity between the APP and the MP platform owner on the APP's participation decision is weakened.

When complementors have a better relationship with the platform owner, they face lower barriers to participation and receive more resources. This enables complementors to exercise more independent thinking. By leveraging their strong relationship with the platform owner, complementors gain confidence in establishing their own competitive advantage by differentiating themselves from other complementors. Therefore, this paper proposes the hypothesis:

H4b: When an APP has a better relationship with the MP platform owner, the positive effect of positioning similarity between the APP and other apps within the same category of the MP platform on the APP's participation decision is weakened.

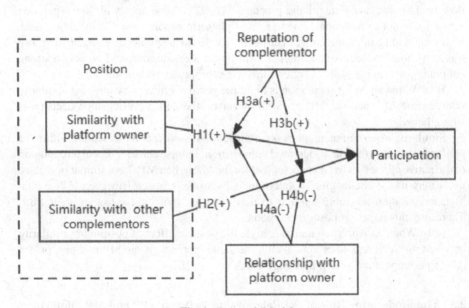

Fig. 1. Research Model

3 Methodology

3.1 Data

To ensure data availability and sample representativeness, the complementor aspect of the study focuses on APPs, while the platform aspect includes four major platforms: WeChat, Alipay, Baidu, and Douyin. These platforms were selected due to their extensive range of MPs, large user bases, and diverse positioning. The corresponding MPs on the sample platforms were retrieved using keywords from the top 200 apps listed in both the free and best-seller categories provided by Qimai. If an app had participated in one or more MP platforms, it was included in the sample pool. To minimize the likelihood of complementors abstaining from participation due to platform scrutiny, the study excluded the "financial" and "medical" categories, which Alipay and Douyin clearly indicated as "directional invitation." Additionally, categories with a particularly low number of participating complementors were also excluded. As a result, the study obtained samples from 16 subcategories: Life, Tool, Entertainment, Shopping, Education, News, Tourism, Social Networking, Health and Fitness, Gourmet Food, Photography, Business, Books, Efficiency, Sport, and Reference Materials. After eliminating invalid data, the study ultimately obtained 2792 App-platform samples, consisting of 698 App samples across the four platforms.

3.2 Model and Variables

Since the dependent variables in this paper are dichotomous variables, this paper mainly adopts the Probit model to analyze the effect of complementarians' positioning on participation decisions.

Dependent Variable. There's only one dependent variables, *Part*, which represents participation, with APP having participated in the sample platform marked as 1 and not participated in as 0.

Independent Variable. There are two independent variables, namely *Sim1* and *Sim2*. In this paper, we use developer instructions of APPs to measure the explanatory variable. We use natural language processing methods to perform word splitting, remove deactivated words, vectorize the processed text, and calculate the cosine values. *Sim1* is measured by the cosine values between complementors and MP platforms. Similarly, calculate the mean vector of the intra-platform category to which the complementor belongs, and then calculate the cosine values between complementors and the average vectors, which is *Sim2*.

Moderating Variable. There are two moderating variables, *Fame* and *Rela*. *Fame* is measured by the mean of APP review and APP rating [20]. Each category was ranked from highest to lowest by the number of reviews in each of the 16 categories, and each 20% was assigned a rank and a value. In terms of app ratings, the average of the ratings of both the Android app market and the Apple iOS app market was taken. *Rela* represents the relationship between complementor and platform owner, we assign a value of 0–3 to indicate the relationship between the two, 0 = no relationship, 1 = platform investment, and 2 = platform self-management, information is collected from Qichacha.

Control Variable. APP level: *Category*, we use 16 dummy variables represent 16 categories; *Word*, App description's length; *Fee*, whether the APP has internal purchase items; *Age*, length of time the App has been on sale, taking a logarithmic number; *Exp*erience, number of apps developed by the developer, taking a logarithmic number. Platform level: *Plact*, representing the rate of platform activity, collected from Talking Data platform; Plsc, representing the number of platform users, collected from IRindex platform, taking a logarithmic number.

4 Results

4.1 Descriptive Statistics

Table 1 gives the descriptive statistics of the variables. As can be seen from Table 1, *Sim1* and *Sim2* are significantly and positively correlated to *Part*, which provides initial support for the main hypothesizes proposed in this study. In addition, there are no variables with correlation coefficients greater than 0.6 and significant in Table 1, and the variance inflation factor (VIF) test was conducted, the mean value of VIF is 1.22 and the maximum value of VIF is 1.53, which can be regarded as there is no multicollinearity problem.

Table 1. Descriptive statistics

Variable	Mean	SD	(1)	(2)	(3)	(4)
sim1	0.063	0.040	1			
sim2	0.099	0.059	0.044**	1		
Part	0.451	0.498	0.049***	0.391***	1	
fame	3.502	1.059	0.037*	0.104***	0.050***	1
rela	0.067	0.319	-0.005	0.067***	0.180***	0.077***
word	491.0	332.0	0.017	0.122***	0	0.290***
fee	0.491	0.500	0.038**	0.005	0.092***	0.266***
age	7.658	0.766	0.018	0.121***	0.087***	0.499***
exp	1.084	1.028	0.056***	0.031	−0.005	0.282***
plsc	11.34	0.209	0.016	0.021	0.583***	0.005
plact	0.737	0.117	0.070***	−0.004	0.411***	−0.003

Variable	(5)	(6)	(7)	(8)	(9)	(10)	(11)
rela	1						
word	0.021	1					
fee	0.005	0.244***	1				
age	0.069***	0.230***	0.045**	1			
exp	0.137***	0.108***	0.186***	0.184***	1		
plsc	0.127***	−0.002	0.002	−0.003	0	1	
plact	0.064***	-0.003	0.003	−0.003	0.010	0.504***	1

Significance level: * p < 0.1, ** p < 0.05, *** p < 0.01.

4.2 Regression Results

The regression results are shown in Table 2 and Table 3. Model 1 tests the main effect, model 2 and model 3 test the moderating effect, and model 4 adds all variables. As

Table 2 shows, from model 1, it can be seen that the positioning similarity between the APP and the MP platform owners has a significant positive effect on the APP's participation decision ($\alpha1 = 1.820$, $p < 0.01$), which supports H1. From model 2, it can be seen that the APP with high reputation tends to have stronger relationship between positioning similarity with the MP platform owner and participation decision ($\alpha2 = 1.545$, $p < 0.05$), supporting H3a. From Model 3, it can be seen that the better the APP's relationship with the platform owner, the more likely the APP chooses to participate in the platform even if its positioning is not as similar as the platform owner's ($\beta3 = -7.844$, $p < 0.05$), supporting H4a.

Table 2. Regression results of *Sim1*

Variable	Model1	Model2	Model3	Model4
sim1	1.820^{***}	1.739^{***}	1.501^{**}	1.438^{**}
	(0.007)	(0.010)	(0.029)	(0.036)
fame		0.060^{*}		0.052
		(0.075)		(0.123)
sim1 × fame		1.545^{**}		1.673^{***}
		(0.016)		(0.009)
rela			0.738^{***}	0.736^{***}
			(0.000)	(0.000)
sim1 × rela			-7.844^{**}	-7.614^{**}
			(0.012)	(0.015)
word	0.000	0.000	0.000	0.000
	(0.315)	(0.434)	(0.284)	(0.372)
fee	-0.169^{**}	-0.203^{***}	-0.164^{**}	-0.195^{**}
	(0.021)	(0.007)	(0.028)	(0.010)
lnage	0.180^{***}	0.146^{***}	0.170^{***}	0.140^{***}
	(0.000)	(0.004)	(0.000)	(0.006)
lnexp	-0.009	-0.017	-0.027	-0.035
	(0.775)	(0.577)	(0.378)	(0.265)
lnplsc	3.988^{***}	4.002^{***}	3.910^{***}	3.923^{***}
	(0.000)	(0.000)	(0.000)	(0.000)
plact	2.007^{***}	2.004^{***}	2.056^{***}	2.052^{***}
	(0.000)	(0.000)	(0.000)	(0.000)
_cons	-48.399^{***}	-48.472^{***}	-47.458^{***}	-47.538^{***}
	(0.000)	(0.000)	(0.000)	(0.000)

(*continued*)

Table 2. (*continued*)

Variable	Model1	Model2	Model3	Model4
N	2792.000	2792.000	2792.000	2792.000
Pseudo R2	0.3346	0.3366	0.3473	0.3493

Application category dummies have been included in the analysis but not shown in the table. Significance level: * $p < 0.1$, ** $p < 0.05$, *** $p < 0.01$.

As Table 3 shows, from model 1, it can be seen that the positioning similarity between the APP and other APPs within the same category of the MP platform has a significant positive effect on the APP's participation decision ($\alpha1 = 0.35, p < 0.01$), which supports H2. From Model 2, it can be seen that the APP with high reputation tends to have stronger relationship between positioning similarity with other APPs within the same category of the MP platform and participation decision ($\alpha2 = 2.347, p < 0.01$), which supports H3b. From Model 3, it can be seen that, the better the APP's relationship with the platform's owner, the more likely the APP will choose to participate in the platform even if it is not so similar to other APPs' positioning within the platform category ($\beta3 = -10.419, p < 0.01$), supporting H4b (Table 4).

Table 3. Regression results of *Sim2*

Variable	Model1	Model2	Model3	Model4
sim2	0.350***	0.350***	0.351***	0.352***
	(0.000)	(0.000)	(0.000)	(0.000)
fame		0.051		0.050
		(0.227)		(0.244)
sim2 × fame		2.347***		2.437***
		(0.005)		(0.004)
rela			0.749***	0.749***
			(0.000)	(0.000)
sim2 × rela			−10.419***	−9.711**
			(0.009)	(0.014)
word	−0.001***	−0.001***	−0.001***	−0.001***
	(0.000)	(0.000)	(0.000)	(0.000)
fee	0.006	−0.029	0.021	−0.013
	(0.953)	(0.764)	(0.831)	(0.897)

(*continued*)

Table 3. (*continued*)

Variable	Model1	Model2	Model3	Model4
lnage	0.157***	0.123*	0.145**	0.112*
	(0.006)	(0.057)	(0.011)	(0.085)
lnexp	−0.028	−0.034	−0.054	−0.061
	(0.471)	(0.383)	(0.179)	(0.134)
lnplsc	6.052***	6.071***	5.993***	6.011***
	(0.000)	(0.000)	(0.000)	(0.000)
plact	2.085***	2.095***	2.146***	2.156***
	(0.000)	(0.000)	(0.000)	(0.000)
_cons	−75.105***	−75.238***	−74.415***	−74.543***
	(0.000)	(0.000)	(0.000)	(0.000)
N	2792.000	2792.000	2792.000	2792.000
Pseudo R2	0.6237	0.6257	0.6314	0.6335

Table 4. Regression results of IV

Variable	Model1	Model2	Model3	Model4
IV1	0.223**	0.225**	0.231**	0.233**
	(0.043)	(0.041)	(0.041)	(0.039)
fame		0.060*		0.053
		(0.074)		(0.121)
IV1 × fame		1.654***		1.733***
		(0.010)		(0.007)
rela			0.772***	0.766***
			(0.000)	(0.000)
IV1 × rela			−9.865***	−9.472***
			(0.003)	(0.005)
N	2792.000	2792.000	2792.000	2792.000
Pseudo R2	0.3341	0.3363	0.3475	0.3496

Control variable have been included in the analysis but not shown in the table.

Significance level: * $p < 0.1$, ** $p < 0.05$, *** $p < 0.01$.

Application category dummies have been included in the analysis but not shown in the table.

Significance level: * $p < 0.1$, ** $p < 0.05$, *** $p < 0.01$.

4.3 Endogeneity Test

However, due to the difficulty of data acquisition, there may be a potential endogeneity problem, so we try to solve this problem by using an instrumental variable Probit model. We choose whether the complementor and the platform owner are in the same category as the instrumental variable for *Sim1*, we choose the logarithmic value of *Sim2* as the instrumental variable for *Sim2*. In this paper, we adopt the endogeneity test of binary choice model. P-values of AR and Wald for *IV1* are significant at the 10% level, and the weak instrumental test passes; the p-value of the Hausman test is 0.0465, and the hypothesis of the non-existence of endogeneity is rejected at the 5% level which means endogeneity exists. The weak instrumental test for *IV2* also passes, and the p-value of Hausman test is 0.5980, which shows that there is no endogeneity problem, so only the estimation results of the Probit model for *IV1* are shown, all the regression results are consistent with the original model, indicating that Hypotheses 1, 3a, and 4a still hold.

5 Conclusions

Drawing upon the Optimal Distinctiveness theory, this study investigates the relationship between positioning similarity and an APP's decision to participate in an MP platform. Specifically, we examine both the similarity with the MP platform owner and other complementors within the same category of the MP platform. Overall, our findings indicate that greater similarity between an APP and the MP platform owner increases the likelihood of the APP participating in the platform. Similarly, when an APP aligns closely with the positioning of other APPs in the same category of the MP platform, it is more inclined to participate in the platform. Moreover, complementor reputation positively moderates this relationship, while the relationship with the platform owner negatively moderates it.

This paper examines the impact of positioning similarity on complementors' decision to participate in the platform, taking into account both platform owners and complementors' frameworks, which aligns with the multilateral architecture characteristic of platforms [9]. Additionally, it delves into the motivations behind complementors' participation in the platform, thereby expanding the real-world contexts of complementor research and Optimal Distinctiveness research. The MP platform explored in this study stands out as significantly different from other platforms, offering valuable real-world insights. For platform owners, the research findings suggest that complementors on MP platforms prioritize consistency over differentiation. This indicates that the platform owner's positioning imposes constraints and pressures on complementors. To excel in the competition, platform owners should adapt their policies and resource allocation strategies to attract complementors with diverse positionings, ultimately aiming to become a more comprehensive platform. Regarding APPs, choosing to participate in fields that closely align with their own positioning can be a strategic move. However, they should also consider whether the platform owner's product has already entered that field since the platform tends to allocate resources to self-management products. APPs should avoid blindly following the crowd and instead make adjustments based on the specific circumstances. If resources permit, adopting a differentiation strategy can capture consumer attention more effectively.

This paper acknowledges several limitations that provide valuable directions for future research. Firstly, due to data availability challenges, the impact of MP platform supervision on APPs' participation was not thoroughly examined. Future studies should strive to gather relevant data to better understand this aspect. Secondly, APPs' participation is a multifaceted process influenced by various factors. Future research can explore the influence of additional factors on APPs' participation decisions, such as the size of the APP and its past performance. Furthermore, investigating the diversity of participation strategies and their impact on outcome performance would provide deeper insights to guide the MP ecosystem effectively. Thirdly, the focus of this paper was primarily on APPs due to sample availability. To broaden the scope of this study, future research should consider including a more diverse range of complementors on the MP platform. This expansion would enhance the comprehensive understanding of the topic.

Acknowledgement. The authors gratefully acknowledge financial support from the National Social Science Foundation of China (Grant No. 21BGL033), Principal Scholar/Excellent Team of Instructors of Qinglan Project of Universities in Jiangsu, Postgraduate Research & Practice Innovation Program of Jiangsu Province and Innovation Team Project "Internet Platform Strategy and Governance (KYCTD202201)" sponsored by Nanjing University of Finance and Economics.

References

1. Cheng, K., Schreieck, M., Wiesche, M., Krcmar, H.: Emergence of a post-app era – an exploratory case study of the WeCchat mini-program ecosystem. In: WI2020 Zentrale Tracks, pp. 1444–1458 (2020)
2. Schreieck, M., Ou, A., Krcmar, H.: Mini-app ecosystems, business & information. Syst. Eng. **65**(1), 85–93 (2022)
3. Cenamor, J.: Complementor competitive advantage: a framework for strategic decisions. J. Bus. Res. **122**, 335–343 (2021)
4. Kapoor, R., Agarwal, S.: Sustaining superior performance in business ecosystems: evidence from application software developers in the iOS and android smartphone ecosystems. Organ. Sci. **28**(3), 531–551 (2017)
5. Zhao, E.Y., Ishihara, M., Jennings, P.D., Lounsbury, M.: Optimal distinctiveness in the console video game industry: an exemplar-based model of proto-category evolution. Organ. Sci. **29**(4), 588–611 (2018)
6. Taeuscher, K., Rothe, H.: Optimal distinctiveness in platform markets: leveraging complementors as legitimacy buffers. Strateg. Manag. J.. Manag. J. **42**(2), 435–461 (2020)
7. Taeuscher, K., Bouncken, R., Pesch, R.: Gaining legitimacy by being different: optimal distinctiveness in crowdfunding platforms. Acad. Manag. J.Manag. J. **64**(1), 149–179 (2021)
8. Barlow, M.A., Verhaal, J.C., Angus, R.W.: Optimal distinctiveness, strategic categorization, and product market entry on the Google Play app platform. Strateg. Manag. J.. Manag. J. **40**(8), 1219–1242 (2019)
9. Evans, D.S.: Some empirical aspects of multi-sided platform industries. Rev. Netw. Econ.Netw. Econ. **2**(3), 191–209 (2004)
10. Wang, J., Qu, Q., Qiu, Y.: How to implement platform mosaic strategy for startups in digital ecology? J. Foreign Econ. Manage. **43**(09), 24–42 (2021). in chinese
11. Haunschild, P.R., Miner, A.S.: Modes of Interorganizational Imitation: the effects of outcome salience and uncertainty. Adm. Sci. Q. **42**(3), 472–500 (1997)

12. DiMaggio, P.J., Powell, W.W.: The iron cage revisited institutional isomorphism and collective rationality in organizational fields, Economics Meets Sociology in Strategic Management, pp. 143–166 (2000)
13. Podolny, J.M.: Market uncertainty and the social character of economic exchange. Adm. Sci. Q. **39**(3), 458–483 (1994)
14. Erratum, The relationship of reputation and credibility to brand success, Pricing Strategy and Practice 5(1), pp. 25–29 (1997)
15. Floyd, K., Freling, R., Alhoqail, S., Cho, H.Y., Freling, T.: How online product reviews affect retail sales: a meta-analysis. J. Retail. **90**(2), 217–232 (2014)
16. Elsenmann, T., Parker, G., Vanalstyne, M.: Platform envelopment. Strateg. Manag. J.. Manag. J. **32**(32), 1270–1285 (2011)
17. Zhu, F., Liu, Q.: Competing with complementors: an empirical look at Amazon.com. Strategic Manage. J. **39**(10), 2618–2642 (2018)
18. Wang, R.D., Miller, C.D.: Complementors' engagement in an ecosystem: a study of publishers' e-book offerings on Amazon Kindle. Strateg. Manag. J.. Manag. J. **41**(1), 3–26 (2019)
19. Zenger, T.R., Felin, T., Bigelow, L.: Theories of the firm–market boundary. Acad. Manag. Ann.Manag. Ann. **5**(1), 89–133 (2011)
20. Windrum, P.: Leveraging technological externalities in complex technologies: microsoft's exploitation of standards in the browser wars. Res. Policy **33**(3), 385–394 (2004)

Pricing Product Data for Manufacturing Enterprises: A Bargaining Model

Ting Yang[1], Meishu Zhang[1,2], Yu Jia[1(✉)], Nianxin Wang[1], and Shilun Ge[1]

[1] School of Economics and Management, Jiangsu University of Science and Technology, Zhenjiang 212003, Jiangsu, China
jiayu@just.edu.cn

[2] Department of Humanities and Social Sciences, Jiangsu University of Science and Technology, Zhenjiang 212003, Jiangsu, China

Abstract. Pricing is the pivotal aspect in the commercialization of data elements, serving as the fundamental mechanism of the data element market. In this study, we focus on the product data and aim to set reasonable prices for the product data trading in manufacturing enterprises. Specifically, we identify key factors such as production cost and market loss for the product data owner, R&D investment, market return, and equipment cost for demander, and develop a three-stage one-to-one bargaining pricing model between owners and demanders. Results indicate that, (1) the equilibrium price of product data is positively correlated with the owner's discount factor, market loss rate, and demander's market rate of return, and negatively associated with the demander's discount factor and equipment cost rate. (2) the owner's equilibrium return is positively correlated with the owner's discount factor and the demander's market rate of return, and negatively correlated with the owner's market rate of loss, the demander's discount factor, and the equipment cost rate. (3) the demander's equilibrium returns are positively associated with the demander's discount factor and market rate of return and inversely related to the owner's discount factor, market loss rate, and demander's equipment input cost rate. This study provides a novel perspective on trading strategy for product data in manufacturing enterprises and expands existing studies that mainly focused on pricing of domain data.

Keywords: Product Data · Pricing Models · Bargaining Mode · Manufacturing Enterprises

1 Introduction

At present, data has emerged as the most distinctive factor of production, evolving into the core driving force behind the further development of the digital economy and the advancement of digital transformation in both corporate and social governance in China [1, 2]. Pricing plays a crucial role in the formation of a data factor market, acting as the essential driver that propels its growth and development [3, 4]. The pricing of data products has gained significant attention from both academic and industry circles, and numerous studies have delved into different aspects such as pricing methods, models, mechanisms, and strategies for data products [4–7]. For instance, Pei [8] examined the data pricing problem from an economic perspective, categorizing data products into different versions based on their characteristics or user requirements, and implementing various pricing methods accordingly. Koutris [9] developed the version-based pricing method and introduced a query-based data pricing strategy. Additionally, several studies have also examined the influencing factors, challenges, and characteristics of data product pricing. Liang et al. [7] postulated that data serve as digital commodities and their prices are influenced by the structure of the data market. Tang et al. [10] conducted an empirical analysis and compiled 18 key factors that impact the market price of data elements. Huang et al. [11] examined the characteristics and transaction patterns of data products throughout their circulation process, paving the way for establishing transaction pricing for data products.

Despite the fruitful results achieved in the pricing studies of data products, there are still some gaps in the literature. First, numerous pricing models and methods have been developed at the theoretical level, making it challenging to effectively guide the practical application of data product pricing. Most studies centered on the fundamental distinctions between data products and conventional products, considering the distinctive characteristics of data products (diversity, timeliness, repeatability, etc. [6]), transaction models (customer-led, supplier-led, platform-led, etc. [11]), pricing strategies (free, user-based, package pricing, etc. [7]), and various application scenarios from diverse perspectives. Second, most pricing methods are limited to specific data types, models, and scenarios. Additionally, the value of data products or data elements is primarily determined using market-based, income-based, or cost-based methods, or by evaluating the significance weight of the application scenario [4, 12]. However, evidence suggests that the challenges in quantifying the cost of data products, estimating their potential value, and determining their business value have hindered the trading and circulation of data products [13]. Third, prior studies focus on the Internet platform, finance, power grid, personal health, and government open data products [5], aiming to construct transaction pricing models that cater to various competitive scenarios and ideal conditions. In contrast, lack of studies explores how traditional enterprises harness the value of their data and facilitate data transaction flows, especially for manufacturing enterprises. As a cornerstone of China's economic development, promoting and enabling data circulation in manufacturing enterprises carries significant theoretical importance and strategic value.

In practice, the digital applications in manufacturing enterprises have accumulated a substantial amount of data encompassing different facets of production, operations, and management, and documenting the complete lifecycle of enterprise activities [14, 15]. Product data, as the most important and valuable data in manufacturing enterprises, comprises core information such as product structure, design techniques, and manufacturing processes. Product data offers a comprehensive and detailed representation of the product's manufacturing process. Thus, devising appropriate pricing strategies for product data within manufacturing enterprises, and facilitating their transaction and circulation, holds significant research importance and economic value.

The purpose of this study is to address the intricate issue of pricing product data in manufacturing enterprises. Drawing upon existing data product transaction pricing models, we consider the production costs and potential market losses borne by product data owners, and the research and development investments, market returns, and equipment investment costs incurred by demanders. We develop a three-stage one-on-one bargaining model for pricing product data transactions within manufacturing enterprises. This model aids in determining the equilibrium price of product data and the balanced revenue accrued by both parties.

The structure of this study is as follows. In Sect. 2, we provide a comprehensive review of the relevant studies conducted in this field. Section 3 focuses on the problem description and model development, including the construction and analysis of the pricing model. Finally, in Sect. 4, we present our conclusions.

2 Literature Review

Data products encompass data sets that are valued as standalone products or information services derived from such datasets [2]. The efficient circulation and trading of these data products hold the promise of delivering substantial economic and social benefits to enterprises as well as the broader society. The distinctive properties of data products, including their non-exclusivity, non-scarcity, ease of replication, and value-added sharing, give rise to numerous unresolved issues and challenges in pricing and trading circulation. Notably, data product pricing serves as a crucial link in the process of data marketization [3] and is essential for facilitating the circulation of data transactions and ensuring their value realization. The existing pricing studies on data products primarily center on various types of data based on their unique characteristics, including personal data, financial data, real estate data, geographic mapping data, Internet data, and Internet of Things data [5].

However, there is a paucity of studies focusing on the pricing of product data in manufacturing enterprises. Product data encompasses all the information generated and utilized throughout various stages of a product's life cycle, including research and development, manufacturing, sales, and after-sales service. It serves as the fundamental resource for production organization and management within manufacturing enterprises. Product data, as the most essential and valuable asset of manufacturing enterprises, encompasses core information such as product structure, manufacturing process, manufacturing technology, materials, labor hours, and production. It provides a comprehensive and detailed representation of product structure, manufacturing process, manufacturing methods, and manufacturing equipment. Unlocking the value of product data in manufacturing enterprises and fostering the exchange of product data transactions are essential for realizing the full potential of data in these enterprises, leveraging the rich resources of manufacturing enterprises' data elements, and supporting the development, preservation, and enhancement of their data assets.

Determining reasonable prices is paramount in facilitating the circulation of data transactions, especially given the increasingly intricate and diverse nature of data products [3]. Currently, scholars have conducted extensive research on pricing models for product data. Yu et al. [16] independently evaluated metrics across various quality dimensions and accounted for the influence of consumer heterogeneity. They posited that platforms should devise multi-variant data assets and prices tailored to distinct consumer groups. Lin et al. [17] have developed a comprehensive multi-dimensional factor pricing model that caters to consumers with diverse utility sensitivities, taking into account factors such as data quality, quantity, and their interactions. Additionally, Luong et al. [18] developed an IoT data trading model in which all data owners engage in transactions competitively. Liu et al. [19] introduced a two-stage Stackelberg game to address the data trading challenges between data platforms and data consumers.

Based on the research presented above, several key findings emerge. Firstly, while numerous data product pricing strategies and transaction methods have been proposed, a standardized and orderly transaction pricing mechanism remains lacking, leading to a relatively complex data product pricing system. Secondly, the current transaction pricing methods exhibit diverse focuses, with some solely relying on data characteristics to determine prices, disregarding external factors like market supply and demand relationships. Thirdly, the current data product transaction pricing strategies and methods tend to be tailored to specific types of data products, limiting their broader applicability. While existing research has primarily focused on personal and government public data products, it has paid less attention to the context of manufacturing enterprises. Consequently, further research is required to establish reasonable prices for manufacturing enterprise product data transactions.

3 Problem Description and Model

3.1 Problem Description

This study delves into the intricate matter of determining the optimal pricing strategy for product data in manufacturing enterprises. It specifically examines the one-on-one transaction model, where only one product data owner and one product data demander participate in the transaction. The product data owner is a manufacturer of a unique or highly advantageous product or series of products that holds a certain or strong competitive edge in the market. On the other hand, the product data demander is a manufacturer interested in purchasing this data to produce the product.

In comparison to preexisting data product transaction models, the exchange of product data within manufacturing enterprises exhibits the following distinguishing features.

(1) Product data demanders acquire product data for specific products, enabling them to quickly integrate it into the design, production, and manufacturing of the product. This process allows for a swift entry into the market, reducing R&D investment in the product while increasing market opportunities and generating sales revenue. Nevertheless, during the application of product data, new equipment requirements may arise due to the inability of existing production equipment to meet its application requirements. This necessitates additional equipment investment costs.

(2) The owner of the product data meticulously extracts and refines data pertinent to product development, design, and production, thereby generating the product data for

the given product. By selling this data, they reap financial benefits. Simultaneously, the demander of this product data introduces the identical product into the market, encroaching on the owner 's market share. Consequently, in addition to earning revenue from selling the product data, the owner must also contend with the market losses incurred by the demander's entry into the market with the acquired product data.

According to the problem description, this study targets product data transaction pricing as its primary area of exploration. It delves into the factors that shape the price of product data, from the perspectives of both product data owners and demanders. This study proceeds to establish psychological retention prices and revenue functions for both parties, taking into account these influencing factors. It also constructs a one-to-one bargaining game model, aiming to determine a price that satisfies both parties, thus facilitating the efficient transaction and circulation of product data. The pricing model developed is illustrated in Fig. 1.

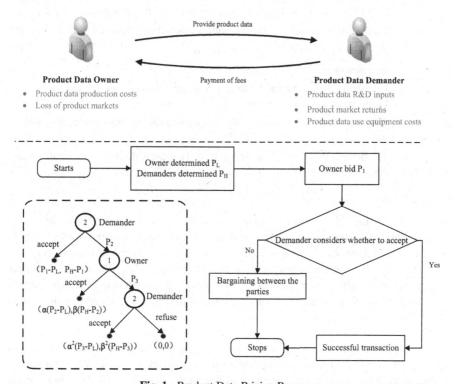

Fig. 1. Product Data Pricing Process

3.2 Bargaining Model

Symbol Description. The reference symbol settings used in this study are comprehensively outlined in Table 1.

Table 1. Parameter Symbol Setting

Symbols	Variable description
P_L	Owner's minimum reservation price for product data
P_H	Demanders' maximum reservation price for product data
Q	The sales volume over a contract period
R	Profit per unit of product
C	Total value of equipment used for product data
C_S	Owners' processing costs for product data
r_S	Owner's product market loss rate in a contract period, $r_S \in (0, 1)$
C_D	Total cost of inputs required by the demander to develop product data
r_D	The market rate of return on the demander's product in a contract period, $r_D \in (0, 1)$
t	Cost ratio of additional equipment required to use the product data
P_i	Stage i bids for product data, following a uniform distribution, $i = 1, 2, 3$
S_i	Benefits to product data owners at stage i, $i = 1, 2, 3$
D_i	Benefits for product data requesters in stage i, $i = 1, 2, 3$
p_i	Probability that the demander in stage i accepts the owner's offer, $p_i \in (0, 1)$, following a uniform distribution
α	Owner's discount factor α, $\alpha \in (0, 1)$, reflecting the owner's transaction costs or patience
β	The demander's discount factor β, $\beta \in (0, 1)$, reflects the demander's transaction costs or patience

Model Assumption. The following modeling assumptions are established in this study.

Assumption 1: The market for the product that corresponds to the product data is currently in an under-served state, making it profitable for new producers to enter.

Assumption 2: Over the course of a contract period, the sales volume of the product that corresponds to the product data is Q, generating a profit per unit of R. This results in a total profit of RQ during the contract period. Additionally, the equipment utilized for the product data has a total value of C.

Assumption 3: The owner's cost of production for the product data is denoted as C_S. Since the demander acquires the product data and manufactures the product, it will claim a portion of the product market, resulting in market losses for the owner. The rate of product market loss during a contract period is denoted as r_S, $r_S \in (0, 1)$. It is assumed that the owner's minimum reservation price for the product data is P_L. Therefore, the owner's minimum reservation price should take into account both the cost of production the product data and the market losses, which is denoted as $P_L = C_S + r_S RQ$.

Assumption 4: The maximum reservation price set by the demander for the product data is P_H, if $P_H < P_L$, there is no possibility of negotiation between the two parties.

Therefore, we assume that $P_L \leq P_H$. Simultaneously, for the demander, the comprehensive expenses associated with generating the product data, designated as C_D, must be taken into account. Additionally, the market return rate of the product obtained during the contract period, designated as r_D, $r_D \in (0, 1)$, and the extra equipment investment cost rate, designated as t, required for utilizing the product data must be considered. Consequently, the maximum reservation price for the demander is $P_H = C_D + r_D RQ - tC$.

Assumption 5: The product data market operates in a setting of incomplete information, where neither party has knowledge of the other's reservation prices. During the negotiation process, bidding turns alternate between the owner and the demander. At the ith stage of the product data bid $P_i (i = 1, 2, 3)$, P_i follows a uniform distribution. If the owner bids, $P_i \geq P_L$, if the demander bids, $P_i \leq P_H$. Consequently, when the price of the product data is $P_i \in [P_L, P_H]$, there is an increased likelihood of a successful transaction, and $[P_L, P_H]$ represents the feasible strategy space for both parties.

Assumption 6: At the ith stage, the owner and the demander receive respective payoffs of S_i and $D_i (i = 1, 2, 3)$. The probability of the demander accepting the owner's offer at the ith stage, denoted as p_i, $p_i \in (0, 1)$, follows a uniform distribution. The discount factors in the bargaining process between the owner and the demander are denoted by α and β, respectively, $\alpha, \beta \in (0, 1)$.

Assumption 7: We assume that both parties involved are rational economic agents who take the game process seriously, pursue revenue maximization, engage in a dynamic game with incomplete information and that the owner makes the initial offer in the game process. Additionally, it is assumed that the value of the product data remains unchanged throughout the buying and selling process.

Model Construction. For the demander, the sooner they acquire product data and initiate production, the more substantial profits they stand to gain from the product market. Similarly, the earlier the owner sells the product data, the greater the revenue they will acquire. Given the low degree of patience on both sides during the bargaining process, this study introduces a one-to-one bargaining game model based on a three-stage process to determine the equilibrium price of the product data.

In the initial stage, the owner offers a price of P_1, at which point their gain is $S_1 = P_1 - P_L$. The demander then evaluates this proposed price, deciding whether to accept it. If the demander accepts, their gain is $D_1 = P_H - P_1$, bringing the bargaining process to an end and establishing the price of the product data as P_1. If the demander rejects the offer, the process proceeds to the next stage.

In the second stage, the demander counters with an offer of P_2. At this point, the demander's gain is calculated as $D_2 = \beta(P_H - P_2)$. The owner then considers the demander's counteroffer and decides whether to accept it. If the owner accepts, their gain is $S_2 = \alpha(P_2 - P_L)$, which brings the bargaining process to an end with the agreed price of the product data P_2. However, if the owner rejects the offer, the negotiations proceed to the next stage.

In the third stage, the owner makes a bid P_3, and their payoff at this point is calculated as $S_3 = \alpha^2(P_3 - P_L)$. Whether the demander accepts or rejects the price, the game reaches its conclusion. If the demander accepts, their payoff is $D_3 = \beta^2(P_H - P_3)$. However, if the demander rejects the offer, the payoffs for both parties are zero.

Model Solution. According to the backward induction method, we first analyze the third stage of the game.

In the third stage, the owner bids P_3, which maximizes its own revenue while also satisfying the demander's revenue requirement of being greater than or equal to 0, yielding:

$$\max S_3 = \alpha^2(P_3 - P_L) * p_3 + (1 - p_3) * 0$$
$$\text{s.t. } D_3 = \beta^2(P_H - P_3) \geq 0 \tag{1}$$
$$P_L \leq P_3$$

During this stage, there is a likelihood that the demander will accept the price if $P_H \geq P_3$. Simultaneously, due to the second stage of the game, the owner's minimum reservation price has shifted from P_L to P_2, thereby narrowing the price range to $[P_2, P_H]$. Consequently, $p_3 = \frac{P_H - P_3}{P_H - P_2}$, the owner's third stage of the benefits of the first-order optimality conditions for solving have:

$$P_3 = \frac{P_H + P_L}{2} \tag{2}$$

Stage 2: The demander proposes a counteroffer with a price of P_2, and to persuade the owner to accept this price and finalize the transaction, they strive to optimize their own profit. However, they also ensure that the condition $S_2 \geq S_3$ is fulfilled. That is, it needs to meet:

$$\max D_2 = \beta(P_H - P_2)$$
$$\text{s.t.}\alpha(P_2 - P_L) \geq \alpha^2(P_3 - P_L) \tag{3}$$

So when $S_2 = S_3$, take the price P_2 and get:

$$P_2 = \alpha\frac{P_H - P_L}{2} + P_L \tag{4}$$

Stage 1: The owner offers a bid of P_1, and to finalize the deal as much as possible, they aim to maximize their revenue while ensuring that $D_1 \geq D_2$. Consequently, there is:

$$\max S_1 = (P_1 - P_L) * p_1 + (1 - p_1) * 0$$
$$\text{s.t.} P_H - P_1 \geq \beta(P_H - P_2) \tag{5}$$

From the constraints:

$$P_H \geq \beta(1 - \frac{\alpha}{2})(P_H - P_L) + P_1 \tag{6}$$

Let $k = \beta(1 - \frac{\alpha}{2})(P_H - P_L) + P_1$, if the demander accept the offer with probability $p_1 = \frac{P_H - k}{P_H - P_L}$, the first-order optimality condition solution for solving the problem of maximizing $\max S_1 = (P_1 - P_L) * p_1$ is:

$$P_1 = \frac{1}{2}(P_H + P_L) - \frac{1}{2}\beta(1 - \frac{\alpha}{2})(P_H - P_L) \tag{7}$$

At this point, if the demand side opts to accept, both parties stand to gain as follows:

$$S_1 = \frac{1}{2}(1 - \beta(1 - \frac{\alpha}{2}))(P_H - P_L) \tag{8}$$

$$D_1 = \frac{1}{2}(1 + \beta(1 - \frac{\alpha}{2}))(P_H - P_L) \tag{9}$$

Substitute the values of P_L and P_H into P_1, S_1 and D_1 to obtain:

$$P_1 = \frac{1}{2}(1 - \beta(1 - \frac{\alpha}{2}))(C_D + r_D RQ - tC) + \frac{1}{2}(1 + \beta(1 - \frac{\alpha}{2}))(C_S + r_S RQ) \tag{10}$$

$$S_1 = \frac{1}{2}(1 - \beta(1 - \frac{\alpha}{2}))(C_D + r_D RQ - tC - C_S - r_S RQ) \tag{11}$$

$$D_1 = \frac{1}{2}(1 + \beta(1 - \frac{\alpha}{2}))(C_D + r_D RQ - tC - C_S - r_S RQ) \tag{12}$$

Model Analysis. Proposition 1: The equilibrium price P_1 is directly proportional to the owner's discount factor α, the market rate of loss r_S, and the demander's market rate of return r_D, and inversely proportional to the demander's discount factor β, and the rate of equipment cost t.

Proof: To derive Eq. (10) for the bargained equilibrium price P_1 with respect to α, β, r_S, r_D and t, we note that $\frac{\partial P_1}{\partial \alpha} \geq 0$, $\frac{\partial P_1}{\partial \beta} \leq 0$, $\frac{\partial P_1}{\partial r_S} \geq 0$, $\frac{\partial P_1}{\partial r_D} \geq 0$ and $\frac{\partial P_1}{\partial t} \leq 0$. Proposition 1 is thereby established.

Proposition 2: The owner's equilibrium return S_1 is directly proportional to the owner's discount factor α and the demander's market rate of return r_D, and inversely proportional to the owner's market rate of loss r_S and the demander's discount factor β, the rate of cost of equipment t.

Proof: To derive Eq. (11) for the owner's equilibrium return S_1 with respect to α, β, r_S, r_D and t, we note that $\frac{\partial S_1}{\partial \alpha} \geq 0$, $\frac{\partial S_1}{\partial \beta} \leq 0$, $\frac{\partial S_1}{\partial r_S} \leq 0$, $\frac{\partial S_1}{\partial r_D} \geq 0$ and $\frac{\partial S_1}{\partial t} \leq 0$. Proposition 2 is thereby established.

Proposition 3: The equilibrium return D_1 to the demander is directly proportional to the demander's discount factor β and the demander's market rate of return r_D, and inversely proportional to the owner's discount factor α, the market rate of loss r_S, and the demander's rate of cost of equipment t.

Proof: To derive Eq. (12) for the demander's equilibrium return D_1 with respect to α, β, r_S, r_D and t, we note that $\frac{\partial D_1}{\partial \alpha} \leq 0$, $\frac{\partial D_1}{\partial \beta} \geq 0$, $\frac{\partial D_1}{\partial r_S} \leq 0$, $\frac{\partial D_1}{\partial r_D} \geq 0$ and $\frac{\partial D_1}{\partial t} \leq 0$. Proposition 3 is thereby established.

4 Conclusion

This study suggests a solution to the problem of pricing product data in manufacturing companies with incomplete information by establishing a one-to-one bargaining model. Initially, the primary considerations affecting the pricing of product data are comprehensively examined, considering both the owner's and demander's perspectives. The owner's minimum acceptable reservation price and the demander's maximum willing reservation price are then established. Subsequently, by developing a three-stage bargaining model and engaging in a dynamic game with incomplete information, we determine the revenue functions for both parties at each stage. Using the backward induction method, we derive the equilibrium price in the bargaining process, thereby determining the transaction price of the product data and the revenue earned by both parties. It is found that (1) the equilibrium price of product data is positively correlated with the owner's discount factor, the market loss rate, and the demander's market rate of return, and negatively correlated with the demander's discount factor and the rate of equipment input cost. (2) The owner's equilibrium return is positively correlated with the owner's discount factor and the demander's market rate of return, and negatively correlated with the owner's market rate of loss, the demander's discount factor, and the equipment input cost rate. (3) The demander's equilibrium return is positively related to the demander's discount factor and the market rate of return, and inversely related to the owner's discount factor, the market rate of loss, and the demander's equipment input cost rate.

This study offers three significant contributions to the existing literature. Firstly, it expands the scope of research on pricing product data for manufacturing enterprises. While prior studies have primarily concentrated on data originating from the personal, financial, and Internet sectors, they have often overlooked the product data of manufacturing enterprises. By focusing on manufacturing enterprise product data and exploring its pricing mechanisms, this paper establishes a theoretical framework that supports the efficient circulation of such data within the manufacturing industry. Secondly, existing studies tend to approach pricing from the perspective of the data owner, aiming to maximize their benefits. However, they overlook the intricate decision-making process involved when the demand side purchases the data. This paper takes a more comprehensive approach, considering the factors that influence the price of manufacturing enterprise product data from both the seller and buyer's perspectives. By dynamically determining the product data price through negotiation, we ensure the rationality and fairness of the pricing process. Lastly, through a meticulous analysis of the relationship between the influencing factors and the price, this paper delves into the dynamics of equilibrium price and equilibrium income in response to varying factors. This provides theoretical support for both parties involved in the transaction, enabling them to make informed decisions and arrive at a reasonable price. Overall, this study offers a comprehensive and nuanced understanding of pricing mechanisms for manufacturing enterprise product data, contributing significantly to the field of data pricing and management.

This study delves into the pricing challenges of product data in manufacturing enterprises, drawing from the framework of data product pricing models. It emphasizes the significance of this research for facilitating the circulation of product data. Especially for products with high R&D costs, procuring product data not only expedites entry into the market but also elevates the overall technological standards in the manufacturing industry. This advancement plays a pivotal role in bolstering the country's comprehensive strength. Nonetheless, numerous avenues for further exploration exist. For instance, in scenarios where a single owner faces multiple demanders, the study could expand the one-to-one bargaining model to a one-to-many framework. This approach would consider the optimal sales quantity and pricing of product data, aiming to maximize revenue. Such an approach broadens the scope of research on product data pricing.

Acknowledgments. This research is partly supported by the National Natural Science Foundation of China [72372060, 71972090, 72272066, and 71971101], General Project of Philosophy and Social Science Research in Universities in Jiangsu Province [2022SJYB2238], Jiangsu University of Science and Technology Youth Science and Technology Innovation Project [1042922212].

References

1. Liu, J.Z., Wang, S.Y.: Dilemmas and suggestions on market-based data allocation. Bulletin of Chinese Academy of Sciences **37**(10), 1435–1443 (2022). (in Chinese)
2. Huang, L.H., Guo, M.K., Shao, Z.Q., et al.: Thoughts on national unified data asset registration system. Bull. Chin. Acad. Sci. **37**(10), 1426–1434 (2022). (in Chinese)
3. Wu, B.Y., Huang, L.H.: The dual dimension of data pricing: from product price to asset value. Price: Theory & Practice (07), 70–75 (2023). (in Chinese)
4. Wang, J.Z., Dou, Y.F., Huang, L.H., et al.: Data product pricing: a review of research progress and comparison of pricing methods. Price: Theory & Practice (04), 22–27 (2023). (in Chinese)
5. Cai, L., Huang, Z.H., Liang, Y., et al.: Survey of Data Pricing. J. Front. Comput. Sci. Technol. **15**(09), 1595–1606 (2021). (in Chinese)
6. Jiang, D., Yuan, Y., Zhang, X.W., Wang, G.R.: Survey on data pricing and trading research. Ruan Jian Xue Bao/J. Softw. **34**(3), 1396–1424 (2023). (in Chinese)
7. Liang, F., Yu, W., An, D., et al.: A survey on big data market: Pricing, trading and protection. IEEE Access **6**, 15132–15154 (2018)
8. Pei, J.: A Survey on Data Pricing: From Economics to Data Science. IEEE Trans. Knowl. Data Eng.Knowl. Data Eng. **34**(10), 4586–4608 (2022)
9. Koutris, P., Upadhyaya, P., Balazinska, M., et al.: Query-based data pricing. J ACM **62**(5), 44 (2015)
10. Tang, Q., Shao, Z., Huang, L., et al.: Identifying influencing factors for data transactions: a case study from shanghai data exchange. J. Syst. Sci. Syst. Eng. **29**, 697–708 (2020)
11. Huang, L.H., Dou, Y.F., Guo, M.K., et al.: Features and transaction modes of data products in data markets. Big Data Res. **8**(03), 3–14 (2022). (in Chinese)
12. Short, J., Todd, S.: What's your data worth? MIT Sloan Manag. Rev. **58**(3), 17 (2017)
13. Ou, Y.R.H., Du, Q.Q.: Research Progress on the pricing mechanism of data. Econ. Perspect. **02**, 124–141 (2022). (in Chinese)
14. Jia, Y., Ge, S., Liang, H., et al.: Incorporating use history in information system remodularization. IEEE Trans. Eng. Manage. **71**, 1394–1408 (2024)
15. Jia, Y., Ge, S., Wang, N.: Analyzing enterprise information system's feature use: a data-driven perspective. Inf. Technol. People **34**(1), 375–398 (2021)
16. Yu, H.F., Zhang, M.X.: Data pricing strategy based on data quality. Comput. Ind. Eng. **112**, 1–10 (2017)
17. Lin J J, Huang Z G, Tang Y.: Data Quality, Quantity and Data Asset Pricing: Based on the Perspective of Consumer Heterogeneity. Chin. J. Manag. Sci, 1–12 (2023). (in Chinese)
18. Luong, N.C., Hoang, D.T., Wang, P., et al.: Data collection and wireless communication in Internet of Things (IoT) using economic analysis and pricing models: a survey. IEEE Commun. Surv. Tutorials **18**(4), 2546–2590 (2016)
19. Liu, K., Qiu, X., Chen, W., et al.: Optimal pricing mechanism for data market in blockchain-enhanced internet of things. IEEE Internet Things J. **6**(6), 9748–9761 (2019)

The Influence of the Similarity of Digital Transformation Orientation Between Enterprises and Large Customers on Customer Dependence

Jiang Wu[✉] and Yunxu Wang

Wuhan University, Wuhan 430072, China
`liuyun@xmut.edu.cn`

Abstract. In recent years, the market has been depressed and large customers have frequently experienced black swan events, posing significant challenges for enterprises' survival and development. Therefore, it is crucial to enhance the stability of large customers. Leveraging text analysis technology, this study empirically examines the impact of digital transformation orientation similarity on customer dependence and its underlying mechanism using data from Shanghai-Shenzhen A-share listed enterprises spanning 2016 to 2021. The findings reveal that: (1) Adopting a digital transformation orientation similar to key customers strengthens customer dependence and enhances customer stability. (2) Trust levels are enhanced, product enterprise standards are standardized and unified, and bargaining power is improved as intermediate mechanisms through which digital-transformation-oriented similarity positively influences customer dependence. (3) Heterogeneity tests considering external environmental factors and internal characteristics of enterprises show that in developed regions with low profitability or non-state-owned status, the positive impact of digital-transformation-oriented similarity on customer dependence becomes more prominent. These conclusions remain robust even after conducting endogenous tests. This paper not only provides new insights into exploring the similarity between enterprises' digital transformation orientations and those of their major customers but also offers empirical evidence supporting the notion that an effective digital transformation strategy can facilitate rapid enterprise development.

Keywords: The Similarity of Digital Transformation Orientation · Customer Dependence · Trust Level · Product Enterprise Standard · Bargaining Power

1 Introduction

Currently, in this era of unprecedented "great changes," China's economic environment is characterized by volatility, uncertainty, ambiguity, and complexity. The frequent disruptions from major customers pose a severe threat to enterprise supply chain security and hinder high-quality enterprise development [1]. Therefore, it is crucial to enhance stability among key customers and strengthen their reliance on enterprises.

Y. P. Tu and M. Chi (Eds.): WHICEB 2024, LNBIP 516, pp. 350–360, 2024.
https://doi.org/10.1007/978-3-031-60260-3_29

The present study utilizes Python text analysis technology to capture and construct the key word frequency vector of enterprise digital transformation in A-share listed enterprises from 2016 to 2021 in Shanghai and Shenzhen stock markets. Subsequently, the cosine similarity method measures the similarity of key word frequency vectors between enterprises and large customers, enabling measurement of digital transformation orientation similarity. Empirical testing explores the relationship between this similarity and customer dependence among enterprises and key customers. Furthermore, this paper delves into three paths - trust level, product enterprise standard, and bargaining power - through which positive impacts are observed regarding the influence of similarities in digital transformation orientation on customer dependence. The findings can be summarized as follows: (1) There is a positive correlation between similarities in digital transformation orientation and customer dependence; (2) Higher levels of digitally-transformed-oriented similarity enhance customer dependence by improving trust levels, product enterprise standards, and bargaining power; (3) Low profitability among large customers along with backward trends in local digital technology environments may amplify customer dependence within an enterprise context.

The marginal contribution of this paper is mainly in the following aspects. (1) Through the introduction of customer dependence, it provides a new Angle for exploring the consequences of the similarity of digital transformation orientation between enterprises and large customers. Previous studies on the similarity of digital transformation orientation between enterprises and large customers mainly focus on the antecedents, but rarely on the consequences. (2) This paper finds that the impact of digital-transformation-oriented similarity on customer dependence is mainly realized through three paths: trust level, product enterprise standards, and bargaining power, providing more multidimensional empirical evidence for revealing the internal mechanism of digitalization affecting the real economy. (3) It has enriched and expanded enterprises' understanding of digital transformation strategy. Digital transformation is a complex system project involving the whole business and cross-functions, and the transformation is difficult, high cost and long cycle. The limitation is that it is impossible to evaluate whether the path mechanism of digital transformation orientation similarity affecting customer dependence is the optimal three paths, and some potential variables in the regression model may not be fully considered.

2 Literature Review and Theoretical Analysis

2.1 Literature Review

The reference to customer dependence in this article pertains to the reliance of large customers on enterprises, and should be distinguished from "large customer dependence", which refers to the dependency of enterprises on large customers.

Since the concept of enterprise digital transformation emerged, extensive research has been conducted on various dimensions, primarily focusing on influencing factors [2], processes [3], outcomes [4], evaluation systems [5], and theoretical frameworks [6]. Scholars have started to consider whether enterprise digital transformation can mitigate the negative effects of relying heavily on major clients and how to dismantle this mechanism. Qiu Yu's empirical study[1] found that from the perspective of production action mechanisms, sales and pricing links, enterprise digital transformation mainly reduces dependence on major customers through three avenues: enabling product specialization, strengthening channel construction capabilities, and enhancing potential price reduction space. This fresh perspective encourages further investigation into dependency on big customers. In recent years, research focus has shifted towards exploring similarities in digital transformation orientation between enterprises and major customers with a focus on antecedents. Wang Chengyuan's empirical analysis [7] examined the influence of geographical distance between major customers on similarities in digital transformation orientation between enterprises and these key clients. The findings indicate that geographical distance significantly promotes alignment in digital transformation orientation between enterprises and their major customers. The analysis also revealed that increased geographical distance increases risks of supply chain relationship disruption; Thus, prompting enterprises to make more relationship commitments by actively aligning their digital transformation orientations with those of their significant clientele. Wang Zhenjie [8] took A-share listed companies from 2009 to 2020 as samples to empirically study the impact of digital transformation on key customer dependence and its mechanism. The study found that digital transformation can reduce the dependence of enterprises on large customers.

2.2 Theoretical Analysis and Hypothesis Deduction

The mechanism by which the similarity of digital transformation orientation between enterprises and key customers affects customer dependence.

(1) Trust level: Adopting a digital transformation strategy similar to that of major customers can enhance trust and promote cooperation between enterprises. According to Larson's research [9] on trust in self-organizing teams, organizational communication fosters increased trust among members. Elena [10] also suggests that trust gradually develops during cooperation within an organization. Additionally, Johnson-George and Swap [11] propose that trust reflects stakeholders' willingness to take risks in achieving desired goals. The frequency of transactions between an enterprise and its major customers characterizes their level of cooperation and accumulated trust. Therefore, this paper proposes using the transaction ratio as a measure for assessing the level of trust.

Hypothesis 1: The higher the similarity of digital transformation orientation between enterprises and big customers, the higher the level of trust and the stronger the customer dependence.

(2) Product enterprise standard: Enterprise standards are a set of technical, management, and work requirements formulated by an organization to ensure coordination and uniformity within the enterprise. These standards serve as the foundation for organizing production and business activities. Aligning digital transformation strategies with those of large customers leads to consistent product standards. Simultaneously, enterprises enhance their capabilities in digital technology application, operational efficiency, service quality, and product innovation efficiency. This enables them to produce products that better meet the needs of large customers, strengthening customer dependence on enterprises and reducing the likelihood of being

replaced. Therefore, this study proposes using word frequency vector similarity analysis between enterprise and big customer product standards as a measure of their unity.

Hypothesis 2: The higher the similarity of digital transformation orientation between enterprises and big customers, the more unified the product enterprise standard and the stronger the customer dependence.

(3) Bargaining power: Bargaining power is defined as an enterprise's ability to control the funds of key customers within the same industrial chain, where unequal transactions occur between upstream suppliers and downstream customers. This inequality is typically manifested through capital occupation or its impact on pricing power. Challenges faced by enterprises during transactions, such as delayed payments or incomplete transactions, further highlight differences in bargaining power. Liquid assets refer to assets that can be realized or utilized within a business cycle of one year or more, including monetary funds, short-term investments, notes receivable, accounts receivable, and inventories. Current liabilities encompass debts that an enterprise must repay within one year or during a business cycle exceeding one year; these include short-term borrowings, accounts payable, notes payable, wages payable, benefits payable taxes payable dividends payable interest payable accounts received in advance expenses withheld other payables other taxes payable etc. Therefore, this paper will use the ratio of liquid assets to liquid liabilities as a measure reflecting enterprises' bargaining power.

Hypothesis 3: The higher the similarity of digital transformation orientation between enterprises and key customers, the stronger the bargaining power of enterprises and the stronger the customer dependence.

3 Research Design

3.1 Sample Selection and Data Source

The sample used in this paper is derived from the supply chain portfolio disclosed in the annual reports of Shanghai and Shenzhen A-share listed companies in China. The process for constructing and screening the sample is as follows: (1) Gather information on the top five customers reported in Chinese listed companies' annual reports between 2016 and 2021 from the CSMAR database; (2) Identify listed customers and match them with listed companies to establish an initial set of supply chain samples including upstream and downstream entities; (3) Exclude supply chain samples involving finance and insurance enterprises, ST enterprises, data anomalies, or missing data. In total, we obtain 3715 samples consisting of listed enterprises. The management analysis and discussion textual content for this study is sourced from the CNRDS database, while all other data originates from the CSMAR database.

3.2 Definition of Variables

1. The similarity of digital transformation orientation.

The present study employs the keyword frequency similarity method to assess the alignment between enterprises and major clients in terms of digital transformation orientation. Initially, the management discussion and analysis text is tokenized using a Python program, followed by extraction of the key word frequency vectors for enterprise and customer digital transformation based on Wu Fei's digital transformation dictionary [12]. Subsequently, cosine similarity is utilized to gauge the resemblance of these key word frequency vectors pertaining to digital transformation across enterprises and large customers.

The measurement formula is as follows:

$$DC_{ijt} = \frac{S_{it} \times C_{jt}}{\|S_{it}\| \|C_{jt}\|} \tag{1}$$

The DC_{ijt} on behalf of the enterprise i and customer j in first t year digital key word frequency vector cosine similarity transformation, S_{it}, C_{jt} on behalf of the enterprise i and customer j respectively in the first t year the digital transformation of key word frequency vector, $\|Sit\|$ and $\|Cjt\|$ represent the modulus length of the key word frequency vector for the enterprise's and customer's digital transformation respectively. DC_{ijt} is the value range of [0,1]. The greater the value, the higher the similarity between the key word frequency vector of the enterprise and the customer's digital transformation, which also means the higher the similarity between the enterprise and the customer's digital transformation orientation. In addition, when both enterprise and customer digital transformation word frequency vectors are empty, their cosine similarity is set to 0.

2. Control variables.

According to the existing literature [13–15], this paper controls a set of variables related to enterprise characteristics, customer characteristics and the characteristics of the relationship between the two parties, all of which will have an important impact on the enterprise's digital transformation orientation. The definitions of all variables are shown in Table 1.

3. Model setting.

In this paper, the following regression model is used to test the impact of the similarity of digital transformation orientation between enterprises and key customers on customer dependence:

$$CD_{ijt} = \alpha_0 + \alpha_1 DS_{ijt} + \alpha_2 Control_{ijt} + Year + IND + PRO + \varepsilon_{ijt} \tag{2}$$

where CD_{ijt} stands for customer dependence, DS_{ijt} stands for the similarity of digital transformation orientation, $Control_{ijt}$ contains the control variable defined above, and ε_{ijt} is the random disturbance term. Year, IND and PRO represent fixed effects by year, industry and province respectively.

Table 1. Description of main variables

Types of variables	Variable symbol	Variable name	Variable explanation
Dependent Variables	CD	Customer Dependency	A business's percentage of total sales among upstream suppliers to large customers
Independent variable and intermediate variable	DS	Enterprise and large customer the similarity of digital transformation orientation	Cosine similarity of key word frequency vector of enterprise and customer digital transformation
	TL	Trust level	Number of trades to the total number of trades
	PES	Product Corporate Standards	Product enterprise standard word frequency vector similarity
	BP	Bargaining power	Ratio of current assets to current liabilities
Control variables	Lev	Financial Leverage	Asset-liability ratio
	Cos	Digital transformation keyword similarity	Cosine similarity of the frequency vector of key words in digital transformation between the current year and the previous year
	Asset	Enterprise size	The natural logarithm of the total assets of the business
	ROA	Return on assets	The ratio of a firm's net profit to its total assets
	Top1	Ownership concentration	The shareholding ratio of the largest shareholder
	SOE	Nature of business property rights	1 for state-owned enterprises, 0 for others
	Year	Year dummy variable	Annual dummy variable
	IND	Industry dummy variables	Industry dummy variables
	PRO	Province dummy variables	Province dummy variable

4 Empirical Results and Analysis

4.1 Descriptive Statistics

For the descriptive statistics presented in Table 2, the mean value of customer dependence (CD) is 0.309, with a standard deviation of 0.269 and a maximum value of 0.913. This indicates significant variation in customer dependence among different enterprises, where some rely heavily on large customers for their sales revenue. The mean value, standard deviation, and maximum value of the similarity of digital transformation orientation (DS) between firms and big customers are 0.083, 0.174, and 1.000 respectively, suggesting that there is generally low similarity in digital transformation orientation within the sample. The mean trust level (TL) is found to be 0.247 with minimum and maximum values of 0.134 and 0.508 respectively, indicating an overall low level of trust. Regarding Product Enterprise Standard (PES), it has a mean value of 0.384 along with a standard deviation of 0.152 and a maximum value of 0.902; Thus, highlighting substantial variations in product standards across different enterprises with only few having unified standards. Furthermore, the average bargaining power (BP) was determined to be at around 0.452 while reaching its peak at approximately 2.882, signifying that most firms possess weak bargaining power whereas some exhibit strong negotiation capabilities.

Table 2. Descriptive statistics of main variables

Variables	Sample size	Mean	Standard deviation	Minimum	Maximum
CD	3715	0.309	0.269	0.008	0.913
DS	3715	0.083	0.174	0.000	1.000
TL	3715	0.247	0.215	0.134	0.508
PES	3715	0.384	0.152	0.116	0.902
BP	3715	0.452	0.613	0.417	2.882
Lev	3715	0.423	0.301	0.008	1.310
Cos	3715	0.238	0.279	0.000	1.000
Asset	3715	22.256	1.759	16.412	31.191
ROA	3715	0.167	1.424	17.329	56.309
Top1	3715	0.233	0.151	0.004	0.593
SOE	3715	0.320	0.393	0.000	1.000

4.2 Robustness Test

1.This paper uses the measure of replacing key variables to mitigate potential endogeneity problems, specifically as follows:

First, re-evaluate the similarity of digital transformation orientation between enterprises and key customers using different measurement methods for robustness testing. Considering the lag in information transmission, enterprises are likely to align with their customers' previous digital transformation orientation. Therefore, we use the cosine similarity (DC_{ijt-1}) between the enterprise's digital transformation keyword frequency vector at time t and its customer's digital transformation keyword frequency vector at time t-1 as an alternative measurement index. Additionally, we recalculate the similarity using Tanimoto coefficient (Tanimoto_DC) to express it as a deformation of cosine similarity known as Valley coefficient [11], which represents the intersection ratio of two words frequency vector sets on their union. The dependent variables in columns (2) and (3) in Table 3 represent the degree of digital-transformation orientation similarity measured by Gubin coefficient. Among them, Tanimoto_DS is calculated based on the frequency vectors of digital transformation-oriented keywords for both enterprise and customer at time t, while Tanimoto_DS_{ijt-1} is calculated based on enterprise's frequency vector at time t and customer's frequency vector at time t-1. Regression models (1)–(3) respectively utilize these three indicators as main explanatory variables while keeping other variables constant for multiple regression analysis performed on model (2). The regression results show that the conclusions of this paper are still valid after redefining the digital-transformation orientation similarity between enterprises and big customers in various ways.

Second, re-measure customer dependency variables. By referring to Li Shu [17], CusdependH index, which shows the proportion of sales to the top 5 customers of each enterprise, measures the index of corporate big customer dependence. Regression 5 of Table 3 includes CusdependH as the explained variable, with the remaining variables unchanged and re-fitting. Regression results show that the conclusions remain consistent after changing the measurement of the business customer dependency indicator.

Table 3. Changes the measurement method of key variables

Variables	Remeasure explanatory variables			Reweigh the explained variable
	(1)	(2)	(3)	(4)
	CD	CD	CD	CusdependH
DS_{ijt-1}	0.283*** (2.32)			
Tanimoto-DS_{ijt}		0.347*** (3.67)		
Tanimoto-DS_{ijt-1}			0.914*** (4.85)	
DS				0.147*** (4.77)
Constant term	61.288*** (25.72)	63.172*** (23.69)	60.679*** (24.84)	7.698*** (5.12)
Adj.R^2	0.173	0.169	0.182	0.114

Note: All regressions in the table include control variables as well as year, industry and province fixed effects. The sample size was 3,715 for all

5 Analysis of Mechanism of Action

Based on the theoretical analysis above, enhancing the similarity of digital transformation orientation between enterprises and key customers can increase customer dependence by improving trust levels, unifying product standards, and strengthening bargaining power. To test this hypothesis, we construct the following model to examine its action mechanism.

$$Path_{k,t} = a_0 + a_1 \times DS_{k,t} + a_2 \times Control_{k,t} + YEAR + IND + PRO + \varepsilon_{k,t} \quad (3)$$

$$CS_{k,t} = a_0 + a_1 \times DS_{k,t} + a \times Path_{k,t} + a_2 \times Control_{k,t} + YEAR + IND + PRO + \varepsilon_{k,t} \quad (4)$$

where Path represents the enabling mechanism of digital transformation-oriented similarity, encompassing three indicators: trust level (TL), product enterprise standard (PES), and bargaining power (BP). The remaining variables were consistent with the baseline regression. The results of the mechanism of action test are presented in Table 4.

Table 4. Tests the effect of the similarity of digital transformation orientation on customer dependence

Variables	Trust level Enablement		Product enterprise standard enablement		Bargaining power enablement	
	(1)	(2)	(3)	(4)	(5)	(6)
	TL	CS	PES	CS	BP	CS
DS	0.147***	0.139***	0.414***	1.382***	0.034***	1.377***
	(3.83)	(1.42)	(4.27)	(8.78)	(2.21)	(9.12)
TL		1.276***				
		(12.27)				
PES				0.145***		
				(3.19)		
BP						3.483***
						(4.62)
Constant term	40.329***	30.341***	20.032***	45.639***	21.114***	33.098***
	(21.77)	(23.81)	(4.53)	(26.12)	(29.91)	(18.25)
Adj.R2	0.035	0.312	0.081	0.302	0.236	0.109

Note: same as Table 3.
Enabling mechanism: Trust level.

The results of the trust level path test are presented in Table 4, illustrating the regression analysis (1)–(2). In the intermediary factor test of regression (1), a significantly positive regression coefficient at the 1% level is observed for trust level (TL) on digital transformation-oriented similarity (DS), indicating a positive influence. Subsequently, incorporating TL into regression (2) reveals a significantly positive regression coefficient at the 1% level, suggesting that trust level serves as an effective mediator variable for assessing digital transformation orientation similarity between enterprises and large customers. Thus, Hypothesis 1 is confirmed.

Enabling mechanism: Product enterprise standard.

The test results in Table 4 show regression (3) and (4) under product enterprise standards. Regression (3) indicates a significantly positive coefficient of PES to DS at the 1% level, suggesting that digital-transformation orientation similarity positively influences product enterprise standards. Regression (4), incorporating the intermediary factor PES, also demonstrates a significantly positive coefficient of PES at the 1% level. These regression findings support hypothesis 2 by confirming the mediating effect of digital-transformation orientation similarity between enterprises and big customers on customer dependence.

The enabling mechanism: bargaining power.

The results of the bargaining power path are presented in Table 4, specifically regression (5) and (6). In the intermediate factor test of regression (5), it is evident that higher levels of similarity in digital transformation orientation positively influence enterprise bargaining power, as indicated by the significantly positive coefficient for bargaining power (BP) towards digital transformation orientation similarity (DS) at a 5% significance level. Regression (6) includes the intermediary factor BP, and the results demonstrate a highly significant positive coefficient at a 1% significance level. To summarize, there exists an intermediary effect within the positive impact pathway between digital-transformation orientation similarity among enterprises and their big customers on bargaining power, aligning with theoretical expectations outlined in hypothesis 3.

6 Implications

The research conclusions of this paper have the following implications:

(1) Given the rapid advancement in digital technology, enterprises should fully grasp the significant value of digital transformation, devise appropriate strategies, align with national policies, and adhere to contemporary trends. By expediting this process, they can provide a strong foundation for propelling China's economy towards rapid development.

(2) When cultivating customer loyalty, enterprises should carefully consider the influence pathway and incorporate principles such as enhancing trust levels, unifying and standardizing product enterprise standards, and increasing bargaining power into all aspects of production and operation.

(3) Before senior management decides to implement digital technology for driving enterprise development, it is crucial to gather comprehensive digital transformation strategies from key customers and raise awareness about similar orientations. The fundamental objective of digital transformation is to empower enterprises in effectively meeting customer needs and creating value together. Only when enterprises thoroughly understand big customers' orientations can they achieve successful collaboration through their own transformations.

References

1. Qiu, Y., Pan, P.: Enterprise digital transformation and key customer dependence governance. Finance Trade Econ. (2023). (in Chinese)
2. Zhang, H., Huang, Q.: Can overseas executives drive digital transformation?. Res. Sci. Sci. (2023). (in Chinese)
3. Wu, L., Li, S., Wang, H., et al.: Research on advanced mechanism of digital transformation of manufacturing enterprises based on "Corporate governance - Organizational capability" configuration model. Nankai Manag. Rev. (2023). (in Chinese)
4. Zhang, S., Zhang, P., Gu, S.: Enterprise digital transformation and supply chain efficiency. Statist. Decision **39**(18), 169–173 (2023). (in Chinese)
5. Chen, C., Xu, J.: Evaluation system and application of digital transformation capability of manufacturing enterprises. Sci. Technol. Manag. Res. **40**(11), 46–51 (2020). (in Chinese)
6. Wu, J., Chen, T., Gong, Y., et al.: Theoretical framework and research prospects of enterprise digital transformation. J. Manag. 201, 18(12), 1871–1880. (in Chinese)
7. Wang, C., Wang, Q., Luo, B., et al.: The impact of geographical distance of key customers on enterprise digital transformation orientation from the perspective of relationship. China Manag. Sci. (2023) (in Chinese)
8. Wang, Z., Lu, Z.: Whether digital transformation can help enterprises get rid of large customer dependence - an integrated perspective of relationship ecology. Modern Finance Econ. (2023). (in Chinese)
9. Larson, C.E. , LaFasto, F.M.J.:Teamwork: What Must Go Right/What Can Go Wrong. Sage Publications (1989)
10. Elena, R.: Trust breaks down in electronic contexts but can be repaired by some initial face-to-face contact. In: Proceedings of the SIGCHI Conference on Human Factors in computing Systems. Los Angeles, California, United States: ACM Press/Addison-Wesley Publishing Co. (1998)
11. Johnson-George, C., Swap, W.C.: Measurement of specific interpersonal trust: construction and validation of a scale to assess trust in a specific other. J. Pers. Soc. Psychol. **43**(6), 1306–1317 (1982)
12. Wu, F., Hu, H., Lin, H., et al.: Corporate digital transformation and Capital market performance: Empirical evidence from stock liquidity. Management World, 201, 37(07), 130–144. (in Chinese)
13. Chu, Y., Wang, L.: Capital structure along the supply chain: how does customer leverage affect supplier leverage decisions? Q. J. Financ.Financ. **7**(4), 1750014 (2017)
14. Wan, Q., Cheng, X., Yang, M., et al.: Is geographical proximity of key customers enough to inhibit company violations?. China Soft Sci. (08), 100–119 (2019). (in Chinese)
15. Dasgupta, S., Zhang, K., Zhu, C.: Do social connections mitigate hold-up and facilitate cooperation? Evidence from supply chain relationships. J. Financial Quant. Analy. **56**(5), 1679–1712 (2021)
16. Han, J., Pei, J., Tong, H.: Data mining: Concepts and techniques. Morgan kaufmann, Cambridge (2022)
17. Li, S., Li, D., Tian, M., Du, Y.: Can technological innovation reduce the dependence of enterprises on big customers?. Nankai Manag. Rev. (2021). (in Chinese)

An Empirical Study on Influencing Learners' Value Co-creation Intention in Educational Virtual Communities

Xuandi Gong[✉]

Communication University of China, No.1, Dingfuzhuang East Street, Chaoyang District, Beijing, China
gxuandi0720@126.com

Abstract. Compared with the traditional education environment, the new generation of information technology-enabled Educational Virtual Community (EVC) breaks the boundaries between learners and knowledge, transforming them from passive recipients of information to the main participants in the acquisition of knowledge. EVC not only empowers learners with the initiative to acquire, experience and share knowledge, but also provides learners with rich perceived value during the process, building an important carrier for learners to co-create value. Based on the theoretical framework of S-O-R (Stimulate-Organize-Response), this paper considers the interactions between learners and organizational characteristics, and innovatively constructs a technology acceptance model integrating TAM and VAM to explain learners' value co-creation intention in EVC. 357 valid samples were collected through an online questionnaire platform, which were analyzed and tested by structured equation modeling to clarify the influencing factors of user participation in value co-creation in EVC. The results of the study reveal the influence mechanism of EVC characteristics on learners' intention to participate in value co-creation on the theoretical level, enriching the study of the driving factors of learners' participation in EVC value co-creation; and provide corresponding references and suggestions for promoting and incentivizing learners to participate in value co-creation activities in EVC on the practical level, which provides managerial insights into high-quality development of EVC.

Keywords: Educational virtual community · Intelligence education · Learner perception · Empirical research

1 Introduction

With the application and rise of artificial intelligence (AI), big data, and other advanced information technologies in the smart era, newly online atmosphere for human learning have emerged, namely educational virtual community (EVC). The emergence of EVC has significantly disrupted the traditional education industry. This disruption is evident in various forms, including educational service products that leverage digital content and technology, such as MOOCs, mobile libraries, and intelligent subject service platforms.

© The Author(s), under exclusive license to Springer Nature Switzerland AG 2024
Y. P. Tu and M. Chi (Eds.): WHICEB 2024, LNBIP 516, pp. 361–373, 2024.
https://doi.org/10.1007/978-3-031-60260-3_30

Aligned with the principles of openness and freedom, the EVC allows learners to engage with the mobile information environment whenever and wherever they choose. Educational resources become accessible as learners interact and collaborate with community platforms and other participants. Simultaneously, EVC enhances the intelligence of knowledge services by employing smart technology to comprehend learners' behavioral patterns within the community. This enables the provision of personalized learning services based on educational big data.

Studies have highlighted the importance of the emergence of the EVC, such as achieving the objective of empowering learners in education, reflecting the human-centered approach of the smart era, and so on [1]. In the field of EVCs, learners exhibit diverse knowledge needs. They can select required services and engage in cross-disciplinary interactions, accessing, sharing, discussing knowledge, analyzing and solving problems. Consequently, EVC transforms the traditional value co-creation approach by stimulating value co-creation through the collision of various knowledge sets, driven by the increasing diversity of learner interactions. The development of EVC hinges on knowledge accessibility. Collaborative value creation among learners is pivotal for sustainable development in the EVC. Therefore, the establishment and growth of the EVC rely not only on technology but also on learning activities and social interactions within the online space. Therefore, it is necessary to further study the subdivision of the characteristics of the EVC, studying the interplay among organizational characteristics and learners' value co-creation attitudes.

This study explores the correlation between EVC characteristics and learners' intention for value co-creation. The main goal is to identify strategies that enhance learners' participation in value co-creation within the EVC, thereby promoting its advancement.

2 Theoretical Foundation

2.1 Virtual Education Community

The term "virtual community" was initially coined by Howard Rheingold in his book *The Virtual Community*, defining it as "a social community of people of a certain size that has emerged from the Internet and engages in open discussion with an abundance of emotion in cyberspace". The "educational virtual community" extends this concept, existing within an inter-temporal, open, and free network virtual environment. It forms a community of ecological social relations characterized by a shared culture and mentality. Interaction, cooperation, and resource sharing among community members influence and promote each other.

Various EVCs have surfaced over time, falling into three distinct categories: platforms for daily information sharing, platforms for course teaching and management, and platforms for academic exchange. Presently, the rapid evolution of mobile internet technology has introduced information technology, including AI and big data, into the educational landscape. This integration provides notable benefits such as emotional communication, a sense of presence, interactivity, enriched teaching resources, and personalized learning experiences.

These advantages contribute to creating a closely-knit community among its members, and promoting mutual support and interdependence through diverse community activities. This dynamic enhances learners' motivation and sense of responsibility for learning while reducing the feeling of isolation in the learning process. Additionally, it deepens learners' comprehension of their studies by collectively solving problems encountered during learning and exchanging their learning experiences.

2.2 Value Co-creation

Bateson (1985) introduced the idea of value co-creation from a product-centric viewpoint, asserting that users contribute value by engaging in the creation and production of a product, constituting the essence of value creation. In alignment with the Service-Dominant Logic (S-D), Lusch and Nambisan (2004) underscored the significance of users, exchanges, interactions, and relationships in the context of value co-creation. In the EVC, the manifestation of value co-creation behavior results from effective interactions among learners, knowledge contributors, and platforms. Learner value co-creation involves knowledge sharing, interpersonal interaction, and on-demand feedback to boost participation in community activities. Moreover, the synergy between learners and the platform in value co-creation includes providing technical support, developing functionalities, advocating for learners, and engaging in behaviors that foster sustained usage of the community.

3 Research Model and Hypothesis

3.1 Theory and Research Framework

The S-O-R (Stimulus-Organism-Response) theoretical model comprises stimulus, organism, and response. Stimulus refers to the factor evoking a response from the receiver, impacting it. Organism pertains to an individual's psychological cognition and emotional state, involving the acquisition, processing, and retention of information post-stimulus, subsequently influencing behavior. Response involves psychological processes wherein an individual adopts an inherent or external behavioral reaction to a received stimulus. The inherent response typically reflects attitude, while the external response involves approach or avoidance behavior [9]. Drawing on existing literature, it is evident that the S-O-R model provides a concise and structured framework for substantiating the impact of environmental characteristics within the EVC. Additionally, it addresses features of published information as external stimuli affecting learners' perceived value. Consequently, this perception influences their intention to actively engage in value co-creation.

Drawing from the ongoing evolution of the Theory of Planned Behavior (TPB) and the Theory of Rational Behavior (TRB), the Technology Acceptance Model (TAM) emerged to scrutinize learners' behaviors regarding the acceptance, use, or rejection of new technologies. However, scholars have highlighted that learners' attitudes and behaviors concerning information system use are influenced by various external variables, including intrinsic motivation, warranting comprehensive consideration. To address this, Kim et al. (2007) introduced the Value Acceptance Model (VAM), building on TAM and perceived value theory. In the VAM model, perceived value comprises two dimensions:

perceived benefit and perceived cost. Perceived benefit encompasses the learner's perception of future benefits, including usefulness and hedonic aspects, while perceived cost includes the learner's perception of future costs, such as the time and effort consumed to become familiar with and master new technologies. According to the underlying logic of the VAM model, learners carefully weigh the costs and benefits of using the service, making a comprehensive evaluation of the obtained value, ultimately influencing their behavior. In today's diverse range of options, learners' behavior in online communities is shaped by factors beyond just the ease of use and usefulness of technology. Considerations of the cost and benefit of technology play a crucial role. Therefore, the VAM model is more suitable for studying learner behavior in online network platforms. Furthermore, the VAM model can be expanded to investigate the willingness of learners to engage in value co-creation behaviors within the EVC environment.

This study integrated perceived usefulness and perceived ease of use from the TAM model into its own framework, recognizing their role in fostering positive behavioral willingness through learner acceptance. However, focusing solely on these factors overlooks external variables, like online community characteristics, which alone are insufficient to explain learners' behavioral intention. To address this gap, additional variables are incorporated into the VAM model, aligning with the S-O-R model's theoretical framework. This results in the development of a research model illustrating the factors influencing learners' intention to participate in value co-creation within the EVC (see Fig. 1) (Table 1).

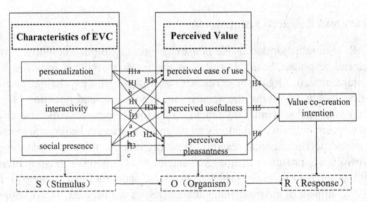

Fig. 1. Model of the factors influencing learners' value co-creation intention in the EVC

3.2 Research Hypothesis

Impacts of EVC's Characteristics on Perceived Value

The rapid development of new-generation information technology and the ubiquitous use of smart devices have facilitated the integration of technology into education. This integration enables personalized teaching, valuing individual worth and fostering holistic human development. Previous research indicates that the information quality of personalized customization systems positively influences perceived ease of use and significantly

Table 1. Definitions of variables.

Variable	Definition	Reference Percentage
personalization	the ability of EVC in providing knowledge and services meeting learners' specific needs	Kaptein & Parvinen, 2015 [2]
interactivity	the ability to engage in real-time two-way information exchange through EVC	Janlert & Stolterman, 2017 [3]
social presence	learners' warm, intimate, and social feeling by receiving and sharing knowledge in the EVC	Sun et al., 2019 [4]
perceived ease of use	learners' assessment of whether there has difficulty in learning and adopting the EVC	Rahmi et al., 2018 [5]
perceived usefulness	learners' adjustment whether EVC will improve the overall quality of their study	Alsabawy et al., 2016 [6]
perceived pleasantness	learners' subjective happiness and pleasure during the process of the EVC	Horng & Hsu, 2020 [7]
value co-creation intention	likelihood or intention of individuals collaboratively creating value through the services exchange and resources integration	Kamali et al., 2021 [8]

impacts perceived usefulness [9]. Simultaneously, personalized content enhances user enjoyment and positively influences perceived pleasure [10]. Therefore, the following hypotheses are proposed:

H1a: Personalization of EVC positively influences perceived ease of use.
H1b: Personalization of EVC positively influences perceived usefulness.
H1c: Personalization of EVC positively influences perceived pleasantness.

Interactivity includes both direct user-platform interaction and user-user interaction [11]. Studies have shown that interactivity not only improves perceived usability but also positively affects user satisfaction, playing a crucial role in determining their engagement level [12]. Learners can readily acquire needed knowledge through diverse forms of interaction and share information with others, thereby enhancing perceived usefulness. Therefore, the following hypotheses are proposed:

H2a: The interactivity of EVC positively influences perceived ease of use.
H2b: The interactivity of EVC positively influences perceived usefulness.
H2c: The interactivity of EVC positively influences perceived pleasantness.

Social presence can enhance emotional connections among users, bringing people and information closer together and consequently influencing the level of online user engagement. In online collaborative environments, social presence has demonstrated a significant improvement in perceived usefulness and pleasantness [13]. Heightened levels of social presence can enhance perceptions of others in communication, fostering an authentic sense in face-to-face interactions. This contributes to a more enjoyable experience for learners when using the EVC, positively impacting their perception and bolstering trust in the community. Therefore, the following hypotheses are proposed:

H3a: The social presence of EVC positively influences perceived ease of use.
H3b: The social presence of EVC positively influences perceived usefulness.
H3c: The social presence of EVC positively influences perceived pleasantness.

Influence of Perceived Value on Value Co-creation Intention
The ease with which learners access online information can significantly diminish online information asymmetry. In the context of electronic value co-creation, learners produce subjective evaluations and feedback post-use, considering factors like service provision, problem-solving capabilities, knowledge acquisition timeliness, and personalized needs fulfillment. The greater convenience learners experience in accessing information and using the process, the more inclined they are to engage in value co-creation behavior. Therefore, the following hypotheses are proposed:

H4: Learner's perceived ease of use positively impact their value co-creation intention.

According to the Technology Acceptance Model (TAM), perceived usefulness positively affects adoption intention, a relationship affirmed by numerous researchers. Some scholars have extended the concept of perceived usefulness to the examination of value co-creation, demonstrating its positive influence on learners' intention to share. Additionally, perceived benefits significantly and positively impact learners' intention to participate in continuous value creation [14]. When learners believe that value co-creation brings them greater benefits, their willingness to participate in value co-creation strengthens. Therefore, the following hypotheses are proposed:

H5: Learner's perceived usefulness positively impact their value co-creation intention.

Environmental stimuli are perceived by learners not only cognitively but also emotionally. Meaningful activities can yield significant positive psychological effects, generating feelings of pleasure. Perceived pleasantness serves as an emotional gauge for a learner's perception during interactions with a platform, particularly in online virtual environments [10]. The perceived pleasantness significantly influences learners' attitudes toward use. The greater the pleasure experienced by learners when engaging in value co-creation within the EVC, the more willing they are to participate in value co-creation. Therefore, the following hypotheses are proposed:

H6: Learner's perceived pleasantness positively impact their value co-creation intention.

The Mediating Impact of Perceived Value

The rapid development of EVC transforms learners from passive recipients of information into active consumers and contributors of information. The personalization capability of EVC influences how well learners' diverse needs are addressed. Mastery of new technologies in EVC enables learners to interact in various ways, facilitating knowledge exchange and problem-solving. Social presence enhances learners' immersion in the application scenario, improving their ability to grasp knowledge and, consequently, increasing the efficiency of community use. Therefore, the following hypotheses are proposed:

H7a: Learner's perceived ease of use plays an intermediary role between personalization and value co-creation intention.
H7b: Learner's perceived ease of use plays an intermediary role between interactivity and value co-creation intention.
H7c: Learner's perceived ease of use plays an intermediary role between social presence and value co-creation intention.

Personalization increases users' satisfaction and indirectly influences their willingness to use the platform by shaping their perceived attitudes. Learners' perception of the usefulness of EVC's personalization and interactivity is tied to how well their knowledge needs are met and whether the community values a learner-centered operational mindset. This, in turn, influences learners' intention to participate in value co-creation. Moreover, social presence positively affects perceived usefulness [15], reinforcing learners' sense of identification and trust, promoting EVC adoption, and creating the intention to engage in value co-creation. Therefore, the following hypotheses are proposed:

H8a: Learner's perceived usefulness plays an intermediary role between personalization and value co-creation intention.
H8b: Learner's perceived usefulness plays an intermediary role between interactivity and value co-creation intention.
H8c: Learner's perceived usefulness plays an intermediary role between social presence and value co-creation intention.

Users experience complex emotional reactions when adopting new technology. Personalization primarily addresses the issue of information overload, aiming to provide learners with pleasant experiences through personalized recommendations. Additionally, interactivity affects learners' cognition and emotion. As learners engage more in EVC interactions, trust builds, creating a positive emotional connection between learners and the community. This, in turn, influences their intrinsic motivation to use EVC. Moreover, a high level of social presence is likely to bring learners closer, strengthening emotional bonds, enhancing the sense of belonging, and leading to more active participation in value co-creation. Therefore, the following hypotheses are proposed:

H9a: Learner's perceived pleasantness plays an intermediary role between personalization and value co-creation intention.
H9b: Learner's perceived pleasantness plays an intermediary role between interactivity and value co-creation intention.
H9c: Learner's perceived pleasantness plays an intermediary role between social presence and value co-creation intention.

4   Study Procedure

4.1   Scale Design

The questionnaire comprises three sections: (1) demographic information, covering gender, age, education, occupation, etc.; (2) inquiries about learners' EVC experience, average browsing time, main behaviors, etc., aimed at pinpointing the relevant target population for this paper's content; and (3) survey instruments adapted from established scales, modified as necessary for this study. It includes 21 items rated on a five-point Likert scale, ranging from 1: "strongly disagree" to 5: "strongly agree".

4.2   Data Collection

This study uses the multistage cluster sampling method to gather a sample of college and university students. We conduct an initial survey on EVC learners, optimizing the questionnaire based on reliability, validity, difficulty, and discriminability tests. Next, we collect data through the professional survey platform wxj.cn. A questionnaire is considered effective under three conditions: (1) respondents have experience using EVC; (2) there are non-identical options for all questions; (3) respondents spend no less than 180 s completing the questionnaire. Out of 408 surveys collected, 357 are deemed valid (i.e. 87.5% effective rate). We then utilize IBM® SPSS® Amos™ and IBM® SPSS® Statistics for data analysis. The number of valid questionnaires collected is more than five times the measurement items, meeting the standard that Nunally and Berstein proposed in 1994.

5   Data Analysis and Results

5.1   Sample Descriptive Statistic

We possess descriptive statistics of the survey respondents. An analysis of the investigators' basic information reveals that the majority of participants align with the sample target population. They possess a certain period of experience using EVC, allowing them to better comprehend relevant topics and provide objective answers based on practical experience. Meanwhile, results indicate that the mean of each item is around 3.5, suggesting that respondents have a moderate level of agreement with the items. The standard deviations for all factors hover around 1, indicating a relatively tight distribution of each item. Additionally, the absolute values of skewness and kurtosis are within 3, signifying that the sample data generally follow a normal distribution and meet the prerequisites for further analysis.

5.2   Reliability and Validity Tests

We assess the internal consistency reliability of each measurement variable using Cronbach's α, with criteria established by Zaichkowsky (1985) to gauge good internal consistency. The results indicate that the Cronbach's α coefficient for each variable exceeds 0.7, and the Cronbach's α coefficient for the entire questionnaire surpasses 0.9, signifying a high overall reliability of both the questionnaire and its individual items. Additionally, a Kaiser-Meyer-Olkin (KMO) test for sampling adequacy yields a value of 0.892, indicating highly adequate sampling suitable for factor analysis. In addition, the Bartlett's test is significant at the 0.001 significance level.

Moreover, the factor loadings of each potential variable corresponding to the topic are greater than 0.7, signifying their high representativeness. Additionally, the average variance extracted (AVE) for each latent variable exceeds 0.5, and the composite reliability (CR) surpasses 0.7, indicating good convergent validity.

Table 2 displays the results of the discriminant validity test. The square root of the AVE for each variable is greater than the absolute value of its correlation coefficient, indicating good discriminant validity.

Table 2. Specific data on discriminant validity.

	PER	IN	SP	PE	PU	PP	VCI
PER	**0.847**						
IN	0.339**	**0.731**					
SP	0.361**	0.444**	**0.817**				
PE	0.306**	0.396**	0.446**	**0.865**			
PU	0.361**	0.412**	0.405**	0.440**	**0.849**		
PP	0.395**	0.493**	0.493**	0.416**	0.460**	**0.803**	
VCI	0.312**	0.425**	0.377**	0.374**	0.422**	0.395**	**0.770**

5.3 Structural Equation Modeling

Bentler (1992) suggests that acceptable model fit should satisfy the following criteria: the degree of agreement no greater than 3.0, the root mean square error of approximation (RMSEA) greater than 0.05 and the comparative fit index (CFI) no less than 0.9. By using IBM® SPSS® Amos™ software for confirmatory factor analysis, we find that $\frac{\chi^2}{df} = 1.229$, RMSEA = 0.025, CFI = 0.990, IFI = 0.990, TLI = 0.988. All these results show high construct validity of our model.

5.4 Hypothesis Testing

There are 12 hypotheses in this paper. We perform path analysis using IBM® SPSS® Amos™ (see Fig. 2). Results indicate that only one hypothesis fails to pass the test, while the other 11 hypotheses meet the significance level of 0.01.

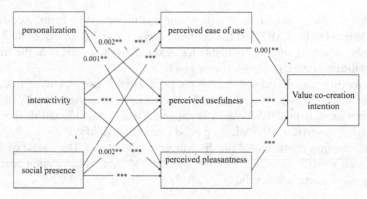

Fig. 2. Hypothesis path test

Note: *, **, *** denote significant levels p < 0.05, p < 0.01, p < 0.001, respectively, and dashed lines indicate that the hypotheses are not supported (Table 3).

Table 3. Bootstrap mediation effect test.

Hypothesis	Estimate	Bias-corrected 95% CI			Mediating test effect
		Lower	Upper	P-value	
PER-PE-VCI	0.019	−0.110	0.059	0.216	Insignificant
PER-PU-VCI	0.059	0.140	0.119	0.006	Significant
PER-PP-VCI	0.046	0.120	0.098	0.008	Significant
IN-PE-VCI	0.057	0.015	0.111	0.003	Significant
IN-PU-VCI	0.101	0.036	0.180	0.001	Significant
IN-PP-VCI	0.087	0.026	0.169	0.002	Significant
SP-PE-VCI	0.061	0.014	0.123	0.004	Significant
SP-PU-VCI	0.064	0.008	0.132	0.030	Significant
SP-PP-VCI	0.070	0.020	0.132	0.004	Significant

6   Conclusion and Insight

6.1   Research Findings

Several crucial findings emerge from empirical tests. We observe that the personalization of the EVC significantly influences learners' perceived usefulness and perceived pleasantness, albeit without a substantial impact on perceived ease of use. Moreover, in the context of EVC, interactivity is the most important factor in learners' perceived usefulness. Furthermore, social presence emerges as a potent factor positively influencing learners' perceived ease of use and perceived pleasantness. Meanwhile, our findings reveal that learners' value co-creation is positively influenced by perceived ease of use, perceived pleasantness, and perceived usefulness, with the latter two exerting a more robust and significant impact.

The operational logic of EVC content prioritizes the actual needs of learners, emphasizing user needs over platform-centric considerations. Swiftly bringing together learners with shared values, common educational backgrounds, and interests, the content ensures a rapid and tailored response to their needs. Additionally, interactivity serves as the catalyst, enabling learners to access timely and effective content that aligns with their requirements. Fruthermore, diverging from traditional perspectives that emphasize the collaboration between customers and firms, the EVC places learners as the primary architects of value. In this context, learners actively engage in activities and mutual interactions to fulfill diverse needs, fostering an exchange of knowledge that deepens their immersive experience of the community. As perceived value increases, learners develop a stronger sense of existence and participation, motivating them to share knowledge.

6.2 Theoretical and Practical Implications

This study developed a novel user value co-creation model, drawing inspiration from the S-O-R framework and emphasizing the interactions among the environment, individual, and behavior. The research reveals that perceived usefulness and perceived ease of use contribute to explaining user acceptance behavior, leading to positive behavioral intentions post-acceptance. However, solely considering these two factors, without incorporating external variables (e.g., online environment characteristics), provides insufficient explanatory power for learners' behavioral intentions. In EVCs, learners function as both recipients and creators, bearing the cost of using the platform voluntarily. Bearing this in mind, this study integrates supplementary variables from the VAM to elucidate and validate learners' perceived behaviors to varying degrees, extending the application of TAM and VAM to the exploration of value co-creation.

Moreover, this study contributes to the literature on value co-creation under the perspective of users' experiences. Previous research on value co-creation has primarily focused on the product value level, often neglecting the nuanced psychological needs of users. However, in environments like EVC, characterized by learners' autonomous behaviors and intentions, interpersonal interaction plays a foundational role in value co-creation. Particularly, the role of information interaction in the value creation process is increasingly significant. This study analyzes the factors influencing learners' perceived value at the benefit level, outlining the pathways that impact their intention to participate in value co-creation.

At a practical level, research findings can serve as a foundation for attracting and guiding learners to actively participate in value co-creation, thereby enhancing the quality of relationships within the learner community. For knowledge content creators, prioritizing the fulfillment of learners' personalized needs, highlighting unique content, and maintaining a robust knowledge interaction network are crucial. This approach promotes effective and in-depth relationship interactions among learners, encouraging value co-creation behaviors in the network information era. Moreover, EVC operators, to enhance learner participation, should improve the community interface's friendliness, create an enjoyable community atmosphere, and establish an environment conducive to learner interaction. Addressing cognitive bias caused by information asymmetry through an enhanced internal search mechanism aids learners in efficiently finding relevant information. This contributes to the sustainable development of the EVC.

6.3   Limitations and Future Work

This study was not free of limitations. Future scholars are encouraged to provide detailed and in-depth insights into the mechanisms by which learners in EVC participate in value co-creation, based on empirical testing of the influencing factors identified in this study. Additionally, it is suggested to incorporate demographic variables, such as gender, age, and education, as moderator variables to explore inter-group variances in value co-creation participation. Furthermore, more sophisticated analyses and comparisons can be conducted across different segmented categories of EVC in future research.

References

1. Wachter, R.M., Gupta, J.N.D., Quaddus, M.A.: IT takes a village: virtual communities in support of education. Int. J. Inf. Manag. **20**(6), 473–489 (2000)
2. Kaptein, M., Parvinen, P.: Advancing e-commerce personalization: process framework and case study. Int. J. Electron. Commer. **19**(3), 7–33 (2015)
3. Janlert, L.E., Stolterman, E.: The meaning of interactivity—some proposals for definitions and measures. Hum.-Comput. Interact. **32**(3), 103–138 (2017)
4. Sun, Y., Shao, X., Li, X., et al.: How live streaming influences purchase intentions in social commerce: an IT affordance perspective. Electron. Commer. Res. Appl. **37**, 100886 (2019)
5. Rahmi, B., Birgoren, B., Aktepe, A.: A meta analysis of factors affecting perceived usefulness and perceived ease of use in the adoption of e-learning systems. Turk. Online J. Dist. Educ. **19**(4), 4–42 (2018)
6. Alsabawy, A.Y., Cater-Steel, A., Soar, J.: Determinants of perceived usefulness of e-learning systems. Comput. Hum. Behav. **64**, 843–858 (2016)
7. Horng, J.S., Hsu, H.: A holistic aesthetic experience model: creating a harmonious dining environment to increase customers' perceived pleasure. J. Hosp. Tour. Manag. **45**, 520–534 (2020)
8. Kamali, M., Zarea, H., Su, Z., et al.: The influence of value co-creation on customer loyalty, behavioural intention, and customer satisfaction in emerging markets. AD-Minist. **39**, 5–24 (2021)
9. Park, M.S., Shin, J.K., Ju, Y.: Social networking atmosphere and online retailing. J. Glob. Scholars Market. Sci. **24**(1), 89–107 (2014)
10. Benlian, A.: Web personalization cues and their differential effects on user assessments of website value. J. Manag. Inf. Syst. **32**(1), 225–260 (2015)
11. Wang, W., Chen, R.R., Ou, C.X., et al.: Media or message, which is the king in social commerce?: an empirical study of participants' intention to repost marketing messages on social media. Comput. Hum. Behav. **93**, 176–191 (2019)
12. Animesh, A., Pinsonneault, A., Yang, S.B., et al.: An odyssey into virtual worlds: exploring the impacts of technological and spatial environments on intention to purchase virtual products. MIS Q. 789–810 (2011)

13. Ogonowski, A., Montandon, A., Botha, E., et al.: Should new online stores invest in social presence elements? the effect of social presence on initial trust formation. J. Retail. Consum. Serv. **21**(4), 482–491 (2014)
14. Lee, A.R., Kim, K.K.: Customer benefits and value co-creation activities in corporate social networking services. Behav. Inf. Technol. **37**, 675–692 (2018)
15. Gefen, D., Karahanna, E., Straub, D.W.: Trust and TAM in online shopping: an integrated model. MIS Q. **27**(1), 51–90 (2003)

Research on the Peer Effect of Digital Innovation in Manufacturing Enterprises

Haiyan Ma, Tianyi Zhou, Ying Chen, and Maomao Chi[✉]

China University of Geosciences, Wuhan, Hubei, China
chimaomao111@sina.com

Abstract. Based on the peer effect perspective, we establish a digital innovation linkage between the same group enterprises and the focal enterprise, and explore the existence of the peer effect of digital innovation, as well as the cross-layer boundary conditions of executives' digital background (micro), status (meso), and intellectual property protection (macro), and their substitution relationships among the three. Using the data of Chinese listed companies from 2012 to 2022, we find that: (1) Digital innovation has the peer effect, that is, The level of digital innovation in focal enterprise can be influenced by the average level of digital innovation among firms in the same industry; (2) Executives' digital background positively influences the peer effect of digital innovation. With the improvement of the status, the peer effect of digital innovation shows a trend of strengthening first and then weakening. The intensity of intellectual property protection positively affects the peer effect of digital innovation; (3) The moderating effect of status takes precedence over intellectual property protection, and the moderating effect of intellectual property protection is prioritized over executives' digital background.

Keywords: Digital Innovation · Peer Effect · Executives' Digital Background · Status · Intellectual Property Protection

1 Introduction

Digital innovation is defined as the creation of (and consequent change in) market offerings, business processes, or models that result from the use of digital technology [1]. It fundamentally changes the nature and structure of new products and services, spurs new value creation and value distribution pathways, diversifies the innovation subjects, and even changes the development of the entire industry [1]. Existing literature mainly explores the antecedents of corporate digital innovation from the perspectives of corporate resource capabilities (e.g. digital infrastructure, customer and user knowledge [2], dynamic capabilities [3]) and market characteristics (e.g. market integration [4]), but mostly ignores the external interference triggered by the value contribution of digital innovation and the transferability and assimilation of its outcomes by other peer enterprises on the focal enterprise.

Compared to traditional innovation, digital innovation can help enterprises quickly seize the future market and establish long-term competitive advantages through

© The Author(s), under exclusive license to Springer Nature Switzerland AG 2024
Y. P. Tu and M. Chi (Eds.): WHICEB 2024, LNBIP 516, pp. 374–385, 2024.
https://doi.org/10.1007/978-3-031-60260-3_31

economies of scale and creative destruction effects in the era of digital economy [4]. However, where the probability of "creative destruction" is higher and market entry opportunities are more abundant, risks also follow. Therefore, when making digital innovation decisions, enterprises tend to observe and imitate the behavior of other organizations facing similar environments in order to reduce the risk uncertainty faced by individuals due to limited information and resources. In addition, the unique characteristics of digital innovation, such as non-competitiveness, self-growth, and boundarylessness, make the decision-making context for enterprises to implement this form of innovation ambiguous. However, there has been little literature on this topic.

Therefore, this paper will test the existence of digital innovation peer effect. And it will also explore the boundary conditions of digital innovation peer effect and the substitution relationship between them by considering three levels of contextual factors: executives' digital backgrounds (micro), status (meso), and intellectual property protection (macro). Our main research contributions are as follows: First, we extend the relevant research on peer effect to digital innovation activities, providing a new theoretical explanation for the decision-making process of digital innovation for enterprises based on inter-organizational social relationships and behavioral influences. Second, we incorporate cross-level boundary conditions into the research framework, clarifying the specific situational factors of digital innovation peer groups, and further opening up the black box of the generation mechanism of digital innovation peer effect. Third, we compare the priority ranking of multi-level situational factors, identifying key elements that are more instructive and influential for identifying the peer effect of digital innovation.

2 Theoretical Basis and Research Hypothesis

2.1 The Existence of Peer Effect in Enterprises Digital Innovation

Literature Review on Peer Effect[1]. The related hypothesis of the peer effect breaks the assumption of independent decision-making of micro enterprises, and holds that the decision-making behavior of enterprises will not only be affected by their own characteristics, but also by organizations or groups with similar environments [5]. Previous literature on the peer effect of corporate behavior has primarily focused on internal corporate governance (e.g. capital structure, executive compensation, and excessive debt) and strategic decision-making (e.g. innovation decisions, mergers and acquisitions decisions, information disclosure, etc.). With the advent of the digital economy era, topics related to digital transformation peer effect have begun to emerge. However, research on peer effect in digital innovation, which serves as a fundamental barrier to the digital transformation of manufacturing enterprises, still needs to be supplemented. Although some scholars have attempted to unpack the black box of digital innovation peer effect from the perspective of the external environment using dynamic competition theory, the complexity of the peer effect driving mechanisms and the ambiguity of digital innovation decision-making scenarios make it challenging to accurately explore the driving mechanisms and boundary conditions of digital innovation peer effect from a single theory or perspective.

---

[1] Due to space limitations, the detailed literature review and references for this section are available upon request.

The Triggering Mechanism of Peer Effect in Digital Innovation. Companies in the same field may be either "competitors" with unequal exchange of interests or "symbiont" with equal cooperation [6]. The dual identity of enterprises can trigger the peer effect of digital innovation through different channels.

The Motivation of "Pursuit of Profit" as Competitors. On the one hand, from the perspective of dynamic competition theory, inter-organizational connections and interactions can affect companies' defensive responses to competitors' innovation activities, avoiding the loss of competitiveness due to the establishment of barriers [7]. Due to the greater economies of scale and higher probability of "creative destruction" in digital innovation, it is likely to result in a situation of "winner takes all", which may put incumbents at risk of losing the entire market. Therefore, when the digital innovation level of peer enterprises is relatively high, in order to avoid being severely impacted by innovation lagging, the focal enterprise will passively imitate the digital innovation behaviors of competitors to firmly occupy the position of "players" and maintain a competitive balance. On the other hand, from the perspective of social learning theory, when observing that competitors have improved their resource integration and collaboration efficiency and have changed the individual's ability status in the entire value creation system through the integration of digital technology into new products and innovation processes, the focal enterprise will actively imitate the digital innovation behavior of other companies in the same group to reduce the cost and risk of corporate decision-making, leveraging the value-added effect of digital innovation.

The Motivation of "Avoiding Harm" as a Symbiont. Institutional theory points out that when a sufficient number of individuals adopt a certain behavior, the behavior may be seen as a matter of course or institutionalized factors, and the remaining individuals are more likely to also take the same action in order to gain organizational legitimacy [8]. This means that when the overall level of digital innovation in the industry is high or tends to move towards a high level, corporate normative legitimacy and cognitive legitimacy will increase simultaneously, and focal enterprise will be forced by social expectations and normative pressures to choose to engage in digital innovation with a high probability. Based on the above analysis, we propose the following hypothesis:

H1: Digital innovation has the peer effect, which means it is influenced by other companies in the same group.

2.2 The Moderating Effect of Multilevel Scenarios

The Moderating Effect of Executives' Digital Background. The demand for senior executives with a digital background as a new role of "digital communicator" can not only cultivate the digital thinking of senior executives [9], but also help to enhance the enthusiasm of organizational members to participate in digital transformation. When the senior management team has a digital background, it will show stronger digital affinity, better identify and understand the potential digital innovation opportunities and internal logic in the market [9], capture the positive signals of peer enterprise digital innovation behavior, and timely adjust and improve their own digital strategic decisions, promoting the peer effect of digital innovation. Based on the above analysis, we propose the following hypothesis:

H2: Executives' digital background positively affects digital innovation peer effect.

The Moderating Effect of Status. Derived from sociological research, when exploring whether enterprises choose to comply with or deviate from popular activities [10], the role of status is often considered. When status is relatively low, it has little chance of being the first choice of consumers, and it also lacks the motivation to comply with regulatory management in the industry, as it does not gain any benefits from compliance and does not lose anything by not complying with regulations [11]. At this time, the "avoid harm" motivation of digital innovation peer effect is weakened. However, due to the favorable signals released by peer enterprises' digital innovation and the low entry threshold of digital innovation itself [4], low-status enterprises still actively observe and learn from the digital innovation behaviors of peer enterprises because of the "profit-seeking" motivation, creating the possibility for the enterprise to overtake its competitors. As the status improves, middle-status enterprises on the one hand want to maintain their competitive advantages in the industry, and on the other hand, from a middle-status conformity perspective, they will pay particular attention to industry consistency pressure and social expectations. Therefore, enterprises at this stage will show strong peer motivation. However, as the status continues to climb, both the "profit-seeking" and "avoid harm" motivations of digital innovation peer effect will gradually fade away. This is because the selection benefits and endorsement benefits brought by high status enable enterprises not only to maintain their dominant position as standard setters, but also to effectively enhance high-quality signals, making their digital innovation activities more easily recognized by the market and in line with public digital expectations [12], thereby reducing decision-making risks. Additionally, the resource benefits provided by high status enable enterprises to obtain more scarce digital resources from the outside world, optimize their resource allocation, and enhance their confidence in digital innovation. Based on the above analysis, we propose the following hypothesis:

H3: The moderating effect of status has a phased characteristic. As status increases, the peer effect of digital innovation first increases and then decreases.

The Moderating Effect of Intellectual Property Protection. As an important institutional arrangement to protect the rights and interests of enterprise innovation achievements, intellectual property protection can not only enhance the actual benefits brought by digital innovation to enterprises, but also effectively restrain gray competition among enterprises in the same group caused by low violation costs. When the intensity of intellectual property protection in the region is low, enterprises may choose to hide their R&D information to avoid digital innovation income losses caused by information leakage [13]. This will increase the cost of information exchange between enterprises and establish information barriers, which will hinder the focal enterprise from following and imitating the peer enterprises. Based on the above analysis, we propose the following hypothesis:

H4: Intellectual property protection positively affects digital innovation peer effect.

2.3   Comparative Analysis of Cross-Layer Boundary Conditions

Compared with the single channel impact of executives' digital background and intellectual property protection, status can jointly affect the peer effect of digital innovation through multiple channels, including internal resource endowments and external environmental legitimacy pressure perception.In addition, unlike the executives' digital background reflecting digital thinking and digital insight of enterprises, intellectual property protection, as an external mandatory and uncontrollable institutional regulation, determines the expected return of digital innovation investment of enterprises, and is more guiding for enterprises to balance patents and technical secrets. It directly relates to the acquisition of external resource information. Based on the above analysis, we propose the following hypothesis:

H5: The moderating effect of status has the highest priority and the intellectual property protection is prioritized over executives' digital background.

3   Research Design

3.1   Sample Selection and Data Sources

Based on the "Guidelines on classification of listed companies in China" (2012), we select manufacturing listed companies from 2012 to 2022 as the research sample. On this basis, ST and *ST companies and companies with significant data missing are excluded. In addition, we draw on reference [5] to define enterprises at the same industry as peer groups. At the same time, considering that the sample size within the same industry is too small to produce a peer effect, manufacturing industries with fewer than 10 samples are excluded. Finally, a balanced panel database of 719 listed companies from 2012 to 2022 was constructed, with a total of 7909 valid samples. Among them, digital innovation is derived from the State Intellectual Property Office of China (SIPO), which was manually collated by the author. The remaining data sources are the China Statistical Yearbook, China Stock Market Accounting Research (CSMAR), China Center for Economic Research (CCER), and Wind Database.

3.2   Research Variables

Dependent Variable. *Digital Innovation (DI).* Draw on reference [4] and reference [12], we choose the number of patents identified as digital innovation and authorized patents plus one logarithm as the measurement index of enterprise digital innovation. Specifically, firstly, based on the relevant digital economy industry classification standards established in the "Statistical Classification of Digital Economy and Its Core Industries (2021)", we used the pre-trained language model SBERT in the field of machine learning methods, and used Python to calculate the text similarity between patent abstract texts and descriptions of each category to identify patents belonging to digital innovation. At the same time, two researchers independently coded and verified to ensure the accuracy of screening. Secondly, following the research of Boeing et al. (2016), we matched the identified patents with listed companies. Finally, we screened out authorized digital innovation patents.

Independent Variable. *Peer Firms' Digital Innovation (DI_peer).* Referring to the calculation method in reference [5], we construct formula (1) to measure the core explanatory variable. Where i, j, and t represent enterprise, industry, and year, respectively, and N represents the number of enterprises in the industry to which enterprise i belongs. The formula is as follows.

$$DI\_peer_{i,j,t} = \frac{1}{N-1}\left(\sum_{i=1}^{N} DI_{i,j,t} - DI_{i,j,t}\right) \tag{1}$$

Moderating Variables. *Status.* Considering that the list of the top 500 Chinese manufacturing enterprises cannot cover all manufacturing enterprises, we refer to the approach in reference [12], using the weighted average of total assets, total operating income, and net profit to form highly significant predictors for the ranking of the top 500 Chinese manufacturing enterprises. The weighted average ranking is used to determine the status of an enterprise in the industry. In addition, formula (2) is used to standardize the ranking to improve comparability across industries, where $Rank_{i,j}$ represents the rank of company i in industry j, and $Rank_{max,j}$ represents the maximum number of ranks within industry j. The formula is as follows:

$$Status_{i,j} = 1 - \frac{Rank_{i,j}}{Rank_{max,j}} \tag{2}$$

Executives' Digital Background (EDB). Combining reference [9], we observe whether the education or employment experience of executives includes descriptions such as "CIO, CTO, information computing, software, e-commerce, IT, and technology". If it does, it indicates that the executives of the enterprise have digital knowledge, and the value is 1. Otherwise, it is 0.

Intellectual Property Protection (IP). Referring to the approach in reference [14], we use the ratio of technology market turnover to GDP as a measure of the intensity of intellectual property protection.

Control Variables. In line with the research designs in reference [15], we control the enterprise-level variables of firm size, total asset turnover rate, asset-liability ratio, total asset net profit ratio, Tobin's Q value, firm age, proportion of independent directors, top three executive compensation, R&D intensity[2], and individual and year factors. Based on the peer effect research, we also control the relevant indicators of the above enterprise characteristics variables based on the peer level, with the calculation method similar to formula (1). In addition, in order to exclude the interference of regional peers, we also include the average digital innovation of other enterprises located in the same region as the focal enterprise (*DI_city*) as a control variable.

---

[2] Due to the serious missing values in the R&D intensity, we refer to the practices of Flannery and Rangan (2006), and take the R&D intensity of the sample with undisclosed R&D expenses as 0, and includes a dummy variable for whether or not to disclose R&D expenses as a control variable to control possible sample selection bias.

3.3 Model Setting

We use model (3) to test the existence of peer effect in digital innovation and the moderating role of status, and uses model (4) to test the moderating role of executives' digital background and intellectual property protection.

$$DI_{i,j,t} = \alpha 0 + \alpha 1 DI\_peer_{i,j,t} + \alpha_2 DI\_city_{i,j,t} + \alpha_3 CV_{i,j,t} + \alpha_4 CV\_peer_{i,j,t} + \theta_i + \mu_t + \varepsilon_{i,t} \quad (3)$$

$$DI_{i,j,t} = \alpha 0 + \alpha 1 DI\_peer_{i,j,t} + \beta_1 boundary_{i,j,t} + \beta_2 DI\_peer_{i,j,t} \times boundary_{i,j,t}$$
$$+ \alpha_2 DI\_city_{i,j,t} + \alpha_3 CV_{i,j,t} + \alpha_4 CV\_peer_{i,j,t} + \theta_i + \mu_t + \varepsilon_{i,t}$$
$$\quad (4)$$

where, i, j and t represent the enterprise, industry and year respectively. *boundary* represents the executives' digital background (EDB) and intellectual property protection (IP). CV represents the control variables at the focal enterprise level, and CV_peer represents the control variables at the peer enterprises level. θ_i and μ_t are individual and year fixed effects, respectively, and $\varepsilon_{i,t}$ is a random disturbance term.

4 Results

4.1 The Existence Test of Digital Innovation Peer Effect and the Moderating Effect Test of Executives' Digital Background

The regression results in column (1) of Table1 show that the coefficient of peer enterprises' digital innovation is $0.3195 > 0$, which is significant at the 0.01 level, indicating that the peer effect of digital innovation exists. H1 is confirmed.

To verify the impact of the executives' digital background on the peer effect of digital innovation, we construct a cross-term of peer enterprises' digital innovation and executives' digital background into the regression equation. The results show that the coefficient of the cross-term in column (2) is $0.1096 > 0$ and significant, indicating that the executives' digital background positively affects the peer effect of digital innovation, thus supporting H2.

4.2 The Moderating Effect Test of Status

To test the impact of status on the peer effect of digital innovation, we categorize the focal enterprises based on their industry status. Enterprises with a status higher than the upper quartile are defined as high-status groups, those lower than the lower quartile are low-status groups, and the remaining are middle-status groups. The results in columns (3)–(5) of Table1 indicate that under the premise of passing the pairwise matched group coefficient difference test, status can affect the peer effect of digital innovation in enterprises. Specifically, when enterprises are in the middle, low, and high status groups, the significance of DI_peer decreases successively. The coefficient of the low-status group is smaller than that of the middle group ($0.2066 < 0.3702$). In the high-status group, there is no peer effect. It indicates that when the market ranking status of enterprises is relatively low, as status increases, the peer effect of digital innovation in enterprises gradually strengthens. However, when the status is relatively high, as status increases, the peer effect of digital innovation in enterprises weakens or even disappears. H3 is confirmed.

Table 1. The results of the existence of peer effect of digital innovation and the moderating mechanism of executives' digital background and status.

			Low-status	Middle-status	High-status
	(1)	(2)	(3)	(4)	(5)
DI_peer	0.3195***	0.3257***	0.2066*	0.3702***	0.3315
	(3.96)	(4.05)	(1.81)	(3.40)	(1.54)
EDB		0.0324			
		(0.86)			
DI_peer × *EDB*		0.1096**			
		(2.26)			
DI_city	0.0141	0.0185	−0.0060	−0.0210	0.1756
	(0.16)'	(0.21)	(−0.04)	(−0.17)	(0.85)
CV/CV_peer	Y/Y	Y/Y	Y/Y	Y/Y	Y/Y
Individual/Year	Y/Y	Y/Y	Y/Y	Y/Y	Y/Y
R^2	0.115	0.117	0.075	0.128	0.184
N	7909	7909	1977	3953	1979
The test of the difference in coefficient between groups in the regression of status grouping:					
Low and Middle groups	45.32**				
Middle and High groups	57.00***				
Low and High groups	56.41***				

Note: *** $p < 0.01$, ** $p < 0.05$, * $p < 0.1$ and the t-values are shown in brackets. The standard errors of all regression coefficients have been clustered at the enterprise level. The regression results have omitted control variables (*CV* and *CV_peer*) and constant terms. The test of differences in coefficients between groups uses the seemingly unrelated regression test. The same applies to the following tables

4.3 The Moderating Effect Test of Intellectual Property Protection

The results in Table 2 show that in column (1), the coefficient of *DI_peer* × *IP* is significantly positive, indicating that intellectual property protection can positively affect the peer effect of digital innovation. H4 is preliminarily confirmed. In addition, as the level of intellectual property protection that enterprises receive has distinct regional characteristics and exhibits systematic heterogeneity, we further employ a grouped regression approach to supplement the verification of H4 and provide a grouping basis for comparing the priority order of intellectual property protection and executives' digital background in the following text. We classify sample into weak, medium, and strong intellectual property protection groups based on the ranking of intellectual property protection intensity in the regions. The results in columns (2)–(4) are basically consistent with those in the previous text, and H4 is again confirmed.

Table 2. The test of the moderating effect of intellectual property protection.

		Weak-IP	Medium-IP	Strong-IP
	(1)	(2)	(3)	(4)
DI_peer	0.2926***	0.2056*	0.3451*	0.3707***
	(6.10)	(1.67)	(1.83)	(2.91)
IP	−3.8335***			
	(−3.26)			
DI_peer × IP	1.2094**			
	(2.17)			
DI_city	−0.0039	−0.0891	−0.0032	−0.2010
	(−0.06)	(−0.57)	(−0.02)	(−1.25)
CV/CV_peer	Y/Y	Y/Y	Y/Y	Y/Y
Individual/Year	Y/Y	Y/Y	Y/Y	Y/Y
R^2	0.117	0.138	0.157	0.111
N	7909	2888	2325	2696
The test of differences in intellectual property protection between groups:				
Weak and Medium groups	67.59***			
Medium and Strong groups	48.58**			
Weak and Strong groups	67.15***			

4.4 The Comparative Results of the Priority of Moderating Variables

The results in Table 3 indicate that when the full samples are grouped by status, the interaction terms between executives' digital background and peer digital innovation are not significant. As status increases, the significance of the interaction term coefficient between intellectual property protection and peer firms' digital innovation decreases significantly. In the middle and high status groups, intellectual property protection no longer has a moderating effect. It can be seen that the moderating effect of status on the peer effect of digital innovation has priority over executives' digital background and intellectual property protection. Similarly, as intellectual property protection intensity increases, in the medium and high intellectual property protection groups, executives' digital background no longer has a moderating effect. It indicates that the moderating effect of intellectual property protection has priority over executives' digital background. H5 is confirmed.

Table 3. The comparative results of the priority among the three moderating variables.

group	Status-EDB			Status-IP			IP-EDB		
	Low	Middle	High	Low	Middle	High	Weak	Medium	Strong
DI_peer	0.21^{**}	0.37^{***}	0.25	0.17^{*}	0.37^{***}	0.32	0.23^{*}	0.34^{*}	0.38^{***}
	(2.13)	(3.43)	(1.42)	(1.66)	(3.35)	(1.42)	(1.87)	(1.82)	(3.03)
EDB	0.02	0.02	0.07				0.12^{*}	0.02	−0.00
	(0.31)	(0.36)	(0.69)				(1.74)	(0.26)	(−0.05)
$DI\_peer \times EDB$	0.05	0.04	0.19				0.27^{***}	0.01	0.10
	(0.90)	(0.72)	(1.61)				(2.88)	(0.13)	(1.28)
IP				−2.15	−4.15	-7.98^{**}			
				(−0.85)	(−1.37)	(−2.21)			
$DI\_peer \times IP$				2.38^{**}	0.21	−0.18			
				(1.98)	(0.16)	(−0.10)			
DI_city	−0.00	−0.02	0.21	−0.04	−0.04	0.13	−0.06	−0.00	−0.20
	(−0.03)	(−0.15)	(0.99)	(−0.26)	(−0.35)	(0.65)	(−0.41)	(−0.03)	(−1.23)
CV/CV_peer	Y/Y	Y/Y	Y/Y	Y/Y	Y/Y	Y/Y	Y/Y	Y/Y	Y/Y
Individual/Year	Y/Y	Y/Y	Y/Y	Y/Y	Y/Y	Y/Y	Y/Y	Y/Y	Y/Y
R^2	0.076	0.128	0.207	0.073	0.129	0.189	0.149	0.157	0.113
N	1977	3953	1979	1977	3953	1979	2888	2325	2696

Note:Due to table width limitations, the coefficients in Table 3 are rounded to two decimal places

4.5 Robustness Test[3]

To validate the robustness of the results, we conduct the following six tests: (1) *Placebo test.* We first use the placebo test to exclude the results bias caused by unobservable common factors. (2) *Propensity score matching (PSM).* To alleviate the endogeneity problem caused by sample selection bias, we perform 1:1 non-replacement matching on the samples using the median of peer firms' digital innovation as the dividing line, and use the matched samples for regression. (3) *Instrumental variable method.* The endogenous problem caused by reverse causality may exist in the existence test of peer effect. Therefore, we construct instrumental variables using "peer's peer"[4] [16], and conduct instrumental variable regression based on this. (4) *Lagged regression.* Considering that

---

[3] Due to space limitations, the results of robustness tests are not presented. Please contact the author for further information.

[4] "Peer's peer" in this paper is defined as the enterprises located in the same region as the peer enterprises, and manually excludes enterprises in the same industry and region as the focal enterprise to ensure the exogeneity of the instrumental variables.

there is a certain period for enterprises to transmit and react to information, using current variables to test the existence of peer effect may cause endogeneity problems caused by reverse causality. Therefore, we further lag the core explanatory variables and control variables by one to three periods and conduct regression. (5) *Changing the regression method.* Considering that the digital innovation of an enterprise in a given year may be related to the digital innovation levels of the previous and next years. We use two-step system GMM to overcome such inertia issues. (6) *Changing the measurement method of variables.* We use the average number of citations and the maximum number of citations for each enterprise's digital innovation patents, and take the logarithm after adding 1 to measure the level of digital innovation. At the same time, considering the problem of "right truncation", we only use the 5-year window period after authorization to calculate citations [4]. The results of the above robustness tests all confirm that there is indeed a peer effect in digital innovation.

5 Conclusion and Implications

Based on dynamic competition theory, social learning theory, and institutional theory, this paper examines the existence and cross-level boundary conditions of digital innovation peer effect as well as their substitution relationship. The research findings indicate that: (1) Based on the motivation of "seeking benefits and avoiding harm", digital innovation peer effect exists. This conclusion responds to reference [5] from the perspective of enterprise digital innovation, arguing that there is inevitable interdependence among peer enterprises in enterprise decision-making. Unlike the research of Li et al. (2022) which studied the peer effect of innovation, this paper combines the unique characteristics of digital technology to reveal another new idea for enterprises to enhance their competitive advantages. (2) From a micro perspective, this paper is the first to examine the positive moderating effect of executives' digital backgrounds on digital innovation peer effect; from a meso perspective, as the status improves, the peer effects of digital innovation initially increase and then decrease. This conclusion differs from reference [15] which studied the heterogeneity of status in the same industry. Our research categorizes the status of enterprises more meticulously, combining the middle-status conformity perspective, and believes that the moderating effect of status on peer effect is not a single weakening relationship, but a more complex and phasic coexistence relationship; from a macro perspective, intellectual property protection has a positive moderating effect on digital innovation peer effect, providing evidence at the regional institutional level for research on digital peer effect. (3) There is substitutability between cross-layer boundary conditions, that is, the priority of status's moderating effect is the highest, followed by intellectual property protection, and finally executives' digital background.

The above research findings provide three management implications for enterprises: (1) In the digital economy, enterprises should focus on enhancing their own digital capabilities and knowledge, cultivate digital thinking and awareness among organizational members, and fully leverage the guidance and incentive role of executives on organizational members. (2) Focal enterprises should pay attention to their own status in the industry hierarchy and keep abreast of the trends of digital innovation in the industry. In particular, low-status enterprises should actively embrace the digital wave, leverage the resource information and favorable signals released by peer enterprises, and improve their digital innovation capabilities through the low threshold and self-growth characteristics of digital innovation, in order to catch up with their competitors. (3) Local governments should enhance their awareness and protection of property rights, ensure the digital innovation benefits of enterprises, continuously deepen the reform of intellectual property rights distribution, and help build a good digital innovation ecosystem in the industry.

Acknowledgement. We are grateful to the editor and anonymous reviewers for their constructive comments and suggestions. And this work was supported by the National Natural Science Foundation of China under Grant 72272138 and 71973130 and the National Social Science Foundation of China under Grant 22AZD126.

References

1. Nambisan, K., Lyytinen, A., Majchrzak, M.: Song Digital innovation management: reinventing innovation management research in a digital world. MIS Q. **41**(1), 223–238 (2017)
2. Abrell, T., Pihlajamaa, M., Kanto, L., et al.: The role of users and customers in digital innovation, insights from B2B manufacturing firms. Inf. Manag. **53**(3), 324–335 (2016)
3. Warner, K.S., Wager, M.: Building dynamic capabilities for digital transformation, an ongoing process of strategic renewal. Long Range Plann. **52**(3), 326–349 (2019)
4. Hu, Z.X., Ma, S.Z.: The impact of market integration on firm digital innovation: an analysis on digital innovation measurement methods. Econ. Res. J. **58**(06), 155–172 (2023). (in Chinese)
5. Leary, M.T., Roberts, M.R.: Do peer firms affect corporate financial policy? J. Finance **69**(1), 139–178 (2014)
6. Yang, J.Y., Peng, Q.P., Ge, Z.T.: Spillover effect of digital transformation along the supply chain-the perspective of supplier innovation. China Ind. Econ. **8**, 156–174 (2022). (in Chinese)
7. Hsieh, K.Y., Tsai, W., Chen, M.J.: If they can do it, why not us? competitors as reference points for justifying escalation of commitment. Acad. Manag. J. **58**(1), 38–58 (2015)
8. March, J.G.: Decisions in organizations and theories of choice. J. Mater. Sci. **40**(7), 1763–1765 (1981)
9. Firk, S., Gehrke, Y., Hanelt, A., Wolf, M.: Top management team characteristics and digital innovation: exploring digital knowledge and TMT interfaces. Long Range Plan. **55**(3), 102166 (2022)
10. Prato, M., Kypraios, E., Ertug, G., Lee, Y.G.: Middle-status conformity revisited, the interplay between achieved and ascribed Status. Acad. Manag. J. **62**(4), 1003–1027 (2018)
11. Phillips, D.J., Zuckerman, E.W.: Middle-status conformity, theoretical restatement and empirical demonstration in two markets. Am. J. Social. **107**(2), 379–429 (2001)
12. Liu, Y., Dong, J.Y., Ying, Y., et al.: Status and digital innovation: a middle-status conformity perspective. Technol. Forecast. Soc. Change **168**(3), 12781 (2021)
13. Raut, L.K.: R & D spillover and productivity growth: evidence from Indian private firms. J. Dev. Econ. **48**(1), 1–23 (1995)
14. Ang, J.S., Cheng, Y., Wu, C.: Does enforcement of intellectual property rights matter in China? evidence from financing and investment choices in the high-tech industry. Rev. Econ. Stat. **96**(2), 332–348 (2014)
15. Li, Z.Z., Li, Z.B.: Research on the peer effect of enterprise ESG information disclosure. Nankai Bus. Rev. 1–22 (2024). (in Chinese)
16. Zhang, A.C., Fang, J., Jacobsen, B., et al.: Peer effects, personal characteristics and asset allocation. J. Bank. Finan. **90**(1), 76–95 (2018)

Cryptocurrency Transaction Fraud Detection Based on Imbalanced Classification with Interpretable Analysis

Wenlong Jiang[1], Pei Yin[1,2(✉)], and Wangwei Zhu[1]

[1] Business School, University of Shanghai for Science and Technology, Shanghai 200093, China
pyin@usst.edu.cn

[2] School of Intelligent Emergency Management, University of Shanghai for Science and Technology, Shanghai 200093, China

Abstract. Given the significant distribution disparity between normal and fraudulent transaction data in cryptocurrency samples, as well as the complex high-dimensional nature of transaction data with non-linear relationships, this study introduces an interpretable imbalanced data classification method for detecting cryptocurrency transaction fraud. We address data imbalance using SMOTE over-sampling and data augmentation through contrastive learning. Next, we introduce a Transformer-based deep learning model that learns sample relevance. The model undergoes pre-training with a contrastive loss and fine-tuning through Bayesian optimization to effectively extract high-dimensional, higher-order, and fraud-related features. We employ a SHAP-based interpreter along with attention scores to elucidate the role of various transaction features in fraud detection. Comparative results demonstrate the model's remarkable recall performance in identifying cryptocurrency transaction fraud. Furthermore, it achieves an excellent F1 value, striking a balance between accuracy and recall. Ablation experiments affirm the necessity of the proposed data balancing and pre-training-fine-tuning strategies, highlighting their effectiveness in addressing imbalanced data classification issues. This research not only enriches financial fraud detection but also enhances cryptocurrency transaction security, promotes market development, and contributes to economic stability and social security.

Keywords: cryptocurrency · fraud detection · extremely imbalanced data classification · interpretable analysis

1 Introduction

The cryptocurrency market, established in 2008, has seen remarkable growth, primarily driven by digital currencies like Bitcoin and Ether, acclaimed for their decentralized nature based on blockchain technology. These attributes have enhanced cryptocurrency credibility while simultaneously fostering opportunities for fraudulent activities, including money laundering, phishing, Ponzi schemes, and ICO scams. The vast scale and limited regulation of cryptocurrency transactions, relative to traditional currencies, coupled

Y. P. Tu and M. Chi (Eds.): WHICEB 2024, LNBIP 516, pp. 386–398, 2024.
https://doi.org/10.1007/978-3-031-60260-3_32

with the anonymity and complexity of smart contracts, intensify challenges in fraud detection. To address this problem, machine learning-based financial fraud detection research has made significant progress [1]. Deep learning models, particularly neural networks, have gained attention for their high accuracy, adaptability, and scalability [2]. Despite advancements, such as the use of graph neural networks to enhance fraud detection accuracy by modeling transaction network structures, there remains a need for a thorough analysis of inter-user and inter-transaction similarities, as well as transaction feature interactions [3].

Fraud detection research in cryptocurrency is still emerging. The distinctive characteristics of blockchain technology contribute to the complexity of cryptocurrency data, making it challenging to identify fraudulent features accurately. Decentralization in blockchain transactions hinders access to fraudulent data, creating a substantial imbalance between normal and fraudulent transactions. Additionally, cryptocurrency markets' high volatility can lead to misinterpretations of routine price fluctuations as fraud, further complicating fraud detection. Furthermore, achieving a reasonable balance between accuracy and recall is crucial, prioritizing the identification of fraudulent transactions over pinpoint accuracy. Compliance with regulations like the European Union's GDPR mandates explanations for fraud detection results to enhance the transparency of these models.

Therefore, this paper is motivated to tackle the problems above and try to answer the following research question:

Should cryptocurrency transaction fraud detection be regarded as a classification task? How can we address the challenge of handling highly imbalanced data to achieve effective classification? What is the significance of transaction features in the context of fraud detection?

This paper contributes in several ways: Firstly, it enhances data balance through a method that combines SMOTE oversampling and data augmentation in contrast learning. Secondly, it employs contrast loss-based pre-training and Bayesian optimization-based fine-tuning strategies, enhancing the model's focus on high-dimensional, high-order features related to fraud, thereby improving fraud detection performance. Experimental results demonstrate the method's high accuracy, recall, and F1-score in cryptocurrency fraud detection. Lastly, by combining the attention mechanism and the SHAP method, the paper enhances the interpretability of the fraud detection model, revealing the significance of cryptocurrency transaction features in fraud detection.

2 Related Work

2.1 Financial Fraud Detection

Financial fraud is an issue that can have serious implications in finance and life, and there has been a large body of literature examining various types of fraud, such as financial statement, credit card, insurance, and cryptocurrency fraud. Earlier rule-based fraud detection methods relied on expert knowledge, which made it difficult to capture complex and changing patterns and were vulnerable to attacks [5]. To overcome these limitations, recent research has used machine learning models to automatically discover potential fraud patterns in data. These methods extract statistical features from multiple aspects such as user profiles and historical behaviors, and use traditional classifiers such as SVMs and tree-based methods to determine the presence of fraud [6]. However, as the amount of real-world data increases and the structure of relationships becomes more complex, more powerful learning models are needed to deal with fraud [7]. In recent years, some studies have begun to utilize graph structures for fraud detection, such as the graph convolutional network approach of FdGars [8], but these approaches have not yet fully considered the similarities between users or transactions and the interactions between transaction features.

2.2 Cryptocurrency Fraud Detection

In the current digital age, cryptocurrencies and blockchain technology are gradually transforming the global economy, and digital currencies have dramatically changed the way transactions are conducted [9]. Due to the decentralization of blockchain technology and the anonymity of digital currencies, exchanges are relying more on digital currencies than traditional currencies [10]. Although blockchain features such as decentralization, invariance, and anonymity have increased the credibility of cryptocurrencies, they have also provided a ground for fraudulent activities such as money laundering, phishing, Ponzi schemes, and Initial Coin Offering (ICO) scams [11]. Therefore, fraud detection research aims to detect these fraudulent scams using various methods to successfully identify and respond to them.

There are significant differences between cryptocurrencies and traditional currencies in terms of fraud detection, including anonymous transactions, technical complexity, and market volatility [12]. While the authentication and traceability of the traditional financial system makes fraud easier to track, cryptocurrencies make it more difficult. Cryptocurrencies involve complex technology such as smart contracts, providing fraudsters with more sophisticated and harder to detect means of committing fraud. Increased market volatility makes normal price fluctuations easy to mischaracterize as fraud, adding to the challenge of accurately identifying fraudulent features. Ponzi schemes are widespread in the cryptocurrency space, and deep learning frameworks such as SCSGuard detect various types of Ponzi schemes based on analyzing code features of smart contracts [13]. Detection models for money laundering activities are typically trained using account features [14], while models for phishing scams are analyzed primarily for the structure of the transaction network [15]. However, improving model accuracy is also challenged by decreasing interpretability, so explaining model decisions becomes more important.

2.3 Research Review

In general, the existing researches on cryptocurrency transaction fraud detection have limitations in the following aspects:

1. Most scholars view cryptocurrency transaction fraud detection as a classification problem. This is because in cryptocurrency transaction fraud detection, data with known labels are usually available and therefore can be classified using supervised learning methods without relying on anomalous patterns in the data.

2. Early methods of manual rules and feature engineering was limited by expert knowledge and could not capture complex and changing patterns. Traditional machine learning models were insufficient to handle larger data volumes and more complex relationship structures. And existing deep learning models need to take more account of the similarities between users and transactions.

3. It is challenging for the extent researches when dealing with extremely unbalanced classification problems like cryptocurrency trading.

4. There is an urgent need to develop methods to interpret deep learning "black box" models and increase their transparency.

3 Models

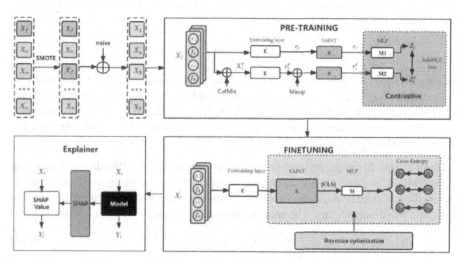

Fig. 1. Figure 1 shows the overall process architecture including oversampling, pre-training and fine-tuning modules using SMOTE.

To address these issues, this paper proposes an interpretable imbalanced data classification method for identifying fraudulent transactions on cryptocurrency platforms. Firstly, SMOTE oversampling and data augmentation techniques in contrastive learning are utilized to data balancing. Then, the Transformer-based deep learning model SAINT [4] concentrating on inter-sample attention is introduced and pre-trained by designing a contrastive loss function so as to better extract the high-order features that are truly related to the fraud by deferentiating normal and fraud samples, and subsequently, this paper applies a Bayesian optimization method to fine-tune the pre-trained model to further improve the effect of fraud recognition. Finally, the model is interpreted by combining the attention score and SHAP methods to calculate the contribution of each feature to fraud detection.

3.1 SMOTE and Random Noise Based Data Balancing Method

Data Coding. Assuming that $D = \{X_i, Y_i\}_{i=1}^{k}$ is that there are k number of samples of transaction data, where X_i is an n-dimensional feature vector, and Y_i is the label marked as normal or fraudulent. Meanwhile, the *[CLS]* token is added as an embedding into the feature vector of each sample. The feature vector of X_i can be expressed as $X_i = \{[CLS], f_1, f_2, ..., f_n\}$.

SMOTE Oversampling. The SOMTE algorithm balances the distribution of categories in the dataset by adding samples from a small number of categories while maintaining information about the topology of the data.

For each minority class fraud sample, compute its k nearest-neighbors minority class samples, and then randomly select a sample from its k nearest-neighbors samples and randomly select a sample from its nearest-neighbors samples. Then the newly generated fraud sample can be represented as follows:

$$X_{f(new)} = X_f + rand(0, 1) * d\left(X_f, X_f'\right) \tag{1}$$

where $rand(0, 1)$ denotes a value randomly selected from the uniform distribution of $[0, 1]$, and $d\left(X_f, X_f'\right)$ denotes the selected sample X_f and one of its nearest neighbors samples X_f' the difference between it and one of its nearest neighbors. Finally, the generated synthetic samples are added to the dataset such that the number of few fraudulent samples in the dataset increases.

Adding Noise. In this paper, considering that the structure of the data after oversampling using SMOTE is relatively homogeneous, in order to increase the diversity of samples, the method of adding normally distributed random noise is used to simulate real-life authentic fraud sample data. The specific method of adding noise is as follows:

$$X_{2i} = X_{f(new)} + noise_n \tag{2}$$

where $noise_n$ denotes the normally distributed random noise, the $i = 1, 2, \ldots, k/2$.

Then the final simulation data set can be expressed as:

$$D = X_i, Y_{i(i=1)}^{k} \tag{3}$$

where X_i denotes the set of fraudulent and normal samples after oversampling, and Y_i is the label labelled as normal or fraudulent, k denotes the number of samples with k transactions.

3.2 Pre-training Method Based on Contrastive Learning

Data Enhancement. In this paper, the data enhancement strategy in contrast learning is used to do further data balancing. CutMix is used to perform random mixing of features on the original input data, and then mixup is used to perform random mixing on the vector representations that have gone through the embedding layer; the combination of the two methods can enhance the sample diversity more effectively, thus improving the overall contrast learning.

In Fig. 1 E denotes the embedding layer, S denotes SAINT, the M_1 and M_2 denote the two fully connected layers that act as projection heads. Denote the enhancement probability of CutMix as p_{CutMix}, the parameters of mixup are denoted as a, for the original input X_i, its representation after the embedding layer can be written as $e_i = E(X_i)$, then the representation of the data after enhancement is as follows:

$$X' = X_i * M + X_a * (1 - M) \tag{4}$$

$$e'_i = \alpha^* E(X'_i) + (1 - \alpha)^* \left(E(X'_b) \right) \tag{5}$$

Which X_a, X_b is a random sample of the current batch, and $X_{b'}$ is a random sample of the X_b CutMixed version, M is a vector of binary masks sampled from a probability of p_{CutMix} the binary mask vector sampled from the Bernoulli distribution with probability, and α is the parameter of mixup. First, the CutMix version of each data point in the same batch is obtained by randomly selecting the original samples to be mixed. Then, a new mixed sample is selected for mixup among the samples after passing through the embedding layer.

After obtaining the embedded representation without data enhancement e_i and the embedded representation after data-enhanced mixing $e_{i'}$. After that, they are fed into the SAINT model separately, and then fed into two fully connected layers as projection heads for dimensionality reduction, each of which consists of a hidden layer and a ReLU activation function. Finally, the contrast loss is computed for the two sets of vector representations after dimensionality reduction.

Transformer Variant - SAINT Model. SAINT is a variant of the transformer encoder, modeled by L identical modules, each consisting of a self-attention module and an inter-sample attention module. The self-attention module is the same as in the transformer encoder, while the inter-sample attention module is similar to the self-attention module. Specifically, inter-sample attention is the process of connecting the embeddings of each feature of a single sample, and then computing the attention of the sample (rather than the feature), which allows the model to improve the representation of the current sample by comparing it to other samples.

Contrastive Loss Functions. In pre-training the SAINT model, InfoNCE loss in metric learning is used to compare two different vector representations Z_i and $Z_{i'}$ obtained from the same sample and shrink their distances, for different samples Z_i and Z_j (i is not equal to j) are then made to move away from each other, and the loss function is expressed as follows:

$$L_{pretraining} = -\sum_{i=1}^{k} log \frac{exp(z_i * z'_i / \tau)}{\sum_{m=1}^{k} exp(z_i * z'_i / \tau)} \tag{6}$$

where $Z_i = M_1(r_i), Z'_i = M_2(r'_i)$ is the temperature parameter, which is used to regulate the scaling of the similarity scores.

3.3 Fine-Tuning Method Based on Bayesian Optimization

Bayesian Optimization. In this paper, we search for model-optimal hyperparameters through Bayesian optimization, which is a tuning method that models the objective function by continuously using previous model performance information in conjunction with a Gaussian process model and searches for possible optimal solutions in unexplored regions. The method is evaluated by selecting the most promising points in the parameter space, which leads to a fast convergence to the global optimum of the objective function in a finite number of iterations.

Fine-tuning Strategies. As shown in Fig. 1, all unlabeled data complete the pre-training on SAINT before the labelled data are used to fine-tune the SAINT model. For the original input data, a vector representation containing global information is obtained through the embedding layer and SAINT, and then the *[CLS]* tokens in the vectors are used as embeddings to do the final prediction through a fully-connected layer, and the predicted values are compared with the true values, and then the cross-entropy loss is used to evaluate the classification effectiveness of fraudulent samples and normal samples. And, in this paper, the hyperparameters of the model are searched and optimized by using Bayesian optimization, including the learning rate, the learning step, the number of iterations and the batch size to obtain the highest performance of the prediction model.

3.4 SHAP-Based Interpreter

In this paper, the SHAP (SHapley Additive exPlanations) method is used to interpret the fraud detection model over the Shapley values to quantify the marginal contribution of the features in the fraud detection task, which is calculated as follows:

$$\varphi_i(f) = \sum_{S \in N \setminus i} \frac{|S|!(|N| - |S| - 1)!}{|N|!} [f(S \cup i) - f(s)] \tag{7}$$

where $\varphi_i(f)$ is the feature i of the SHAP value, and f is the prediction function of the model, and N is the total number of features, and S is a subset of the feature index, denoting the exclusion of the feature i combinations of features, and $f(S \cup i)$ denotes a combination of features that includes the features i of the combination of features predicted by the model, and $f(S)$ denotes a model prediction that does not include the feature i the model prediction of the combination of features. For the feature i SHAP values, for all feature combinations that do not include the feature i combinations of features are considered to calculate the model prediction of the combination of features added i and without the feature i the difference in model predictions with and without the inclusion of features, and consider all possible combination weights.

4 Experimental Setup and Evaluation

4.1 Experimental Data

In this paper, we use the Ethereum transaction fraud detection data provided by Kaggle, with a total sample size of 12,147, of which 11,232 are normal samples and 915 are fraudulent samples, with a total of 33 features. Since the data is labeled, we likewise define the cryptocurrency transaction fraud detection task as a binary classification problem. However, the proportion of normal samples and fraud samples is seriously unbalanced, to solve this problem, SMOTE oversampling method is used to balance the data, and random noise is introduced into the balanced data to simulate the real data. The total number of balanced samples is 22464, and the category ratio is close to 1:1.

We divide the data into training set, validation set and test set in 8:1:1 ratio. First, the training set is pre-trained to learn higher-order features, and then fine-tuned by the training and validation sets, where the validation set accuracy is used as an objective function for Bayesian optimization to improve the model's performance on the validation set. Finally, the detection performance of the model is evaluated using the test set.

4.2 Evaluation Methodology

In this paper, Precision, Recall and F1 are used as the evaluation indexes of the model. $Precision = TP/(TP + FP)$, $Recall = TP/(TP + FN)$, $F1 = 2*(Precision*Recall)/(Precision + Recall)$. Where TP is the sample that is correctly predicted as positive class, and FP is the sample that was incorrectly predicted to be positive class, and FN is the sample that is actually positive but not predicted as positive.

5 Analysis of Experimental Results

5.1 Sensitivity Experiments

In this paper, sensitivity experiments are conducted to find the optimal parameters of the model and through the same pre-training and fine-tuning steps, the experimental results are shown in the table below (Table 1):

Table 1. Results of sensitivity experiments.

blocks	heads	input dim	Precision	Recall	F1
2	4	16	0.7495	0.8502	0.7966
4	8	32	0.8473	0.927	0.8854
8	16	64	0.7611	0.8653	0.8099

For the SAINT model used in this paper, the optimal model parameters are: the number of layers of self-attention is set to 4, the attention head is set to 8, and the input dimensions are set to 32. When pre-training the model, the optimizer is chosen to be AdamW, the learning rate is 0.0001, and the batch size is 64. When fine-tuning the model, a set of hyperparameters is obtained after 100 experiments on Bayesian optimization to make the model hyperparameters with the best performance, a learning rate of 0.00069, an iteration number of 20, a batch size of 64, a learning step of 5, and an optimizer of AdamW.

5.2 Ablation Experiments

In order to examine the effectiveness of different modules on the detection results, ablation experiment is conducted to compare different module combinations, and the experimental results are shown in the following figure (Fig. 2):

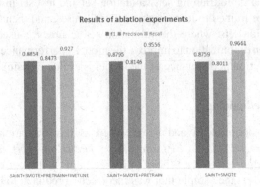

Fig. 2. Histogram of ablation experiment results.

As can be seen from the figure, the complete model exhibits a high recall rate, indicating that it is effective in capturing fraud and reducing underreporting. Meanwhile, the high F1 value indicates a balance between recall and precision.

After removing the pre-training and fine-tuning seperately, the model is able to predict fraud samples more accurately, leading to an increase in recall. However, the model incorrectly predicts more normal samples as fraudulent, reducing the precision rate. In addition, the F1 value decreases, indicating that the balance between recall and precision is disrupted and the overall performance deteriorate. Thus, the necessity and the effectiveness of the pre-training strategy and fine-tuning strategy proposed in this paper is proved.

5.3 Comparative Experiments

The baseline methods compared in this paper are as follows:

Random Forest: It is an integrated learning method for solving classification and regression problems.

LightGBM: It is a gradient boosting framework, an efficient machine learning algorithm developed by Microsoft.

XGBoost: It is also a gradient boosting algorithm that solves classification and regression problems by combining multiple weak learners to build a powerful integrated model.

TabTransformer: It is a deep learning model for tabular data designed to process structured information from tabular data (Table 2).

In evaluating cryptocurrency transaction fraud detection methods, our analysis reveals distinct performance characteristics. XGBoost demonstrates high precision but low recall, effectively identifying a majority of fraudulent transactions within its limited

Table 2. Comparison of cryptocurrency transaction fraud detection performance.

Metric	Precision	Recall	F1
LightGBM	0.6723	0.5067	0.5779
Random Forest	0.8776	0.6376	0.7386
XGBoost	**0.9664**	0.3561	0.5205
TabTransformer	0.733	**0.9783**	0.8381
Model	0.8473	0.927	**0.8854**

predicted sample size. Conversely, TabTransformer exhibits high recall yet low precision, marking a broader range of transactions as fraudulent with less accuracy. Overall, our model outperforms these and four other baseline models in overall efficacy.

Key findings from our experiments are:

Machine learning models typically underperform relative to deep learning models in handling large, complex datasets. This is evidenced by the comparative performance of TabTransformer (a deep learning model) and SAINT, with the latter showing superior fraud detection ability. This suggests that SAINT's inter-sample attention mechanism, which assesses similarities between fraudulent and normal transactions, enhances its capability to identify fraud.

Contrastive learning-based pre-training enables the model to grasp a comprehensive feature representation of both fraudulent and normal transactions. This learning approach significantly boosts the model's performance in subsequent classification tasks. Furthermore, hyperparameter optimization is crucial for model refinement. Bayesian optimization, in this context, has proven more effective and efficient than manual tuning or grid search methods, offering better results in optimizing model parameters.

5.4 Interpretable Analyses

Interpretable Analyses Based on Attention Mechanisms

Table 3. Eigenvalues and attention weights for a sample of frauds (top 5).

Features	lifetime	giniRec	dailyMax	totalEtherBalance	activityDays
Values	776	0.85256	12	−1.546	122
Weights	0.03634	0.03521	0.03520	0.03331	0.03176

In this paper, we analyze the impact of transaction characteristics in the fraud prediction process based on the attention scores computed by the Transformer model, and select the top 5 significant characteristics for explanatory analysis. The model found that new user registration, abnormally high number of bought currencies, use of multiple small transactions to circumvent monitoring, mismatch between buying and selling, and short active days have a significant impact on fraud prediction (Table 3).

Interpretable SHAP-Based Analyses

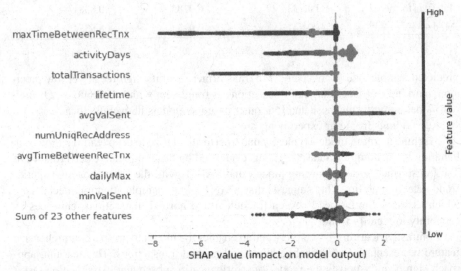

Fig. 3. SHAP swarm diagram

In this study, we conduct an advanced analysis of transaction features for fraud prediction using the SHAP (SHapley Additive exPlanations) interpretive framework. We visualize SHAP values for each feature and sample via SHAP swarm plots (Fig. 3) to intuitively decipher model outputs. The graph highlights the five most critical features influencing fraud prediction: maximum time interval between receiver transactions, account activity duration, total transaction count, account registration length, and average currency sale value. Key observations include:

1. Longer intervals between recipient transactions typically indicate normal activity.
2. Account activity duration, total transactions, and registration length exhibit an inverse correlation with fraud; active, long-standing accounts are less likely to engage in fraudulent activities.
3. Higher average sale values of currency, associated with increased SHAP values in the model, potentially indicate fraudulent behavior. Normal transactions predominantly involve currency purchases, making large-scale sales anomalous. Our model identifies fraudulent behaviors in cryptocurrency transactions primarily through these dimensions:

1. New, less active users are more susceptible to fraud, possibly due to their limited understanding of cryptocurrency operations, making them easy targets.

2. Fraudulent transactions often feature low individual amounts but high frequency and aggregate sums, aiming to evade detection by minimizing each transaction's visibility while accumulating significant total values.
3. Unlike typical transactions where bought currency amounts surpass sold amounts (reflecting the rising market value of cryptocurrencies), fraudulent transactions often exhibit a reverse trend. This suggests a pattern where users are coerced into selling cryptocurrencies to fraudulent entities at a loss.

6 Conclusion

To address cryptocurrency transaction fraud detection complexity, this study introduces an interpretable imbalanced data classification method. It utilizes SMOTE oversampling, contrast learning for data enhancement, and employs contrast loss pre-training and Bayesian optimization-based fine-tuning for the Transformer-based deep learning model SAINT to extract fraud-related high-order and high-dimensional features in order to better distinguish the fraud sample from the normal sample. Additionally, a SHAP-based interpreter incorporating attention scores aids in model interpretation.

Experimental results demonstrate the model's strong recall performance and its superior F1 value. They also underscore the necessity of the proposed data balancing and pre-training-fine-tuning strategies. Furthermore, interpretable analysis shows the importance of various transaction features in fraud detection. This research enriches financial fraud detection and fosters cryptocurrency market development. However, real-world validation is crucial for assessing the model's feasibility and effectiveness in actual cryptocurrency trading environments. Future studies can explore enhancing the model's cross-platform applicability to accommodate diverse trading platforms and cryptocurrencies.

Acknowledgement. Funding: This work was supported by Key Lab of Information Network Security, Ministry of Public Security (C23600). The financial support is gratefully acknowledged.

References

1. Chandradeva, L.S., Amarasinghe, T.M., de Silvam, M., et al.: Monetary transaction fraud detection system based on machine learning strategies. In: Proceedings of the 4th International Congress on Information and Communication Technology, pp. 385–396 (2020)
2. Sürücü, O., et al.: A survey on ethereum smart contract vulnerability detection using machine learning. In: Proceedings SPIE 12117, Disruptive Technologies in Information Sciences VI, 121170C (2022)
3. Kurshan, E., Shen, H., Yu, H.: Financial crime & fraud detection using graph computing: application considerations & outlook. In: Proceedings of the 2020 Second International Conference on Transdisciplinary AI (TransAI), pp. 542–549 (2020)
4. Somepalli, G., Goldblum, M., Schwarzschild, A., Bruss, C.B., Goldstein, T.: SAINT: improved neural networks for tabular data via row attention and contrastive pre-training (2021). arXiv:2106.01342v1 [cs.LG]
5. Dazeley, R.P.: To the knowledge frontier and beyond: a hybrid system for incremental contextual-learning and prudence analysis. PhD thesis (2006)

6. Ryman-Tubb, N.F., Krause, P., Garn, W.: How Artificial Intelligence and machine learning research impacts payment card fraud detection: a survey and industry benchmark. Eng. Appl. Artif. Intell. **76**, 130–157 (2018)
7. Ravisankar, P., Ravi, V., Rao, G.R., et al.: Detection of financial statement fraud and feature selection using data mining techniques. Decis. Supp. Syst. **50**, 491–500 (2011)
8. Whiting, D.G., Hansen, J.V., McDonald, J.B., et al.: Machine learning methods for detecting patterns of management fraud. Comput. Intell. **28**, 505–527 (2012)
9. Iansiti, M., Lakhani, K.R.: The truth about blockchain. Harv. Bus. Rev. **95**, 118–127 (2017)
10. Tharani, J.S., Charles, E.Y.A., Hóu, Z., Palaniswami, M., Muthukkumarasamy, V.: Graph based visualisation techniques for analysis of blockchain transactions. In: Proceedings of the 2021 IEEE 46th Conference on Local Computer Networks (LCN), Edmonton, AB, Canada, 4–7 October 2021, pp. 427–430 (2021)
11. Yuan, Y., Wang, F.Y.: Blockchain and cryptocurrencies: model, techniques, and applications. IEEE Trans. Syst. Man Cybern. Syst. **48**, 1421–1428 (2018)
12. Mukherjee, S., Larkin, C.: Cryptocurrency ponzi schemes. In: Corbet, S. (ed.) Understanding Cryptocurrency Fraud, pp. 111–120. De Gruyter, Berlin (2022)
13. Yuan, Q., Huang, B., Zhang, J., Wu, J., Zhang, H., Zhang, X.: Detecting phishing scams on ethereum based on transaction records. In: Proceedings of the 2020 IEEE International Symposium on Circuits and Systems (ISCAS), Sevilla, Spain, 10–21 October 2020, pp. 1–5 (2020)
14. Wu, J., et al.: Who are the phishers? phishing scam detection on ethereum via network embedding. IEEE Trans. Syst. Man Cybern. Syst. **52**, 1156–1166 (2020)
15. Wen, H., Fang, J., Wu, J., Zheng, Z.: Transaction-based hidden strategies against general phishing detection framework on ethereum. In: Proceedings of the 2021 IEEE International Symposium on Circuits and Systems (ISCAS), Daegu, Republic of Korea, 22–28 May 2021, pp. 1–5 (2021)

Does Port Smartization Policy Affect Port Carbon Emission Efficiency? -Validation Based on PSM-DID

Chaohui Zhang, Nianxin Wang, and Yuxue Yang[(✉)]

School of Economics and Management, Jiangsu University of Science and Technology,
Zhenjiang 212100, China
yangyuxue1224@163.com

Abstract. Port smartization is increasingly used by many ports nowadays to promote efficient port development and improve the quality of the environment. To
evaluate the effect of port smartization on carbon emission, this study regards the
initiation of port smartization policies at each port as a quasi-natural experiment.
Based on the panel data of 39 major ports in China from 2013 to 2021, the impact
of port smartization construction on the carbon emission efficiency of ports in
China is explored through a multi-period PSM-DID model. The findings of this
study indicate that port smartization construction significantly improves the carbon emission efficiency of ports. The results pass parallel trend tests and remain
valid after a series of robustness tests, including placebo tests, the substitution of
the explained variable, the double difference with propensity score matching, etc.
Moreover, heterogeneity analysis indicates that ports in the Yangtze River Delta
and southeast coastal regions can more efficiently utilize smartization policies to
enhance port carbon emission efficiency. Factors such as operational mode, transportation method, and energy consumption affect port carbon emission efficiency,
and there is no direct correlation with port size.

Keywords: Port Smartization · Carbon Emission Efficiency · Multi-period
PSM-DID

1 Introduction

Climate change and its impacts have become one of the world's most severe environmental problems today[1]. As the country with the world's largest population and carbon
emitter, China faces the greatest challenge in achieving the basic goal of socialist modernization, which is addressing climate change [2]. To proactively address the climate
crisis and make a greater contribution to the global carbon reduction process, China
has put forward goals for carbon peaking and carbon neutrality. The task of reducing
greenhouse gas emissions has been incorporated into the national '14th Five-Year Plan'
and the 2035 long-term objectives. For China, achieving a low-carbon transformation is
an intrinsic requirement for high-quality economic development.

© The Author(s), under exclusive license to Springer Nature Switzerland AG 2024
Y. P. Tu and M. Chi (Eds.): WHICEB 2024, LNBIP 516, pp. 399–410, 2024.
https://doi.org/10.1007/978-3-031-60260-3_33

The transportation industry is a crucial sector in our country, accounting for about 15% of the national carbon emissions. Among them, port-related carbon emissions make up approximately 6.5% of the overall transportation industry. In recent years, our country's port development has achieved remarkable results, gradually establishing world-class port clusters such as the Yangtze River Delta, Bohai Rim, and Guangdong-Hong Kong-Macao. The throughput of port cargo and container has consistently ranked first in the world for consecutive years. According to statistics, in 2022, the cargo throughput of China's ports reached 15.68 billion tons, and the container throughput reached 300 million TEU. The overall port throughput showed a steady increase. Ports undertake crucial operations such as the entry and exit of vessels, berthing, cargo loading and unloading, and transshipment. They serve as vital transportation hubs, and their high cargo throughput contributes significantly to energy consumption within the entire transportation sector [3]. Therefore, strengthening the energy-saving and emission reduction, green and low-carbon development of ports [4], and improving the carbon emission efficiency of ports is of crucial significance for achieving China's dual-carbon goals.

In recent years, various ports along the coast of China have continuously advanced the use of AI technology and 5G technology in automated terminals, consistently promoting intelligent production. Against the backdrop of accelerating the construction of a transportation powerhouse, the construction of port smartization is considered a crucial means to enhance the core competitiveness of ports [5]. The promotion of the intelligent upgrade of ports is a significant support for the transformation of a major port country into a powerful port nation. However, in the process of port transformation and upgrading, does port smartization play a crucial role in affecting the carbon emission efficiency of the port? Is there heterogeneity in the impact of port smartization on the carbon emission efficiency of ports in different regions? Does port smartization have different effects on the carbon emission efficiency of ports of different scales? The resolution of these issues is not only related to the low-carbon construction of the port but also directly affects the path selection for the port's transformation and upgrading [6]. To this end, this article starts from the perspective of carbon emission efficiency, combining the national major strategy of peak carbon and carbon neutrality. It selects 39 major ports in China from 2013 to 2021 as the research objects, taking the initiation of smart port policies as a quasi-natural experiment. It employs a propensity score matching - double difference model to empirically test the impact of port smartization on port carbon emission efficiency. The heterogeneous effects of smart port policies on carbon emission efficiency in different regions and different-sized ports are also compared and analyzed.

2 Literature Review

With the expansion of research in the field of carbon emission efficiency, scholars are studying the dynamic carbon emission efficiency across multiple sectors within the total factor productivity framework. For example, Zhou et al. [7] proposed the Malmquist Carbon Emission Efficiency Index (MCPI) and conducted a comparative study on the dynamic changes in carbon emission efficiency in 18 major carbon-emitting countries globally. Zhang et al. [8] established a non-radial Malmquist Carbon Emission Efficiency

Index (NMCPI) for the transportation industry, revealing decreased carbon emission efficiency in the transportation sector. Liu et al. [9] applied the Malmquist index model to the dynamic measurement of carbon emission efficiency in regional agriculture and industry. Furthermore, research has mainly focused on industries such as agriculture, manufacturing, and industry, with few scholars delving into ports' carbon emission efficiency issues.

Scholars have consistently focused on the impact of technological advancements on carbon emissions, conducting numerous fruitful studies. They propose that enhancing technological capabilities is a crucial pathway to reducing energy consumption and CO_2 emissions [6]. Some scholars believe that technological progress positively influences carbon reduction [10], driving advancements in clean production technologies and improving the efficiency of carbon emission processing and transformation [11]. However, another perspective contends that technological progress hinders the carbon reduction process [12], as it lowers unit product costs and prices [10], leading to increased energy consumption and consequently raising carbon emissions. Existing research has already elucidated the impact of technological advancements on carbon emissions, while port smartization refers to the use of intelligent and digital technologies in port operations to reduce costs and waste, and enhance efficiency. However, there is still a lack of in-depth exploration and research on the impact of port smartization technologies on port carbon emissions.

From the above discussion, scholars have extensively explored the issue of carbon emissions. However, existing research lacks empirical assessment of the policy effects of port smartization construction on carbon emissions, and further research on the impact of port smartization policies on carbon emissions is needed. Therefore, this study uses a multi-period PSM-DID model to investigate the impact of port smartization construction on the carbon emission efficiency of Chinese ports. The results of the study will contribute to a better understanding of the actual situation of coastal ports in China and provide more targeted emission reduction strategy recommendations and improvement plans. At the same time, it will help the port industry more effectively reduce carbon emissions in response to the challenges of climate change and sustainable development.

3 Methods and Data

3.1 PSM-DID Model

According to the basic principle of PSM-DID model establishment, this study sets up two dummy variables, namely group dummy variables *treat* and time dummy variables *period*, and the core explanatory variables *did* are represented by the interaction terms of the two dummy variables *treat* $\times$ *period*. Secondly, the research object of this paper is the major ports in China, considering the different time when different ports started to be smart, this paper sets up the following multi-temporal DID model to identify the impact of port smartization on port carbon emission efficiency, as shown in Eq. (1):

$$CEE_{it} = \alpha_0 + \alpha_1 did_{it} + \sum_{i=1}^{N} b_j X_{ij} + \varepsilon_i + \mu_t + \eta_{it} \tag{1}$$

where i and t are the port and time, respectively, and CEE denotes the carbon emission efficiency of the port. In addition, considering that the difference in carbon emission efficiency between the experimental group and the control group before and after the port started to be smart may have a potential impact on the assessment of the effectiveness of port smartization, this paper controls for some other variables that may affect the carbon emission efficiency of the port, which is represented by X. ε、μ、η represent the port individual fixed effects, time fixed effects and random error terms, respectively. According to the basic principle of PSM-DID model establishment, this paper focuses on the coefficient α_1 of the core explanatory variable did after controlling other factors, which represents the net effect of port smartization on port carbon emission efficiency CEE. The coefficient of α_1 should be significantly positive if port smartization enhances port carbon emission efficiency.

3.2 Variable Definition

The data required for the empirical analyses consisted of three main categories: measuring port carbon emissions, input-output variables measuring the efficiency of the port's carbon emissions, and control variables required for conducting PSM-DID analyses.

Explained Variables. This study interprets the dependent variable as port carbon emission efficiency. The calculation of carbon emission efficiency refers to the research of Ge and Wang [13]. The comprehensive energy consumption per unit throughput of the port is obtained by the consumption of major energy sources such as gasoline; diesel, heavy oil, coal, and electricity in Chinese coastal ports, combined with the port cargo throughput. The carbon emission of the port is obtained by combining different energy sources and carbon emission coefficients with the port cargo throughput, indirectly measuring the port's carbon emission. The formula is

$$Z_i = W_i \cdot Q_i \cdot \lambda_{CO_2} \tag{2}$$

In the formula: i is for different years, Z_i is the total carbon emission of the port in year i (t); W_i is the comprehensive energy consumption of the port per unit of throughput (t standard coal/ 10,000 t of throughput); Q_i is the cargo throughput of the port in year i (t); and λ_{CO_2} is the carbon emission coefficient of energy, which is taken as 2.4589.

Explanatory Variables. The core explanatory variable did of this study is whether the port has implemented a smart policy or not, defining $treat$ as 1 for the port where port smartization started and 0 for the other ports to describe the difference between the experimental and control groups, and $period$ as 1 for the year after the start of port smartization, and 0 for the year before the start of port smartization, to differentiate the difference between before and after the start of port smartization.

Control Variables. Drawing on the studies of Sun et al.[14], Wang et al. [15] and Wen et al.[16], this paper selected eight factors as the control variables affecting carbon emissions from ports, namely, the level of economic development ($pgdp$), the population size (pop), the level of urbanisation (urb), the industrial structure (ind), the level of science and technology ($tech$), the stock of human capital (sto), the environmental regulation ($envir$), and the infrastructure ($infra$). Table 1 presents descriptive statistics for the controlled variables.

Table 1. Descriptive statistics of variables

Variable	Obs	Mean	Std. Dev	Min	Med	Max
CEE	351	0.6722	0.1694	0.3968	0.6511	1.02
pgdp	351	6.1174	0.6927	4.5326	6.2315	8.13
pop	351	11.328	0.4493	10.268	11.365	12.14
urb	351	0.6797	0.122	0.41	0.6713	1.00
ind	351	0.4849	0.1011	0.2698	0.4752	0.77
tech	351	0.03264	0.02317	0.002246	0.02834	0.13
sto	351	206,199	262,237	3,620	96,519	1,077,100
envir	351	89.473	12.712	36.72	94.61	100
infra	351	208.46	650.71	19	72	5,799

3.3 Data Sources

Considering the availability of data and the heterogeneity of statistical caliber, we adopt panel data with the time span of 2013–2021, and the decision unit is 39 major ports in China. The port data are obtained from China Port Yearbook, China Statistical Yearbook and local yearbooks of various regions in the past years. In the specific measurement, the super-efficiency SBM model is selected for analysis[17], which facilitates the comparative ranking of the efficiency value of the decision unit, i.e., port DMUs; some ports do not have berths above 10,000 tons, and the MIN-MAX standardization method is adopted to standardize the data.

4 Analysis of Empirical Results

4.1 Empirical Results and Analyses of PSM-DID

PSM Results Analysis. To eliminate the selection bias problem and ensure the accuracy of DID analysis, we first conducted a PSM on the 39 ports. Based on the carbon emission efficiency calculation data of the Super-SBM model, we utilize the Logit model to estimate the propensity scores of the model's control variables. Kernel matching is then applied to estimate whether the remaining ports in the control group have no difference with the treated group in terms of the matching variables we select. Table 2 provides details of matching variables before and after the PSM. We can see that the differences between the experimental group and the control group significantly decreased. After matching, the standardized deviations of all variables were less than 10%. Moreover, the t-test results for all variables are non-significant after matching, indicating that there is no significant difference between the treatment and control groups.

From Fig. 1 and Fig. 2, it can be observed that after core matching, the absolute values of standardization deviation are concentrated within 20%. The kernel density curves of the experimental group and the control group essentially overlap, indicating a good match. The matched data can be further used for multi-period DID analysis in the subsequent text.

Table 2. Comparison of balance test results

Variable	Sample category	Mean		%Bias	% Reduct |Bias|	T-Test	
		Treated	Control			T	P > |T|
pgdp	Unmatched	6.2331	6.088	21.1	85.4	1.46	0.145
	Matched	6.2613	6.2825	−3.1		−0.16	0.872
pop	Unmatched	11.553	11.281	63.6	83.6	4.26	0.000
	Matched	11.588	11.543	10.5		0.60	0.548
urb	Unmatched	0.74163	0.66694	62.6	83.5	4.39	0.000
	Matched	0.7475	0.75982	−10.3		−0.56	0.576
ind	Unmatched	0.5154	0.47623	33.8	54.7	2.60	0.010
	Matched	0.51459	0.53232	−15.3		−0.81	0.420
tech	Unmatched	0.0379	0.03158	25.1	71.9	1.89	0.059
	Matched	0.03948	0.0377	7.1		0.38	0.704
sto	Unmatched	3.0e + 05	1.9e + 05	41.5	74.6	3.18	0.002
	Matched	3.1e + 05	3.4e + 05	−10.5		−0.48	0.634
envir	Unmatched	90.338	89.336	8.5	81.4	0.54	0.589
	Matched	91.597	91.784	−1.6		−0.11	0.914
infra	Unmatched	660.75	151.57	34.6	99.5	3.89	0.000
	Matched	199.38	202.13	−0.2		−0.07	0.948

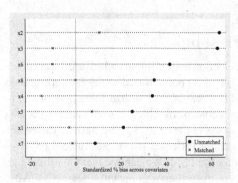

Fig. 1. Scatterplot

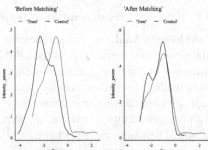

Fig. 2. Kernel density function plot after propensity score matching

Empirical Results and Analyses of PSM-DID. To assess the impact of port smartization on port carbon emission efficiency, this paper uses the port carbon emission efficiency calculated by the super-efficiency SBM model as the explanatory variable for the baseline regression. The results show that the coefficient of the core variable did is 0.069, and it has passed the 1% significance level test. This indicates that the port smartization construction can effectively improve port carbon emission efficiency. Taking into account other factors, this policy makes the carbon emission efficiency of ports that have started the smartification process approximately 6.9% higher on average compared to ports that have not initiated smartification (Table 3).

Table 3. Benchmark regression results

Variable	Mixed OLS regression	Fixed effects model	
		Panel regression	High-dimensional regression
did	0.066***	0.069***	0.069***
	(0.024)	(0.019)	(0.021)
Constant	0.511	0.107	0.096
	(0.483)	(1.200)	(1.177)
Observations	311	311	311
R-squared		0.234	0.788
Year fix	YES	YES	YES
Id fix	YES	YES	YES

Note: ***, ** and * indicate that the variable passed the 1%, 5% and 10% significance level tests, respectively, with robust standard errors in parentheses

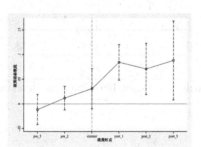

Fig. 3. Parallel trend test for two-way difference models

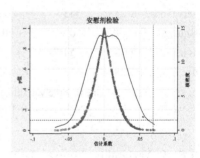

Fig. 4. Placebo test

Parallel Trend Test. The precondition for estimating the double difference method is that, before the occurrence of policy shocks, the experimental group and the control group have parallel trends. This article borrows from the parallel trend test method and event study method used by Beck et al. [18] to construct a statistical test. From the results of the parallel trend test, the results before the implementation of the policy are not significant, indicating that before the port's smart implementation, the experimental group and the control group had consistent changing trends, with no significant differences. However, after the policy implementation, the port carbon emission efficiency of the experimental group significantly increased compared to the control group. Therefore, the sample passed the parallel trend test required for estimation through the difference-in-differences method (Fig. 3).

4.2 Heterogeneity Analysis

Port Regional Differences. To further clarify the impact of port areas on port carbon emission efficiency, we divided the samples into six groups based on the geographical location of the ports. The results in Table 4 show that the core explanatory variable coefficients for the Yangtze River Delta region and the southeast coast have passed the significance test at a 10% level, suggesting that ports in the Yangtze River Delta and southeast coast regions can more efficiently utilize port smartization policies to enhance port carbon emission efficiency.

Table 4. Baseline regression results for harbour zoning

Variable	Bohai Economic Circle	Yangtze River Delta	Pearl River Delta	South-eastern seaboard	South-west coast	Yangtze river basin
did	0.027	0.074*	−0.091	0.049*	−0.076**	0.005
	(0.023)	(0.033)	(0.052)	(0.025)	(0.011)	(0.038)
Constant	−5.053	−50.027**	0.703	0.950	−1.688***	−2.647
	(5.541)	(16.603)	(4.198)	(1.014)	(0.150)	(3.299)
Observations	66	43	29	52	27	128
R−squared	0.898	0.955	0.911	0.498	0.994	0.833
Year fix	YES	YES	YES	YES	YES	YES
Id fix	YES	YES	YES	YES	YES	YES

Note: ***, ** and * indicate that the variable passed the 1%, 5% and 10% significance level tests, respectively, with robust standard errors in parentheses

Port Scale Variability. To examine whether the smartization of ports has an equal impact on the carbon emission efficiency of ports of different scales, we classified the port sizes into five categories based on the port cargo throughput. The regression results are shown in Table 5, where R represents the throughput of goods. The findings reveal that the core variable *did* is positively correlated with the carbon emission efficiency of the port. Ports with a throughput of more than 40,000 million tons have passed the significance test at the 5% level. This indicates that for larger ports, the implementation of port smartization policies has a more pronounced effect on improving their carbon emission efficiency. This may be because large ports are more centralized and efficient in transportation and logistics. In addition, large ports usually pay more attention to sustainable development and environmental protection, taking various measures to reduce the impact of operations on the environment. However, ports with throughputs between

20,000 million tons and 40,000 million tons, as well as those with less than 5,000 million tons, did not pass the significance test. This suggests that there may not be a direct correlation between port scale and carbon emission efficiency. The efficiency is also influenced by various factors, such as the port's operating mode, transportation method, and energy consumption.

Table 5. Baseline regression results for harbour sizing

Variable	R ≥ 4 0000	20000 ≤ R ≤ 4 0000	10000 ≤ R ≤ 2 0000	5000 ≤ R ≤ 1 0000	R ≤ 5000
did	0.082**	0.019	0.052*	0.049*	0.045
	(0.035)	(0.034)	(0.030)	(0.025)	(0.056)
Constant	−9.775**	−1.203	−0.471	0.950	−1.299
	(3.688)	(1.434)	(2.059)	(1.014)	(13.174)
Observations	56	83	76	52	44
R-squared	0.653	0.157	0.666	0.498	0.524
Year fix	YES	YES	YES	YES	YES
Id fix	YES	YES	YES	YES	YES

Note: ***, ** and * indicate that the variable passed the 1%, 5% and 10% significance level tests, respectively, with robust standard errors in parentheses

4.3 Robustness Test

Placebo Test. To examine to what extent the above results are influenced by omitted variables, random factors, etc., we refer to the practices of La Ferrara et al. [19]. In line with this, the paper conducted a placebo test by randomly assigning smart port activations, performing 500 independent and sufficient samples. Regression was carried out according to formula (2), and finally, a distribution chart of the estimated coefficient *did* was plotted. This was done to verify whether the carbon emission efficiency of ports is significantly affected by factors other than smartization and related variables. Figure 4 shows the distribution of regression estimated coefficients for independently repeated experiments. From the kernel density distribution of the coefficient estimates and P-values, it can be seen that the regression coefficients are close to 0, and the majority of P-values are greater than 0.1. This indicates that there is no serious issue of omitted variables in the model setup, and the core conclusion remains robust.

Re-testing Based on PSM-DID. We conduct several tests to check the robustness of the positive effect of port smartization policies on the carbon emission efficiency. We adjust the k-nearest neighbor matching value and use a 1:3 matching approach for robust re-examination based on PSM-DID. Subsequently, a Logic regression model is constructed. After obtaining matched samples, DID estimation is performed, and the results are shown in the first column of Table 6, as indicated in (1). The coefficients of the core explanatory variables are significantly positive at the 1% level, indicating the robustness of the PSM-DID results.

Other Methods. We then employ robustness testing using the replacement of the explained variable. The PSM-DID estimation is conducted with carbon emission efficiency calculated by the SBM model as the explained variable, as shown in the second column of Table 6, passing the significance test at the 5% level. In addition, to ensure that the conclusions are not influenced by outliers, this article truncates the explained variable, truncating at 1% and 5%, and reconducts the PSM-DID regression. The results, as shown in the third and fourth columns of Table 6, indicate that after excluding extreme values, the coefficient estimates all pass the significance test at the 1% level, demonstrating the robustness of the PSM-DID results.

Table 6. Baseline regression results after shrinkage treatment

Variable	(1)	(2)	(3)	(4)
did	0.067***	0.031**	0.068***	0.066***
	(0.024)	(0.013)	(0.019)	(0.018)
Constant	−0.453	−2.609**	−1.275	−1.141
	(1.261)	(1.203)	(1.626)	(1.567)
Observations	311	311	311	311
Number of id	36	36	36	36
R-squared	0.794	0.810	0.241	0.245
Year fix	YES	YES	YES	YES
Id fix	YES	YES	YES	YES

Note: ***, ** and * indicate that the variable passed the 1%, 5% and 10% significance level tests, respectively, with robust standard errors in parentheses

5   Conclusions and Policy Implications

5.1   Research Conclusion

As a crucial manifestation of technological innovation, port smartization construction plays a pivotal role in promoting the green and low-carbon development of ports. However, there is still a lack of extensive research on the port smartization construction, and further in-depth studies are urgently needed. In this regard, this paper considers the construction of port smartization as a quasi-natural experiment. Using panel data from 2013 to 2021 for 39 major ports in China, the ports are divided into experimental and control groups. The impact of port smartization construction on the carbon emission efficiency of Chinese ports is explored through a multi-period PSM-DID model. Firstly, the study found that port smartization construction significantly improves the carbon emission efficiency of ports. The results pass parallel trend tests and remain valid after a series of robustness tests, including placebo tests, replacement of the explained variable, double difference with propensity score matching, and more. Secondly, heterogeneity analysis indicates that, compared to the five major port groups, ports in the Yangtze River Delta and southeast coastal regions can more efficiently utilize smart policies to enhance port carbon emission efficiency. Port carbon emission efficiency is influenced by various factors such as operating models, transportation methods, and energy consumption, and there is no direct correlation with port size.

The contribution of this article is mainly reflected in three aspects: Firstly, this research addresses the carbon emission efficiency of Chinese ports based on geographical location, contributing to the promotion of the intensive development of ports and enhancing the level of regional economic cooperation. Secondly, the study explores the impact of port smartization policies on port carbon emission efficiency, helping to clarify the influence of smart technologies on port carbon emissions and prompting relevant industries to pay more attention to the application of smart technologies. Finally, the empirical analysis in this article evaluates the impact of smart policies on port carbon emission efficiency, providing valuable reference for better implementation of smart port strategies and optimizing related policies.

5.2 Policy Recommendations

Based on the above conclusions, the following policy recommendations are proposed: Firstly, the empirical results of this article indicate that port smartization significantly improves port carbon emission efficiency. Therefore, efforts should be intensified in constructing smart ports, and policy implementation should be increased. For the government, further encouragement and guidance should be provided to ports for intelligent construction, through means such as policy support and subsidies, encouraging enterprises to innovate in technology and port smartization construction. For enterprises, investment in green and low-carbon technologies should be increased to promote the green and low-carbon development of ports. Secondly, the heterogeneous results of this article indicate differences in the use of intelligence to improve carbon emission efficiency among ports in different regions. Therefore, when carrying out port intelligent construction, the actual situation of each region should be fully considered, and differentiated implementation of port intelligent construction should be carried out, formulating smart strategies that conform to local characteristics.

Acknowledgement. This research is supported by Postgraduate Research & Practice Innovation Program of Jiangsu Province (Project Title: Research on the Impact of Smartization on Port Carbon Emission Efficiency and Dynamic Evolution Analysis).

References

1. Wang, Y., et al.: Carbon emissions efficiency in China: key facts from regional and industrial sector. J. Clean. Prod. **206**, 850–869 (2019)
2. Liu, L.-C., et al.: Using LMDI method to analyze the change of China's industrial CO2 emissions from final fuel use: an empirical analysis. Energy Policy **35**(11), 5892–5900 (2007)
3. Yang, B., et al.: Analyzing land use structure efficiency with carbon emissions: a case study in the Middle Reaches of the Yangtze River, China. J. Clean. Prod. **274**, 123076 (2020)
4. Xu, B., Lin, B.: How industrialization and urbanization process impacts on CO2 emissions in China: evidence from nonparametric additive regression models. Energy Econ. **48**, 188–202 (2015)
5. Schiavone, F., Paolone, F., Mancini, D.: Business model innovation for urban smartization. Technol. Forecast. Social Change (2019)
6. Wang, S., Zeng, J., Liu, X.: Examining the multiple impacts of technological progress on CO2 emissions in China: a panel quantile regression approach. Renew. Sustain.Energy Rev. **103**, 140–150 (2019)
7. Zhou, P., Ang, B., Han, J.: Total factor carbon emission performance: a Malmquist index analysis. Energy Econ. **32**(1), 194–201 (2010)
8. Zhang, N., Wei, X.: Dynamic total factor carbon emissions performance changes in the Chinese transportation industry. Appl. Energy **146**, 409–420 (2015)
9. Liu, B., Shi, J., Wang, H., Su, X., Zhou, P.: Driving factors of carbon emissions in China: a joint decomposition approach based on meta-frontier. Appl. Energy **256**, 113986 (2019)
10. Fu, Y., He, C., Luo, L.: Does the low-carbon city policy make a difference? empirical evidence of the pilot scheme in China with DEA and PSM-DID. Ecol. Ind. **122**, 107238 (2021)
11. Wang, Y., et al.: Spatial correlation of factors affecting CO2 emission at provincial level in China: a geographically weighted regression approach. J. Clean. Prod. **184**, 929–937 (2018)
12. Chen, Y., Lee, C.-C.: Does technological innovation reduce CO2 emissions? cross-country evidence. J. Clean. Prod. **263**, 121550 (2020)
13. Yanyan, G., Shanshan, W.: Analysis of total factor productivity and influencing factors of ports considering carbon emissions. J. Transport. Syst. Eng. Inf. Technol. **21**(02), 22–29 (2021). (in Chinese)
14. Sun, L., Li, W.: Has the opening of high-speed rail reduced urban carbon emissions? empirical analysis based on panel data of cities in China. J. Clean. Prod. **321**, 128958 (2021)
15. Wang, L., Shao, J., Ma, Y.: Does China's low-carbon city pilot policy improve energy efficiency? Energy **283**, 129048 (2023)
16. Wen, S., Liu, H.: Research on energy conservation and carbon emission reduction effects and mechanism: quasi-experimental evidence from China. Energy Policy **169**, 113180 (2022)
17. Sun, P., Liu, L., Qayyum, M.: Energy efficiency comparison amongst service industry in Chinese provinces from the perspective of heterogeneous resource endowment: analysis using undesirable super efficiency SBM-ML model. J. Clean. Prod. **328**, 129535 (2021)
18. Beck, T., Levine, R., Levkov, A.: Big bad banks? the winners and losers from bank deregulation in the United States. J. Finan. **65**(5), 1637–1667 (2010)
19. Ferrara, E.L., Chong, A., Duryea, S.: Soap operas and fertility: evidence from Brazil. Am. Econ. J. Appl. Econ. **4**(4), 1–31 (2012)

Is it Always Better to Be Distinctive? Optimal distinctiveness in the Sharing Economy Platform Market to Maintain Active User

Mengsi Zhu, Nianxin Wang, and Yuxue Yang[⊠]

School of Economics and Management, Jiangsu University of Science and Technology,
Zhenjiang 212100, China
yangyuxue1224@163.com

Abstract. In today's competitive app market, developers must provide a range of user-oriented features to improve app performance. This study extends the theory of optimal differentiation to the sharing economy domain to investigate whether there exists an optimal feature heterogeneity that makes apps perform at their highest. Based on the panel data of eight categories of app information in the sharing economy domain from September 2021 to September 2023, machine learning methods as well as fixed-effects models are used to explore the effect of app functional heterogeneity on app user activity. It is found that there is a significant "inverted U-shaped" relationship between functional heterogeneity and user activity, and we elaborate on the contribution of this finding to the theory of the sharing economy and the competitive strategies of sharing platforms. We also discuss implications for practice and make suggestions for future work.

Keywords: Sharing Economy Platform · Optimal Distinctiveness · Functional Heterogeneity

1 Introduction

In recent years, the sharing economy has had an increasingly important impact on human production, life, consumption, and other economic behaviors in various fields, such as transportation and travel, short-term rental of housing, labor, capital, skill sharing, etc. [1]. According to the sharing economy development report of China's National Information Centre, the transaction scale of the sharing economy market in 2022 will be about 3,832 billion yuan, with a year-on-year growth of about 3.9%, and the scale of China's sharing economy market continues to expand. From the perspective of the development of the sharing economy itself, the sharing economy has become an important economic model worldwide. Sharing platforms play a key role in this emerging field, as they provide a convenient interaction platform for both supply and demand, promoting the efficient use of resources and sustainable economic growth. However, with increasing competition, sharing platforms not only need to attract more users but also need to keep these users active to maintain the platform's ecological balance and long-term sustainable development.

© The Author(s), under exclusive license to Springer Nature Switzerland AG 2024
Y. P. Tu and M. Chi (Eds.): WHICEB 2024, LNBIP 516, pp. 411–422, 2024.
https://doi.org/10.1007/978-3-031-60260-3_34

The development process of a sharing economy platform can be divided into three stages: start-up, development, and maturity. In the first two stages of platform development, the main task of the platform is to attract as many users as possible to the platform, so that when the users reach a certain level, a network effect can be formed, laying the foundation for the formation of the platform's subsequent profit model. In the first two stages, enterprises often use a "burning money" strategy or differentiation strategy to attract users and promote the growth of the platform, such as Uber, DiDi, Airbnb and other platforms at the beginning of the high subsidies, a large number of marketing and other ways to capture the market, but the platform will suffer huge losses, long-term burning money strategy is not conducive to the sustainable development of the platform, the platform enters into a new phase of the platform. The sustainable development of the platform, after the platform enters the stable operation period, there is a stable user base, and the target is transferred from the user to the platform itself, we should pay attention to the platform's competitive strategy, profit model and other issues, such as DiDi will focus on technological innovation and business layout, to maximize the breadth of the platform's business development, and greatly improve the degree of differentiation of the platform, which makes it difficult for the competitors to copy and improves the user's Stickiness.

In past studies on the relationship between differentiation strategy and firm performance in traditional industries, most scholars believe that differentiation strategy is positively correlated with competitive advantage or performance [2–4]. However, a high degree of differentiation may be accompanied by some challenges and risks while bringing advantages, in addition to this, more and more studies focus on the curvilinear relationship between differentiation strategy and performance, and a large number of studies related to platform markets have explored how firms can achieve optimal uniqueness through behaviors such as narration and strategic positioning through optimal differentiation theory [5–9], but there are almost no studies that have applied optimal differentiation theory to the sharing economy domain. Optimal differentiation theory emphasizes that an optimal differentiation can be found to balance the tension between differentiation and consistency, i.e., to balance the competitive pressure and institutional pressure. At present, the sharing economy is booming and the market competition is fierce, sharing platforms need to continuously optimize their differentiation strategies to succeed in the market; at the same time, the compliance level of platform enterprises continues to improve, and compliance has become a new focus of competition, the governance rules and institutional norms continue to be perfected, law enforcement efforts are intensified, and the market order continues to be regulated. As a result, the sharing economy faces high competitive and institutional pressures, and the measure of the degree of differentiation is crucial to platform development.

Based on the above analysis, our research question is posed: *Is there an optimal platform functional heterogeneity that maximizes user activity?* To address this question, we develop a research model that explains how sharing economy platforms can improve user activity during stable operation periods. The research model is validated with a unique panel dataset of 4494 monthly observations collected from multiple sources of 188 sharing economy platforms in China.

2   Literature Review

The optimal differentiation theory originated from the study of individual identity and has been applied cross-disciplinary by researchers to scholars in the field of strategy. Based on social identity theory, Brewer emphasised how individuals can shape their uniqueness in the face of the pressure to conform to norms [10]. Further, Deephouse introduced the concept of strategic tradeoff, which creatively integrates the frameworks of competitive differentiation and institutional analysis of isomorphism, and for the first time introduced the concept of optimal differentiation into the field of strategy [11]. Specifically, what optimal differentiation needs to address is the tension between differentiation-consistency. Strategic management scholars emphasize that differentiated positioning provides firms with a competitive advantage because of reduced competitive pressures; in contrast, organizational scholars argue that differentiation leads to a lack of coherence and thus affects firm legitimacy. Optimal differentiation theory therefore stresses that an optimal level of differentiation can be found to balance this set of tensions, i.e. to balance competitive and institutional pressures.

A large number of studies on platform markets have also explored how firms can achieve optimal distinctiveness through narrative, strategic positioning, and other behaviors through optimal differentiation theory. Platforms often adopt "get big fast" strategies and differentiation strategies to facilitate platform growth, with differentiation strategies being an important way to achieve platform firms' distinctive positioning [12]. Snihur et al. [13] explored how disruptive business model innovators in ecosystems can achieve optimal differentiation through the tension between uniqueness narrative frameworks and leadership narrative frameworks. Tension between uniqueness narrative frames and leadership narrative frames to achieve optimal differentiation. Based on optimal differentiation theory, Song Lifeng et al. [14] explored how knowledge payment platforms can achieve optimal differentiation of business model groupings through differentiation and legitimacy dimensions. Taeuscher and Rothe [8] focused on positioning at the level of complementary portfolios based on previous research on platform competition and conceptualized strategic positioning uniqueness as the deviation of a platform's product portfolio from the market's average product mix by collecting information on competitive platforms' product mixes at large scale and by collecting information on competing platforms' product mixes. Portfolio, measured uniqueness by collecting data related to competing platforms in the massive open online course (MOOC) market, and found that platform uniqueness only has an impact on user growth at a specific legitimacy threshold, and that high-status complements have a compensatory mechanism for uniqueness.

3   Research Design

3.1   Data Collection

The dataset used in this study is iPhone application information publicly available in the iOS App Store in the Chinese market. When collecting data, the first step is to identify and filter app samples in the sharing economy field, and exclude apps that do not belong to the sharing economy category from the application classification. The final dataset includes 188 apps, and these apps are divided into 8 sub-categories according to their respective sharing economy fields: shared travel, shared accommodation, shared healthcare, freight delivery, Second-hand platforms, skills, knowledge education and online travel.

The data of this study includes application information of the iOS App Store from September 2021 to September 2023, capturing content such as application name, icon, description, rating, release date, user comments, and update logs. The monthly user activity of the app comes from Yiguan Qianfan, and the monthly download volume is from Qimai Database and Diandian Database, both of which are well-known data service providers, including monitoring and analyzing app performance in the iOS and Android app stores in the Chinese market.

3.2   Identification and Classification of Functions

In order to access the functionality of the app, this study performed text mining on the app's application description. Firstly, the app descriptions were subjected to clause and word segmentation using the pyltp toolset, followed by text pre-processing including tokenization, stop word removal and lexical tagging. Secondly, dependent syntactic analysis was performed to obtain the syntactic parse tree of the functional description statements, and functional candidate phrases were extracted using a text pattern-based approach. Finally, we select the $BERT_{Base}$ model for Chinese processing, fine-tune the model with token data to adjust the model parameters, and classify the functional candidate phrases into functional and non-functional descriptive phrases, and finally obtain the function set of the app. In order to ensure the comprehensiveness and accuracy of the app functions, the functions possessed by each app were manually observed to supplement and correct the obtained function set.

Subsequently, we classified these features into different categories to measure the heterogeneity of App features. App features are designed to attract customers. An initial assessment of the classification framework for the identified features revealed that the types of features of sharing apps have similarities with the types of features provided by e-commerce platforms, and thus the App features were categorised drawing on the coding process documented by Tan et al. Functionality categories were classified based on the customer service lifecycle (CSLC) model, with features focusing on sales incentives and price reductions (e.g., coupons, membership services, etc.) categorised as pricing-oriented features; features related to users' personal property (e.g., one-click alarms, trip sharing, etc.) categorised as security-related features; features related to users' viewing of specific content (e.g., detailed information, multiple images, etc.) categorised as product display-oriented functions; third-party payment and UnionPay payment functions provide users with diversified payment options, which are classified as payment-oriented functions; in the after-sales stage, functions such as feedback and complaints are classified as after-sales service functions; apps in different areas of the sharing economy platform provide different types of service content, which are categorised as core functions, value-added services, etc., as functions related to user experience Functions. To sum up, we classify the functions of apps into 6 categories, and Table 1 summarises the results of the 6 categories.

Table 1. APP Functions

Categories	Definitions
Payment-Oriented Functions	Provides online customers with diverse payment options in the acquisition stage of CSLC
Security-Related Functions	Functions related to user's personal and property
Product Presentation-Oriented Functions	Provides detailed product information to mitigate the lack of "touch and feel" in the e-marketplace
Pricing-Oriented Functions	Allows sellers to specify the degree of, and time period for, product discounts
After-Sales Service-Oriented Functions	Supports the customer along and after the sales process
User Experience-Related Functions	Provide core services, value-added services, and interactions with third parties

3.3 Variable Description

To measure app activity, we obtained App Monthly Active User Number (MAU) from the eView Chifan database, which indicates the number of unique users who have used the app at least once in a month. A higher MAU indicates that users have sustained interest and engagement in the app, which is crucial for building user stickiness and increasing user lifecycle value.

Functional heterogeneity refers to the extent to which the type of functionality an app has differs from industry norms[15]. It is measured by referring to the formula for calculating heterogeneity in the competitive action literature, which is as follows:

$$Heterogeneity_{it} = \sqrt{\frac{\left(f_{i1}-\bar{f}_1\right)^2+\left(f_{i2}-\bar{f}_2\right)^2+\left(f_{i3}-\bar{f}_3\right)^2+\left(f_{i4}-\bar{f}_4\right)^2+\left(f_{i5}-\bar{f}_5\right)^2+\left(f_{i6}-\bar{f}_6\right)^2}{6}} \tag{1}$$

The f_{ij} represents the number of functions in each function type j undertaken by App i in the past month, $i = 1, 2, 3, \ldots, 188, \bar{f}_j = \sum(f_{1j}, f_{2j}, \ldots, f_{188j})/188$ (where $j = 1, 2, 3, 4, 5, 6$). A high functional heterogeneity score indicates that the functions that an App deploys are very different from its rivals, while a low score denotes that the App's functions are similar to its rivals. Table 2 lists the major variables and their measures.

To rule out other possible explanations, we add several control variables that may also affect app activity. App downloads are directly related to the app's share of the user market, reflecting the number of users who use the app. Apps with high downloads typically have higher user activity. We use the natural logarithm of downloads (plus one) to reduce the skewness of this variable. App age refers to the number of months since the app was released. In order to control the quality of apps, a weighted average of user ratings from one to five stars given to apps in the App Store is used to obtain the App score. The greater the number of features an app has, the more it may satisfy diversified user needs to a certain extent, which in turn affects user activity. In addition, due to the

Table 2. Measurements of All Variables

Variables	Measurements
MAU	Number of independent users who have used the Application at least once within a month
Heterogeneity	$Heterogeneity_{it}=$ $$\sqrt{\frac{(f_{i1}-\bar{f}_1)^2+(f_{i2}-\bar{f}_2)^2+(f_{i3}-\bar{f}_3)^2+(f_{i4}-\bar{f}_4)^2+(f_{i5}-\bar{f}_5)^2+(f_{i6}-\bar{f}_6)^2}{6}}$$ f_{ij} represents the number of functions in each function type j undertaken by App i in the past month, i = 1, 2,...,188, $\bar{f}_j=\sum(f_{1j},f_{2j},\ldots,f_{188j})/188$ (where j = 1,2,3,4,5,6)
Download	Number of people downloading Apps per month
App age	Number of months after Application release
Number of functions	The number of features in the App
Epidemic situation	Observe whether the period of App data is in the period of the COVID-19 epidemic, and code it as 0 before the end of the epidemic and 1 after the end of the epidemic
App score	Weighted average of one to five-star ratings from users in the App Store for the App

special nature of the sharing economy, the supplying parties must have communication or get along with each other, which may be affected by the new crown epidemic, and thus the variable of whether the epidemic is over or not needs to be controlled.

3.4 Empirical Models

We developed a fixed-effects model (FE) to analyze the longitudinal observation dataset because the result of the Hausman test that we ran suggested that estimates of the FE are consistent, while the estimates of a random-effects model are not. We specified the following FE:

$$y_{it} = \beta_0 + \beta_1 H_{it} + \sum_{k=1}^{n} \beta_k C_{it} + +\sigma_i + \gamma_t + \varepsilon_{it} \tag{2}$$

where y_{it} represents the logarithm of dependent variable MAU for App i at time t; β_0, β_1, β_k denote the coefficients for all variables; H denotes heterogeneity, and C denotes other control variables, download, App age, number of functions, epidemic situation, and App score; σ_i and γ_t denote the unobservable individual and time effects of the model respectively; and ε_{it} is the error term. As download is very different from the independent variables in terms of means and standard deviations, log transformation is used to improve the model fit.

In order to further verify the "inverted U-shape" effect of app functional heterogeneity on the number of monthly active users, a quadratic term of functional heterogeneity is introduced on the basis of Eq. (3):

$$y_{it} = \beta_0 + \beta_1 H_{it} + \beta_2 H_{it}^2 + \sum_{k=1}^{n} \beta_k C_{it} + + \sigma_i + \gamma_t + \varepsilon_{it} \tag{3}$$

where H^2 denotes the quadratic term of functional heterogeneity, and β_2 is the coefficient to be estimated.

4 Analysis and Results

4.1 Base Regression Results

In order to investigate the "inverted U-shape" effect of app functional heterogeneity on the number of monthly active users of apps, regression estimation based on Eq. (2) and Eq. (3) was carried out by using Stata 18.0 software, respectively. We conducted descriptive statistics and binary correlation analysis on key variables, and the results show that the highest correlation coefficient is 0.585, which is below the critical threshold of 0.7. In addition, the data were tested for multicollinearity using Variance Inflation Factor (VIF) and the highest Variance Inflation Factor was 1.21, which is well below the threshold of 10 (see Table 3), indicating that there is no problem of multicollinearity between the variables.

The results of the FE regressions with robust standard errors for all variables are given in Table 4. Model 1 is the base model for investigating the effect of control variables on the number of monthly active users, where the control variables work to a greater extent in the expected way. For example, the number of monthly active users of an app increases when the number of downloads of the app increases and when the number of features of the app increases. Model 2 introduces the independent variable functional heterogeneity and Model 3 introduces the square of functional heterogeneity.

Model 2 and model 3 are used to verify whether there is an "inverted U-shaped" relationship between app functional heterogeneity and the number of monthly active users of an app. From the regression results of the model, it can be observed that when the quadratic term of functional heterogeneity is not introduced, the main effect of heterogeneity is positive and significant (b = 0.031, SE = 0.015, p < 0.001). When the quadratic term of functional heterogeneity is introduced, the heterogeneity is significantly positive at the 1% level (b = 0.193, SE = 0.031, p < 0.001), and the squared coefficient of heterogeneity is negative and significant (b = - 0.030, SE = 0.005, p < 0.001), which suggests that there is a significant "inverted U-shape" between the functional heterogeneity of the app and the number of monthly active users of the app. This indicates that there is a significant "inverted U-shaped" relationship between the functional heterogeneity of apps and the number of monthly active users of apps. After calculation, the inflection point value of functional heterogeneity is 3.25301, that is, when the functional heterogeneity of App is less than 3.25301, there is a promotion effect of heterogeneity on MAU; when the functional heterogeneity of App is greater than 3.25301, the effect of heterogeneity on MAU changes from promotion to inhibition. The "inverted U-shaped" curve of functional heterogeneity and MAU is shown in Fig. 1.

Table 3. VIF Values

Variables	VIF	1/VIF
Number of functions	1.21	0.8235164
App age	1.18	0.845458
Download	1.13	0.881632
App score	1.08	0.924089
Epidemic situation	1.04	0.958645
Mean VIF	1.12	

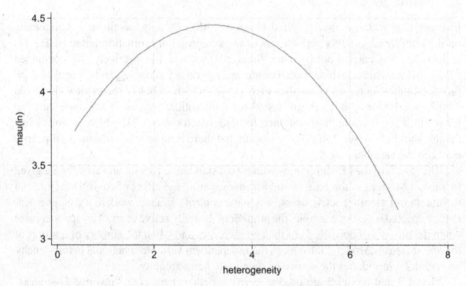

Fig. 1. Functional heterogeneity and the inverted U-shaped curve of MAU

Table 4. Results of Fixed-Effects Model with Robust Standard Errors

	Model1	Model2	Model3
Heterogeneity		0.031** (0.015)	0.193*** (0.031)
Heterogeneity^2			−0.030*** (0.005)
Download(ln)	0.175*** (0.025)	0.174*** (0.010)	0.176*** (0.009)

(continued)

Table 4. (*continued*)

	Model1	Model2	Model3
App age	0.044**	0.061**	0.063**
	(0.020)	(0.022)	(0.024)
Number of functions	0.009**	0.009**	0.009**
	(0.004)	(0.004)	(0.009)
Epidemic situation	−1.034**	−1.419**	−0.989**
	(0.488)	(0.524)	(0.071)
App score	0.002	0.001	0.002
	(0.014)	(0.014)	(0.014)
Constant	2.699***	2.547***	2.091***
	(0.167)	(0.182)	(0.197)
F test	1192.07***	1187.42***	1191.50***
R-square	0.9836	0.9836	0.9837
R-square Change	–	0	0.0001

Notes: The dependent variable is Ln(MAU); Number of observations = 4494; Number of App = 188; Robust Standard Errors in parentheses. * $p < 0.1$, ** $p < 0.05$, *** $p < 0.001$

Table 5. Results of U-test

	Lower bound	Upper bound
Interval	0.3636849	7.410749
Slope	0.1739892	-0.2503705
t-value	5.678284	-6.902526
P > |t|	0.000	0.000

4.2 Non-linear Relationship Test

In the previous section, we proved the "inverted U-shaped" nonlinear relationship between functional heterogeneity and app user activity by introducing the quadratic term of functional heterogeneity and simply calculated the inflection point value according to the characteristics of the quadratic equation. In order to verify the existence of the inflection point and the robustness of the nonlinear relationship, we do the Utest test and regress the heterogeneity primary and secondary terms, and the regression estimation results are shown in Table 5. We observe that at the lowest point of heterogeneity (0.3636849), the slope is positive and significant ($b = 0.174$, $p < 0.001$), and at the highest point of heterogeneity (7.41079), the slope is negative and significant ($b = -0.25$, $p < 0.001$). In addition, the extreme point of heterogeneity corresponding to the highest user activity was 3.25301, with a 95% confidence interval between 2.7510827 and 3.7077109, and the value of the extreme point fell within this range. Therefore, this further validates the robustness of the "inverted U-shaped" relationship between functional heterogeneity and app user activity.

5 Discussion

5.1 Conclusion

This study focuses on the impact of app feature heterogeneity on user activity. The current sharing economy market in China is booming, and platforms face tense competition when iterating features. On the one hand, it is necessary to seek consistency with other platforms in the same category to reduce users' learning costs, make it easier for users to accept and use new features, and reduce the risks caused by excessive innovation; on the other hand, to avoid competitive pressures and attract new users, the features should be different from those of apps in the same category. How companies manage these tensions while pursuing performance excellence is an ongoing debate in traditional industries. The purpose of this study is to further explore the generality of the optimal distinction by examining the relationship between functional heterogeneity and user activity of apps. Our study confirms an "inverted U-shaped" relationship between the functional heterogeneity of apps and app user activity, suggesting that there exists an optimal functional heterogeneity that results in apps with the highest user activity, which is consistent with our expectations and provides evidence for our previously proposed theory.

5.2 Implications

Based on the optimal differentiation theory, this study investigates the heterogeneity of sharing platforms, which can enrich the theories of sharing economy theory and sharing platform competition strategy, combine the theoretical study of sharing economy with the actual economic situation, and put forward the thinking and suggestions of sharing economy platforms, which is of great significance at the theoretical level and the practical level.

Our work makes several major theoretical contributions. First, our study contributes to the sharing economy literature by advancing scholarly understanding of the role of functional heterogeneity in improving user activity from an optimal distinctiveness perspective. Second, our study contributes to optimal distinctiveness by extending it to the sharing economy context. Prior distinctive research has focused on traditional industries. This extension contributes to the optimal distinctiveness by treating the functional characteristics of Apps as objects of study and showing to what extent heterogeneity optimally affects user activity. Third, this study contributes to the literature on user behavior by exploring the relationship between functional heterogeneity and user activity, and by providing a deeper understanding of users' behavioral patterns and decision-making processes on sharing economy platforms. Finally, our work broadens the scope of the extant operation management literature on the sharing economy and contributes to our understanding of how sharing economy platforms increase user activity during the smooth operation period, a crucial aspect to maintaining the long-term sustainability of the platform.

On a practical level, understanding the different needs of users for features can lead platforms to customize the user experience and provide more personalized services, thus increasing user retention and loyalty; by understanding how different users react to platform heterogeneity, platforms can better segment and position themselves in the market. This helps to identify target user groups and develop more precise marketing strategies; it can support the business strategies of sharing economy platforms, which can adjust their functions according to user needs, optimize user experience, increase user activity, and ultimately promote business growth.

5.3 Limitations and Future Research

Like all studies, ours has limitations. Firstly, the app data we collected was from the iOS App Store, which only focuses on the performance of apps in the Apple App Store and does not take into account the context of other platforms such as Google Play; future research could explore how our results would be different under the premise of covering multiple app shops. Second, in addition to the functionality that an app has, factors such as the interface characteristics of the app such as the depth of the interface hierarchy can have an impact on the usability of the app, which in turn may play a role in user activity, and future research should consider adding this variable. Third, our results suggest that a significant amount of App functional heterogeneity is not optimal, and given the motivation for making optimal choices, this result deserves further consideration, and future research could explain this result.

References

1. Barta, K., Neff, G.: Technologies for sharing: lessons from quantified self about the political economy of platforms. Inf. Commun. Soc. **19**(4), 518–531 (2016)
2. Chen, Q., Eriksson, T., Giustiniano, L.: Leading well pays off: mediating effects and multigroup analysis of strategic performance. Manag. Decis. **55**(2), 400–412 (2017)
3. González-Benito, J., Suárez-González, I.: A study of the role played by manufacturing strategic objectives and capabilities in understanding the relationship between Porter's generic strategies and business performance. Br. J. Manag. **21**(4), 1027–1043 (2010)
4. Leitner, K.-H., Güldenberg, S.: Generic strategies and firm performance in SMEs: a longitudinal study of Austrian SMEs. Small Bus. Econ. **35**, 169–189 (2010)
5. Barlow, M.A., Verhaal, J.C., Angus, R.W.: Optimal distinctiveness, strategic categorization, and product market entry on the Google Play app platform. Strat. Manag. J. **40**(8), 1219–1242 (2019)
6. Khanagha, S., et al.: Mutualism and the dynamics of new platform creation: a study of cisco and fog computing. Strateg. Manag. J. **43**(3), 476–506 (2022)
7. Taeuscher, K., Bouncken, R., Pesch, R.: Gaining legitimacy by being different: optimal distinctiveness in crowdfunding platforms. Acad. Manag. J. **64**(1), 149–179 (2021)
8. Taeuscher, K., Rothe, H.: Optimal distinctiveness in platform markets: leveraging complementors as legitimacy buffers. Strateg. Manag. J. **42**(2), 435–461 (2021)
9. van Angeren, J., et al.: Optimal distinctiveness across revenue models: performance effects of differentiation of paid and free products in a mobile app market. Strateg. Manag. J. **43**(10), 2066–2100 (2022)

10. Brewer, M.B.: The social self: on being the same and different at the same time. Pers. Soc. Psychol. Bull. **17**(5), 475–482 (1991)
11. Deephouse, D.L.: To be different, or to be the same? It's a question (and theory) of strategic balance. Strateg. Manag. J. **20**(2), 147–166 (1999)
12. Cennamo, C., Santalo, J.: Platform competition: strategic trade-offs in platform markets. Strateg. Manag. J. **34**(11), 1331–1350 (2013)
13. Sinha, N., Singh, N.: Revisiting expectation confirmation model to measure the effectiveness of multichannel bank services for elderly consumers. Int. J. Emerg. Mark. (2022)
14. Song, L., Yang, Z, Lu, Y.: Optimal differentiation between institutional entrepreneurship and differentiated competition in the field of weak legitimacy: a multi-case study based on knowledge payment Manage comments. **32**(05), 321–336 (2020). (in Chinese)
15. Li, H., et al.: Platform-based function repertoire, reputation, and sales performance of e-marketplace sellers. MIS Q. **43**(1), 207–236 (2019)

How Digital Transformation Influences Firm Performance: A Configurational Perspective

Yuqin Liang and Yiwei Gong[✉]

School of Information Management, Wuhan University, Wuhan 430072, China
yiweigong@whu.edu.cn

Abstract. In the new era of the digital economy, traditional manufacturing firms are stepping up their digital transformation to remain competitive. Digital transformation might impact firm performance, resulting in a need to investigate the complex relationships between firm performance and various conditions in digital transformation. Based on resource orchestration theory (ROT), this study provided a configurational analysis of the multiple paths of organizational capability (i.e., innovation capability), organizational resources (i.e., relational resources and regional resources), and organizational characteristics (i.e., firm size and digital transformation strategy) to achieve high firm performance using a mix of fuzzy-set Qualitative Comparative Analysis (fsQCA) and Necessary Conditions Analysis (NCA) methodologies. Using data from listed companies in China's manufacturing industry, the findings identify six configurations that generate high firm performance, demonstrating the diversity in the mechanisms achieving high firm performance in Chinese-listed manufacturing firms, which can guide the implementation of digital transformation in the manufacturing industry.

Keywords: Digital transformation · Firm performance · Fuzzy-set Qualitative Comparative Analysis (fsQCA) · Necessary Condition Analysis (NCA)

1 Introduction

The new era of the digital economy is bound up with digital technologies (e.g., artificial intelligence, big data, and cloud computing). To remain competitive in such an environment, traditional manufacturing firms are stepping up their digital transformation to radically respond to the disruptive potential of digital technology demands. Digital transformation refers to a process that aims to improve an entity by triggering significant changes to its properties including its business models, organizational structure, and business processes [1]. Despite new opportunities for product and service innovation, digital transformation is frequently perceived as a threat to firms' well-established business operations, consequently influencing firm performance. While more and more traditional manufacturing firms have started their digital transformation most of them only have a diffuse understanding about the nature and impact of digital transformation, resulting in challenges to sustain their performance during transformation. Therefore, investigating the relationship between digital transformation and firm performance is of great significance for traditional manufacturing firms to succeed in their digital transformation.

The extant literature on the relationship between digital transformation and firm performance is dominated by linear regression analysis [2, 3], which outputs 'one best solution' with multiple factors. However, it's difficult for the 'one best solution' to cover kinds of success stories in reality, because firms often achieve high performance in several pathways. Arguably, influencing factors do not operate independently; rather, they work in combination with others to collectively contribute to the overall performance of firms. However, few studies have examined how these influencing factors in combination lead to improvements in firm performance. To address the above gap, this study investigates the influencing factors and their configurations to reveal the complex relationship between digital transformation and firm performance. It seeks to answer the research question: Which configurations of factors lead to the achievement of high firm performance in digital transformation? This study employs fuzzy-set Qualitative Comparative Analysis (fsQCA) and Necessary Conditions Analysis (NCA) to comprehensively analyze data from Chinese-listed manufacturing firms. The findings identify six strategic paths to achieve high firm performance from three dimensions (i.e., capability, resources, and characteristics), which can guide the implementation of digital transformation in the manufacturing industry and provide support for governments to formulate policies.

2   Theoretical Background and Research Framework

The relationship between digital transformation and firm performance involves various factors, such as innovation capability [4], cooperative partners [5], and digital transformation strategy [6]. These factors and their interrelationships reflect the inherent complexity associated with explaining digital transformation and performance outcomes, prompting a need for a suitable theoretical framework.

2.1   Resource Orchestration Theory

Derived from the Resource-based View, the resource orchestration theory (ROT) argues that the causal complexity of firm performance is relative to not only the firm's capabilities and resources, but also the configuration of organizational capabilities, resources, and managerial decisions in response to the internal and external environments [7]. ROT can be an excellent foothold for understanding the configuration of resources and other factors. For example, the superior operational performance outcomes can be attributed to lean with inter-firm resources, as well as similarly agility with idiosyncratic resources [8]. Based on previous studies, this study adopts a configurational perspective to examine the complex relationship between firm performance and various conditions, namely, organizational capability (i.e., Innovation capability), organizational resources (i.e., relational resources and regional resources), and organizational characteristics (i.e., firm age and digital transformation strategy).

2.2 Capability

Innovation capability can be characterized as the ability to create or absorb new knowledge for generating new processes, products, and services [9]. Innovation capability is the point to building and maintaining a competitive advantage in a digital transformation environment. As an essential component of innovation capacity, research and development (R&D) can provide cost-effective technology to maximize resource utilization, which reduces costs, designs differentiated products or services, and optimizes business processes [10], thereby enhance firm performance. R&D indicators primarily comprise R&D expenditures and R&D employees, which are the variables of innovation capability in this study.

2.3 Resources

This study involves two types of firms' organizational resources, namely relational resources and regional resources. Relational resources refer to inter-organizational relationships between a firm and its external partners who specialize in the firm's digital transformation. The relationships with partners aim to leverage the digital technology capabilities of partners to obtain high benefits, such as sharing R&D costs to diminish risks, reducing repetitive R&D activities, and obtaining complementary resources [11]. Regional resources correlate with the degree of regional digitization. Regional resources serve as the technological foundation and driving force behind firms' digital transformation [12]. Consequently, regional resources can provide local firms with basic digital equipment and service support, accelerating the pace of firms' digital transformation.

2.4 Characteristics

In a digital environment, organizational characteristics include two aspects, namely firm age and digital transformation strategy. Firm age has been widely acknowledged as an essential determinant for converting organizational resources into firm performance [13]. In general, the effects of age might lead to organizational rigidity and routinization. Digital transformation strategy is important for firms to help them allocate resources and competence in the face of digital challenges. A digital transformation strategy is a prerequisite for high firm performance [6].

2.5 Research Framework

On the above three dimensions, this study identifies six antecedent variables, namely R&D expenditures, R&D employees, relational resources, regional resources, firm age, and digital transformation strategy. A theoretical framework for this study was developed based on the ROT (see Fig. 1).

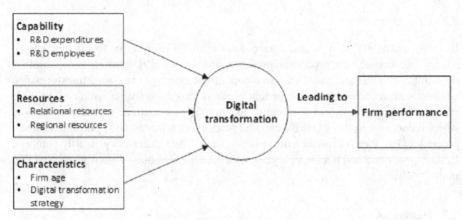

Fig. 1. Theoretical framework.

3 Methods

3.1 FsQCA Combined with NCA

Qualitative comparative analysis (QCA) conducts sufficient and necessary research on causality based on Set Theory and has the characteristics of both qualitative and quantitative analysis [14]. There are three types of QCA, namely csQCA, fsQCA, and mvQCA. Compared with the other two, fsQCA is more advantageous in terms of solving the degree and affiliation problem and focusing on individual cases to explain causality in detail. Therefore, this article chooses fsQCA as the research method.

NCA is a novel method of analyzing complex causality. Different from QCA, it can identify the necessary conditions from result variables, and quantify the effect size and bottleneck level of the necessary conditions [15]. As a result, NCA can be a complementary tool for QCA necessity analysis. Combining NCA and fsQCA can analyze the necessary and sufficient complex causal relationships fully, contributing to more robust conclusions.

3.2 Sample and Data Collection

This study takes the relevant data of Chinese manufacturing firms in 2022 as the research sample, which are obtained from the CSMAR database, firms' annual reports, firms' official websites, and firms' WeChat official accounts. The data excludes the following three types of firms: (1) financial-related firms, (2) ST and *ST firms, and (3) firms with mass abnormal data as well as missing relevant data. Finally, this article obtains a sample set containing 160 manufacturing firms.

3.3 Measures

Firm Performance. This is the outcome variable in this study. Given the large number of indicators reflecting the performance of firms, this study selects 14 financial indicators (see Table 1) in five aspects, including firm development ability, profitability, operating ability, solvency, and cash ability, utilizing the entropy value method to construct comprehensive indicators reflecting the firm performance.

Table 1. Financial indicators for the firm performance.

Dimension	Indicators	Calculation method
Development capacity	Revenue growth rate	(Current year's operating income - Last year's operating income) / Last year's operating income
	Total assets growth rate	(Current year's total assets - Last year's total assets) / Last year's total assets
	Operating profit growth rate	(Current year's operating profit - Last year's operating profit) / Last year's operating profit
Profitability	Return on net assets	Net profit / Owners' equity (average of beginning and end of year)
	Return on total assets	Net profit / Total assets (average of beginning and end of year)
	Operating profit ratio	Operating Profit / Operating Income
Operating capacity	Total assets turnover ratio	Operating Income / Total Assets (average of beginning and end of year)
	Current assets Turnover ratio	Operating Income / Current Assets (average of beginning and end of year)
	Accounts receivable turnover ratio	Operating income / Accounts receivable (average of beginning and end of year)
Solvency	Current ratio	Current assets / Current liabilities
	Quick ratio	Quick assets / Current liabilities
	Gearing ratio	Total Assets / Current Liabilities
Cash Capacity	Net cash from operations	Net cash flow from operations / Operating income
	Total cash recovery ratio	Net cash flow from operations / Total assets (average of beginning and end of year)

Innovation Capability. A firm's Innovation capability is measured by two R&D indicators: the ratio of R&D expenditures to operating revenues and the ratio of the number of R&D employees. The bigger the firms R&D indicators, the stronger its innovation capability.

Relational Resources. It indicates whether a firm cooperates with other firms to promote its digital transformation process. The study obtained relevant cooperation information from multiple sources, using 1 to mean that the firm has cooperated with others in its digital transformation process, and 0 to mean no cooperation.

Regional Resources. The higher the regional digitization level, the more regional resources the firm has for digital transformation. Referring to Gu ct al. [16], combined with the actual situation, this study constructed a regional digitization level evaluation system that includes two levels of indicators, namely, basic capabilities, and core capabilities. The basic capabilities indicators measure the infrastructure capacity and the degree of data usage, mainly reflecting the digital infrastructure of the region. Core capabilities measure the digitalization capacity of firms, information business revenue, investment in innovation platforms, and the level of development of the information society, reflecting the region's technological capacity, technological environment, and social environment for digital transformation. This study uses again the entropy weight method to calculate the regional digitization level.

Firm Age. It is measured as the number of years since the firm establishment.

Digital Transformation Strategy. It is related to the firms digital transformation index. To obtain this data we first used Python software to conduct textual analysis on the annual reports of the manufacturing firms and identified the keywords related to digital transformation. Then, we summed up the number of occurrences of each keyword to create the total number of occurrences in every annual report of manufacturing firms. In addition, this study denoted the digital transformation index as the natural logarithm of 1 plus the total number of occurrences.

3.4 Calibration

Before fsQCA and QCA, it is necessary to convert the variables to set concepts, in other words, to fuzzy set variables of 0–1. To ensure the objective accuracy of the calibration process, this study adopted the direct calibration method and used the 95%, 50%, and 5% quantiles of each variable as anchor points, which are set as "fully in", "cross-over", and "fully out" (see Table 2). Following established practices, add a small constant (0.001) for all exact 0.5 membership scores to recalibrate [17].

Table 2. Variable calibration.

Set	Fully out	Cross-over	Fully in
Firm performance	0.286346027	0.375058204	0.489408359
R&D expenditures	2.966	5.03	12.151
R&D employees	7.727	15.76	35.631
Relational resources	0	0	1
Regional resources	0.207289051	0.507968304	0.798575997
Firm age	14	21	30
Digital transformation strategy	1.322219295	1.812913357	2.41532911

4 Empirical Results

4.1 Necessary

Before exploring the complex paths toward high performance driven by multiple factors, it is important to test the consistency of every antecedent condition. If the consistency of an antecedent condition is over 0.9, it means that this condition is the necessary condition for the outcome [18]. This study conducted a necessity test on the individual antecedent conditions of achieving high firm performance and low firm performance (see Table 3). The results show that the consistency of all single antecedent conditions are less than 0.9, indicating that there is no necessary condition for generating high or low firm performance.

Table 3. The necessity test of a single condition for high firm performance in fsQCA.

Sets of conditions	high firm performance		low firm performance	
	Consistency	Coverage	Consistency	Coverage
R&D expenditures	0.607929	0.633419	0.642002	0.690275
~R&D expenditures	0.702739	0.655439	0.659054	0.634318
R&D employees	0.664426	0.655439	0.660838	0.67271
~R&D employees	0.668222	0.65627	0.661519	0.670428
Relational resources	0.350283	0.498364	0.341676	0.501636
~Relational resources	0.649717	0.488856	0.658324	0.511144
Regional resources	0.736643	0.693784	0.567586	0.551628
~Regional resources	0.523929	0.540051	0.684924	0.728538
Firm age	0.642752	0.618487	0.680194	0.67541

(continued)

Table 3. (*continued*)

Sets of conditions	high firm performance		low firm performance	
	Consistency	Coverage	Consistency	Coverage
~Firm age	0.662675	0.667555	0.615785	0.640122
Digital transformation strategy	0.630931	0.627714	0.671723	0.689633
~Digital transformation strategy	0.688042	0.670085	0.637382	0.640563

In addition, the NCA method is used for necessity testing and bottleneck-level analysis. Among the necessary conditions, two conditions had to be fulfilled at the same time: the effect size should be more than the threshold value($d > 0.1$) and the Monte Carlo simulation replacement test should show that the effect size is significant ($P < 0.05$) [15]. The results (see Table 4) show that only the regional resources condition has an effect size greater than 0.1 in the CR measure, but its P-value is not less than 0.05, which cannot be considered a necessary condition for high firm performance; while the other five conditions are all insignificant. Therefore, there is no necessary condition for high firm performance, which is consistent with the fsQCA results above.

Table 4. Results of necessary condition analysis.

Sets of conditions	Method	Scope	Celling	Accuracy (%)	Effect size (d)	P value
R&D expenditures	CR	0.98	0.074	89.30%	0.075	0.197
	CE	0.98	0.018	100%	0.018	0.439
R&D employees	CR	0.98	0.008	98.70%	0.008	0.78
	CE	0.98	0.006	100%	0.007	0.851
Relational resources	CR	1.00	0.005	100%	0.005	0.352
	CE	1.00	0.01	100%	0.01	0.352
Regional resources	CR	0.93	0.125	91.80%	0.135	0.061
	CE	0.93	0.031	100%	0.033	0.093
Firm age	CR	0.99	0.01	97.50%	0.011	0.7
	CE	0.99	0.01	100%	0.01	0.739
Digital transformation strategy	CR	0.98	0.018	98.10%	0.019	0.611
	CE	0.98	0.008	100%	0.008	0.862

The next is the CR estimation method for bottleneck-level analysis in NCA (see Table 5). It shows that when the level of firm performance is below 40%, no antecedent condition is the necessary condition. Moreover, to achieve 100% firm performance of manufacturing firms, it needs at least 55.5% level of R&D expenditures, at least 33.4% level of R&D employees, at least 23.9% level of digital transformation strategy, at least 9% level of firm age, and at least 47.6% level of Regional resources.

Table 5. Results of bottleneck-level analysis under the NCA method

Firm performance/%	R&D expenditures	R&D employees	Relational resources	Regional resources	Firm age	Digital transformation strategy
0	NN	NN	NN	NN	NN	NN
10	NN	NN	NN	NN	NN	NN
20	NN	NN	NN	NN	NN	NN
30	NN	NN	NN	NN	NN	NN
40	NN	NN	NN	NN	NN	NN
50	NN	NN	NN	5.6	NN	NN
60	NN	NN	NN	14	NN	NN
70	NN	NN	NN	22.4	NN	NN
80	14.5	NN	NN	30.8	1.3	NN
90	35	NN	NN	39.2	5.2	8.7
100	55.5	33.4	NA	47.6	9	23.9

4.2 Configuration Analysis

After the aforementioned data calibration and necessity analysis, this study sets the minimum case threshold to 1, the consistency threshold to 0.8, and the PRI consistency threshold to 0.5 [19]. The results of fsQCA software show three solutions, namely a complex solution, a minimalist solution, and an intermediate solution. In QCA research, intermediate solutions supplemented by the the minimalist solutionS are often chosen for the interpretation of configuration analysis results. The fsQCA analysis results (see Table 6) adopt the symbolic representation of Ragin and Fiss (i.e., the Fiss configuration diagram) [18].

The results show that there are six paths promoting the high performance of manufacturing firms, and the consistency of the six paths is higher than the commonly accepted consistency threshold of 0.8. The overall solution coverage is 0.588937 and the solution consistency is 0.845671, indicating that the six configurations of high firm performance have an explanatory power of 84.56% and can explain 58.89% of the digital-transformation firm cases. The regional resources factor presents as the core condition of all solutions for firm performance, so to achieve high firm performance, getting more regional resources is necessary.

In S1, firm performance is promoted by fully utilizing R&D employees and regional resources under a high digital transformation strategy. With insufficient R&D expenditures for digital innovation, firms can focus on digital transformation, let R&D employees conduct innovative activities, and utilize regional digital resources for high firm

Table 6. Configuration analysis results.

Configuration	S1	S2	S3	S4	S5	S6
R&D expenditures	⊗		⊗	●		
R&D employees	●	●		●	⊗	⊗
Relational resources			⊗	⊗	●	●
Regional resources	●	●	●	●	●	●
Firm age		⊗	⊗			●
Digital transformation strategy	●	●	●	⊗	⊗	
Raw coverage	0.340217	0.349743	0.19555	0.19851	0.160197	0.160492
Unique coverage	0.0285069	0.0514864	0.029026	0.0499433	0.0368822	0.0186726
Consistency	0.89679	0.860545	0.880599	0.855968	0.8894	0.943894
Overall solution consistency	0.588937					
Overall solution coverage	0.845671					

● represents that the core condition is present, ⊗ represents that the core condition is absent, ● represents that the edge condition is present, and ⊗ represents that the edge condition is absent. A space indicates that the condition can or cannot exist. S means "Solution".

performance. For example, with only 4.39% of the ratio of R&D expenditures, Guangdong Shenling Environmental Systems Co., Lt, forms its digital factory model at an early stage. With the efforts of the company's employees, its digitalization construction has achieved significant results, forming a digital application of the whole process from customer demand to product design, process, manufacturing, testing, logistics, and delivery.

S2 and S3 highlight the influence of low firm age, high regional resources, and high digital transformation strategy on high firm performance. S2 and S3 have the same core conditions, while S2 has high R&D employees as the auxiliary condition but S3 has low R&D expenditures and low relational resources as the auxiliary condition. Compared to mature firms, emerging firms with low firm age usually do not have enough capital, people, technology, and relationships, less able to win in the marketplace and achieve high performance. Therefore, emerging firms pay more attention to digital transformation and take advantage of regional resources to reduce the costs of digital transformation, then have high firm performance. Like Yizumi Holdings Co., Ltd. Founded in 2002, it has a third factory with the goal of building a "smart factory", which surely significantly enhances the firm's core competitive advantages.

S4 fosters higher firm performance through innovative capability and regional resources. Even if a firm has a weak digital transformation strategy and is not partnering with other companies for digital transformation, its sufficient R&D funding, R&D staff, and regional resources are enough for the firm to get high performance. For example, since 2020, Shenzhen United Winners Laser Co., Ltd. Has spared no effort in the construction of intelligent manufacturing. The company specifically set up an intelligent software research and development center to coordinate the construction of intelligent manufacturing, and with the demand of each department as the guide, data as the core, focusing on research and development, manufacturing, marketing, management, and supply chain and other areas to develop a clear intelligent manufacturing construction planning and intelligent manufacturing implementation goals and paths.

S5 and S6 demonstrate that firms with enough relational and regional resources will have higher performance. This is a group of firms that, despite having insufficient R&D and innovation staff, can still achieve high business performance by relying on sufficient partnership resources and regional digital resources. For example, Zhejiang Windey Co., Ltd, cooperates with a firm named sangfor, takes advantage of digitization resources in Zhejiang, builds a digital operation and management platform for the whole lifecycle of wind power, and pushes forward the firm's leapfrog development from informatization to digitization and then to intelligentization.

4.3 Robustness Test

To verify the robustness of the fsQCA result, this study chooses varying frequency and consistency thresholds to test the robustness of the configurations that produce high firm performance. When the case frequency threshold increases from 1 to 2 or the PRI consistency is increased from 0.5 to 0.6, the solutions are the subset of the present configurations. The above robustness tests show that the results are resilient.

5 Discussion

Based on ROT, this study conducted a configurational analysis of the multifarious paths of organizational capability (i.e., innovation capability), organizational resources (i.e., relational resources and regional resources), and organizational characteristics (i.e., firm size and digital transformation strategy) to promote high firm performance using a mix of fsQCA and NCA methods. The findings reveal that improving regional resources is critical for realizing high firm performance. This study identified six configurations that generate high firm performance, demonstrating the diversity in the mechanisms for achieving high firm performance.

5.1 Implications

This article makes several contributions to the research stream on firm performance. First, many previous studies have explored the effect of critical factors on firm performance.

However, this study contradicts the fact that achieving firm performance requires the interaction of multiple factors. This study identified six equivalent pathways to boost firm performance. The six solutions show how a combination of organizational capability, resources, and characteristics can achieve high firm performance, helping us understand the mechanisms for achieving high firm performance.

Second, this study provides practical implementation route for manufacturing firms that aim to high firm performance via digital transformation. According to their characteristics, firms can then utilize their capabilities and invest their resources into the configurations that best suit them to achieve high firm performance. First of all, firms must leverage regional digital resources as much as possible. In addition, firms with Insufficient funding for R&D and innovation can focus on digital transformation strategies and encourage employees to innovate and reform (S1). Emerging firms should also focus on digital transformation as their growth strategy (S2 and S3). Firms with adequate funding and staffing hold a great advantage in digital transformation by themselves and achieving high performance (S4). Otherwise, firms can achieve high performance by partnering with other digital service providers (S5 and S6).

Third, this article also provides practical implications for governments that cultivate local firms to achieve high performance through digital transformation. This study shows that regional resources are the core condition of all solutions for high firm performance, which requires governments to promote the digital economy and business environment to create resources for firms' digital transformation. For example, governments can increase investment in digital infrastructure, introduce relevant digitization guidelines and policies to encourage enterprises to undergo digital transformation.

5.2 Limitations and Future Research

Two limitations in this study should be addressed in future research. On the one hand, this study is based on static data. However, as the capability, resources, and characteristics of any firm do not remain constant, firm performance may vary. Future studies could make use of time series data and dynamic QCA methods. On the other hand, other elements also influence firm performance, and variables such as managers' characteristics, firm type, and market competition can be added to broaden the future research.

Acknowledgement. This research was supported by the National Natural Science Foundation of China under Grant 72174150.

References

1. Vial, G.: Understanding digital transformation: a review and a research agenda. J. Strateg. Inf. Syst. **28**(2), 118–144 (2019)
2. Zhai, H., Yang, M., Chan, K.C.: Does digital transformation enhance a firm's performance? evidence from China. Technol. Soc. **68**, 101841 (2022)
3. Kristoffersen, E., et al.: The effects of business analytics capability on circular economy implementation, resource orchestration capability, and firm performance. Int. J. Prod. Econ. **239**, 108205 (2021)

4. Zhang, Y., et al.: The impact of digital transformation of manufacturing on corporate performance—the mediating effect of business model innovation and the moderating effect of innovation capability. Res. Int. Bus. Finan. **64**, 101890 (2023)
5. Imran, F., et al.: Digital transformation of industrial organizations: toward an integrated framework. J. Chang. Manag. **21**(4), 451–479 (2021)
6. Yu, J., Moon, T.: Impact of digital strategic orientation on organizational performance through digital competence. Sustainability **13**(17), 9766 (2021)
7. Kauppila, O.-P.: Alliance management capability and firm performance: using resource-based theory to look inside the process black box. Long Range Plan. **48**(3), 151–167 (2015)
8. Iyer, K.N.S., Srivastava, P., Srinivasan, M.: Symbiotic association of resources and market-facing capabilities in supply chains as determinants of performance: a resource orchestration perspective. Eur. J. Mark. **57**(11), 2893–2917 (2023)
9. Lawson, B., Samson, D.: Developing innovation capability in organisations: a dynamic capabilities approach. Int. J. Innov. Manag. **03**(5), 377–400 (2001)
10. Peng, J., Quan, J., Qin, Q.: R&D investment, intellectual capital, organizational learning, and firm performance: a study of Chinese software companies. Total Qual. Manag. Bus. Excell. **34**(9–10), 1196–1216 (2022)
11. Lei, H., et al.: Enterprise digitalization, employee digital literacy and R&D cooperation: the moderating role of organizational inertia. Chin. Manag. Stud. **18**, 479–505 (2023)
12. Li, S., et al.: Exploring the effect of digital transformation on Firms innovation performance. J. Innov. Knowl. **8**(1), 100317 (2023)
13. Coad, A., et al.: Firm age and performance. J. Evol. Econ. **28**(1), 1–11 (2017)
14. Fiss, P.C.: A set-theoretic approach to organizational configurations. Acad. Manag. Rev. **4**(32), 1180–1198 (2007)
15. Dul, J., van der Laan, E., Kuik, R.: A statistical significance test for necessary condition analysis. Organ. Res. Methods **23**(2), 385–395 (2018)
16. Gu, R., et al.: The impact of industrial digital transformation on green development efficiency considering the threshold effect of regional collaborative innovation: evidence from the Beijing-Tianjin-Hebei urban agglomeration in China. J. Clean. Prod. **420**, 138345 (2023)
17. Fiss, P.: Building better causal theories: a fuzzy set approach to typologies in organization research. Acad. Manag. J. **54**, 393–420 (2011)
18. Ragin, C.C.: Redesigning Social Inquiry: Fuzzy Sets and Beyond. University of Chicago Press (2009)
19. An, W., et al.: Configurations of effectuation, causation, and bricolage: implications for firm growth paths. Small Bus. Econ. **54**(3), 843–864 (2019)

Author Index

Printed in the United States
by Baker & Taylor Publisher Services